Proceedings

International Database Engineering & Applications Symposium

   Concordia
UNIVERSITY

Proceedings

Seventh International
Database Engineering and
Applications Symposium

July 16 – 18, 2003, Hong Kong, SAR

Editors: Bipin C. Desai and Wilfred Ng

IEEE
COMPUTER
SOCIETY
http://computer.org

Los Alamitos, California

Washington • Brussels • Tokyo

IEEE Computer Society Order Number PR01981
ISBN 0-7695-1981-4
ISSN Number 1098-8068

Additional copies may be ordered from:

IEEE Computer Society	IEEE Service Center	IEEE Computer Society
Customer Service Center	445 Hoes Lane	Asia/Pacific Office
10662 Los Vaqueros Circle	P.O. Box 1331	Watanabe Bldg., 1-4-2
P.O. Box 3014	Piscataway, NJ 08855-1331	Minami-Aoyama
Los Alamitos, CA 90720-1314	Tel: + 1-732-981-0060	Minato-ku, Tokyo 107-0062
Tel: + 1-714-821-8380	Fax: + 1-732-981-9667	JAPAN
Fax: + 1-714-821-4641	http://shop.ieee.org/store/	Tel: + 81-3-3408-3118
E-mail: cs.books@computer.org	customer-service@ieee.org	Fax: + 81-3-3408-3553
		tokyo.ofc@computer.org

Individual paper REPRINTS may be ordered at: reprints@computer.org

Editorial production by Bob Werner
Cover art production by Joe Daigle/Studio Productions
Printed in the United States of America by The Printing House

Table of Contents

Seventh International Database Engineering and Applications Symposium (IDEAS 2003)

Data and Database Modelling

Data Mining I

XML Data Management

Data Mining II

Advanced Database Techniques I

Advanced Database Techniques II

Imprecise and Temporal Databases

Querying XML Data and Web Issues

Database Applications I

Database Applications II

Database Reliability/Stability and Security

Message from the General Chair

IDEAS'03 is the seventh in a series of meetings to address the continuing need for engineering databases for complex applications requiring security, reliability and high availibility. Previous symposiums were held in Canada, France, Japan and the U.K. at Concordia University (Montreal, '97 and '98), Cardiff University (Cardiff, '98) Keio University (Yokohama, '00), Grenoble Universities (Grenoble, '01), and University of Alberta (Edmonton, '02).

I wish to express my gratitude to the many people in Hong Kong and Montreal, particularly Wilfred Ng (Chair, Local Organizing Committee), Hong Va Leong (Chair, Publicity), and Qing Li (Chair, Publication). They have all worked hard providing active support for IDEAS'03 particularly during the times when the SARS epidemic created doubt as to the holding of the meeting in Hong Kong. In addition, Wilfred and the local organizing committee were resourceful in arranging this meeting and providing excellent facilities for it. I would also like to take this opportunity to thank the people at Concordia including Alison Parson, Martha Smith and Drew. I would also like to express my appreciation to Bob Werner, our IEEE editor; it is always a pleasure to work with him.

As in the previous years, the Program Committee and the external referees have ensured the quality of the symposium through meticulous refereeing of the submitted papers.

I would also like to thank IEEE Hong Kong, KC Wong Education Foundation for the financial support and the cooperation of IEEE Computer Society for making IDEAS'03 possible.

Bipin C. Desai
IDEAS'03 General Chair

Preface

The aim of the IDEAS series of symposia is to address issues on the engineering and application of databases. The IDEAS symposium is scheduled annually and has been held since 1997 in North America, Europe and Asia. It has attracted participants from governmental and non-governmental agencies, industry, and academia to exchange ideas and share experiences. IDEAS2003 is hosted by the Department of Computer Science of HKUST and takes place at HKUST, Hong Kong.

Following the tradition, IDEAS2003 includes quality papers describing original ideas and new findings on applied technological and theoretical aspects of database engineering and applications. The Program Committee and the referees have ensured this quality for the symposium through careful referring of the submitted papers. In summary, we received a total of 86 submissions; four referees reviewed each paper. Twenty-four of the papers with the highest score were selected as full papers. We also accepted 20 short papers and 5 poster papers, so as to include good papers in application and applied areas. The symposium thus provides an international forum for discussion of the problems of engineering database systems involving not only database technology, but also the related areas of information retrieval, multimedia, human machine interface and communication.

We wish to express our gratitude to the many people at the Hong Kong University of Science and Technology and Concordia University, and the local organizing committee members, particularly Professor Qing Li from City University and Professor Hon Va Leong from the Hong Kong Polytechnic University. We would like to thank all the authors who submitted their work to the symposium and especially those who are willing to come to Hong Kong to participate in the meeting. We would also like to thank IEEE Computing Society and KC Wong Education Foundation for their financial support for IDEAS2003.

Bipin C. Desai and Wilfred Ng
Program Co chairs

Organization Committees

General Chair
Bipin C. Desai (Concordia University, Canada)

Program Co-chairs
Bipin C. Desai and Wilfred Ng (Hong Kong University of Science & Technology, Hong Kong)

Local Organization
Wilfred Ng (Chair)
Hong Va Leong (Hong Kong Polytechnic University, Hong Kong) (Publicity)
Qing Li (City University of Hong Kong, Hong Kong) (Publication Chair)

Program Committee

Agma Traina (USP at Sao Carlos, Brazil)

Asuman Dogac (Middle East Tech. Univ., Turkey)

Bala Iyer (IBM Silicon Valley Lab, USA)

Beng-Chin Ooi (NUS, Singapore)

Bettina Kemme (McGill Univ., Canada)

Brigitte Kerherve (University of Montreal, Canada)

David Wai-lok Cheung (Univ. of Hong Kong, Hong Kong)

Dik Li (Hong Kong Univ of Sci and Tech, Hong Kong)

Dimitris Papadias (Hong Kong Univ of Sci and Tech, Hong Kong)

Domenico Sacca (Universite della Calabria, Italy)

Elisa Bertino (Univ. of Milano, Italy)

Esther Pacitti (Univ. Paris5, France)

Fabio Casati (HP, USA)

Feng Ling (University of Twente)

Frederick Lochovsky (Hong Kong Univ of Sci and Tech, Hong Kong)

Gonzalo Navarro (Univ. of Chile, Chile)

Gottfried Vossen (University of Münster, Germany)

Hongjun Lu (Hong Kong Univ of Sci and Tech, Hong Kong)

Isabel Cruz (Univ. of Illinois at Chicago, USA)

Jari Veijalainen (University of Jyväskyl, Finland)

Jeffery Yu (Chinese Univ. of H. Kong, Hong Kong

Jiawei Han (Simon Fraser Univ., Canada)

Joerg Sander (Univ. of Alberta, Canada)

Karl Aberer (EPFL, Switzerland)

Ke Wang (Simon Fraser Univ., Canada)

Ken Barker (Univ. of Calgary, Canada)

Klemens Boehm (ETH, Switzerland)

Luc Bouganim (Univ. of Versailles, France)

Maria Orlowska (Univ. of Queensland, Australia)

Mark Levene (Univ. of London, England)

Martin Kersten (CWI, Netherlands)

Masaru Kitsuregawa (Univ. of Tokyo, Japan)

Michael H. Böhlen (Aalborg University)

Michel Adiba (Univ. of Grenoble, France)

Nematollaah Shiri (Concordia University)

Nick Koudas (AT&T Labs, USA)

Qiang Yang (Hong Kong Univ of Sci and Tech, Hong Kong)

Ralf H. Gueting (Fern Univ. of Hagen, Germany)

Richard McClatchey (CERN/UWE)

Roger Barga (Microsoft, USA)

Theo Haerder (Univ. of Kaiserlautern, Germany)

Tore Risch (Uppsala Univ., Sweden)

Yannis Theodoridis (Computer Technology Inst., Patras)

External Reviewers

Masayoshi Aritsugi

Edgard-Ivan Benitez-Guerrero

Roberto Figueira Santos Filho

Filippo Furfaro

Alfredo Garro

Gianluigi Greco

Haibo Hu

Mei Jie

Ho Lam Lau

Yan Hong Li

Kaiyang Liu

Qiong Luo

Giuseppe Manco

Alexey Mazhelis

Anirban Mondal

Tadashi Ohmori

Iko Pramudiono

Mahmudur Rahman

Krishina Reddy

Pasquale Rullo

Patricia Serrano-Alvarado

Yufei Tao

Caetano Traina Jr

Domenico Ursino

Jiying Wang

Tao Wang

Tongyua Wang

Jianliang Xu

Bei Hua Zhang

Jun Zhang

Baihua Zheng

Manli Zhu

Wei Zou

Data and Database Modelling

A Model for Schema Integration in Heterogeneous Databases

Avigdor Gal*

Technion — Israel Institute of Technology, Israel

avigal@ie.technion.ac.il

Alberto Trombetta

Università dell'Insubria, Italy

alberto.trombetta@uninsubria.it

Ateret Anaby-Tavor

Technion — Israel Institute of Technology, Israel

ateret@techunix.technion.ac.il

Danilo Montesi[†]

Università di Camerino, Italy

danilo.montesi@unicam.it.

Abstract

Schema integration is the process by which schemata from heterogeneous databases are conceptually integrated into a single cohesive schema. In this work we propose a modeling framework for schema integration, capturing the inherent uncertainty accompanying the integration process. The model utilizes a fuzzy framework to express a confidence measure, associated with the outcome of a schema integration process. In this paper we provide a systematic analysis of the process properties and establish a criterion for evaluating the quality of matching algorithms, which map attributes among heterogeneous schemata.

*Partially supported by Technion V.P.R. Fund - New York Metropolitan Research Fund and the IBM Faculty Award for 2002/2003 on "Self-Configuration in Autonomic Computing using Knowledge Management." Also, supported by the Ministry of Science, Culture, and Sport in Israel and by the CNR in Italy.

[†]Partially funded by MURST Project "Algorithms to index and query semistrucrured data" RSO ex-60% and by MIUR as part of the SAHARA Project. Also, partially supported by the Ministry of Science, Culture, and Sport in Israel and by the CNR in Italy.

1 Introduction and motivation

Schema integration is the process by which schemata from heterogeneous databases are conceptually integrated into a single cohesive schema. In this work we propose a modeling framework for schema integration, capturing the inherent uncertainty accompanying the integration process. We assert that the proposed formal model provides a solid foundation for analyzing the quality of a schema integration process. To substantiate our claim, we provide a systematic analysis of the process properties and establish a criterion for evaluating the quality of matching algorithms, which map attributes among heterogeneous schemata. This criterion (dubbed *monotonicity*) demonstrates the usefulness of the model and can serve in a comparative empirical analysis of various algorithms. Our research is motivated by the shift from manual schema integration, as was proposed in [23, 15] to semiautomatic schema integration [12] and fully automatic schema integration [18]. The latter is of particular importance in supporting the reasoning capabilities of software agents in the Semantic Web. The proposed model, to be given in details in Section 2, utilizes a fuzzy framework to model a confidence measure, associated with the outcome of a schema integration process. For example, given two attribute sets $\mathcal{A}$ and $\mathcal{A}'$, the model associates a similarity measure, normalized between 0 (total dissimilarity) and 1 (equivalence) with any mapping among attributes of $\mathcal{A}$ and $\mathcal{A}'$. Therefore, given two attributes $A \in \mathcal{A}$ and $A' \in \mathcal{A}'$, A and A' are μ-similar (denoted $A \backsim_{\mu_{att}} A'$), specifying a confidence measure for the mapping. We assume that a manual matching is a perfect process, resulting in a *crisp* mapping, with $\mu_{att} = 1$. As for automatic matching, a hybrid of algorithms, such as those presented in [7, 18, 21] or adaptation of relevant work in proximity queries (*e.g.*, [5, 2]) and query rewriting over mismatched domains (*e.g.*, [6]) can determine the level of μ_{att}. Identifying a similarity measure μ, in and by itself, is insufficient for matching purposes. One may claim, and justly so, that the use of syntactic means to identify semantic equivalence, may be misleading in that a mapping with a high μ can be less precise, as conceived by an expert, than a mapping with a lower μ. We therefore propose a family of "well-behaved" mappings (termed *monotonic mappings*), for which one can safely interpret a high similarity measure as a good semantic mapping. An immediate consequence of this result is the establishment of a corroboration for the quality of mapping techniques, based on their capability to generate monotonic mappings.

Despite a vast body of research on heterogeneous schemata matching (MOMIS [3], DIKE [22], Clio [20], Cupid [18], and OntoBuilder [21], to name a few), there is sparse academic literature on appropriate evaluation tools for proposed algorithms and matching methods in this area. A recent work on representing mappings between domain models was presented in [17]. This work provides a model representation and inference analysis. Managing uncertainty was recognized as the next step on the research agenda in this area and was left open for a future research. Our work fills this gap in providing a framework that models and enables reasoned analysis of uncertainty. In [19], a model for estimating information loss in a matching process was introduced. The model computes precision and recall of substitutions of terms in a generalization-specialization hierarchy. The proposed metrics (and their combination, as suggested in [19]) serve as alternatives to the μ-similarity measure we propose in this paper. However, no evaluation of the correspondence of these measures with the "goodness" of the mapping, as perceived by an expert, are available. Our work shows that μ-similarity can be correlated with mapping quality. Our approach was inspired by works of Fagin [10], who proposed a method of combining answers to queries over different data sources using simple fuzzy set theory concepts and a method for allowing users to weight different parts of their queries. This work extends imprecision to metadata and identifies a family of mappings for which imprecision calculations is meaningful. An alternative to the fuzzy sets framework exists in the form of probabilistic methods (*e.g.*, [9]). A probabilistic-based approach assumes that one has an incomplete knowledge on the portion of the real world being modeled. However, this knowledge can be encoded as probabilities about events. The fuzzy approach, on the other hand, aims at modeling the intrinsic imprecision of features of the modeled reality. Therefore, the amount of knowledge at the user's disposal is of little concern. Our choice, in addition to philosophical reasoning, is also based on pragmatic reasoning. Probabilistic reasoning typically relies on event independence assumptions, making correlated events harder to assess. Our approach is supported by the results presented in [8], where a comparative study of the capabilities of probability and fuzzy methods is presented. This study shows that although probabilistic analysis is intrinsically more expressive than fuzzy sets, fuzzy methods demonstrate higher computational efficiency.

The rest of the paper is organized as follows. Section 2 introduces the proposed schema integration model. We formally define similarity relations (primitive and compound) as fuzzy relations and demonstrate these concepts by defining similarities among data values, domains, individual attributes, and mappings. We next define a class of monotonic mappings in Section 3, for which we show that fuzzy matching reflects the precision of the mapping itself. In Section 4 we analyze some properties of compound similarity relations. In particular, we provide a justification, in retrospect, for the common use of weighted bipartite matching in identifying the best mapping. The paper is concluded in Section 5 with a discussion of the model applicability and directions for future research.

2 The model

In this section we provide a formal model for computing similarities among attribute sets, based on fuzzy relations [4], as follows. A *fuzzy set* A over a domain $\mathcal{D}$ is a set, characterized by a membership function $\delta_A : \mathcal{D} \to [0, 1]$, where $\delta_A(a) = \mu$ is the fuzzy membership degree of the element a in A. In what follows we use $\mu^{A,a}$ to specify the elements of interest whenever it cannot be clearly identified from the context. Given domains $\mathcal{D}_1, \mathcal{D}_2, \ldots, \mathcal{D}_n$ and their Cartesian product $\mathbf{D} = \mathcal{D}_1 \times \mathcal{D}_2 \times \cdots \times \mathcal{D}_n$, a *fuzzy relation* R over the domains $\mathcal{D}_1, \mathcal{D}_2, \ldots, \mathcal{D}_n$ is a fuzzy set of elements (tuples) of $\mathbf{D}$. We next introduce two types of similarity relations. Primitive similarity relations are introduced in Section 2.1. Section 2.2 introduces compound similarity relations.

2.1 Primitive similarity relations

Given domains $\mathcal{D}$ and $\mathcal{D}'$, a *primitive similarity relation* is a fuzzy relation over $\mathcal{D} \cup \mathcal{D}'$, denoted $\sim_\mu$, where μ is a membership function such that the following properties hold:

- (ref) For every $d \in \mathcal{D} \cup \mathcal{D}'$, $d \sim_\mu d$ (using an infix notation) with $\mu = 1$.

- (sym) For $d \in \mathcal{D}$, $d' \in \mathcal{D}'$, $d \sim_\mu d' \to d' \sim_\mu d$.

4

- (trin) For $d \in \mathcal{D}$, $d' \in \mathcal{D}'$ and $d'' \in \mathcal{D}''$ (where $\mathcal{D}''$ is a third domain and the similarity relation is defined over $\mathcal{D} \cup \mathcal{D}' \cup \mathcal{D}''$), $(d \sim_\mu d' \wedge d' \sim_{\mu'} d'') \rightarrow d \sim_{\mu''} d''$ such that $\mu'' \leq \mu + \mu'$.

A primitive similarity relation is a fuzzy relation (over $\mathcal{D}, \mathcal{D}'$) whose membership degree is computed using some distance metric among domain members. We can also require the partition of the domain such that for $d \neq d'$, if $\{d, d'\} \subseteq \mathcal{D}$ or $\{d, d'\} \subseteq \mathcal{D}'$, then $d \sim_\mu d'$ with $\mu = 0$. Such partitioning is natural in our case, given that our aim is to match elements of different domains. We annotate by $\mu^{d,d'}$ the similarity between d and d'. As an example, consider two non-negative numeric domains $\mathcal{D} = \{0, 15, 30, 45\}$ and $\mathcal{D}' = \{0, 10, 20, 30, 40, 50\}$, both representing a fraction of an hour in which a car will be picked up. Assume that the similarity of elements $d \in \mathcal{D}$ and $d' \in \mathcal{D}'$ is measured according to their Euclidean distance, normalized between 0 and 1:

$$\mu^{d,d'} = 1 - \frac{|d - d'|}{\max_{d_i, d_j \in \mathcal{D} \cup \mathcal{D}'} \{|d_i - d_j|\}} \qquad (1)$$

Therefore, the similarity score between 15 (in $\mathcal{D}$) and 30 (in $\mathcal{D}'$) is 0.7. $\mu^{d,d'}$, as defined in Equation 1, is a primitive similarity relation.

The properties of primitive similarity relations are desirable properties when it comes to schema integration. Reflexivity ensures that exact matching receives the highest possible score (as in the case of two attributes with the same name). Symmetry ensures that the order in which two schemata are compared has no effect on the final outcome. Finally, the triangular property enables the generation of similarity classes, sets of attributes (one of each

schema) that are synonymical. This last property enables a desirable learning feature for automatic schema integration.

2.2 Compound similarity relations

Compound similarity relations use similarity measures (either primitive or compound) to compute new similarity measures. In this section we introduce compound similarity relations via an example. We defer the formal analysis of such relations to Section 4. As an example, we can compute the similarity of two numeric domains, based on the similarity of their values. Let $\mathcal{D}$ and $\mathcal{D}'$ be the domains. Let μ_{dom} be a function, termed the *domain similarity measure*. Then, $\sim_{\mu_{dom}}$ is a *domain similarity* relation (over a set of domains) and $\mathcal{D} \sim_{\mu_{dom}} \mathcal{D}'$ is the domain similarity of the domains $\mathcal{D}$ and $\mathcal{D}'$. μ_{dom} is a function of the similarities of every pair of elements from $\mathcal{D}$ and $\mathcal{D}'$. For example, one may compute μ_{dom} as:

$$\mu_{dom}^{\mathcal{D},\mathcal{D}'} = \min_{d \in \mathcal{D}, d' \in \mathcal{D}'} \left(\mu^{\mathcal{D},d'}, \mu^{\mathcal{D}',d} \right) \qquad (2)$$

where for all $d' \in \mathcal{D}'$, $\mu^{\mathcal{D},d'} = \max_{d \in \mathcal{D}} \left(\mu^{d,d'} \right)$ and for all $d \in \mathcal{D}$, $\mu^{\mathcal{D}',d} = \max_{d' \in \mathcal{D}'} \left(\mu^{d,d'} \right)$. That is, each value in $\mathcal{D}$ is matched with the "best" value in $\mathcal{D}'$, and vice versa, and the strength of μ_{dom} is determined by the strength of the "weakest link." Our use of min and max is in line with fuzzy logic conventions, where max is interpreted as disjunction and min is interpreted as conjunction. We shall discuss alternative operators in Section 4, providing constraints on the possible operator selection. As a concrete example, consider $\mathcal{D}$ and $\mathcal{D}'$ given above. Computing $\mu_{dom}^{\mathcal{D},\mathcal{D}'}$ according to Equation 2 yields a matching of 0 with 0, 10 and 20 with 15, etc. $\mu_{dom}^{\mathcal{D},\mathcal{D}''} = 0.9$, since each element in $\mathcal{D}'$ has a corresponding element in $\mathcal{D}$ which is at most 5 minutes apart (and $1 - \frac{5}{50} = 0.9$). It is worth noting that the similarity measure given by Equation 2 is both reflexive and symmetric.

3 Monotonic mappings: measuring matching quality

In this section we aim at modeling the relationship between a choice of a mapping, based on similarity of attributes, and a choice of a mapping, as performed by a human expert. The more correlated these mappings are, the more effective would an automatic mapping process be. In order to compare the effectiveness of various choices of mappings and operators, we introduce the notion of mapping *imprecision*, which follows common IR practice for retrieval effectiveness (*e.g.*, [11]). Assume first that among all possible mappings between two attribute sets of cardinality n ($n!$ such mappings for $1 : 1$ matching), we choose one and term it the *exact mapping* (denoted $\bar{F}$). Intuitively, the exact mapping is the best possible mapping, as conceived by a human expert. Having selected the exact mapping between $\mathcal{A}$ and $\mathcal{A}'$, we measure the imprecision of any other mapping G simply by counting how many arguments of $\bar{F}$ and G do not coincide. We next present a formal definition of mapping imprecision.

Definition 1 *Let $\mathcal{A} = \{A_1, \ldots, A_n\}$ and $\mathcal{A}' = \{A'_1, \ldots, A'_n\}$ be attribute sets of cardinality n. Also, let F and G be two mappings over $\mathcal{A}$ and $\mathcal{A}'$ and $A_i \in \mathcal{A}$ an attribute. F discord with G over A_i if*

$F(A_i) \neq G(A_i)$. $\mathcal{D}^{F,G}$ *denotes the set of attributes of $\mathcal{A}$ over which F discord with G .*

Definition 2 *Let $\bar{F}$ be an exact mapping over $\mathcal{A}$ and $\mathcal{A}'$ and let G be a mapping over $\mathcal{A}$ and $\mathcal{A}'$ such that there are $m \leq n$ attributes in $\mathcal{A}$ over which $\bar{F}$ discord with G. Then G is m-imprecise (with respect to $\bar{F}$). We denote by i_G the imprecision of G.*

Definition 3 *Let F and G be mappings over attribute sets $\mathcal{A}$ and $\mathcal{A}'$. F and G are similarity preserving on an attribute $A \in \mathcal{A}$ if $i_F < i_G$ implies $\mu_{att}^{A,F(A)} > \mu_{att}^{A,G(A)}$. $\mathcal{M}^{F,G}$ denotes the set of attributes of $\mathcal{A}$ on which F and G are similarity preserving.*

Definition 4 *Let $\mathcal{F} = \{F_1, F_2, \ldots, F_m\}$ be a set of mappings over attribute sets $\mathcal{A}$ and $\mathcal{A}'$, and let $\bar{\varpi} = (\varpi_1, \ldots, \varpi_n)$ be a weight vector that sums to unity, associating with each attribute $A_i \in \mathcal{A}$ a weight ϖ_i. $\mathcal{F}$ is monotonic if the following inequality holds for any pair $\{F_i, F_j\} \subseteq \mathcal{F}$ such that $i_{F_i} < i_{F_j}$:*

$$\sum_{A_k \in \mathcal{D}^{F_i,F_j} \cap \mathcal{M}^{F_i,F_j}} \left(\varpi_k \left(\mu_{att}^{A_k,F_i(A_k)} - \mu_{att}^{A_k,F_j(A_k)} \right) \right) >$$

$$\sum_{A_k \in \mathcal{D}^{F_i,F_j} \setminus \mathcal{M}^{F_i,F_j}} \left(\varpi_k \left(\mu_{att}^{A_k,F_j(A_k)} - \mu_{att}^{A_k,F_i(A_k)} \right) \right)$$

The sum on the left represents the benefit of switching from F_j to F_i. $\mathcal{D}^{F_i,F_j} \cap \mathcal{M}^{F_i,F_j}$ represents those attributes over which F_i discord with F_j, yet are similarity preserving. Since $i_{F_i} < i_{F_j}$, each term in the sum adds to the overall similarity. The sum on the right represents the loss involved in switching from F_j to F_i. $\mathcal{D}^{F_i,F_j} \setminus \mathcal{M}^{F_i,F_j}$ represents those attributes over which F_i discord with F_j, and that are not similarity preserving. These attributes lower the overall similarity by switching from F_j to F_i. If the benefit of switching from F_j to F_i surpasses the cost for all pairs $\{F_i, F_j\} \subseteq \mathcal{F}$ such that $i_{F_i} < i_{F_j}$, we consider the set to be monotonic. If the exact mapping is chosen among monotonic mappings, then the following holds: if $\bar{F} \in \mathcal{F}$ and $\mathcal{F}$ is monotonic then $\bar{F}$'s overall similarity measure is greater than the overall similarity degrees of i-imprecise mappings in $\mathcal{F}$, even if such mappings yield better similarity degrees on some pairs of domain elements and on some pairs of attribute names. If all one wishes to obtain is the ability to identify the exact mapping through the use of similarity, one needs a weaker notion of monotonicity, as defined next.

Definition 5 *Let* $\mathcal{F} = \{F_1, F_2, ..., F_m\}$ *be the set of all possible mappings over attribute sets* $\mathcal{A}$ *and* $\mathcal{A}'$. $\mathcal{F}$ *is monotonic with respect to the exact mapping* $\bar{F} \in \mathcal{F}$ *if the following inequality holds for any* $F_i \in \mathcal{F}$:

$$\sum_{A_k \in \mathcal{D}^{F_i, \bar{F}} \cap \mathcal{M}^{F_i, \bar{F}}} \left(\varpi_k \left(\mu_{att}^{A_k, \bar{F}(A_k)} - \mu_{att}^{A_k, F_i(A_k)} \right) \right) >$$

$$\sum_{A_k \in \mathcal{D}^{F_i, \bar{F}} \setminus \mathcal{M}^{F_i, \bar{F}}} \left(\varpi_k \left(\mu_{att}^{A_k, F_i(A_k)} - \mu_{att}^{A_k, \bar{F}(A_k)} \right) \right)$$

4 Compound similarity properties

Having defined the framework for expressing schema mapping similarity, we turn our attention to compound similarity properties. In Section 4.1, we discuss the set of alternative operators we have at our disposal and their inter-relationship. Section 4.2 presents some interesting properties of monotonic mappings. The main result of this section states

that, under appropriate hypotheses made explicit in Section 4.2, a monotonic set of mappings orders mappings according to their imprecision level.

4.1 Similarity operators

In this section we present two families of similarity operators, namely triangular norms and fuzzy aggregate operators, and compare their properties. Operators from both families are typically used in fuzzy-based applications to combine various fuzzy membership degrees. Since the study of different ways of combining similarities is crucial to this work, we provide a brief introduction of their main properties.

The min operator was introduced in Section 2.1 for computing the similarity degree of two domains. This operator is the most well-known representative of a large family of operators called *triangular norms* (t-norms, for short), routinely deployed as interpretations of fuzzy conjunctions. In the following, we define t-norms and discuss their relevant properties. We refer the interested reader to [16] for an exhaustive treatment of the subject.

A *triangular norm* $T : [0, 1] \times [0, 1] \rightarrow [0, 1]$ is a binary operator on the unit interval satisfying the following axioms for all $x, y, z \in [0, 1]$:

- (boundary condition) $T(x, 1) = x$,

- (monotonicity) $x \leq y$ implies $T(x, z) \leq T(y, z)$,

- (commutativity) $T(x, y) = T(y, x)$,

- (associativity) $T(x, T(y, z)) = T(T(x, y), z)$.

Examples of t-norms that are typically used as interpretations of fuzzy conjunctions include minimum ($Tm(x,y) = \min(x,y)$), product ($Tp(x,y) = x \cdot y$), and the Lukasiewicz t-norm ($Tl(x,y) = \max(x + y - 1, 0)$). It is worth noting that Tm is the only idempotent t-norm. That is, $Tm(x,x) = x$. This becomes handy when comparing t-norms with fuzzy aggregate operators. Also, it can be easily proven (see [14]) that $Tl(x,y) \leq Tp(x,y) \leq Tm(x,y)$ for all $x, y \in [0,1]$.

The *average* operator that is typically used for the computation of the similarity of attribute sets does not satisfy the t-norm axioms. Rather, it belongs to another large family of operators termed *fuzzy aggregate operators* [16]. A fuzzy aggregate operator $H : [0,1]^n \rightarrow [0,1]$ satisfy the following axioms for every $x_1, \ldots, x_n \in [0,1]$:

- (idempotency) $H(x_1, x_1, \ldots, x_1) = x_1$.

- (increasing monotonicity) for every $y_1, y_2, \ldots, y_n \in [0,1]$ such that $x_i \leq y_i$. $H(x_1, x_2, \ldots, x_n) \leq H(y_1, y_2, \ldots, y_n)$.

- H is a continuous function.

Let $\bar{x} = (x_1, \ldots, x_n)$ be a vector such that for all $1 \leq i \leq n$, $x_i \in [0,1]$ and let $\bar{\varpi} = (\varpi_1, \ldots, \varpi_n)$ be a weight vector that sums to unity. Examples of fuzzy aggregate operators include the *average* operator $Ha(\bar{x}) = \frac{1}{n} \sum_1^n x_i$ and the *weighted average* operator $Hwa(\bar{x}, \bar{\varpi}) = \bar{x} \cdot \bar{\varpi}$. Clearly, *average* is a special case of the *weighted average* operator, where $\varpi_1 = \cdots = \varpi_n$. It is worth noting that Tm (the min t-norm) is also a fuzzy aggregate operator, due to its idempotency (its associative property provides a way of defining it over any number of arguments). However, Tp and Tl are not fuzzy aggregate operators. T-norms and fuzzy

aggregate operators are comparable, using the inequality $\min(x_1, \ldots, x_n) \leq H(x_1, \ldots, x_n)$ for all $x_1, \ldots, x_n \in [0,1]$ and function H satisfying idempotency, increasing monotonicity and continuity axioms.

4.2 Monotonic mappings revisited

In this section we present some relevant properties of compound similarity operators. In particular, we show that for a monotonic set of mappings, the use of a weighted average to compute mapping similarity orders mappings according to their imprecision level.

Theorem 1 *Let $\mathcal{F}$ be a monotonic set of mappings and let $\{F_i, F_j\} \in \mathcal{F}$ be mappings over attribute sets $\mathcal{A}$ and $\mathcal{A}'$ with imprecision i_{F_i} and i_{F_j}, respectively, such that $i_{F_i} < i_{F_j}$. If the corresponding similarity measures are combined using the Hwa (weighted average) operator yielding respectively μ^F and μ^G, then $\mu^F > \mu^G$.*

Theorem 1 requires that similarities are combined using the Hwa (weighted average) operator. We now show that the use of weighted average is preferred over any t-norm operator to compute mapping similarity. For simplicity sake, we restrict our discussion to similarity among attribute pairs and their combination into similarities among schemata. The following result can be easily generalized to any similarity measure method. We denote by $X_1 X_2$ a particular selection of operators for computing attribute similarity (X_1), and mapping similarity (X_2). We next show that, in most cases, a selection of type $X_1 Ha$ is superior to any selec-

8

tion of type $X_1 T$, where T stands for any t-norm operator.

Definition 6 *Let* $\mathcal{A} = \{A_1, \ldots, A_n\}$ *and* $\mathcal{A}' = \{A'_1, \ldots, A'_n\}$ *be attribute sets of cardinality n.* $\mathcal{A}$ *and* $\mathcal{A}'$ *are* closely related *if for any mapping F over* $\mathcal{A}$ *and* $\mathcal{A}'$, *if* $(A, A') \in F$, *then* $\mu_{att}^{A,A'} > 0$.

Closely related attribute sets consist of attributes that may map well in various combinations. Our experience show that this is hardly ever the case, since attributes tend to vary in names and domains. We next present a proposition arguing that t-norms are not suitable for modeling attribute sets that are not closely related.

Proposition 1 *Let* $\mathcal{A} = \{A_1, \ldots, A_n\}$ *and* $\mathcal{A}' = \{A'_1, \ldots, A'_n\}$ *be attribute sets of cardinality n. If* $\mathcal{A}$ *and* $\mathcal{A}'$ *are* **not** *closely related, any selection of operators of type* $X_1 T$ *yields a non monotonic mapping set.*

An immediate corollary to Proposition 1 relates to mappings using weighted bipartite graph matching. Given two attribute sets, $\mathcal{A}$ and $\mathcal{A}'$, one may construct a weighted bipartite graph $G = (V, E)$, such that $V = \mathcal{A} \cup \mathcal{A}'$, and $(v_i, v_j) \in E$ if $v_i \in \mathcal{A}$, $v_j \in \mathcal{A}'$. The weight function $\varpi : \mathcal{A} \times \mathcal{A}' \to [0, 1]$ is defined to be $\varpi(v_i, v_j) = \mu_{att}^{v_i, v_j}$. The weighted bipartite graph matching algorithm yields a $1 : 1$ mapping F with maximum weight $\Omega^F = \sum_{(v_i, v_j) \in F} \varpi(v_i, v_j)$. Given that $\mathcal{A}$ and $\mathcal{A}'$ are attribute sets of cardinality n, that are not closely related, and assuming a selection of operators of type $X_1 Ha$, such mapping yields $\mu^F = \frac{1}{n} \Omega^F$. Therefore, the use of weighted bipartite graph matching is

equivalent to a selection of operators of type $X_1 Ha$, which yields results as good as any selection of operators of type $X_1 T$, and possibly better.

5 Conclusion and future work

We have presented a formal model for schema matching, capturing the inherent uncertainty of the outcome of automating the process. The model presentation is followed by an analysis of the model properties and the identification of a sufficient condition for the correlation of the automatic process outcome with that of a manual process. The formal model borrows from fuzzy set theory in modeling uncertainty. The theoretical analysis of the model have yielded that for monotonic mappings one may correlate similarity measure with precision, as conceived by a human expert. While monotonicity is a strong notion, weaker notions, such as monotonicity with respect to an exact match suffices for practical purposes (such as identifying the exact mapping within a small number of iterations). Therefore, matching algorithms that generate monotonic mappings (in any form) are well suited for automatic semantic reconciliation. Unless attributes in schemata are closely related, mapping similarity cannot utilize any t-norm as its computation vehicle. A preferred operator would come from the fuzzy aggregate operator family, *e.g.*, the *average* operator. This result provides a theoretical support for the use of variations of the weighted bipartite graph matching for computing schema mapping.

We have performed initial experiments, aiming at verifying empirically the correlation between a similarity measure (generated by a given algorithm) on the one hand and monotonicity on the other hand, using imprecision level as the experimentation tool. A full report of the experiments is available in [13].

We envision multitude of applications for automatic schema matching. For example, the research is likely to aid in the design of smart agents that will negotiate over information goods using schema information and provide them with some practical tools to combat schema heterogeneity. Towards this end, we shall conduct a thorough analysis of schema usability, to enable a realistic evaluation of the outcomes of a top-K algorithm [1] on a practical level. The top-K algorithm, presented in [1], enables an efficient identification of K mappings with the highest similarity measure. The outcome of the analysis would be the development of robust methods for assessing the usability of mappings to a user. Using these methods, an agent performing on behalf of a user will be able to filter out non-usable matchings from the top-K group, so that the remaining results, that are to be presented to the user, would be of the best quality.

References

[1] A. Anaby-Tavor, A. Gal, and A. Moss. Efficient algorithms for top-k matchings. Submitted for publication. Available upon request from avigal@ie.technion.ac.il, 2003.

[2] W.G. Aref, D. Barbará, S. Johnson, and S. Mehrotra. Efficient processing of proximity queries for large databases. In P.S. Yu and A.L.P. Chen, editors, *Proceedings of the IEEE CS International Conference on Data Engineering*, pages 147–154. IEEE Computer Society, 1995.

[3] S. Bergamaschi, S. Castano, M. Vincini, and D. Beneventano. Semantic integration of heterogeneous information sources. *Data & Knowledge Engineering*, 36(3), 2001.

[4] P. Ciaccia, D. Montesi, W. Penzo, and A. Trombetta. Imprecision and user preferences in multimedia queries: A generic algebraic approach. In *Lecture Notes on Computer Science, 1762*, pages 50–71. Springer, 2000.

[5] L.S. Davis and N. Roussopoulos. Approximate pattern matching in a pattern database system. *Information systems*, 5(2):107–119, 1980.

[6] L. G. DeMichiel. Performing operations over mismatched domains. In *Proceedings of the IEEE CS International Conference on Data Engineering*, pages 36–45, Los Angeles, CA, February 1989.

[7] A. Doan, P. Domingos, and A.Y. Halevy. Reconciling schemas of disparate data sources: A machine-learning approach. In Walid G. Aref, editor, *Proceedings of the ACM-SIGMOD conference on Management of Data (SIGMOD)*, Santa Barbara, California, May 2001. ACM Press.

[8] J. Drakopoulos. Probabilities, possibilities and fuzzy sets. *International Journal of Fuzzy Sets and Systems*, 75(1):1–15, 1995.

[9] T. Eiter, T. Lukasiewicz, and M. Walter. Extension of the relational algebra to probabilistic complex values. In B. Thalheim K.-D. Schewe, editor, *Lecture Notes on Computer Science, 1762*, pages 94–115. Springer, 2000.

[10] R. Fagin. Combining fuzzy information from multiple systems. *J. of Computer and System Sciences*, 58:83–99, 1999.

[11] W.B. Frakes and R. Baeza-Yates, editors. *Information Retrieval: Data Structures & Algorithms*. Prentice Hall, Englewood Cliffs, NJ 07632, 1992.

[12] N. Fridman Noy and M.A. Musen. PROMPT: Algorithm and tool for automated ontology merging and alignment. In *Proceedings of the Seventeenth National Conference on Artificial Intelligence (AAAI-2000)*, pages 450–455, Austin, TX, 2000.

[13] A. Gal, A. Trombetta, A. Anaby-Tavor, and D. Montesi. A framework for evaluating similarity-based schema matching. Submitted for publication. Available upon request from avigal@ie.technion.ac.il, 2003.

[14] P. Hajek. *The Metamathematics of Fuzzy Logic*. Kluwer Acad. Publ., 1998.

[15] R. Hull. Managing semantic heterogeneity in databases: A theoretical perspective. In *Proceedings of the ACM SIGACT-SIGMOD-SIGART Symposium on Principles of Database Systems (PODS)*, pages 51–61. ACM Press, 1997.

[16] G.J. Klir and B. Yuan, editors. *Fuzzy Sets and Fuzzy Logic*. Prentice Hall, 1995.

[17] J. Madhavan, P.A. Bernstein, P. Domingos, and A.Y. Halevy. Representing and reasoning about mappings between domain models. In *Proceedings of the Eighteenth National Conference on Artificial Intelligence and Fourteenth Conference on Innovative Applications of Artificial Intelligence (AAAI/IAAI)*, pages 80–86, 2002.

[18] J. Madhavan, P.A. Bernstein, and E. Rahm. Generic schema matching with cupid. In *Proceedings of the International conference on very Large Data Bases (VLDB)*, pages 49–58, Rome, Italy, September 2001.

[19] E. Mena, V. Kashayap, A. Illarramendi, and A. Sheth. Imprecise answers in distributed environments: Estimation of information loss for multi-ontological based query processing. *International Journal of Cooperative Information Systems*, 9(4):403–425, 2000.

[20] R.J. Miller, M.A. Hernàndez, L.M. Haas, L.-L. Yan, C.T.H. Ho, R. Fagin, and L. Popa. The clio project: Managing heterogeneity. *SIGMOD Record*, 30(1):78–83, 2001.

[21] G. Modica, A. Gal, and H. Jamil. The use of machine-generated ontologies in dynamic information seeking. In C. Batini, F. Giunchiglia, P. Giorgini, and M. Mecella, editors, *Cooperative Information Systems. 9th International Conference, CoopIS 2001, Trento, Italy, September 5-7, 2001, Proceedings*, volume 2172 of *Lecture Notes in Computer Science*, pages 433–448. Springer, 2001.

[22] L. Palopoli, L.G. Terracina, and D. Ursino. The system DIKE:towards the semi-automatic synthesis of cooperative information systems and data warehouses. In *PADBIS-DASFAA*, pages 108–117, 2000.

[23] A. Sheth and J. Larson. Federated database systems for managing distributed, heterogeneous, and autonomous databases. *ACM Computing Surveys*, 22(3):183–236, 1990.

A Hybrid Model for Data Synchronism in Data Warehouse Projects

Isabel Cristina Italiano
Instituto de Matematica e Estatistica
Universidade de Sao Paulo – SP – Brazil
ici@ime.usp.br

Joao Eduardo Ferreira
Instituto de Matematica e Estatistica
Universidade de Sao Paulo – SP – Brazil
jef@ime.usp.br

Abstract

A data warehouse can be viewed as a set of portions of information from transactional systems (OLTP – On-Line Transaction Processing) with different business characteristics and used by analytical applications (OLAP – On-Line Analytical Processing) with different user requirements. As the concept of real time enterprise evolves, the synchronism between transaction data and data warehouse, statically implemented, has been reviewed. This paper proposes a hybrid synchronism model for the data warehouse. In this model, portions of information are analyzed by a set of parameters and searching functions.

With the parameters and searching functions in mind we can go on to choosing the most suitable synchronism option for each portion of information.

1. Introduction

The use of a data warehouse has been increasing significantly over the past few years. It plays a role of fundamental importance, based on decision support processes and the use of analytical applications, both in the commercial and academic environment.

Using the concept of real time enterprise, some business areas require increasingly faster and more accurate decision processes [7]. As a result, the model of synchronism between the transactional and analytical environment, normally implemented through periodical loadings, becomes a critical point. On the other hand, some business models require dynamic synchronism – maintaining transactional data and data warehouse synchronized in real time or intermittent periods, shorter than those implemented by static loadings performed from time to time [8,9,10]. The objective of this paper is to introduce a framework that allows defining the most suitable synchronism option for a certain business model. This analysis is based on a function that uses a set of parameters to define the most suitable synchronism option for each of the data portions.

The data warehouse can implement a hybrid synchronism model where its portions are synchronized in

different time intervals, depending on the characteristics of the transaction environment from where the information has originated and the requirements of the analytical application has been used. This analysis will therefore result in a domain classification.

Section 2 shows the characteristics of the transaction and analytical environment that affects the choice of the synchronism option. Section 3 shows a formalization of the analysis function to be applied to each of the data warehouse portions. Section 4 describes the implementation of this function with a prototype to be used in practical cases and section 5 contains the conclusion with a list of contributions and future works.

2. A classification of transactional and analytical domains

The frequency of a data warehouse loading process is used to define the points of synchronism between the transaction systems and the data warehouse with its analytical applications. To implement a dynamic warehouse synchronized in real time with the transactional systems, the interval between the points of synchronism must be reduced. To achieve that dynamic synchronism, the updates on transactional data must be reflected immediately on an analytical database system.

Under these circumstances, data warehouse loading process is divided among various maintenance transactions, so real-time synchronism is executed in the shortest possible time interval, taking into account the operational conditions required for processing and conveying information.

Choosing the most suitable synchronism option for each part of the data warehouse enables the optimization of the maintenance resources available, decreasing its complexity.

Defining the synchronism model that better suits a data warehouse requires an analysis of the domains of both the transactional and analytical applications. Thus, the following sections will cover the most important aspects of the analysis and evaluation of a synchronism model.

2.1. Analysis of the transactional environment characteristics

The transactional environment we are interested in is the set of functions that generates the information to be stored in the data warehouse portions. This evaluation requires that transactional applications are divided into sets of functions that handle each portion of the data. Where these data portions or subsets must be regarded as a functional unit within the transactional environment. Each of these functional units may have distinct behaviors related to its synchronism with the data warehouse.

In this context, some factors should be evaluated in order to define the implementation of the synchronism level.

2.1.1. The need for dynamic maintenance.
The first point is related to the functional characteristics of the transactional systems, source of data warehouse information. Because of functional characteristics, some systems are regarded as typically static. Classical cases are found in systems that work based on periodic closing points of processing, no matter if they occur every day, weekly, , fortnightly, monthly etc.

Other systems may require a small synchronism interval preferably immediately, in real time. Maybe the most typical example of this class of application is the data webhouse. A webhouse keeps the click stream of each user for an analysis of the user's behavior in certain Internet environment. In these cases, the applicability of the dynamic loading may be imperative.

Possible values for this parameter are:

- **Typically static** – the transactional system has characteristics that require a typically static loading, with no requirement for implementing dynamic updates;
- **Dynamic** – because of its functional characteristics, the transactional system requires a data warehouse dynamic update, considering the analyzed set of transactions.

2.1.2. The adaptation capacity of the transactional environment.
This point is related to the possibility of applying a dynamic approach to the transactional system being analyzed. We call this **adaptability** or capability of adaptation. The dynamic loading implementation requires some control over the transactional system and the possibility of changing its process for adding the functions required for the dynamic loading process implementation. Any system that does not allow these changes cannot be adapted to the real-time dynamic synchronism process. In these cases, the data warehouse works as a systemic integrator to access data, updated statically.

In these situations changes can be made directly in the transactional application or using database resources, such as triggers, logs or some other procedures that frequently check the changes and sends the new information to the analytical environment.

Obviously, we should also consider the cases where none of the above options is possible, either because of limitations of the database system used or because it is impossible to change the transactional application. That situation limits the synchronism to the static option only.

The values that can be assumed by this parameter are as follows:

- **Dynamic loading is allowed to be implemented** – the requirements could be added for gathering and propagating information to the data warehouse and the transactions involved;
- **Dynamic loading is not allowed to be implemented** – there is not a minimum control level to implement the functions.

2.1.3. The desirable time interval for the synchronism
Another factor to be evaluated is the desirable **time interval** for the synchronism. One should evaluate the real need for dynamic synchronism, in real time or in a short time interval, because the cost generated by this type of implementation can be too high for the benefits provided. In the scope of this paper, the possible values are:

- **Minimum possible** (Real Time) – the data warehouse synchronism with the transactional data must be in real time, keeping only the minimum time required for the information transmission and processing;
- **Determined interval** – the application requires synchronism in a certain period of time, longer than required for real time, but shorter than the static loading frequency;
- **Postponed Synchronism** – the synchronism can be kept at regular intervals determined by the data warehouse update static process during its periodic loading (eg.; day-1, day-2, month, etc.).

2.1.4. Complexity in the transactional environment.
The **complexity** of the transactional environment must be taken into account. When the information is updated in the operational base and transferred to the data warehouse, here is a cost involving that process. If the data warehouse uses information at the transactional environment lowest level of granularity, the loading process becomes simpler and minimizes the complexity involved in the loading sub processes and, consequently, the time limit required for its execution. This parameter can be analyzed from two distinct points of view:

Complexity in the propagation: Propagation complexity is related to the number of different objects involved in the transaction during a transactional database update. Obviously, the larger the number of objects involved in the transactional process, the more complex the propagation of information will be to the data warehouse.

The value intervals considered in this assignment version rely on empirical and experimental approaches and are classified as follows:

- **Low** – the number of distinct objects involved in the update is small, 1 or 2;
- Average – from 3 to 5 distinct objects involved;
- **High** – the number of distinct objects involved is high, more than 5 objects involved.

Complexity in the consistency: Consistency complexity is directly related to the complexity of the check and validation operations that must be performed by the transaction, immediately after the transactional base update. Even if a few different objects are involved in the update, the transaction may require a high degree of complexity in order to check the consistency of the information to be propagated. Considering, for example, the operations in the relational model, using the Structured Query Language (SQL), the possible values are:

- **Low** – there isn't or it is too small the need to validate or check other **elements** in addition to the information being handled during the transaction. These are the cases of simple selection with no more complex operations, such as, a *joining*, for example;
- **Average** – there is an average level of complexity involved in *joining*-related selection operations when preparing the information for loading;
- **High** – because of its complexity, the transaction also requires highly complex checks and validations when the information is prepared to be transmitted to the data warehouse. That is the case of selection operations involving an information joining and the use of *group by* and *having* operators.

2.2. Analysis of the analytical environment characteristics

Also important to the synchronism level definition, the types of queries to be performed on the data warehouse must be analyzed. Different types of users require different types of queries, which involve a variety of views of the data warehouse in numerous combinations of aggregations and detailed data.

Since most of the queries on the data warehouse are related to aggregation functions, such as *sum*, *count* and *group by*, among others, the complexity of analytical applications depends on the aggregation levels involved in

each query. Several strategies can be implemented to speed up the response time. These strategies are used when precomputing portions of the information that can be aggregated at different levels according to the queries.

Some of the common techniques related to aggregation use in data warehouses are:

- Dynamic aggregations calculated at the time the query is performed [1];
- Development of views with the required aggregation functions. They are called "aggregation views" and are used and computed during the query execution [2];
- Aggregation views are stored in caches and used when answering later queries [3];
- Summarization Tables representing aggregation views implemented as materialized views [4] [5];
- Results from queries on the data warehouse. They can be used again for similar queries performed later;
- Multidimensional aggregates, stored in cubes, which are physical structures separated from the central data warehouse. Its generation is performed from time to time [6].

These techniques optimize execution time of the analytical applications, whose complexity depends on the aggregation level used in the queries.

An option to evaluate the analytical environment behavior is based on two parameters: *a query classification based on their aggregation level* and *the type of the aggregation implemented in the data warehouse*. The following two parameters must be analyzed in order to define the most suitable synchronism option.

2.2.1. The use of aggregates in analytical queries. Some queries only use data at the most detailed level, while others only use aggregated values or a combination of details and aggregations. As a result, the analytical queries can be classified as follows:

- **Just detail** – the queries involved do not use aggregates and, therefore, can only access information at a lower granularity level;
- **Aggregates** – the queries perform functions such as *sum*, *count*, *group by* and others, supplying aggregate information to the user.

2.2.2. Aggregates implementation procedure. This parameter describes the way the **aggregates are implemented** in the analytical base. The possible values are:

- **None** – analytical database does not contain any pre-aggregated information. Any aggregated value requirement has to be computed while the query is performed;

- **Virtual views with aggregates** – the analytical database has unmaterialized aggregation views that can be used by the queries, but they are computed when the queries are performed;
- **Materialized views with aggregates** – the analytical database contains tables or views of the materialized aggregations, which contain the aggregated information required by the inquiry. These tables must reflect any changes affecting the source tables;
- **Cubes** – all the aggregation levels required by the queries have been previously prepared and stored in cubes.

2.3. Synchronism model parameters evaluation

The transactional and analytical characteristics described in Sections 2.1 and 2.2 must now be regarded as parameters and be jointly evaluated. This first version of parameters was defined based on the author's many years of database and data warehouse use experience. This evaluation shows the interference of the parameters for the purpose of providing guidelines to define the data warehouse synchronism model.

The following is a summary of the parameters and their possible values:

Transactional environment parameters:

P1 – Applicability:
   Typically static
   Dynamic

P2 – Adaptability
   Dynamic loading is allowed to be implemented
   Dynamic loading is not allowed to be implemented

P3 – Time interval
   Minimum possible (real time)
   Determined interval
   Postponed synchronism (periodic loading)

P4 – Complexity in the propagation
   Low
   Average
   High

P5 – Complexity in the consistency
   Low
   Average
   High

Analytical environment parameters:

P6 – Use of aggregates
   Just detail
   Aggregates

P7 – Aggregates implementation
   None
   Virtual views with aggregates
   Materialized views with aggregates
   Cubes

The parameters are displayed as decision trees (figures 1, 2 and 3) representing all possible combinations. There is one tree to evaluate analytical environment parameters and another for the transactional environment parameters.

The leaves of each tree represent the selected synchronism model, based on the decision path and according to the values shown. The model selected is the one that requires the shortest possible time interval for the synchronism. The values used to represent the synchronism options are:

- **Dr** – dynamic model with real-time synchronism considering only the time required for data selection and transmission;
- **Ddt** – dynamic model with synchronism in a certain time interval (Δt);
- **St** – static model with synchronism based on periodic loadings.

The decision to represent two options for the dynamic model (Dr and Ddt) results from the fact that the data warehouse dynamic update may allow variations in the time interval for synchronism. Within the limits are the **Dr** option, which represents the dynamic synchronism in real time, and the **St** option, which represents the synchronism based on the periodic static loading. The **Ddt** alternative represents the dynamic synchronism with a time interval (Δt), which varies according to the complexity and need for applications. This Δt is longer than the one used for the real-time synchronism option and shorter than the one used for the periodic loading.

A certain tree path may be invalid because of a certain set of values. This happens when the value combination of two or more parameters is incompatible. In the decision trees, these values are represented by ´--´.

2.3.1. The transactional environment decision tree. In figure 1, this tree is represented in a summarized way. Figure 2 shows some of the paths in detail.

Some remarks to figure 1 (summarized view) are:

- Paths (1) and (2) were regarded as not applicable, since according to the P1 parameter definition, a transactional system considered as typically static does not require the implementation of dynamic updates. Thus, it does not make sense to require a time interval (P3) as a real time or a determined interval, which are specific requirements for the dynamic synchronism;
- Path (3) leads to a static implementation with postponed synchronism, regardless of the parameters found at lower levels (P4 and P5 not shown on the summarized tree);
- Remark 1 above is also applicable to paths (4) and (5);
- Remark 2 above is also applicable to path (6);
- Paths (7) and (8) are the only paths that require a combined evaluation with P4 and P5 parameters.

The above summarized tree is not enough to show any result;

- In the representation of path (9), despite the fact that the application shows functional characteristics for the implementation of the dynamic synchronism (P1) and allows the implementation of the dynamic loading (P2), the time interval required is for the postponed synchronism, leading to a more suitable option – which is the update based on a periodic static loading that does not require the evaluation of P4 and P5 parameters (not shown on the summarized tree);
- Paths (10), (11) and (12) also lead to a typically static solution, since the transactional environment does not have an adaptation capacity that allows the dynamic maintenance implementation, thus

restricting the options available. Also in this case, the values indicated by the P4 and P5 parameters are irrelevant.

The tree on figure 2 shows path (7) and (8) of the summarized tree (fig. 1), including all the parameters (P1, P2, P3, P4 and P5).

The important remarks on the partial tree shown on figure 2 are:

- All the paths lead to a dynamic solution since P1 and P2 indicate that this type of synchronism is applicable and there are means of implementing it;
- As the complexity of parameters P4 and P5 increases, the time interval required for transmitting and processing information also increases. This indicates that the real-time synchronism is only possible when the complexities are lower.

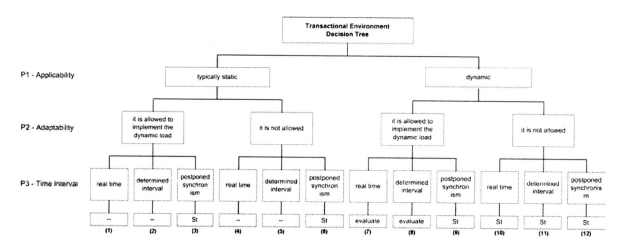

Figure 1. Summarized transactional environment decision tree

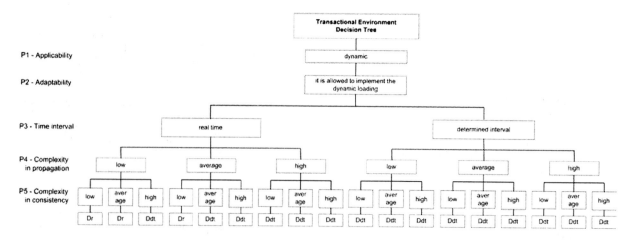

Figure 2. Detailed transactional environment decision tree

16

2.3.2. The analytical environment decision tree. The analytical environment decision tree can be represented as in figure 3.

Some remarks on this tree are relevant:

- Δt of path (4) can be regarded as longer than Δt of path (3), since the information cube loading normally requires a time longer than that of the

materialized view update, when the same set of information is evaluated. The same situation applies to paths (7) and (8);

- Path (5) is regarded as invalid, because the application uses aggregates (as per Parameter P6). However, there is no implementation of the required aggregates (as per Parameter P7).

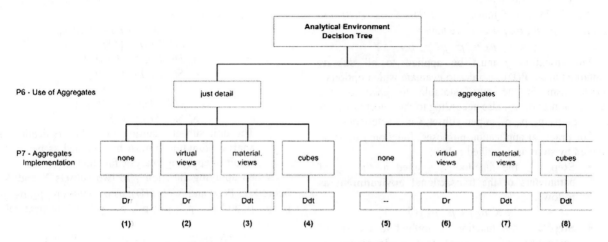

Figure 3. Analytical Environment Decision Tree

3. The parameter analysis function formalization

The parameters analysis must be made on information subsets contained in the data warehouse. Each of these subsets contains information from one or more business functions of the transactional environment applications. Thus, when defining a portion of the data warehouse information, one should assume that the analysis will be made considering this portion, also taking into account characteristics of the transactional environment from which the information was originated.

To formalize this analysis function, the definitions outlined below are required.

(i) **D** is a set that represents all the elements (information atomic value) belonging to a data warehouse defined as:
$$D = \{x \mid x \text{ is the data warehouse element}\}$$

(ii) **P(D)** set with all the subsets that represent portions of the data warehouse information, identified by **X** and represented as follows:
$$P(D) = \{X \mid X \subset D\} \text{ and}$$
$$(\forall x)\ (x \in X \rightarrow x \in D) \text{ that is, } X \subset D$$
Those portions of data warehouse elements make up an application and evaluation unit for the analysis function.

(iii) Domains to parameters P1, P2, P3, P4, P5, P6 and P7, as defined in Section 2.3, are:

$P1 = \{\text{'typically static', 'dynamic'}\}$;
$P2 = \{\text{'it is allowed to implement the dynamic loading', 'it is not allowed'}\}$;
$P3 = \{\text{'minimum possible', 'determined interval', 'postponed synchronism'}\}$;
$P4 = \{\text{'low', 'average', 'high'}\}$;
$P5 = \{\text{'low', 'average', 'high'}\}$;
$P6 = \{\text{'just detail', 'aggregates'}\}$;
$P7 = \{\text{'none', 'virtual views with aggregates', 'materialized views with aggregates', 'cubes'}\}$.

(iv) **A** is a set containing a combination of values applicable to parameters P1, P2, P3, P4, P5, P6 and P7, respectively, so that:
$$A = \{(p_1, p_2, p_3, p_4, p_5, p_6, p_7) \mid p_1 \in P1, p_2 \in P2, p_3 \in P3, p_4 \in P4, p_5 \in P5, p_6 \in P6, p_7 \in P7\}$$

(v) **B** is a set that represents the possible levels of synchronism, as per Section 2.3, so that:
$$B = \{\text{'Dr', 'Ddt', 'E'}\}$$
Just like in definition *(ii)*, the **P(B)** set is made up of all the subsets that represent combinations of the **B** set elements, so that:
$$P(B) = \{Y \mid Y \subset B\} \text{ and}$$
$$(\forall y)\ (y \in Y \rightarrow y \in B) \text{ that is, } Y \subset B$$

The **analysis function** and **parameter evaluation** are designated by γ and are applied to a portion of the data warehouse information, having the following definition:
$$\gamma(\mathbf{P(D)},\mathbf{A}) \rightarrow \mathbf{P(B)}$$
where:

P(D) represents the set containing the portions of information selected for the analysis process defined in *(ii)*;

A is a set of combinations of applicable values to parameters P1, P2, P3, P4, P5, P6 e P7, defined in *(iv)* and

P(B) is the **set** of values that represent possible levels of **synchronism** defined in *(v)*.

This is done as follows $X \subset P(D)$, $Y \subset P(B)$ and $(p_1, p_2, p_3, p_4, p_5, p_6, p_7) \in A$, we have:

$$\gamma(X, p_1, p_2, p_3, p_4, p_5, p_6, p_7) \to Y$$

This function γ must be applied to all subsets contained in set **P(D)**, in order to evaluate which option of synchronism is the most suitable to each of the information portions, also according to the selected values $p_1, p_2, p_3, p_4, p_5, p_6, p_7$, as per subset **X** characteristics.

For practical application purposes, function γ must be applied by steps as described below:

- **Step 1** – the function is applied to the set of parameters of the transactional **environment** as follows:

$$\gamma(X, p_1, p_2, p_3, p_4, p_5) \to Y_1$$

- **Step 2** – the function is applied to the set of parameters of the **analytical environment** as follows:

$$\gamma(X, p_6, p_7) \to Y2$$

- **Step 3** – the following function is applied over resulting sets **Y₁** and **Y₂**:

$$\delta: P(B) \times P(B) \to P(B)$$

so that δ determines, in P(B), the **unit subset** that contains the minimum implementation option. Function δ establishes the **precedence of complexity** among the synchronism options. The complexity definition of each option is related to the number of transactions that perform message exchanges between the transactional and analytical environments when the selected synchronism model is implemented. The complexity precedence among the options defined in item *(v)* of this section can be represented as:

$$St < Ddt < Dr$$

which indicates that synchronism option **St** is less complex, making less message exchanges than the others. That is because the static loading of a certain information portion is normally implemented in a set of batch processes, in which the information gathered from the transactional base is processed and later sent to the analytical environment as a batch. The most complex synchronism option is **Dr**, which processes the information gathered from the transactional systems and sends it synchronously to the analytical environment with the change in the source bases. We can image that, in certain

systems, the number of message exchanges between the transactional and the analytical environments – when this synchronism model is implemented – is very high. Based on the above reasoning, we conclude that option **Ddt** remains at an intermediate level in the precedence of complexity implemented by function δ.

Thus, it is possible to define the results of applying function δ as being:

$$\delta('St', 'Ddt', 'Dr') = \{'St'\};$$
$$\delta('St', Ddt') = \{'St'\};$$
$$\delta('Dr', Ddt') = \{'Ddt'\};$$
$$\delta('St', 'Dr') = \{'St'\};$$
$$\delta('Dr', 'Dr') = \{'Dr'\};$$
$$\delta('Ddt', 'Ddt') = \{'Ddt'\};$$
$$\delta('St', 'St') = \{'St'\};$$

The unit subset resulting from the application of analysis function δ must be regarded as being the result of applying analysis function γ.

When applying function γ to two subsets X and X', being $X \subset P(D)$ and $X' \subset P(D)$, using values $p_1, p_2, p_3, p_4, p_5, p_6, p_7$ and $p_1', p_2', p_3', p_4', p_5', p_6', p_7'$, respectively, we have:

$$\gamma(X, p_1, p_2, p_3, p_4, p_5, p_6, p_7) \to Y \text{ and}$$
$$\gamma(X', p_1', p_2', p_3', p_4', p_5', p_6', p_7') \to Y'$$

It may then happen that:

1. $X \cap X' = \varnothing$ that is, X and X' are disjoined sets or
2. $X \cap X' \neq \varnothing$

In situation (1), where the sets are disjoined, the synchronism model to be implemented in **X** and **X'** is the one defined by function γ, **Y** and **Y'**, respectively.

In situation (2), that is, in the event the portions are nondisjoined sets, after the application of the analysis function γ, we must proceed with the choice of the most suitable option, given the characteristics of the subsets of information involved. In this case, some options must be assessed, namely:

1. Establishment of three distinct portions of information:

   Portion X - (X ∩ X'), whose synchronism option will be of that initially defined by γ, that is, **Y**;

   Portion X' - (X ∩ X')}, whose synchronism option will be of that initially defined by γ, that is, **Y'**;

   Portion (X ∩ X'), whose synchronism option will be chosen according to the contents and form of use of the set of information. In this case, one should take into account that a certain synchronism option, different from **Y** or **Y'** may lead to temporary inconsistencies in the analytic base, until the three portions are again synchronized. Even so, this is a feasible alternative since this temporary alternative may not be relevant to the analytical applications involving this information portion.

2. Establishment of two information portions:

Portion X, whose synchronism option will be that initially defined by γ, that is, **Y**;

Portion X', whose synchronism option will be that initially defined by γ, that is **Y'**.

In this case, the strategies already defined are kept, but it is necessary to control the synchronism competition with regard to the information contained in (X ∩ X'). The reason for this is that this information will be updated by the synchronism processes for **X** and by the processes for **X'**, since they belong to both sets.

3. Establishment of just one information portion:

Portion (X ∪ X'), whose synchronism option must be decided by choosing the one causing less impact, which is considered here to be the one with less complexity. This can be achieved with the application of function δ to the unit subsets resulted from the application of analysis function γ to **X** and **X'**, that is, δ must be applied to subsets **Y** and **Y'**. Thus, the resulting final synchronism option in this case is defined by:

$$\delta(\gamma(\mathbf{X}, p_1, p_2, p_3, p_4, p_5, p_6, p_7), \gamma(\mathbf{X'}, p_1{}', p_2{}', p_3{}', p_4{}', p_5{}', p_6{}', p_7{}')) \rightarrow \mathbf{Y''}$$

it is being that Y'' = Y or Y'' = Y'.

4. The application of transactional and analytical classification of domains using a prototype

A prototype has been developed to implement the evaluation function described in Section 3 with the purpose of assessing real situations.

Another important aspect is that, over time, the transactional environment and the analytical environment characteristics change and may require a more suitable synchronism option.

In the transactional environment, for example, changes in the business requirements may happen, because of economic aspects. In the analytical environment, new users with new analysis requirements cause significant changes in the profile of the queries on this base. An increase in the data volume in the data warehouse may require different aggregation strategies, and new queries may require information that is more aggregate than the original one.

For this reason, the parameters used for choosing the synchronism option must be monitored frequently to identify possible changes in the behavior of the transactional and analytical environments. This should be like a behavior history record.

In addition to the choice of the most suitable synchronism, the prototype has also the purpose of simulating the gathering of analysis parameters and assessing their history record. This will be useful in the

data warehouse modeling with regard to the most suitable level of synchronism and will make it possible to have an adaptive system based on the history record of the adopted synchronism options.

The following sections describe the data structure used and the main functions implemented in this prototype.

4.1. The implementation of decision trees

The decision trees described in Sections 2.3.1 and 2.3.2 have been implemented as tables in a relational database. One table represents the transactional environment tree and the other the analytical environment tree. The choice of this implementation results from the ease of making queries on these tables by varying the parameter values according to the data portion profile being evaluated.

Each path of the decision tree, including the leaf, with the synchronism option has been implemented as a table line.

The prototype has functions for maintenance and loading of these tables.

4.2. The parameter evaluation function

A function has been implemented in the prototype that, after the parameters are supplied, it will search the decision tree for valid path(s) for the set of parameters supplied and will show the resulting synchronism option.

The algorithm used was based on functions γ and δ, whose descriptions are in Section 3.

Besides the values applicable to these parameters and shown in Section 2.3, the *any* option that has been added to indicate the ignoring of the value of a certain parameter or when this value is not unique. If the *any* value is chosen for one or more parameters, the decision tree search will cover the various paths, including, as a search argument, all the values that are possible for that (those) parameter(s).

Figure 4 shows the application of the analysis function to a certain set of specified values.

4.3. The evaluation of the information portion behavior

As referred to in the beginning of Section 3, the choice of a synchronism option is not definitive, since the characteristics of the transactional environment and the analytical environment will change over time. For this reason, a routine has been developed to simulate the periodic gathering of the parameter values. This will make it possible to identify the need for changing the implemented synchronism option later.

The prototype will gather the parameter values for the identified data portions and will apply the analysis function to obtain the synchronism option that results from the parameter tree path. It may happen that there is more than one valid path for that set of parameters. In this case, the prototype will store the distinct synchronism options found and the data will remain stored for a later analysis, identified by the portion code, gathering date and time. This information will form a history record of the changes occurred in the behavior of a certain data portion, making it possible to analyze in detail, the variations of the characteristics of the transactional and analytical environments over time.

Another routine has been developed to analyze the behavior history of a portion. As a result, it is possible to view all the data gathered for a certain portion. With the help of this function, the person responsible for the definition of the data warehouse synchronism model may assess the behavior variations that occur in certain time intervals in the transactional and analytical environments and change the synchronism option, if applicable. Figure 5 represents this function.

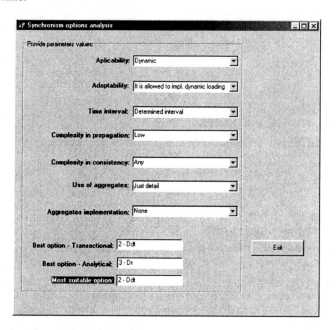

Figure 4. Prototype – choice of the synchronism option based on the analysis function

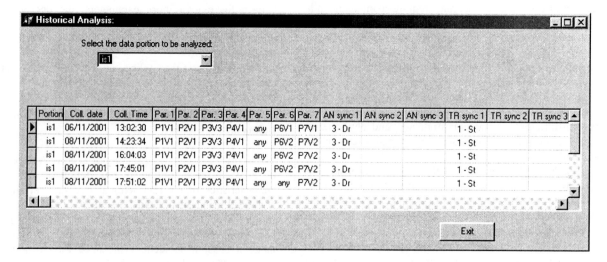

Figure 5. Prototype – analysis of the behavior history of an information portion.

5. Conclusion

In this paper, we have presented a customized solution for the differentiated processes of data update between the transactional and analytical environments. We have started from the assumption that both the data update processes and the data availability requirements are homogeneous in a data warehouse project.

Thus, we have proposed a hybrid data synchronism model for the data warehouse projects. To make such a hypothesis feasible, we have developed guidelines for classifying the transactions, both in the transactional and analytical environments. These guidelines have resulted in the definition of parameters according to Section 2.3 and its respective formalism is shown in Section 3. To validate such formalism, a prototype has been developed and is also shown in Section 3.

The result of this research shows that the existence of a hybrid data model for data warehouse projects is feasible. This feasibility makes the data synchronism processes more efficient and helps decrease the synchronism time between the transactional and analytical systems and also reduces the exaggerated hardware resources required for keeping an acceptable data synchronism for the environments at issue.

Our ongoing work includes:
1) The incorporation of the prototype developed for this paper through the data transfer tools available from the market; 2) the evaluation and extent of the hybrid data model for heterogeneous databases; 3) the elaboration of a methodology for use of hybrid models for data synchronism in data warehouse projects.

References

[1]   J. Albrecht et al.. "Management of Multidimensional Aggregates for Efficient Online Analytical Processing". *In: Proc. International Database Engineering and Applications Symposium (IDEAS'99)*, 1999.

[2]   Information Advantage, Decision Path™ Implementation Methodology. MyEureka!™ data warehouse requirements guide, 1999

[3]   P. M. Deshpande, K. Ramaswamy, A. Shukla, and J. F. Naughton. "Caching Multidimensional Queries Using Chunks". *In Proc. ACM SIGMOD Conference on Management of Data*, Seattle, WA, 1998.

[4]   I. Mumick, D. Quass and B. Mumick, "Maintenance of Data Cubes and Summary Tables in a Warehouse". *In Proc. ACM SIGMOD Conf. on Management of Data*, Arizona, May 1997

[5]   N. Stefanovic, J. Han, and K. Koperski. "Object-Based Selective Materialization for Efficient Implementation of Spatial Data Cubes". *In IEEE Transaction on Knowledge and Data Engineering*, 2000.

[6]   S. Agarwal, R. Agrawal, P. M. Deshpande, A. Gupta, J. F. Naughton, R. Ramakrishnan, and S. Sarawagi. "On the Computation of Multidimensional Aggregates". *In Proc. 22nd VLDB*, pages 506--521, Mumbai, Sept 1996

[7]   J. Han, J. Pei, G. Dong, and K. Wang, "Efficient Computation of Iceberg Cubes with Complex Measures", *In: Proc. ACM SIGMOD Int. Conf. on Management of Data (SIGMOD'01)*, Santa Barbara, CA, May, 45-56, 2001.

[8]   Y. Zhuge, H. Garcia-Molina, and J. L. Wiener, "Consistency Algorithms for Multi-source Warehouse View Maintenance", *In: Journal of Distributed and Parallel Databases, vol. 6, n. 1, 7-40*, 1998.

[9]   J. Chen, S. Chen, and E. Rundensteiner, "A Transactional Model for Data Warehouse Maintenance", *In Proc. ER 2002*, Tempere, Finland, September, 2002.

[10]   K. Salem, K. S. Beyer, R. Cochrane, and B. G. Lindsay, "How to Roll a Join: Asynchronous Incremental View Maintenance", *In Proc. ACM SIGMOD International Conference on management of Data*, Dallas, Texas, USA, May, 2000.

A Multi-resolution Block Storage Model for Database Design

Jingren Zhou
Columbia University
jrzhou@cs.columbia.edu

Kenneth A. Ross*
Columbia University
kar@cs.columbia.edu

Abstract

We propose a new storage model called MBSM (Multi-resolution Block Storage Model) for laying out tables on disks. MBSM is intended to speed up operations such as scans that are typical of data warehouse workloads. Disk blocks are grouped into "super-blocks," with a single record stored in a partitioned fashion among the blocks in a super-block. The intention is that a scan operation that needs to consult only a small number of attributes can access just those blocks of each super-block that contain the desired attributes. To achieve good performance given the physical characteristics of modern disks, we organize super-blocks on the disk into fixed-size "mega-blocks." Within a mega-block, blocks of the same type (from various super-blocks) are stored contiguously. We describe the changes needed in a conventional database system to manage tables using such a disk organization. We demonstrate experimentally that MBSM outperforms competing approaches such as NSM (N-ary Storage Model), DSM (Decomposition Storage Model) and PAX (Partition Attributes Across), for I/O bound decision-support workloads consisting of scans in which not all attributes are required. This improved performance comes at the expense of single-record insert and delete performance; we quantify the trade-offs involved. Unlike DSM, the cost of reconstructing a record from its partitions is small. MBSM stores attributes in a vertically partitioned manner similar to PAX, and thus shares PAX's good CPU cache behavior. We describe methods for mapping attributes to blocks within super-blocks in order to optimize overall performance, and show how to tune the super-block and mega-block sizes.

1 Introduction

The I/O behavior between main-memory and secondary storage is often a dominant factor in overall database system performance. At the same time, recent architectural advances suggest that CPU performance on memory-resident

data is also a significant component of the overall performance [14, 2, 3, 8]. In particular, the CPU cache miss penalty can be relatively high, and can have a significant impact on query response times [2]. Therefore, modern database systems should be designed to be sensitive to both I/O performance and CPU performance.

In this paper, we focus in particular on the storage model used to place data from relational tables on disk. Our goal is to create a scheme that yields good performance for workloads in which operations such as table scans are frequent relative to single-record insertions and deletions.

I/O transfers between memory and disk are performed in units of *blocks* (sometimes also called *pages*). I/O volume, measured in blocks, is a simple measure of an algorithm's I/O complexity. More detailed cost models take into account the physical characteristics of disk devices. For example, sequential I/O is faster than random I/O because the disk head usually does not need to seek.

Relational DBMSs typically pack records into slotted disk pages using the N-ary Storage Model (NSM). NSM stores records contiguously starting from the beginning of each disk page, and uses an offset (slot) table at the end of the page to locate the beginning of each record [11]. Given access to the page identifier (say via an index), a record can be retrieved using a single page of I/O. On the other hand, scans that access just a few columns must retrieve from the disk *all* blocks of the table, even though most of the transferred data is not relevant to the query. NSM has poor cache behavior because it loads the cache with unnecessary data [1].

The Decomposition Storage Model (DSM) [4] was proposed to minimize unnecessary I/O for those queries which only use a small number of attribute values in each record. DSM vertically partitions an *n*-attribute relation into *n* sub-relations, each of which is accessed only when the corresponding attribute values are needed. An extra record-id field (surrogate) is needed in each component sub-relation, so that records can be pieced together. Sybase-IQ uses vertical partitioning combined with bitmap indices for data warehouse applications [10]. For table scans involving just a few attributes, DSM requires considerably less I/O than

---

*This research was supported by NSF grant IIS-01-20939.

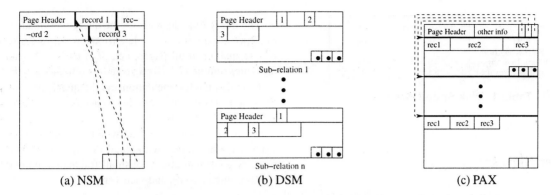

Figure 1. Three Data Placement Schemes

NSM. On the other hand, queries that involve multiple attributes from a relation must spend additional time to join the participating sub-relations together; this additional time can be significant [1]. Single-record insertions and deletions also require many pages of I/O rather than one for NSM (assuming no overflow).

To address the issue of low cache utilization in NSM, Ailamaki et al. introduce Partition Attributes Across (PAX), a new layout for data records [1]. Unlike NSM, within each page, PAX groups all the values of a particular attribute together on a minipage. During a sequential data access, PAX fully utilizes the cache resources, because only a number of the required attribute's values are loaded into the cache. However, compared with DSM, PAX doesn't optimize the I/O between disk and memory. Like NSM, PAX loads all the pages belonging to the relation into the memory for scans, regardless of whether the query needs *all* or only several of the attributes. Unnecessary attributes' values waste the I/O bandwidth between disk and memory and decrease the efficiency of database buffer pool management. The challenge is to design a storage model with better I/O performance without compromising the nice cache behavior.

In this paper, we introduce a new storage model called MBSM (Multi-resolution Block Storage Model) which takes care to address both the I/O performance and cache utilization in main-memory. It is similar to PAX in that attributes are stored columnwise as physically contiguous array segments. As a result, it shares PAX's good cache behavior. It is different from PAX in that it only loads pages with referenced attributes' values from disk. It also considers disk characteristics by placing the data carefully on disk to facilitate fast sequential I/O.

Disk blocks are grouped into "super-blocks," with a single record stored in a partitioned fashion among the blocks in a super-block. The intention is that a scan operation that needs to consult only a small number of attributes can access just those blocks of each super-block that contain the desired attributes. To achieve good performance given the

physical characteristics of modern disks, we organize super-blocks on the disk into fixed-size "mega-blocks." Within a mega-block, blocks of the same type (from various super-blocks) are stored contiguously. The cost of reconstructing a record from its partitions is small.

Experiments show that MBSM outperforms competing approaches such as NSM, DSM and PAX, for I/O bound decision-support workloads consisting of scans in which not all attributes are required. The average scan query cost for a workload based on the TPC-H benchmark is 70% less with MBSM than with either PAX or NSM, and comparable with DSM, which has high record reconstruction cost. For insertions and deletions of single records into the Lineitem table of TPC-H, the cost is 40% less for MBSM than for DSM.

The rest of this paper is organized as follows. Section 2 surveys current disk technology. Sections 3 and 4 explain our new storage model in detail and analyze it storage requirements. Section 5 lists the changes required of conventional database systems to use MBSM. Section 6 evaluates MBSM on both a synthetic workload and a workload based on the the TPC-H decision-support benchmark. We conclude in Section 7.

2 Disk Technology

Access time is the metric that represents the composite of all specifications reflecting random performance positioning in the hard disk. The most common definition is that access time is the sum of *command overhead time*, *seek time*, *settle time* and *rotational latency*. The *Track-to-Track Seek Time* is the amount of time that is required to seek between adjacent tracks. It is much smaller than the *Average Seek Time* from one random track (cylinder) to any other.

For the experimental results in this paper, we are using two state-of-the-art SCSI Ultra160 disks: the Seagate Cheetah X15 and the Quantum Atlas 10K II. Table 1 lists some of the specifications of both disks. Detailed descriptions can

	Seagate Cheetah	Quantum Atlas
Capacity (GB)	18.35	36.7
RPM	15K	10K
Avg. Rot. Latency (ms)	2	3
Avg. Seek Time (ms)	3.9	4.7
Adjacent Track Seek (ms)	0.5	0.6

Table 1. Disk Specifications

be found in [13, 9].

3 Super-Blocks

In this section, we introduce our new strategy for placing tables on disk for fast I/O performance. We assume we have a relation with n attributes, each attribute having size $s_i, 1 \leq i \leq n$. We assume for now that each attribute is fixed-sized. We will discuss variable-sized attributes in Section 3.3 and Section 7.

3.1 A First Step

As a starting point, imagine that we use a super-block with n component pages, one attribute per page. We place values for an attribute in one and only one of the n pages. Within each page, the values are stored contiguously, with an array of bits stored at the end of the page to keep track of free slots. The page structure is similar to a fixed-sized DSM page, except that we don't have surrogates for records. The record reconstruction cost is low since matching attributes can be found from their offsets, and there is no join needed. We stop inserting new records into a super-block once one of the component pages is full. Figure 2(a) shows a filled four-page super-block for a relation with four attributes. The shaded region represents empty space and the dashed lines within a page represent value boundaries. The super-block contains 3 records. The super-block is full only because the first page, which stores the largest attribute, is full.

Pages in a super-block can be accessed independently. With proper information, the database can access only the pages for the required attributes. The super-block has good cache behavior due to the high value density. The record reconstruction cost is low since matching attributes can be found from their offsets, and there is no join needed.

We measure the quality of this solution in terms of the average query time and the space needed to represent the relation. The space *overhead* is easily measured as the proportion of wasted space in a page that is lost due to fragmentation. In Figure 2(a), suppose we have R records to store. Then the space needed for the whole table is $4R/3$ pages. Since the data can actually fit in $3R/4$ pages without fragmentation (Figure 2(c)), the fragmentation overhead is $4R/3 - 3R/4 = 7R/12$ pages total, and the fragmentation constitutes 7/16 of each super-block.

The query time depends on the query workload. In Figure 2(a), a scan of any single attribute requires the reading of one quarter of all pages, i.e., $R/3$ pages. A scan of k attributes requires $kR/3$ pages in this scheme, $1 \leq k \leq 4$.

Note that the fragmentation and the query time are positively correlated. Although disk space is cheap these days, the issue is that the extra space resulting from fragmentation consumes precious I/O bandwidth. As a result, we expect that a solution with small average query time (our primary goal) will also have small fragmentation overhead (our secondary goal), and vice-versa.

3.2 A Second Step

The method of Section 3.1 works when s_i is roughly the same for all i. If not, it could yield a large fragmentation within many blocks of each super-block. For example, if $s_i + s_j \leq s_k$, it would better to put both the ith and jth attributes' values in one page and construct a super-block with $n - 1$ pages.

As shown in Figure 2(b), the reorganized super-block has less fragmentation. In particular, the fragmentation now constitutes just $1/4$ of each super-block. This reorganization does not change the time required for any single-attribute queries. However, a query that requires both attributes 2 and 3 is now significantly cheaper. For example, such scan query takes $R/3$ pages rather than $2R/3$ pages.

Suppose that p is the number of pages available in a super-block. The optimization problem is "Given different s_i, how does one place attribute values into a p-page super-block in a balanced way to get the least fragmentation?". Unfortunately, this is a well-known NP-complete problem. For a given p, this problem is usually referred to as parallel machine scheduling [6] (the attributes are jobs, the attribute sizes are processing time, the goal is to minimize the schedule length). There are several approximation algorithms for this problem. If we first sort the attributes (largest size first), and repeatedly place the next attribute on the least loaded page, we get a 4/3-approximation [7]. Note that in addition to performing the optimization described above, we are also able to optimize p to find a good layout scheme. We defer the discussion of how to choose p until Section 4. We remark that even when the number of attributes u is small, exhaustive search takes time of the order of $min(u, p)^u$, which is likely to be infeasible; when we consider splitting attributes in the next section, the search space becomes even larger.

In subsequent sections, we use this 4/3-approximation algorithm as the basis for a heuristic attribute placement method. As our optimization criteria become more complex, it becomes much more difficult to give theoretical bounds on the quality of the solutions. Our expectation is that even though the optimization criteria become more

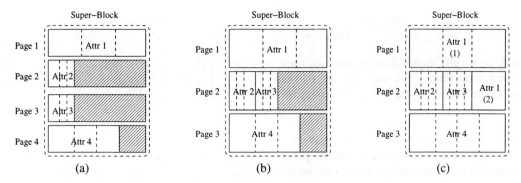

Figure 2. Super-Block Structure

complex, the underlying nature of the optimization remains the same, and so extensions of the 4/3-approximation algorithm will generate good solutions.

3.3   A Third Step

If one attribute size is much larger than the total size of the rest of the attributes, even the optimal placement can not guarantee small fragmentation. For example, in the TPC-H database benchmark [15], some relations have very large "comment" attributes. In Figure 2(b), the first attribute size is large, meaning that when the first page is full, there is still much empty space in the rest of the pages.

In this case, we may choose to place the largest attribute's value in more than one page in a super-block. For a given p and $S = \sum_{i=1}^{n} s_i$, we first divide any attribute whose size is larger than $\frac{S}{p}$ into several $\lceil \frac{S}{p} \rceil$-sized sub-attributes, plus one extra smaller sub-attribute if necessary. Then, we use the 4/3-approximation algorithm to place the resulting attributes.

Although we split large attributes into small sub-attributes in choosing plans, the real attribute values are not split vertically. Those pages which are designed to store an attribute's values are filled in order. During the insertion, the attribute's values are first placed into the first page until it is full, then we move to the next page, and so on. The order is important. As we will discuss in Section 5, the database uses the order information to compute in which page a specific record's attribute is stored.

Figure 2(c) shows the results of the previous relation after such a reorganization. The first attribute's values are stored in the first two pages (the first page is filled first). The super-block now stores four records, instead of three. As a result, there is zero fragmentation overhead. A scan of attribute 4 now takes $R/4$ pages rather than $R/3$, and a similar observation holds for a query that scans both attributes 2 and 3. On the other hand, a query that scans attribute 1 becomes more expensive, requiring $R/2$ pages rather than $R/3$, since both pages 1 and 2 need to be

consulted. The net effect on average query time depends on the query workload. We will formulate average query time as our optimization criterion in Section 3.4.

For variable-length attributes, we choose the largest possible size as the size of the attribute, since we don't have any prior-knowledge of its size distribution. By using the largest sizes of variable-length attributes, we know in advance how many records will be placed in each super-block, and we can avoid having to deal with overflows. On the other hand, we waste some space when variable-length attributes are large and are often smaller than their maximum size.

3.4   Cost-Based Super-Block

We now change our optimization criterion from fragmentation to average query time. For decision-support applications, we can optimize the super-block placement based on known workloads. Existing algorithms [4, 5] partition each relation based on an attribute affinity graph, which connects pairs of attributes based on how often they appear together in queries. These algorithms cannot be used directly to guide our super-block placement because they may generate sub-relations of different size, thus incurring much fragmentation in a super-block. Sometimes, it is impossible to compose a plan with both optimal attribute affinity and optimal fragmentation. Instead, we use attribute affinity heuristics to guide our partition.

First we develop a score function for each placement plan for the given workload. We assume that the workload consists of queries whose access patterns amount to scans of the referenced tables for the referenced attributes. This choice is reasonable for a decision-support application, where such queries are common, and are generally the most expensive. Suppose the cost of sequential data access is proportional to the number of disk pages read. Given the number of records in the relation, the total cost to read one page from each super-block is given by

$$disk\,pages_{read} = \frac{total\ number\ of\ records}{records\ per\ page}$$

$$records\ per\ page = \frac{page\ size}{\max_i(\sum attribute\ sizes\ in\ page_i)}$$

We define M as the maximum sum of the attribute sizes in any page of a super-block. The total I/O cost is thus M multiplied by the number of pages required from each super-block.

Let q_i equal the number of pages in a super-block referenced by the ith query in the workload. If one attribute's values are stored in more than one page, all the pages should be counted. Let p_i equal the probability of the ith query in the workload. The score function is defined as $M * \sum_i(q_i * p_i)$. Note that both M and q_i vary as the placement scheme varies. Our revised algorithm is given below:

- We define a affinity threshold. Any pair of attributes having affinity larger than the threshold are merged into a larger attribute with the size of the sum of the two attributes' sizes. More than two attributes may be merged in this way.

- Use the 4/3-approximation method to place attributes for each p (the range of p is discussed in Section 4.2).

- Split large attributes as described in Section 3.3. However, if an attribute actually consists of several attributes merged using the affinity criterion, and it is too big, undo one step of the merge procedure for this attribute, and rerun the placement algorithm.

- Choose the plan with minimal score.

4 Mega-Blocks

How do we organize the super-blocks on disk? Suppose we have a single-attribute scan query and the referenced attribute values are all in the first page of a super-block. If we place super-blocks contiguously, the database needs to read a page in one super-block, skip another $p - 1$ pages, then read a page and so on. What is the disk performance for this kind of access method, compared with sequential access?

We simulate this kind of interleaved reading on the Seagate Cheetah X15 disk[1] when $p = 4$. We define a reading-block as the number of blocks read per sequential access. The simulation reads a reading-block, skips another 3 reading-blocks, then reads a reading-block and so on. The simulation varies the reading-block size from 1 disk page to 100 disk pages, but the total number of pages read is kept the same. Figure 3 shows the results for reading 10,000 blocks. For reference, it takes 2 seconds to sequentially read 10,000 blocks.

---

[1] Similar results were obtained for the Quantum disk.

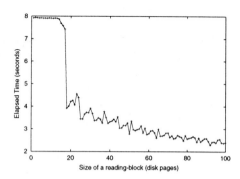

Figure 3. Simulation of Interleaved Reading

When the reading-block size is one disk page, we are simulating the case of a single-attribute scan over a 4-page super-block. The time taken is only a little less than sequentially reading all of the super-blocks. The time drops significantly when the reading-block is larger than one track (about 20 pages in this case). This is because when the reading-block is smaller than one track, the dominant cost is rotational latency; we have lost the benefit of sequential I/O optimization. As the reading-block size increases, the number of skip operations decreases and there is more sequential reading *within* each reading-block, so the time drops.

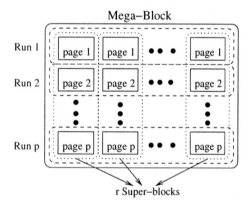

Figure 4. Mega-Block Structure

As we see, it is not a good idea to place super-blocks contiguously on disk. Instead, we group super-blocks into a *mega-block*. Corresponding pages are stored in one contiguous *run*. Figure 4 shows the structure of a mega-block. The size of a run is r disk pages. As we see in Figure 3 a lower bound on the run length should be the track size. The total size of a mega-block is $p * r$ disk pages.

If one attribute is stored in more than one page in a super-block, we try to arrange these pages in adjacent runs so that a single-attribute scan query can be answered by sequentially reading one or more runs in each mega-block. We also define the affinity of any two distinct pages in a

26

super-block as the largest affinity of any two attributes, one from each of the two pages. A pair of pages with higher affinity are more likely to be accessed in the same query. Thus, we also try to arrange such pages into adjacent runs.

4.1 Mega-Block Performance Issues

Disk Prefetching. Consider a query which involves a few (more than one) attributes. Database systems typically require that all the referenced attributes for the same record are available before performing any operations. A naive scan operator would have some drawbacks. For example, a two-attribute scan operator might first get the first block in the first run which stores the first required attribute, then seek to the first block in the second run which stores the second required attribute. After that, the scan operator goes back to the first run and reads the second block there. The disk head *thrashing* damages the performance.

Disk prefetching in buffer pool management can be useful in this case. During a sequential read, when we come to the first super-block of a mega-block, all blocks in the current run, instead of just one block, are read each time and buffered in memory. Disk heads move to the other run (or somewhere else) only after reading one run of blocks.

Updates and Lookups. Modifying a single attribute under MBSM requires one *random* disk write for the block containing the attribute value. Inserting or deleting a record requires $min(u, p)$ block writes, where u is the number of attributes in the relation. Those blocks belong to a single super-block and are stored on different runs of a mega-block. Fortunately, runs on a mega-block are close to each other, within a few tracks. Thus the update cost is 1 *random* disk write plus $min(u, p) - 1$ *nearby* disk writes. Under DSM, inserting or deleting a record requires u *random* disk writes because different sub-relations are not necessarily stored in an interleaved fashion. Note that MSBM handles bulk appends efficiently, since many records can be placed into a super-block, and data may be written one run at a time.

Lookups of a single record under MBSM require a number of page reads that depends on the number of attributes required. Lookups for a single attribute require one page of I/O. Lookups for v attributes require at most $min(v, p)$ pages, and even fewer if several of the requested attributes reside on the same page within a super-block.

4.2 Choosing p and r

We defined the size of a mega-block as $r * p$ (r is the size of a run and p is the size of a super-block). It is tempting to make mega-blocks large in order to get better performance. However, we will be forced to allocate disk space in mega-block sized units. The allocation unit on disk cannot be arbitrarily large, since disk fragmentation will result. Further, a large mega-block means that more disk pages have to be prefetched during sequential data access, which increases the memory requirements and decreases the efficiency of database buffer pool management. Different systems may have different mega-block sizes, according to their resources. Within a single system, the mega-block size may be different for different tables. In our experiments, we set 4 MBytes as the upper bound for mega-block size.

A larger run size r improves sequential I/O performance. The minimum r should be larger than a disk track size, as suggested by Figure 3. A larger super-block size p gives more opportunities for attribute placement, potentially improving query time and/or fragmentation. But increasing p increases the cost of insertion or deletion (until p exceeds the number of attributes, at which point the cost of insertions and deletions remains constant). Given the upper bound on $r * p$, there is a trade-off in choosing r and p.

In our experiments, we are considering a decision-support workload, which would have relatively few single-record insertions and deletions. Considering that different disk zones have different track sizes, we choose r as 30 disk pages, a little more than the average track size (23 disk pages). This gives an upper bound on p of 17 pages. We vary p from 1 to 17, and choose the plan of placement with minimum score. Ties are broken by choosing the plan with smaller p.

5 Database Implementation

Under MBSM, a record is identified by using the pair $<$ *superblock id, offset* $>$, instead of using the pair $<$ *page id, offset* $>$ in conventional database systems. A super-block is identified by the page id of its first block. Given the super-block size p and the run size r of the mega-block which stores it, the p blocks in a super-block are addressed by $pageid_{first\ block} + i * r$, $(0 \leq i \leq p - 1)$. These numbers p and r are stored in the catalog for each table that uses the MBSM format. Since the super-block id itself is a page-id, the query execution engine doesn't have to change record representations. All the address mapping happens in a layer just above the buffer manager. Layers above this address mapping are essentially unchanged; they simply have the illusion of a larger "page" size equal to the super-block size. The buffer manager itself still deals with pages. Indexes can also be built using MBSM addresses without knowing the mapping.

When an operator opens an MBSM-organized table for subsequent access, it is provided with a *descriptor*. In addition to the conventional arguments to open, the operator supplies a list of attributes to be referenced, and a flag to indicate whether the operator is performing a scan (or scan-like, sequential) operation. The descriptor remembers the flag. The descriptor also records the set of pages within each super-block that are needed to include all of the requested attributes. (This information is derived from the catalog.)

Subsequent operator requests include the record identifier (pg, $offset$) together with the descriptor d. If d indicates a sequential operation, and pg is the first super-block in the mega-block, then all runs for the pages identified in d are read into the buffer sequentially. (If those pages are already in the buffer, no actual I/O happens.) Otherwise, just the pages for the single super-block corresponding to the required pages specified in d are read into the buffer.

A subtle point in this latter operation is that there may be several pages in the super-block containing attribute values specified in the open operation. In that case, d records the offset boundaries corresponding to switches from one page to the next. The value of $offset$ is compared against these boundaries to locate the single page containing the attribute for the requested record.

Unlike the improved version of DSM [12], our method can support query plans involving the intersection of physical pointers (ie. $<$ $superblock\ id$, $offset$ $>$). Such plans are often useful when multiple indexes are available.

We now describe additional changes in behavior of other components of a database system.

Buffer Manager. There is little change in the buffer manager. The request to the buffer manager is still the page id. Under MBSM, the buffer manager needs to be able to allocate at least one mega-block to the scanned table to avoid thrashing. A buffer replacement policy that was aware of sequential MBSM access patterns would be desirable.

Disk Space Manager. The disk space manager needs to respond to requests for allocations of mega-blocks at a time. Note that not all tables need to use MBSM, so the disk space manager may be allocating space at several granularities. Mega-blocks should be allocated in a contiguous sequence where possible, but this is not required. MBSM can adapt itself to data striping (such as RAID) by increasing the run size. Operations on each data disk in the array still maintain good sequential I/O performance.

Lock and Recovery Manager. Attributes of a record are stored in different pages in a super-block. Traditional page-level locking could become super-block-level locking under MBSM. Generally, under MBSM, updates on records touch more pages because attributes are stored across pages. Thus, there might be less concurrency under page-level locking. (This issue is relatively unimportant for data warehousing workloads.)

Query Optimizer. The cost model should be revised, considering the efficiency of sequential scans under MBSM. Catalog information can be used during optimization. The I/O cost is (essentially) the cost of retrieving just the referenced pages.

6 Experimental Evaluation

In this section, we evaluate and compare four data placement schemes: MBSM, NSM, DSM and PAX on both synthetic and TPC-H based workloads. We conduct the experiments on a Dell Precision 330 PC, with a 1.8Mhz Pentium 4 CPU and 1G Rambus Memory. This computer is running the RedHat Linux 7.1 operating system. We treat the two SCSI disks as raw devices. Our experiments read or write directly from or directly to the devices independent of the filesystem. Before operations, we clear both the disk cache and the operating system buffer caches. The size of a memory page and a disk page is 8KB.

MBSM stores attributes in a vertically partitioned manner similar to PAX, and thus shares PAX's good CPU cache behavior (which is thoroughly studied in [1]). PAX saves at least 75% of NSM's cache stall time, and it is also better than DSM. Due to space limitations, we do not show cache-related experiments. [1] also demonstrates that DSM incurs high reconstruction cost. Our experiments directly simulate the I/O behavior by generating I/O operations on raw disk devices; we do not employ a database system.

6.1 Projectivity Analysis

To demonstrate how MBSM works for different query projectivity, we create a workload consisting of one relation R and variations of queries which involve different numbers of attributes. Relation R contains eight 8-byte attributes and is populated with 10 million records. The super-block in MBSM has eight pages. Values for one attribute go to one page in a super-block. This is a synthetic "best-case" for MBSM because there is no fragmentation. This example is used for illustration of the potential performance benefits.

We vary the query projectivity from one attribute to all eight attributes. Figure 5(a) shows the disk volume requested to answer different queries. MBSM has the least disk volume requested for each query. For NSM and PAX, all the disk pages must be requested for all the queries. DSM has the most disk volume request when the query involves more than six out of eight attributes. Note that the final columns of Figure 5(a) show the disk space used for each scheme. DSM uses the most space because there is a 4-byte logical record ID for each record in every sub-relation. Our scheme used slightly less space than PAX because we save the space of pointers to minipages within PAX pages.

To gain better I/O performance, we assume both NSM and PAX pages are stored contiguously on disk. For DSM, each sub-relation is stored as a contiguous big file and sub-relations are stored one after another. This disk organization actually favors DSM. In practice, DSM sub-relations can be stored at different locations on disk. MBSM stores the records in mega-blocks of size 4 MB, which translates into a

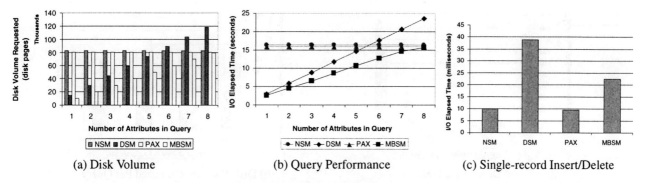

| (a) Disk Volume | (b) Query Performance | (c) Single-record Insert/Delete |

Figure 5. Synthetic Workloads

run length r of 64 pages. Figure 5(b) compares the speed of four schemes as a function of the number of attributes in the query for an implementation on the Seagate disk. Although MBSM requests the fewest disk pages for all the queries, it is about the same as DSM at first. This is because for the first query, all the pages requested for DSM are from one sub-relation and that sub-relation is stored contiguously and is accessed sequentially. In MBSM, records are stored in mega-blocks. It reads one run in a mega-block, skips the remaining runs and goes to the next mega-block and so on. This slows the throughput of the disk slightly. As the number of attributes increases, MBSM reads more tracks in a mega-block and the speed overhead is less important than the fewer disk pages transferred. (Similar results were observed on the Quantum disk.) We don't include the record reconstruction cost for DSM in the comparison. As the number of attributes increases, we expect the overall cost of DSM to be much higher [1].

Figure 5(c) compares the performance of inserting or deleting a record in the four schemes. Under NSM and PAX, only one random disk write for the block containing the new or old record is required. Both MBSM and DSM require eight disk writes. However, the performance is different in that MBSM has one random disk write and the remaining writes are in adjacent or nearby tracks.

6.2 TPC-H Workloads

This section compares the different storage models when running a decision-support workload based on TPC-H. We conducted experiments on a factor 1 TPC-H database, generated using the *dbgen* software distributed by the TPC [15]. The database includes attributes of type integer, floating point, date, fixed-length string and variable-length string. We convert variable-length attributes to fixed-length attributes by allocating space equal to their maximum size. The workload consists of all 22 TPC-H queries and we assume each of them has the same probability of execution.

We do not actually execute the 22 queries. Instead,

we reformulate the actual queries into "abstract" queries. This reformulation allows us to focus on the aspects of the query most relevant to MBSM, namely which relations are scanned, and which attributes are accessed in the same query. An abstract query is a set of entries of the form "table-name.column-name". (We omit the table name when the table is clear.) For a TPC-H query, every column syntactically mentioned in the query is part of this set. For example, Query Q14 from TPC-H is reformulated as {p_type, p_partkey, l_partkey, l_extendedprice, l_discount, l_shipdate}.

We interpret an abstract query as requiring a single scan through all records in the referenced tables, accessing at least the attributes mentioned in the set. That the queries require scans is reasonable since we are assuming a decision-support workload in which a large fraction of all records are touched by most queries. Index-based access is usually not competitive due to random I/O. That the queries require *single* scans is an approximation. It is conceivable that the data is sufficiently large that multiple scans would be required for hash joins, for example. Nevertheless, we believe that abstract queries are sufficiently descriptive to capture important aspects of the workload.

We generate the attribute affinity for each relation from the workload. The attribute affinity threshold is set empirically as 4: if any two attributes from the same relation appear together in more than 4 out of the 22 queries, we try to assign them into one page in the super-block. For variable-length attributes, we use their maximum size as the attribute size. Table 2 shows the super-block size p chosen by the optimization algorithm for the six largest TPC-H tables. (The tables NATION and REGION are too small to be partitioned further.) Recall that we varied p from 1 to 17, as discussed in Section 4.2. Details of some of the assignments can be found in [16].

Figure 6(a) shows the disk space required for the six largest TPC-H tables in the different storage models. DSM uses significantly more space than the others for table LINEITEM because the table consists of 16 relatively small

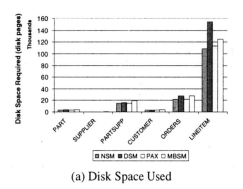

(a) Disk Space Used

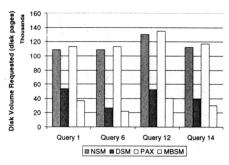

(b) Disk Volume Requested Per Query

Figure 6. Storage Performance for TPC-H Workloads

Table	Columns	Pages per Super-Block	Frag. Overhead
PART	9	17	3.53%
SUPPLIER	7	17	4.62%
PARTSUPP	5	11	0.45%
CUSTOMER	8	13	4.7%
ORDERS	9	15	4.67%
LINEITEM	16	17	5.27%

Table 2. TPC-H Table Partitions

attributes, so the 4-byte surrogate overhead cannot be ignored. Our scheme uses a little more space than NSM and PAX for two reasons. First, there could be some fragmentation within the super-blocks because we cannot guarantee each page within a super-block is exactly full. Second, we use the maximum possible size for variable-length attributes. The actual average size is smaller than the maximum size, and all of PAX, DSM and NSM use only the space required by the actual attribute value.

The layouts of Table 2 are optimized for the overall workload of all 22 queries. We choose four TPC-H queries, Q1, Q6, Q12 and Q14, as examples to demonstrate individual query performance on this layout. Queries 1 and 6 are range queries on the LINEITEM table, with multiple aggregates and predicates. Queries 12 and 14 are equijoins of LINEITEM with another table; they involve additional selection predicates, and they compute conditional aggregates.

Figure 6(b) shows the disk volume requested for the four queries in the different schemes. Figure 7(a) shows the I/O elapsed time for the four queries. Figure 7(c) shows the average I/O elapsed time for the 22 queries. Both DSM and MBSM read fewer disk pages and perform faster, compared to NSM and PAX. While DSM looks competitive, remember that we have excluded the record reconstruction cost. If this cost is included, the overall cost of DSM is much higher than MBSM. Figure 7(b) shows the performance of single-record insert/delete operation on the biggest table LINEITEM. Both NSM and PAX requires only one block write, while DSM and MBSM each require for 16 block writes. MBSM is faster than DSM due to the proximity of

the block that need to be written.

Figure 7(d) shows how the quality of the layout varies as we adjust p and r, keeping $p * r$ (i.e., the mega-block size) bounded by 4MB. Given a run size, the y-axis shows the workload average I/O elapsed time for the best table layouts. With larger r, the potential I/O speed increases. But smaller p means that more attributes could be stored in one page in a super-block. Queries which involve only a few attributes may end up requiring more disk pages than necessary. As we can see, $r = 30$ seems to balance the competing aims; this is the value used for the previous experiments.[2]

7 Conclusion and Future Work

We have proposed a new storage model called MBSM, which stores records in a partitioned way in a super-blocks, and then organizes super-blocks on disk into mega-blocks. MBSM is most suitable for decision-support workloads that frequently execute table scans.

- Compared to NSM and PAX, MBSM requests fewer disk pages and uses 70% less I/O processing time for a decision-support workload involving table scans. MBSM shares PAX's good CPU cache behavior.

- Compared to DSM, MBSM's scan performance is comparable. However, MBSM's cache performance is better because no surrogates are involved and MBSM has better insert/update I/O performance. Further, MBSM doesn't require a join to reconstruct the records while DSM has high reconstruction cost [1].

We plan to investigate several directions in future research. Queries seldom use large variable-length attributes, such as "comment" etc. It could be a better idea to store these attributes separately in DSM, and to use MBSM for

---

[2]The results were qualitatively similar for the Quantum disk, but a larger value of r was optimal.

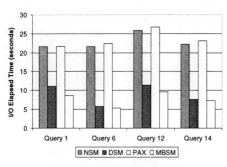

(a) Query Performance

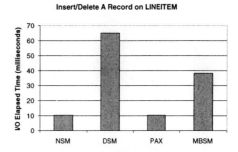

(b) Single-record Insert/Delete Performance

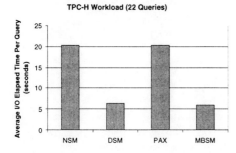

(c) Average Query Performance

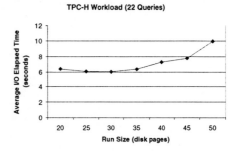

(d) Mega-Block Design Trade-off

Figure 7. Performance for TPC-H Workloads

the fixed-sized attributes (with one surrogate). Alternatively, one could store variable-length attributes in a pointer-based way using a heap to avoid wasted space. For this second option, one needs a method to handle page overflows, and one may not be able to uniquely identify the physical page containing the required attribute. It is conceivable that a probabilistic analysis of attribute size and query reference patterns could do a reasonable job of ensuring good performance without wasting space.

References

[1] A. Ailamaki, D. J. DeWitt, M. D. Hill, and M. Skounakis. Weaving relations for cache performance. In *Proceedings of VLDB Conference*, 2001.

[2] A. Ailamaki, D. J. DeWitt, M. D. Hill, and D. A. Wood. DBMSs on a modern processor: Where does time go? In *Proceedings of VLDB conference*, 1999.

[3] P. Boncz, S. Manegold, and M. Kersten. Database architecture optimized for the new bottleneck: Memory access. In *Proceedings of VLDB Conference*, 1999.

[4] G. P. Copeland and S. F. Khoshafian. A decomposition storage model. In *Proceedings of ACM SIGMOD Conference*, pages 268–279, 1985.

[5] D. W. Cornell and P. S. Yu. An effective approach to vertical partitioning for physical design of relational databases. *IEEE Transactions on Software Engineering*, 16(2), 1990.

[6] R. Graham, E. Lawler, J. Lenstra, and A. Kan. Optimization and approximation in deterministic sequencing and scheduling: a survey. *Annals of Discrete Mathematics*, 5:287–326, 1979.

[7] R. L. Graham. Bounds on multiprocessing timing anomalies. *SIAM Journal of Applied Mathematics*, 17(2):416–429, 1969.

[8] S. Manegold, P. Boncz, and M. Kersten. What happens during a join? Dissecting CPU and memory optimization effects. In *Proceedings of VLDB Conference*, 2000.

[9] Maxtor Corp. Atlas 10K II overview, 2002. Available from http://www.maxtor.com/.

[10] P. O'Neil and D. Quass. Improved query performance with variant indexes. In *Proceedings of ACM SIGMOD Conference*, 1997.

[11] R. Ramakrishnan and J. Gehrke. *Database Management Systems*. McGraw-Hill, 2 edition, 2000.

[12] R. Ramamurthy, D. J. DeWitt, and Q. Su. A case for fractured mirrors. In *Proceedings of VLDB conference*, 2002.

[13] Seagate Corp. Cheetah X15 product manual, volume 1, 2002. Available via http://www.seagate.com/.

[14] A. Shatdal, C. Kant, and J. F. Naughton. Cache conscious algorithms for relational query processing. In *Proceedings of VLDB Conference*, pages 510–521, 1994.

[15] Transaction Processing Performance Council. TPC Benchmark H. Available via http://www.tpc.com/tpch/.

[16] J. Zhou and K. A. Ross. A multi-resolution block storage model for database design. *Technical Report CUCS-007-03, Department of Computer Science, Columbia University*, 2003.

Data Mining I

Bitmap Techniques for Optimizing Decision Support Queries and Association Rule Algorithms

Xiaohua Hu
College of Info. Science
Drexel University
Philadelphia, PA 19104
thu@cis.drexel.edu

T.Y.Lin
Dept. of Computer Science
San Jose State University
San Jose, California 95192
tylin@cs.sjsu.edu

Eric Louie
IBM Almaden Research Center
650 Harry Road
San Jose, CA 95120
ewlouie@almaden.ibm.com

Abstract

In this paper, we discuss some new bitmap techniques for optimizing decision support queries and association rule algorithm. We first show how to use a new type of predefined bitmap join index (pre-join_bitmap_index) to efficiently execute complex decision support queries with multiple outer join operations involved and push the outer join operations from the data flow level to the bitmap level and achieve significant performance gain. Then we discuss a bitmap based association rule algorithm. Our bitmap based association rule algorithm Bit-AssocRule doesn't follow the generation-and-test strategy of Apriori algorithm and adopts the divide-and-conquer strategy, thus avoids the time-consuming table scan to find and prune the itemsets, all the operations of finding large itemsets from the datasets are the fast bit operations. The experimental results show Bit-AssocRule is 2 to 3 orders of magnitude faster than Apriori and AprioirHybrid algorithms. Our results indicate that bitmap techniques can greatly improve the performance of decision support queries and association rule algorithm, and bitmap techniques are very promising for the decision support query optimization and data mining applications.

1. Introduction

In this paper we present some novel bitmap techniques in two new areas. We first present a new method to use bitmap join indexes to efficiently execute complex DSS queries with multi-tables with outer join conditions, and then we discuss a bitmap-based algorithm in finding association rules from large databases. In DSS application, for multi-table joins with outer join operations, no work is done to use the performance advantages of the bitmap

indexes, all the execution of the complex queries with outer join operations are done in the data flow level in an "as written" manner. With the outer join operations are becoming more and more frequent in the DSS and DM queries, it is very important to push down part of the join operations to the bitmap join indexes level to take the advantage of the efficiency of the bitmap join indexes to efficiently execute common multi-table joins with outer join operation involved. In our method, a predefined join table (prejoin table) is created for multi-table join based on the full outer join conditions. A set of prejoin_bitmap_indexes is created corresponding to the full outer join conditions in the multi-table joins. An efficient method to calculate the foundset for the multi table outer joins by using prejoin_bitmap_indexes for multiple outer join operations is proposed. Our method uses prejoin_bitmap_indexes, which can resolve join predicates using the bitmap indexes to determine a found set very efficiently. Next we present a bitmap-based algorithm Bit-AssocRule for finding association rules from large databases. Traditional Apriori algorithms require multiple full table scans and generates and tests the itemsets in order to find association rules from large database. Our Bit-AssocRule avoids these time-consuming operations and relies on the fast bit operations to find the large itemsets. With bitmap techniques, we can greatly improve the performance of the association rule algorithms.

The rest of the paper is organized as follows: we give an overview of bitmap indexes and introduce the new bitmap techniques in Section 2. In Section 3 we present the prejoin_bitmap_index based algorithm for outer join DSS queries optimization with some examples. In section 4 we present the bitmap-based association algorithm Bit-AssocRule and the comparison results of Bit-AssocRule with Apriori and AprioriHybrid. Section 5 concludes the paper with some discussions

2. Bitmap Indexes and New Bitmap Techniques

Various bitmap techniques have been studied extensively and applied successfully in various application domains [5,12,14,15,16,19,20,22,23,27,28,30,31,32].

In our study we noticed that there is a relationship between a column's cardinality (i.e., the number of distinct values) and its usage within the SQL language and the DSS & DM usage model. A column that has a low cardinality tends to be used most frequently in DSS within SQL WHERE clauses and GROUP BY clause. When use in SQL WHERE clause, a high cardinality column is usually a range predicate []. Based on this consideration, we propose a hybrid bitmap technique which uses projection indexes, B-Tree indexes, traditional bitmap indexes, and advanced high-cardinality bitwise indexes to store and manipulate all data.

Our implementation of the low cardinality indexing technique differs from other implementation in several ways. Most implementations, including the one used by Oracle, are only useful at the very low end. This is because as the cardinality increases, so does the size of the index. What basically occurs is that the number of zero bits in the bitmaps increases with the cardinality. The number of 1 bits increases with the number of rows. Hence, as the cardinality increases with the same number of rows, more and more zero bits occur with the same number of 1 bit. The increasing popular zero bits allow the compression to get better and better. Using this technique we have been able to extend the range of usable cardinality to a very large number.

A problem with using bitmap indexes for a column with high cardinality is its high storage costs and potentially high expression evaluation costs. One method for dealing with the problem of using bitmap index on high-cardinality attributes is to compress the bitmap. The form of compression is the most crucial aspect of such an implementation, since it must be designed both to save disk space for sparse bitmaps, and also to efficiently perform the operations AND, OR, NOT and COUNT. [21]. We have two types of bitmap indexes: index for high cardinality column with symbolic values, index for high cardinality column with numeric values. In this approach, the data column is broken up into N

number of separate bitmaps. One bitmap for each bit of precision in the quantity being indexed. Organizing the data in this way greatly reduces the size of the data. A considerable body of work has been devoted to the study of bitmap index compression. The use of bitmap compression has many potential performance advantages: less disk space is required to store the indexes, the indexes can be read from disk into memory fast, and more indexes can be cached in memory. A wide variety bitmap representations and compressions have been proposed, such as Verbatim, Run Length Encoding (RLE), Gzip, ExpGol and BBC [4]. Our bitmap techniques extend the range of the unique value of a column to > 10000, by combining bitmap and compression. As the number of values increases, the amount of compression increases. The bitwise index proposed by O'Neil [21] is close to our High cardinality indexes

3. A Prejoin_Bitmap_Index Based Algorithm for Outer Join DSS Query Optimization

In this section we will discuss our new prejoin_bitmap_index based algorithm for outer join DSS queries optimization and the integration of it into a commercial data flow based query engine. For explanation purpose, we use a Volcano style data flow based query engine [12] as the underlying query engine to implement our algorithm. Each query plan in the query engine is a tree of operators, all operators are implemented as iterators, i.e., they support a simple open-next-close protocol, but our algorithm is easily extended to any other data flow based query engine.

We have implemented various types of bitmap indexes based on the cardinality of the data columns described in Section 2. Based on the query at hand, the best index can be chosen to run the query fast. The factors in choosing the proper bitmap index for attributes depend on the number of distinct values of the attribute, type of the queries the attributes will most likely to be involved [3]. Optimizer will choose the correct index when evaluating a query. The type of indexes chosen would be based on how a column will be used in general and not on specific queries.

3.1 Some Limitations of the Current Database Systems for DSS Queries Optimization

Currently there are two approaches to process complex decision support queries with multi-table joins to improve query performance: (1) to create join indexes or/and (2) to store the join result of two or more tables in advance which is often used in the queries. Join index [20,23,30] can be used to avoid actual joins of tables, or to greatly reduce the volume of the data. This join technique speeds join processing by processing multiple bit vector indexes and has been used in some commercial RDBMS. For example, Informix/Red Brick (now part of IBM) RDBMS adopts the first approach to create STARindex [27,28] for multi table joins and dramatically accelerate join performance. These two approaches work very well in multi table joins without multi outer join operations because outer join operations need to reserve those rows even though they don't satisfy the join conditions. If these tables are joined together through outer join conditions, then these methods will not generate the correct answers because all of them rely on AND or OR the bitmap indexes involved in the join conditions (inner join, natural joins and so on), but the semantic meaning of outer joins is so different, just ANDed or ORed these bitmap indexes is not enough to get the correct answer.

To enable the current RDBMS to support outer join operations through bitmap indexes, some modifications and extensions are needed because of the following limitations of the current data flow based query engine:

(1) In the current data flow engine; the execution order of the predicate is not exactly the same sequence as predicates appear in the query statement. The execution order of the predicates is determined by the cost of selectivity in most systems. This is fine and actually can improve query performance in a lot of circumstances without outer join involved because changing the execution orders of predicates would not affect the semantic meaning of the query, so the results are the same. But for multi table joins with outer join conditions, the story is totally different. It is essential to reserve the predicate orders in order to guarantee the correct results because outer joins are not commutative, so we need to find the found set for the outer joins based on the strictly order of the join conditions in the query plan tree. For multi table joins with outer join operations, the order of the join indexes access must have the same order as the outer joins in the original join sequences.

(2) For join conditions on an outer join, these will be bitmap join indexes, which are the bitmaps for that join conditions for inner, right outer and left outer. These are then ANDed and ORed with the current found set. The

rules for ANDing and Oring these bitmap indexes for the leaf joins in the join tree and for higher level joins need to be different to not lose outers from earlier joins in the join sequences. This requires that a bitmap join index need to know whether its child at each side is another join or base table. But of the current bitmap indexes for join nodes, there is no mechanism to tell the difference and store the essential information. All current bitmap join indexes such as STARindex of Informix and bitmap join index of O'Neil [20] point to two base tables only, thus could not deal with multiple outer join operations. For all commercial RDBMSs products, complex queries with outer joins are executed by the query engine in an "as written" manner. This requires that a bitmap join index needs to know whether its child at each side is another join or a base table.

3.2 Predefined Join Table and Prejoin_Bitmap_Indexes

A new type of bitmap join index called prejoin_bitmap_index is proposed to solve the problems discussed above. A predefined join table (**prejoin table** for short) is a full denormalized table of all columns from participating tables from full outer joins. A prejoin table can join more than two tables in a single operation, so it overcomes the problems that plaque traditional OLTP RDBMS products. All the predicates local to the prejoin table can be solved using the prejoin_bitmap_indexes.

Definition 1: A Prejoin Table is a denormalized table storing and indexing the full denormalized result set of all columns from participating tables from full outer join.

The prejoin table has the following characteristics:

- Join more than two tables
- Support full outer joins in a star relationship as well as linear join chain
- Multi-column join keys
- Multi-table join queries with more than one outer joins.

For each join relation in the prejoin table, a set of prejoin_bitmap_index is created. Since the results of a full outer join of two tables can be perceived as three parts: INNER, LEFT and RIGHT. The INNER part is those rows from both tables which match the join conditions, The LEFT part is those rows from the first table which fails the join conditions while the RIGHT part is those rows from the second table. So it is natural to define three bitmap indexes for a full outer join relation. If there are multiple join relations, the join relation should tell whether the tables involved in the join relation are base tables or not because this information determines the semantic meaning of how the bitmap indexes of this join relation should be used. A prejoin_bitmap_index is able to point to the derived tables, not just the base table. This is one of the advantages of our prejoin_bitmap_index over STARindex or the bitmap index proposed in [3,20,23,30,31, 32].

Each prejoin_bitmap_index consists of three bitmaps as follow:

IJIndex: The inner join of the result of the two tables with all conditions applied.

LJIndex: All rows from the left table not included in the IJIndex, extended with NUL values for each column of the right table.

RJIndex: All rows from the right table not included in the IJIndex, extended with NULL values for each column of the left table.

Suppose we have a Create Prejoin Table command as follow: **Create Prejoin Table FT_1T_2 as ((F Full Outer Join T_1 On $A_2=A_1$) Full Outer Join T_2 on $A_3=A_6$)**

For this prejoin table FT_1T_2, two prejoin_bitmap_indexes are created (Table 3). Jindex1 corresponds the join relation between base tables F and T_1 on join condition $A_2=A_1$, Jindex2 corresponds to the join relation between the derived table (the result of F Full Outer Join T_1 on join condition $A_2=A_1$) and the base table T_2 on join condition $A_3=A_6$. For each type of outer join (left, right, full), just put the proper "pieces" together using UNION All by using the corresponding prejoin_bitmap_index.

Example 3.1: to compute the foundset FS of (F Left Outer Join T_1 On $A_2=A_1$), just ORed the two bitmaps LJIndex of Jindex1: FS=LJIndex OR IJIndex = (0 0 0 0 0 1 1 0 0) OR (1 1 1 1 1 0 0 0 0) = (1 1 1 1 1 1 1 0 0). For foundset of (F Full Outer Join T_1 On $A_2=A_1$), just ORed all the three bitmaps of Jindex1: FS=(0 0 0 0 0 1 1 0 0) OR (1 1 1 1 1 0 0 0 0) OR (0 0 0 0 0 0 1 0)=(1 1 1 1 1 1 1 0)

A_1
a
b
d
e

Table T1

A_6	A_7
2	4
3	2
3	5
8	1

Table T_2

A_8
u
v
w
x

TableT_3

A_2	A_3	A_4	A_5
a	1	u	o
b	2	v	o
d	3	w	p
d	4	x	q
f	5	z	t
g	7	z	s

Table F

No.	A_2	A_3	A_4	A_5	A_1	A_6	A_7
1	a	1	u	o	a	null	null
2	b	2	v	o	b	2	4
3	d	3	w	p	d	3	2
4	d	3	w	p	d	3	5
5	d	4	x	q	d	null	null
6	f	5	z	t	null	null	null
7	g	7	z	s	null	null	null
8	null	null	null	null	e	null	null
9	null	null	null	null	null	8	1

Table 2: FT_1T_2

0	1	0	1	0	0
0	1	0	0	1	0
0	1	0	0	1	0
0	1	0	0	1	0
0	1	0	1	0	0
1	0	0	1	0	0
1	0	0	1	0	0
0	0	1	1	0	0
0	0	0	0	0	1

LJIndex	IJIndex	RJIndex	LJIndex	IJIndex	RJIndex

Table 3: Prejoin_bitmap_index **Jindex1** & **Jindex2**

3.3 Finding the Prejoin Table in the Query Execution Plan

In order to use prejoin_bitmap_index in the data flow query engine, we simply add a new type of data flow node, called prejoin table node, which also follows the open-next-close interface of Volcano style engine [12]. In the query execution plan, a prejoin table is a subclass of the table node, but a table node only refers to one base table while a prejoin table can refers to two or more tables depending on the number of tables involved in the full outer join. Also there is an additional member for the prejoin table node: **Join_Relation_Tree.** Join_Relation_Tree is the join sequence tree, which matches the join order specified in the prejoin table command and is used to control the construction of the foundset bitmap (FSBM) for the prejoin table node. For each join node in the Join_Relation_Tree, there is a prejoin_bitmap_index, which consists of 3 parts: **IJIndex, LJIndex** and **RJIndex.** Four different join results can be derived based on the different combinations of these three bitmap indexes. For example, the IJIndex is the inner join result of this join node, the union of LJIndex and IJIndex is the left outer join of this join node, the union of the IJIndex and RJIndex are the right outer join while the union of IJIndex, LJIndex and RJIndex are the full outer join of the join node.

For each join node in the query execution plan, we associate it with three members: **Join_Key_Type, Join_Predicate_Vector** and **Join_Operator,** which will help us to find whether the join node is part of a prejoin table or not. The Join_Key_Type is set to Table_Table if the join node links two base tables. It is set to Join-Table if the left child of the join node is a join node (also called derived table) and the right child is a base table. If the left child is a Table node and the right child is a join node, the Join_Key_Type is set to Table-Join. The Join_Predicate_Vector is used to store the join predicates. A prejoin match is found if the Join_Key_Type, Join_Predicate_Vector of the join

nodes matches with the prejoin table definition. The Join_Operator is set to Inner, LOuteror ROuter or FOuter if the join node type is inner join, left outer join and full outer join respectively.

Example 3.2: Suppose we have a query Select * from ((F Left Outer Join T_1 On $A_2=A_1$) Right Outer Join T_2 On $A_3=A_6$) Full Outer Join T_3 On $A_4=A_8$)

The query plan tree for this query is shown in Figure 4:

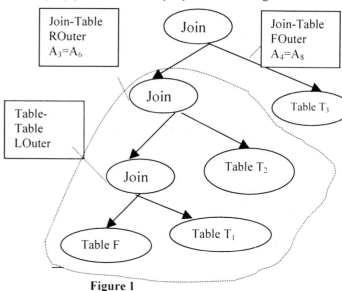

Figure 1

Our optimizer can identify that part of the outer join operations (F Left Outer Join T_1 On $A_2=A_1$) Right Outer Join T_2 On $A_3=A_6$) involved in the multi-table joins matches with our prejoin table FT_1T_2, so we can replace that part in the plan tree with the prejoin table node FT_1T_2. A modified plan tree is as follow (Figure 2).

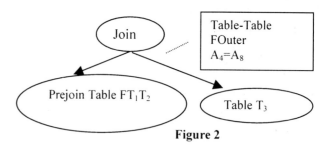

Figure 2

Since the prejoin table is based on the full outer join condition, the prejoin table node FT1T2 contains more rows than (F Left Outer Join T_1 On $A_2=_{A1}$) Right Outer Join T_2 On $A_3=A_6$, so we need to get rid of the extra rows introduced by the full outer join in order to get the correct answer. We can use the prejoin_bitmap_indexes associated with the Join_Relation_Tree of the prejoin table, the Join_Operator of the join nodes in the Join_Relation_Tree and put the proper "Pieces" together to construct the correct foundset bitmap for the prejoin table node in the modified plan tree. These are then ANDed and ORed with the current foundset. The rules for ANDing and Oring these bitmaps for the leaf joins in the join tree and for higher level joins are different in order to reserve outers from earlier joins in the join sequence.

Algorithm 1: Executing the Prejoin Table Node in the Query Execution Plan

traverse the Join_Relation_Tree of the prejoin table in breadth first order {
df_joinnode * current_node= node of the Join_Relation_Tree
  IF current_node is a join node {
    Bitmap I_index = current_node→IJIndex
    Bitmap L_index = current_node→LJIndex
    Bitmap R_index = current_node→RJIndex
    IF the current_node is the root of the Join_Relation_Tree) {
      Case (Join_Operator) {
        Inner: FSBM = I_index
        LOuter: FSBM = I_index OR L_index
        ROuter: FSBM = I_index OR R_index
        FOuter: FSBM = I_index OR L_index OR R_index }}
Else {
    Case (Join_Operator) {
      Inner: FSBM = FSBM AND (NOT (L_index OR R_index))
      LOuter: FSBM = FSBM AND (NOT R_index)
      ROuter: FSBM = FSBM AND (NOT L_index)
      FOuter: no change }}}
current_node = next node of the Join_Relation_Tree }

Example 3.3: For the modified plan tree in Figure 2, we compute the found set FSBM for prejoin table node FT1T2 starting form the top node of the Join_Relation_Tree (the part inside the dash curve in Figure 1). The root join node is a right outer join (the corresponding join index is Jindex2), then we combine the two pieces IJIndex and RJIndex: $FSBM_1$ = IJIndex OR RJIndex = (0 1 1 1 0 0 0 0 0) OR (0 0 0 0 0 0 0 0 1) = (0 1 1 1 0 0 0 0 1), the next join node is a left outer join (the corresponding join index Is Jindex1), we should remove those extra rows introduced from the right side (use the RJIndex of Jindex1). $FSBM_2$ = $FSBM_1$ AND (NOT (RJIndex)) = FSBM1 and (NOT (0 0 0 0 0 0 1 0) = FSBM1 AND (1 1 1 1 1 1 0 1) = (0 1 1 1 0 0 0 0 1) AND (1 1 1 1 1 1 0 1) = (0 1 1 1 0 0 0 0 1), so foundset bitmap corresponding to ((F Left

Outer Join T1 On $A_2=A_1$) Right Outer Join T2 On $A_3=A_6$) is (0 1 1 1 0 0 0 0 1), then we can project out the corresponding rows of the foundset (as shown in Table 4) and pass the rows to the join node above

A_2	A_3	A_4	A_5	A_1	A_6	A_7
b	2	v	o	b	2	4
d	3	w	p	d	3	2
d	3	w	p	d	3	5
null	null	null	null	null	8	1

Table 4: Rows of Prejoin Table Node

We can choose any one of the join algorithms (like nested-loop join, hash-join, sort-merge join and so on) and apply it to the Table T_3 and then we obtain the final result Table 5 for the query.

The prejoin table match method and prejoin_bitmap_index based outer join optimization techniques have been implemented in a commercial database's query engine. It took only 6 man-months to have our techniques seamlessly integrated into the existing system. The initial test on TPCD benchmark data set using query **Q5** and **Q8** [29] showed an average **30** times fast on scale **10** (10 Gigabytes).

A_2	A_3	A_4	A_5	A_1	A_6	A_7	A_8
b	2	v	o	b	2	4	v
d	3	w	p	d	3	2	w
d	3	w	p	d	3	5	w
null	null	null	null	null	8	1	null
null	null	null	null	null	null	null	u
null	null	null	null	null	null	null	x

Table 5: Result of the Query.

4. A Bitmap-Based Association Rule Algorithm Bit-AssocRule

Though most of data mining algorithms assume all data are stored in a flat relation, in reality data are stored in various normal forms. So the techniques of previous sections are extremely important in supporting data mining; we rely on them to generate a virtual flat relation. We have adopted the layered view, so in this section, we will only discuss the algorithms based on the flat relation without examining the detail interaction; we will defer it on later papers on data warehouse. Our focus in this section is to present a bitmap-based algorithm Bit-AssocRule to find association rule efficiently from large databases.

Given a set of transaction D, the problem of mining association rules is to generate all associations that meet certain user-specific minimum support and confidence. The problem can be decomposed into two subproblems: (1) finding all combinations of items that have transaction support above the minimum support, (2) use the large itemsets to generate the desired rules. The challenging issues of association rule algorithms are multiple scans of transaction databases and huge number of candidates. There have been many association rule algorithms [1,2,5,13,24,27,33] developed to reduce passes of transaction database scans and shrink number of candidates, which can be classified into two categories: (1) candidate-generation-and-test approach such as Apriori [2,5,13], (2) pattern-growth approach [24,27,33]. The most influential algorithm Apriori developed by Rakesh etc [1,2] generates the k-candidate by combining two (k-1)-itemsets. A new k-candidate becomes a k large itemset if every (k-1)-subset of the k-candidate is a large itemset otherwise it is removed, the process is very time consuming.

The use of bitmaps improves the performance to find association rules. The bit representation of bitmaps offers efficient storage while the intersection of bitmaps offers fast computation in finding association rules. The AND, SHIFT, and COUNT operations among bitmaps are extremely fast. Unlike the traditional Apriori algorithm which generates k-candidate by combining two (k-1) large itemset. Our Bit-AssocRule algorithm generates k-candidate by intersecting the bitmap of 1 attribute value with bitmaps of other (k-1) attribute values. The algorithm starts with a list L_1, which contains attribute values (also called 1-itemset, all the counts of the bitmaps of these 1-itemset are greater than the minimal counter number). The k-candidates consist of k attribute values $(X_{1,t1}, X_{2,t2}, ..., X_{k-1,tk-1}, X_{ij})$ from k attributes. Using bitmap techniques, the candidate is a large itemset if the bit count on the intersection of all the bitmaps $B_1 \cap B_2 \cap ... \cap B_k$ (suppose B_j is the bitmap of the $X_{k,tj}$) is equal or greater than the minimal count. The bit count is the number of 1's in the bitmap indexes from the result of the intersection of the bitmaps.

During each cycle, combinations of length k, or in short, k-candidates are generated. When intersecting the bitmaps, the size of the bitmaps may be large. Thus, slices of the bitmaps are read and processed until all slices of the bitmaps are done. In the end, if the intersection of bitmaps in the k-candidate results in a count that meets or exceeds the minimal count, the candidate is a large itemset, and it is saved. At the end of the cycle, if any k-candidates are declared as large itemsets, new candidates of length k+1 are generated for the next cycle. The cycle stops when no k-candidates are found to be large itemset or if no new (k+1)-candidate can be generated from the discovered k large itemset. When making k-candidates, all the 1-itemsets in the list L_1 are verified if they exist as elements in any (k-1)-itemset. If a 1-itemset does not exist in any (k-1)-itemset, it is removed from the list L_1. Next, new k-candidates are created by joining a (k-1)-itemset with 1-itemset in L_1 that has an attribute index greater than all attribute indexes of elements in that (k-1)-itemset. Only the new k large itemset are kept. Below is the algorithm

Algorithm 2: Bit-AssocRule

L_1 = {bitmaps of large 1-itemset}
For (k=2; $L_{k-1} \neq \phi$; k++) **Do Begin**
    Remove those 1-itemsets in L_1 which are not included in any itemset of L_{k-1} //prune L_1
    C_k = { Join the 1-itemset in L_1 that is larger than any elements in the (k-1) large item set
        with the itemset in L_{k-1}} // new candidate
    L_k = {c $\in$ C_k | bitmap count of c >= minsup}
End
Answer = $\cup_k L_k$

Theorem 1: **If the count of the intersection of the bitmap of 1-itemset X_{ij} with the bitmap of (k-1)-itemset $(X_{1,t1}, X_{2,t2}, ..., X_{k-1,tk-1})$ is large (namely greater than or equal to the minimum support count C), then it is guaranteed that the newly k-candidate $(X_{1,t1}, X_{2,t2}, ..., X_{k-1,tk-1}, X_{ij})$ is a large item.**

Proof: Suppose B_k denotes the bitmap of the 1-itemset X_{ij} and $B_1, B_2, ...B_{k-1}$ bitmaps of $X_{1,t1}, X_{2,t2}, ..., X_{k-1,tk-1}$ respectively. If the count of the intersection of the bitmap B_k of 1-itemset X_{ij} with the bitmaps $B_1 \cap B_2 ... \cap B_{k-1}$ of (k-1)-itemset $(X_{1,t1}, X_{2,t2}, ..., X_{k-1,tk-1})$ is large (namely greater than or equal to the minimum support count C), that means: Count($B_1 \cap B_2 \cap B_3 ... \cap B_{k-1} \cap B_k$) > C . Based on the logical bit **And** operations, it means that there must exists at least C positions (suppose these positions are $p_1, p_2, p_3,..p_C$) in the bitmaps $B_1, B_2, ...B_{k-1}, B_k$ such that

$B_1[p_1] = B_2[p_1] = ... B_{k-1}[p_1] = ... = B_k[p_1] = 1$

$B_1[p_2] = B_2[p_2] = ... B_{k-1}[p_2] = ... = B_k[p_2] = 1$

....

$B_1[p_C] = B_2[p_C] = \dots B_{k-1}[p_C] = \dots = B_k[p_C] = 1$

Then based on the bit **And** operation, for any (k-1) subset from the k-candidate $(X_{1,t1}, X_{2,t2}, \dots, X_{k-1,t-1}, X_{ij})$, the count of their bitmap intersection must be also greater than or equal to C, thus any (k-1) subset is a large item set, so the newly k-candidate is a large item set.

This theorem says that Our Bit-AssocRule algorithm doesn't need to check the (k-1)-subset of the new k-candidate. If the count of the bitmap of $(X_{1,t1}, X_{2,t2}, \dots, X_{k-1,tk-1}, X_{ij})$ is greater than C, there is no need to check whether any (k-1)-subset of $(X_{1,t1}, X_{2,t2}, \dots, X_{k-1,tk-1}, X_{ij})$ is also a large item set because we are sure the newly k-candidate is an k large item set. This property of our Bit-AssocRule algorithm is a significant improvement over the Aprior algorithm because the Apriori algorithm spends a huge amount of time to check all the (k-1) subsets of the newly k-candidate. Only after all the (k-1)-subsets of the k-candidate is checked then it can decide whether the new k-candidate is a large itemset or it should be removed. Our Bit-AssocRule eliminates this expensive step in the procedure, thus saves a lot of running time.

Four synthetic data sets are generated to compare the run time on these algorithms to find association rules. The program for Apriori and AprioriHybrid are our honest implementations of the algorithms in [2]. In the implementation, we use some buffer scheme to speedup read/write for all algorithms. The tests were conducted using an IBM PC with 933Mhz CPU, 512MB memory under Window 2000. The program is coded in C++.

Data set	Rows	Column	#of items	Table size	Bitmap size	Min Sup
DS1	400K	16	199	25.6MB	10.6MB	20K
DS2	800K	20	247	64MB	25.0MB	40K
DS3	1.6M	30	709	140MB	62MB	50K
DS4	3.0M	30	303	361MB	91MB	80K

Table 6: 4 data sets

Data set	Length of candidate	# of candidates	#of itemsets	Bit-AssocRule	Apriori Hybrid	Apriori
DS1						
	1	199	188	3.966s	4.106s	4.105s
	2	16333	103	18.426s	1402.977s	1403.438s
	3	92	10	0.111s	1.833s	5.979s
	4	0	0	0s	0s	0
	Total time			22.503s	1408.916s	1413.522s
DS2						
	1	247	235	10.375s	10.275s	10.786s
	2	26033	88	56.371s	4496.245s	4496.405s
	3	0	0	0s	0.01s	0s
	Total time			66.746s	4506.530s	4507.191s
DS3						
	1	303	303	24.816s	9.894s	9.904s
	2	43996	2681	99.162s	11245.120s	11231.390s
	3	614	924	46.117s	5368.569s	9391.324s
	4	0	0	0.03	25.487s	1658.455s
	Total time			171.401s	16649.070s	22291.073s
DS4						
	1	244	244	49.021s	25.557s	20.059
	2	28430	3920	153.080s	13979.431s	13682.575s
	3	55467	2586	308.593s	28294.946s	45159.676s
	4	3152	108	20.109s	455.155s	58274.374s
	5	0	0	0	0.000s	180.209s
	Total time			530.803s	42755.089s	117316.893s

Table 7: Experimental Run of 4 Data Sets

Here are some observations and explanations on the results

(1). The total time of our comparison includes the time to write the association rules to a file; Bit-AssocRule is 2 to 3 orders of magnitude faster than the various Apriori algorithms (64-221 times faster). The big the test data set, the big the time difference between the Bit-AssocRule and the various Apriori algorithms. We haven't compared our algorithm with some of the other association rule algorithms such as VIPER [27], CHARM [33], CLOSE [13,24] (CHARM and CLOSE are based on the closed frequent itemsets concept), but based on their published comparison results with Apriori, our Bit-AssocRule is very competitive compared to them and a direct comparison will be conducted and reported in the near future.

(2) Bit-AssocRule takes the same or litter longer time than the various Apriori algorithms in constructing the 1-itemsets because of the extra cost of building the bitmaps for the 1-itemsets. But after the 1-itsemtset is done, Bit-AssocRule is significant faster than the Apriori algorithms in constructing large frequent itemsets because it only uses the fast bit operations (AND, COUNT and SHIFT) and doesn't need to test the subsets of the newly candidate

(3) Bit-AssocRule only stores the bitmaps of the frequent items, and the bitmap storage (uncompressed) is less than the original data set (1/2 to 1/4 of the original data size).

The main reasons that Bit-AssocRule algorithm is significant faster than Apriori and its variations are

(1) Bit-AssocRule adopts the divide-and-conquer strategy, the transaction is decompose into vertical bitmap format and leads to focused search of smaller domain. There is no repeated scan of entire database in Bit-AssocRule.

(2) Bit-AssocRule doesn't follow the traditional candidate-generate-and test approach, thus saves significant amount of time to test the candidates

(3) In Bit-AssocRule, the basic operations are bit Count and bit And operations, which are extremely faster than the pattern search and matching operations used in Apriori and its variations

5. Conclusion

The contributions of this paper are in two aspects: we extend the application domains of bitmap techniques and introduce the bitmap techniques for complex DSS query optimization and association algorithm. We present a bitmap based query optimization algorithm to optimize complex query with multiple table join based on outer join operations and push the outer join operations from the data flow level to the bitmap level and achieve significant performance gain. We introduce a novel algorithm to calculate the foundset for those tables involved in the prejoin table by using prejoin_bitmap_indexes and integrate this algorithm into the current commercial data flow based query engine seamlessly. Our query optimization can achieve an order of magnitude faster than conventional query engine. Secondly we introduce the bitmap technique to the data mining procedure and develop a bitmap-based algorithm Bit-AssocRule to find association rules. Our Bit-AssocRule avoids the time-consuming table scan to find and prune the itemsets, all the operations of finding large itemsets from the datasets are the fast bit operations. The experimental result of our Bit-AssocRule algorithm with Apriori and AprioirHybrid algorithms shows Bit-AssocRule is2 to 3 orders of magnitude faster. This research indicates that bitmap technique can greatly enhance the performance for decision support queries and finding association rule, and bitmap techniques are very promising for the decision support query optimization and DM applications.

Bitmap technique is only one way to improve the performance of complex DSS queries and DM algorithm. Parallelism is another crucial factor to improve the performance of DSS and data mining. We are currently working on paralleling the bitmap-based algorithms and hope to report our findings in the near future.

6. References

[1] Agrawal R. Srikant R., "Fast algorithm for mining association rules", Prod. of the 20th VLDB Conf. 1994

[2] Agrawal R., Mannila H., Srikant R., Toivonen H., Verkamo A., "Fast discovery of association rules", in Advances in Knowledge Discovery and Data Mining, MIT 1996

[3] AIPD Technical Publications. In Sybase IQ Administration Guide, Sybase IQ Release 11.2 Collection, Sybase Inc

[4] Amer-Yahia S., Johnson T., "Optimizing queries on compressed bitmaps", Prod. of the 20th VLDB Conf.

[5] Bayardo R.J.Jr., Agrawal, R., Gunopulos D., "Constraint-based rule mining in large, dense databases", Proc. of the 15th Int'l Conf. on Data Engineering (ICDE1999)

[6] Bertino E., Ooi B.C., Sacks-Davis R. etc, "Indexing techniques for advanced database systems", Kluwer Academic Publishers.

[7] Chan C., Ioannidis Y., "Bitmap index design and evaluation", Prod of the SIGMOD-96

[8] Chatziantoniou D., Akinde M, Johnson T, Kim S, "The md-join: an operator for complex olap". Prod of the 18th Int'l Conference on Data Engineering (ICDE2001)

[9] Data, C.J., "The outer join", Prod. of the 2nd International Conf. on Databases,

[10] French C., " 'One size fits all' database architecture do not work for dss", Prof of the SIGMOD-95

[11] Galindo-Legaria, C and Rosenthal, A., "Outer join simplification and reordering for query optimization", ACM TODS, 22(1), 1997

[12] Graefe G., "Volcano, an extensible and parallel query evaluation system", IEEE Transaction on Knowledge and Data Engineering, 6(6), 1994

[13] Han, J. Pei, J. Yin. Y., "Mining frequent patterns without candidate generation", Prod of the SIGMOD-2002

[14] Hanusa R., "A lesson in outer joins (learned the hard way!)", Teradata Review, Spring 1998

[15] Jermaine C., Data A, "A novel index supporting high volume data warehouse insertion" Prod. of the 25th VLDB Conf.

[16] Johnson T , "Performance measurements of compressed bitmap indices" Prod. of the 25th VLDB conf

[17] Lin T.Y., "Data mining and machine oriented modeling: a granular computing approach", Journal of Applied Intelligence, Oct. 2000

[18] Louie E., Lin T.Y., "Finding association rules using fast bit computation: machine-oriented modeling" ISMIS-2000

[19] Morzy T., Zakrzewicz M., "Group bitmap index: a structure for association rules retrieval", Prod. of the 4th Int'l Conf. on Knowledge Discovery and Data Mining (KDD-98)

[20] O'Neil P., Graefe G., "Multi-table joins through bitmapped join indexes", SIGMOD September 1995, 8-11

[21] O'Neil P., Quass D., "Improved query performance with variant indexes", Prod of the SIGMOD-1997

[22] O'Neil P., Informix and indexing support for data warehouses, Informix Whitepaper

[23] Oracle 9i bitmap join index , http://technet.oracle.com/products/oracle9i/daily/apr09.html

[24] Pei, J. Han, H. Lu, S. Nishio, S. Tang, and D. Yang. "H-mine: hyper-structure mining of frequent patterns in large databases", Proc. The 2001 IEEE Int'l Conference on Data Mining

[25] Rinfret D, O'Neil P., O'Neil E., "Bit-Sliced Index Arithmetic", Prod of the SIGMOD-2001

[26] Savasere , A. Omiecinski E., Navathe S., "An efficient algorithm for mining association rules in large databases", in Prod. of the 21st VLDB conf.

[27] Shenoy P., Bhalotia G., Haritsa J., Bawa M., Sudarshan S., Shah D., "Turbo-charging vertical mining of large database", Prod. of the SIGMOD-2000

[28] "Star schema processing for complex queries", Red Brick/Informix White Paper

[29] "Star schemas and starjoin technology" Red Brick/Informix White Paper

[30] TPC benchmark d (decision support) standard specification, Release 2.2. (Transaction Processing Performance Council (TPC)

[31] Valduriex P., "Join indexes" ACM TODS, 12(2), 1987

[32] Wu M., Buchmann A., "Encoding bitmap indexing for data warehouse", Proc. of the 14th Int'l Conference on Data Engineering, 220-231, 1998

[33] Zaki., M., Gouda K., "Fast vertical using diffsets", Tech report, Dept. of computer science, RPI

[34] Zhao Y., Deshpande P., Naughton J., Shukla A., "Simultaneous optimization and evaluation of multiple dimensional queries", SIGMOD-98, 271-282

Modeling and Efficient Mining of Intentional Knowledge of Outliers

Zhixiang Chen*, Jian Tang[+], Ada Wai-Chee Fu[+],
Department of Computer Science, University of Texas-Pan American,
Edinburg TX 78539 USA.
email:chen@cs.panam.edu
[+] Department of Computer Science, Chinese University of Hong Kong,
Shatin, N.T., Hong Kong.
email:tang@cse.cuhk.edu.hk, email:adafu@cse.cuhk.edu.hk

Abstract

In this paper, we study in a general setting the notion of outliered patterns as intentional knowledge of outliers and algorithms to mine those patterns. Our contributions consist of a model for defining outliered patterns with the help of categorical and behavioral similarities of outliers, and efficient algorithms for mining knowledge sets of distance-based outliers and outliered patterns. Our algorithms require only very limited domain knowledge, and no classified information. We also present an empirical study to show the feasibility of our algorithms.

keywords*: outlier detection, knowledge sets, categorical similarity, behavioral similarity, outliered patterns*

1 Introduction

Outliers are those data records that do not follow any pattern in an application. In some applications detecting outliers is more significant than detecting general patterns. For instance, calling card fraud in telecommunications [8], credit card fraud in banking and finance [14], computer intrusion in information systems [6], to name a few. In these applications, outliers may cause tremendous damages at the individual, business or even national level such as terrorist attacks, and therefore the methodologies to detect them are of crucial importance.

Extensive research has been done on the discovery of patterns [7, 11, 13, 16]. Although in principle these methods can also generate outliers as by-products, for efficiency and flexibility reasons, independent methods for outlier detections are in general more favorable. Most of the early schemes for outlier detection have been done in the field of statistics. These methods normally assume that the distribution of a data set is known in advance and try to detect outliers by examining the deviations of individual data objects based on such a distribution. In reality, however, a priori knowledge about the distribution of a data set is not always obtainable. Besides, these methods do not scale well for even modest number of dimensions as the size of data set increases.

Recent progresses in outlier detection include, among many others, the distance-based scheme (called $DB(d, n)$-outlier) proposed by Knorr and Ng in [9], the density-based scheme by Breuning, et al, in [4]; and the connectivity-based scheme by Tang et al, in [15]. All the above work considers outliers as being conceptually disjoint with patterns. In reality, however, some outliers themselves can be patterned. For example, consider a database that contains records for mobile phone calls. An outlier may result from an occasional action taken by a legal owner in an exceptional circumstance, or a malicious behavior of a thief. While in the former case the kind of behavior may be sporadic, in the latter case the thief may repeat the similar actions over time and as a result generate a pattern. In many cases, identifying the patterns of the outliers is of practical significance. For instance, for the above mobile phone database, discovering the unusual calling patterns may assist in revealing the illegal activities by thieves. The simplest method, of course, is to find all the outliers first and then apply any general clustering algorithm on the set of the outliers. The problems of this strategy are twofold. Firstly, any existing clustering algorithm essentially is based on the distributions of the data as being presented in the application. Thus its effectiveness depends on the accuracy that these distributions reflect the nature of the data. Since the number of outliers is usually small, their distributions as being presented to the user in general cannot be accurate for reflecting their true nature. Secondly, in the clustering algorithms, objects and their attributes are un-interpreted, and similarities between objects are evaluated based solely on their distances. On the other hand, outliers are semantically more meaningful. (They are outliers.) In order to model effectively the pattern in this context, we should make use of these semantics. Also, a user should be allowed to deal with patterns objectively, so that only those patterns that are to his/her interest will be discovered. In summary, we need different paradigm for the modeling of outliered patterns and algorithms to discover them in the applications.

To the best of our knowledge, no existing work has considered this problem with adequate generality. Although some application-specific mechanisms have been proposed [8], they deal only with isolated instances, and require a priori domain knowledge and some classified information in order to be trained in discovering the patterns of abnormal behaviors. In case the required knowledge is not available, these mechanisms do not work. Naturally, none of these approaches characterize the concept in a general setting, and hence do not offer insights into understanding the problem in the general case.

In this paper, we study in a general setting the notion of outliered patterns and methods to tackle them. Our contributions consist of a model for outliered pattern and several algorithms to identify them. Our algorithms require only very limited domain knowledge, and no classified information. We also present an empirical study to show the feasibility of our method.

2 A Model

2.1 Roles of Subspaces

The work [1] realized that in most cases, for the objects in a high dimensional space, it makes sense only to consider outliers for their projections on lower dimensional subspaces. On the other hand, the work in [10] noticed that an outlier is most meaningful in the minimal subspaces where it is an outlier. The above work suggests the important roles subspaces may play in outlier formulation. We observe that in the context of outliered patterns, all the subspaces do not play the same role, and it is necessary to categorize them based on the roles they play in outlier detection. We shall now substantiate the mobile phone database given in the previous section, and use it as an illustrating example in the subsequent discussions.

Example 1 *A mobile phone call is recorded by a vector of eight attributes* <acct_num, home, from, to, time, date, duration, times>. *Each phone must set up a unique account number before it can be used. The city where the account is set up is called the "home" of the phone. While the call can be made from/to anywhere, the rate is the lowest if it is from the home. The attribute* times *indicates the total number of calls made from* acct_num *in* date. *Intuitively, a legal call is likely to follow the following pattern: its* from *is its* home *city, its* time *is not very late at night, its* duration *is not very long if* time *is during office hours, and the number of* times *is not too high. Here the attributes* from, to, time, duration *and* times *can be viewed as indicators for normal/abnormal behaviors of calls. On the other hand, we usually do not use* acct_num *and* home *to distinguish normal calls from abnormal ones. Instead, we simply use them to identify the calls so that those that share the same account number and/or set up cities can be related. In addition, we note that the attribute* date *can neither indicate the status (i.e., normal or abnormal), nor provide identities of calls. Its role is for observation. For example, if a thief periodically makes long distance calls late at night with a long duration, this is observed at different* dates.

We will use the following notations. $\mathcal{D} = \{A, \ldots, A_d\}$ is called a d-dimension set, where each A_i is the name of a dimension. Define $P_{+\mathcal{D}} = domain(A_1) \times domain(A_2) \times \ldots \times domain(A_d)$. That is, $P_{+\mathcal{D}}$ is the d-dimensional space defined on the dimensions in $\mathcal{D}$. R denotes an arbitrary set such that $R \subseteq P_{+\mathcal{D}}$. For any dimension set A such that $A \subseteq \mathcal{D}$, and any object $o \in P_{+\mathcal{D}}$, $\prod_A(o)$ denotes the projection of o on P_{+A}. Define $\prod_A(R) = \{\prod_A(o) : o \in R\}$.

Definition 1 *The quadruple (I, C, O, idc) is a role arrangement for $\mathcal{D}$ if I, C and O constitute a partition of $\mathcal{D}$. The sets P_{+I}, P_{+C} and P_{+O} respectively are called identification, indication and observation subspaces of $P_{+\mathcal{D}}$. idc is a predicate defined on $2^{P_{+I}}$. We call idc an identification condition.*

Definition 2 *R is identified by idc if $\forall R_1 \subseteq R, [idc(\prod_I(R_1)] = true]$. R is fully identified by idc if R is identified by idc and for all $S \supset R$, S is not identified by idc.*

Thus for the mobile phone call database, a possible role arrangement is $I = \{acct_{num}, home\}$, $C = \{from, to, duration, time, times\}$, $O = \{date\}$, and $idc(X) = true$ iff $\forall x, y \in X, \prod_I(x) = \prod_I(y)$. The identification condition here identifies any set of phone calls made from the same phone device. In the following discussions, the symbols I, C, O, idc are used exclusively for role arrangement.

Definition 3 *An observation sequence for R is a sequence $T = <T_1, \ldots, T_u>$ where $\cup_{i=1}^u T_i = \prod_O(R)$ and for all $1 \leq i < j \leq u, T_i \cap T_j = \emptyset$. Each element set in T is called an observation spot. For any R_1, R_1 is observed at T_i if $\prod_O(R_1) \subseteq T_i$. For any $o \in R_1$, o is an outlier observed at T_i with respect to R_1 if R_1 is observed at T_i and $\prod_C(o)$ is an outlier with respect to $\prod_C(R_1)$.*

It is worth noting here that the three kinds of roles of the subspaces stated above in general belong to domain knowledge. Our model to be introduced in the next subsection will assume that users have this knowledge. We argue that this assumption is reasonable since for any application, if a user is interested in detecting outliers, he/she must have

ideas of what his/her concern is. This means that he/she has some idea about the nature of attributes. In other words, he/she has some basic understanding of the meaning of the attributes, and the attributes that contribute to the abnormal behaviors.

2.2 Knowledge Sets of Outliers

We first review some concepts introduced in [10] that will be used in our model. Let $X \subseteq \mathcal{D}$ be any given nonempty set of attributes. Let U be a set of objects in P_{+X}, and $o \in U$ be an outlier. We say that o is a **non-trivial outlier** in the attribute set X if for all proper subset $Y \subset X$, $\prod_Y(o)$ is not an outlier in $\prod_Y(U)$, otherwise it is a trivial outlier in X. For a trivial outlier in X, the attributes in X do not give an accurate qualification for the outlier. For example, suppose a thief makes a call after midnight for one hour, while in general many legal calls are also made after mid-night, but last only a few minutes, and many calls last for more than one hour but earlier than mid-night. In this case the attribute set $\{time, duration\}$ accurately describe the nature of the illegal call, since, when viewed separately, neither "calling at midnight" nor "lasting for one hour" is special. On the other hand, if very few legal calls are made after midnight, then the same attribute set is not accurate in describing the nature of the unusual call. In this case the singleton set $\{time\}$ is more accurate. In this paper, if o is a non-trivial outlier in an attribute set X then we say that X is a *knowledge attribute set* of o (or *knowledge set* if no confusion is possible). Note that an outlier may have multiple knowledge sets. For example, if in addition to very few calls being made after midnight, we also have that very few calls last more than one hour, then both $\{times\}$ and $\{duration\}$ are knowledge sets for that unusual call.

2.3 Similarities

We are interested in the similarities based on which the repetitive nature of the outliered patterns can be established. In our model, the repetitive nature is observed at the observation spots. Thus the similarities are defined only on the objects that are observed at different observation spots. Depending on the applications, different kinds of similarities can be defined. We will introduce two kinds of similarities that fit different expectations of users. We first introduce some notations relating to knowledge sets of outliers.

Let o be an outlier. We define the **knowledge attribute class** for o as $KAClass(o) = \{X : X \text{ is a knowledge set for } o\}$. Let U be a set of outliers. We define the **knowledge attribute cartel** on U as $KACartel(U) = \cup_{o \in U} KAClass(o)\}$. Namely, the knowledge attribute cartel on U is the set of all the knowledge attribute sets of outliers in U.

Let S be the set of database objects from which we want to find the outliered patterns, and $T = < T_1, \ldots, T_n >$ be the observation sequence for S. Let $S = \cup_{i=1}^n S_i$ where for all i, $1 \le i \le n$, S_i is observed at T_i, and Q_i be the set of all the outliers observed at T_i with respect to S_i. Assume $Q \subseteq Q_1 \cup \cdots \cup Q_n$ such that Q is fully identified by idc in $Q_1 \cup \cdots \cup Q_n$. For all i, $1 \le i \le n$, let $G_i = Q \cap Q_i$. Let $G = \{G_1, G_2, \ldots, G_n\}$. For any $X \in KACartel(G_i)$, let $G_i(X) = \{p : p \in G_i \ \& \ X \in KAClass(p)\}$. Namely, $G_i(X)$ is the set of all outliers in G_i with knowledge set X.

Definition 4 *Let $Z = KACartel(G_i) \cap KACartel(G_j)$ for any two outlier groups G_i and G_j in G. G_i and G_j are categorically similar with respect to a predefined positive threshold $\alpha > 0$, if*

$$\frac{|\cup_{X \in Z} G_i(X)|}{|G_i|} \ge \alpha \quad and \quad \frac{|\cup_{X \in Z} G_j(X)|}{|G_j|} \ge \alpha.$$

We call the fractions categorical rates.

In each categorical rate, the numerator is the number of outliers in group $G_i(G_j)$ that share some knowledge sets with some members in $G_j(G_i)$. Roughly speaking, two outlier groups are categorically similar with respect to a given threshold, if each group has sufficiently large number of members that share some knowledge sets with the members in the other group. Since a knowledge set essentially categorizes the outliers based on the minimal information that can describe them, in each of the categorically similar groups, most outliers can find some outliers in the same category in the other group.

Categorical similarity uses attribute names only. It addresses only the natures of the outliers, not their precise behaviors. To address the behaviors, it is necessary to use not only attribute names, but also the attribute values.

Let S, T and G be the same as defined above. Further let $Center(Y)$ be the center for any set of outliers Y.

Definition 5 *Let $Z = KACartel(G_i) \cap KACartel(G_j)$. For any two outlier groups G_i and G_j in G and any $\delta > 0$, let*

$$B_i =$$
$$\bigcup\nolimits_{X \in Z}\{G_i(X) : dist(Center(G_i(X)), Center(G_j(X)))$$
$$\le \delta\} \ and$$

$$B_j =$$
$$\bigcup\nolimits_{X \in Z}\{G_j(X) : dist(Center(G_j(X)), Center(G_i(X)))$$
$$\le \delta\}$$

G_i and G_j are behaviorally similar with respect to three predefined positive thresholds α, β and δ, if G_i and G_j are categorically similar with respect to α, and

$$\frac{|\cup_{W \in B_i} W|}{|G_i|} \ge \beta \quad and \tag{1}$$

$$\frac{|\cup_{W \in B_j} W|}{|G_i|} \ge \beta, \tag{2}$$

We call the fractions the behavior rates.

The condition (1) indicates the following property: G_i has a high percentage of outliers forming a set of subgroups; each of those subgroups is characterized by a common knowledge attribute set of G_i and G_j; and the center of each subgroup in G_i is very close to the center of the corresponding subgroup in G_j. Condition (2) indicates the similar property for G_j. Intuitively, the behavioral similarity is meant to reveal the property that the two outlier groups have not only a very high percentage of common "categories" as characterized by their categorical similarity, but also a very high percentage of outliers in one of the two groups that lie very close to their corresponding outliers sharing the same knowledge set in the other group.

An issue here is how to determine the parameters. Like any other outlier detection schemes, these should be determined in an iterative try-and-refine manner. A detailed discussion on this issue is beyond the scope of this paper.

Example 2 *Consider the telephone call database described in* EXAMPLE 1. *Suppose the identification condition is defined as "all calls in the group have the same home", and the observation sequence contains two consecutive Saturdays, each observing the data records in the preceding seven days. Let us consider the fully identified group of unusual phone calls that have Hong Kong as their homes. Assume that during the first seven-day period, 50% of the calls are long lasting late night calls, with the center, (i.e., average), at (2 pm, 1.5 hours), 20% are made at day-time with high daily frequency, with the center at (15 times), and 30% are from overseas. Assume calls from overseas are always centered at (overseas)[1].*

During the second seven-day period, 10% are day-time high frequency calls centering at (6 times), 40% are made late at night with long duration with the center of around (3 am, 2 hours), 35% are from overseas and 15% are to Tibet. Let Y_1 and Y_2 respectively be the outlier groups observed at the first and the second observation spots.

Thus
$$KACartel(Y_1) = \{\{time, duration\}, \{times\}, \{from\}\}$$
and
$$KACartel(Y_2) =$$
$$\{\{time, durations\}, \{times\}, \{from\}, \{to\}\}.$$
Suppose $\alpha = 80\%$,
$\beta = 70\%$,
and the value of δ makes the following true:
$$dist((2pm, 1.5hours), (3am, 2hours)) < \delta,$$
$$dist((15times), (6times)) > \delta.$$
We also have $dist((overseas), (overseas)) = 0$.

Thus the categorical rate for Y_1 is 100%, and for Y_2 is 85%. Y_1 and Y_2 are categorically similar. The behavior rate for Y_1 is 80%, and for Y_2 is 75%. They are behaviorally similar, too. Observe that although the day-time high frequency calls in each group contribute to the categorical similarity, they do not contribute to the behavior similarity: they can be described by the same minimal set of attributes, but are not considered very close in the behavior. Another fact is that the calls to Tibet observed at the second observation spot do not contribute to either kind of similarities, since no call to Tibet has be observed at the first observation spot.

---
[1]For simplicity, assume these groups do not overlap.

This example shows how the similarities reveal the natures/behaviors of the unusual phone calls at 'home' level. By varying the identification condition, one can refine/coarsen this level. For example, by defining the idc as "all calls with the same account number", one can detect the similarities among the unusual phone calls with the same account.

2.4 Category and Behavior Patterns of Outliers

Based on the categorical and behavior similarities introduced in the previous two subsections, we can now formulate the corresponding patterns. Let S, T and G be the same as defined in Section 2.3. We have

Definition 6 *A category pattern of outliers for G and T is a maximum sequence $G_{i_1}, G_{i_2}, \ldots, G_{i_k}$ such that $1 \leq i_1 \leq i_2 \leq \cdots \leq i_k \leq n$, and any two consecutive outlier groups in the sequence are categorically similar.*

Analogously, we define behavior patterns of outliers as follows.

Definition 7 *A behavior pattern of outliers for G and T is a maximum sequence $G_{i_1}, G_{i_2}, \ldots, G_{i_k}$ such that $1 \leq i_1 \leq i_2 \leq \cdots \leq i_k \leq n$, and any two consecutive outlier groups in the sequence are behaviorally similar.*

```
Algorithm Mine-Knowledge-Set(o, r, n)
1.  C_1 = K_1 = ∅;
2.  for i = 1, 2, ..., d do
3.      find L_i^{o,r};   //all L_i^{o,r} can be found
            via scanning database once
4.      if (|N_r^{{A_i}}(o)| < n)   //N_r^{{A_i}}(o)| ⊆ ∏_{A_i} L_i^{o,r}
5.          K_1 = K_1 ∪ {A_i};
6.      else C_1 = C_1 ∪ {L_i^{o,r}};
7.  for k = 2, ..., d do
8.      C_k = Knowledge-Set-Gen(C_{k-1})
9.      if (C_k = ∅) exit;
10.     for each L_{i_1,...,i_k}^{o,r} ∈ C_k
11.         if (|N_r^{{A_{i_1},...,A_{i_k}}}(o)| < n)
                //N_r^{{A_{i_1},...,A_{i_k}}}(o) ⊆ ∏_{A_i} L_{i_1,...,i_k}^{o,r}
12.             K_k = K_k ∪ {A_{i_1},...,A_{i_k}};
13.             C_k = C_k - {L_{i_1,...,i_k}^{o,r}};
14  return ∪_k K_k;
```

Fig. 1. Algorithm KSAPriori

3 Finding Knowledge Sets of Outliers

The problem of finding knowledge sets of outliers is different from that of finding "strong outliers" studied in [10]. Strong outliers are defined with respect to *strong knowledge sets* (or *strong outlying spaces*). From [10], a knowledge set is strong if it contains at least one outlier but any of its subset contains no outliers. (Refer to Section 2.2.) In our context, we want to find all knowledge sets for every individual outlier, not just strong ones. A super set of a strong knowledge set (or strong outlying space) is not interesting in [10], but may be interesting in our context. E.g., given a strong knowledge set X and a group of strong outliers in it, X may have some super sets that are knowledge sets of some other outliers, and therefore those super sets contain valuable information that describes patterns of outliers in them. The approach in [10] ignores such information, and is therefore not applicable in our context.

It is worth noting here that our similarity model in the previous section is applicable to any existing outlier models. In the following, we will use distance-based outlier model proposed in [9] due to its simplicity, and develop algorithms for pattern discovery. We first design an innovative algorithm for mining knowledge sets of distance-based outliers in Fig. 1.

The distance-based outlier model specifies two parameters, a radius r and a cardinality n. An object o is an outlier with respect to r and n if $|\{p : dist(p,o) \leq r\}| < n$. In our algorithm, we assume that each attribute A_i has an interval domain V_i. Given any outlier $o = (o_1, o_2, \ldots, o_d)$ and a radius r, let $V_i^{o,r}$ be the subset interval of V_i with o_i as its center and r as radius. Furthermore, let $L_i^{o,r}$ be the set of all the objects in the subspace $V_1 \times \cdots \times V_{i-1} \times V_i^{o,r} \times V_{i+1} \times \cdots \times V_d$. In general, for any k attributes $A_{i_1}, A_{i_2}, \ldots, A_{i_k}$ with $i_1 < i_2 < \cdots < i_k$, let $L_{i_1,i_2,\ldots,i_k}^{o,r}$ be the set of objects in the subspace $V_1' \times \cdots \times V_d'$ such that for $j = 1, \ldots, d$,

$$V_j' = \begin{cases} V_j, & if\ j \notin \{i_1, i_2, \ldots, i_k\}, \\ V_j^{o,r}, & otherwise. \end{cases}$$

As can be seen easily, algorithm Mine-Knowledge-Set() resembles the well-known *apriori* algorithm in nature. The difference is that in our case, C_k can not be generated from K_{k-1} directly. It is obtained from projections in C_{k-1}. Procedure *Knowledge-Set-Gen()* also resembles the procedure *apriori-gen()* in the *apriori* algorithm. Like the procedure *apriori-gen()*, Knowledge-Set-Gen(C_{k-1}) first generates the set

$$\{L_{i_1,\ldots,i_k}^{o,r} : L_{i_1,\ldots,i_{k-1}}^{o,r} \in C_{k-1}\&$$
$$L_{i_2,\ldots,i_{k-1},i_k}^{o,r} \in C_{k-1}\&$$
$$i_1 < i_2 < \cdots < i_k < i_{k+1}\}.$$

Next, in the *prune* step, it deletes all $L_{i_1,\ldots,i_k}^{o,r}$ such that for some $(k-1)$-subset $\{i_{j_1}, \ldots, i_{j_{k-1}}\}$ of $\{i_1, \ldots, i_k\}$, $L_{i_{j_1},\ldots,i_{j_{k-1}}}^{o,r} \notin C_{k-1}$. The prune step requires testing that all $(k-1)$-subsets of a newly generated k-candidate-attribute set are contained in C_{k-1}. As in the *apriori* algorithm, we can use *hash-tree* to represent C_k to speed up such membership testing. At step 4, we need to find $N_r^{\{A_i\}}(o)$, the r-neighborhood of o in $\{A_i\}$. Since $N_r^{\{A_i\}}(o) \subseteq \prod_{\{A_i\}} L_i^{o,r}$, this can done with the help of $L_i^{o,r}$. Similarly, at step 11, we need to find $N_r^{\{A_{i_1}, \ldots, A_{i_k}\}}(o)$, the r-neighborhood of o in $\{A_{i_1}, \ldots, A_{i_k}\}$. Because $N_r^{\{A_{i_1}, \ldots, A_{i_k}\}}(o) \subseteq \prod_{\{A_i\}} L_{i_1,\ldots,i_k}^{o,r}$, this can done with the help of $L_{i_1,\ldots,i_k}^{o,r}$

Algorithm Mine-Knowledge-Set() finds all knowledge sets for any given outlier o with respect to r and n. It serves as the kernel of our algorithm FindKS (Find Knowledge Sets) as described in Fig. 2.

Algorithm FindKS($\mathcal{D}, r, n$)
1. $\mathcal{S} = \emptyset$;
2. $\mathcal{O} = findOutlier(\mathcal{D}, r, n)$;
3. for every $o \in \mathcal{O}$ do
4. $\mathcal{S} = \mathcal{S} \cup \{< Mine - Knowledge - Set(o, r, n), o >\}$;
5. return $\mathcal{S}$

Fig. 2. Algorithm FindKS

The procedure *findOutlier* finds outliers in the indication subspace of $\mathcal{D}$ with respect to r and n. We can use the efficient algorithms in [10] for this procedure. Mine-Knowledge-Set.

4 Discovering Patterns of Outliers

Since we have studied the problem of mining knowledge sets for outliers in the previous section we assume in this section that the knowledge set (and hence the knowledge attribute class) for each outlier is given. For each outlier o, let $m(o)$ denote a knowledge set of o. Recall that an outlier may have multiple knowledge sets. Because we assume that all the knowledge sets of the outlier groups are known, we can represent any outlier group G_i as a list of pairs

$$G_i = [<o_{i_1}, m(o_{i_1}) >, \ldots, <o_{i_{s_1}}, m(o_{i_{s_1}}) >].$$

Without loss of generality, we can further assume that attributes in each knowledge set are sorted according to some order.

The central part is to determine, for any given pair of outlier groups G_i and G_j, whether they are similar or not based on definitions 4 and 5. A straightforward method would be for each common knowledge set to the two groups, we scan each group to construct the maximal set of the outliers with that knowledge set. These maximal sets are then used to evaluate the two formulas. A more clever method is to use a counting tree where nodes are attributes and paths are knowledge sets. For each item $< o, m(o) >$ in the above list, we traverse the path $m(o)$. At the leaf node o is stored, together with the group id where o belongs. This structure allows us to store at the leaf node of each path a triple of the form $< G, O, c >$ where G is the group id, O is the set of all the outliers which share the path as one of their knowledge sets, and c is the center of O. (See [5] for more detail.)

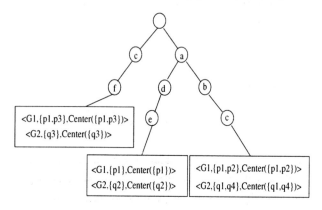

Figure 3. A Knowledge Set Counting Tree

Example 3 *Consider a set of attributes* $\{a, b, c, d, e, f\}$ *and two outlier groups* $G_1 = [< p1, \{a, b, c\} >$

$, < p1, \{a, d, e\} >, < p1, \{c, f\} >, < p2, \{a, b, c\} >$
$, < p3, \{c, f\} >]$ *and* $G_2 = [< q1, \{a, b, c\} >, < q2, \{a, d, e\} >, < q3, \{c, f\} >, < q4, \{a, b, c\} >]$. *A knowledge set counting tree for* G_1 *and* G_2 *is illustrated in Fig. 4.*

Note that in reality, in addition to the patterns themselves, the algorithm should also present to users the knowledge sets for the outliers in the patterns, and the center of each group of outliers that share the same knowledge set. This information serves as descriptions of the patterns that will assist users in analysing the patterns and revealing the causes for the repetitive behaviors of the outliers involved.

5 Empirical Analysis

Because our algorithms are the first in the study of mining outliered patterns, we have no other algorithms to compare with ours. As pointed out in section 3, algorithms in [10] for mining strong outliers and outlying space is related to our work, but they are not applicable to our context. Since the kernel of our algorithms is Mine-Knowledge-Set, we will focus on this algorithm to conduct our empirical analysis. The computing environment of our experiments is a Dell Precision 530 Workstation with dual Xeon 1.5 GHz processors. In order to have fair comparisons, all implementations are based on the same basic data structure.

As in [2], we use Poisson distributions to create synthetic data. First we consider a set of 20 attributes and generate 40 potential knowledge sets for an outlier. Note that those 20 attributes can form 1,048,575 non-empty knowledge sets. The size of a knowledge set is determined by a Poisson distribution with mean equal to 1, 2, 3, 4, 5, or 6, and attributes are randomly assigned to the set. To model that a knowledge set is *"maximal"* in the sense that it contains no other knowledge sets, some fraction of attributes in subsequent knowledge sets are chosen from attributes not contained in previous knowledge sets generated. Next, we generate 10k 20-dimensional data points to form a data sets. The data points are generated with a uniform distribution outside subspaces consisting of the potential knowledge sets. However, in order to smooth the over all distribution of data points, a small fraction of data points are generated within the subspaces consisting of the potential knowledge sets. In general, we use PxDySzk to denote a data set $\mathcal{D}$ with the following properties: it has 40 potential knowledge sets whose size follows a Poisson distribution with mean equal to x; its dimension is y, and it have $z \times 1,000$ many data points.

The performance results of algorithm Mine-Knowledge-Set for the six datasets are shown in Fig. 4 In our experiments, we choose $n = \alpha\%$ of N, where N is the total number of data points. In each of the first six illustrations of Fig. 4 the x-axis indicates decreasing values of α (hence it indicates decreasing values of n), the y-axis indicate execution times of algorithm Mine-Knowledge-Set with $r = 40, 60$, and 80. Three curves are plotted accordingly, which show trends of execution times for a fixed r value and variable decreasing n values.

The last two illustration in Fig. 4 show the scale-up performance of algorithm Mine-Knowledge-Set with respect to the size and the dimension of a dataset. We used the same Poisson distribution with mean equal to 4 to generate datasets and conducted experiments with three parameter settings $(40, 1)$, $(60, 0.75)$ and $(80, 0.5)$, where in each setting the first is the value of r and the second is the percentage α used to compute n. The execution times are normalized with respect to the times for dataset P4D20S10k in the seventh illustration, and for dataset P4D10S10k in the last illustration. As can be seen, the execution times scale linearly in both illustrations.

6 Discussion and Conclusion

Our model assumes that the user has an idea about the roles the attributes play so that he/she is able to subdivide the entire attribute set into the three required subsets. We have argued that this assumption in general is not too strong to be realistic. On the other hand, different users may divide the attribute set differently. In general, these will generate different results. To maximize the satisfaction toward the results, a user may want to use different division schemes and refine the results iteratively. Similarly, the decision on how to define an observation sequence, in particular, the size of an observation spot, is also an iterative process. If the observation spot is too small, the pattern may be hard

to find since the number of outliers observed at each spot is not sufficiently large to contribute to a pattern. On the other hand, if it is too large, the pattern found may not reflect the reality.

The task of outlier detection has traditionally taken the view that the outliers are isolated events. This view ignores the possibilities that some outliers be related and form a pattern. In this paper, we propose a framework for modeling outliered patterns. We introduce two kinds of similarities that may exist among outliers, and propose algorithms that can be used to detect patterns based on these similarities.

In the future, we shall apply our model and algorithms on some real data and the results will be reported in the full version of the paper.

ACKNOWLEDGMENTS. Jian Tang is on leave from Memorial University of Newfoundland, Canada. Part of work was done while Zhixiang Chen was visiting Chinese University of Hong Kong. This research was supported by the Hong Kong RGC Research Grant Competitive Bids, Ref: 4179/01E, and the Hong Kong RGC Research Grant Direct Allocation, ID 2050279.

References

[1] C. Aggarwal and P.S. Yu: Outlier detection for high dimensional data, SIGMOD, 2001, pp 37-46.

[2] R. Agrawal, H. Mannila, R. Srikant, H. Toivonen, and A.I. Verkamo: Fast discovery of association rules, in U.M. Fayyad, et al., eds., *Advances in Knowledge Discovery and Data Mining*, pp 307-328, 1996.

[3] A. Arning, R. Agrawal, P. Raghavan: "A Linear Method for Deviation detection in Large Databases", KDD, 1996, pp 164 - 169.

[4] M. Breuning, Hans-Peter Kriegel, R. Ng, J. Sander: "LOF: Identifying density based Local Outliers", SIGMOD, 2000.

[5] Z. Chen, A. Fu, J. Tang, "Detection of Outliered Patterns", Tech. Report, Dept. of CSE, Chinese University of Hong Kong, 2002.

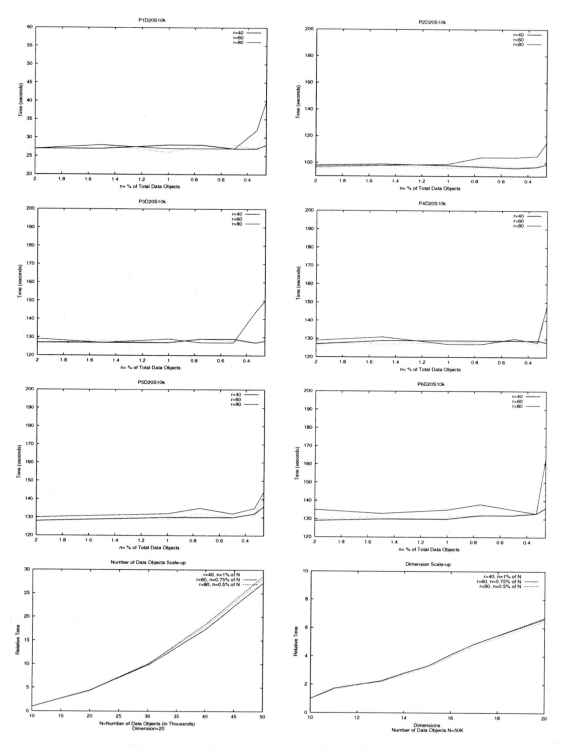

Figure 4. Execution Time and Scale-up Performance

[6]   W. DuMouchel, M. Schonlau: "A Fast Computer Intrusion Detection Algorithm based on Hypothesis Testing of Command transition Probabilities", KDD, 1998, pp. 189 - 193.

[7]   M. Ester, H. Kriegel, J. Sander, X. Xu: "A Density-Based Algorithm for Discovering Clusters in Large Spatial Databases with Noise", KDD, 1996, pp 226 - 231.

[8]   T. Fawcett, F. Provost: "Adaptive Fraud Detection", Data Mining and Knowledge Discovery Journal, Kluwer Academic Publishers, Vol. 1, No. 3, 1997, pp 291 - 316.

[9]   E. Knorr, R. Ng: "Algorithms for Mining Distance based Outliers in Large Datasets", VLDB, 1998, pp 392 - 403.

[10] E. Knorr, R. Ng: "Finding Intensional Knowledge of Distance-based Outliers", VLDB, 1999, pp 211 - 222.

[11] R. Ng, J. Han: "Efficient and Effective Clustering Methods for Spatial Data Mining", VLDB, 1994, pp 144 - 155.

[12] S. Ramaswamy, R. Rastogi, S. Kyuseok: "Efficient Algorithms for Mining Outliers from Large Data Sets", SIGMOD, 2000, pp 427 - 438.

[13] G. Sheikholeslami, S. Chatterjee, A. Zhang: "WaveCluster: A   multi-Resolution   Clustering Approach for Very Large Spatial Databases", VLDB, 1998, pp 428 - 439.

[14] S. Stolfo, W. Fan, W. Lee, A. Prodromidis, P. Chan: "Cost-based Modeling for Fraud and Intrusion Detection: Results from the JAM Project", In Proc. of DARPA Information Survivability Conference & Exposition - Vol. 2, 2000, pp 1130 - 1144.

[15] J. Tang, Z. Chen, A. Fu, D. Cheung, "A Robust Outlier Detection Scheme in Large Data Sets", PAKDD, 2002.

[16] T. Zhang, R. Ramakrishnan, M. Linvy: "BIRCH: An Efficient Data Clustering Method for Very Large Databases", SIGMOD, 1996, pp 103 - 114.

Algorithms for Balancing Privacy and Knowledge Discovery in Association Rule Mining

Stanley R. M. Oliveira[1,2]
[1]Embrapa Informática Agropecuária
Av. André Tosello, 209
13083-886 - Campinas, SP, Brasil
oliveira@cs.ualberta.ca

Osmar R. Zaïane[2]
[2]Department of Computing Science
University of Alberta
Edmonton, AB, Canada T6G 2E8
zaiane@cs.ualberta.ca

Abstract

The discovery of association rules from large databases has proven beneficial for companies since such rules can be very effective in revealing actionable knowledge that leads to strategic decisions. In tandem with this benefit, association rule mining can also pose a threat to privacy protection. The main problem is that from non-sensitive information or unclassified data, one is able to infer sensitive information, including personal information, facts, or even patterns that are not supposed to be disclosed. This scenario reveals a pressing need for techniques that ensure privacy protection, while facilitating proper information accuracy and mining. In this paper, we introduce new algorithms for balancing privacy and knowledge discovery in association rule mining. We show that our algorithms require only two scans, regardless of the database size and the number of restrictive association rules that must be protected. Our performance study compares the effectiveness and scalability of the proposed algorithms and analyzes the fraction of association rules which are preserved after sanitizing a database. We also report the main results of our performance evaluation and discuss some open research issues.

1 Introduction

The recent advance of data mining technology to analyze vast amount of data has played an important role in marketing, business, medical analysis, and other applications where pattern discovery is paramount for strategic decision making. Despite its benefits in such areas, data mining also opens new threats to privacy and information security if not done or used properly. Recent advances in data mining and machine learning algorithms have introduced new problems in privacy protection [6, 2]. The main problem is that from non-sensitive data, one is able to infer sensitive information, including personal information, facts, or even patterns that are not supposed to be disclosed.

The current status in data mining research reveals that one of the current technical challenges is the development of techniques that incorporate security and privacy issues. The main reason is that the increasingly popular use of data mining tools has triggered great opportunities in several application areas, which also requires special attention regarding privacy protection.

In this paper, we focus on privacy preserving association rule mining. We start by considering a motivating example discussed in [3, 4]. Suppose a situation exists in which one supplier offers products in reduced prices to some consumers and, in turn, this supplier receives permission to access the database of the consumers' customer purchases. The threat becomes real whenever the supplier is allowed to derive highly sensitive knowledge from unclassified data that is not even known to the database owners (consumers). In this case, the consumers benefit from reduced prices, whereas the supplier is provided with enough information to predict inventory needs and negotiate other products to obtain a better deal for his consumers. This implies that the competitors of this supplier start losing business.

The simplistic solution to address the problem of our motivating example is to implement a filter after the mining phase to weed out/hide the restricted discovered association rules. However, in the context of our research, the users are provided with the data and not the association rules and are free to use their own tools, and thus the restriction for privacy has to be applied before the mining phase on the data itself. For this reason, to address this particular problem, we need to develop mechanisms that will enable data owners to choose an appropriate balance between privacy and precision in discovered association rules. Such mechanisms can lead to new privacy control systems to convert a given database into a new one in such a way to preserve the general rules mined from the original database. The released database is called sanitized database.

The procedure of converting an original database into a sanitized one is called the sanitization process and it was initially introduced in [1]. To do so, a small number of transactions have to be modified by deleting one or more items from them or even adding noise to the data by turning some items from 0 to 1 in some transactions. This approach relies on boolean association rules. On one hand, this approach slightly modifies some data, but this is perfectly acceptable in some real applications [3, 4, 9]. On the other hand, such an approach must hold the following restrictions: (1) the impact on the non-restricted data has to be minimal and (2) an appropriate balance between a need for privacy and knowledge discovery must be guaranteed.

To accomplish these restrictions, we introduce new algorithms for balancing privacy and knowledge discovery in association rule mining. Our sanitizing algorithms require only two scans regardless of the database size and the number of restrictive association rules that must be protected. The first scan is required to build the index (inverted file) for speeding up the sanitization process, while the second scan is used to sanitize the original database. This represents a significant improvement over the previous algorithms presented in the literature [4, 9], which require various scans depending on the number of association rules to be hidden. One major novelty with our approach is that we take into account the impact of our sanitization not only on hiding the association rules that should be hidden but also on accidentally hiding legitimate rules that should not be hidden. Other approaches presented in the literature focus on the hiding of restrictive rules but do not study the effect of their sanitization on accidentally concealing legitimate rules or even generating artifact rules (i.e. rules that do not exist in the original database).

Our algorithms are integrated with the framework for enforcing privacy in association rule mining presented in [7, 8]. The framework is composed of a transaction retrieval engine relying on an inverted file and Boolean queries for retrieving transaction IDs from a database, a set of sanitizing algorithms, and performance measures that quantify the fraction of association rules which are preserved after sanitizing a database. Our experiments demonstrate that our algorithms are effective and achieve reasonable results when compared with the other approaches presented in [4, 9].

This paper is organized as follows. In Section 2, we provide the basic concepts to understand the issues addressed in this paper. In addition, the problem definition is given. We present the idea behind our framework in Section 3. In Section 4, we introduce new sanitizing algorithms. In Section 5, we present the experimental results and discussion. Related work is reviewed in Section 6. Finally, Section 7 presents our conclusions and a discussion of future work.

2 Basic Concepts

In this section, we briefly review the idea behind transactional databases and association rules. After that, we present the formulation of the research problem.

2.1 Transactional Databases

A transactional database is a relation consisting of transactions in which each transaction t is characterized by an ordered pair, defined as $t = \langle TID, list\_of\_elements \rangle$, where TID is a unique transaction identifier number and $list\_of\_items$ represents a list of items making up the transactions. For instance, in market basket data, a transactional database is composed of business transactions in which the list of elements represents items purchased in a store.

2.2 The Basics of Association Rules

Association rules provide a very simple but useful form of rule patterns for data mining. A rule consists of a left-hand side proposition (the antecedent or condition) and a right-hand side (the consequent). Both the left and right-hand side consist of Boolean statements (or propositions). The rules state that if the left-hand side is true, then the right-hand side is also true.

Formally, association rules are defined as follows: Let $I = \{i_1,...,i_n\}$ be a set of literals, called items. Let D be a database of transactions, where each transaction t is an itemset such that $t \subseteq I$. A unique identifier, called TID, is associated with each transaction. A transaction t supports X, a set of items in I, if $X \subset t$. An association rule is an implication of the form $X \Rightarrow Y$, where $X \subset I, Y \subset I$ and $X \cap Y = \emptyset$. Thus, we say that a rule $X \Rightarrow Y$ holds in the database D with *confidence* φ if $\frac{|X \cup Y|}{|X|} \geq \varphi$, where $|A|$ is the number of occurrences of the set of items A in the set of transactions D. Similarly, we say that a rule $X \Rightarrow Y$ holds in the database D with *support* σ if $\frac{|X \cup Y|}{|N|} \geq \sigma$, where N is the number of transactions in D.

Association rule mining algorithms rely on support and confidence and mainly have two major phases: (1) based on a support σ set by the user, frequent itemsets are determined through consecutive scans of the database; (2) strong association rules are derived from the frequent item sets and constrained by a minimum confidence φ also set by the user.

2.3 Privacy Preservation: Problem Definition

The scenario we address in this paper is one which deals with two parties A and B, A owning a transactional database and B wanting to mine it for association rules. The problem is how can A make some restrictive rules hidden regardless of which minimum support threshold B would use. Note that A does not know which association rule mining algorithm or support threshold B would use.

In this context, the database owner A needs to look for some sensitive association rules in order to prevent them from being disclosed. So A, the owner of the transactional database, has full access to the database and would know what should be restricted based on the application and the database content, whether these rules to restrict exist in the database or not. A only knows that if these rules exist they should not be disclosed to B. The user B has no knowledge that some rules were hidden. Once B gets access to the sanitized database, B can mine any available rule. The restricted rules, if they existed in the original database, are supposedly removed by the sanitization process by changing some transactions in the database. In other words, the user B does not have to know about the rules, and A only needs to know which rules (existing or not) should not be disclosed.

Given these facts, the specific problem addressed in this paper can be stated as follows: If D is the source database of transactions and R is a set of relevant association rules that could be mined from D, the goal is to transform D into a database D' so that the most association rules in R can still be mined from D' while others, representing restricted knowledge, are hidden. In this case, D' becomes the released database.

3 The Framework for Privacy Preservation

As depicted in Figure 1, our framework encompasses a transactional database (modeled into a text database), an inverted file, a set of sanitizing algorithms used for hiding restrictive association rules from the database, a transaction retrieval engine for fast retrieval of transactions, and performance measures that quantify the fraction of association rules which are preserved after sanitizing a database. We describe the inverted file, the transaction retrieval engine, and the performance measures in this section, and the new algorithms in Section 4.

3.1 The Inverted File Index

Sanitizing a transactional database consists of identifying the sensitive transactions and adjusting them. To speed up this process, we model transactions into documents in which the items simply become terms. This model preserves all the information and provides the basis for our indexing (inverted file), borrowing from the information retrieval domain. We index the transactional database with the purpose of speeding up the sanitization process.

In our framework, the inverted file's vocabulary is composed of all different items in the transactional database,

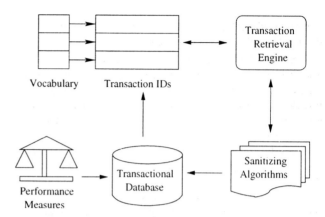

Figure 1. Privacy Preservation Framework

and for each item there is a corresponding list of transaction IDs in which the item is present. Figure 2 shows an example of an inverted file corresponding to the sample transactional database shown in the figure.

Docs	Items/Terms
T1	A B C D
T2	A B C
T3	A B D
T4	A C D
T5	A B C
T6	B D

Items	Freq	Transaction IDs
A	5	T1, T2, T3, T4, T5
B	5	T1, T2, T3, T5, T6
C	4	T1, T2, T4, T5
D	4	T1, T3, T4, T6

Vocabulary   Transaction IDs

Figure 2. An example of transactions modeled by documents and the corresponding inverted file

We implemented the vocabulary based on a perfect hash table [5], with no collision, insertion, or deletion. For a given item, one access suffices to find the list of all transaction IDs that contain the item.

3.2 The Transaction Retrieval Engine

To search for sensitive transactions in the transactional database, it is necessary to access, manipulate, and query transaction IDs. The transaction retrieval engine performs these tasks. It accepts requests for transactions from a sanitizing algorithm, determines how these requests can be filled (consulting the inverted file), processes the queries using a query language based on Boolean model, and returns the results to the sanitizing algorithm. The process of searching for sensitive transactions through the transactional database works on the inverted file. In general, this process follows three steps: (1) *Vocabulary search*: each restrictive association rule is split into single items. Isolated items are transformed into basic queries to the inverted index; (2) *Retrieval of transactions*: The lists of all transaction IDs of transactions containing each individual item respectively are retrieved; and (3) *Intersections of transaction lists*: The lists of transactions of all individual items in each restrictive association rule are intersected using a conjunctive Boolean operator on the query tree to find the sensitive transactions containing a given restrictive association rule.

3.3 Performance Measures

In this section, we introduce our privacy performance measures related to the problems illustrated in Figure 3.

Problem 1 occurs when some restrictive association rules are discovered. We call this problem **Hiding Failure**, and it is measured in terms of the percentage of restrictive association rules that are discovered from D'. Ideally, the hiding failure should be 0%. The hiding failure is measured by $HF = \frac{\#R_R(D')}{\#R_R(D)}$ where $\#R_R(X)$ denotes the number of restrictive association rules discovered from database X. In our framework, the proportion of restrictive association rules that are nevertheless discovered from the sanitized database can be controlled with the disclosure threshold ψ, and this proportion ranges from 0% to 100%. Note that ψ does not control the *hiding failure* directly, but indirectly by controlling the proportion of sensitive transactions to be sanitized for each restrictive association rule.

Problem 2 occurs when some legitimate association rules are hidden by accident. This happens when some non-restrictive association rules lose support in the database due to the sanitization process. We call this problem **Misses Cost**, and it is measured in terms of the percentage of legitimate association rules that are not discovered from D'. In the best case, this should also be 0%. The misses cost is calculated as follows: $MC = \frac{\#\sim R_R(D) - \#\sim R_R(D')}{\#\sim R_R(D)}$ where $\#\sim R_R(X)$ denotes the number of non-restrictive association rules discovered from database X. Notice that there is a compromise between the misses cost and the hiding failure. The more association rules we hide, the more legitimate association rules we miss.

Problem 3 occurs when some artificial association rules are generated from D' as a product of the sanitization process. We call this problem **Artifactual Patterns**, and it is measured in terms of the percentage of the discovered association rules that are artifacts. This is measured as: $AP = \frac{|R'| - |R \cap R'|}{|R'|}$ where $|X|$ denotes the cardinality of X.

4 Sanitizing Algorithms

In this section, before we introduce our sanitizing algorithms, we present our heuristic approach to sanitize a transactional database.

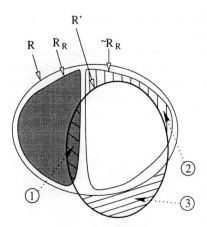

Figure 3. (A): Visual representation of restrictive and non-restrictive association rules and the rules effectively discovered after transaction sanitization.

4.1 Heuristic Approach

The goal of our heuristic is to facilitate proper information accuracy and mining, while protecting a group of association rules which contains highly sensitive knowledge. We refer to these rules as restrictive association rules and define them as follows:

Definition 1 (Restrictive Association Rules): Let D be a transactional database, σ the minimum support threshold, R be a set of all association rules that can be mined from D based on a minimum support σ, and $Rules_H$ be a set of decision support rules that need to be hidden according to some security policies. A set of association rules, denoted by R_R, is said to be restrictive if $R_R \subset R$ and if and only if R_R would derive the set $Rules_H$. $\sim R_R$ is the set of non-restrictive association rules such that $\sim R_R \cup R_R = R$.

Figure 3 illustrates the relationship between the set R of all association rules in the database D, the restrictive and non-restrictive association rules, as well as the set R' of patterns discovered from the sanitized database D'. 1, 2, and 3 are potential problems that respectively represent the restrictive association rules that were failed to be hidden, the legitimate rules accidentally missed, and the artificial association rules created by the sanitization process. We provide performance measures for these potential problems in Section 3.3.

A group of restrictive association rules is mined from a database D based on a special group of transactions. We refer to these transactions as sensitive transactions and define them as follows:

Definition 2 (Sensitive Transactions): Let T be a set of all transactions in a transactional database D and R_R be a set of restrictive association rules mined from D. A set of transactions is said to be sensitive, as denoted by S_T, if $S_T \subset T$ and if and only if all restrictive association rules can be mined from S_T and only transactions in S_T contain items involved in the restrictive association rules.

In most cases, a sensitive transaction derives more than one restrictive association rule. We refer to such transactions as conflicting transactions, since modifying one of them causes an impact on other restrictive transactions or even on non-restrictive ones. The *degree of conflict* of a sensitive transaction is defined as follows:

Definition 3 (Degree of Conflict of a Sensitive Transaction): Let D be a transactional database and S_T be a set of all sensitive transactions in D. The degree of a sensitive transaction t, denoted by degree(t), such that $t \in S_T$, is defined as the number of restrictive association rules that have items contained in t.

To illustrate the presented concepts, let us consider the sample transactional database in Figure 2. Suppose that we have a set of restrictive association rules $R_R = \{$A,B→D; A,C→D$\}$. This example yields the following results: the sensitive transactions S_T containing the restrictive association rules are $\{$T1, T3, T4$\}$. The degrees of conflict for the transactions T1, T3 and T4 are 2, 1 and 1 respectively. Thus, the only conflicting transaction is T1, which covers both restrictive association rules at the same time. An important observation here is that any association rule that contains a restrictive association rule is also restrictive. Hence, if A,B→D is a restrictive association rule but not A,C→D as above, any association rule derived from the itemset ABCD will also be restrictive since it contains ABD. This is because if ABCD is discovered to be a frequent itemset, it is straightforward to conclude that ABD is also frequent, which should not be disclosed. In other words, any superset containing ABD should not be allowed to be frequent.

Our sanitizing algorithms, presented in Section 4.2, act on the original database taking into account the degree of conflict of sensitive transactions.

4.2 Sanitizing Algorithms

Unlike algorithms that hide restrictive rules by modifying existing information in the database, our algorithms solely remove information by reducing the support of some items. This creates a smaller impact on the database since they do not generate artifacts such as association rules that would not exist had the sanitizing not happened. These artifactual rules are generated by a noise addition approach,

i.e., by adding some items in certain transaction. Such algorithms create the possibility of discovering some association rules that are not supposed to exist.

For our hiding strategies: Round Robin and Random algorithms, the inputs are a transactional database D, a set of restrictive association rules R_R, and a disclosure threshold ψ, while the output is the sanitized database D'. To sanitize a database, each sanitizing algorithm requires only two scans of the original database: one initial scan to build the inverted index, and an additional scan to alter some sensitive transactions, while keeping the other transactions intact.

All our sanitizing algorithms have essentially four major steps: (1) Identify sensitive transactions for each restrictive association rule; (2) For each restrictive association rule, identify a candidate item that should be eliminated from the sensitive transactions. This candidate item is called the *victim item*; (3) Based on the disclosure threshold ψ, calculate for each restrictive association rule the number of sensitive transactions that should be sanitized; and (4) Based on the number found in step 3, identify for each restrictive association rule the sensitive transactions that have to be sanitized and remove the victim item from them.

Our sanitizing algorithms mainly differ in step 2 in the way they identify a victim item to remove from the sensitive transactions for each restrictive rule, and in step 4 where the sensitive transactions to be sanitized are selected. Steps 1 and 3 remain essentially the same for all approaches.

The complexity of our sanitization algorithms in main memory is $O(n \times NlogN)$, where n is the number of restrictive association rules and N the number of transactions in the database. The proof of this is given in [7].

In section 5, we compare the effectiveness and scalability of Round Robin and Random algorithms with those ones proposed in [4, 9], and with the Item Grouping Algorithm, our best algorithm so far published and presented in [8]. The main idea behind the Item Grouping Algorithm, denoted by IGA, is to group restricted association rules in groups of rules sharing the same itemsets. If two restrictive rules intersect, by sanitizing the conflicting sensitive transactions containing both restrictive rules, one would take care of hiding these two restrictive rules in one step and consequently reduce the impact on the released database. However, clustering the restrictive rules based on the intersections between rules leads to groups that overlap since the intersection of itemsets is not transitive. By solving the overlap between clusters and thus isolating the groups, we can use a representative of the itemset linking the restrictive rules in the same group as a victim item for all rules in the group. By removing the victim item from the sensitive transactions related to the rules in the group, all sensitive rules in the group would be hidden in one step [8]. This again minimizes the impact on the database and reduces the potential accidental hiding of legitimate rules.

58

4.2.1 The Round Robin Algorithm

The main idea behind the Round Robin Algorithm, denoted by RRA, is: rather than selecting a unique victim item per given restrictive association rule, we select different victim items in turns starting from the first item, then the second and so on in each sensitive transaction. The process starts again at the first item of the restrictive rule as a victim item each time the last item is reached. The rationale behind this selection is that by removing one item at a time from the sensitive transactions it would alleviate the impact on the sanitized database and the legitimate association rules to be discovered, since this strategy tries to balance the decreasing of the support of the items in restrictive association rules. Selecting the sensitive transactions to sanitize is simply based on their degree of conflict. Given the number of sensitive transactions to alter, based on ψ, this approach selects for each restrictive rule the sensitive transactions whose degree of conflict is sorted in descending order. The rationale is that by sanitizing the conflict sensitive transactions that share a common item with more than one restrictive rule, this optimizes the hiding strategy of such rules in one step and, consequently, minimizes the impact of the sanitization on the discovery of the legitimate association rules. The sketch of the Round Robin Algorithm is given as follows:

Round_Robin_Algorithm
Input: D, R_R, ψ
Output: D'
Step 1. For each association rule $rr_i \in R_R$ do
    1. $T[rr_i] \leftarrow$ Find_Sensitive_Transactions(rr_i, D);
Step 2. For each association rule $rr_i \in R_R$ do
    1. $Victim_{rr_i} \leftarrow item_v$ such that $item_v \in rr_i$ and
        if there are k items in rr_i, the ith item is
        assigned to $item_v$ mod k in round robin fashion
Step 3. For each association rule $rr_i \in R_R$ do
    // $|T[rr_i]|$ is the number of sensitive transactions for rr_i
    1. $NumbTrans_{rr_i} \leftarrow |T[rr_i]| \times (1 - \psi)$
Step 4. $D' \leftarrow D$
    For each association rule $rr_i \in R_R$ do
    1. Sort_Transactions($T[rr_i]$); //in descending order of
        degree of conflict
    2. $TransToSanitize \leftarrow$ Select first $NumbTrans_{rr_i}$
        transactions from $T[rr_i]$
    3. in D' foreach transaction $t \in TransToSanitize$ do
        3.1. $t \leftarrow (t - Victim_{rr_i})$
End

The four steps of this algorithm correspond to the four steps described above in the beginning of this section. The first step builds an inverted index of the items in D in one scan of the database. In step 2, the victim item $Victim_{rr_i}$ is selected in a round robin fashion, for each restrictive association rule. Line 1 in step 3 shows that ψ is used to compute the number $NumbTrans_{rr_i}$ of transactions to sanitize. This means that the threshold ψ is actually a measure on the impact of the sanitization rather than a direct measure on the restricted association rules to hide or disclose. Indirectly, ψ does have an influence on the hiding or disclosure of restricted association rules. There is actually only one scan of the database in the implementation of step 4. Transactions that do not need sanitization are directly copied from D to D', while the others are sanitized before copied to D'. In our implementation, the sensitive transactions to be cleansed are first marked before the database scan for copying. The selection of the sensitive transactions to sanitize, $TransToSanitize$ is based on their degree of conflict, hence the sort in line 1 of step 4. When a transaction is selected for sanitization, only the victim items are removed from it (line 3.1 in step 4).

4.2.2 The Random Algorithm

The intuition behind the Random Algorithm, denoted by RA, is to select as a victim item, for a given restrictive association rule, one item of such rule randomly. Like the Round Robin Algorithm, the rationale behind this selection is that removing different items from the sensitive transactions would slightly minimize the support of legitimate association rules that would be available for being mined in the sanitized database. Selecting the sensitive transactions to sanitize is simply based on their degree of conflict. We evaluated the sanitization through the Random Algorithm by selecting sensitive transactions sorted in ascending and descending order. The approach based on descending order, in general, yielded the best results. That is why we have adopted such an approach for our algorithm. The sketch of the Random Algorithm is given as follows:

Random_Algorithm
Input: D, R_R, ψ
Output: D'
Step 1. For each association rule $rr_i \in R_R$ do
    1. $T[rr_i] \leftarrow$ Find_Sensitive_Transactions(rr_i, D);
Step 2. For each association rule $rr_i \in R_R$ do
    1. $Victim_{rr_i} \leftarrow item_v$ such that $item_v \in rr_i$ and
        if there are k items in rr_i, the item assigned to
        $item_v$ is random(k)
Step 3. For each association rule $rr_i \in R_R$ do
    // $|T[rr_i]|$ is the number of sensitive transactions for rr_i
    1. $NumbTrans_{rr_i} \leftarrow |T[rr_i]| \times (1 - \psi)$
Step 4. $D' \leftarrow D$
    For each association rule $rr_i \in R_R$ do
    1. Sort_Transactions($T[rr_i]$); //in descending order of
        degree of conflict
    2. $TransToSanitize \leftarrow$ Select first $NumbTrans_{rr_i}$
        transactions from $T[rr_i]$
    3. in D' foreach transaction $t \in TransToSanitize$ do
        3.1. $t \leftarrow (t - Victim_{rr_i})$
End

The four steps of this algorithms correspond to those in the Round Robin Algorithm. The only difference is that the Random Algorithm selects the victim item randomly, while the Round Robin Algorithm selects the victim item taking turns.

5 Experimental Results

We performed two series of experiments: the first to measure the effectiveness of our sanitization algorithms and the second to measure the efficiency and scalability of the algorithms. All the experiments were conducted on a PC, AMD Athlon 1900/1600 (SPEC CFP2000 588), with 1.2 GB of RAM running a Linux operating system. To measure the effectiveness of the algorithms, we used a dataset generated by the IBM synthetic data generator to generate a dataset containing 500 different items, with 100K transactions in which the average size per transaction is 40 items. The effectiveness is measured in terms of the number of restrictive association rules effectively hidden, as well as the proportion of legitimate rules accidentally hidden due to the sanitization. We selected for our experiments a set of ten restrictive association rules from the dataset ranging from two to five items in length with support ranging from 20% to 42% and confidence ranging from 80% to 100% in the database.

We ran the Apriori algorithm to select such association rules. The time required to build the inverted file in main memory was 4.05 seconds. Based on this inverted file, we retrieved all the sensitive transactions in 1.02 seconds. With our ten original restrictive association rules, 94701 rules became restricted in the database since any association rule that contains restrictive rules should also be restricted.

5.1 Measuring effectiveness

In this section, we measure the effectiveness of our algorithms taking into account the performance measures introduced in Section 3.3. We compare our algorithms with a similar one proposed in [4] to hide rules by reducing support, called Algo2a. The algorithm GIH designed by Saygin et al. [9] is similar to Algo2a. The basic difference is that in Algo2a some items are removed from sensitive transactions, while in GIH a mark ? (unknowns) is placed instead of item deletions.

Figure 4 shows a special case in which the disclosure threshold ψ is set to 0%, that is no restrictive rule is allowed to be mined from the sanitized database. In this situation, 30.16% of the legitimate association rules in the case of RRA and RA, 24.76% in the case of Algo2a, and 20.08% in the case of IGA are accidentally hidden.

While the algorithms proposed in [4, 9] hide rules reducing their absolute support in the database, in our frame-

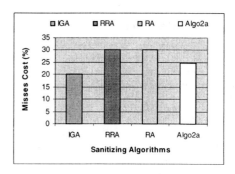

Figure 4. Effect of ψ on misses cost

work the process of modifying transactions satisfies a disclosure threshold ψ controlled by the database owner. This threshold basically expresses how relaxed the privacy preserving mechanisms should be. When $\psi = 0\%$, no restrictive association rules are allowed to be discovered. When $\psi = 100\%$, there are no restrictions on the restrictive association rules. The advantage of having this threshold is that it enables a compromise to be found between hiding association rules while missing legitimate ones and finding all legitimate association rules but uncovering restrictive ones.

Figure 5 shows the effect of the disclosure threshold ψ on the hiding failure and the misses cost for all three algorithms, considering the minimum support threshold $\sigma = 5\%$. Notice that RRA and RA yielded basically the same results. That is why their curves are very identical at the scale of the figure. As can be observed, when ψ is 0%, no restrictive association rule is disclosed for all three algorithms. However, 30.16% of the legitimate association rules in the case of RRA and RA, and 20.08% in the case of IGA are accidentally hidden. When ψ is equal to 100%, all restrictive association rules are disclosed and no misses are recorded for legitimate rules. What can also be observed is that the hiding failure for RA is slightly better than that for the other approaches. On the other hand, the impact of IGA on the database is smaller and the misses cost of IGA is the lowest among all approaches before $\psi = 75\%$. After this value, all the algorithms yield similar results.

Regarding the third performance measure, artifactual patterns, one may claim that when we decrease the frequencies of some items, the relative frequencies in the database may be modified by the sanitization process, and new rules may emerge. However, in our experiments, the problem artifactual pattern AP was always 0% with all algorithms regardless of the values of ψ. Our sanitization, indeed, does not remove any transaction. The same results can be observed for the algorithms presented in [4, 9].

We could measure the dissimilarity between the original and sanitized databases by computing the difference between their sizes in bytes. However, we believe that this

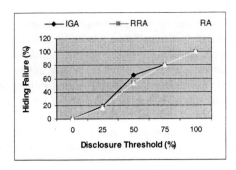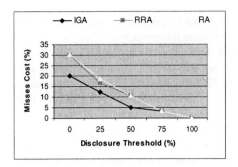

Figure 5. Effect of ψ on the hiding failure and misses cost

dissimilarity should be measured comparing their contents, instead of their sizes. Comparing their contents is more intuitive and gouges more accurately the modifications made to the transactions in the database.

To measure the dissimilarity between the original and the sanitized datasets we simply compare the difference of their histograms. In this case, the horizontal axis of a histogram contains all items in the dataset, while the vertical axis corresponds to their frequencies. The sum of the frequencies of all items gives the total of the histogram. So the dissimilarity between D and D', denoted by $dif(D, D')$, is given by:

$$dif(D, D') = \frac{1}{\sum_{i=1}^{n} f_D(i)} \times \sum_{i=1}^{n} [f_D(i) - f_{D'}(i)]$$

where $f_X(i)$ represents the frequency of the ith item in the dataset X.

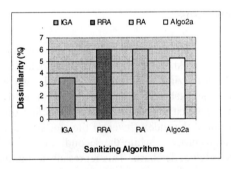

Figure 6. Difference in size between D and D'

Figure 6 shows the differential between the initial size of the database and the size of the sanitized database when the disclosure threshold $\psi = 0\%$. To have the smallest impact possible on the database, the sanitization algorithm should not reduce the size of the database significantly. As can be seen, IGA is the one that impacts the least on the database. In this particular case, 3.55% of the database is lost in the case of IGA, 6% in the case of RRA and RA, and 5.24% in the case of Algo2a.

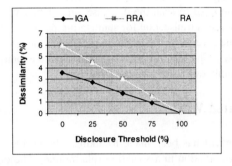

Figure 7. Difference in size between D and D'

Figure 7 shows the differential between the initial size of the database and the size of the sanitized database for our three algorithms with respect to the disclosure threshold ψ. Again, IGA is the one that impacts the least on the database for all values of the disclosure threshold ψ. Thus, as can be seen, the three algorithms slightly alter the data in the original database, while enabling flexibility for someone to tune them.

5.2 CPU Time for the Sanitization Process

We tested the scalability of our sanitization algorithms vis-à-vis the size of the database as well as the number of rules to hide. Our comparison study also includes the algorithm Algo2a.

We varied the size of the original database D from 20K transactions to 100K transactions, while fixing the disclosure threshold ψ and the support threshold to 0%, and keeping the set of restrictive rules constant (10 original patterns). Figure 8A shows that IGA, RRA, and RA increase CPU time linearly with the size of the database, while the CPU time in Algo2a grows fast. This is due the fact that Algo2a requires various scans over the original database, while our algorithms require only two. Note that our algorithms yield almost the same CPU time since they are very similar. Although IGA sanitizes less sensitive transactions, it has an overhead to group restrictive association rules that share the same items and optimizes this process.

We also varied the number of restrictive rules to hide from approximately 6000 to 29500, while fixing the size of the database to 100K transactions and fixing the support and disclosure thresholds to $\psi = 0\%$. Figure 8B shows that our algorithms scale well with the number of rules to hide. The figure reports the size of the original set of restricted rules, which varied from 2 to 10. This makes the set of all restricted rules range from approximately 6097 to 29558. This scalability is mainly due to the inverted files we use in our approaches for indexing the transactions per item and indexing the sensitive transactions per restrictive rule. There is no need to scan the database again whenever we want to access a transaction for sanitization purposes. The inverted file gives direct access with pointers to the relevant transactions. The CPU time for Algo2a is more expensive due the number of scans over the database.

6   Related Work

Some effort has been made to address the problem of privacy preservation in association rule mining. The class of solutions for this problem has been restricted basically to randomization, data partition, and data sanitization. In this work, we focus on the latter category.

The idea behind data sanitization was introduced in [1]. Atallah et al. considered the problem of limiting disclosure of sensitive rules, aiming at selectively hiding some frequent itemsets from large databases with as little impact on other non-sensitive frequent itemsets as possible. Specifically, the authors dealt with the problem of modifying a given database so that the support of a given set of sensitive rules, mined from the database, decreases below the minimum support value. The authors focused on the theoretical approach and showed that the optimal sanitization is an NP-hard problem.

In [4], the authors investigated confidentiality issues of a broad category of association rules and proposed some algorithms to preserve privacy of such rules above a given privacy threshold. Although these algorithms ensure privacy preservation, they are CPU-intensive since they require multiple scans over a transactional database. In addition, such algorithms, in some way, modifies true data values and relationships by turning some items from 0 to 1 in some transactions.

In the same direction, Saygin et al. [9] introduced a method for selectively removing individual values from a database to prevent the discovery of a set of rules, while preserving the data for other applications. They proposed some algorithms to obscure a given set of sensitive rules by replacing known values with unknowns, while minimizing the side effects on non-sensitive rules. These algorithms

also require various scans to sanitize a database depending on the number of association rules to be hidden.

Oliveira and Zaïane [8] introduced a unified framework that combines techniques for efficiently hiding restrictive patterns: a transaction retrieval engine relying on an inverted file and Boolean queries; and a set of algorithms to "sanitize" a database. In this framework, the sanitizing algorithms require two scans regardless of the database size and the number of restrictive patterns that must be protected.

The work presented here differs from the related work in some aspects, as follows: First, we extended our previous work presented in [8] by adding two new algorithms (Round Robin and Random) to the set of sanitizing algorithms. Second, the hiding strategies behind our algorithms deal with the problem 1 and 2 in Figure 3, and most importantly, they do not introduce the problem 3 since we do not add noise to the original data. Third, we study the impact of our hiding strategies in the original database by quantifying how much information is preserved after sanitizing a database. So, our focus is not only on hiding restrictive association rules but also on maximizing the discovery of rules after sanitizing a database. Another difference of our algorithms from the related work is that our algorithms require only two scans over the original database, while the algorithms presented in [4, 9] require various scans depending on the number of association rules to be hidden. This is due the fact that our sanitizing algorithms are built on indexes and, consequently, they achieve a reasonable performance.

7   Conclusions

In this paper, we have introduced two algorithms for balancing privacy and knowledge discovery in association rule mining. Our sanitizing algorithms require only two scans regardless of the database size and the number of restrictive association rules that must be protected. This first scan is required to build the index (inverted file) for speeding up the sanitization process, while the second scan is used to sanitize the original database. This represents a significant improvement over the previous algorithms presented in the literature [4, 9].

Our algorithms are integrated to the framework presented in [8], which combines three advances for efficiently hiding restrictive rules: inverted files, one for indexing the transactions per item and a second for indexing the sensitive transactions per restrictive association rule; a transaction retrieval engine relying on Boolean queries for retrieving transaction IDs from the inverted file and combining the resulted lists; and a set of sanitizing algorithms.

The experimental results revealed that our algorithms for sanitizing a transactional database can achieve reasonable

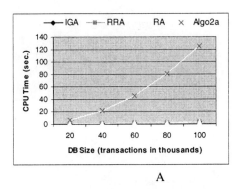 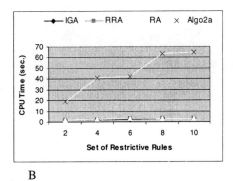

A   B

Figure 8. Results of CPU time for the sanitization process

results when compared with the other approaches in the literature. Such algorithms slightly alter the data while enabling flexibility for someone to tune them. In particular, the IGA algorithm reached the best performance, in terms of dissimilarity and in terms of preservation of legitimate association rules. On the other hand, the results suggested that RA is slightly better than the other algorithms for hiding failure.

Although our algorithms guarantee privacy and do not introduce false drops to the data, an extra cost is payed because some rules would be removed accidentally since there are functional dependencies between restricted and non-restricted rules. The rationale behind this is that privacy preserving association rule mining deals with a trade-off: privacy and accuracy, which are contradictory, i.e., improving one usually incurs a cost for the other.

It is important to note that our sanitization methods are robust in the sense that there is no de-sanitization possible. The alterations to the original database are not saved anywhere since the owner of the database still keeps an original copy of the database intact while distributing the sanitized database. Moreover, there is no encryption involved. There is no possible way to reproduce the original database from the sanitized one.

Currently, we are investigating new optimal sanitization algorithms that minimize the impact in the sanitized database, while facilitating proper information accuracy and mining. In addition, we are working on the optimization of the algorithms RRA and RA, specially in terms of preservation of legitimate association rules, since their results revealed they are promising.

8 Acknowledgments

Stanley Oliveira was partially supported by CNPq (Conselho Nacional de Desenvolvimento Científico e Tecnológico) of Ministry for Science and Technology of Brazil, under Grant No. 200077/00-7. Osmar Zaïane was partially supported by a Research Grant from NSERC, Canada. We would like to thank Yücel Saygin and Elena Dasseni for providing us the code of their respective algorithms for our comparison study.

References

[1] M. Atallah, E. Bertino, A. Elmagarmid, M. Ibrahim, and V. Verykios. Disclosure Limitation of Sensitive Rules. In *Proc. of IEEE Knowledge and Data Engineering Workshop*, pages 45–52, Chicago, Illinois, November 1999.

[2] C. Clifton. Using Sample Size to Limit Exposure to Data Mining. *Journal of Computer Security*, 8(4):281–307, November 2000.

[3] C. Clifton and D. Marks. Security and Privacy Implications of Data Mining. In *Workshop on Data Mining and Knowledge Discovery*, pages 15–19, Montreal, Canada, February 1996.

[4] E. Dasseni, V. S. Verykios, A. K. Elmagarmid, and E. Bertino. Hiding Association Rules by Using Confidence and Support. In *Proc. of the 4th Information Hiding Workshop*, pages 369–383, Pittsburg, PA, April 2001.

[5] M. Dietzfelbinger, A. R. Karlin, K. Mehlhorn, F. M. auf der Heide, H. Rohnert, and R. E. Tarjan. Dynamic Perfect Hashing: Upper and Lower Bounds. *SIAM Journal on Computing*, 23(4):738–761, 1994.

[6] D. E. O'Leary. Knowledge Discovery as a Threat to Database Security. In G. Piatetsky-Shapiro and W. J. Frawley (editors): Knowledge Discovery in Databases. AAAI/MIT Press, pages 507-516, Menlo Park, CA, 1991.

[7] S. R. M. Oliveira and O. R. Zaïane. A Framework for Enforcing Privacy in Mining Frequent Patterns. Technical report, TR02-13, Computer Science Department, University of Alberta, Canada, June 2002.

[8] S. R. M. Oliveira and O. R. Zaïane. Privacy Preserving Frequent Itemset Mining. In *Proc. of the IEEE ICDM Workshop on Privacy, Security, and Data Mining*, pages 43–54, Maebashi City, Japan, December 2002.

[9] Y. Saygin, V. S. Verykios, and C. Clifton. Using Unknowns to Prevent Discovery of Association Rules. *SIGMOD Record*, 30(4):45–54, December 2001.

XML Data Management

Extending XML-RL With Update

Guoren Wang, Mengchi Liu, and Li Lu
School of Computer Science, Carleton University
Ottawa, Ontario, Canada, K1S 5B6
{wanggr, mengchi}@scs.carleton.ca, llu@math.carleton.ca

Abstract

With the extensive use of XML in applications over the Web, how to update XML data is becoming an important issue because the role of XML has expanded beyond traditional applications, in which XML is used as a mean for data representation and exchange on the Web. This paper presents a novel declarative XML update language which is an extension of the XML-RL query language. Compared with other existing XML update languages, it has the following features. First, it is the only XML data manipulation language based on a higher data model. All of the other update languages adopt so-called graph-based or tree-based data models. Therefore, update requests can be expressed in a more intuitive and natural way in our language than in the other languages. Second, our language is designed to deal with ordered and unordered data. Some of the existing languages cannot handle the order of documents. Third, our language can express complex update requests at multiple level in a hierarchy in a simple and ¤at way. Some existing languages have to express such complex requests in nested updates, which is too complicated and nonintuitive to comprehend for end users. Fourth, our language directly supports the functionality of updating complex objects while all other update language do not support these operations. Lastly, most of existing languages use rename *to modify attribute and element names, which is a different way from updates on value. Our language modi£es tag names, values, and objects in a uni£ed way by the introduction of three kinds of logical binding variables:* object variables, value variables, *and* name variables. *The powerful ability of our language is shown by various examples.*

1. Introduction

As the emerging standard for data representation and exchange on the Web, XML is adopted by more and more applications. How to update XML data is becoming an im-

portant issue as the role of XML has been expanded beyond its traditional applications.

So far, several languages for pure querying and extracting XML data have been proposed, such as *XML-GL* [5], *XPath* [4], *Quilt* [6], *XML-QL* [8], *XQuery* [9], *XML-RL* [14] and *XQL* [11]. Also, several languages for both querying and manipulating XML data have been proposed, such as *Lorel* [2], *CXQuery* [7] and *XPathLog* [15]. However, all these XML query and manipulation languages adopt low-level graph-based or tree-based data models, which makes query statements and update requests unnecessarily a complicated and unnatural from database point of view.

In the Lorel data model [2], XML data are modeled as a directed graph with labelled edges. A node represents an XML element using a pair *<eid, value>*, where *eid* is a unique *element identi£er*, and *value* is either an atomic text string or a complex value. Although Lorel was originally designed for querying and updating semistructured data, it has now been extended to support XML data. XML-QL [8] uses an XML *Graph* to represent an XML document, in which each node is associated with an object identi£er and each edge is labelled with an element tag identi£er. Each XML *Graph* has a root. XML-GL [5] adopts an XML Graphical Data Model (XML GDM) to represent both XML DTDs and actual documents, in which XML elements are represented as rectangles and attributes and atomic values are represented as circles. Actually, these three data model are equivalent [3]. The other query and update languages except for *XML-RL* use tree-based data models, in which XML documents are modeled as node-labelled, tree-shaped graphs. The W3C consutium proposed a data model [10] for *XQuery*, *Quilt* and *XPath*, which represents XML data as a tree that contains seven types of nodes. In XQL [11], it was assumed that XML implied data model. Actually the data model used in XQL can be regarded as tree-structured. *CXQuery* [7] and *XPathLog* [15] are rule-based XML data manipulation languages, and the data model used is tree structured because they follow the query facilities of *XPath*.

The Lore system [2] has a simple declarative update language with the functions of creating and deleting database names, creating a new atomic or complex object, modifying the value of an existing atomic or complex object. Update requests are mainly expressed using a simple operator (+|-|:)=, where they are used to create, remove, or update the parent-child relationship between two existing objects. In addition, bulk loading a database is supported by the update language. However, it does not support update requests on ordered data. The syntax of value update requests is different from that of tag name updates (label in the Lore system). XPathLog [15] is a rule-based data manipulation language. When used in the head of rules, the "/" operator and the "[ ]" construct are used to specify which properties should be added or updated. But XPathLog only supports creation and modification of elements. CXQuery [7] is also a rule-based data manipulation language and it's update language is similar to XPathLog, but simpler than XPathLog's update language. XUpdate [12] is an XML update language and is a working draft of W3C. It allows users to create, insert, update and remove selected elements and attributes, and uses the expression language defned by XPath to locate elements or attributes to be updated. Update requests on ordered or unordered data are considered in XUpdate. The unique feature of XUpdate is that its syntax complies with the XML specifcation. Tatarinov et al. [17] extends *XQuery* with update, including *deletion*, *insertion*, *replacement* and *rename* of component elements or attributes. Update requests on ordered or unordered data are also considered and complex updates at multiple levels within a hierarchy are supported and specifed using nested update operations. All the existing update languages do not support updates of complex objects or expressed them with a more complicated and unnatural way due to the adoption of lower level data models.

Because the graph-based or tree-based data models are too low-level, the query and data manipulation languages based on them are not powerful enough, and query statements and update requests are expressed in a complicated, non-intuitive and unnatural way. Therefore, a novel data model for XML is proposed in [13], in which XML data is modeled in a way similar to complex object models [1, 16]. Based on this higher level data model, a rule-based declarative XML query language, XML-RL, is suggested in [14]. In this paper, we extend the query language with the functionality of data manipulation including *insertion*, *deletion* and *replacement*. It has the following advantages over other XML update languages.

(1) It is the only update language supporting the high level data model. Therefore, it can represent update requests in a simple, natural, and powerful way. (2) It is designed to deal with ordered and unordered data. (3) It can express complex multiple level update requests in a hierarchy in a simple and ¤at way. Some existing languages have to use nested updates to express such complex requests, which are

too complicated and non-intuitive to comprehend. (4) Most of existing languages use *rename* to modify tag names in a far different way from updating values. Our language modifes tag names, values and objects in a unifed syntax by using three kinds of logical binding variables: *object variables*, *value variables*, and *name variables*. (5) Our language directly supports the functionality of updating complex objects while all other update language do not support these operations.

The remainder of this paper is organized as follows. Section 2 gives an overview of XML-RL including the data model and the query language. Section 3 describes the update language proposed in this paper, including *insertion*, *deletion* and *replacement* of element and attribute objects, and demonstrates them with a lot of examples. Section 4 presents the architecture of the XML-RL system. Finally, Section 5 concludes this paper.

2 Overview of XML-RL

In this section, we give an overview of *XML-RL* by using the sample XML document in Figure 1. Its meaning is straightforward so no more explanation is necessary. We discuss brie¤y the data model and query language of *XML-RL* [13, 14] in sections 2.1 and 2.2, respectively.

2.1 Data Model

The *XML-RL* data model represents an XML document in a natural way as in complex object data models. In order to model basic concepts of XML specifcation, the following £ve kinds of objects are proposed in the *XML-RL* data model.

(1) An *element object* represents an element with tag and value pair, for example, $name \Rightarrow (firstname \Rightarrow Ayse, lastname \Rightarrow Alaca), faculty \Rightarrow null$. Symbol '$\Rightarrow$' is used to separate the name of object from the value of the object.

(2) An *attribute object* represents an attribute with name and value pair, for example, $@id \Rightarrow S200, @supervisor \Rightarrow F200$.

(3) A *tuple object* represents the relationship among elements and attributes in XML, for example,
$$[@id \Rightarrow S100, @supervisor \Rightarrow F100,$$
$$name \Rightarrow [firstname \Rightarrow Alisar, lastname \Rightarrow Smith],$$
$$program \Rightarrow Software\ Engineering]$$
where the pair '[' and ']' is used to construct a tuple object.

(4) A *list object* represents multiple values of an attribute or element, for example, $\{S100, S200\}$. The pair of '{' and '}' is used to construct a list object.

```
<department dname = "Computer Science">
    <faculty id = "F100", supervisee = "S100">
        <name> <firstname> Ayse </firstname> <lastname> Alaca </lastname> </name>
        <position> Associate Professor </position> <salary> $50,000 </salary>
    </faculty>
    <faculty id = "F200">
        <name> <firstname> Bob </firstname> <lastname> Smith </lastname> </name>
        <position> Associate Professor </position> <salary> $40,000 </salary>
    </faculty>
    <faculty> </faculty>
    <student id = "S100", supervisor = "F100">
        <name> <firstname> Alisar </firstname> <lastname> Smith </lastname> </name>
        <program> Software Engineering </program>
    </student>
    <student id = "S200">
        <name> <firstname> Mary </firstname> <lastname> Lee </lastname> </name>
        <program> Hardware Engineering </program>
    </student>
</department>
```

Figure 1. Sample XML document

(5) A *lexical object* represents the constant value of an element or an attribute, for example, *Marry*, *databases*.

Next we discuss briefly how to convert an XML document to the complex object model. From the XML document in Figure 1, we can see that there are five kinds of basic concepts, *string data*, *simple attribute*, *complex attribute* (i.e. IDREFS attribute), *simple element* and *complex element*. Correspondingly, there are five kinds of objects defined in the XML-RL complex data model, *lexical object*, *attribute object*, *list object*, *element object* and *tuple object*. The informal mapping rules from the XML document to the complex object model is as follows.

(1) A *string data* is mapping into a lexical object, for example, string data *Computer Science* is mapping to lexical object *Computer Science*.

(2) A *simple attribute* is mapped into an attribute object, for example, an attribute @*id*="*S100*" of element *student* is mapping to an attribute object @*id*⇒*S100*. Note that the symbol @ in font of *id* is used to distinguish attributes from elements.

(3) A *complex attribute* is mapped into an attribute object with a value of lexical list object, for example, an IDREFS attribute @*supervisee*="*S100*" of the first *faculty* element is mapping to an attribute object @*supervisee*⇒{*S100*}.

(4) A *simple element* is mapped into an element object, for example, <*name*> *Jones Gillmann* </*name*> is mapping to *name*⇒*Jones Gillmann*.

(5) A *complex element* is mapped into an element object with a value of tuple object that is composed of other simple objects or nested complex objects, for example,

$$<addr> <street> 708D \ Somerset </street>$$
$$<city> \ Ottawa </city>$$
$$<state> \ Ontario </state>$$
$$<zip> \ K2B \ 7Q8 </zip>$$
$$</addr>$$

is mapping to

$$addr \Rightarrow [street \Rightarrow 708D \ Somerset, city \Rightarrow Ottawa,$$
$$state \Rightarrow Ontario, zip \Rightarrow K2B \ 7Q8].$$

Using the above mapping rules, the XML document in Figure 1 can be naturally and straightforward converted into the complex object model shown in Figure 2.

2.2 Query Language

XML-RL [13, 14] is the only query language based on a higher data model, consisting of a *query* clause, which is used to extract data from XML documents based on a rule-based path expressions, and a *construct* clause, which is used to construct query results, as shown in the following.

Query $qexp_1, ..., qexp_n$
Construct cexp

where $qexp_1, ..., qexp_n$ are query expressions and *cexp* is resulting construct expression.

For more details about *XML-RL*, see [13, 14]. Because logical variables are closely associated with the extended

```
department⇒[@dname⇒Computer Science,
          faculty⇒[@id⇒F100, @supervisee⇒{S100},
                   name⇒[firstname⇒Ayse,lastname⇒Alaca],
                   position⇒Associate Professor, salary⇒$50,000],
          faculty⇒[@id⇒F200,
                   name⇒[firstname⇒Bob,lastname⇒Smith],
                   position⇒Associate Professor, salary⇒$40,000],
          faculty⇒null,
          student⇒[@id⇒S100,@supervisor⇒F100,
                   name⇒[firstname⇒Alisar,lastname⇒Smith],
                   program⇒Software Engineering],
          student⇒[@id⇒S200, name⇒[firstname⇒Mary,lastname⇒Lee],
                   program⇒Hardware Engineering]]
```

Figure 2. Complex object model

update language, here we first introduce them. *XML-RL* supports rich types of logical variables and restrictions on them: *object* variables, *name* variables and *value* variables. An object variables is used to hold an object including the name and the value of it. Consider the expression

(url)/department[@dname⇒Computer Science]/$f

where $f holds all component objects of the *Computer Science* department object, including one @dname attribute object, three *faculty* objects and two *student* objects. If we only want to hold one of the *faculty* objects, then we can apply a restriction on the logical variable: (url)//$f(faculty⇒[name⇒[last-name⇒Smith]]), where $f binds a *faculty* object. If we do not care about the value of the object variable, then we can use an anonymous variable $ in the restriction to match any value, i.e., (faculty⇒$). Also, the restriction can be simplified to (*faculty*). Of course, we can apply a restriction only on the value of the object variable. Consider the expression: (url)//$f($⇒[name⇒[lastname⇒Smith]]), where anonymous variable $ in the expression matches any tag name. The results of this query are the second *faculty* object and the first *student* object. A name variable is used to hold the names of objects. Consider the expression: (url)/department/$n⇒$, $n≠*student*, where the variable $n holds the names of *faculty* object. A value variable is used to hold the values of objects. Consider the expression: (url)/department/$⇒$v, where the variable $v is used to hold the values of a *faculty* object or a *student* object. Of course, a restriction can be applied to both name variables and value variables in a way similar to object variables.

Example 1. Consider the sample XML document in Figure 1, the following query is to find all faculties whose salary is more than $45,000 and position is *Associate Professor*. Assume that corresponding XML document is located at `http://www.scs.carleton.ca/`

`depcomputer.xml`.

Query (http://www.scs.carleton.ca/depcomputer.xml)/
     department/$f(faculty⇒[salary⇒>$45,000,position⇒
     Associate Professor])
Construct (http://www.scs.carleton.ca/result.xml)/
     department/$f

where $f matches element objects with tag name *faculty*. The result of the above query is the first *faculty* in the document of Figure 1.

For the sake of saving space, we do not use a real url address but (URL) in statements in the remainder of this paper in the case that no confusion occurs.

3 Update Language

In this section, we discuss our extension to XML-RL with updates, including *insertion*, *deletion* and *replacement* of atomic and complex XML objects in a straightforward way.

An update statement has the following form:

Query $qexp_1, \cdots, qexp_m$
     $uexp_1, \cdots, uexp_n$

where $qexp_1, \cdots, qexp_m$ are query expressions and $uexp_1, \cdots, uexp_n$ are update expressions that may be one of the following five basic forms.

(1) **Insert** *content* **into** $v;

(2) **Insert** *content* **before** $v;

(3) **Insert** *content* **after** $v;

(4) **Delete** $v;

(5) **Replace** $v **with** *content*;

where $v is a binding variable appearing in the *query* part while *content* can be either query expression or a *term* defined in [14]. The query result could be bound to variables to hold XML objects. These variables can be used in an update operation as an object to be updated and the *content* of the update. A binding variable may be used in several update expressions.

We describe the *insertion*, *deletion*, *replacement* operations below, and also discuss some exotic features of our update languages.

3.1 Insertion

Insertion operations are designed to deal with ordered and unordered data. There are three primitive insertion operations, *insert into*, *insert before* and *insert after*. The *insert before* operation is used to insert an XML object to the selected XML object as its preceding sibling for ordered XML data. Similarly, the *insert after* operation is used to insert an XML object to the selected XML object as its following sibling for ordered XML data. The *insert into* operation is used to insert an XML object as a child at arbitrary position of the selected XML object for unordered data, or as a last child for ordered XML data. We can use these three operations to do an insertion for simple objects and complex objects, including attribute, IDREFS attribute, simple element, and complex element.

First we discuss the insertion of simple attributes, then discuss the insertion of simple elements. Because attributes are unordered, the *insert into* operation is designed to insert attributes while the *insert before* and *insert after* are not applicable.

Example 2. The following update statement inserts an attribute @*supervisor* that points to faculty *Bob Smith* into the *student* element whose name is *Mary Lee*.

Query (URL)/department/$s(student⇒[name⇒
[$firstname$ ⇒Mary,lastname⇒Lee]])
(URL)//faculty⇒[@id⇒$id,name⇒
[$firstname$ ⇒Bob,lastname⇒Smith]]
Insert @supervisor⇒$id **into** $s

where variable $s is used to hold the *student* object whose name is *Mary Lee* and variable $id is used to hold the value of @id attribute object of the *Bob Smith* faculty object. If an attribute object with name @id is already contained in the selected element object $s, then the insertion operation is prohibited. It is possible that there might be more than one *student* whose name is *Mary Lee* in the XML document. In this case, the new attribute is inserted into each *Mary Lee student* object.

Note that although it is natural to use the *insert into* operation for unordered data, it can also be used for ordered data. In this case, the object is simply inserted into the target object as its last child.

Example 3. The following update statement adds an element *address* to each student element as the last child.

Query (URL)/department/$s(student)
Insert address⇒311 Bell St **into** $s

If we want to add the object to each student as the following sibling object of the *name* object. Then we can use the *insert after* operation as follows.

Query (URL)/department/student/$n(name)
Insert address⇒311 Bell St **after** $n

The case for *insert before* operation is similar.

The other existing update languages also provide the insertion operation to insert simple objects. But they need two primitive operations for this purpose. One is for the node object creation and the other is for the edge object linking, because they use graph-based or tree-based data models to represent XML data. Our update language just needs one primitive operation for such kind of updates.

Now we discuss the insertion of complex objects, including IDREFS attribute insertion, IDREFS entry insertion and complex element insertion. An IDREFS attribute insertion is similar to a simple attribute except that value expression of IDREFS attribute objects is different from that of simple attribute objects.

Example 4. The following update statement adds a new attribute *supervisee* that contains the id of student *Alisan Smith* to faculty *Bob Smith*.

Query (URL)/department/$f(faculty⇒[name⇒
[$firstname$ ⇒Bob,lastname⇒ Smith]]),
(URL)/department/student⇒[@id⇒$id,name⇒
[$firstname$ ⇒Alisar, lastname⇒Smith]]
Insert @supervisee⇒{$id} **into** $f

where {$id} is used to construct a list object. Variable $id holds the value of the @id attribute object of the selected *student* object and variable $f holds the selected *faculty* object. Therefore, the above statement inserts the object @supervisee⇒{S100} into the *faculty* object.

If we use the *insert into* operation to insert an entry to a list object, then the entry is inserted at the end of the list. We can also use the *insert before* or *insert after* operation to insert an entry at proper position in the list of IDREFS since an IDREFS is a named ordered list of IDs [17].

Example 5. The following update statement adds the id of the *student* object whose name is *Mary Lee* to an IDREFS attribute of the *faculty* object whose name is *Ayse Alaca*.

Query (URL)//faculty⇒[@supervisee⇒{$s}, name⇒
[$firstname$ ⇒Ayse,lastname⇒Alaca]],
(URL)//student⇒[@id⇒$id, name⇒
[$firstname$ ⇒Mary,lastname⇒Lee]]
Insert $id **after** {$s}.position(0)

where the list value variable {$s} holds a list of student ids, the single value variable $id holds another student *id* to be inserted. {$s}.*position(0)* is a built-in function to indicate the £rst reference. Like most programming languages, we use 0 to represent the £rst member of a list.

The following example discusses the insertion of complex elements.

Example 6. Insert a new faculty *Charis Adson* after *Bob Smith*.

Query (URL)/department/$f(faculty⇒[name⇒
                    [*firstname*⇒Bob, lastname⇒Smith]])
Insert faculty⇒[@id⇒F300,
            name⇒[*firstname*⇒Charis,lastname⇒Adson],
            position⇒Professor,
            salary⇒$70,000]
after $f

where the variable *$f* holds a *faculty* element for *Bob Smith*. After the update operation, a new *faculty* element is added after *Bob Smith*.

Although some other update languages provide the functions of insertions involving in IDREFS attributes, non of them can directly support the insertion of complex elements because they cannot directly express complex element object due to the data models used are too lower. In order to insert the above complex element object, most update languages needs 12 node object creation primitive operations and 12 edge linking primitive operations as shown in Figure 3, where complex elements are represented as *solid rectangles*, simple elements as *blank rectangles*, attributes as *circles*, and string data as *triangles*. This demonstrates our update language is quite powerful.

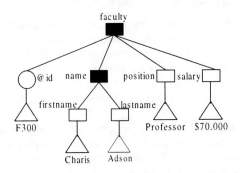

Figure 3. An example of complex element object

3.2   Deletion

The *delete* operation allows users to remove objects from an XML document. The deleted objects are usually the ones returned by the *query* part, either objects or their values. We cannot remove the name of an existing object. When the value of an element is deleted, the value of object will be set to *null*.

Example 7. The following update statement deletes the value of salary for a faculty whose *id* is *F200*.

Query (URL)/department/faculty⇒
                    [@id⇒F200,salary⇒$s]
Delete $s

where $s holds the value of *salary* objects of the *faculty* object whose *id* is *F200*. So deleting $s means the values of the selected *salary* objects are set to *null*.

Deleting a complex object or value will typically remove all of nested simple and complex objects within the deleted complex object or value. Because they may be references to the deleted objects, we assume that a reference is allowed to dangle. The same assumption is done in XQuery and its extended update language [17].

Example 8. The following update statement deletes a student whose name is *Alisar Smith* from the database.

Query (URL)/department/$s(student⇒
                    [name⇒[*firstname*⇒Alisar,lastname⇒Smith]])
Delete $s

where the variable $s is used to hold the *student* object whose name is *Alisar Smith*. The *student* object to be deleted contains two attribute objects, *@id⇒S100* and *@supervisor⇒F100*, and a complex element object, *name⇒(firstname⇒, lastname⇒Smith)*, and a simple element object *program⇒Software Engineering*. All these nested objects are also removed. So the reference to the deleted *student* object in the *faculty* object whose *id* is *F100* dangles.

3.3   Modi£cation

The modi£ed object must be returned by the *query* part before the *replace* operation can be applied. The *replace* operation can be used to modify tag names, values and objects, which depends on what the binding variable refers to. When the *replace* operation is used to change tag names, its function is equivalent to the *rename* operation designed in some other XML update languages.

Example 9. The following update statement changes the name of @id of all student objects to @sid.

Query (URL)/department/student⇒[@$id⇒$], $id=id
Replace $id **with** sid

where the variable $id holds the name of attribute @id objects of student objects. So the *replace* clause is used to change attribute name @id to @sid. Some update languages, such as the extended XQuery update language [17] and XUpdate [12], use *rename* primitive operation for change of tag names. Some languages such as lorel [2] do not support the operation directly. Object name updating can be indirectly supported in these languages in a two-steps way. First, select value from existing object and assign it to a new object name; second, delete the existing object. This is actually a combination of creation and deletion operations. While our language supports the change of tag names in the same syntax with value and object updates. So our language does not need an extra *rename* primitive operation.

Example 10. The following update statement adds some new data for faculty objects whose value is *null*.

Query (URL)/department/faculty$\Rightarrow$\$fv,\$fv=null
Replace \$fv
with [@id$\Rightarrow$0278,
name$\Rightarrow$[$firstname\Rightarrow$Nency, lastname$\Rightarrow$White],
position$\Rightarrow$Instructor, salary$\Rightarrow$\$35,000]

In the above update statement, the value of all *null* faculty objects is replaced with a complex values. Of course, the *replace* operation can also be used to update complex objects. For example,

Query (URL)/department/\$f(faculty$\Rightarrow$null)
Replace \$f
with faculty$\Rightarrow$[@id$\Rightarrow$0278,
name$\Rightarrow$[$firstname\Rightarrow$Nency, lastname$\Rightarrow$White],
position$\Rightarrow$instructor, salary$\Rightarrow$\$35,000]

This update statement has the same function as the above one, but it updates the *null faculty* objects rather than the *null* value of the *faculty* objects because \$f is used to hold the *null faculty* objects rather than their values. Similar to the insertion of complex objects, all other XML update languages cannot support the replacement of complex objects and their values because they cannot express complex objects and complex values due to the low level data models used.

3.4 Exotic Updates

In the above sections, we have discussed the *insertion*, *deletion* and *replacement* operations, and shown using some examples some unique features of our update language, such as insertion and replacement of complex objects, replacement of tag names and object values. In this section, we discuss some other exotic features of our update language, including *mixed update*, *multiple level update* and *copy semantics*.

In our update language, one and more insertions, deletions and replacements on tag names, objects and values can be performed together within one update statement.

Example 11. The following update statement changes the attribute name *ID* to *SID* and the value of *program* from *software engineering* to *hardware engineering* for student

elements, and inserts element *address* after element *program*.

Query (URL)//student$\Rightarrow$[@\$id$\Rightarrow$\$,\$p(program$\Rightarrow$\$a),
name$\Rightarrow$[$firstname\Rightarrow$Alisar,lastname$\Rightarrow$Smith]],
\$@id=@id
Replace \$id **with** SID,
Replace \$a **with** Hardware Engineering,
Insert address$\Rightarrow$440 Albert St **after** \$p

where the variable \$id is used to hold the name of attribute @id object, \$p is used to hold the program element object and \$a is used to hold the value of the program element object of the student object whose name is *Alisar Smith*. Three different update requests are mixed together within one update statement.

Sometimes we need to update multiple level elements in a hierarchy. Most update languages do not supports such kind of updates. In the extended XQuery update language [17], updating multiple level objects must use a complicated nested FOR WHERE UPDATE form. This make it too complicated to comprehend for users. However, our update language supports multiple level update requests in a ¤at and natural but powerful way based on the logical variables.

Example 12. The following update statement changes all attribute names of all department from @*dname* to @*id* and raise all Associate Professors' salary by 5%. The update statement is as follows.

Query (URL)/department$\Rightarrow$[@\$n$\Rightarrow$\$]/faculty$\Rightarrow$
[salary$\Rightarrow$\$s, position$\Rightarrow$Associate Professor],
\$@n=@dname
Replace \$n **with** id,
Replace \$s **with** \$s + (\$s $\times$ 5%)

where variable \$n holds the name of @*dname* attribute under *department* level while variable \$s holds the value of *salary* of the applicable *faculty* under *faculty* level. The update operations apply to the binding variables that refer to different level objects.

The following is another example of multiple level update.

Example 13. Insert an element *middlename* with value *Pears* for faculty *Ayse* and insert element *age* with value *20* for student *Alisar*. This is a multiple-levels update. The update statement is as follows.

Query (URL)/department/faculty/name/\$f
($firstname\Rightarrow$Ayse),
(URL)/department/student/\$n(name$\Rightarrow$
[$firstname\Rightarrow$Alisar])
Insert middlename$\Rightarrow$Pear **after** \$f,
Insert age$\Rightarrow$20 **after** \$n

where the £rst query expression gets faculty *Ayse*'s £rst name element and binds the result with variable *\$f* while the second query expression gets student *Alisar*'s full name and binds the result with variable $n. The update expressions add a middle name after f and add an *age* element after $n.

Besides reference semantics, the XML-RL data model supports copy semantics. Therefore, our update language also supports update operations based on copy semantics. If an existing object is used as part of *content* of an update operation, then the copy of the existing object rather than reference is used for this update. All other XML update languages do not support this kind of updates by copying objects from one document to another one or from one place to another place in the same document.

Example 14. Suppose a faculty *Cantor Cliton* is working in *Math* department, and his data is at `http://www.carleton.ca/depmath.xml`. Now assume that he is also working in the *computer science* department. Therefore, we need to copy his data from the site of *math* department to the site of *computer science* department after Professor *Bob Smith*.

Query (http://www.carleton.ca/depmath.xml)/
    department/$fm(faculty⇒[name⇒
    [*firstname*⇒Cantor, lastname⇒Cliton]]),
(http://www.carleton.ca/depcomputer.xml)/department/
    $fc(faculty⇒name⇒[*firstname*⇒Bob,
    lastname⇒Smith]])

Insert $fm **after** $fc

After updating, the data about *Cantor Cliton* is copied into the XML document of *computer science* department as the following sibling of Professor *Bob Smith*.

4   Architecture of XML-RL Update System

XML-RL is an XML query system that is currently being implemented at Carleton University, under Linux using Java 1.3.1, JCUP 0.10 for generating parsers and JLEX 1.25 for generating a lexical analyzer. The architecture of the update sub-system is shown in Figure 4.

The XML-RL update system consists of three main parts: the *XML Document Loader*, the *Language Processor* and the *Result Processor*. The *XML Document Loader* loads involved XML documents into the *XML-RL* system while the *Result Processor* constructs the £nal query results and stores them at corresponding site or display them in standard output in XML format. The *Language Processor* is the core part of the XML-RL system, which is in charge of analyzing language, processing query and update requests and managing XML-RL data model. These three parts are described as follows.

The *XML Document Loader* is in charge of parsing XML documents and transforming them to XML-RL data model. Therefore, it consists of two modules: *XML Parser* and *Model Transformer*. An XML document, which can

be either local or in elsewhere on the Internet, is parsed by the *XML Parser* and a *DOM tree* is generated. Then the *Model Transformer* converts the *DOM tree* into an in-memory internal representation of XML-RL data model. The tool *JAXP*, which is JAVA API XML Parser developed by SUN Company, is chosen as the appropriate XML parser for XML-RL's implementation. In addition, DOM API is chosen for XML-RL implementation because DOM API makes query and transformation easy since it generates an in-memory parser tree while event-based SAX API makes query and transformation dif£cult since it deals with XML documents piece by piece sequentially. The processing in the *Language Processor* is not done directly on XML document or DOM tree rather than the XML-RL data model, the DOM tree needs to be transformed to an in-memory internal representation of XML-RL data model. The transformation rules are described in Section 2.1 that are straightforward because the XML-RL data model provides a natural way to represent XML data.

The *Language Processor* is mainly in charge of processing query and update requests. It consists of £ve parts: the *User Interface*, the *Language Analyzer*, the *Query Processor*, the *Update Processor* and the *XML-RL Data Model Manager*. The *User Interface* receives user queries, constructs query statements, and passes them to the *Language Analyzer*. Three kinds of user interfaces are provided: textual user interface, graphic user interface, and web interface. They provides different kinds of environment for users to query and update XML documents. The *Language Analyzer* is in charge of handling user requests, including parsing the statements, checking the syntactic correctness, performing semantic validation with the assistance of the *Query Processor* and the *XML Parser*, and rewriting the user query and update requests into standard internal representation form. In the current implementation of XML-RL, JCUP and JLEX tools are chosen for the *Language Analyzer*. JLEX is a lexical analyzer generator, written for Java. It takes a speci£cation £le, then creates a Java source £le for the corresponding lexical analyzer. The lexical analyzer works as the scanner for parser. JLEX is used to construct a lexical analyzer to break characters up into meaningful tokens. JCUP is used to generate a LALR parser based on the speci£cation of our XML-RL update language grammar. When the *Query Processor* receives valid user query requests from the *Language Analyzer*, it calls the *XML Document Loader* to load involved XML documents. It processes the query requests according to the XML-RL data model, gathers the structural information for the *Language Analyzer* to check semantics. Calculations happen in the *Query Processor* when necessary, for example when a query has predicate or deductive operations. Finally, the *Query Processor* stores the query results to the *Variable Repository*, which bridges between the *Query Processor* and the *Update Processor* and between

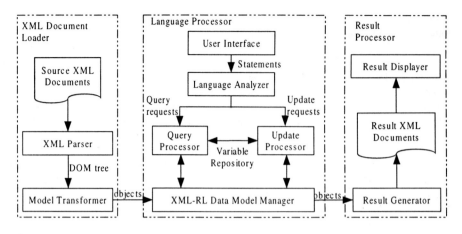

Figure 4. Architecture of XML-RL Update system

the *Query Processor* and the *Result Processor*.

Because variables are used in the *construct* part of a query request and in primitive operations of an update request, they play an important role in the XML-RL language. From the functional view of point, we just need a list of variables with their correspondingly possible values. However, XML allows elements to be nested and there can be more than one sub-elements contained inside an element. Also, there may be such kind of nested hierarchical relationship amongst the variables and these hierarchical information are very important for result constructing and update performing. Therefore, we designed two important data structures for the *Variable Repository*: *Variable Guide* and *Result Repository*. The *Variable Guide* is used to describe the hierarchical information appeared in the query. As shown in Figure 5, it is implemented as a *general tree*. Each node contains two part: the variable's path and variable's name. Actually, the *Variable Guide* only keeps track of the relationships between variables, which is used to construct the *Result Repository* and guide the performing of update operations.

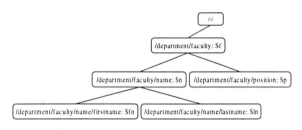

Figure 5. Variable Guide

The *Result Repository* is used to keep possible values of variables satisfying the query predicates. Also it keeps the hierarchical relationships amongst the values of the vari-

ables, which play an important role for result constructing and update performing. As shown in Figure 6, which corresponds to the Variable Guide in Fugure 5, the *Result Repository* is also implemented as a *general tree*. There are two kinds of nodes: variable nodes representing as bold rounded rectangles and value nodes representing as shadowed rounded rectangles. The variable nodes are ordered in the Result Repository based on the precedence they appear in the query. The value node contains two pointers: parent pointer and sibling pointer. Each variable value in a value node is a *reference* to corresponding XML-RL objects rather than a real object value.

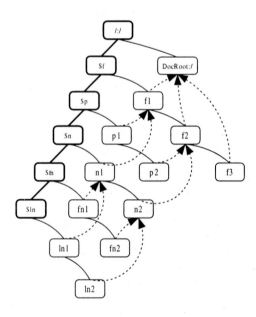

Figure 6. Result Repository

The *Update Processor* is in charge of performing primitive update operations. It may call the *Query Processor* to determine the corresponding objects involved in the update before performing the update. Then, it performs the semantic check based on the *Variable Repository* and the structural information gathered by the *Language Analyzer*. The updates with incorrect semantics will be prohibited by the *Update Processor*. It interacts with the *XML-RL Data Model Manager* to perform actual updates on corresponding objects stored in the memory. The *XML-RL Data Model Manager* is in charge of managing in memory objects represented in the XML-RL data model, including object location and basic object update primitives.

The *Result Processor* is in charge of result generation and result display and therefore consists of the *Result Generator* and the *Result Displayer*. After the query or update request is performed by the *Query Processor* or the *Update Processor*, the *Variable Repository* is then sent to the *Result Processor*. For the query request, the *Result Generator* constructs the £nal XML document based on the *Variable Repository* and the *construct rules*. For the update request, the £nal XML document is generated from the updated XML-RL data model. The *Result Displayer* modi£es the target XML document £le or displays it on the standard output.

5 Conclusions

We have described a declarative XML update language which is based on the XML-RL data model and query language, and demonstrated insertion, deletion and replacement primitive operations by various examples. Our update language has several unique features over other languages, such as the high level data model support, complex object insertion and replacement, multiple level update support in a ¤at way, copy semantics support. We are implementing the XML-RL system including query and update at Carleton University.

Acknowledgement. Guoren Wang's research is partially supported by the Teaching and Research Award Programme for Outstanding Young Teachers in Post-Secondary Institutions by the Ministry of Education, China (TRAPOYT) and National Natural Science Foundation of China under grant No. 60273079. Mengchi Liu's research is partially supported by National Science and Engineering Research Council of Canada.

References

[1] S. Abiteboul, R. Hull, and V. Vianu. *Foundation of Databases*. Addison Wesley, 1995.

[2] S. Abiteboul, D. Quass, J. McHugh, J. Widom, and J. Wiener. The lorel query language for semistructured data. *Int'l Journal on Digital Libraries*, 1(1):68–88, 1997.

[3] A. Bonifati and S. Ceri. Comparative analysis of £ve xml query languages. *SIGMOD Record*, 29(1):68–79, 2000.

[4] J. Cark and S. DeRose. Xml path language (xpath), ver. 1.0. tech. report rec-xpath-19991116, w3c. Technical report, November 1999.

[5] S. Ceri, S. Comai, E. Damiani, P. Fraternali, S. Paraboschi, and L. Tanca. Xml-gl: A graphical language for querying and restructuring xml documents. In *Proceedings of the 8th Int'l World Wide Web Conference, Toronto, Canada*, 1999.

[6] D. Chamberlin, J. Robie, and D. Florescu. Quilt: An xml query language for heterogeneous data sources. In *Proceedings of Third Int'l Workshop WebDB*, pages 1–25, May 2000.

[7] Y. Chen and P. Revesz. Cxquery: A nodel xml query language. Internet document. `http://citeseer.nj.nec.com/539624.html`.

[8] A. Deutsch, M. Fernandez, D. Florescu, A. Levy, and D. Suciu. A query language for xml. In *Proceedings of the Eighth International World Wide Web Conference, Toronto, Canada*, May 1999.

[9] P. Fankhauser. Xquery formal semantics: State and challenges. *SIGMOD Record*, 30(3):14–19, 2001.

[10] M. Fernandez, A. Malhotra, J. Marsh, M. Nagy, and N. Walsh. Xquery 1.0 and xpath 2.0 data model. W3c working draft: `http://www.w3.org/TR/2002/WD-query-datamodel-20021115/`, November 2002.

[11] H. Ishikawa, K. Kubota, and Y. Kanemasa. Xql: A query language for xml data. In *W3C Workshop on Query Language, Boston, Massachussets, USA*, 1998.

[12] A. Laux and L. Martin. Xupdate - xml update language. W3c working draft: `http://www.xmldb.org/xupdate/xupdate-wd.html`, 2000.

[13] M. Liu. A logical foundation for xml. In *Proceedings of the 14th International ConferenceAdvanced Information Systems Engineering(CAiSE'02), Toronto, Canada*, pages 568–583, May 2002.

[14] M. Liu and T. Ling. Towards declarative xml querying. In *Proceedings of The 3rd International Conference on Web Information Systems Engineering(WISE'02), Singapore*, December 2002.

[15] W. May. Xpathlog: A declarative, native xml data manipulation language. In *Proceedings of International Database Engineering & Applications Symposium(IDEAS'01)*, pages 123–128, July 2001.

[16] T. Ruhl and H. E. Bal. The nested object model. In *Proceedings of 6th ACM SIGOPS European Workshop on Matching Operating Systems to Application Needs*, pages 134–137, Dagstuhl Castle, Germany, September 1994.

[17] I. Tatarinov, Z. Ives, A. Halevy, and D. Weld. Updating xml. In *Proceedings of 2001 SIGMOD International Conference on Management of Data, Santa Barbara, CA, USA*, May 2001.

Dynamic Tuning of XML Storage Schema in VXMLR*

Zhengchuan Xu   Zhimao Guo   Shuigeng Zhou
Aoying Zhou
Department of Computer Science and Engineering
Fudan University, Shanghai, 200433, China
{zcxu, zmguo, sgzhou, ayzhou}@fudan.edu.cn

Abstract

This paper reports the techniques of dynamic tuning of XML storage schema in VXMLR, which is a XML management system based on RDBMS. With two different tuning strategies, VXMLR can dynamically adjust its storage schema based on the latest query records to improve its query processing efficiency. When a tuning event is triggered, VXMLR first derives from its history queries the initial mapping rules that map XML DTD to relational schemas; then by vertically partitioning the relational tables or redundantly storing the data relevant to history queries, some candidate storage schemas are generated; following that, the benefit and cost of each candidate schema is estimated; and finally a cost-driven approach is proposed to select the final storage schema from the candidate schemas under a certain space constraint. Experimental results validate the practicability and effectiveness of the proposed techniques.

Keywords *XML data management, storage schema, dynamic tuning, VXMLR*

1. Introduction

Extensible Markup Language (XML) is fast emerging as the dominant standard for representing and exchanging data on the Internet. As the amount of XML data increases, There is a growing interest in storing XML in relational databases so that the well-developed features of these systems (e.g. concurrency control, crash recovery and query optimizer) can be re-used.

Currently, there are mainly two classes of approaches to map XML into RDBMS: model based approaches and structure based approaches[1]. The former uses a fixed database schema to store the structures of all XML documents. For example, Florescu and Kossmann[2] proposed six simple mapping strategies to map the relationship between nodes and edges of DOM into the relational schema based on the DOM model of XML document. The latter derives relational schemas from the structures of XML documents. For example, Deutsch *et al.*[3] presented a declarative language, STORED, which allows user to define mappings from the structure of semistructured data to relational schemas; and Shanmugasundaram *et al.*[4] introduced two ways to map DTDs into relational schemas, namely SHARED and HYBRID respectively. HYBRID inlines all of the descents not attached by * in DTD graph into their parents, while SHARED maps the nodes with multiple parents (*i.e.*, in-degree greater than 1) into independent relations. The different manners to deal with these nodes with in-degree greater than 1 consist of the only difference between SHARED and HYBRID. Comparing with the model based approaches, the structure based approaches, like the inlining techniques presented in [4], produce fewer document fragments, hence require less joins for path traversal, and subsequently outperform the model based approaches. Tian *et al.*[5] compared the performance of alternative mapping approaches, including relational and non-relational ones, and showed that structural mapping approach is the best one when DTD is available.

While generating storage schema, approaches mentioned above take only the processed XML documents into account, without considering the queries information. Those approaches may not generate efficient storage schema for an arbitrary XML document and a workload composed of an expected set of queries.

Recently, some scholars have started to address the problem of designing efficient XML storage schema by using user's query information. Bohannon *et al.*[6] presented a framework to design XML storage for a given application (defined by XML Schema, XML data statistics, and an XML query workload); Zheng *et al.*[7] studied storage schema selection based on the cost of given user queries.

*This work is supported by the National Natural Science Foundation of China under Grant No. 60228006 and the Fok Ying Tung Education Foundation under Grant No. 81062.

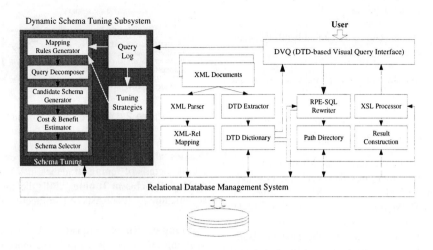

Figure 1. The architecture of VXMLR

The major difference between their papers is the applied algorithms of schema selection.

Note that for a running XML documents management system, user's queries may change along with time and may not be fully expected. In such a situation, it is better that the system can dynamically adjust its storage schema based on changing user queries. According to Zipf's law[8], the relative probability of the i'th most frequent query is proportional to $1/i$. So we can roughly expect user's queries based on the query records. That is to say, we can dynamically adjust XML storage schema based on user's query records to exploit the potential of system's query processing efficiency as a whole.

In this paper, we present the techniques of dynamic storage schema tuning in VXMLR(*Visual XML-R*elational database system). VXMLR is a visual and RDBMS based XML documents management system developed in Fudan University, it had been demonstrated in VLDB 2001 [9]. Initially, VXMLR adopts inlining techniques of [4] to map DTDs into relational schemas, then it can dynamically tuning its storage schema according to user's history workload. Our work is distinct from that of [6] and [7] at least in the following aspects:

- Our focus is *dynamic tuning* of XML storage schema according to user's query records.

- We adopt different approach to select storage schema. The knapsack algorithm is adapted to schema selection under given space constraint.

- To further improve system efficiency, we allows some relevant data to be stored redundantly.

- Our techniques have been fully implemented in a running system, *i.e.* VXMLR.

Major contributions of this paper are as follows:

1. Concrete algorithms are proposed for XML storage schema tuning based on user's history queries under given space constraint.

2. Two dynamic tuning strategies are given. One is based on query efficiency, the other is based on query content.

3. Proposed techniques (algorithms and strategies) are fully implemented in VXMLR.

4. Experiments are conducted to validate the practicability and effectiveness of the proposed techniques.

The remainder of this paper is organized as follows. Section 2 introduces briefly the VXMLR system, including its architecture and storage method. Section 3 provides the techniques of XML storage schema tuning based on history queries. Section 4 presents two dynamic tuning strategies of XML storage schema. Section 5 gives some experimental results of VXMLR. Section 6 concludes the paper.

2. VXMLR and its Storage Method

2.1. Introduction to VXMLR

VXMLR is a visual XML-relational database system for managing XML documents by relational databases. The system has the following features:

- XML documents are mapped to relational tables and stored in a relational database.

- XML Storage Schema can be dynamically adjusted according to the latest query records.

- A visual query interface provides an easy way to query XML data stored in relational databases.

- A query rewriting module was developed to transform a path expression query into a set of SQL statements.

Figure 1 shows the architecture of VXMLR. XML documents are stored in a relational database system, managed by a relational DBMS. An input XML document is first parsed into a DOM tree. At the same time, DTD for the document is extracted. The document tree is then mapped to relational tables and stored in the database. Both DTD structure and mapping information are maintained in a DTD Directory, which is used for rewriting XML queries and constructing results. To access XML data stored in the database, VXMLR supports a visual querying interface. Through the interface, DTD structures of stored XML documents are displayed, and users can form queries by clicking the relevant data elements and entering conditions. Such queries are first expressed as path expression queries, then they are transformed into SQL statements to be submitted to the underlying relational DBMS. To generate efficient SQL statements from path expression queries, a path directory are used in the query rewriting process to reduce the number of SQL statements and simplify join conditions. The returned query results are constructed and expressed using XSL, which are then delivered to the user through the querying interface.

With two different tuning strategies, VXMLR can dynamically adjust its storage schema based on the latest query records to improve its query processing efficiency. When a tuning event is triggered, VXMLR first derives from its history queries the initial mapping rules that map DTD to relational schemas; then by vertically partitioning the relational tables or redundantly storing the data relevant to history queries, some candidate storage schemas are generated; following that, the benefit and cost of each candidate schema is estimated; and finally a cost-driven approach is proposed to select the final storage schema from the candidate schemas under a certain space constraint.

In VXMLR, the **Dynamic Storage Schema Tuning** subsystem is responsible for XML storage schema tuning task. It consists of three modules: **Query Log**, **Dynamic Tuning Strategies**, and **Schema Tuning**. **Query Log** is responsible for recoding the query information submitted by user, which includes query statements, query frequency and time cost for query processing. This information will be used for storage schema tuning. **Dynamic Tuning Strategies**

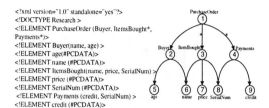

Figure 2. DTD(Purchase.dtd) and DTD Graph

decides when to trigger schema tuning event. We will delay the details of tuning strategies in VXMLR till Section 4. Module **Schema Tuning** fulfills the concrete process of schema tuning, it consists of five functional components as follows.

Mapping Rules Generator. Used for generating the mapping rules, *i.e.* generating the mapping rules for the nodes with in-degree greater than 1 based on the affinity between them and their parents in history queries.

Query Decomposer. Used for decomposing every query in query log into a series of SQL statement which only access a single table and joins between them.

Candidate Schema Generator. Used for deriving candidate schemas by using overlapping independent storage and non-overlapping independent storage,

Benefit and Cost Estimator. Used for estimating the query benefit and space cost of every candidate schema, and computing the ratio of benefit to cost.

Schema Selector. Used for selecting the final schema from all candidate schemas by trading off between query benefit and storage cost.

2.2. The Storage Method of VXMLR

The basic storage approach in VXMLR is structure-based approach: by mapping DTDs into relational schemas, XML documents will be mapped to relational databases by using these schemas. The structure of XML documents is described by their DTDs, There are two major issues that must be addressed before generating relational schemas from XML DTDs. The first is the conflict between the two-level nature of relational schemas and the arbitrary nesting of XML DTD schemas, and the second is the set-value attributes and recursions in DTDs.

The first issue is dealt with by mapping root nodes and separate nodes into separate relations and inlining the child nodes into the relations where their parents reside. The second issue is tackled by mapping the set-value nodes into separate relations, and as to the recursive nodes, one of them is made a separate relation. Concretely, first simplifying the DTD as a DTD graph, in which elements are nodes linked by directed edges from elements to their subelements; then mapping the following three types of nodes into separate relations:

1. nodes with in-degree zero (the separate nodes).

2. nodes with at least one incoming edge labelled with * operator (the set-value nodes).

3. one of the nodes with in-degree of one that are mutually recursive.

And the nodes with in-degree one and not in a recursive path, are flatten and inlined into the relation corresponding to its nearest ancestor.

As for the nodes with multiple parents (*i.e.* in-degree greater than 1), in structure-based approaches, SHARED maps these nodes into separate relations, while HYBRID inlines them into the relational tables where their parents are put.

Figure 2 shows an example DTD and its DTD graph about the purchase order information. According to the mapping rules above, the nodes *PurchaseOrder, ItemBought, Payments* of this DTD will be made separate relations, and the nodes *age, price, credit* will be inlined into the relational tables *PurchaseOrder, ItemBought* and *Payments* respectively. In this DTD Graph, only nodes *name* and *SerialNum*'s in-degree is greater than 1 and they are not set-value nodes. If we inline these nodes into the relational tables where their parents situate, that is HYBRID approach, the node *name* is inlined into relational tables *PurchaseOrder* and *Itembought*, and the node *SerialNum* is inlined into relational tables *Itembought* and *Payments*. We call the relational schema generated by this approach Hybrid schema, shown in Figure 3.

> *PurchaseOrder (ID, Buyer_age, Buyer_name, PID);*
> *ItemBought (ID, name, price, SerialNum, PID);*
> *Payments (ID, SerialNum, credit, PID);*

Figure 3. Hybrid schema

Otherwise we map them into separate tables respectively (we call it outline technique in this paper), that is SHARED approach, the relational schema generated by this approach is called Shared schema. For example, the node *name* is mapped into a separate relational table *name*, and the node *SerialNum* is mapped into another separate relational table *SerialNum*.

For the need of query transformation and reconstruction, we must preserve the join information in every separate relation by two attributes *ID* and *PID* (shown in Figure 3).

For the nodes with in-degree greater than 1, if the queries access these nodes and their parents simultaneously, inlining these nodes is better than outlining them, because inlining them reduces the number of joins required in the SQL queries. But if the queries only access these nodes or their subnodes, outlining them is better than inlining them, because inlining them causes these queries to access all ta-

bles where these nodes' parents reside and union all results, while these queries only need access one table if these nodes are outlined. So we should determine to inline or outline the nodes with in-degree greater than 1 according to the information of expected queries.

3. Tuning of Storage Schema

We state the problem of tuning XML storage schema in VXMLR as follows. VXMLR system has a history workload consisting of queries $\{Q_i | 1 \leq i \leq N\}$, the weight of Q_i be W_i, which is the execution time of the query over the initial storage schema (The initial schema can be Shared or Hybrid, it doesn't affect our tuning process), and the frequency of Q_i be F_i (or the query's occurrence). Suppose storage space be M, we adjust the storage schema to make the cost of the history queries as minimal as possible.

3.1. Mapping Rules for Nodes with In-degree Greater Than 1

As mentioned in section 2, inlining or outlining the nodes with in-degree greater than 1 indiscriminatingly will deteriorate the performance in some cases. For example a query requesting all serial numbers of purchase orders, if node SerialNum is inlined (just like in Figure 3), this query must access the two tables *ItemBought* and *Payments*, and union the results. But if it is outlined, it only need access the table *SerialNum*. So here we should outline the node SerialNum. At the same time the other query requests all buyers' name. If we inline the node *name*, this query only need access the table *PurchaseOrder*, but if the node is outlined, it must access the two tables *PurchaseOrder, name* and join them. In this case the node *name* should be inlined into the tables where its parents are. Therefore based on these two queries, we map the DTD into the new schema shown in Figure 4.

> *PurchaseOrder (ID, Buyer_name, Buyer_age, PID);*
> *ItemBought (ID, Item_name, price, PID);*
> *Payments (ID, credit, PID);*
> *SerialNum (ID, SerialNum, PID);*

Figure 4. The tuned relational schema

So we can determine to inline or outline a node with in-degree greater than 1, according to the affinity between these nodes and their parents based on history queries.

Definition 1. The queries where the nodes and their parents appear simultaneously are called **affinitive queries** for these nodes, other queries are called **non-affinitive queries**.

Definition 2. A node's **affinity** is measured by the sum of product of each affinitive query's weight and its frequency. And the sum of product of each non-affinitive query's weight and its frequency equals to **non-affinity**.

For one node if its affinity is bigger than its non-affinity, we inline it, otherwise we outline it. Assuming that the set of nodes with in-degree greater than 1 is $\{N_j|1 \leq j \leq m\}$, based on the set of history queries mentioned above, we design the algorithm MappingDegree2Node to determine the mapping manners of these nodes. Figure 5 gives the pseudo-code for the algorithm MappingDegree2Node.

Using this algorithm and inlining techniques, we can get an improved relational schema. And the execution time of this algorithm scales with the number of queries and the size of DTD. Next, we adjust the relational schema further.

```
Algorithm MappingDegree2Node
Input:Set of nodes with in-degree greater than 1
{N_j} and history queries {Q_i}.
Output:Outline or inline the node N_j
    For each N_j {
        W_inline = 0; W_outline = 0;
        For each {Q_i} {
            If N_j and its parents co-exist in Q_i
                W_inline + + = W_i * F_i;
            Else W_outline + + = W_i * F_i;
        }
        if W_inline > W_outline
            inline N_j;
        else outline N_j;
    }//End
```

Figure 5. Algorithm MappingDegree2Node

3.2. Query Decomposition

An XML query is a query with simple path expressions or regular path expressions. We can transform the query with regular path expressions into several queries with simple path expressions using the transforming rules in [4]. And using the rewriting rules we can rewrite XML queries with simple path expressions as the SQL queries over tables after we store the XML data in relational databases [4]. So every XML query in the set $\{Q_i|1 \leq i \leq N\}$ can be transformed into a series of sub-queries over relational tables, each of which only accesses a single table, and the joins between them. For further discussion, we list the notation used in this paper in Table 1, where the R is a relation.

If there is a query Q_i accessing the tables $R_1 \cdots R_n$ with the frequency F_i and the weight W_i, we decompose it into $SubQ_1 \cdots SubQ_n$ and the joins between them, the sub-query $SubQ_i$ only accesses the table R_i.

We represent every sub-query as a set of relative attributes, just like $SubQ_i := \{Attr_j|1 \leq j \leq k\}$ where $Attr_j$ is an column accessed by the query in the relational table. The data size relative to this sub-query is represented

Table 1. Notation

Symbol	Definition
$|R|$	Number of pages of relation R
$\|R\|$	Total number of instances of R
$Attr_j$	The attributes of R, $1 \leq j \leq k$. k is the total number of attributes of R
$Sizeof(Attr_j)$	The data size of the type of $Attr_j$
$|R's\ join\ info|$	Sum of data size for joins between R and other tables, equals $(Sizeof(ID) + Sizeof(PID)) * \|R\|$

as $|SubQ_i|$, and its computing formula is as follows:

$$|SubQ_i| = \left(\sum_{j=1}^{k} (Sizeof(Attr_j) * \|R_i\|) \right)$$
$$+ |R_i's\ join\ info|. \qquad (1)$$

We assume that $SubQ_i's$ frequency is $SubF_i$, and its weight is $SubW_i$. Then

$$SubF_i = F_i. \qquad (2)$$

$$SubW_i = \left(\frac{|R_i|}{|R_1| + \cdots + |R_n|} \right) * W_i. \qquad (3)$$

If we decompose all queries in the set $\{Q_i|1 \leq i \leq N\}$, we can get a new set of sub-queries $\{Q_{ij}|1 \leq i \leq N, 1 \leq j \leq m\}$. All identical sub-queries in this set can be represented by one of them whose frequency equals to the sum of their frequencies and weight equals to the biggest one among them, then we get the set of sub-queries $\{SubQ_i|1 \leq i \leq n\}$. Further, we can get a lot of candidate storage schemas on the basis of this set. Next, we give the analysis of XML query cost.

3.3. XML Query Cost

In this paper, we only want to select the candidate storage schema with highest benefit/cost ratio, so we only pay attention the different efficiencies of different storage schemas, and don't care about the accurate computation of query cost.

It is well known that the cost of a query grows with the size of the accessed table [10]. If a query accesses a relation R, its cost can be viewed as a monotonic function of $|R|$.

A join's cost is the monotonic function of data size accessed by it too. In this paper we consider 3 types of classic joins, i.e. nested-loop join, sort merge join and hash join. Suppose there are two relations R and S, Sel_R and Sel_S are their selectivity respectively. The cost models of these 3 types of joins between S and R [11] are as follows:

Nested-Loop join:
$$C_{nest} = |R| + (|R| * |S|) + Sel_R * Sel_S * |R|$$
Sort-Merge join:
$$C_{merge} = 2 * |R| * \log|R| + 2 * |S| * \log|S| + |R| + |S| + Sel_R * Sel_S * |R|$$
Hash join:
$$C_{hash} = 3 * (|R| + |S|) + Sel_R * Sel_S * |R|$$

It is clear that the cost of all these joins is the monotonic function of the size of the tables accessed. As mentioned above, the query on XML documents can be transformed into a series of sub-queries and the joins between them, and each sub-query only accesses a separate table. Therefore the XML query cost equals to the sum of all sub-queries cost and the joins cost between them. According to the analysis of the query's cost in relational database, we must minimize every relational table accessed to reduce the query cost, as a result the efficiency is improved.

So to tune the storage schema is to make the data irrelevant to sub-queries in tables as small as possible. Therefore, we put the data relevant to a sub-query into a separate table, i.e. only store the data of attribute columns relevant to a sub-query into a new table. We call this technique **independent storage** of the sub-query. Independently storing a sub-query results in a new candidate schema, so by independently storing sub-queries, we can get a lot of candidate schemas. And the benefit and cost of independently storing a sub-query equal to the benefit and cost of the new schema generated from this adjustment. We give the computing formulas of benefit and cost in next section.

3.4. Estimation of Query Benefit and Storage Cost

We present some notations in this paper as follows. The query benefit of storing $SubQ_i$ independently is $B(SubQ_i)$, the storage cost is $C(SubQ_i)$. The original table accessed by $SubQ_i$ is R_i, $SubQ_i's$ frequency is $SubF_i$, and its weight is $SubW_i$. And the new relational table created for independently storing $SubQ_i$ is R_i', and $|R_i'|$ equals to $|SubQ_i|$.

We define the benefit of a query's independent storage as the reduction of the size of the accessed table. The computing formula of query benefit is as follows:

$$B(SubQ_i) = (|R_i| - |R_i'|) * SubF_i * SubW_i$$
$$= (|R_i| - |SubQ_i|) * SubF_i * SubW_i. \quad (4)$$

And the storage cost is the extra space that is used to store the data relevant to the sub-query independently. There are two methods for independent storage. One is **overlapping independent storage**, namely creating a new table and copying the relevant data into it, while the relevant data still remains in the original table. The other is **non-overlapping independent storage**, i.e., moving the relevant data from the original table into a new table, that is

```
for $s in document("Purchase.xml") //PurchaseOrder
    where $s/Buyer/name/text() = "Tom"
        and $s/ItemBought/price/text() = "$1000"
return $s/ItemBoght/name/text()
```

Figure 6. A query example

vertical partition of the original table. Note that the join information, i.e. the data in columns ID and PID, still must be copied into the new table and redundantly stored.

The storage cost of these two approaches are different. The storage cost of overlapping independent storage is the size of the new table, its computing formula is as follows:

$$C_{overlapping}(SubQ_i) = |R_i'| = |SubQ_i|. \quad (5)$$

And the non-overlapping independent storage cost is only the size of redundant part which is the join information, thus its computing formula is as follows:

$$C_{non-overlapping}(SubQ_i) = |R_i's\ join\ info|. \quad (6)$$

We illustrate the computation of query benefit and storage cost by the following example.

Example 1. Consider a query on the XML document Purchase.xml conforming the DTD in Figure 2. It requests the names of items which are bought by Tom and whose prices are $1000. Suppose that the frequency and weight of this query are F_i and W_i respectively, and the relational schema to store XML data is the schema in figure 4. We present this query in XQuery(shown in Figure 6).

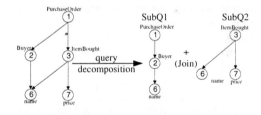

Figure 7. Decomposition of a sample query

The query path is illustrated in the left part of Figure 7, and this query can be decomposed into two sub-queries SubQ1, SubQ2 and the join between them. The table accessed by SubQ1 is *PurchaseOrder (ID, Buyer_name, Buyer_age, PID)*. The table accessed by SubQ2 is *ItemBought (ID, name, price, SerialNum, PID)*. Here SubQ1 is to request the purchase orders whose buyer name is Tom, represented as {*Buyer_name*}, while SubQ2 is to request the names of items whose price is $1000, represented as {*name, price*}. The sub-queries are illustrated in the right part of figure 7. And their frequencies are all equal to the XML query's frequency F_i, their weights are assumed to be SubW1 and SubW2 respectively. So according to formula 1,3 we can get:

$$|SubQ1| = Sizeof(ID + Buyer\_name + PID) * \\ \|PurchaseOrder\|$$

$$|SubQ2| = Sizeof(ID + name + price + PID) * \\ \|ItemBought\|$$

$$SubW1 = W_i * \left(\frac{|PurchaseOrder|}{|PurchaseOrder|+|ItemBought|}\right);$$

$$SubW2 = W_i * \left(\frac{|ItemBought|}{|PurchaseOrder|+|ItemBought|}\right);$$

According to the formula 4,5,6, we can compute the query benefit and storage cost of these two sub-queries' independent storage as follows:

For SubQ1:

$$B(SubQ_1) = (|PurchaseOrder| - |SubQ1|) * \\ F_i * SubW1 = 0.$$

$$C_{overlapping}(SubQ_1) = |SubQ1|.$$

$$C_{non-overlapping}(SubQ_1) = \\ |PurchaseOrder's\ join\ info|.$$

For SubQ2:

$$B(SubQ_2) = (|ItemBought| - |SubQ2|) * F_i * \\ SubW2.$$

$$C_{overlapping}(SubQ_2) = |SubQ2|.$$

$$C_{non-overlapping}(SubQ_2) = \\ |ItemBought's\ join\ info|.$$

3.5. Independent Storage

As far as storage cost is concerned, non-overlapping independent storage is better than overlapping independent storage. But if there are some common attributes between sub-queries, non-overlapping independent storage of some sub-queries may deteriorate the performance of the other sub-queries.

For example, there are two sub-queries $SubQ1, \{Attr1, Attr2, Attr3\}$ and $SubQ2, \{Attr3, Attr4, Attr5\}$. They all access $R(Attr1, Attr2, Attr3, Attr4, Attr5, Attr6...)$, and their common attribute is $Attr3$. Their frequencies are F_1 and F_2, their weights are W_1, W_2 respectively, and $W_1 > W_2$. If we non-overlapping independently store $SubQ1$, then R is separated into two relations, $R_1(Attr1, Attr2, Attr3)$ and $R_2(Attr4, Attr5, Attr6...)$. $SubQ1$ only need access R_1, at the same time $SubQ2$ need access R_1 and R_2, the query cost increases instead.

So when we non-overlapping independently store the sub-queries having common attributes with others, the data in common attributes must be stored redundantly. Assuming the common attributes is $Attr_j(1 < j < c)$, the computing formula of storage cost must be modified as follows:

```
Algorithm: MergeSubQueries
Input: {SQ_k}, 1 ≤ k ≤ j.
Output: {MQ}.
MergeSubQueries{
    {MQ} = φ;
    for (k = 1; k ≤ j; k + +){
        GreedyMerge(SQ_k);
    }// end of mergence of all subqueries
    return{MQ} ;
}//end of the MergeSubQueries

//merge sub-queries for highest benefit/cost ratio.
GreedyMerge( {SQ_k} ){
    msq = msqt = φ;
    While ( SQ_k ≠ φ ){
        for each sq ∈ SQ_k{
            msqt = (msq ∪ sq);
            R_B/C = B(msqt)/C_non-overlapping(msqt);
            if( R_B/C > B(msq)/C_non-overlapping(msq)
                and R_B/C > B(sq)/C_overlapping(sq)
                msq = msqt;
                SQ_k = SQ_k - {sq};
        }
        if (msq ≠ φ){
            {MQ} = {MQ} ∪ {msq};
            msq = φ;
        }
        else END While;
    }
    return{MQ};
}//end of GreedyMerge
```

Figure 8. Algorithm MergeSubQueries

$$C_{non-overlapping}(SubQ_i) = (\sum_{j=1}^{c}(Sizeof(Attr_j)$$

$$*\|R_i\|)) + |R_i's\ join\ info|. \quad (7)$$

In order to get a good trade-off between query benefit and storage cost, we merge the sub-queries with common attributes into a new sub-query and non-overlapping independently store the new sub-query. So the size accessed by all these sub-queries is reduced, the performance is improved.

For example, in the example above we can merge $SubQ1$ and $SubQ2$ as $SubQ'$, and $SubQ' = SubQ1 \cup SubQ2 = \{Attr1, Attr2, Attr3, Attr4, Attr5\}$. F', the frequency of $SubQ'$, is the sum of these two sub-queries' frequencies, that is $F' = F_1 + F_2$. The weight of $SubQ'$ is W_1, the bigger one of two sub-queries' weights. The query benefit of its independent storage is equal to $((|R| - |SubQ'|) * W_1 * F')$, and the storage cost is the data space to non-overlapping independently store the $SubQ'$, namely $|R's\ join\ info|$.

To merge the Sub-queries, we decompose the set $\{SubQ_i\}$ into the set $\{IndSubQ_i\}$ where sub-queries have no common attributes between each other, and the set $\{CorSubQ_j\}$ where sub-queries have common attributes among them, i.e. $\{SubQ_i\} = \{IndSubQ_i\} \cup \{CorSubQ_j\}$, s.t. $\forall q \in \{CorSubQ_j\}, \exists q' \in \{CorSubQ_j\}, q' \neq q$, and $q \cap q' \neq \phi$. While $\forall q, q' \in \{IndSubQ_i\}, q \cap q' = \phi$.

We divide the set $\{CorSubQ_j\}$ into a series of small sets $\{SQ_k\}, 1 \leq k \leq j$, s.t. $\forall q, q' \in \{CorSubQ_j\}$ if $q \cap q' \neq \phi$, then $\exists SQ_k$ and $q, q' \in SQ_k$, while if $q \in SQ_k, q' \notin SQ_k$, then $q \cap q' = \phi$.

We merge the sub-queries in every set SQ_k using a greedy algorithm, that is we only merge the sub-queries to achieve highest benefit/cost ratio. We put the new merged sub-queries into the set $\{MQ\}$. The complete algorithm to merge sub-queries is given in Figure 8. Here we assume that $B(\phi) = 0$ and $C_{non-overlapping}(\phi) = C_{overlapping}(\phi) = 1$.

Because the sub-queries selected from $\{IndSubQ_i\}$ or $\{MQ\}$ have no common attributes among them, we will non-overlapping independently store them. And overlapping independently store the sub-queries selected from $\{SQ_k\}$, which have common attributes among them. Then according to the computing formula above, we can compute query benefit and storage cost of independently storing all elements in the sets $\{IndSubQ_i\}$, $\{MQ\}$ and $\{SQ_k\}$.

By computing the benefit and cost of independently storing every sub-query, we get the query benefit set $\{P_i\}$ and storage cost set $\{C_i\}$ for all candidate schemas. Now the problem becomes how to select out the schema with highest benefit under the space constraint M. This problem belongs to the knapsack problem, in which one tries to "maximize" the obtained "profit" without exceeding the knapsack capacity [12]. We give the corresponding algorithm in 3.6.

3.6. Schema Selection

The knapsack problem is defined in its simplest form as follows: a hitch-hiker wants to fill up his knapsack, selecting among various objects. Each object has a particular weight (w_i) and obtains a particular profit (p_i). The knapsack can be filled up to a given maximum weight (M). How can he choose objects to fill the knapsack maximizing the obtained profit? [12]

The mathematical formulation of knapsack problem is as follows: For given $M > 0, W_i > 0, P_i > 0$, find a vector $(x_1, x_2, \cdots, x_n)(0 \leq x_i \leq 1, 1 \leq i \leq n)$ that maximizes the objective function $(profit) \sum_{i=1}^{n} p_i x_i$, while satisfying the constraint $\sum_{i=1}^{n} w_i x_i \leq M$. When x_i is restricted to be integer 0 or 1, this problem is called the 0-1 knapsack problem. Sahni[12] proposes an increasingly accurate, polynomial time-bounded approximation algorithms for this problem, which is named APPROXIMATE KNAPSACK. This algorithm can obtain a solution that is within a factor $\varepsilon > 0$

```
Algorithm: TuneStorageSchema
Input: DTD, history queries {Q_i}, space constraint M, and the
   approximate parameter ε
Output: the result storage schema
TuneStorageSchema{
   1. call MappingDegree2Node; //determine mapping rule
   2. map DTD into relational schema S;
   3. Transform {Q_i} into {SubQ_i};
   4. Divide {SubQ_i} into {IndSubQ_i},and {SQ_k};
   5. {MQ} = MergeSubQueries({SQ_k});
   6. {P_i} = Comp_Benefit({IndSubQ_i}, {MQ}, {SQ_k});
   7. {C_i} = Comp_Cost({IndSubQ_i}, {MQ}, {SQ_k});
   8. (x_1, x_2, ···, x_n) = AppKnap({P_i}, {C_i}, n, M, ε);
   9. for each SubQ_i{
          if x_i = 1 then {
             if SubQ_i ∈ {SQ_k} then
                overlapping independently store SubQ_i;
             else non-overlapping independently store SubQ_i;}
      }//store the sub-queries selected independently
} //End
```

Figure 9. Algorithm TuneStorageSchema

of the optimal, and the ε is a input parameter of this algorithm.

Accordingly, the tuning of storage schema can be transformed into 0-1 knapsack problem. $\{P_i\}$ corresponds P_i of 0-1 knapsack problem, $\{C_i\}$ corresponds to W_i, and the space constraint is the knapsack capacity M. We use APPROXIMATE KNAPSACK (abbreviated as AppKnap() in algorithm) to compute the n-ary vector$(x_1, x_2, \cdots, x_n)$, $x_i = 0, 1$. When $x_i = 1$, the corresponding $SubQ_i$ is selected to be stored independently. The method of independently storing a sub-query depends on the set to which it belongs. As mentioned in 3.5, if it belongs to the set $\{IndSubQ_i\}$ or $\{MQ\}$, we non-overlapping independently store it, otherwise we overlapping independently store it. In this way we select out the result storage schema with highest benefit under the space constraint M. The complete algorithm TuneStorageSchema is described in the Figure 9, it is polynomial time-bounded.

4. Dynamic Tuning Strategies

In Section 3 we introduced the techniques of storage schema tuning, here we will give two different dynamic tuning strategies of XML storage schema: *efficiency based tuning strategy* and *content based tuning strategy*. Tuning strategy decides when a tuning event should be triggered. We implemented both tuning strategies in VXMLR. The default tuning strategy of VXMLR is the efficiency based strategy, but user can select either as the tuning strategy of the running system.

4.1. Efficiency Based Tuning Strategy

Let users' queries be seen as a sequence of queries: $q_1, q_2, q_3, q_4, \cdots$. Suppose the query sequence starts from the first query covered by the last tuning event, and extends to the last query of the incoming tuning event. c_i is denoted as the time cost of query q_i. Creating a sliding window on the queries sequence, its length is w, which means the number of queries covered by the sliding window. Denote the first sliding window on the query sequence W_0, its corresponding queries segment is: $q_1, q_2, \ldots q_w$. These queries included in W_0 is the history queries used for the last schema tuning. The sliding window moves forward by step size of k(i.e. k queries consecutively distributed on the queries sequence), then queries in ith sliding window W_i are: $\{q_{ik+1}, q_{ik+2}, \ldots q_{ik+w}\}$. The averaged processing time for all queries in W_i is:

$$\bar{c}_i = (\sum_{j=1}^{w} c_{ik+j})/w \qquad (8)$$

Definition 3. The *Efficiency Degradation Factor* of Window W_i is defined as:

$$EDF(i) = \bar{c}_i/\bar{c}_0 \qquad (9)$$

Above, $\bar{c}_0$ is the averaged processing time of queries in the first windows W_0. Based on the definition above, we give the *efficiency based tuning strategy* as follows.

Definition 4. Let Max_EDF be a pre-specified query efficiency degradation threshold value, if there is a sliding window W_i whose efficiency degradation factor $EDF(i) > Max\_EDF$, then after the latest query q_{ik+w} in W_i is processed, system triggers a new schema tuning by using queries: $q_{ik+1}, q_{ik+2}, \ldots, q_{ik+w}$.

4.2. Content Based Tuning Strategy

Analogously, we treat the users' queries as a sequence of queries, and check the content difference between queries in the current window $W_i, \{q_{ik+1}, q_{ik+2}, \ldots q_{ik+w}\}$ and queries in the window W_0, corresponding to the last schema tuning event. We represent this difference with *distance*, denoted as $Dist(W_0, W_i)$. So content based schema tuning can be defined as follows.

Definition 5. Let Max_Dist be a pre-specified query content distance threshold value, if there is a sliding window W_i, the distance of content between W_i and W_0 fulfills $Dist(W_0, W_i) > Max\_Dist$, then after the last query q_{ik+w} in window W_i is processed, system triggers a new storage schema tuning event by using $q_{ik+1}, q_{ik+2}, \ldots q_{ik+w}$.

Now the problem lies in how to compute $Dist(W_0, W_i)$. First we consider *similarity* $Sim(P, Q)$ between two arbitrary query sequences $P = \{p_1, p_2, \ldots, p_n\}$ and $Q = \{q_1, q_2, \ldots, q_m\}$. We use $Sim(p, q)$ to represent the similarity between two queries p and q.

$$Dist(W_0, W_i) = 1 - Sim(W_0, W_i). \qquad (10)$$

Definition 6. Given $p_i \in P (1 \leq i \leq n)$ and $q_k \in Q (1 \leq k \leq m)$, if p_i, q_k is the *most similar queries pair* in P and Q, then $\forall p_j \in P$ and $q_l \in Q$, $Sim(p_i, q_k) \geq Sim(p_j, q_l)$. Here p_i and q_k are abbreviated as $P(1)$ and $Q(1)$.

Definition 7. Let $P^1 = P - \{P(1)\}$ and $Q^1 = Q - \{Q(1)\}$. According to the definition 6, $P^1(1)$ and $Q^1(1)$ is the *most similar queries pair* in P^1 and Q^1, then we defined $P^1(1)$ and $Q^1(1)$ as 2th *most similar query pair*, and are abbreviated as $P(2)$ and $Q(2)$. Analogously, the kth $(1 \leq i \leq Min(n, m))$ *most similar queries pair* in P and Q, $P(k)$ and $Q(k)$ are abbreviation of $P^{k-1}(1)$ and $Q^{k-1}(1)$.

Definition 8. $Sim(P, Q)$ is computed according to the following formula:

$$Sim(P, Q) = 2 \sum_{k=1}^{Min(n,m)} \frac{Sim(P(k), Q(k))}{n + m} \qquad (11)$$

That is,

$$Dist(P, Q) = 1 - 2 \sum_{k=1}^{Min(n,m)} \frac{Sim(P(k), Q(k))}{n + m} \qquad (12)$$

For $|W_0| = |W_i| = w$, we obtain

$$Dist(W_0, W_i) = 1 - \sum_{k=1}^{w} \frac{Sim(W_0(k), W_i(k))}{w} \qquad (13)$$

Now, we give the computing formula for similarity between any two queries p and q, that is $Sim(p, q)$. For simplicity, we can regard a XML query as either a text string or a query tree.

a) If we treat XML query as text string, we can compute the similarity between two queries by comparing the content of two strings. Here we use the keyword set to represent query content. The keywords are the words that reflect the structure (or schema) of XML documents. So the similarity between queries p and q can be represented as:

$$Sim(p, q) = (|p \cap q|)/(|p \cup q|) \qquad (14)$$

b) If we use query tree to represent XML query, the similarity between XML queries can be measured by the similarity between two query trees. And similarity between trees has been extensively studied [13], here we directly use the research results in related literature. Due to space limitation, we give no more details about this problem.

5. Experiments

We conducted a series of experiments to evaluate the performance of VXMLR in schema tuning and compare the performance of the original schema with that of the tuned schema.

Table 2. The elapse time of history queries

Query	Shared	Tuned	Query	Shared	Tuned
Q1	1603	811	Q10	861	641
Q2	480	326	Q11	125240	111370
Q3	2364	2333	Q12	441	160
Q4	841	371	Q13	1182	650
Q5	170	170	Q14	721	721
Q6	932	321	Q15	1101	351
Q7	421	301	Q16	892	681
Q8	22292	1593	Q17	701	682
Q9	53287	5107			

Shanmugasundaram *et al.* pointed out that the difference between SHARED and HYBRID isn't significant for the general DTD, and Tian *et al.* argued that SHARED is the representative of structure-based approaches, so we implemented the original schema with SHARED. The storage space constraint is set to 110% of the original data space, *i.e.* the storage overhead of the tuned schema must be less than 110% of the original schema's storage overhead. XMark is a benchmark database containing synthetic auction data intended as a benchmark suite[14], We use the 133M auction data generated from XMark, and test the 17 pieces of Benchmark queries, which are used to evaluate the performance of XML query. We set the frequency of every query in our experiments to 1, and set every query's weight to its execution time over the original schema. The experiments are conducted on a 500MHZ Pentium computer with 128M memory running WINDOWS 2000 Sever. We choose SQL Server 2000 as the background RDBMS. The results of our experiments are shown in table 2, Figure 11 and 12.

In the table 2 and Figure 11, *Shared* indicates t_{shared}, which is the execution time when the XML document being stored in the relational database using Shared schema, or the execution time over the original schema; *Tuned* means t_{tun}, the execution time over the tuned schema. The evaluation formula for efficiency improvement factor is: $Eff = \frac{t_{shared}-t_{tun}}{t_{shared}}$. From table 2, we can compute the total execution time of all queries. we can see that using tuned schema, up to 41% of total efficiency improvement is achieved.

From table 2, we can see that almost every query's execution time is reduced over the tuned schema. As for the query Q11, its execution efficiency is not significantly affected. This is because most of Q11's execution time is spent on the joins (The semantic and SQL statement of Q11 is shown in the Figure 10). From its query plan, we can see

---

> **Query Q11:** For each person, list the number of items currently on sale whose price does not exceed 0.02% of the person's income
>
> **select** xben_person.person_profile_income,count1 **from**
>   (**select** xben_personid,count(xben_openauctionid)
>   **from** xben_person,xben_site,xben_openauction
>   **where** xben_siteid = xben_person.parentid
>   **and** xben_siteid = xben_openauction.parentid
>   **and** openauction_initial * 5000>
>   person_profile_income
>   **group by** xben_personid)
>   **as** tempTable(id1,count1), xben_person
> **where** xben_personid = temptable.id1

Figure 10. The semantic and SQL statement of Q11

that the execution time of a hash join occupies 80% of the Q11's total time cost. However the algorithm in this paper is designed to improve the efficiency accessing the separate relations, and has little effect on joins . While ignoring Q11, the total time cost of 16 pieces of queries is shown in Figure 11, and the total efficiency improvement factor is by 82.8%. This indicates that our approach can improve system's efficiency significantly without causing apparently increasing of storage overhead.

To evaluate the performance of dynamic storage schema tuning, we split the 17 queries into two group, Q1 to Q9 are assigned to the first group, and the rest lie in the second group. First,we tune storage schema based on the first group queries, then we tune storage schema based on the second group queries. The test results are illustrated in Figure 12. Here, the curve labelled *first* indicates execution time of the 17 queries after the first tuning, and the curve labelled *second* corresponds to the results of second tuning. For the first tuning, queries in the first group (from Q1 to Q9) have higher efficiency than queries in the second group; On the contrary, for the second tuning, queries in the second group outperform queries of the first group. This shows that the current queries in query log will have higher efficiency after the storage schema is tuned according to the current query log. When some new queries are added, the query log

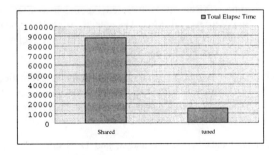

Figure 11. Total Elapse Time Without Q11(ms)

is updated, and the existing storage schema maybe be not suitable for the new queries, then system efficiency may get degraded. So VXMLR can adaptively improve its efficiency by dynamically tuning its storage schema based on latest query records.

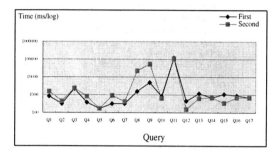

Figure 12. The performance of two group queries after tuning storage schema

6. Conclusion

This paper presents techniques of dynamic tuning of XML storage schema based on user query records in VXMLR. Concrete algorithms for XML storage schema tuning are given, and two dynamic schema tuning strategies are introduced. The proposed techniques are implemented in VXMLR, a RDBMS based XML documents management system developed in Fudan University. Experiments are conducted, which validate the practicability and effectiveness of the proposed techniques. The future research includes considering adapting our method to other platforms, such as native storage, text storage, and hybrid storage XML management systems etc. We are also interested in using clustering methods to tune XML storage schema.

References

[1] M. Yoshikawa, T. Amagasa, T. Shimura and S. Ue-mura, "XRel: A Path-Based Approach to Storage and Retrieval of XML Documents using Relational Databases", ACM Transactions on Internet Technology, August 2001, pp. 110-141.

[2] D. Florescu D. Kossmann, "A Performance Evaluation of Alternative Mapping Schemes for Storing XML Data in a Relational Database", Technical Report 3684 INRIA March 1999, pp. 27-34.

[3] A. Deutsch, M. Fernandez, and D. Suciu, "Storing semi-structured data with STORED", Proc. of SIGMOD, 1999, pp. 431-442.

[4] J. Shanmugasundaram K. Tufte C. Zhang and et al, "Relational Databases for Querying XML Documents: Limitations and Opportunities", Proc. of VLDB, Edinburgh, September 1999, pp. 302-314.

[5] F.Tian, D.DeWitt, J.Chen, C.Zheng, "The Design and Performance Evaluation of Alternative XML Storage Strategies", SIGMOD Record special issue on "Data Management Issues in E-commerce", March 2002, pp. 5-10.

[6] P. Bohannon, J. Freire, P. Roy, J. Simeon, "From XML Schema to Relations:A Cost-based Approach to XML Storage", ICDE 2002.

[7] S. Zheng, J. Wen and H. Lu, "Cost-Driven Storage Schema Selection for XML", DASFAA 2003, Kyoto, Japan, March, 2003, pp. 26-28.

[8] L. Breslau, P. Cao, L. Fan, G. Philips and S. Shenker, "Web Caching and Zipf-like Distributions: Evidence and Implications", Proc. of IEEE Infocom, NY, 1999, pp. 126-134.

[9] A. Zhou, H. Lu, S. Zheng, Y. Liang, L. Zhang, W. Ji, Z. Tian, "VXMLR: A Visual XML-Relational Database System", VLDB 2001, PP. 719-720.

[10] P. Selinger, M. Astrahan, D. Chamberlin, "Access Path Selection in a Relational Database Management System", Proc. ACM SIGMOD 1979, pp. 23-34.

[11] Y. Yang, M. Singhal, "A Comprehensive Survey of Join Techniques in Relational Databases", http://citeseer.nj.nec.com/yang97comprehensive.html ,1997.

[12] S. Sahni, "Approximate algorithms for 0/1 knapsack problem", Journal of the ACM, v.22, 1975, pp. 115-124.

[13] S. Flesca, F. Furfaro, and E. Masciari, "Meaningful change detection on the Web", In Proc. of DEXA, LNCS, vol. 2113, 2001, pp. 22-31.

[14] A. Schmidt, F. Waas, M. Kersten, D. Florescu, I. Manolescu, M. Carey, R. Busse, "The XML Benchmark Project", Technical Report INS-R0103, CWI, Amsterdam, April 2001.

Query Translation from XSLT to SQL

Jixue Liu   Millist Vincent

School of Computer and Information Science, The University of South Australia

Email: {jixue.liu, millist.vincent}@unisa.edu.au

Abstract

XML has been accepted as a universal format for data interchange and publication. It can be applied in the applications in which the data of a database needs to be viewed in XML format so that the data being viewed takes more semantics and is easily understood. In these applications, the user of the data to be viewed sees only XML data, not the database. He may use XML query languages such as XSLT to query data and the retrieved data is presented in XML format to them. We are interested in the connection between the data that the user sees and the data in the database. More specifically, we are interested in translating XSLT queries to SQL queries.

Keywords: *XML, XSL/XSLT, SQL, query translation*

1. Introduction

The eXtensible Markup Language (XML) [5] has been accepted as a universal format for data interchange and publication on the internet [2]. It can be applied in the applications in which the data of a database needs to be viewed in XML format so that the data being viewed takes richer semantics, allows more flexibility in syntax, and is easily understood. These types of applications can rise in two ways. In the first, initial data is defined in XML format and is then mapped and stored in a database to achieve better access efficiency as done in [9, 6]. In the other way, the data in a database needs to be wrapped in XML format for interchange or publication purpose. In both situations, the user who views the data through *XML glass* [8] will see only XML data, not the database and so may use XML query languages such as XSLT [1], XQuery and XML-QL to query the data. In such scenarios, one issue of utmost importance is to provide techniques and tools for converting XML queries to SQL queries on the underline database. Without such techniques and tools, the use of XML as a data interchange language in the applications just mentioned can not be implemented. The work done on this important problem up to now is not thorough and systematical. This motivates

our research of our paper.

We choose to use the XML query XSLT (XSL Transformation) in our research. XSL was first defined as a language to transform XML data to HTML documents. However, after variables and parameter passing are added to the language, XSL has become a powerful XML query language [4]. There are two reasons we have chosen XSLT as our query language. The first is the expressive power of XSLT. The study in [4] has show that XSLT is a more powerful language than other XML languages such as XML-QL. The second reason for choosing XSLT is that a wide range of implementation support is available in comparison to other languages. We have noticed that although our focus of this paper is on XSLT, the techniques and ideas developed in this paper are applicable to the translation of queries in some other XML languages to SQL queries.

Translating XML queries to SQL queries is was initially investigated in [7]. However, the method proposed in [7] is example-based and lack of generality. Furthermore, the method proposed in [7] translates XSLT queries by using information not only from the quires themselves. Therefore, the automation of the method becomes a problem. In contrast to [7], our paper solve the problem translating XSLT queries to SQL queries in a general and systematical manner. The approach used in our paper is syntax based and does not need information from outside of a query. Similar work on XML query translation is done in [6]. The method proposed in [6] is for translating XML-QL queries to SQL ones via an intermediate language called RXL. Data to be queried by XML-QL queries are organized in RXL virtual views. An XML-QL query over these virtual views is translated to a RXL query and the latter is further translated to a number of SQL queries. The differences of our work to that of [6] is that the XSLT language we choose to use is more expressive than XML-QL and we do not employ any intermediate language. Furthermore, we do not limit users to views predefined as basis of queries.

The focus of this paper is to develop a framework for translating XSLT queries to SQL queries. We firstly investigate how to map an XML DTD (Document Type Definition) to a relational database by borrowing ideas from [9] and how to generate an XML DTD from a relational database based on theory of [3]. After DTD is known, we then take an arbitrary XSLT query, parse it, translate it to a number of SQL queries. In doing so, we consider XML DTDs that do not contain loops and XSLT queries that may contain all XSLT 1.0 statements [1] and functions, including aggregation functions, except for the order function $position()$ of XPath 1.0. In addition, we also translate the grouping statement proposed in XSLT 2.0 which is the major improvement compared to XSLT 1.0.

We do the translation by firstly building up a list of expressions called *T-expressions*. A T-expression corresponds to an XSLT statement that may produce output. It is gradually constructed as the XSLT query is parsed and its final value represents all semantics of the element in the whole XSLT query. A final T-expression is then translated to a SQL query.

2. XML and XSLT

In this section, we review the features of the XML model and of XSLT language, as defined in [4], which are relevant to our research.

2.1 XML DTD and documents

An XML DTD defines data types for the elements of XML documents [5]. An XML DTD can be represented by a directed graph [2, 9]. The elements and the attributes of the DTD are mapped to the **names** of the nodes of the graph. The edges of the graph map the parent-children relationships among the elements. If an edge goes from node n_1 to node n_2, n_2 is called the **child** and n_1 is called the **parent**. Because a DTD is a graph, a child may have multiple parents and a parent may have multiple children. The node **root** of the graph is the node that does not have a parent. The **leaf nodes** of the graph are those that do not have children. In this paper, we exclude loops in DTDs because recursion is not supported by relational databases.

We use symbolic notation in the graph to show the occurrence indicators of elements and also to to distinguish attributes from elements. The symbol "@" is put on top of a node name to mean that the node is an attribute. The symbol "+" or "*" is put on top of a node name to mean that the node is an element and the element is allowed to appear multiple times under its parent in an XML document that conforms to the DTD.

A node in a DTD graph is a **complex node** if it is either an internal node or a leaf node with the occurrence indicator of "+" or "*". A node is an **simple node** if it is either an

---

[1] In XSLT terms, these are called *elements*. Here we use *statements* to avoid the confusion of XSLT elements from XML elements.

attribute node a leaf text node that is allowed only to appear once within its parent node.

Figure 1 shows a DTD graph defined for a bibliography XML document. Figure 2 gives an XML document that conforms to the DTD defined in Figure 1. Note that an XML document is always a tree.

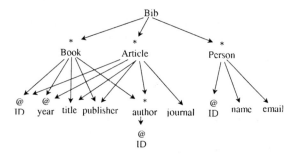

Figure 1. DTD of XML data

```
<Bib>
  <Book id="b1" year="2000">
    <author id="p2"/>    <author id="p1"/>
    <title> Java </title>
    <publisher> Wiley </publisher>    </Book>
  <Book id="b2" year="1990">
    <author id="p1"/>    <author id="p2"/>
    <title> C </title>
    <publisher> Wilson </publisher>    </Book>
  <Article id="a1" year="2002">
    <author id="p1"/> <title> XML </title>
    <journal> TODS </journal>
    <publisher> Wiley </publisher>    </Article>
  <Person id="p1">
    <name> John </name>
    <email> john@uni </email>        </Person>
  <Person id="p2">
    <name> Tom </name>
    <email> tom@hotmail </email>      </Person>
</Bib>
```

Figure 2. An example XML document conforming to the DTD in Figure 1

2.2 XSLT

An XSLT program (also called a query) is a collection of templates where each template is comprised of a matching pattern and a template definition. An XSLT program p is executed against an XML input document t by starting at the root node of t. When a node u of t is processed as the current context node and if the XSLT statement for processing the current context node is *xsl:apply-templates*, u is used to match match patterns of all templates. If a match is successful, the definition of the matched template is applied to each child of *u*. With the *xsl:apply-templates* statement, any nodes of the XML document can be processed recursively and as desired. A variable definition, if it is parallel to templates, can be seen as a special template that has a matching pattern but does not have a definition. Such variables are executed before templates.

Figure 3 illustrates an example of an XSLT query which retrieves data from an XML document conforming to the DTD in Figure 1. The output of the query is given in Figure 4 when the input data is Figure 2.

```
1: <xsl:variable name="bkjnl"
        select="//*[title]" />
2:
3: <xsl:template match="Person[@ID]">
4:     <xsl:variable name="psn" select="."/>
5:     <xsl:for-each select=
        "$bkjnl[author/@ID=$t/@ID]">
6:         <xsl:sort select="@year"/>
7:             <xsl:if test="contains
                (publisher,'Wi')">
8:                 <xsl:copy-of select="title"/>
9:             </xsl:if>
10:     </xsl:for-each>
11:     <numberOfItems> === <xsl:value-
            of select="count($bj)"/>
        </numberOfItems>
12: </xsl:template>
13:
14: <xsl:template match="/">
15:     <xsl:apply-templates/>
16: </xsl:template>
```

Figure 3. An example XSLT query

```
    Java      Wiley
    C         Wilson
    XML       TODS         Wiley
<title> C </title>
<title> Java </title>
<title> XML </title>
<numberOfItems> === 3 </numberOfItems>
<title> C </title>
<title> Java </title>
<numberOfItems> === 3 </numberOfItems>
```

Figure 4. The output of the XSLT query in Figure 3

3. Architecture of the transformation system

The architecture of the transformation system that we propose is given in Figure 5. The round cornered boxes in the diagram show the processes in the architecture and arrows in the diagram show the information flow. The box DTD in the diagram is an important component. It is the

basis for users to compose XSLT queries. A user's XSLT query, after composition, is converted by using the DTD to a SQL query for the relational database and at the same time a wrapping schema is generated. In the diagram, we include a component called Data Wrapping to make the architecture complete. However, we will not discuss the details of the component and leave it as future work. The Data Wrapping component will serve wrapping the returned data from the execution of the SQL query by using the wrapping schema to get XML data which is then presented to the user. Thus, to the user of the system, he/she has posed an XSLT query and received XML data and thus the fact that the XML document is only a view over the database is hidden to the user.

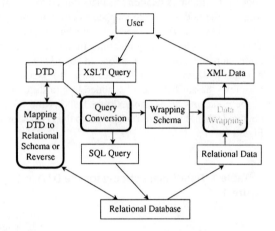

Figure 5. Architecture of the transformation system

4. Mapping between DTD and relational schema

The DTD and the relational database schema in Figure 5 are two important components in the architecture for query translation. They are convertible from each other. In this section, we present the methods for the conversion. More specifically, we discuss how an XML DTD can be mapped into a relational database schema and how a DTD can be exported from a relational database. For mapping an XML DTD to a relational database schema, we use the method proposed in [9] with some modifications. For exporting a relational database schema to a DTD, we review the idea of XML DTD design in [3] which leads to a design without redundancy if the relational design is in Boyce-Codd Normal Form.

Mapping DTD to relational schema We use the method proposed in [9] to map an XML DTD graph to a relational database schema with modifications. The method proposed in [9] suggests that a leaf node of a DTD graph be mapped into a relation. We modify this by not mapping every leaf node to a relation. Instead, we only map the leaf nodes that have the "*" or "+" occurrence indicator to reduce the number of relations. We use an attribute "text" in a relation when a node is allowed to have text. This enables us to handle internal nodes that may have mixed values (both text and sub elements) and to handle leaf nodes with multiple occurrence. The details of our improved method are as follows.

Given a DTD graph, a relation is created for each complex node (see Section 2.1) and let n represent a complex node of the graph. A relation r is then created for n and the simple child nodes of n are mapped as attributes of r. If r does not have an ID attribute, an ID attribute is added to r. This ID attribute uniquely identifies tuples in the relation. For each parent node p of n, a foreign key pID is added to r so that pID references ID values of p. If n is allowed to have text, the attribute "text" is added to r to store the text of the node. As an example, Table 1 shows the relations obtained when this method is applied to the DTD shown in Figure 1.

Table 1. Relational schema for the DTD in Figure 1

(a) Bib

ID
r01

(b) Book

ID	year	title	publisher	pID
b1	2000	Java	Wiley	r01
b2	1990	C	Wilson	r01

(c) Author

ID	pID
p2	b1
p1	b1
p1	b2
p2	b2
p1	a1

(d) Article

ID	year	title	journal	publisher	pID
a1	2002	XML	TODS	Wiley	r01

(e) Person

ID	name	email	pID
p1	John	john@uni	r01
p2	Tom	tom@hotmail	r01

Mapping relational schema to a DTD As suggested in [3], a relational database schema can be easily mapped to an XML DTD D. The initial graph of D only contains the root node. Then for each relation R in the relational database, a new element e is created and added right under the root node. The attributes of R are mapped into attributes of e. In this way, an XML DTD is generated for the relational database schema. All elements and attributes of the DTD are within three levels including the root. If the relational database schema is in Boyce-Codd Normal Form, the XML DTD does not have redundancy [3]. Note that in this paper, we do not consider the translation of relational constraints into XML.

5. Calculation of the wrapping schema

In this section, we propose our approach of translating XSLT statements to SQL queries. The approach deals with all XSLT statements in two phases. In the first phase, all those XSLT statements that have the potential to produce output such as *xsl:value-of* and *xsl:copy-of* are considered. In the second phase, those XSLT statements that control the execution flow, such as *xsl:for-each*, *xsl:if*, *xsl:for-each group*, *xsl:apply-template* etc. are considered. Note that some statements have to be considered in both phases for the reason that they could produce output and at the same time, they could also work as a flow control statement. For example, *xsl:apply-templates* produces output if no other templates match current node. Otherwise, it works as a flow control statement to combine the matched templates to the current node.

We call these statements that have potential to produce output **O-statements**. They include *xsl:value-of, xsl:copy-of, xsl:variable, xsl:apply-templates* and *xsl:call-template without parameters* [2]. We include **constant texts** and **constant statements** in an XSLT program as O-statements because they generate output. For example, the string "===" in Line 11 of Figure 3 is a constant text and $<numberOfItems>$ in Line 3 is a constant statement. Both of these two are O-statements. It is obvious that an O-statement e is definitely enclosed in a template. Between the template statement and e, there can be other **flow control statements** such as *xsl:for-each*, *xsl:if* and *xsl:when*. We call these statements that inholding e **enclosing statements** and denote it by $enclose(e)$. Generally, $enclose(e)$ is a list which can be represented by $[e_1, e_2, \cdots, e_n]$ where e_1 is the template, every statement is enclosed in all its preceding statements, and e is enclosed in all $e_1, e_2, ..., e_n$.

The basic idea of translating an XSLT query to SQL queries is to create a translation expression for each O-statement of the XSLT query. A **translation expression (T-expression for short)** is an expression (defined later) with similar syntax to XSLT that is mainly the concatenation of the selection and the test expressions of all enclosing statements of the O-statement. More specifically, a T-expression combines expressions in the *match* clause of xsl:template, in the *test* clauses of *xsl:if* and *xsl:when*, and in the *select* clauses of other enclosing statements, if any. The order of the concatenation matters. For an O-statement e and its enclosing statements $enclose(e) = [e_1, e_2, ..., e_n]$ obtained by parsing the XSLT query, the T-expression of e is achieved by concatenating the conditions in $enclose(e)$ in a backward manner. That is, e_n is processed first, then

---

[2]The case of *xsl:call-template* with parameters is similar to the case of variable processing.

$e_{n-1}, \cdots$, and finally e_1. As the concatenation proceeds, T-expressions are updated.

After the updating of T-expressions completes, a T-expression becomes **final**. This means that the T-expression should be headed with the root element of the DTD and should have no wildcards. Then the final T-expression can be translated into a SQL query. The translated SQL query joins all tables corresponding to all complex elements involved in the T-expression and uses all the filters of the T-expression as conditions. Note that the two properties of the final T-expression are important. If a T-expression is not headed by the root element, the translated SQL query would not give correct result because an XSLT query is evaluated from the root element and from parent nodes to child nodes of the DTD while the translated SQL query would not contain the table of the root element. If a T-expression has wildcards, it can not be converted to a SQL query. Wildcards in XSLT can mean multiple elements and paths which are not name specific. It is not possible to find the relational database tables for these wildcards if we do not know the names of the elements.

The general format of a T-expression is $E = /s_1/ \cdots /s_n$ where $s_1, \cdots, s_n$ are called sections of E. Each section s_i, $1 \le i \le n$, has the format of

$$p_i\{\forall \}\{E\}\{A\}\{CE\}\{CT\}[<filter>]\{group : g\}\{sort : p_o\}\{select : simpleNames\}$$

where p_i is an element name or a constant text and all other subsections are optional:

- The flags $\{\forall\}$, $\{E\}$, $\{A\}$, $\{CE\}$, and $\{CT\}$ are exclusive and only one of them can appear before p_i.

  $\{\forall \}$ indicates that p_i is the current context node. This flag is needed because the statements *xsl:for-each*, *xsl:template*, and *xsl:for-each-group* change the current context node.

- $\{E\}$ shows that p_i is a name that is generated by the *xsl:elemet* statement;

- $\{A\}$ indicates that p_i is a name that is generated by the *xsl:attribute* statement;

- $\{CE\}$ means p_i is a constant statement name defined in the XSLT query; and

- $\{CT\}$ means p_i is a constant text defined in the XSLT query. Note the difference between a constant statement and a constant string we defined before.

- The subsection $[<filter>]$ indicates a filter applying to p_i.

- The subsection $\{group : g\}$ is used to map the grouping statement of XSLT where g is the group key.

- The subsection $\{sort : p_o\}$ means the output is sorted based on the sorting key p_o.

- The subsection $\{select : simpleNames\}$ can only appear in the last section s_n and when p_n is a complex node element. This subsection is used to express the columns to be selected from a relational database. So the names in $simpleNames$ are names for the leave node of the DTD graph.

We now use an example to show the meaning of a T-expression. Let a T-expression be $E = /bib/book\{\forall \}[@id]\{sort : year\}/publisher\{select : name, address\}$. This T-expression means that for every node *book* under the root *bib*, if it has an *id* attribute, then its publisher's name and address are selected and the output of T-expression is sorted based on the year in which the book is published. Note that the DTD implied in this example is different from the DTD defined in Figure 1.

To distinguish the symbol "/" used for root element and the same symbol used for path delimiter, we employ "¶" for the root element in the T-expression. This is necessary because sometimes the root element can appear in the middle of a T-expression when the *select* clause of a statement selects from the root element, not from the current element. For a path p, we define a function $replroot(p)$ for this purpose. The function replaces the heading "/" with "¶" if the former appears.

To obtain final T-expressions, we define a data structure called a wrapping schema to control the T-expression update procedure.

5.1 The wrapping schema

The wrapping schema is a table containing the columns of line number L, element type T, execution order O, T-expression E, SQL-query Q, and return set S as shown in Table 2 (a). A tuple in the table stores schema information for an O-statement e. For presentation reasons in the following, when we say an O-statement e, we also mean the tuple for e. The notation $X(e)$ means the X value for e. Thus, $L(e)$ is the line number of e in the XSLT query. We use this number to distinguish one O-statement from others if they have the same name. If there are more than one O-statement in a line, a sequential number is appended after the line number to distinguish them. $T(e)$ is the type of the O-statement. The type for each O-statement is given in Table 2 (b). $O(e)$ is an integer number indicating an order in which all the O-statements are executed and in which the return sets of the corresponding SQL queries are to be wrapped to XML data. The initial value of $O(e)$ is 0 if the O-statement is a variable element and is 1 otherwise. $E(e)$ is the T-expression. The initial value of $E(e)$ is p' where p' is constructed from $replroot(p)$ and p is the path of the *select* clause of e; at the same time $\{\forall\}$ is added after the last element of p if the element is not a leaf node name and not '.' (the current node). If there is no condition, an empty string is set to $E(e)$. $Q(e)$ will be used to store the SQL query translated from the T-expression for the O-statement. The last column $S(e)$ is a set containing tuples returned from executing the SQL query $Q(e)$. As an example, Table 2 (c) gives the initial wrapping schema of the XSLT query in Figure 3.

Table 2. The wrapping schema

(a) A general template

L	T	O	E	Q	S
...	...	...	...	...	...

(b) Type values for O-statements

O-statement	Type value
xsl:value-of	*value*
xsl:copy-of	*copy*
xsl:variable	<variable name>
xsl:call-template	*call*
xsl:apply-templates	*apply*
constant string	*const*

(c)Initial wrapping schema for the query in Figure 3

L	T	O	E	Q	S
1	$bkjnl	0	//*{$\forall$}[title]		
4	$psn	0	.		
8	*copy*	1	title		
11.1	const	1	{CT}===		
11.2	value	1	count($bkjnl)		
15	*apply*	1			

The following sub sections will update the initial wrapping schema until the T-expressions in the schema become final.

5.2 Updating of T-expressions

The aim of updating T-expressions is to combine the selection and the test conditions of all enclosing statements of an O-statement so that all these conditions are put together in one T-expression to enable the generation of a SQL query for the O-statement. Let e be an O-statement and $enclose(e) = [e_1, \cdots, e_n]$ be the list of enclosing statements of e as defined before. The update is done by checking the enclosing statements from the closest enclosing statement e_n of e to the furthest enclosing statement e_1, i.e., the *xsl:template* statement. For example, for the *xsl:copy-of* O-statement in Line 8, we check Line 7, Line 6, and so on until the checking reaches Line 3. For the *xsl:value-of* in Line 11, there are two statements to be checked, i.e., the constant statement $<numberOfItems>$ and the statement *xsl:template* Line 3.

During the above process, we check those statements which control the execution flow. They include *xsl:if*, *xsl:when* and *xsl:for-each*, *xsl:for-each-group*, *xsl:sort*,

xsl:element,*xsl:attribute*, and constant statements defined in the XSLT query. Checking T-expressions terminates if there is no more enclosing statements existing. For example, Line 1 in Figure 3 is not surrounded by any enclosing statement, so the checking of $bkjnl$ terminates at that line. Similarly, the checking of the *xsl:copy-of* in Line 8 of Figure 3 terminates at Line 3. We now show how T-expressions are checked against each type of enclosing statements in the following subsections.

5.2.1 *xsl:if* and *xsl:when*

Both *xsl:if* and *xsl:when* statements have a *test* clause which tests if a condition is satisfied. The test clause is mapped to a filter in the T-expression of the enclosed O-statement. Let e be the current enclosed O-statement under discussion and $E(e)$ be the current T-expression of e. Then $E(e)$ is updated as $E(e) = $ "[" $+ replroot(t) + $ "]" $+ dlmtr + E(e)$ where $+$ is the string concatenation operation, t denotes the condition in the *test* clause of *xsl:if* or *xsl:when*, and $replroot()$ function has been defined before. $dlmtr$ takes one of two values. If the heading character of the left $E(e)$ is "[", $dlmtr$ is empty; otherwise, it is "/". Note that if there are more than one filter in a subsection of current T-expression, the filters can be combined using logic *and*.

5.2.2 *xsl:for-each* and *xsl:template*

The general form of the *xsl:for-each* statement is $<xsl:for-each select="p">$. It selects p children of the current context node. For each p child n, n becomes the new context node and is processed by the statements inside the *xsl:for-each* statement. In other words, the *xsl:for-each* statement changes the current context node and causes the processing of input XML tree down to each p child. Based on this observation, the T-expression is changed using $E(e) = p' + dlmtr + E(e)$ where $dlmtr$ is empty if the first letter after it is "[" and otherwise $dlmtr$ is "/". p' is constructed from $replroot(p)$ by adding $\{\forall\}$ right after the last element of $replroot(p)$ where $\{\forall\}$ indicates the name of current context node. Note that the "for-each" semantic of this statement is automatically taken by the T-expression because all element instances will be selected from the relational database after the T-expression is translated to a SQL query.

Similarly, if the enclosing statement is $<xsl:template$ $match="p">$, $E(e) = p' + dlmtr + E(e)$. However, if $p = /$, we do not use $\{\forall\}$ because there is only one root node in an XML document.

5.2.3 *xsl:for-each-group*

The basic form of the grouping statement is $<xsl:for-each-group select = p$ $group-by = g>$ where p is a path to select elements to be grouped; g is a path which is the grouping key of the selected elements. Note that we do not deal with other formats of the grouping statement. To map this statement to the T-expression, we use $E(e) = p'\{group : g\} + dlmtr + E(e)$ where $E(e)$, p' and $dlmtr$ are defined in the same way as above and $\{group : g\}$ maps the grouping key of the statement. We note that this statement also changes the current context node as the *xsl:for-each* statement. So the flag $\{\forall\}$ is used indicate the new context node. Because every enclosed O-statement of *xsl:for-each-group* contains this mapping in its T-expression, the semantic of "for each group" and "for each group member" has been automatically applied to the O-statement when the SQL query of the T-expression is executed. Note that the function $current - group$ is often used inside *xsl:value-of* when the grouping statement is used. As indicated above, there is no need to translate this function. Note also that we do not deal with the *separator* clause of *xsl:value-of* (XSLT version 2) because the clause causes the concatenation of values from parallel elements which is equivalent to concatenating relational tuples and has no direct SQL counterpart.

5.2.4 *xsl:sort*

The general form of the *xsl:sort* statement is *<xsl:sort select="p_o">* where p_o defines the sorting key. We deal with this statement simply by putting a special string at the beginning of the T-expression as $\{sort : p_o\}$.

5.2.5 *xsl:element*, *xsl:attribute* **and constant statements**

For an O-statement e, if an enclosing statement is *<xsl:element name="n">*, $E(e) = n\{E\}/ + E(e)$ where the flag $\{E\}$ means n is defined as a constant element name. If an enclosing statement is *<xsl:attribute name="n">*, $E(e) = n\{A\}/ + E(e)$ where the flag $\{A\}$ means the name following is defined as an attribute. If an enclosing statement is a constant statement, say *<n>*, $E(e) = n\{CE\}/ + E(e)$ where $\{CE\}$ indicates that the name n is element name and defined in a constant statement. Similarly, for a constant string t, it is mapped to $E(e) = t\{CT\}/ + E(e)$.

Note that the aim of including constant statements into the T-expression is to allow the T-expression to be used to wrap data into XML output after translated SQL queries are executed. The subsections of the T-expression that are flagged as constants will not be translated into SQL.

By applying the above processes to all enclosing statements of each O-statement, we have updated the T-expressions in the wrapping schema.

After the completing of updating, the T-expressions in the wrapping schema may contain wildcards and the first character of the T-expressions may not be "¶" (the root element). In other words, the T-expressions may not be final. Non-final T-expressions can not be translated to SQL queries as discussed before. For this reason, we have to process the T-expressions further.

5.3 Processing wildcards

Wildcards contained in XSLT path expressions can be one or more of ".", "..", "//", "|", "/*/", and "/@*". We process them as the followings.

"." The wildcard "." refers to the current context node. This wild card is processed by removing it together with the "/" before it (if there is a "/" before it) from the T-expression.

".." The wildcard ".." refers to the parent node of the current context node. If it appears in a T-expression as $p/q/../s$, we remove $q/..$ and get p/s. If ".." appears at the beginning of a filter like $p/q[../s]$, we move the filter one level up and get $p[s]/q$. Note that it is a syntax error if a T-expression updated up to now is preceded with ".." as $../p/q$.

"$p_a//p_b$" The wildcard "$p_a//p_b$" means all paths between elements p_a and p_b. If p_a is empty, p_a is set to the root of the DTD. We deal with this wildcard by searching through DTD D to find all paths starting from p_a and ending to p_b and denote all found paths by a set $P = \{p_1, \cdots, p_n\}$. Then the original T-expression containing the wildcard is translated to a set of of T-expressions as $p_a/p_1/p_b$, $\cdots$, $p_a/p_n/p_b$ which are additional to the wrapping schema. These n additional rows are added to the schema by creating n new rows. The line number of a new added row is constructed from the line number of the original row by appending '.i' where i is the sequential number of the new T-expression in P. The type value and the order value of the new rows are the same as the original row. The Q and S column of the new rows are set to empty. After the new rows are created, the original row is deleted from the schema. An example will be given later.

"$p_a|p_b$" The wildcard "|" means the logical 'or' relationship . The T-expression containing this wildcard is processed by producing two T-expressions: one is p_a and the other is p_b. New rows are constructed to store the two expressions, as discussed above, and the old row is deleted.

"$p_a/ * /p_b$" The wildcard "*" means all children of p_a or all patents of p_b in the DTD. We search through the DTD to find all elements that are children of p_a or parents of p_b and denote all found elements by $e_1, \cdots, e_n$. The original T-expression $p_a/ * /p_b$ is translated to a set of new T-expressions $p_a/e_1/p_b$, $\cdots$, $p_a/e_n/p_b$. New rows in the schema are added to store all these T-expressions. Here p_a and p_b can be empty. If both of them are empty, the wildcard matches any element. Then for each element, a

T-expression is produced.

"$p_a/@*$" The wildcard "@*" means all attributes of p_a. This is processed in the same way as "*" is processed.

We now use T-expression $//*[title]$ as an example. This T-expression is to select any elements that have a title child element no matter on which level the elements are. We go through the DTD given in Figure 1 to find parents of the element $title$ and get two elements $Book$ and $Article$. So the wildcard "*" is replaced by two T-expressions $//Book[title]$ and $//Article[title]$. We further process the wildcard "//" by searching all ancestors of $Book$ and $Article$ and we get $\P Bib$. So the T-expressions become $\P Bib/Book[title]$ and $\P Bib/Article[title]$.

5.4 The statements of 'apply' and 'call'

The *xsl:apply-templates* statement in XSLT uses the current context node to match patterns of templates. If a match is successful, the matched template is applied to this context node. If no templates match the current context node, a default template will be used to print all texts of the current context node and all its descendants. The key point of the matching is that the type of the current context node has to be the same as the match pattern of the template. When we translate queries, we do not know what is the type of the current context node. So a direct translation of the query is not possible. We need DTD to get more information for the translation. Before we present algorithms, we define global and local T-expressions. A T-expression is global if the first character of the expression is the root element "$\P$". A T-expression is local if it is not global. Let L be the set of all local T-expressions in the wrapping schema.

The *apply* statement is processed by starting with the shortest global T-expression. By shortest, it means that it has the least number of levels from the root. Usually, this global T-expression is the root element. If there is no such a global expression in the wrapping schema, we add an *apply* statement to the wrapping schema and set its T-expression value to "$\P$", set its line number to a number that is larger than any line number in the table, and set order number to 1. Then the new added *apply* statement is the one to start with the processing in the wrapping schema.

The basic idea of the process is to search recursively for the paths from the root of the DTD to the starting element of local T-expressions. If such paths are found, local T-expressions then can be updated to global ones. This search also aims to find those paths starting from the root that do not match any local paths. For example in Figure 6, because c_1 matches the heading elements of l_1 and l_2, so l_1 and l_2 become global. On the second level, l_3 and l_4 become global because c_{i1} matches l_3 and l_4. The remaining paths $e/c_i/c_{i2}$ and e/c_n do not match any local T-expressions.

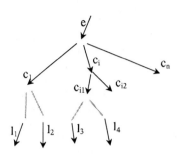

Figure 6. Complexity of joining templates

They corresponds to the default template of XSLT.

The above algorithm is used repeatedly until all local T-expressions become global. Note that variable T-expressions are handled in later.

The processing of *xsl:call-template* is much simpler because the call is based on a template name. Let $E(e)$ be the T-expression of the element $e=xsl:call-template$. Let TP be the template that is called by e. Let T be the set of all T-expressions generated in TP. For each T-expression $e' \in T$, $E(e')$ is updated as $E(e') = E(e) +$ "/" $+ E(e')$. Finally, the order number of e is set to 0.

5.5 Variable replacement

We now consider variables in T-expressions. Generally a variable may have multiple T-expressions defined in different rows in the wrapping schema. The T-expression of each row of the variable is called **a definition** of the variable. We handle a variable $\$x$ in a T-expression e by replacing $\$x$ in e with the definitions of $\$x$. If $\$x$ is defined in m rows, the row in which e contains $\$x$ is duplicated to have m copies so that a definition of $\$x$ replaces $\$x$ in one of e's copies. After the replacement, the O-numbers of the copies are changed to the longest O-number among all the variable definitions plus 1. After that, if $\$x$ in all T-expressions is replaced, the O-numbers of $\$x$ are set to 0.

When duplication is made, there is one exception if a variable is inside an aggregation function like $count(\$x)$. we apply the function to each T-expression of the variable and then add the returned values of the function together. If the aggregation functions are $min()$ or $max()$, similar processing can be employed. This will be demonstrated in the example given later.

After all variable replacements are completed, we delete those rows in the schema that have 0 O-number.

We further delete those $\{\forall\}$ symbols that are in filters and in functions. Then we number the remaining $\{\forall\}$ by adding a subscript to them. The subscripts are sequential numbers with the one to the most left being 1.

5.6 Last element names of T-expressions

The last element of some T-expressions (including the path expressions inside functions) may correspond to an internal node in the DTD. In this case, the *xsl:value-of* and the *xsl:copy-of* statements would print the text of the node and the texts of all descendants of the node. To translate the semantics in this situation, we need to check the last element of T-expressions. If the last element of a T-expression is an internal node, we need to get all descendants of the element.

We check the T-expression E of each row of the wrapping schema. If the last element $end(E)$ of that row corresponds to an internal node of the DTD, we calculate all descendants of $end(E)$. If $end(E)$ is a leaf node of the DTD, we replace $end(E)$ and the slash "/" before it with $\{select : end(E)\}$.

After all these operations, we re-order the rows of the wrapping schema based on the O-number.

Table 3 gives the final T-expressions after all update processes have been applied to the initial wrapping schema.

Table 3. The wrapping schema after processing $[select :]$

L	T	O	E	Q	S
15.1	value	1.1	$E_{1.1}$		
15.2	value	1.2	$E_{1.2}$		
8.1	copy	1.3.1.1	$E_{1.3.1.1}$		
8.2	copy	1.3.1.2	$E_{1.3.1.2}$		
11.1	value	1.3.2	$E_{1.3.2}$		
11.2	value	1.3.3	$E_{1.3.3}$		

where
$E_{1.1}$=¶bib/book{select:title,publisher}
$E_{1.2}$=¶bib/article{select:title,journal,publisher}
$E_{1.3.1.1}$=¶bib/Person{∀ 1}[@id]/book{∀ 2}[title][author/@id=
   ¶bib/person[@id]/@id and contains(publisher,'wi')]
   {sort:year}{select:title}
$E_{1.3.1.2}$=¶bib/Person{∀ 1}[@id]/article{∀ 2}[title][author/@id=
   ¶bib/person[@id]/@id and contains(publisher,'Wi')]{sort:year}
   {select:title}
$E_{1.3.2}$=¶bib/person{∀ 1}[@id]/numberOfItems{CE}/==={CT}
$E_{1.3.3}$=¶bib/person{∀ 1}[@id]/numberOfItems{CE}/count(¶bib/book
   [title]{select:*})+count(¶bib/article[title]{select:*})

6. Translation of final T-expressions to SQL queries

Each final T-expression in the wrapping schema is translated to a SQL query. As presented before, a T-expression contains a list of names including those names inside path expressions in the filters and functions. Some of them are elements of complex nodes in the DTD graph. These elements have corresponding tables in the relational database. The other names in the T-expression are either simple node names of the DTD graph or the constant names preceded with flags of $\{E\}$, $\{A\}$, $\{CE\}$, and $\{CT\}$. The simple node names correspond to columns of tables. The constant names will not be involved in the translation. They will be added to XML data when the returned relational data is wrapped. Let

- $t = \{t_1, ..., t_n\}$ be the set of all tables corresponding to all the names of complex nodes of the T-expression in the DTD graph;

  $g = \{t_{g_1}, ..., t_{g_h}\}$ be a sub set of t containing all the tables corresponding to all the names flagged by $\{\forall_k\}$ with the order of the names being the order of the current node number k in $\{\forall_k\}$;

- $grpNames = t_{g_1}.ID, ..., t_{g_h}.ID$;

- $sortNames$ be constructed by inserting the tailing names of p_o in all $\{sort : p_o\}$ of the T-expression right the closest current node name in front of them;

- $selectNames$ be defined in $\{select : selectNames\}$ with with the table name being added in front of each name;

- c be a condition translated from all filters of the T-expression.

Then a T-expression can be translated to the following SQL query.

```
SELECT sortNames, selectNames
FROM t₁,t₂,···,tₙ
WHERE t₁.ID = t₂.parentID AND
    ···
    tₙ₋₁.ID = tₙ.parentID AND
    c
GROUP BY sortNames, selectNames
SORT BY sortNames
```

Note that the join condition $t_{j-1}.ID = t_j.parentID$ is added only if t_{j-1} is a parent of t_j. In other words, if "¶" is between t_{j-1} and t_j, no join conditions are added. This query joins all tables corresponding to complex node elements. It selects ID values of all tables corresponding to the current node names and selects the values for $sortNames$ and $selectNames$. The ID values and the $sortNames$ values will be used for rearranging the order of the retrieved data so that the wrapped data is in the order of its XSLT counterparts.

The translation of filters to c in the above discussion can be further elaborated as the following. If there is more than one filter in the T-expression, the logic 'and' operator is used to connect them. Functions in the filter are translated to similar SQL keywords. For example, the function

$contains(x,y)$ can be translated to x LIKE '%y%'. A filter like $[x]$ can be translated to x IS NOT NULL. Note that we do not allow the $position()$ function in the XSLT query. This is because the $position()$ function does not have a direct counterpart in the relational database.

As an example, we apply the above process to Expression $E_{1.3.3}$ and obtain the following two SQL queries.

$Q_{1.3.3}(a)$:
```
SELECT person.id, count(*)
FROM bib, book, person
WHERE bib.id=book.parentID and
      bib.id=person.parentID and
      person.id is not null and
      Book.title IS NOT NULL
GROUP BY person.id
SORT BY Person.id
```

$Q_{1.3.3}(b)$:
```
SELECT person.id, count(*)
FROM bib, article, person
WHERE bib.id=article.parentID and
      bib.id=person.parentID and
      person.id is not null and
      artciel.title IS NOT NULL
GROUP BY person.id
SORT BY Person.id
```

Table 4. Retrieved data by running the SQL queries

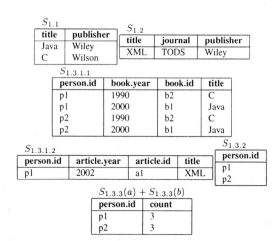

databases are retrieved through XML views. The basic idea of our method is to parse XSLT queries into a set of T-expressions. Each T-expression is then translated to a SQL query. Future research includes developing algorithms for wrapping the data returned from the execution of the SQL queries, analyzing performances on all the algorithms, and developing the way of processing specific XSLT functions.

References

[1] W3C Working Draft 16 August 2002. Xsl transformations (xslt) version 2.0. Technical report, 2002. http://www.w3.org/TR/2002/WD-xslt20-20020816/.

[2] Serge Abiteboul, Peter Buneman, and Dan Suciu. *Data on the Web - From Relations to Semistructured Data and XML*. Morgan Kayfman Publisher, 2000.

[3] Marcelo Arenas and Leonid Libkin. A normal form for xml documents. *PODS*, 2002.

[4] Geert Jan Bex, Sebastian Maneth, and Frank Neven. Expressive power of xslt. *http://citeseer.nj.nec.com/bex00expressive.html*.

[5] Tim Bray, Jean Paoli, and C. M. Sperberg-McQueen. Extensible markup language (xml) 1.0. Technical report, http://www.w3.org/TR/1998/REC-xml-19980210, 1998.

[6] Mary F. Fernandez, Wang Chiew Tan, and Dan Suciu. Silkroute: trading between relations and xml. *Computer Networks*, 33(1-6), 2000.

[7] Sushant Jain, Ratul Mahajan, and Dan Suciu. Translating xslt programs to efficient sql queries. *WWW2002*, 2002.

[8] Arnaud Sahuguet and Fabien Azavant. Looking at the web through xml glasses. *International Conference on Coorperative Information Systems*, pages 148–159, 1999.

[9] Jayavel Shanmugasundaram, Kristin Tufte, Hang He, Chun Zhang, David DeWitt, and Jeffrey Naughton. Relational database for querying xml documents: limitations and opportunities. *VLDB*, pages 302–314, 1999.

7. Conclusion

In this paper, we proposed methods of translating XSLT queries to SQL queries. This is used when relational

96

Data Mining II

Frequent itemsets mining for database auto-administration

Kamel Aouiche, Jérôme Darmont
ERIC/BDD, University of Lyon 2
5 avenue Pierre Mendès-France
69676 Bron Cedex, FRANCE
{kaouiche, jdarmont}@eric.univ-lyon2.fr

Le Gruenwald
School of Computer Science
University of Oklahoma
Norman, OK 73019, USA
ggruenwald@ou.edu

Abstract

With the wide development of databases in general and data warehouses in particular, it is important to reduce the tasks that a database administrator must perform manually. The aim of auto-administrative systems is to administrate and adapt themselves automatically without loss (or even with a gain) in performance. The idea of using data mining techniques to extract useful knowledge for administration from the data themselves has existed for some years. However, little research has been achieved. This idea nevertheless remains a very promising approach, notably in the field of data warehousing, where queries are very heterogeneous and cannot be interpreted easily. The aim of this study is to search for a way of extracting useful knowledge from stored data themselves to automatically apply performance optimization techniques, and more particularly indexing techniques. We have designed a tool that extracts frequent itemsets from a given workload to compute an index configuration that helps optimizing data access time. The experiments we performed showed that the index configurations generated by our tool allowed performance gains of 15% to 25% on a test database and a test data warehouse.

1 Introduction

Large-scale usage of databases requires a Database Administrator (DBA) whose principal role is data management, both at the logical level (schema definition) and the physical level (files and disk storage), as well performance optimization. With the wide development of Database Management Systems (DBMSs), minimizing the administration function has become critical to achieve acceptable response times even at load peaks [22]. One important DBA task is the selection of suitable physical structures to improve the system performances by minimizing data access time [10].

Indexes are physical structures that allow a direct access to the data. From the DBA's point of view, performance op-

timization lies mainly in the selection of indexes and materialized views [4, 12]. These physical structures play a particularly significant role in decision-support databases such as data warehouses due to their huge volume and complex queries.

The problem of selecting an optimal index set for a database has been studied since the seventies. The most recent studies regarding index selection use the DBMS' query optimizer to estimate the cost of various configurations of candidate indexes [3, 7, 8, 11]. However, the idea of using data mining techniques to extract useful knowledge for administration from the data themselves has been around for some years [6]. Little work has been done, though. In this paper, we designed and coded a tool that exploits data mining to recommend a relevant index configuration.

Assuming that index utility is strongly correlated to the usage frequency of the corresponding attributes within a given workload, the search for frequent itemsets [1] appeared well adapted to highlight this correlation and facilitate index selection. Our tool parses the transaction log file (the set of queries executed by the DBMS) to build a context for mining frequent itemsets. This context connects queries from the input workload to the attributes that may be indexed. The output frequent itemsets are sets of attributes forming a configuration of candidate indexes. Finally, various strategies can be applied to select the indexes to effectively build from within this configuration.

In the remainder of this paper, we present our proposal in Section 2 and some preliminary experimental results in Section 3, and then finally conclude the paper and present future research perspectives in Section 4.

2 Frequent itemsets mining for index selection

2.1 Principle

Our approach exploits the transaction log to extract an index configuration. The queries from the transaction log

```
Q1: SELECT * FROM T1, T2 WHERE A BETWEEN 1 AND 10 AND C=D
Q2: SELECT * FROM T1, T2 WHERE B LIKE '%this%' AND C=5 AND E<100
Q3: SELECT * FROM T1, T2 WHERE A=30 AND B>3 GROUP BY C HAVING SUM(E)>2
Q4: SELECT * FROM T1 WHERE B>2 AND E IN (3, 2, 5)
Q5: SELECT * FROM T1, T2 WHERE A=30 AND B>3 GROUP BY C HAVING SUM(E)>2
Q6: SELECT * FROM T1, T2 WHERE B>3 GROUP BY C HAVING SUM(E)>2
```

Figure 1. Sample workload

constitute a workload that is treated by an SQL query analyzer. The SQL query analyzer extracts all the attributes that may be indexed (indexable attributes). Then, we build a "query-attribute" matrix, the rows of which are the workload queries, and the columns are the indexable attributes. The role of this matrix is to link each indexable attribute to the workload queries it appears in.

This matrix represents the extraction context for frequent itemsets. To compute these frequent itemsets, we selected the Close algorithm [17, 18], because its output is the set of the frequent closed intemsets (closed regarding the Galois connection [18]), which is a generator for all the frequent itemsets and their support. In most cases, the number of frequent closed itemsets is much lower than the total number of frequent itemsets obtained by classical algorithms such as Apriori [2]. In our context, using Close enables us to obtain a smaller (though still significant) configuration of candidate indexes faster.

Finally, we select from the configuration of candidate indexes (that corresponds to the input workload) the most relevant indexes and create them.

2.2 Workload extraction

We assume that a workload similar to the one presented in Figure 1 is available. Such a workload can be easily obtained either from the DBMS' transaction logs, or by running an external application such as Lumigent's Log Explorer [14].

2.3 Indexable attributes extraction

To reduce response time when running a database query, it is best to build indexes on the very attributes that are used to process the query. These attributes belong to the WHERE, ORDER BY, GROUP BY, and HAVING clauses of SQL queries [7].

We designed a syntactic analyzer that is able to operate on any SQL query type (selections and updates — subqueries are allowed), and extracts all the indexable attributes. This process is applied to all the queries from the workload.

2.4 Building the extraction context for the frequent closed itemsets

We build a matrix (Figure 2) the rows of which represent the workload queries, and the columns represent the set of all the indexable attributes identified in the previous step. This "query-attribute" matrix links each query to the indexable attributes within it. Attribute presence in a query is symbolized by 1, and absence by 0.

Queries	Attributes				
	A	B	C	D	E
Q1	1	0	1	1	0
Q2	0	1	1	0	1
Q3	1	1	1	0	1
Q4	0	1	0	0	1
Q5	1	1	1	0	1
Q6	0	1	1	0	1

Figure 2. Sample extraction context

2.5 Frequent closed itemsets mining

The Close algorithm scans in breadth first a lattice of closed itemsets in order to extract the frequent closed itemsets and their support. Its input is an extraction context such as the one presented in Figure 2.

Intuitivelty, a closed itemset is a maximal set of items (attributes) that are common to a set of transactions (queries). For instance, in Figure 2's extraction context, the BCE itemset is closed because it is the largest set of common attributes for the set of queries {Q2, Q3, Q5, Q6}. On the other hand, the BC itemset is not closed since all the queries containing attributes B and C (Q2, Q3, Q5, and Q6) also contain attribute E. Eventually, a closed itemset is said frequent when its support is greater or equal to a threshold parameter named *minsup* (minimal support).

The application of Close on the context presented in Figure 2 outputs the following set of frequent closed itemsets (and their support) for a minimal support equal to 2/6: {(AC, 3/6), (BE, 5/6), (C, 5/6), (ABCE, 2/6), (BCE, 4/6)}.

We consider this set as our configuration of candidate indexes.

2.6 Indexes construction

The higher the size of the input workload is, the higher the number of candidate indexes obtained with our approach becomes. Thus, it is not feasible to build all the proposed indexes. Index creation time, and later update time, would both be too costly. Hence, it is necessary to devise filtering methods or processes to reduce the number of indexes to generate.

The first naive method is to build all the candidate indexes. This method is only applicable when the number of indexes is relatively small. In that particular case, creation and update times remain acceptable.

In the context of decision-support databases, and more particularly, of data warehouses, building indexes is a fundamental issue because of the huge volume of data stored in fact tables and some dimension tables. Thus, it is more critical to build indexes on large tables. Index contribution on small tables can indeed prove negligible, and even sometimes, costly.

Statistical input, such as the cardinality of the attributes to be indexed, may also be exploited to build indexes. An attribute's cardinality is the distinct number of values for this attribute within a given relation. Depending on the cardinality, indexing may be more or less efficient. If the cardinality is very large, an index degenerates toward a sequential scan (of the index structure itself); and if it is very small, an index might not bring a very significant improvement [21]. Hence, the best choice might be to build indexes on attributes with an "average" cardinality.

In this first study, we took a particular interest in table sizes. We indeed established two strategies to build indexes from the union of the frequent closed itemsets provided by Close. The first strategy systematically builds all the proposed indexes (naive method). In this case, each frequent closed itemset corresponds to an index to be created. The second strategy takes the size of the tables an index refers to into account. In this case, the DBA must define whether a table is large or not, and only indexes on attributes from these large tables are built.

2.7 Comparison with the existing methods

Unlike the index selection methods that have been recently developed, the tool that we propose does not communicate with the DBMS' query optimizer. The communication between the index selection tool and the optimizer is usually costly and must be minimized. An index configuration computing time is indeed proportional to the size of the workload, which is typically large. Our method based on frequent itemsets mining is also greedy in terms of computing time, but it is currently difficult for us to determine which approach generates the heaviest overhead for the system.

However, we are more interested in the quality of the generated indexes. For instance, the *Index Selection Tool* (IST) developed by Microsoft within the SQL Server DBMS [7] exploits a given workload and provides a configuration of mono-attribute candidate indexes. A greedy algorithm selects the best indexes from this configuration, using estimated costs computed by the query optimizer. The process then reiterates to generate two-attribute indexes using the mono-attribute indexes, and similarly, to generate multi-attribute indexes of higher order. By mining frequent closed itemsets, our tool directly extracts a set of mono-attribute *and* multi-attribute indexes. Hence, we do not build an initial mono-attribute index configuration *a priori*, and we do not need to use any heuristic to build multi-attribute candidate indexes by successive iterations like IST. We believe that this approach avoids the generation and cost evaluation of irrelevant indexes.

3 Experiments

In order to validate our approach, we have applied it on a test database and a test data warehouse. Our objective here is more to find out whether our proposal makes sense in practice than to perform true performance tests.

We have chosen the TPC-R decision-support benchmark [20] for our experiments on a relational database because it is a standard that should allow us to easily compare our approach to the other existing methods in the future. We have generated the TPC-R 1 GB database and used the benchmark's 22 read-only queries (labeled Q1 to Q22). In this first experiment, we suppose refresh operations occur off-line. However, in order to take index management overhead into account, future performance tests will also include TPC-R's RF1 and RF2 refresh functions.

On the other hand, to the best of our knowledge, there is no standard benchmark for data warehouses yet (TPC-DS is still in development [19]). Hence, we worked on a small datamart that had been previously developed in our laboratory. This accidentology datamart is composed of an *Accident* fact table and four dimension tables: *Place, Condition, Date* and *PersonResponsible*. It occupies 15 MB on disk. Starting from our previous analyses on this datamart, we also designed a realistic decision-support workload that is specifically adapted to it. This workload includes both selection and update operations. We cannot present it in detail here due to lack of space; interested readers are referred to [5].

Both the TPC-R database and the accidentology datamart have been implanted within the SQL Server 2000

```
// Cold run (no timing)
FOR each query in the workload DO
      Execute current query
END FOR
// Warm run
FOR i = 1 TO number_of_replications DO
      FOR each query in the workload DO
            Execute current query
            Compute response time for current query
      END FOR
END FOR
Compute global mean response time and confidence interval
```

Figure 3. Test protocol

DBMS.

The test protocol we adopted is presented in Figure 3. This algorithm has been executed for various values of the Close *minsup* (minimal support) parameter. In practice, this parameter helps us limiting the number of indexes to generate by selecting only those that are the most frequently used by the workload. At each step corresponding to a value of *minsup*, we compute the mean response time for the input workload.

3.1 Experiments on TPC-R

The results we obtained are presented in Figure 4 and 5. The results from Figure 4 correspond to the creation of all the candidate indexes obtained with Close, while the results of Figure 5 correspond to a filter on this configuration (indexes on large tables only; cf. Section 2.6).

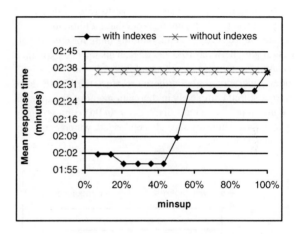

Figure 5. TPC-R results — Indexes on large tables

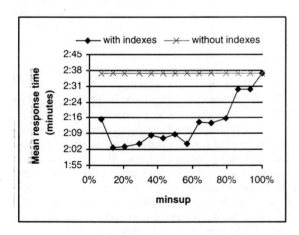

Figure 4. TPC-R results — All indexes

Figure 4 and 5 show that, in comparison with a sequential scan with no indexes, we achieve a gain in performance for the two strategies regardless of the value of *minsup*. The maximum response time gain, which is computed as the difference between the mean response time without indexes and the lowest mean response time with indexes, is close to 22% in the first case and 25% in the second case. The average response time gains computed over all values of minsup are 14.4% and 13.7% in the first and second case, respectively. In the first case, the response time improves until *minsup* reaches 15%, and then degrades at a steady rate, while in the second case, it remains at its lower value in a broader range (from 20% *minsup* to 50% *minsup*) before degrading abruptly. The large number of indexes to be generated in the first case can explain this behavior. Considering only indexes associated with large tables helps reducing the number of generated indexes and avoids index creation for small tables (since they induce a low benefit).

Finally, for high values of *minsup*, the mean response time becomes close to that obtained without generating any index in both cases. This was predictable since for a very high *minsup*, no or very few indexes are actually generated. In the second case, this state is reached sooner since fewer indexes are built, which explains the lower average gain.

3.2 Data warehouse experiments

For this series of experiments, we applied the same protocol (Figure 3). However, we did not employ the large table index creation strategy since all the tables in our test datamart have similar sizes.

The results we obtained are presented in Figure 6. The maximum gain in performance is close to 15% while the average gain is 6.4%. Figure 6 shows that building indexes is actually more costly than not building them for *minsup* values ranging between 10% and 25%. This may be explained by the high number of generated indexes, and thus a high index generation time. Furthermore, since the 15 MB datamart is stored completely in the main memory, the indexes are useful only when it is first loaded. In this context, many sparsely used indexes must also be loaded, which penalizes global performance.

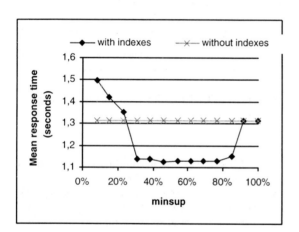

Figure 6. Accidentology datamart results

The best gain in response time appears for *minsup* values ranging between 30% and 85%, when the number of indexes is such that the index generation overhead is lower than the performance increase achieved when loading the datamart. Beyond that point, response time degrades and becomes close to that obtained without indexes because there are a few or no indexes to generate.

Another possible explanation to the lower performances obtained for our datamart, in comparison to the results achieved on the TPC-R database, may come from the structure of the created indexes. Bitmap and star-join indexes are best adapted to data warehouses [15, 16], while the default indexes in SQL Server are variants of B-trees.

4 Conclusions and perspectives

We presented in this paper a novel approach for automatic index selection in DBMSs. The originality of our study rests on the extraction of frequent itemsets to determine an index configuration. Indeed, we assume that the importance of an indexable attribute is strongly correlated with its frequency of appearance in the workload's queries. In addition, the use of a frequent itemsets mining algorithm such as Close enables us to generate mono-attribute and multi-attribute indexes on the fly, without having to implement an iterative process that successively creates increasingly large multi-attribute indexes based on an initial set of mono-attribute indexes.

Our first experimental results show that our technique indeed allows response time improvements of 20% to 25% for a decision-support workload applied to a relational database (TPC-R benchmark). We also proposed two strategies to carry out an index selection among the candidate indexes: the first strategy systematically creates all the candidate indexes, while the second only creates the indexes that are related to so-called large tables. The second strategy allows better performance improvements because it proposes a better compromise between the space occupied by the indexes (the number of created indexes is limited to those that are defined on attributes from large tables) and the use of creating an index (it is not beneficial to create an index on a small table).

We also performed tests on an accidentology datamart, on which we applied an ad hoc decision-support workload. The gain in response time, about 14%, is less significant than in the case of TPC-R. This can be explained by the fact that the default indexes created by SQL Server are B-tree variants and not bitmap or star-join indexes, which would be better adapted for a data warehouse.

Our study shows that using data mining techniques for DBMS auto-administration is promising. However, it is only a first approach and it opens up many prospects for research. Our first research perspective is to improve index selection by designing more elaborated strategies than the exhaustive use of a configuration or the exploitation of relatively basic information relating to table sizes. A more accurate cost model regarding table features (other than size), or a strategy for weighting the workload's queries (by type of query: selection or update), could help us. The use of other unsupervised data mining methods such as clustering could also provide smaller sets of frequent itemsets.

It also appears essential to test our method further to better evaluate the overhead it generates, both in terms of indexes generation time and maintenance time. In particular, it is necessary to apply it on large data warehouses, while exploiting adapted indexes. It would also be very interesting to compare it in a more systematic way to the IST tool that has been developed by Microsoft, either through complexity computations of the index configuration generation heuristics (overhead), or by experiments aiming at evaluating the quality of these configurations (response time improvement and overhead due to index maintenance).

Extending or coupling our approach with other performance optimization techniques (materialized views, buffer management, physical clustering, etc.) also constitutes a promising research perspective. Indeed, in the context of data warehouses, it is mainly in conjunction with other physical structures (primarily materialized views) that indexing allows the most significant performance gains [3, 4, 12].

Finally, it would also be interesting to study how algorithms for mining functional dependencies [13] or inclusion dependencies [9] in databases might be exploited in our context. Many join operations (natural joins) are indeed carried out following inclusion dependencies (concept of foreign key). Discovering hidden dependencies within the data could thus help us generating relevant indexes or materialized views without needing an input workload.

References

[1] R. Agrawal, T. Imielinski, and A. N. Swami. Mining association rules between sets of items in large databases. *SIGMOD Record*, 22(2):207–216, 1993.

[2] R. Agrawal and R. Srikant. Fast algorithms for mining association rules. In *20th International Conference on Very Large Data Bases (VLDB 1994), Santiago, Chile*, pages 487–499, 1994.

[3] S. Agrawal, S. Chaudhuri, and V. R. Narasayya. Automated selection of materialized views and indexes in SQL databases. In *26th International Conference on Very Large Data Bases (VLDB 2000), Cairo, Egypt*, pages 496–505, 2000.

[4] S. Agrawal, S. Chaudhuri, and V. R. Narasayya. Materialized view and index selection tool for Microsoft SQL Server 2000. *2001 ACM SIGMOD International Conference on Management of Data, Santa Barbara, USA*, 2001.

[5] K. Aouiche. Accidentology datamart schema and workload. http://bdd.univ-lyon2.fr/download/charge-accidentologie.pdf, 2002.

[6] S. Chaudhuri. Data mining and database systems: Where is the intersection? *Data Engineering Bulletin*, 21(1):4–8, 1998.

[7] S. Chaudhuri and V. R. Narasayya. An efficient cost-driven index selection tool for Microsoft SQL Server. In *23rd International Conference on Very Large Data Bases (VLDB 1997), Athens, Greece*, pages 146–155, 1997.

[8] S. Chaudhuri and V. R. Narasayya. Autoadmin 'what-if' index analysis utility. In *1998 ACM SIGMOD International Conference on Management of Data, Seattle, USA*, pages 367–378, 1998.

[9] F. De Marchi, S. Lopes, and J.-M. Petit. Efficient algorithms for mining inclusion dependencies. In *8th International Conference on Extending Database Technology (EDBT 2002), Prague, Czech Republic*, volume 2287 of *LNCS*, pages 464–476, 2002.

[10] S. J. Finkelstein, M. Schkolnick, and P. Tiberio. Physical database design for relational databases. *TODS*, 13(1):91–128, 1988.

[11] M. R. Frank, E. Omiecinski, and S. B. Navathe. Adaptive and automated index selection in RDBMS. In *3rd International Conference on Extending Database Technology (EDBT 1992), Vienna, Austria*, volume 580 of *LNCS*, pages 277–292, 1992.

[12] H. Gupta. *Selection and maintenance of views in a data warehouse*. PhD thesis, Stanford University, 1999.

[13] S. Lopes, J.-M. Petit, and L. Lakhal. Efficient discovery of functional dependencies and Armstrong relations. In *7th International Conference on Extending Database Technology (EDBT 2000), Konstanz, Germany*, volume 1777 of *LNCS*, pages 350–364, 2000.

[14] Lumigent Technologies. Log Explorer for SQL Server. http://www.lumigent.com/products/le_sql/le_sql.htm, 2002.

[15] P. O'Neil and G. Graefe. Multi-table joins through bitmapped join indices. *SIGMOD Record*, 24(3):8–11, 1995.

[16] P. O'Neil and D. Quass. Improved query performance with variant indexes. *SIGMOD Record*, 26(2):38–49, 1997.

[17] N. Pasquier, Y. Bastide, R. Taouil, and L. Lakhal. Discovering frequent closed itemsets for association rules. In *7th International Conference on Database Theory (ICDT 1999), Jerusalem, Israel*, volume 1540 of *LNCS*, pages 398–416, 1999.

[18] N. Pasquier, Y. Bastide, R. Taouil, and L. Lakhal. Efficient mining of association rules using closed itemset lattices. *Information Systems*, 24(1):25–46, 1999.

[19] M. Poess, B. Smith, L. Kollar, and P.-A. Larson. TPC-DS: Taking decision support benchmarking to the next level. In *2002 ACM SIGMOD International Conference on Management of Data, Madison, USA*, 2002.

[20] Transaction Processing Council. *TPC Benchmark R Standard Specification*, 1999.

[21] S. Vanichayobon and L. Gruenwald. Indexing techniques for data warehouses' queries. Technical report, University of Oklahoma, School of Computer Science, 1999.

[22] G. Weikum, A. Monkeberg, C. Hasse, and P. Zabback. Self-tuning database technology and information services: from wishful thinking to viable engineering. In *28th International Conference on Very Large Data Bases (VLDB 2002), Hong Kong, China*, 2002.

Efficiently Mining Maximal Frequent Sets
For Discovering Association Rules

Krishnamoorthy Srikumar, Bharat Bhasker
Indian Institute of Management, Prabandh Nagar, Lucknow – 226 013. INDIA.
Phone: 091-0522-361 889 to 091-0522-361 897
Fax: 091-0522-361 843
E-mail: **srikumar@iiml.ac.in**, **bhasker@iiml.ac.in**

Abstract

We present Metamorphosis, an algorithm for mining Maximal Frequent Sets (MFS) using novel data transformations. Metamorphosis efficiently transforms the dataset to Maximum Collapsible and Compressible (MC²) format and employs a top down strategy with phased bottom up search for mining MFS. Using the chess and connect dataset [benchmark datasets created by Univ. of California, Irvine], we demonstrate that our algorithm offers better performance in mining MFS compared to dGenMax (an algorithm that offers better performance compared to other known algorithms) at higher support levels. Furthermore, we evaluate our algorithm for mining Top-K maximal frequent sets in chess and connect datasets. Our algorithm is especially efficient when the maximal frequent sets are longer.

1. Introduction

Mining frequent itemsets is a fundamental and essential operation in many data mining applications including discovery of association rules, strong rules, correlations, sequential rules, episodes, multi-dimensional patterns [6]. In general, frequent itemset mining problem is formulated as follows: Given a large database of transactions, our task is to identify frequent itemsets, where frequent itemsets are those itemsets that occur in at least a user-specified percentage of the database [10].

Most of the current itemset mining algorithms are variants of Apriori and it has been demonstrated that such algorithms are inadequate on data sets with long patterns [4]. As Apriori based algorithms employ a pure bottom-up, breadth first search, mining a frequent pattern of length m require mining all its $2^m - 2$ subsets, which would be computationally expensive if m is very large (> 30). Hence, there has been recent interest in mining

Maximal Frequent Sets (MFS). MFS are frequent itemsets whose supersets are infrequent and all its subsets are frequent.

Recent approaches to MFS mining include Pincer-Search [7] algorithm that uses a mixed search strategy to enumerate MFS. MaxMiner [4] performs a breadth first traversal of the search space with look-ahead. GenMax [10] uses vertical data representation and tidset intersections to mine quickly the MFS. dGenMax[10] is an improved version of GenMax which uses a novel vertical data representation called diffsets that only keeps track of differences in the tids of a candidate pattern. DepthProject [3] utilizes depth first search of a lexicographic tree. It employs a transaction projection mechanism for counting the support of itemsets quickly. Mafia [5] uses three pruning strategies to remove non-maximal sets. They are look-ahead pruning, superset frequency pruning, and parent equivalence pruning. A top-down algorithm proposed in [9] uses a novel concept of dominancy factor for efficiently mining MFS.

Our primary motivation in this paper is to demonstrate that it is possible to mine quickly the entire set of MFS by employing a top-down strategy with phased bottom-up search in dense domains. Additionally, we employ novel data transformation techniques to mine quickly the entire set of MFS.

The organization of the rest of paper is as follows: In the next section we introduce the model, notations, and pruning properties used in our algorithm. Section 3 gives the implementation details of our algorithm in various phases. In Section 4, we present our experimental results. Finally, in section 5, we conclude with a discussion of future work.

2. Model And Notations

The mining algorithm introduced in this paper presumes a dataset consisting of transactions that contain multiple items in each transaction. A set of items present in a transaction is referred to as an itemset. We assume that the items in the transaction are ordered sequence of numbers as per IBM artificial data set generator format [2].

Let $I = \{i_1, i_2, ...i_m\}$ be a set of distinct items. A set $X \subseteq I$ is called an itemset. An itemset X with k items (X_k) is succinctly referred as k-itemset.

A transaction, $T_i = \{x_\lambda \mid \lambda = 1, 2...N_i; x_\lambda \in I\}$, where N_i is the number of items in transaction T_i. A transaction T_i is said to support an itemset $X \subseteq I$ if and only if $X \subseteq T_i$. The support of an itemset X, denoted by Sup (X), is the total number of transactions in the dataset that supports X. The user defined minimum support is denoted as minsupport. An itemset $X \in \Im$(Frequent itemsets) if and only if Sup (X) $\geq$ minsupport.

In order to assist in identifying the unique transactions, we define a hash value of transaction T_i as follows:

Let LogP be an array containing a set of logarithm of prime numbers. The hash value of transactions T_i, denoted as Hval (T_i), is defined as

$$\text{Hval}(T_i) = \sum\nolimits_{\lambda=1}^{Ni} \text{LogP}[x_\lambda], \forall x_\lambda \in T_i.$$

We know that the product of prime numbers is unique and log (m*n) = log (m) + log (n). Hence, it can be easily verified that the computed hash values would be unique only for unique transactions. In earlier passes of the algorithm we collapse the duplicate set of transactions using computed hash values. For more details regarding hash value computation and its usage in collapsing duplicate transactions, the reader is referred to [8].

The dataset or transaction list, D, is an ordered set of triplet,

$D = \{(T_i, N_i, Sup_i) \mid i = 1, 2...L$; where,

  T_i is the ith transaction containing itemset x_λ;

  N_i is the number of frequent 1-items in T_i;

  $Sup_i = Sup(T_i)$;

} Where L is the total number of unique transactions in the dataset.

Table 1 gives a bird's eye view of the transaction list, D.

Table 1. Transaction List, D

TID	$T_i (x_\lambda)$	N_i	Sup_i
T_1	1 2 3 4 5	5	1
T_2	1 2 4 5	4	2
T_3	1 2 3 5	4	1
T_4	2 3 5	3	1
T_5	2 3 4	3	1

Note: Sup (1) = 4; Sup (2) = 6; Sup (3) = 4;

  Sup (4) = 4; Sup (5) = 5

We define TSUP as the set of supports of transactions in D. That is,

TSUP = {Sup_i, i=1, 2, 3...L}.

For example, the transaction list D in Table 1 has TSUP = {1, 2, 1, 1, 1}.

We denote NumF1 as the number of frequent 1-itemsets in the dataset at the user defined minimum support. The set of all frequent 1-itemsets (in ascending order of 1-item support) is denoted as

$\Im_1 = \{x_\lambda \mid \lambda = 1, 2...$ NumF1; Sup (x_λ) >= minsupport;

  Sup(x_i) $\leq$ Sup(x_{i+1}) and i=1,2...(NumF1-1)}.

For the transaction list D in Table 1, assuming a user defined minimum support of 3,

  NumF1 = 5 and $\Im_1 = \{1,3,4,5,2\}$.

Similarly, the set of frequent 2-itemsets is denoted as $\Im_2$. As frequent 2-itemsets has just two items, each item in $\Im_1$ will have set of other items (in $\Im_1$) with whom it is frequent. We refer to this as set of extensions of an item, denoted as Extension (x_λ). For the example in Table 1, assuming a user defined minimum support of 3,

  Extension (1) = {2, 5} as (1,2) and (1,5) are frequent.

  Extension (2) = {3, 4, 5} as (2,3), (2,4) and (2,5) are frequent.

  Extension (3) = {5} as (3,4) is infrequent and Extension (4) = { } as (4,5) is not frequent.

The maximum number of elements in Extension (x_λ) is denoted as Maxlen. For the above example, Maxlen = 3 as Extension (2) has the maximum number of elements of 3.

To mine the MFS efficiently, we transform the transaction list D to a collapsed and compressed format. In this work, we refer to this format as Maximum Collapsible and Compressible (MC^2) format. We now describe the notations specific to this transformation.

Let us assume W as the Word Size of a computer. That is, for a 32-bit computer W=32 and for a 128-bit computer W=128.

We compress the itemsets in every W transactions of D to a single transaction using vertical bitmaps. Table 2 gives the vertical bitmap compression for the transaction list D in Table 1 with W=3. That is, Table 2 shows the bitmap equivalent for the items in every 3 transactions (i.e. $NewT_1$ for T_1, T_2, T_3 and $NewT_2$ for T_4, T_5).

Table 2. Vertical Bitmap Representation (W=3)

NewTID	Item1	Item 2	Item 3	Item 4	Item 5
$NewT_1$	111	111	101	110	111
$NewT_2$	000	110	110	010	100

Table 3 gives the decimal notations for the bitmaps in Table 2. We transform the dataset in Table 1 to Table 3 and refer it as MC^2 (Maximum Collapsible and Compressible) format. Note that although we store the bitmaps in decimal notations as in Table 3, the numbers are internally stored in computer in binary form as in Table 2. Further, W is taken as 32 in the actual implementation though the illustrations in Table 2 and Table 3 has W=3.

```
Metamorphosis (Data-set DB):
Inputs: 1. Data Set, DB; 2. minsupport; 3. K (number of MFS desired), to be given only for Top-K MFS mining
    1. ℑ₁ = {Frequent 1-itemsets}
    2. For each Tᵢ ∈ DB do begin
    3.      Hvalᵢ = Σλ₌₁ᴺⁱ LogP [xλ];
    4.      Scan D and check for unique Hvalᵢ, if exists increment its support,
                Otherwise, sort items in ascending order of support and add Tᵢ to D
    5. End
    6. Scan D and compute ℑ₂ supports (frequent 2-item supports), Maxlen
    7. Convert D to MC² format and write the result to NewDB
    8. ML={};
    9. Initialize k to Maxlen
    10. For  k = Maxlen to 2 do begin
    11.     Generate k-itemsets, check for maximality and infrequency of subsets using INF_Tree, ℑ₂ supports and
                phased subset frequency checks
    12.        For each NewTᵢ ∈ NewDB do begin
                    Compute support of k-itemset by bit-wise AND operation and if the support crosses minsupport
                        requirement, and if no superset of it are frequent, add it to Maximal List, ML
    13.        End
    14.        If (Top-K MFS mining) do
    15.           If  (ML has at least K maximal frequent set) go to step 18.
    16.        decrement k by 2
    17.    End
    18.    Return Output
```

Figure 1. Pseudo-code for Metamorphosis Algorithm

Table 3. Dataset in Maximum Collapsible and Compressible (MC²) format

NewTID	Item 1	Item 2	Item 3	Item 4	Item 5
NewT₁	7	7	5	6	7
NewT₂	0	6	6	2	4

Our algorithm starts mining the MFS using the dataset in MC² format. Now let us describe the notations specific to MC² format. The transactions number i in MC² format is referred as $NewT_i$.

Bit (x_λ, i) denotes the bitmap for item x_λ in transaction $NewT_i$. Here, by bitmap we refer to the equivalent integers stored for item x_λ in MC² format. For instance, in Table 3, Bit (3, 1) is 5 and Bit (5, 2) is 4.

The bitwise AND of all the items in an itemset X_k in transaction $NewT_i$ is denoted as AND (X_k, i). For instance, when k=2, AND (X_2, i) = Bit (x_1, i) & Bit (x_2, i). Note that the operator & is a bitwise operator.

During the mining process, we check for infrequency of subsets of a k-itemset. For accomplishing this we hold a set of infrequent itemsets in a tree named as INF_Tree.

We store the MFS generated during the mining process in a Maximal List,
ML = {X | X ∈ ℑ and (X ∪ {x_λ}) ∉ ℑ ; λ ≥ 1;}

The itemsets in maximal list are stored in compressed form, similar to the one shown in Table 3 with W=32.

We define the MFS of longest length as LM (Longest Maximal) pattern.

For efficient mining our algorithm uses two pruning properties namely, Apriori [1] and Reverse Apriori [7] for limiting the search space.

We define Top-K MFS mining problem as a set of K MFS of longest length. So, essentially the top-K MFS mined will have very low supports compared to all other MFS.

3. Implementation Of Metamorphosis

Our algorithm follows a top down approach with phased bottom up search for mining MFS. In this section we describe the algorithm in various phases.

3.1 Transaction List Generation

In the first pass, the algorithm scans the dataset and computes support for all 1-itemsets. The infrequent 1-itemsets are removed from further evaluation. In the second scan of the dataset, we compute the hash value for all frequent 1-itemsets in each transaction. Before we add a transaction to the Transaction List D, we check for uniqueness of transactions using hash values [8]. If unique hash value already exists we increment the support of corresponding transaction. Otherwise, we add it as a new transaction in D. A sample transaction list, D is given in Table 1 (assuming a user specified minimum support of 2). We store the support value of transactions in TSUP.

While generating D, we store the support values of transaction in TSUP. After the transaction list, D is generated; we make a pass over D to compute ℑ₂ and Maxlen.

3.2 MC² format Dataset Generation

The algorithm converts the transaction list, D to MC² format by compressing the dataset using vertical bitmaps (with W=32). Once the MC^2 format dataset is generated, we discard the transaction list D. Table 3 gives a bird's eye view of the dataset in MC^2 format. For a machine with W=32, we can logically store vertical bitmaps of 32 transactions. This 32-bit number can be represented as 10 digit unsigned integer. Table 3 shows these vertical bitmaps in decimal form with W=3.

3.3 Subset Generations, and Itemset Pruning

As our algorithm follows a top down approach, we start with generating all itemsets of size, k equal to Maxlen.

Our algorithm generates k-itemsets recursively using the items in $\Im_1$. For the k-itemset generated, we check whether it is subsumed by a previously generated MFS stored in ML. If so, we generate the next k-itemset from $\Im_1$ and repeat the above procedure. Then we check for infrequency of subsets for a k-itemset in three steps. In the first step, we check whether all 2-itemsets present in k-itemset are frequent. If not, generate a new k-itemset and repeat all of the above procedures. In the second step, we check whether the k-itemsets' subset is infrequent by using the infrequent tree, INF_Tree. If infrequent subsets of a k-itemset are present in INF_Tree, generate a new k-itemset and repeat all of the above procedures. In the third step, we evaluate whether the k-itemsets' subsets are frequent in a phased manner. The details of phased subset frequency check are as follows:

1. In phase 1, we check for the frequency of first 4 and first 6 items present in the k-itemset. If it is found to be infrequent, we add the infrequent subsets to INF_Tree and repeat all of the above procedures.

2. In phase 2, we check for the frequency of first 8 and first 10 items present in the k-itemset. If it is found to be infrequent, we add the infrequent subsets to INF_Tree and repeat all of the above procedures.

3. In the next phase, we check for the frequency of first 12 and first 14 items present in the k-itemset. Subsequently for first 16 and first 18 items present and so on till the number of items to be evaluated for subset frequency are less than k. If any of the intermediate phases of subset frequency evaluation fails (that is the subset is infrequent), we add the infrequent subset into the infrequent tree, INF_Tree and repeat all of the above procedures.

4. Compute the support for the k-itemset as well as (k+1) itemset in a single pass. Add the frequent itemsets to ML if it is not subsumed by an existing MFS.

The phased subset frequency evaluation is a heuristics employed to identify the smaller infrequent nodes in the dense domain quickly.

All of the above procedures are repeated by decrementing k by 2 (as the support for a k and k+1 itemsets are

computed in a single pass) till 2. The pseudo-code for Metamorphosis is given in Figure 1. Lines 14 and 15 of the pseudo-code are used when mining Top-K MFS. In Top-K MFS mining, as soon as the total number of MFS crosses the user specified number of MFS (referred as K), our algorithm stops and outputs the result.

3.4 Support Counting

The support for an itemset, X_k is computed by performing a bit-wise AND operation on all the items in the itemset X_k. The resulting number is converted to equivalent binary number, say result, and the support is computed by using the position of 1's in result and the TSUP values. For example, support for an itemset {1,3,5} is computed from Table 3 as follows:

From $NewT_1$: AND ({1,3,5}, 1) = 7 & 5 & 7 = 5. Note that logically this operation would be treated in computer, as equivalent to 111 & 101 & 111. The equivalent binary notation for 5 would be 101. So, result=101. From position of 1's in result, we can infer that the itemset {1,3,5} is supported by transactions T_1 and T_3 in the original transaction list D. As the support values of transaction list, D is contained in TSUP, the support of itemset {1,3,5} in $NewT_1$ is the sum of $TSUP_1$ and $TSUP_3$, which is 2.

From $NewT_2$: AND ({1,3,5}, 2) = 0 & 6 & 4 = 0. The equivalent binary notation is 000. So, result=0. As there are no 1's in result, the support of itemset {1,3,5} in $NewT_2$ is zero.

Hence, the support of the itemset {1,3,5} from Table 3 is the sum of the above two values, which is equal to 2. The results can be easily verified from Table 1.

3.5 Maximality Checking

As soon as a k-itemset is found frequent, after checking if it is subsumed by any other MFS, it is written to ML. The Maximal List, ML stores the itemset in compressed bit-vector form similar to the example in Table 3 with W=32.

4 Experimental Results

All our experiments were performed on a 450MHz Pentium-III PC with 64MB of memory, running RedHat Linux 7.2. We use two benchmark datasets for experimentation viz. chess and connect. The characteristics of chess dataset include: 3196 transactions, 75 items and average transaction size of 37. The characteristics of connect dataset include: 67557 transactions, 129 items and average transaction size of 43.

4.1 Evaluation of Metamorphosis for Mining All the Maximal Frequent Sets

For performance comparisons, we used the original source codes for GenMax [10] provided to us by their au-

due to the fact that the Longest Maximal pattern size is far below Maxlen and the primary search strategy employed by Metamorphosis is top-down.

Figure 3 depicts the graphs of NumF1, Maxlen and LM pattern size against different minimum support levels. As

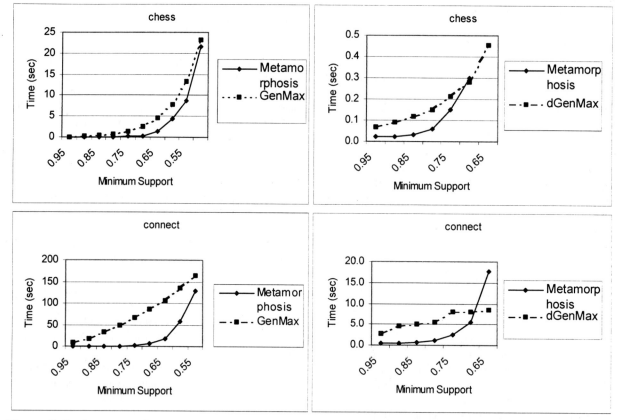

Figure 2. Performance Comparison of Metamorphosis Vs GenMax and dGenMax on chess and connect

thors. The timings reported in this paper include all pre-processing costs (such as time for horizontal-to-vertical conversion in GenMax and transaction collapsing, compressing in Metamorphosis) and doesn't include the output time for displaying MFS for GenMax, dGenMax and Metamorphosis.

Figure 2 shows the performance comparison of Metamorphosis against GenMax and dGenMax on chess and connect datasets. Note that the graphs are plotted for Metamorphosis Vs GenMax and Metamorphosis Vs dGenMax separately to improve the visibility. It is clearly evident from the graph that Metamorphosis outperforms GenMax at supports above 50% (cut-off not shown in the graph) and dGenMax at supports above 71% for the chess dataset. For the connect dataset, Metamorphosis outperforms GenMax at support above 53% (cut-off not shown in the graph) and dGenMax at supports above 68%. At supports below this point Metamorphosis performs poorly

can be evident from the graph, the cleft between the NumF1 and Maxlen as well as Maxlen and LM Pattern Size grows faster as the minimum support decreases. The faster growth of the cleft explains why Metamorphosis performs poorly in mining all the MFS at lower support levels. So, the real application domain of Metamorphosis is on those datasets for which the MFS are much closer to Maxlen as well as NumF1.

4.2 Evaluation of Metamorphosis for Mining Top-K MFS on Benchmark Datasets

Figure 4 gives the mining time required for mining the Top-100 and Top-200 MFS on chess and connect dataset. As can be evident from Figure 4, the time required for mining the Top-100 and Top-200 MFS are significantly lower compared to mining the entire set of MFS.

Top-K MFS mining holds promise on applications in which the total number of MFS generated is exponentially large and mining the entire set of MFS becomes difficult. In general, the characteristics of Top-K MFS include (a) they have much lesser support compared to that of all other MFS, (b) they can be used for generating large number of association rules with very high confidence, especially for large number of items in antecedent of a rule.

5 Summary And Future Research Directions

References

[1] Agrawal, R., Imielinski, T., Swami, A., "Mining association rules between sets of items in large databases", In proceedings of *ACM SIGMOD Conference on Management of Data*, 1993, pp. 207-216.
[2] Agrawal R. et al, "The Quest Data Mining System", Technical report, IBM Almaden Research Center, 1996, Retrieved from http://www.almaden.ibm.com/cs/quest/ in October 2002.
[3] Agrawal R., Aggarwal C., Prasad VVV., "Depth first generation of Long patterns", *7th International conference on Knowl-*

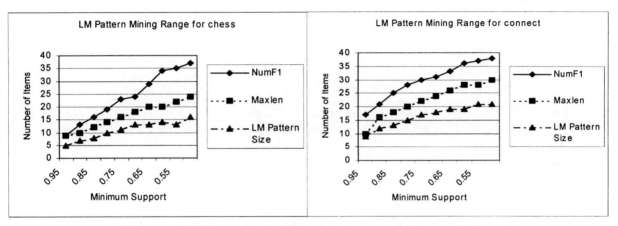

Figure 3. LM Pattern Mining Range for chess and connect datasets

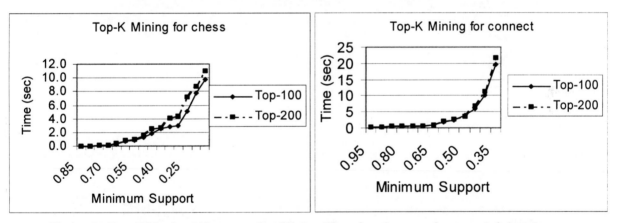

Figure 4. Top-K Maximal Frequent Set Mining Time for chess and connect datasets

edge discovery and Data mining, 2000.
[4] Bayardo R J., "Efficiently mining long patterns from databases", *ACM SIGMOD conference on management of data*, 1998.
[5] Burdick, D., Calimlim, M., Gehrke, J., "MAFIA: A Maximal Frequent Itemset Algorithm for Transactional Databases", In *Intl. Conf. On Data Engineering*, 2001.
[6] Han, J., Kamber, M., "Data Mining: Concepts and Techniques", Morgan Kaufmann Publishers. San Francisco, CA, 2001.

In this paper we presented and evaluated Metamorphosis, an algorithm for mining MFS using novel data transformations.

A hybrid system that invokes the Metamorphosis algorithm at higher support levels and dGenMax at lower support levels can be developed for mining in a real or production environment.

[7] Lin D I., Kedem, Z M., "Pincer Search: A new algorithm for discovering the maximum frequent set", *Intl Conf. on Extending database technology*, 1998.

[8] Srikumar, K., Bhasker, B., "Data Pre-processing for Association Rule Mining", Working Paper Series 2002-19, Indian Institute of Management, Lucknow, 2002.

[9] Srikumar, K., Bhasker, B., "An Algorithm for Mining Maximal Frequent Sets based on Dominancy of Transactions", To To Appear in *Proc. of Intl. Conf. on Enterprise Information Systems*, Angers, France, 2003.

[10] Zaki, M.J., Gouda, K., "Fast vertical mining using diffsets", RPI Technical Report, 01-1, 2001.

Incremental Mining of Frequent Patterns Without Candidate Generation or Support Constraint

William Cheung and Osmar R. Zaïane
University of Alberta, Edmonton, Canada
{wcheung, zaiane}@cs.ualberta.ca

Abstract

In this paper, we propose a novel data structure called CATS Tree. CATS Tree extends the idea of FP-Tree to improve storage compression and allow frequent pattern mining without generation of candidate itemsets. The proposed algorithms enable frequent pattern mining with different supports without rebuilding the tree structure. Furthermore, the algorithms allow mining with a single pass over the database as well as efficient insertion or deletion of transactions at any time.

1. Introduction

One major function of association rules is to analyze large amounts of market basket transactions [1,2,3,4]. Association rules have been applied to many areas including outlier detection, classification, clustering etc [5,6,7,8,9]. The mining process can be broken down into the mining of underlying frequent itemsets and the generation of association rules. Association rule mining is an iterative process [10], thus, in practice, multiple frequent pattern mining processes with different supports are often required to obtain satisfactory results.

This paper introduces Compressed and Arranged Transaction Sequences Tree or CATS Tree and CATS Tree algorithms. Once CATS Tree is built, it can be used for multiple frequent pattern mining with different supports. Furthermore, CATS Tree and CATS Tree algorithms allow single pass frequent pattern mining and transaction stream mining. In addition, transactions can be added to or removed from the tree at any time.

It is assumed that there is no limitation on the main memory. The assumption is realistic for a reasonably large database due to the following reasons: 1) the current trend of modern computing moves towards computers with large amounts of main memory (gigabytes sized); 2) memory management techniques and data compression technique in the CATS Tree reduce memory footprint; 3) the same assumption has been used in other publications [11,12,13,14,15]. In addition, CATS Tree allows removal of transactions concurrently. Even a huge database can be processed by CATS Tree if out-of-date transactions are removed concurrently.

The remainder of the paper is organized as follows. Section 2 surveys related work. Section 3 introduces the CATS Tree structure and the algorithm to build it. CATS Tree based frequent pattern mining algorithm is introduced in Section 4. Section 5 presents some experimental results. Conclusions are given in Section 6.

2. Previous Work

2.1. Apriori-based Algorithms

The very first published and efficient frequent patterns mining algorithm is Apriori [2]. A number of Apriori-based algorithms [1,4,9] have been proposed to improve the performance of Apriori by addressing issues related to the I/O cost.

2.2. Pattern Growth Algorithms

Han et al. propose a data structure, frequent pattern tree or FP-Tree, and an algorithm called FP-growth that allows mining of frequent itemsets without generating candidate itemsets [3]. The construction of FP-Tree requires two data scans.

As pointed out by the designers of FP-Tree, no algorithm works in all situations. A new data structure called H-struct was introduced in [14] to deal with sparse data solely.

3. CATS Tree

In the present study, we have developed a novel data structure, CATS Tree, an extension of FP-Tree[3]. Researchers have proposed to use tree structure in data mining [3,16,17]. However, they are not suitable for interactive frequent pattern mining.

CATS Tree is a prefix tree and it contains all elements of FP-Tree including the header, the item links etc. Paths from the root to the leaves in CATS Tree represent sets of transactions. We use the database in Table 1 to illustrate the construction of a CATS Tree.

Initially, the CATS Tree is empty. Transaction 1 (F, A,C, D, G, I, M, P) is added as it is. As shown in Figure 1, Transaction 2 (A, B, C, F, L, M, O) is added, common items, F, A, C, are extracted from Transaction 2 and are merged with the existing tree. Although item D is not contained in Transaction 2, common items could be found underneath node D. Item M is found to be common. However, Transaction 2 cannot be merged directly at node M because it would violate the structure of CATS tree that the frequency of a parent node must be greater than the sum of its children's frequencies. Node M of CATS Tree is swapped in front of node D as shown in Figure 1 and it is merged with the transaction. After that, there is no more common item. The remaining portion of Transaction 2 is added to node M.

TID	Original Transactions	Projected transactions for FP-Tree
1	F, A, C, D, G, I, M, P	F, C, A, M, P
2	A, B, C, F, L, M, O	F, C, A, B, M
3	B, F, H, J, O	F, B
4	B, C, K, S, P	C, B, P
5	A, F, C, E, L, P, M, N	F, C, A, M, P

Table 1. Sample database

In Figure 1, Transaction 3 (B, F, H, J, O) is added. Item F of Transaction 3 is merged. Since the frequency of node A is the same as that of node F, the search for other possible merge nodes continues along the branch. It passes through node A, C, and M and finally, reaches node B. Even though Transaction 3 also contains an item B, but the frequency of node B is smaller than that of node M, the remaining of the transaction is inserted as a new branch at node F.

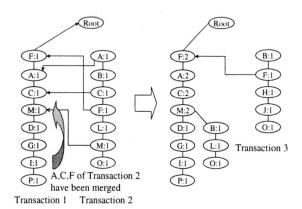

Figure 1. Insertion of Transaction 1, 2 & 3

When Transaction 4 (B, C, K, S, P) is added, there is no common item. Transaction 4 is added as it is. In Figure 2, Transaction 5 (A, F, C, E, L, P, M, N) is added; F, A, C, and M are merged. The search for common

items continues along the path. Item P is common in both the tree path and Transaction 5. This triggers swapping of node P to the front of node D. After item P is merged, there is no more common item. The remainders of Transaction 5 are inserted as a new branch at node P.

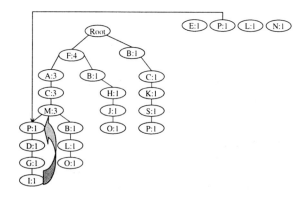

Figure 2. Insertion of Transaction 5

	CATS Tree	FP-Tree
	Contains all items in every transaction	Contains only frequent items
	Sub-trees are locally optimized to improve compression	Sub-trees are not locally optimized
	Ordering of items within paths from the root to leaves are ordered by local support	Ordering of items within paths from the root to leaves are ordered by global support
	CATS nodes of the same parent are sorted in descending order according to local frequencies	Children of a node are not sorted

Table 2. CATS Tree versus FP-Tree.

All CATS Trees have the following properties:
1) The compactness of CATS Tree measures how many transactions are sharing a node. Compactness decreases as it is getting away from the root. This is the result of branches being arranged in descending order.
2) No item of the same kind could appear on the lower right hand side of another item. If there were items of the same kind on the right hand side, they should have been merged with the node on the left to increase compression. Any items on the lower right hand side can be switched to the same level as the item, split nodes as required if switching nodes violates the structure of CATS Tree. After that they can be merged with the item on the left. Because of the above properties, a vertical downward boundary is formed beside each node and a horizontal rightward boundary is formed at the top of each node. The vertical and horizontal boundaries combine to form a step-like individual boundary [18]. As shown in Figure 3, boundaries of multiple items can be

joined together to form a refined boundary for a particular item. Items of the same kind can only exist on the refined boundary. A few major differences between CATS Tree and FP-Tree are listed in Table 2.

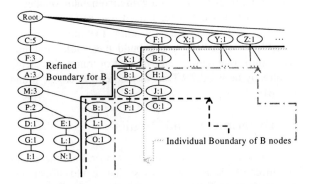

Figure 3. Item boundary in CATS Tree

3.1. CATS Tree Builder

CATS Tree contains all information of a dataset. Its construction requires only a single data scan. Thus, it is not optimal since there is no preliminary analysis before this single data scan. New transactions are added at the root level. At each level, items of the transaction are compared with those of children nodes. If the same items exist in both the new transaction and that of the children nodes, the transaction is merged with the node at the highest frequency. The frequency of the node is incremented. The remainder of the transaction is added to the merged nodes and the process is repeated recursively until all common items are found. Any remaining items of the transaction are added as a new branch to the last merged node. Furthermore, CATS Tree Builder has to consider not only the immediate items of that level, but also all possible descendants. The frequency of a descendant node can become larger than that of its ancestor, once the frequency of the new transaction is added. If the frequency becomes larger, the descendant has to swap in front of its previous ancestor to maintain the structural integrity of CATS Tree. The CATS Tree Builder algorithm cannot afford to search blindly to locate common item. There are few properties of CATS Tree that can be used to prune the search space. 1) Inherited from FP-Tree, the sum of frequencies of all children nodes can only be smaller or equal to that of their parent. 2) Children of a node are sorted. Based on these properties, if a node cannot have local frequency greater than that of its parent, none of its sibling after it or any of its children can. As soon as an invalid node is found, CATS Tree Builder can abort the search and pursue other paths or insert the new transaction as a new branch. Since the frequency of the new transaction is 1,

this implies that the frequency of descendant node must be equal to that of its ancestor. There can only be one node if we need to search downward. If the ordering of sibling node becomes out of order after merging, the offending node is repositioned to maintain the structural integrity of the tree. The algorithm CATS Tree Builder is listed as the following:

Algorithm: CATS Tree Builder
Input: set of transactions
Output: CATS Tree
1. PROCEDURE CATSTreeBuilder(*input_set S*)
2.   for all transactions $t \in S$
3.   for all $i \in t$
4.   i.(frequency in header)++;
5.   *root*.add(*t*);
6. PROCEDURE add(transaction *t*)
7.   if (*this*.children $\cap t \neq \varnothing$)
8.   child node.merge(*t*);
9.   else if (*this*.descendant $\cap t \neq \varnothing$))
10.   swap descendant node and split child node if necessary;
11.   descendant.merge(*t*);
12.   else
13.   *this*.children ← *t*;
14.   Reposition the merged node if necessary;
15. PROCEDURE merge(transaction *t*)
16.   *this*.frequency++;
17.   remove *this*.item from *t;*
18.   node.add(*t*);

Pseudo Code 1. CATS Tree Builder

In general, it is impossible to build a CATS Tree with maximal compression and without prior knowledge of the data. Therefore the compression of a CATS Tree is sensitive to both ordering of transaction and items within the transactions. However based on experiments, the size difference between maximal compressed CATS Tree and a CATS Tree produced by heuristic search is about 5 - 10%. A maximal compressed CATS Tree is an optimal tree where further loss-less compression is not possible. Different CATS Trees from the same database can be converted into a maximal compressed CATS Tree by recursively extracting the most compact item sequentially at each node. Thus, the ordering issues become irrelevant since the maximal compressed CATS Tree is insensitive to the order of input. CATS Tree based frequent patterns mining algorithm, FELINE, produces an identical set of frequent patterns as long as the underlying database remains the same.

4. FrEquent/Large patterns mINing with CATS trEe (FELINE)

Unlike FP-tree, once the CATS Tree is built, it can be mined repeatedly for frequent patterns with different support thresholds without the need to rebuild the tree. Like FP-growth [3], FELINE employs divide and conquer, fragment growth method to generate frequent patterns without generating candidate itemsets. FELINE partitions the dataset based on what patterns transactions have. For a pattern called p, a p's conditional CATS Tree is a tree built from all transactions that contain pattern p. Transactions contained in a conditional CATS Tree can be easily gathered by traversing the item links of pattern p. A conditional condensed CATS Tree is one in which all infrequent items are removed and it is different enough from a conditional FP-Tree that FP-growth cannot be applied. By traversing upward only like FP-growth, the algorithm cannot guarantee that all frequent patterns in a conditional condensed CATS Tree are gathered. In order to ensure all frequent patterns are captured by FELINE, FELINE has to traverse both up and down to include all frequent items. However, this may cause duplications of frequent patterns in different conditional condensed CATS Trees because the same frequent pattern could appear in all trees of the frequent pattern's constituents. While building conditional condensed CATS Tree, items are excluded if the items are infrequent or the items have been mined. A detailed example of FELINE's execution can be found in [18]. The pseudo code for FELINE is given as follows:

Algorithm: FELINE
Input: a CATS Tree and required support
Output: a set of frequent pattern
1. PROCEDURE FELINE(required support ε)
2.   sort(header.frequent items α);
3.   for each frequent item α
4.   build αTree = α's conditional condensed CATS Tree;
5.   mineCATSTree(αTree, ε, null)
6. PROCEDURE mineCATSTree(αTree, ε, stack ps)
7.   if (αtree's support > ε)
8. $ps \leftarrow \alpha$;
9.   frequent pattern $FP \leftarrow ps$;
10. FP's support = αtree's support;
11.   frequent itemsets $\leftarrow FP$;
12.   processed set $s \leftarrow \varnothing$; // prevent duplication
13.   if (αtree.children $\neq\varnothing$)
14.   for all item $i \in \alpha$tree $\wedge i \notin ps \wedge i \notin s$
15. $s \leftarrow i$;
16.   build iTree = i's conditional condensed CATS Tree;
17.   mineCATSTree(iTree, ε, ps);
18.   pop ps; // keep only the path to root

Pseudo Code 2. FELINE

CATS trees can be used with incremental updates of the transactional database. Indeed transactions could be added or deleted on the fly while the mining is still possible without having to rebuild the whole structure. Algorithms that add or remove a set of transactions from an already built CATS Tree, or merge trees can be found in [18].

5. Experiments and Results

The goal of the experiments is to find out the extent of different dataset properties that could affect the performance of CATS Tree algorithms and the relative performance compares with other algorithms. Datasets are generated with the data generator by IBM QUEST. To avoid implementation bias, external Apriori implementation, by Christian Borgelt [19], is used; FP-growth is provided by the original authors. To allow a fair comparison of algorithms, Apriori is also run in cached mode where all transactions are loaded into the main memory. Experiments are performed on a Pentium 4 1.6GHz PC with 512Mb RAM running on Window 2000 server. All programs are complied with the same compiler. They all yield the same patterns with the same dataset and the same parameters. All data files are generated with default parameters: 1 million transactions; average pattern length is 4; average transaction length is 10; number of unique items is 23,890 and the minimum support is 0.15%, unless stated otherwise.

Most of the previous published literature deals with database sized around 100k [3,4,12,14,16,20,21]. In our experiments, our database size is over a million transactions, which is a reasonable size for a respectable department store-like transactional database.

5.1. Scalability

The first experiment measures scalability of CATS Tree algorithms with respect to the number of transactions.

As shown in Figure 4, both CATS Tree Builder and FELINE scale linearly to the number of transactions. FELINE is very efficient while building the CATS Tree may seem expensive. However, the cost of building the CATS tree is quickly amortized in an ad-hoc interactive association rule mining context, since the tree needs only be built once. This matches the design goal: building once and mining multiple times with low overhead.

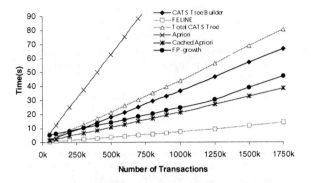

Figure 4. Scalability of CATS Tree with respect to number of Transactions with single run

The goal of the second experiment is to examine the effect of support on CATS Tree algorithms. In addition, the unique characteristic of CATS Tree, that "build once, mine many", is put to the test. A single CATS Tree is built from the data file. Frequent pattern mining iterations with different supports are performed on the same CATS Tree. In Figure 5, for comparison purposes, time required to build CATS Tree is added to the time for Total CATS Tree. In Figure 6, cumulated time from the adding of the first transaction until completion of frequent pattern mining at each data point is calculated. In other words, seven experiments with different supports were done on the same dataset.

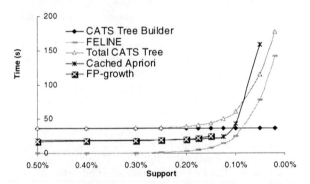

Figure 5. Scalability of CATS Tree with respect to support with single run

Time required by all algorithms increases as the support decreases. However, the rate of increase in Apriori is much faster than that of FELINE. Eventually, CATS Tree algorithms become faster than cached Apriori because FELINE does not generate candidate itemsets. Other than performance, the memory requirement for CATS Tree is smaller than other algorithms when support is low. Apriori and FP-tree runs out of memory at when the support is 0.02% and 0.15% respectively.

Unlike other frequent pattern mining algorithms, CATS Tree algorithms do not require to be started from

scratch when the minimum support is decreased. The same CATS Tree can be used to mine frequent patterns with different supports; only FELINE needs to be rerun. As shown in Figure 6, the benefits of CATS Tree algorithms increase as the number of frequent pattern mining increases.

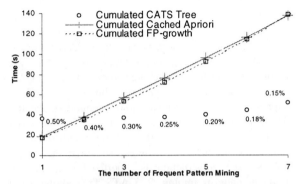

Figure 6. Build once, mine many with CATS Tree: scalability with multiple runs

5.2. Memory Usage

In this experiment, the memory usages of different algorithms are compared. The amounts of memory usage are the peak memory usage reported by the process monitor. In FP-Tree, the theoretical number of nodes is used because the source code of FP growth is not available. Only the executable code was provided to us.

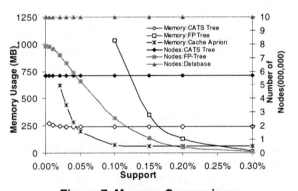

Figure 7. Memory Comparison

As shown in Figure 7, the memory usage of CATS Tree is relatively insensitive to the support while both FP-Tree and Cached Apriori are very sensitive to the support. As the support decreases, the memory consumption of FP-Tree increases exponentially and over takes that of CATS Tree at around 0.16% support.

From the theoretical aspect, CATS Tree is smaller than FP-Tree when the support is low. Because of the local memory management technique, CATS Tree will always consume less memory than a FP-Tree with 0% support. Furthermore, the structure of FP-Tree is based on the frequency list of the items. As soon as a transaction is added, the frequency list could be changed and the FP-Tree may require a significant rearrangement of nodes to maintain the structure.

6. Conclusion

We propose a novel data structure, CATS Tree and an algorithm to build it. The algorithm FELINE is also proposed to mine frequent patterns from CATS Trees.

There are many advantages of CATS Tree algorithms over the existing algorithms. 1) Once a CATS Tree is built, frequent pattern mining with different supports can be performed without rebuilding the tree. The benefit of "build once, mine many" increases with the number of frequent patterns mining performed, i.e., interactive mining with different supports; the cost of CATS Tree construction is amortized over multiple frequent patterns mining. 2) CATS Tree allows single pass frequent pattern mining. 3) CATS Tree algorithms allow addition and deletion of transactions in the finest granularity, i.e., a single transaction. See [18] for more details. Currently, there is no known and published algorithm that can provide the same functionalities efficiently. This makes CATS Tree algorithm suitable for real time transactional frequent pattern mining where modifications and frequent patterns mining are common. Moreover, with the addition and deletion capability, CATS trees algorithms are appropriate to mine transaction streams since one single scan of the data suffices [18].

We have implemented CATS Tree algorithms and compared our approach with other algorithms. CATS Tree algorithms are shown to be efficient and scalable to large amount of transactions and outperform other algorithms in interactive setting.

7. Acknowledgement

We would like to thank Dr. Jian Pei for providing us with the executable code of the FP-growth program that was used in our experiments for comparison purposes. This work was partially supported by the National Science and Engineering Research Council of Canada .

8. References

[1] Savasere, A., Omiecinski, E., and Navathe, S. An Efficient Algorithm for Mining Association Rules in Large Databases. Proceedings of the VLDB Conference. 1995.

[2] Agrawal, R. and Srikant, R. Fast algorithms for mining association rules. VLDB, 487-499. 1994.

[3] Han, J., Pei, J., and Yin, Y. Mining Frequent Patterns without Candidate Generation. SIGMOD, 1-12. 2000.

[4] Brin, S., Motwani, R., Ullman Jeffrey D., and Tsur Shalom. Dynamic itemset counting and implication rules for market basket data. SIGMOD. 1997.

[5] Brin, S., Motwani, R., and Silverstein, C. Beyond market baskets: Generalizing association rules to correlations. SIGMOD 26[2], 265-276. 1997.

[6] Antonie, M.-L. and Zaïane, O. R., Text Document Categorization by Term Association , IEEE ICDM'2002, pp 19-26, Maebashi City, Japan, December 9 - 12, 2002

[7] Han, J., Pei, J., Mortazavi-Asl, B., Chen, Q., Dayal, U., and Hsu, M.-C. FreeSpan: Frequent pattern-projected sequential pattern mining. ACM SIGKDD, 2000.

[8] Beil, F., Ester, M., Xu, X., Frequent Term-Based Text Clustering, ACM SIGKDD, 2002

[9] Orlando, S., Palmerini, P., and Perego, R. Enhancing the Apriori Algorithm for Frequent Set Counting. Proceedings of 3rd International Conference on Data Warehousing and Knowledge Discovery. 2001.

[10] Piatetsky-Shapiro, G., Fayyad, U., and Smith, P., "From Data Mining to Knowledge Discovery: An Overview," in Fayyad, U., Piatetsky-Shapiro, G., Smith, P., and Uthurusamy, R. (eds.) *Advances in Knowledge Discovery and Data Mining* AAAI/MIT Press, 1996, pp. 1-35.

[11] Huang, H., Wu, X., and Relue, R. Association Analysis with One Scan of Databases. Proceedings of the 2002 IEEE International Conference on Data Mining. 2002.

[12] Wang, K., Tang, L., Han, J., and Liu, J. Top down FP-Growth for Association Rule Mining. Proc.Pacific-Asia Conference, PAKDD 2002, 334-340. 2002.

[13] Zaki, M. J. and Hsiao, C.-J. CHARM: An Efficient Algorithm for Closed Itemset Mining. SIAM International Conference on Data Mining. 2002.

[14] Pei, J., Han, J., Nishio, S., Tang, S., and Yang, D. H-Mine: Hyper-Structure Mining of Frequent Patterns in Large Databases. Proc.2001 Int.Conf.on Data Mining. 2001.

[15] Pei, J., Han, J., and Mao, R. CLOSET: An efficient algorithm for mining frequent closed itemsets. SIGMOD. 2000.

[16] Agrawal, R., Aggarwal, C. C., and Prasad, V. V. V. A Tree Projection Algorithm For Generation of Frequent Itemsets. Journal on Parallel and Distributed Computing[(Special Issue on High Performance Data mining)]. 2001.

[17] Goulbourne, G., Coenen, F., and Leng, P. H. Computing association rule using partial totals. In Proceedings of the 5th European Conference on Principles and Practice of Knowledge Discovery in Databases, 54-66. 2001.

[18] Cheung, W., "Frequent Pattern Mining without Candidate generation or Support Constraint." Master's Thesis, University of Alberta, 2002.

[19] Borgelt, C. Apriori. [2.11]. 2001.

[20] Lin, J. L. and Dunham, M. H. Mining association rules: Anti-skew algorithms. The 1998 14th International Conference on Data Engineering, 486-493. 1998.

[21] Zaki, M. J., Parthsarathy, S., Ogihara, M., and Li, W. New Algorithms for Fast Discovery of Association Rules. KDD, 283-286. 1997.

Linear and Sublinear Time Algorithms for Mining Frequent Traversal Path Patterns From Very Large Web Logs

Zhixiang Chen*   Richard H. Fowler*   Ada Wai-Chee Fu[†]   Chunyue Wang*
*Department of Computer Science, University of Texas-Pan American, Texas, USA
chen@cs.panam.edu, fowler@panam.edu, cwang@panam.edu
[†] Department of Computer Science, Chinese University of Hong Kong, Hong Kong
adafu@cse.cuhk.edu.hk

Abstract

This paper aims for designing algorithms for the problem of mining frequent traversal path patterns from very large Web logs with best possible efficiency. We devise two algorithms for this problem with the help of fast construction of "shallow" generalized suffix trees over a very large alphabet. These two algorithms have respectively provable linear time and sublinear complexity, and their performance is analyzed in comparison with the two apriori-like algorithms in [4] and the well-known Ukkonen algorithm for on-line suffix tree construction [13]. It is shown that these two algorithms are substantially efficient than the two apriori-like algorithms and the Ukkonen algorithm. The linear time algorithm has optimal performance in theory, while the sublinear time algorithm has better empirical performance.

1. The Problem Formulation

The Web has a natural graph structure: pages are in general linked via hyperlinks. When a user surfs the Web, she may move forward along the graph via selecting a hyperlink in the current page. She may also move backward to any page visited earlier in the same session via selecting a "backward" icon. A forward reference may be understood as that the user is looking for her desired information. A backward reference may mean that the user has found her desired information and is going to looking for something else. A sequence of consecutive forward references may indicate what the user is looking for. A maximal forward reference is defined as the longest consecutive sequence of forward references before the first backward reference is made to visit some previously visited page in the same session. As thus, the last reference in a maximal forward sequence indicates a content page [4, 5] that is desired by the user.

Under such understanding, when a user searches for desired information, her information needs can be modeled by a set of maximal forward references occurred during her search process.

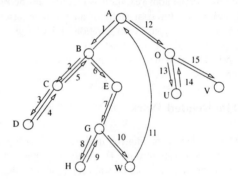

Figure 1. An illustration of traversal path patterns

Suppose, like in [4], the Web log contains the traversal path {A,B,C,D,C,B,E,G,H,G,W, A,O,U, O,V} for a user as shown in Figure 1. Starting at A, we have forward reference sequences AB, ABC and ABCD. Then, at D a backward reference to C is made, meaning that ABCD is a maximal forward reference. Now, some caution shall be paid to C. Here, even though a backward reference is made to B, we shall not consider ABC as a maximal forward reference, because the current backward reference is the second backward reference (the first is D→C). At B, a forward reference is made to E, thus begins new forward reference sequences ABE, ABEG and ABEGH. ABEGH is a maximal forward reference, because the first backward reference occurs at H after the forward reference E. Similarly, one can find the other maximal forward references ABEGW, AOU and AOV. When D, H, W, U and V are the pages desired by the user, the set of the maximal forward references {ABCD, ABEGH, ABEGW,

AOU, AOV} precisely describes the user's needs and her actual search behaviors as well. A *large reference sequence* with respect to some given frequency threshold parameter α is defined as a consecutive subsequence that occurs at least α many times in a set of maximal forward references. A *maximal reference sequence* with respect to α is a large reference that is not contained in any other large reference sequence. In the above example, when the frequency threshold parameter α is 2, we have large reference sequences *A, B, E, G, O, AB, BE, EG, AO, ABE, BEG, ABEG,* and the maximal reference sequences are *ABEG* and *AO*. A maximal reference sequence corresponds to a frequent traversal path pattern, i.e., a *"hot"* access patterns of users. Our goal in this paper is to design algorithms for mining frequent traversal path patterns, i.e., frequent or maximal reference sequences, with best possible efficiency. As pointed out in [4], once large reference sequences are determined, maximal reference sequences can be obtained in a straightforward manner.

The traversal path {*A,B,C,D,C,B,E,G,H,G,W,A,O,U,O,V*} of the user in the above example is recorded in the *referrer log*, and so are traversal paths of all the other users. A *referrer log* is a typical configuration of Web logs, where each traversed link is represented as a pair *(source, destination)*. In this paper, we assume that our Web logs are referrer logs.

2. The Related Work

The problem of mining frequent traversal path patterns was initially investigated in [4]. As the first step, an algorithm for finding maximal forward references from a Web log was designed in that paper. That algorithm works in two phrases. First, the log is sorted according to user IDs to group every user's references as a traversal path. Next, each traversal path is examined to find maximal forward references. The time complexity of the algorithm is $O(N \log N)$, where N denotes the number of records in the log. At the next step, two apriori-like algorithms *FullScan* and *SelectiveScan* were designed for mining large reference sequences from maximal forward references and the performance of these two algorithms were analyzed. [5] has detailed discussions of various data preparation tasks. The maximal forward references, called *"transactions"*, was also examined as a finer level characterization of user access sessions. But no explicit algorithms were given to find maximal forward references, and mining frequent traversal path patterns was not studied there. The work in [15] studied the application of generalized suffix trees to mining frequent user access patterns from Web logs, however the patterns in [15] are not traversal path patterns as considered in the usual settings in many literatures such as [4, 9, 12, 8, 11] and the context of this paper. The patterns in that paper are in essence frequent consecutive subsequences of user access sessions, while traversal paths corresponding to the underlying hyperlink structure were not concerned with. For the example illustrated in Figure 1, that paper concerns with frequent consecutive subsequences of {*A,B,C,D,C,B,E,G,H,G,W,A,O,U,O,V*}, but not frequent consecutive sequences of the maximal forward references {*ABCD, ABEGH, ABEGW, AOU, AOV*}. In other words, it does not concern with the underlying traversal paths as shown in Figure 1. Furthermore, that paper has not studied how to overcome the well-understood obstacles of suffix tree construction (see, e.g., [6], pages 116-119), i.e., the complexity dependence on the size of the underlying alphabet and the lack of good locality properties to support memory paging.

Many researchers have been investigating traversal or surfing path patterns in order to model users' behaviors and interests. The uncovered model can be used in many applications such as prefetching and caching to reduce Web latencies. Examples of such work include [9, 8, 11, 12]. The N-gram approaches were used to find most frequent subsequences of the paths, and sometimes the most frequent longest subsequences are the most interested. Once those subsequences were obtained, methods such as first order or higher order Markov-chains can be applied to predict users' behaviors or interests. Other researchers have also considered user access sessions as ordered sequences, such as in [7]. They also studied how to identify the longest repeating subsequences of the ordered sessions so as to find associations of those sequences. In all those papers, a user's surfing path is considered as an ordered sequences of consecutive references. In other words, a user's surfing path is the user's access session with order. This is different from the maximal forward references studied in [4, 5] and in the present paper.

In [3], optimal algorithms were designed for finding user access sessions from very large Web logs. Since maximal forward references are finer level characterizations of sessions as carefully examined in [5], the algorithms in [3] can not be applied directly to the problem of finding maximal forward references.

3. Properties of Maximal Forward References

We have examined properties of maximal forward references of the five logs *L100MB, L200MB, L300MB, L400MB* and *L500MB*. When the parameters α and β are set to 30 minutes to define interval sessions and gap sessions [3], it is obvious that the length of a maximal forward reference, or the number of URLs in it, is small. Statistical properties of maximal forward references are shown in Figure 2. In summary, we have observed that (1) almost all maximal forward references have a length ≤ 30; more than 90% max-

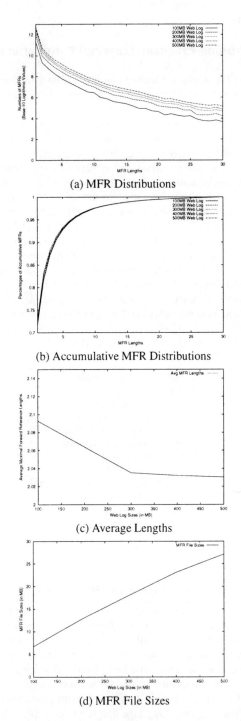

(a) MFR Distributions

(b) Accumulative MFR Distributions

(c) Average Lengths

(d) MFR File Sizes

Figure 2. Properties of Maximal Forward References (MFRs)

imal forward references have lengths less than or equal to 4, and the average length is about 2; and (3) the number of unique URLs is 11,926. In addition, the sizes of five maximal forward reference files corresponding to the five Web logs range from 6.7 megabytes to 27.1 megabytes. we must caution readers that the above three properties are not typical to our Web logs. These are common characteristics of large Web logs. That is, similar properties hold for other large Web logs.

4. "Shallow" Generalized Suffix Trees Over a Very Large Alphabet

Suffix tree are old data structures that become new again and have found many applications in data mining and bioinformatics as well. The first linear-time algorithm for constructing suffix trees was given by Weiner in [14] in 1973. A different but more space efficient algorithm was given by McCreight in [10] in 1976. Almost twenty years later Ukkonen gave a conceptually different linear time algorithm that allows on-line construction of a suffix tree and is much easier to understand. These algorithms build, in their original design, a suffix tree for a single string S over a given alphabet Σ. However, for any set of strings $\{S_1, S_2, \ldots, S_n\}$ over Σ, those algorithms can be easily extended to build a tree to represent all suffixes in the set of strings in linear time. Such a tree that represents all suffixes in strings $S_1, S_2, \ldots, S_n$, is called a *"generalized"* suffix tree. Usually, a set of strings $S_1, S_2, \ldots,$ and S_n, is represented as $S_1\$S_2\$ \ldots \$S_n\$$.

One typical application of generalized suffix trees is the identification of frequent (or longest frequent) substrings in a set of strings. This means that generalized suffix trees can be used to find frequent traversal path patterns of maximal forward references, simply because such patterns are frequent (or longest frequent) substrings in the set of a maximal forward references when maximal forward references are understood as strings of URLs. In Figure 3, we illustrate a generalized suffixed tree *"mississippi\$missing\$sipping\$"*. Notice that in our generalized suffix trees, a counter is used at each internal node to indicate the frequency of the substring labeling the edge pointing to the node.

For any given set of strings $S_1, S_2, \ldots, S_n$ over an alphabet Σ, let $m = \sum_{i=1}^{n} |S_i|$. It is well-understood (see, e.g., [6], pages 116-119) that the linear time (or space) complexity of Weiner, Ukkonen, and McCreight algorithms have all ignored the size of the alphabet Σ, and that memory paging were not considered when trees are large and hence cannot be stored in main memory. Notice that suffix trees or generalized suffix trees do not have nice locality properties to support memory paging. When both m and $|\Sigma|$ are very large, the time complexity of those classical algo-

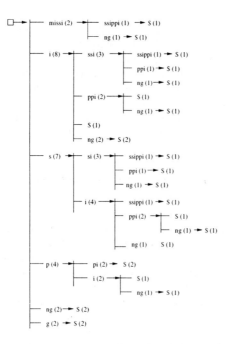

Figure 3. A Generalized Suffix Tree

rithms is $O(m|\Sigma|)$, and the space complexity is $\theta(m|\Sigma|)$. In particular, as pointed in Section 3, the alphabet Σ in our case of mining frequent traversal path pattern is 11,926 (the number of unique URLs) which is too big to be ignored, and m ranges from 6.7 megabytes to 27.1 megabytes and hence the $O(m|\Sigma|)$ space requirement are far beyond the main memory limit of a reasonable computer. Therefore, the challenges of applying generalized suffix trees to efficient mining of frequent traversal path patterns are how to overcome the efficiency dependence on the size of an alphabet in building a generalized suffix tree for a set of maximal forward references, and how to find innovative ways to scale down the space requirement.

As we have learned from Section 3, in our case of mining frequent traversal path patterns, on the one hand the size of the alphabet Σ (the set of all URLs) is very large, and files of maximal forward references are also very large. On the other hand, each maximal forward reference has a short length less than or equal to some small constant (when a threshold is used to delimit sessions); the vast majority have just several URLs; and the average length is even small. Thus, the generalized suffix tree for the sequence of maximal forward references in a Web log is *"shallow"* and very *"flat"*. In the case of our logs, the width of the first level of the tree is $|\Sigma| = 11,926$; the height of each subtree t_i, $1 \le i \le |\Sigma|$, is no more than 30; more than 90% of subtrees have a height ≤ 4; and the average height is just 2. In general, if a generalized suffix tree has a depth bounded

by some constant, then we call it a *"shallow"* generalized suffix tree.

5. Mining Frequent Traversal Path Patterns

In [1], we have designed two linear time algorithms for finding maximal forward references from very large Web logs. We assume in this section that maximal forward references are obtained by either of the two algorithms in [1]. In [2], we have studied fast construction of shallow generalized suffix trees over a very large alphabet. We shall use our techniques developed in [2] to design algorithms with best possible efficiency for mining frequent traversal path patterns. Let Σ be the alphabet of all URLs in maximal forward references. For any maximal forward reference S over Σ with a length of n (i.e., S has n URLs in it), we use $S[1:n]$ to denote S, where $s[i]$ is the ith URL in S. We use RstUkkonen(SuffixTree sft, NewString str) to denote the restricted version of Ukkonen algorithm for building a generalized suffix as follows: it takes an existing generalized suffix tree *sft* and a new string $str[1:n]$ as input and adds the suffix $str[1:n]$ to sft but ignores all the suffixes $str[2:n], str[3:n], \ldots, str[n:n]$. When no confusion arises, we use letters for URLs, and substrings for maximal forward references.

	input: infile, tmpfile, pct, outfile
1.	while (infile is not empty)
2.	readMFR(infile, s)
3.	for $(i = 1; i \le n; i++)$
4.	tmpfile.append(s[i : n])
6.	sort(tmpfile); createSuffixTree(sft)
7.	while (tmpfile is not empty)
8.	readMFR(tmpfile, s)
9.	if (sft.empty() or sft.first() == s[1])
10.	RstUkkonen(sft, s)
11.	else if (sft.first()$\neq$ s[1])
12.	traverseOutput(sft,outfile,pct)
13.	createSuffixTree(sft);
14.	traverseOutput(sft,outfile,pct)

Figure 4: Algorithm SbSfxMiner

Consider a generalized suffix tree *sfx* of a set of strings. For each subtree t of *sfx*, let $t.first()$ denote the first letter occurred at t. As carefully examined in [2], t contains exactly all suffixes starting with the letter $t.first()$, and any two distinct subtrees must have distinct first letters. Furthermore, a simple traversal of the subtree t can generate all the frequent (or longest frequent) substrings starting with the letter $t.first()$. E.g., the first letter occurred at the top subtree in Figure 3 is m, and all suffixes starting with m in the strings *"mississippi\$missing\$sipping\$"* are contained in this subtree. This critical observation leads to the designs of our new algorithms.

120

In the following two subsections, we use N to denote the number of strings in a given set of strings, and a percentage parameter pct to determine the frequency threshold $pct * N$.

5.1. Algorithm SbSfxMiner

In the algorithm, *infile* is the MFR file, *tmpfile* a temporary file, *pct* a frequency threshold parameter, and *outfile* the frequent MFR pattern file. The key idea is as follows. We read strings sequentially from an input file, and for every string $s[1:n]$ we output its n suffixes to a temporary file. We then sort the temporary file to group all the suffixes starting with the same letter together. Next, we build a generalized suffix tree for each group of such suffixes (precisely, our tree here is a subtree of the conventional generalized suffix tree). Finally, we traverse the tree to output all frequent (or frequent longest) substrings. It follows from the properties of maximal forward reference in Section 3 that the size of the temporary file is about $O(N)$. Sorting this file takes $O(N \log N)$ time. By the property of Ukkonen algorithm, building a generalized suffix tree for a group of strings takes $O(N)$. Hence, the whole process is of sublinear time. The description of SbSfxMiner is given in Figure 4.

```
       input: infile, f, pct, outfile
1.     createSuffixTrees(sft, size)
2.     while (infile is not empty)
3.            readMFR(infile, s)
4.            for (i = 1; i ≤ n; i + +)
5.                   RstUkkonen(sft[f(s[i])], s[i:n])
6.     for (i = 0; i < size; i + +)
7.            traverseOutput(sft[i], outfile, pct)
```

Figure 5: Algorithm HbSfxMiner

5.2. Algorithm HbSfxMiner

Here, *infile*, *pct*, and *outfile* are the same as those in algorithm SbSfxMiner, and f is a hash function. The key idea is to eliminate the sorting process to group all suffixes with the same starting letter together. The new approach is to design a fast function to map each letter to a unique integer, and to use this function to map suffixes with the same starting letter into a group. Because URLs have some nice directory path structure, such a function can be designed with constant time complexity. In the general case, we may use a hashing function to replace the function so that it will be more efficient in computing hashing values of letters. The detailed description of the algorithm is given in Figure 5. Because sorting is not required, the time complexity of this algorithm is linear.

5.3. Performance Analysis

We used the five Web logs *L100MB, L200MB, L300MB, L400MB* and *L500MB* to analyze the performance of algorithms SbSfxMiner and HbSfxMiner in comparison with the Ukkonen algorithm [13] and the SelectiveScan algorithm [4]. Since it was known that SelectiveScan is more efficient than FullSacn [4], we decide not to compare our algorithms with FullScan. For SelectiveScan, only times for $pct = 0.2$ is shown. It has much worse performance for other smaller values of pct. The empirical results are shown in Figure 6.

It is clear that our algorithms have the best performance. When carefully examined, algorithm SbSfxMiner performs even better than HbSfxMiner. The reason is that the computing of the underlying hash function, though a constant time for each computation, exceeds the sorting time when accumulated for so many substrings in the file.

6. Conclusions

The problem of mining frequent traversal path patterns from very large Web logs is fundamental in Web Mining. In this paper we design two algorithms for this problem. These two algorithms have respectively linear and sublinear complexity, and have substantially better performance than the two apriori-like algorithms in [4] and the well-known Ukkonen algorithm [13] in the case of mining frequent traversal patterns.

ACKNOWLEDGMENT. The work of the first two and the last authors is supported in part by the the UTPA Computing and Information Technology Center. The work of the third author is supported by the CUHK RGC Research Grant Direct Allocation ID 2050279.

References

[1] Z. Chen, R. Fowler, and A. Fu, Linear time algorithms for finding maximal forward references, Proc. of the IEEE Intl. Conf. on Info. Tech.: Coding & computing (ITCC 2003), 2003.

[2] Z. Chen, R. Fowler, A. Fu, and C. Wang, Fast construction of generalized suffix trees over a very large alphabet, Proceedings of the Intl. Computing and Combinatorics Conf. (COCOON03), 2003.

[3] Z. Chen, A. Fu, and F. Tong, Optimal algorithms for finding user access sessions from very large Web logs, Advances in Knowledge Discovery and Data Mining/PAKDD'02, Lecture Notes in Computer Science 2336, pages 290-296, 2002. (The full version will apear in WWW Journal: Internet and Information Systems, 2003.)

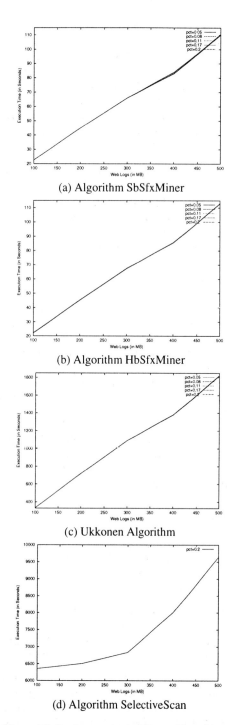

(a) Algorithm SbSfxMiner

(b) Algorithm HbSfxMiner

(c) Ukkonen Algorithm

(d) Algorithm SelectiveScan

Figure 6. Performance of Four Algorithms

[4] M.S. Chen, J.S. Park, and P.S. Yu. Efficient data mining for path traversal patterns. *IEEE Transactions on Knowledge and Data Engineering*, 10:2:209-221, 1998.

[5] R. Cooley, B. Mobasher, and J. Srivastava. Data preparation for mining world wide web browsing patterns. *Journal of Knowledge and Information Systems*, 1:1, 1999.

[6] D. Gusfield, *Algorithms on Strings, Trees, and Sequences*, Cambridge University Press, 1997.

[7] F. Masseglia, P. Poncelet, and R. Cicchetti, An efficient algorithm for Web usage mining, Networking and Information Systems Journal, 2(5-6), pages 571-603, 1999.

[8] V.N. Padmanabhan and J.C. Mogul, Using predictive prefetching to improve World Wide Web latency, Computer Communication Review, 26, 22-36, 1996.

[9] J. Pitkow and P. Pirolli, Mining longest repeating subsequences to predict World Wide Web Surfing, Proc. of the Second USENIX Symposium on Internet Technologies & Systems, pages 11-14, 1999.

[10] E.M. McCreight, A space-economical suffix tree construction algorithm, Journal of Algorithms, 23(2),pages 262-272, 1976.

[11] S. Schetcher, M. Krishnan, and M.D. Smith, Using path profiles to predict HTTP requests, Proc. of the Seventh International World Wide Web Conference, Computer Networks, 30(1-7), 457-467, 1998.

[12] Z. Su, Q. Yang, Y. Lu, and H. Zhang, WhatNext: A prediction system for Web requests using N-gram sequence models, Proc. of the First International Conference on Web Information Systems Engineering, pages 200-207, 2000.

[13] E. Ukkonen, On-line construction of suffix trees, Algorithmica, 14(3), pages 249-260, 1995.

[14] P. Weiner, Linear pattern matching algorithms, Proc. of the 14th IEEE Annual Symp. on Switching and Automata Theory, pages 1-11, 1973.

[15] Y. Xiao and M.H. Dunham, Efficient mining of traversal patterns, Data & Knowledge Engineering, 39, 191-214, 2001.

[16] O. Zaïane, M. Xin, and J. Han. Discovering web access patterns and trends by applying olap and data mining technology on web logs. *Advances in Digital Libraries*, pages 19-29, April, 1998.

Identification of Clusters in the Web Graph Based on Link Topology

Xiaodi Huang , Wei Lai

School of Information Technology, Swinburne University of Technology
PO Box 218. Hawthorn, VIC 3122, Australia
Email: {xhuang, wlai}@it.swin.edu.au

Abstract

The web graph has recently been used to model the link structure of the Web. The studies of such graphs can yield valuable insights into web algorithms for crawling, searching and discovery of web communities. This paper proposes a new approach to clustering the Web graph. The proposed algorithm identifies a small subset of the graph as "core" members of clusters, and then incrementally constructs the clusters by a selection criterion. Two qualitative criteria are proposed to measure the quality of graph clustering. We have implemented our algorithm and tested a set of arbitrary graphs with good results. Applications of our approach include graph drawing and web visualization.

Keywords: Clustering, Web Graph, K-Nearest Neighbor

1 Introduction

The WWW can be considered as a graph where nodes are static html pages and edges are hyperlinks between these pages. This graph is called the web graph. It has been the subject of a variety of recent works aimed at understanding the structure of the World Wide Web [5, 9, 12, 14, 16, 17, 18 and 19].

The main findings about the WWW structure are as follows:

1. A *power-law* distribution of degrees [18, 5]: in-degree and out-degree distribution of the nodes of the Web Graph follows the power law.

2. A *bow-tie* shape[9]: the web's macroscopic structure.

3. The average path length between two web pages: 16 [9] and 19 [5].

4. *Small world phenomenon* [14] [16]: Six degrees of separation between any 2 web pages.

5. *Cyber-communities* [18]: groups of individuals who share a common interest, together with the most popular web pages among them.

6. *Self-similarity structure* [12]: the web shows a fractal structure in many different ways.

Link analysis plays an import role in understanding of the web structure. There are two well known algorithms for ranking pages, such as, Page Rank [8] and HITS [15].

The study of the web graph is not only fascinating in its own right, but also yields valuable insight into web algorithms for crawling, searching and prediction of the web structure. The web graph is actually a special case of a general graph. So, we can employ some exiting graph theoretic approaches to classify the web graph.

This paper is organized as follows. We give the definitions and a formal description of graph clusters in the following section. Our approach is then described in detail in section 3.

In section 4, we provide an empirical evaluation by using our approach for a set of arbitrary graph clustering. Related work is reviewed in section 6. Applications are briefly given in section 6. Finally, we summarize and conclude our work in section 7.

2 Definitions

Suppose a given web graph $G=(V, E)$ and an integer k, we partition G into subgraphs $G_1, G_2, ..., G_k$, such that

$$G=\cup_{i=1}^{k} G_i \text{ and } G_i \cap G_j = \phi, i \neq j$$

An optimization criterion of this partition is the well known Minimum Cuts criterion.

Given a subset T of V, the cut $\delta(T)$ induced by T is the subset of edges $(i, j) \in E$ such that $|\{i,j\} \cap T| = 1$. That is, $\delta(T)$ consists of all those edges with exactly one endpoint in T. Actually, for each edge $e \in E$, if there is a nonnegative cost (or capacity) c_e, the cost of a cut $\delta(T)$ is then the sum of the costs of the edges in that cut:

$$c(\delta(T)) = \sum_{e \in \delta(T)} c_e$$

The minimum cut is to find a cut with minimum cost measured by above formula. In our web graph, all costs are 1, the problem of the minimum cut thus becomes finding a cut with as few edges as possible.

A graph can be partitioned into different clusters in different ways. So, we need a quantitative function to measure the quality of a clustering. Generally speaking, a good clustering algorithm should produce clusters with high "homogeneity (or cohesion)" and low "separation (or coupling)". The nodes in a cluster are highly connected to other nodes in the same cluster, while the nodes in different clusters are separated with a minimum cut.

To measure the homogeneity of a cluster, we give the follow function:

$$\eta(C_i) = \begin{cases} \frac{2}{|C_i|(|C_i|-1)} \sum_{v_i,v_k \in C_i} e_{ik} & |C_i| \neq 1 \\ 1 & |C_i| = 1 \end{cases}$$

(2.1)

according to the above function, if the nodes in C_i are completely connected , then in total there should be $|C_i|(|C_i|-1)/2$ edges in C_i. That is, $\eta(C_i)=1$. Additionally, for a singleton cluster, $|C_i|=1$, we also define the value of its homogeneity as 1.

Definition 1 *Homogeneity of clusters:* Give a graph G $G=(V, E)$ and its subgraphs $G_1, G_2, ..., G_m$, then the weighted average homogeneity of all clusters in G is:

$$C_H(G) = \frac{1}{|S|} \sum_{i}^{S} \eta(C_i)$$

where $|S|$ is the number of clusters in G, $_{|C_i|}$ is the number of nodes the cluster C_i, and $_{\eta(C_i)}$ is determined by equation (2.1). Obviously the value range of homogeneity is [0, 1]. Observe that the bigger the value of $C_H(G)$ is, the more cohesive the nodes in the clusters are.

To measure the separation between two clusters, the value of a function should be used to compare the relative costs of the clustering. Obviously, the sum of the costs of the edges in minimum cut between two clusters is related to the sizes of the separated clusters, so we can use the following function as a measurement of separation in two clusters:

$$\delta(C_i, C_j) = \frac{\delta(T)}{|C_i||C_j|} = \frac{1}{|C_i||C_j|} \sum_{v_l \in C_i, v_k \in C_j} e_{lk}$$
(2.2)

where $i \neq j$, and e_{lk} is the cost of the edge between the nodes v_1 and v_k, with exactly one endpoint in the cut set. In our approach, $e_{jk} = 1$ if the nodes v_1 and v_k are directly connected.

Based on the above function, if a graph is totally unconnected, that is, there is no cost for cut, so $\delta(C_i, C_j) = 0$.

On the other hand, if C_i and C_j are a complete bipartite graph, where every pair of nodes in C_i and C_j are adjacent, then $\delta(C_i, C_j) = 1$.

Definition 2 separation *of clusters: Given a graph G* $G= (V, E)$ and its subgraphs $G_1, G_2, ..., G_k$, we use the arithmetic average as the measurement of the separations among the clusters.

$$C_S(G) = \frac{1}{n} \sum_{1 \leq i, j \leq |S|} \delta(C_i, C_i)$$

where n is the number of pairs of clusters whose member node(s) are directly connected, $0 < n \leq |S||S-1|/2$, and $\delta(C_i, C_i)$ is determined by equation (2.2).

Note that the smaller the value of $C_S(G)$ is, the less cost of the cut. The clustering quality values of graph 1 in The graph clustering problem can be defines as follow.

Definition 3 *Maximum Homogeneity of Graph clustering*: given a connected graph $G= (V, E)$ and an integer m, the G is partitioned into subgraphs $G_1^l, G_2^l, \Lambda, G_m^l$, in the l different ways. If the following conditions hold true

(1) $G = G^l = \cup_{i=1}^m G_i^l$

(2) $G_i^l \cap G_j^l = \phi, for \ i \neq j$

(3) $p = \arg \max_{l=1\Lambda, m} \{C_H(G^l)\}$

(4) $0 \leq C_H(G^l) \leq 1$

Then $G_1^p, G_2^p, \Lambda, G_m^p$ are called *Maximum Homogeneity clusters* of the graph G.

Definition 4 *Minimum coupling of Graph clustering*: given a connected graph $G= (V, E)$ and an integer m, the G is partitioned into subgraphs $G_1^l, G_2^l, \Lambda, G_m^l$, in the l different ways. If the following conditions hold true

(1) $G = G^l = \cup_{i=1}^m G_i^l$

(2) $G_i^l \cap G_j^l = \phi, for \ i \neq j$

(3) $p = \arg \min_{l=1\Lambda, m} \{C_S(G^l)\}$

(4) $0 \leq C_S(G^l) \leq 1$

Then $G_1^p, G_2^p, \Lambda, G_m^p$ are called *Minimum coupling of Graph clusters* of the graph G.

Next, a few definitions used in the following algorithms are given:

Definition 5 *Node degree*. The degree of a node v in a graph, denoted by deg(v), is the number of edges incident with v. The sum of the degrees of G is 2|E|, i.e.,

$$\sum_{i=1}^{|V|} \deg(v_i) = 2 |E|$$

since every edge has exactly two endpoints. So, the average degree of G is $\mu = \overline{Deg}(G) = 2|E|/|V|$. Let σ be the *Standard Deviation* (a statistics term) of the degrees of G.

Definition 6 *Seed nodes* is a set of nodes whose degrees are greater than $\mu + \tau$, denoted by S, where τ is a threshold.

We usually define τ as a value related to σ, because the *standard deviation* σ is a measurement of how spread the distribution of the degrees. In a special case, if G is a fully connected graph, that is, the degree of every node is equal to μ, there will be no seed node. We can then start to construct the clusters from any node in G. In order to introduce the k-nearest neighbor search, we define a distance function as follows:

Definition 7 *A distance function D(v,u)*, where nodes v and $u \in G$, is used to compute the distance between nodes v and u. It is actually the minimum length of all pairs of paths joining them, which is also the number of edges in the shortest path, if such path exists; otherwise $D(v, u) = \infty$. The shortest path can be found by Dijkstra's algorithm.

Definition 8 *k-nearest neighbor search*. For a query node $q \in G$ and a query parameter k, the k-nearest neighbor search returns a set $k\text{-}NN(q) \subset G$ that contains at least k nodes in G, and that the following conditions hold:

$D(u.q) \leq D(w.q), \ \forall u \in k\text{-}NN(q), \ \forall w \in G - k\text{-}NN(q), u \neq w$

Consequently, the result set is $\{w \in G - k\_NN(v) \mid D(w, v) \leq k\}$. For example, 1-NN ($v$) represents a set of nodes with which the node v incidents. Note that the node v is not included in the set of $k\text{-}NN(v)$.

Definition 9 *A Affinity function*: given a connected graph $G= (V, E)$, the affinity of *node v to Cluster C can be measured by*:

$$f(v, C, k) = \frac{|C \cap k\_NN(v)|}{\deg(v)} \quad \text{where } v \notin C$$

Obviously, $0 \leq f(v, C, 1) \leq 1$

We will use these definitions to describe our algorithm in the following section.

3 Algorithms

The algorithm presented here has two steps: find the seed nodes (see Figure 1) and build a cluster around each such node recursively (see Figure 2). It detects the nodes whose degrees have greater than the average degrees of the nodes in the graph as seed nodes previously defined. These nodes are potentially used as initial members of different clusters later. In some cases, however, two or more seed nodes are densely connected and they are not far away in the graph. This suggests they should be within one cluster. Two or more seed nodes will be combined into one seed node, if they share the nodes of their *k-NN*, and if the number of the shared nodes is no less than half a degree of one of them. Each member of the reduced seed node set is a core candidate for each cluster. After this, the algorithm begins by successively adding *1-NN* nodes of seed nodes into corresponding clusters, and then each newly added node in the clusters again expands appropriate nodes in its *1-NN* respectively and so on, until the affinity criterion of a node is not satisfied. Each cluster accepts a node as its member based on a defined affinity function, which measures how the affinity the node is relevant to existing member nodes in the cluster. Specially, the value of a node affinity to a cluster is calculated by the number of the shared nodes in both *1-NN* of the node and the existing member nodes of the cluster. The clusters competitively choose a node as their new member according to the rule: The node is with the highest affinity to a cluster. If the affinities of a node to all the clusters are equal, the node will become a singleton cluster. This procedure processes iteratively until no more nodes can be added to any cluster by following the above rule. Finally, the remaining nodes not belonging to any cluster must belong to a chain. Chains are then divided among their closest clusters, or remain as independent singleton clusters.

The neighboring nodes are found in an incremental manner in our algorithm. In other words, having found the *k* nearest neighbors, in order to find the *k+1st* nearest neighbor, the algorithm does not recompute the set of *k+1* nearest neighbors; it just finds the additional neighbor. The incremental nearest neighbor algorithm ranks the next available unclassified nodes in terms of their affinities to newly classified members of the clusters, and then a cluster chooses the node with highest affinity as its new member. The formal description of the algorithm is given in Figure 1 and Figure 2.

Input: graph $G=(V,E)$; **seed set:** $S \leftarrow \phi$, **threshold :** k and τ

Output: S

Compute the degrees of nodes in G, deg(v).

Compute the average degree μ and stand derivation of the degrees δ

//Find the seed nodes S

for each $v \in V$ **do**

　　if deg(v) $\geq \mu + \tau$ **then**

　　　　$S \leftarrow S \cup \{v\}$

　　end if

end for

for $S = \phi$ **then** STOP

for each $v \in S$ **do**

if $\max_{u \in S - \{v\}} |(k - NN(v) + \{v\}) \cap (k - NN(u) + \{u\})| \geq \deg(u)/2$ **then**

　　　　$S \leftarrow S \setminus \{u\}$

　　end if

end for

Figure 1. A algorithm to find seed nodes

// Construct the clusters around core candidate nodes

Input: seed set $S = \{s_1, s_2, ..., s_m\}$

Output: clusters $C_i (i=1,2,...,m)$

for each $s_i \in S$ **do**

　If $1\_NN(s_i) \neq 1\_NN(s_j)(i \neq j = 1, \Lambda, m)$ **then**

　　　$C_i \leftarrow C_i \cup \{s_i\} \cup 1 - NN(s_i)$

　else

$$k = \arg \max_{i=1,\Lambda,m}\{f(1\_NN(s_i), C_i, 1)\}$$

$$C_k \leftarrow C_k \cup \{s_i\} \cup 1 - NN(s_i)$$

　end if

end for

for $i = 1$ **to** m

　　for each $v \in V - C_i$ **do**

　　　　$k = \arg \max_{i=1,\Lambda,m}\{f(v, C_i, 1)\}$

　　　　if $f(v, C_k, 1) > 0.5$ **then**

　　　　　　$C_k \leftarrow C_k \cup \{v\}$

　　　　end if

　　end for

end for

// This is an optional algorithm for handing the remaining node chain

for each $v \in V - C_i$ **do**

　　　$i = \arg \min_{i=1,...,S}\{D(v,u) | u \in C_i\}$

$C_i \leftarrow C_i \cup \{v\}$

end if

Figure 2 Algorithms to aggregate nodes by local search

The algorithm can be summarized as follows:
1. Identify a small subset S whose members have high degrees in G.
2. Remove the node(s) in S which is (are) highly connected to other node(s). Each remaining node in S is called a core candidate.
3. With a core candidate as its first member, each cluster inclemently classifies available nodes which have the highest affinities to the existing members of the cluster. That is, each member of each cluster continually absorbs the nodes in its *1-NN* until the expansion criterion is not satisfied.

The time complexity of the algorithm is $O(|S|^2)$.

4 Experiments

We have implemented our algorithm in a prototype called PGD (a framework for practical graph drawing) by using Java programming language. In this section, we give the clustering results of a set of arbitrary graphs by applying our approach, and discuss some features. Note that we will use one node to represent all the member nodes in a cluster in the following clustered figures.

The seed node set of Graph 1 in Figure 3 is $\{v_4, v_7, v_9, v_{10}, v_{14}\}$. Because the node v_9 has even affinities to other nodes v_4, v_7, v_{10} and v_{14}, the node v_9 is a singleton cluster. It is actually also a bridge node between clusters v_{1-4}, v_{5-8}, v_{14-17} and v_{10-13}. Note that all members in this seed node set are the core candidates for the clusters.

Graph 2 in Figure 4 is specially designed for testing our algorithm for dealing with remaining node chain during clustering. First, the nodes $v_1 - v_5$ and the nodes $v_6 - v_{11}$ are constructed into two clusters C_1 ($v_1 - v_5$) and C_2 ($v_6 - v_{11}$). The node v_9 then aggregates one member of its 1-NN, node v_{12}, into C_2. That is, the node v_{12} becomes a new member of C_2. However, the node v_{12} can not accept node v_{13} into its cluster, because only one node of 1-NN(v_{13})(v_{12}) is within C_2. So, the aggregation stops at the node v_{12} (See figure 4(b)). Additionally, the remaining node chain $v_{13} - v_{16}$ can optionally be combined into C_2 with the optional algorithm provided (See figure 4(c)). Or just let them remain as different singleton clusters. This is reasonable because the nodes in C_1 and C_2 are densely connected, while the nodes v_{13}- v_{16} are relatively not.

Graph 3 in Figure 5 shows what happens to a remaining node chain with different criteria. C_1 (v_1- v_3) and C_2 (v_4- v_8) are firstly built. (The node v_4 has more affinity to C_2 (v_5 and v_6) than to C_1 (v_3), so v_4 will be put into C_2). Then the remaining node chain v_9- v_{11} is created. With the loose criterion,

$\max\{|1 - NN(v) \cap \{u\,|\,u \in C_2\}|\} \geq \deg(v)/2$, the nodes v_9- v_{11} will be incrementally aggregated into C_2 due to this $v_9 \in 1 - NN(v_6) \to v_{10} \in 1 - NN(v_9) \to v_{11} \in 1 - NN(v_{10})$ (see Figure 5(b)). However, they will be singleton clusters with a strict criterion:

$$\max\{|1 - NN(v) \cap \{u\,|\,u \in C_2\}|\} > \deg(v)/2$$

The result is shown in Figure 5 (c).

Figure 6 and 7 show another two examples of well clustered Graphs 4 and 5 by our approach.

In our experiments, k=1, i.e., 1-NN and τ =0 . If we want to reduce the number of clusters of a given graph, for example, for graph 3 in Figure 5, we should specify $\tau = \sigma$, then $\mu + \tau$ =3.569. So only the node v_6 (see Figure 5 (b)) can be a seed node according to the definition. The nodes v_1 ,v_2 and v_3 will be singleton clusters with the loose criterion.

The experimental results for clustering are reported in Table 1. Some parameters are also illustrated in Figure 8. Our approach has fast running time, and can find a good clustering solution.

Graph	1	2		3		4	5
$|V|$	12	16		11		12	18
$\overline{Deg(G)}$	3.294	3.875		2.363		3.500	3.778
σ	0.470	1.668		1.206		0.978	0.808
$|C|$	5	6	2	2	5	3	2
$C_H(G)$	1	1	0.863	0.511	0.873	0.933	0.642
$C_S(G)$	0.25	0.634	0.018	0.042	0.567	0.095	0.036

Table 1. The parameters for clustering graphs 1-5

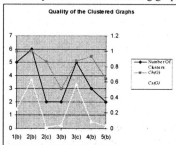

Figure 8. Quality of the clustered graphs

5 Applications

Our approach is based on theoretical properties of the graph, so it potentially has wide application. Here we apply it to web visualization. In our prototype, called PGD, there is a web crawler program that builds the graph of a web. We give a starting address: http://www.it.swin.edu.au, and a depth:5. The program will use a depth-first search algorithm to explore the web and created a graph as shown in Figure 9. Figure 9 is also the clustered graph layout, where the white nodes are the member nodes of the black nearby node. Our approach actually finds the dense subgraph in the web graph and then classifies them. From the clustered web graph, we reach the following conclusions:

1.   The clustered graph can reduce visual complexity. In large graphs, we will only display the clustered nodes and relative edges. Although there are several existing approaches to layout the large graphs, such as Hyperbolic tree [10] and multilevel clustered graphs [11], our approach has a feature of automatically clustering nodes based on the connectivity of the graph.

2.   There is a possible web community around the clustered node. We describe the properties of the web communities derived as two distinct types of dense subgraphs in web graphs, where the link density is greater among members than between members and the rest of the network [22] . A web community is a set of web pages having a common topic and so far various graph theoretical approaches have been proposed to extract web communities from web graph, such as HITS[22] , bipartite graph [21] and Maximum Flow algorithm[23]. All these approaches regard a web community as the dense part of web graph. We can identify a web community by analyzing the member nodes in the clusters in our approach.

3.   Classification of web pages. Hyperlinks contain high-quality semantic clues to the topic of a web page. Pages on the same or related topics tend to be linked more frequently than those on unrelated topics [25].

6 Related Work

Although there are numerous algorithms for cluster analysis in the literatures, we briefly review the approaches that are closely related to the structure of a graph, and compare them with our approach.

Matuala[1,6,7 13] uses a high connectivity in similarity graphs to cluster analysis, which is based on the cohesiveness function. The function defines every node and edge of a graph to be the maximum edge-connectivity of any subgraph containing that element. The k-connected subgraphs of the graph are obtained by deleting all elements with cohesiveness less than k in the graph, where k is a constant value. It is hard to determine the connectivity values in real clustering applications with this approach.

There is recent work related to clustering of a graph. The HCS algorithms [2] use a similarity graph as the input data. The algorithm recursively partitions a current set of elements into two subsets. It then identifies highly connected subgraphs, in which the number of edges exceeds half the number of their corresponding nodes, as kernels among them. A kernel is considered as a cluster. Unfortunately the result of the clustering is not uniquely determined. The CLICK algorithm [4] builds on a statistical model. It uses the same basic scheme as HCS to form kernels, and includes the following processing: singleton adoption, recursive clustering process on the set of remaining singletons, and an iterative merging step. The CAST [3] uses a single parameter t, and starts with a single element. Elements are added or removed from the cluster if their affinity is larger or lower than t, respectively, until the process stabilizes.

The features of our approach differ from previous work in the following ways:

1. The number of clusters is automatically detected based on the distribution of the node degrees of a given graph. It does not need to be specified beforehand (does not like k-means).
2. The number of clusters can be adjusted by specifying different values of the thresholds
3. A proposed simple affinity function , as an expansion condition, is based on the degree of a node
4. The clusters are gradually expanded by local search with k- nearest neighbor.

We also give definitions of homogeneity and separation to measure the quality of a graph clustering .In summary, our approach identifies the number of clusters at a "global" level, and grows the nodes into the clusters by local search.

7 Conclusion

In this paper, we propose a new approach to clustering the web graph. The approach gives good results in our experiments. We also apply it into web visualization. Our approach is a graph theoretic approach, so it has wide applications. For example, if the input graph is a similarity graph, where nodes correspond to elements and edges connect elements with similarity values above some threshold, it can be used to classify the elements. The future improvements may use a weighted web graph, and thus consider clustering the weighted web graph.

References

1. D.W. Matula. The conhsive trength of graphs. In G.Chartrand and S.F. Kapoor, editors, *The many facets of Graph Theory*, (1969) 110.215-221.Lecture Notes in Mathematics
2. Erez Hartuv and Ron Shamir. *A clustering algorithm based on graph connectivity*. Information Processing Letters(2000), 76(4-6):175-181
3. Amir Ben-Dor, Ron Shamir, and Zohar Yakhini. *Clustering gene expression patterns*. Journal of Computational Biology(1999). 6(3/4):281-297
4. R. Sharan and R. Shamir. *CLICK: A clustering algorithm for gene expression analysis*. In S. Miyano, R. Shamir, and T. Takagi, editors. Currents in Compuational Molecular Biology(2000) 6-7. Universal Academy Press
5. A.L. Barabasi and R. Albert, Emergence of scaling in random networks , *Science*(1999) 286
6. D.W. Matula. Cluster analysis via graph theoretic techniques. In R.C Mullin, K.B Reid, and D.p Roselle, editors, Proc. Louisiana Conference on Combinatorics, Graph Theory and Computing(1970)199-212. University of Manitoba. Winnipeg
7. D.W. Matula. K-Components, clusters and slicings in graphs. SIAM J.Appl. Math(1972) 22(3):459-480
8. S.Brin and L.Page. The anatomy of a large-scale hypertextual Web search engines. In Proceedings of the 7th WWW conference(1998)
9. A.Broder, R.Kumar, F. Maghoul, P.Raghavan, S. Rajagopalan, R. Stata, A. Tomkins, J. Wiener, Graph structure in the web, The 9th international WWW Conference(2000) Amsterdam, The Netherlands
10. Tamara Munzner and Paul Burchard Visualizing the Structure of the World Wide Web in 3D Hyperbolic Space, Proceedings of VRML '95, (San Diego, California, December 14-15, 1995), special issue of Computer Graphics, ACM SIGGRAPH, New York (1995)33-38.
11. P. EADES AND Q.–W. FENG, "Multilevel Visualization of Clustered Graphs", *Proceedings of the Symposium on Graph Drawing GD '96*, Springer–Verlag(1997) 101–112
12. S. Dill, R. Kumar, K. McCurley, Sridhar Rajagopalan, D. Sivakumar, A Tomkins. Self-similarity in the web(2001)
13. D.W. Matula. Graph theoretic techniques for cluster analysis algorithms. In J. Van Ryzin, editor , Classification and Clustering (1987) 95-129
14. D.Watts, S. Strogatz, Collective Dynamics of small-world networks, *Nature*(1998) 393 :440-442
15. J. M. Kleinberg. Authoritative sources in a hyperlinked environment. Journal of the ACM(1997) vol. 465: 604-632
16. J.Kleimberg. The Small World Phenomenon: an algorithmic perspective.Technical Report 99-1776(1999), Cornell University
17. R.Kumar, P.Raghavan, S.Rajagopalan, D. Sivakumar, A. Tomkins, E. Upfal. Stochastic models for the web graph. Proceedings of the IEEE symposium on Foundations of Computer Science(2000)
18. S.R. Kumar, P. Raghavan, S. Rajagopalan, and A. Tomkins. Trawling the Web for Emerging Cyber Communities. *Proc. of the 8th WWW Conference*(1999) 403-416
19. C.H. Papadimitriou, Algorithms, Games and the Internet. STOC(2001)
20. G. Pandurangan,P. Raghavan,E. Upfal. Using PageRank to Characterize Web Structure. 8th Annual International Computing and Combinatorics Conference (2002)
21. P.Krishna Reddy and Masaru Kitsuregawa, An approach to relate the web communities through bipartite graphs, in proc. of the Second International Conference on Web Information Systems Engineering (2001)
22. G.W.Flake, S,Lawrence, C.L. Giles, F.Coetzee Self-Organization and Identification of Web Communities, IEEE computers(2002)66-70
23. G.W.Flake, S. Lawrence, C.L,.Giles, Efficient Identification of Web Communities, Proceeding of the Sixth Intreational Conference on Knowledge Discovery and Data Mining(2002)150-160
24. S.Chakrabarti,B. Dom, and P.Indyk, Enhanced Hypertext Classifcaiton Using Hyperlinks. ACM SIGMOD int's Conf. Management of Data, ACM Press, New York(1998)307-318
25. S.Chakrabarti,B.Dom, S.Kumar, P. Raghavan,S.Rajagopalan,A. Tomkins,D.Gibson, J.Kleinberg. Mining the Web's Link Structure. IEEE computers (1999) 60-66

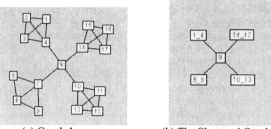

(a) Graph 1   (b) The Clustered Graph 1
Figure 3. Initial and Clustered Graph 1

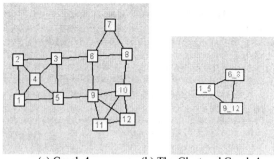

(a) Graph 4   (b) The Clustered Graph 4
Figure 6. Initial and Clustered Graph 4

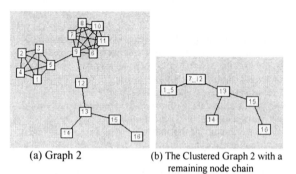

(a) Graph 2   (b) The Clustered Graph 2 with a
                                  remaining node chain

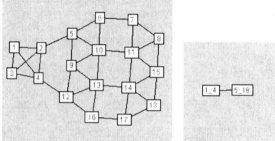

(a) Graph 5   (b) The Clustered Graph 5
Figure 7. Initial and Clustered Graph 5

(c)The Clustered Graph 2 without the remaining node chain

Figure 4. Initial and Clustered Graph 1

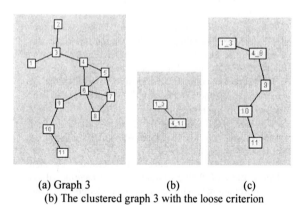

(a) Graph 3   (b)   (c)
(b) The clustered graph 3 with the loose criterion
(c) The clustered graph with the strict criterion

Figure 5. Initial and Clustered Graph 3

Figure 9 Layout of the clustered web graph

Advanced Database
Techniques I

A Stream Segregation Algorithm for Polyphonic Music Databases

Wai Man Szeto   Man Hon Wong*
Department of Computer Science and Engineering
The Chinese University of Hong Kong
Shatin, N.T., Hong Kong
{wmszeto, mhwong}@cse.cuhk.edu.hk

Abstract

Most of the existing algorithms for music information retrieval are based on string matching. However, some searching results are perceptually insignificant in the sense that they cannot really be heard, owing to negligence of how people perceive music. When listening to music, it is perceived in groupings of musical notes called streams. *Stream-crossing musical patterns are perceptually insignificant and should be pruned out from the final results. Stream segregation should be added as a pre-processing or post-processing step in existing retrieval systems in order to improve the quality of retrieval results.*

The key ideas are: (a) representation of music in the form of events, (b) formulation of the inter-event and the inter-cluster distance functions based on the findings in auditory psychology, and (c) application of the distance functions in the adapted single-link clustering algorithm without input of number of clusters. Experiments are performed on real music data to verify our proposed method.

1 Introduction

Music information retrieval is a rapidly growing research discipline. As music can be represented in a series of musical notes, most of the existing methods adapt some general string matching algorithms to search a music database for the occurrences of a musical pattern query [5, 3, 4, 10, 24, 11, 9, 19, 16], in which musical pitches (certain frequencies) are encoded in a finite alphabet set and each alphabet is represented by an integer.

Music databases can be classified according to the type of music stored: monophonic and polyphonic. If only one pitch is played at a time throughout the music, the music is said to be *monophonic*. If the duration of each musical

note is omitted and only the sounding order of pitches is retained, monophonic music can be represented as a pitch sequence $P = (p_1, p_2, \ldots, p_m)$ where p_i is a pitch and is an element of an alphabet set Σ. If several pitches may appear simultaneously, the music is said to be *polyphonic*. The simultaneous pitches are put into a pitch set. Polyphonic music can be represented as a sequence of pitch sets, denoted by $\mathcal{S} = (\mathcal{S}_1, \mathcal{S}_2, \ldots, \mathcal{S}_n)$ where $\mathcal{S}_i = \{s_{i,1}, s_{i,2}, \ldots, s_{i,l_i}\}$ and $s_{i,j} \in \Sigma$. In other words, in the first time interval, the pitches in $\mathcal{S}_1$ are played. In the next time interval, the pitches in $\mathcal{S}_2$ are played and so on. By this definition, most music is polyphonic.

In general, recent contributions on searching in polyphonic music databases mostly focus on the problem below: Given a monophonic query $Q = (q_1, q_2, \ldots, q_m)$ and a polyphonic source $\mathcal{S} = (\mathcal{S}_1, \mathcal{S}_2, \ldots, \mathcal{S}_n)$, the contributors aim at searching for source subsequences $(\mathcal{S}_i, \mathcal{S}_{i+1}, \ldots, \mathcal{S}_{i+m-1})$ that has an occurrence of Q such that $q_k \in \mathcal{S}_{i+k-1}$ for $k = 1, 2, \ldots, m$. In addition to this exact occurrence of a query sequence, some researchers also consider vertical shifting (transposition) and edit distance [24, 10, 11, 9].

However, not all occurrences of a query are perceptually significant, i.e. the occurrences normally cannot be heard. In particular, the repetitive musical pattern discovery algorithm in [17] discovers over 70000 patterns in Sergei Rachmaninov's Prelude in C sharp minor, Op.3 No.2 (about-4-minute piano piece). However, the authors report that probably less than 100 of these are perceptually significant. Some heuristics are suggested to prune out perceptually insignificant patterns but further development are still required to process full-length musical compositions.

The retrieval of perceptually insignificant patterns is a result of negligence of how people perceive music. When listening to music, people perceive music in groupings of musical notes called *streams* which are the perceptual impression of connected series of pitches, instead of isolated sounds. The process of the separation of pitches into streams is called *stream segregation*. For example, a

---

*The authors are partially supported by RGC Earmarked Grant CUHK4437/99E.

melody is usually heard as a single coherent and continuous musical line, that is, a stream. Monophonic musical patterns across streams are perceptually insignificant and should be pruned out from results. Consider the opening theme of Ludwig van Beethoven's Symphony No. 5, i.e. G, G, G, E♭, F, F, F, and D (or mi, mi, mi, doh, ray, ray, ray, and te) as shown in Figure 1, if we we search for any its transposition, an occurrence is found in the bars 1 to 2 of Frederic Chopin's Prelude No. 4 in E minor (Figure 2). However, this occurrence is hardly heard because as shown in Figure 2, there are four streams or musical lines in the opening [21]. We perceive stream 1 as the melody, while the other three streams are combined and formed a single accompaniment. The occurrence is across streams 3 and 4 so it is perceptually insignificant.

Pruning out stream-crossing monophonic patterns is able to be done only when all streams are segregated in music databases. Stream segregation should be added as a pre-processing or post-processing step in existing retrieval systems in order to improve the quality of retrieval results. In this paper, we formalize the stream segregation problem and propose a clustering model based on the findings in auditory psychology. The rest of the paper is organized as follows. Section 2 provides the psychological perspective of stream segregation. Related work is reviewed in Section 3. We will present our method in Section 4. In Section 5, we show our experimental results. Finally, a conclusion is given in Section 6.

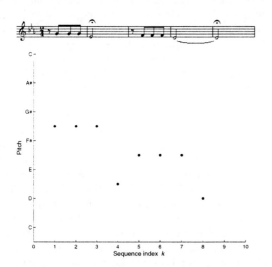

Figure 1. The opening of Beethoven's Symphony No. 5, first movement and its monophonic sequence representation $Q = (q_k)$ for $k = 1 \ldots, 8$.

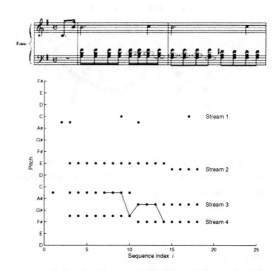

Figure 2. The opening of Chopin's Prelude No. 4 in E minor and its monophonic sequence representation $S = (S_i)$ for $i = 1, \ldots, 18$. The circles in the staff and the solid line in the sequence representation correspond to the Beethoven's symphony.

2 Findings in auditory psychology

Extensive psychological experiments have been being designed to study the factors of stream segregation. The following findings are summarized from the surveys in [6, 22]. Most studies of stream segregation in psychology is influenced by the "Gestalt principles of perception" proposed in the 1920s. It is a set of principles governing the grouping of elements in perception. One is proximity: closer elements are grouped together in preference to those that are spaced further apart. An example is showed in Figure 3a, where the closer dots are perceptually grouped together in pairs. Another is similarity: we tend to group things that are similar. In Figure 3b, we perceive one set of vertical rows formed by filled circles and another set formed by the unfilled circles. The third, good continuation, states that the elements that follow each other in a given direction are perceptually linked together. We group the dots in Figure 3c so as to form the lines AB and CD.

Although demonstrated visually in Figure 3, the Gestalt principles can be applied to music as well. It has been found that the pitch proximity and the temporal proximity are dominant factors in stream segregation. Pitch proximity states that musical notes which are closer in terms of pitch are grouped together. When a sequence of two alternating

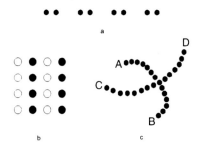

Figure 3. Illustrations of the Gestalt principles of proximity, similarity, and good continuation (adapted from [6]).

pitches is played, the two pitches will seem to fuse into a single stream if they are close together in pitch; otherwise they will seem to form two independent streams. For temporal proximity, it states that musical notes which are closer in terms of time are grouped together. When a sequence of two alternating pitches is played, we tend to perceive them as two separate streams if the alternation speed is high. In addition, other experiments show that a musical note only involves in one stream. Moreover, for a given stream, there will not be more than one musical note at the same time. Although timbre, amplitude, and spatial location may sometimes affect stream segregation, they are often outweighed by pitch and temporal proximities.

3 Related work

Various methods have been proposed for stream segregation and some of which are reviewed in [22]. Based on an analogy with the apparent motion in vision, Gjerdingen proposes a massively parallel, multiplex, feed-forward neural-network system in [7]. In the system, the input is musical notes which are discrete events represented in a pitch-time plane. The "influence" of an event is measured as activation. An event has greatest activation at its pitch value and during its time span. Its influence also "diffuses" to surroundings. A temporal filter smooths the activations of all events in the time dimension. A spatial filter diffuses events over a wider span of pitches with the assumption of a Gaussian distribution of the diffusion. The hill-like activation of all events are summed up. Tracking local maxima of activation along the time dimension can produce a pitch-time graph containing lines which are interpreted as streams. The model can also track more than one line simultaneously. However, the lines in the pitch-time graph may be difficult to interpret.

The McCabe and Denham's model in [15] is similar to Gjerdingen's. Like Gjerdingen's model, the McCabe-Denham model represents music in the dimensions of pitch and time. Two neural networks corresponds to the "foreground" stream and the "background" stream. Musical input is segregated into the two streams. Although the McCabe-Denham model accepts acoustic input, complex acoustic signals have not been tested. Similar to Gjerdingen's model, the output of McCabe-Denham model is difficult to interpret. Moreover, it can track only two streams.

The final model to be considered, developed by Temperley [22], is based on a set of stream segregation preference rules adapted from Lerdahl and Jackendoff [12], and is built on a rule-based stream segregation model in [13]. Its input is also discrete pitch event as in [7]. The model has six preference rules and one optional preference rule. A user is required to input the weight of each rule and the maximum number of streams. Then the system searches for the optimal stream configuration using dynamic programming. However, overlapping notes of the same pitch are disallowed in the input representation.

4 Proposed method

As pitch and temporal proximities are dominant, the attributes of pitch and time of music are taken into account. Each musical note is represented as an *event*. An event $\mathbf{e}$ is a vector (t^s, t^e, p), where t^s is the start time, t^e is the end time, and p is the pitch. The start time and the end time is in the unit of seconds. The pitch is in the unit of MIDI pitch number, which is one of the integers ranging from 0 to 127 inclusively. Middle C is assigned with the value 60. An example is shown in Figure 4.

Intuitively, if musical notes are represented as events in the two-dimensional pitch-time space, the "distance" between two events can reflect the pitch proximity and the temporal proximity of the corresponding musical notes. A stream, a group of events sharing "similar" pitch and time attributes, is in fact a cluster so stream segregation can be modelled as a clustering problem. A stream is thus referred to as a cluster hereinbelow. However, traditional clustering techniques cannot be directly applied to stream segregation because they handle data points rather than events. Moreover, besides the pitch and the temporal proximities, the findings in auditory psychology show that there are preferences to include each event in only one stream and to avoid multiple simultaneous events in one stream. To include these findings, we define two kinds of the relation between two events: *sequential events* and *simultaneous events*.

Definition 4.1 (Sequential events) *Given two events* $\mathbf{e}_1 = (t_1^s, t_1^e, p_1)$ *and* $\mathbf{e}_2 = (t_2^s, t_2^e, p_2)$, *they are* sequential events *if* $t_1^e \leq t_2^s$ *or* $t_2^e \leq t_1^s$, *denoted by* $\mathbf{e}_1 \nparallel \mathbf{e}_2$. *If* $t_1^e \leq t_2^s$, *then* $\mathbf{e}_1 \prec \mathbf{e}_2$. *If* $t_2^e \leq t_1^s$, *then* $\mathbf{e}_1 \succ \mathbf{e}_2$.

Figure 4. A five-event example. The speed is 60 crotchet beats per minute.

Definition 4.2 (Simultaneous events) *If two events* $\mathbf{e}_1$ *and* $\mathbf{e}_2$ *are not sequential events, they are said to be* simultaneous events, *denoted by* $\mathbf{e}_1 \parallel \mathbf{e}_2$.

Example 4.1 *In Figure 4, the event pairs* $\{\mathbf{e}_1, \mathbf{e}_2\}$, $\{\mathbf{e}_1, \mathbf{e}_5\}$, $\{\mathbf{e}_2, \mathbf{e}_3\}$, $\{\mathbf{e}_3, \mathbf{e}_4\}$, $\{\mathbf{e}_3, \mathbf{e}_5\}$, *and* $\{\mathbf{e}_4, \mathbf{e}_5\}$ *are sequential events because they do not overlap with each other in time. The event pairs* $\{\mathbf{e}_1, \mathbf{e}_3\}$, $\{\mathbf{e}_1, \mathbf{e}_4\}$, $\{\mathbf{e}_2, \mathbf{e}_4\}$, *and* $\{\mathbf{e}_2, \mathbf{e}_5\}$ *are simultaneous events.*

After defining the relations between events, we define the distance function between two events. Based on the psychological findings, the distance between any two simultaneous events are set to infinity to ensure each stream containing one event at a time. For sequential events, it is the distance between the tail of the prior event and the head of the posterior event. In order to define the concept formally, we need to address two problems. The first one is the choice of metrics. However, a definitive answer to the most appropriate choice of metrics to "musical" space, to our knowledge, has never been done. Therefore, we use the Euclidean distance, the most common metric. The second problem is the difference of measurement units of pitch and time. We tackle it by assigning weighting factors to the time dimension and the pitch dimension. The weighting factors will be determined empirically. The inter-event distance function is defined below:

Definition 4.3 (Inter-event distance) *Given two events* $\mathbf{e}_1 = (t_1^s, t_1^e, p_1)$ *and* $\mathbf{e}_2 = (t_1^s, t_2^e, p_2)$, *the* inter-event distance *EDIST is*

$$EDIST(e_1, e_2)$$
$$= \begin{cases} \sqrt{(\alpha d)^2 + (\beta(p_1 - p_2))^2} & if\,\mathbf{e}_1 \nparallel \mathbf{e_2}, \\ \infty & if\,\mathbf{e}_1 \parallel \mathbf{e_2}. \end{cases}$$

where α *is the time weighting factor,* β *is the pitch weighting factor, and*

$$d = \begin{cases} t_1^e - t_2^s & if\,\mathbf{e}_1 \prec \mathbf{e}_2, \\ t_2^e - t_1^s & if\,\mathbf{e}_1 \succ \mathbf{e}_2. \end{cases}$$

Example 4.2 *Suppose* $\alpha = 1$ *and* $\beta = 1$. *The inter-event distances between all possible pairs of the events in Figure 4 are shown in Table 1.*

	$\mathbf{e}_1$	$\mathbf{e}_2$	$\mathbf{e}_3$	$\mathbf{e}_4$	$\mathbf{e}_5$
$\mathbf{e}_1$	-	4.00	∞	∞	5.10
$\mathbf{e}_2$	4.00	-	3.35	∞	∞
$\mathbf{e}_3$	∞	3.35	-	1.12	3.20
$\mathbf{e}_4$	∞	∞	1.12	-	3.00
$\mathbf{e}_5$	5.10	∞	3.20	3.00	-

Table 1. The inter-event distances of the events in Figure 4 ($\alpha = 1$; $\beta = 1$).

Before going further, we define some notations adapted from those of the traditional clustering techniques in [23]. A piece of music E consists of N events:

$$E = \{\mathbf{e}_i \mid i = 1, 2, \ldots, N\}$$

A cluster $\mathcal{C}$ has the start time T^s, the end time T^e, and a set of clustered events C:

$$\mathcal{C} = (T^s, T^e, C)$$

where

$$C = \{\mathbf{e}_{i_1}, \mathbf{e}_{i_2}, \ldots\} \subseteq E$$
$$\text{where } \mathbf{e}_{i_k} = (t_{i_k}^s, t_{i_k}^e, p_{i_k}),$$
$$T^s = \min_{i_k}(t_{i_k}^s),$$
$$T^e = \max_{i_k}(t_{i_k}^e).$$

A clustering $\mathfrak{R}$ contains n clusters:

$$\mathfrak{R} = \{\mathcal{C}_j, \quad j = 1, 2, \ldots, n\}$$

As streams have chain-like shapes, we adapt the single-link clustering algorithm to solve the stream segregation problem. The single-link clustering algorithm is a hierarchical clustering method which generates a nested series of partitions of data points. In the single-link method, the distance between two clusters is the minimum of the distances between all pairs of data points drawn from the two clusters (one data point from the first cluster, the other from the second) [8]. We put events equivalent to data points. In order to avoid a cluster from containing any simultaneous events, we define the following two relations between two clusters similar to those between two events.

Definition 4.4 (Sequential clusters) *Given two clusters* $C_1 = (T_1^s, T_1^e, C_1)$ *and* $C_2 = (T_2^s, T_2^e, C_2)$, *they are sequential clusters if* $T_1^e \leq T_2^s$ *or* $T_2^e \leq T_1^s$, *denoted by* $C_1 \nparallel C_2$.

Definition 4.5 (Simultaneous clusters) *If two clusters* C_1 *and* C_2 *are not sequential clusters, they are said to be simultaneous clusters, denoted by* $C_1 \parallel C_2$.

The inter-cluster distance between simultaneous clusters should be set to infinity to ensure that no simultaneous event is in the same cluster. For two sequential clusters, the distance between them is the minimum of the distances between all pairs of events drawn from one cluster and another cluster. We define the inter-cluster distance below:

Definition 4.6 (Inter-cluster distance) *Given two clusters* $C_1 = (T_1^s, T_1^e, C_1)$, $C_2 = (T_2^s, T_2^e, C_2)$, *the* inter-cluster distance $CDIST$ *is*

$$CDIST(C_1, C_2)$$
$$= \begin{cases} \min_{\mathbf{e}_i \in C_1, \mathbf{e}_j \in C_2}(EDIST(\mathbf{e}_i, \mathbf{e}_j)) & \text{if } C_1 \nparallel C_2, \\ \infty & \text{if } C_1 \parallel C_2. \end{cases}$$

There are various methods to implement the single-link clustering algorithm. Here, we adapt the agglomerative algorithm in [23, 14, 8]. For the agglomerative algorithm, the initial clustering $\mathfrak{R}_0$ consists of N clusters, each of which contains one event in E. Among all possible pairs of clusters, find the pair that has the minimum inter-cluster distance over all other pairs. Then the pair of clusters is merged into a larger cluster. Thus, a new clustering $\mathfrak{R}_1$ is formed and the process is repeated. There are two termination conditions. The first condition is that the distances of all possible pairs of clusters are infinity. This means that all pairs of clusters are simultaneous clusters. Noted that during the clustering process, only sequential clusters but not simultaneous clusters can be merged together. Hence, the resulting clusters will not contain any simultaneous events. The second condition is that all events lie in the same cluster, i.e. one large cluster contains all events, in which any two events must be sequential events. This adapted single-link clustering is shown in Algorithm 1.

Applying the algorithm to a music piece yields a *dendrogram*, which represents the nested grouping of events and distances at which groupings change. A dendrogram corresponding to the five-event example in Figure 4 is shown in

---

Algorithm 1 Adapted single-link clustering algorithm

1: Choose $\mathfrak{R}_0 \leftarrow \{C_i = \{\mathbf{e}_i\}, i = 1, 2, \ldots, N\}$ as the initial clustering.
2: $t \leftarrow 0$
3: **repeat**
4:    $t \leftarrow t + 1$
5:    Among all possible pairs of clusters (C_r, C_s) in $\mathfrak{R}_{t-1}$, find C_i, C_j such that $CDIST(C_i, C_j) = \min_{r \neq s} CDIST(C_r, C_s)$
6:    **if** $CDIST(C_i, C_j) = \infty$ **then**
7:       **break**
8:    Merge C_i, C_j into a single cluster C_q and form $\mathfrak{R}_t \leftarrow (\mathfrak{R}_{t-1} - \{C_i, C_j\}) \cup C_q$.
9: **until** $\mathfrak{R}_{N-1}$ clustering is formed, that is, all events lie in the same cluster.

Figure 5. The dendrogram can be broken at different threshold levels to yield different clusterings of the data. According to Algorithm 1, the threshold is equivalent to be set to just above the maximum level except infinity. Hence, users are not required to input the threshold or the number of clusters. The clustering of the five-event example is presented in Figure 6, where $\{\mathbf{e}_1, \mathbf{e}_2\}$ is a cluster and $\{\mathbf{e}_3, \mathbf{e}_4, \mathbf{e}_5\}$ is another.

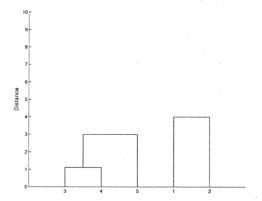

Figure 5. Dendrogram of the five-event example ($\alpha = 1$; $\beta = 1$).

Motivated by the analysis of the general single-link method in [23], the complexity of the adapted algorithm is analyzed as follows. At each level t, there are $N - t$ clusters. Thus, in order to determine the pair of clusters that is going to merged at the $(t + 1)$th level, the number of pairs of clusters to be considered is

$$\binom{N - t}{2} = \frac{(N - t)(N - t - 1)}{2}.$$

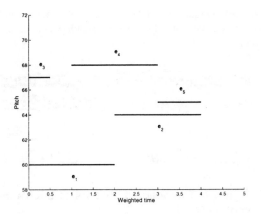

Figure 6. Clustering result: $\{e_1, e_2\}$ **is a cluster and** $\{e_3, e_4, e_5\}$ **is another.**

Therefore, if the number of output clusters is n, the total number of pairs that have to be examined throughout the whole clustering process is

$$
\begin{aligned}
\sum_{t=0}^{N-n} \binom{N-t}{2} &= \sum_{k=n}^{N} \binom{k}{2} \\
&= \sum_{k=0}^{N} \binom{k}{2} - \sum_{k=0}^{n-1} \binom{k}{2} \\
&= \frac{(N-1)N(N+1)}{6} \\
&\quad - \frac{(n-2)(n-1)n}{6}
\end{aligned}
$$

As n is small comparing to N, the total number of operations is proportional to N^3. The calculation of the inter-event distance takes constant time. Therefore, the complexity of the algorithm is $O(N^3)$.

4.1 Clustering quality measurement

Confusion matrix can be used to evaluate the clustering result of the data in which the natural clusters are known [1, 18]. Natural clusters are pre-defined clusters of the data. Usually, the number of natural clusters and output clusters are equal but this property may not be held in our case. We define a generalized version of confusion matrix.

Definition 4.7 (Confusion matrix) *A confusion matrix F (as shown in Table 2) is a $m \times n$ matrix where m is the number of natural clusters while n is the number of output clusters. The entry $F_{i,j}$ is the number of events belonging to the natural cluster C_i^I that is assigned to the output cluster C_j^O.*

	C_1^O	C_2^O	$\cdots$	C_j^O	$\cdots$	C_n^O
C_1^I	$F_{1,1}$	$F_{1,2}$	$\cdots$	$F_{1,j}$	$\cdots$	$F_{1,n}$
C_2^I	$F_{2,1}$	$F_{2,2}$	$\cdots$	$F_{2,j}$	$\cdots$	$F_{2,n}$
$\vdots$	$\vdots$	$\vdots$		$\vdots$		$\vdots$
C_i^I	$F_{i,1}$	$F_{i,2}$	$\cdots$	$F_{i,j}$	$\cdots$	$F_{i,n}$
$\vdots$	$\vdots$	$\vdots$		$\vdots$		$\vdots$
C_m^I	$F_{m,1}$	$F_{m,2}$	$\cdots$	$F_{m,j}$	$\cdots$	$F_{m,n}$

Table 2. Confusion matrix.

The desired output clustering is that there are one-to-one mappings between each natural cluster and each output cluster. However, if the events of a natural cluster map to different output clusters, the natural cluster is considered to be mapped to the output cluster having the maximum number of events in the natural cluster. The events in this output cluster are correctly classified. In other words, the events in other clusters are considered to be misclassified. We define the error rate as below:

Definition 4.8 (Error rate) *An error rate Err is the total number of misclassified events over the total number of events:*

$$
Err = \frac{\sum_{j=1}^{n}(\sum_{i=1}^{m} F_{i,j} - \max_i(F_{i,j}))}{N}
$$

The upper bound of the error rate is shown in Theorem 1. Before proving Theorem 1, we need Lemma 1.

Lemma 1 *Given a real number set $A = \{a_1, a_2, \ldots, a_n\}$, let a_{max} be the maximum number in the set such that $a_{max} \geq a_i$ for all i. Then*

$$
a_{max} \geq \frac{1}{n} \sum_{i=1}^{n} a_i
$$

i.e. the maximum number in a real number set is greater than or equal to the average value.

Proof Assume $a_{max} < \frac{1}{n} \sum_{i=1}^{n} a_i$. Then

$$
n \cdot a_{max} - \sum_{i=1}^{n} a_i < 0
$$
$$
(a_{max} - a_1) + \cdots + (a_{max} - a_n) < 0
$$

There must exist some a_i such that $a_{max} < a_i$. This contradicts $a_{max} \geq a_i$ for all i.

Theorem 1 (Upper bound of error rate)

$$
Err \leq 1 - \frac{1}{m}
$$

Proof

$$Err = \frac{\sum_{j=1}^{n}(\sum_{i=1}^{m} F_{i.j} - \max_{i}(F_{i.j}))}{N}$$

(from Definition 4.8)

$$= \frac{\sum_{j=1}^{n}(\sum_{i=1}^{m} F_{i.j} - \max_{i}(F_{i.j}))}{\sum_{j=1}^{n}(\sum_{i=1}^{m} F_{i.j})}$$

$$= 1 - \frac{\sum_{j=1}^{n} \max_{i}(F_{i.j})}{\sum_{j=1}^{n}(\sum_{i=1}^{m} F_{i.j})}$$

$$\leq 1 - \frac{(1/m)\sum_{j=1}^{n}(\sum_{i=1}^{m} F_{i.j})}{\sum_{j=1}^{n}(\sum_{i=1}^{m} F_{i.j})}$$

(from Lemma 1)

$$= 1 - \frac{1}{m}$$

Definition 4.9 (Normalized error rate) *Normalized error rate $\widetilde{Err}$ is the error rate over its upper bound:*

$$\widetilde{Err} = \frac{Err}{1 - \frac{1}{m}}$$

In the next section, experiments are performed to verify our proposed solution.

5 Experimental results

We implemented our distance functions and adapted the implementation of the single-link clustering algorithm in [14] to demonstrate the capability and usefulness of our proposed method. We collected real polyphonic music data in the MIDI (Musical Instrument Digital Interface) format which is the most common encoding scheme to represent music symbolically.

In the first experiment, Johann Sebastian Bach's two-part Invention No. 1 was collected from [20]. The opening six bars are shown in Figure 7. It is a two-voice keyboard piece, in which the upper voice is played by the right hand and the other by the left. On the facsimile of the title page of the autograph of 1723, Bach wrote that a two-part Invention should be "learned to play cleanly in two parts" [2]. Except the final bar, there is at most two musical notes at a time. Thus, the two parts in the Invention are considered as two streams or two natural clusters in our experiment with the removal of the final bar. We compared the output clusters generated by our method with the natural clusters.

The speed of the Invention was 79.615 crotchet beats per minute which was the average value over 2 editions, 2 commentaries, and 9 recordings from [2]. We set the time weighting factor α to 40 and the pitch weighting factor β to 1. Our method successfully identified that there were two streams. The dendrogram and the clustering result are

depicted in Figures 8 and 9 respectively. The normalized error rate was zero and there was no misclassification of any event.

Figure 7. The opening six bars of Bach's Invention No. 1.

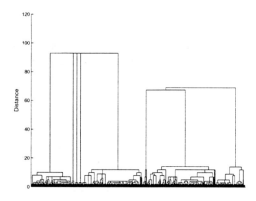

Figure 8. Dendrogram of the complete Bach's Invention No. 1 ($\alpha = 40$; $\beta = 1$).

In the second experiment, we tested our method whether it can identify the four streams in the opening two bars of Chopin's Prelude No. 4 in E minor, the piano piece discussed in Section 1. The natural clusters are the four streams shown in Figure 2. The speed was 64.5 crotchet beats per minute, the average value of 6 performances including Argerich, Bolet, Cherkassky, Cortot, Larocha, and Polini. We also set the time weighting factor α to 40 and the pitch weighting factor β to 1 as in our previous experiment. The dendrogram and the clustering result are depicted in Figures 10 and 11 respectively. Only four output clusters were generated. The normalized error rate was 0.025 and only the first event was misclassified.

In the third experiment, we evaluated the performance of the adapted single-link clustering algorithm in time. Bach's Invention No. 1 was divided into different lengths. The CPU time against the number of events is plotted in Figure

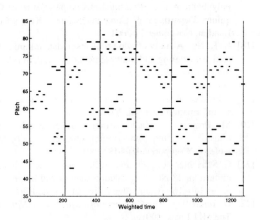

Figure 9. Clustering result: $\widetilde{Err} = 0$ ($\alpha = 40$; $\beta = 1$). **The two continuous lines are the output clusters which are the same as the natural clusters (only the opening six bars are shown).**

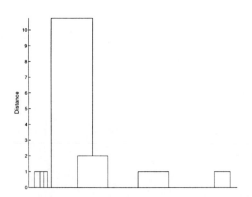

Figure 10. Dendrogram of the opening two bars of Chopin's Prelude in E minor ($\alpha = 40$; $\beta = 1$).

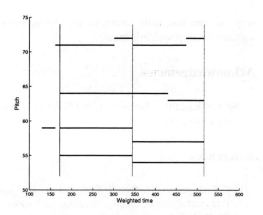

Figure 11. Clustering result: $\widetilde{Err} = 0.025$ ($\alpha = 40$; $\beta = 1$). **The four continuous lines are the output clusters.**

12. Increase in the number of events relates an increase in the CPU time.

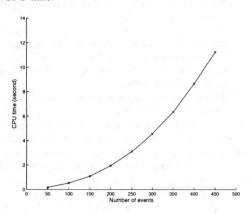

Figure 12. CPU time vs number of events.

6 Conclusion

It is essential to incorporate stream segregation in existing music information retrieval systems in order to improve the quality of retrieval results. In this paper, we tackle the stream segregation problem by representing music in the form of events, formulating the inter-event and the inter-cluster distance functions based on the findings in auditory psychology, and applying the distance functions in the adapted single-link clustering algorithm without input of number of clusters. Supported by the experiments, our proposed method can successfully discover streams with a very low error rate. In the future, we will test our method in a greater set of polyphonic music.

Acknowledgements

We are thankful to Dennis Wu and Eos Cheng for their valuable comments.

References

[1] C. C. Aggarwal, J. L. Wolf, P. S. Yu, C. Procopiuc, and J. S. Park. Fast algorithms for projected clustering. In *Proc. ACM SIGMOD Conference on Management of Data*, pages 61–72, 1999.

[2] J. S. Bach. *Inventions and Sinfonias (Two- and Three-Part Inventions)*. Alfred Publishing Co., 2nd edition, 1991.

[3] D. Byrd and T. Crawford. Problems of music information retrieval in the real world. *Information Processing and Management*, 38:249–272, 2002.

[4] E. Cambouropoulos, T. Crawford, , and C. Iliopoulos. Pattern processing in melodic sequences: Challenges, caveats and prospects. In *Proc. AISB'99 Symposium on Musical Creativity*, pages 42–47, 1999.

[5] T. Crawford, C. Iliopoulos, and R. Raman. String matching techniques for musical similarity and melodic recognition. *Computing in Musicology*, 11:73–100, 1998.

[6] D. Deutsch, editor. *The Psychology of Music*. Academic Press, 2nd edition, 1999.

[7] R. O. Gjerdingen. Apparent motion in music. *Music Perception*, 11:335–370, 1994.

[8] A. K. Jain, M. N. Murty, and P. J. Flynn. Data clustering: a review. *ACM Computing Surveys*, 31(3):264–323, 1999.

[9] K. Lemstrom. *String Matching Techniques for Music Retrieval*. PhD thesis, University of Helsinki, Finland, 2000.

[10] K. Lemstrom and S. Perttu. Semex - an efficient music retrieval prototype. In *First International Symposium on Music Information Retrieval (ISMIR'2000)*, Plymouth, Massachusetts, October 23-25 2000.

[11] K. Lemstrom and J. Tarhio. Searching monophonic patterns within polyphonic sources. In *Proc. Content-Based Multimedia Information Access (RIAO'2000)*, volume 2, pages 1261–1279, Paris, France, April 12-14 2000.

[12] F. Lerdahl and R. Jackendoff. *A Generative Theory of Tonal Music*. The MIT Press, 1983.

[13] A. Marsden. *Computer Representations and Models in Music*, chapter Modelling the perception of musical voices: A case study in rule-based systems, pages 239–263. Academic Press, 1992.

[14] MathWorks. Statistics toolbox version 4, 2002.

[15] S. L. McCabe and M. J. Denham. A model of auditory streaming. *The Journal of the Acoustical Society of America*, 101(3):1611–1621, March 1997.

[16] M. Melucci and N. Orio. Musical information retrieval using melodic surface. In *Proc. ACM International Conference on Digital Libraries*, pages 152–160, 1999.

[17] D. Meredith, G. A. Wiggins, and K. Lemstrom. A geometric approach to repetition discovery and pattern matching in polyphonic music. Presented at Computer Science Colloquium, Department of Computer Science, King's College London, November 21 2001.

[18] K. K. Ng. A study of two problems in data mining: A projective clustering and multiple tables association rules mining. Master's thesis, The Chinese University of Hong Kong, 2002.

[19] J. Pickens. A survey of feature selection techniques for music information retrieval, 2001.

[20] M. Project. Music listing: J. S. Bach's inventions. http://www.mutopiaproject.org/cgibin/maketable.cgi?Composer=BachJS, 2001.

[21] C. Schachter. *Chopin Studies 2*, chapter The Prelude in E minor Op. 28 No. 4: autograph sources and interpretation, pages 140–161. Cambridge University Press, 1994.

[22] D. Temperley. *The Cognition of Basic Musical Structures*. The MIT Press, 2001.

[23] S. Theodoridis and K. Koutroumbas. *Pattern recognition*. Academic Press, 1999.

[24] A. Uitdenbgerd and J. Zobel. Melodic matching techniques for large music databases. In *Proc. ACM International Multimedia Conference*, pages 57–66, 1999.

Efficient Subsequence Matching for Sequences Databases under Time Warping

Teddy Siu Fung Wong, Man Hon Wong *
Department of Computer Science and Engineering
The Chinese University of Hong Kong
Shatin, N.T., Hong Kong, China
Email: {sfwong,mhwong}@cse.cuhk.edu.hk

Abstract

Recently, it has been found that the technique of searching for similar patterns among time series data is very important in a wide range of scientific and business applications. Most of the research works use Euclidean distance as their similarity metric. However, Dynamic Time Warping (DTW) is a more robust distance measure than Euclidean distance in many situations, where sequences may have different lengths or the patterns of which are out of phase in the time axis. Unfortunately, DTW does not satisfy the triangle inequality, so that spatial indexing techniques cannot be applied. In this paper, we present a novel method that supports dynamic time warping for subsequence matching within a collection of sequences. Our method takes full advantage of "sliding window" approach and can handle queries of arbitrary length.

1. Introduction

A time series $X = \langle x_1, x_2, \ldots x_n \rangle$ is a sequence of real numbers, where each number x_i represents a value at a point of time. In the real world, data always appear in the form of time series, e.g. temperature, atmosphere, stock prices, experimental results ... etc. Studying patterns of time series is very important in many areas. For example, in a financial application, we may need to find out some specific patterns in a daily stock price sequence, in order to predict the future trend. In general, similarity queries can be divided into two main categories:

(a) Whole sequence matching: Given a query sequence of length n, and a time series database, we want to find out all the time series from the database that are similar to the query sequence; i.e., given a set of time series $S = \{S_1, \ldots, S_m\}$ and a query sequence

*The authors are partially supported by RGC Earmarked Grant CUHK4437/99E.

$Q = \langle q_1, q_2, \ldots, q_n \rangle$, we want to ask if there is any time series S_i, where $1 < i < m$, such that S_i and Q are similar.

(b) Subsequence matching: Given a query sequence of length n, and a time series database, we want to retrieve all subsequences from the database that are similar to the query sequence; i.e., given a set of time series $S = \{S_1, \ldots, S_m\}$ and a query sequence $Q = \langle q_1, q_2, \ldots, q_n \rangle$, we want to ask if there is any subsequences S' within any S_i, where $1 < i < m$, such that S' and Q are similar.

Most of the research work adopts Euclidean distance as the metric for sequence similarity [15, 4, 19, 8, 7, 12, 9]. Given two sequences $X = < x_1, x_2, \ldots, x_n >$ and $Y = < y_1, y_2, \ldots, y_n >$, the Euclidean distance is defined as follows:

$$D_2(X, Y) = \sqrt[2]{\sum_{i=1}^{n} (x_i - y_j)^2} \qquad (1)$$

Dozens of papers proposed various modifications based on Euclidean distance, such as shifting and scaling elimination [8], noise removal [1], moving average [17] ... etc.

Another technique, called Dynamic Time Warping (DTW) is proposed in [3]. DTW enables matching similar sequences which are out of phase, or even the sequences are of different lengths. Under dynamic time warping, two sequences may be stretched along the time axis. For example, given two sequences $S = < 4, 5, 6, 8, 9 >$ and $Q = < 3, 4, 7, 8, 9, 7 >$ of different lengths, we can stretch the sequences to $S' = < 4, 5, 6, \underline{6}, 8, 9, \underline{9} >$ and $Q' = < 3, \underline{3}, 4, 7, 8, 9, 7 >$, and measure the distance between S' and Q'. In such case, we say that the sequences S and Q "align" with each other. Apparently, there is more than one way to "align" S and Q. The minimum distance among all possible alignments between sequences S and Q is defined as time warping distance, D_{tw}. The DTW technique is actually a well known technique being used in speech recognition [16].

Searching the sequences sequentially can be slow. Obviously, the query process can be speeded up, if an indexing technique is used. When Euclidean distance is used as the similarity measure, a sequence of length n can be transformed into a k-dimensional point, and the point can be indexed with any multi-dimensional indexing structure, such as the R-tree [6] or the R*-tree [11]. Similary, a query sequence can also be transformed into a k-dimensional point, and then a range query search can be performed on the indexing structure. Unfortunately, DTW does not satisfy the triangle inequality, the above method cannot be applied directly.

Nevertheless, a great deal of work is proposed to perform efficient searching and indexing on DTW [2, 13, 18, 14, 5, 10, 20]. In [2], the authors introduce two techniques to speed up the searching process, one is FastMap, which results false dismissals; another one is the lower bound technique. A lower bound function, which the satisfies triangle inequality, is defined by means of lower bound technique. This technique is further used in [18] and [10], in which, DTW can be indexed by any spatial indexing structure [6, 11], whereas the above approaches only accommodate for whole sequence matching. However, subsequence matching is different from whole sequence matching. Note that, when Euclidean metric is used, the distance between any two sequences must be greater than that between their prefixes with the same length. Therefore, given a sequence S, a sliding window approach [4] can be used to extract the prefixes of all the subsequences of S, and then each prefix can be inserted into a multi-dimensional indexing structure. Given a query Q, we can simply extract the prefix of Q and perform a range query on the indexing structure to retrieve the prefixes of all the potential subsequences.

Subsequence matching under time warping distance is more complicated, as the DTW distance between any two sequences may not have a simple relation with that between their prefixes with the same length. Therefore, the above sliding window technique cannot be applied directly.

For subsequence matching, authors in [20] suggest a segment-based approach, but this approach again may cause false dismissals. Another indexing method based on suffix tree is proposed in [13], which guarantees no false dismissals. Unfortunately, the index size of suffix tree is extremely large even for a small data set. As an extension of [18], the authors of [14] proposed to use the prefix querying technique together with the lower bound function suggested in [18] to handle subsequence matching. However, as pointed out in [10], this "lower bound is very loose, and many false alarms are generated".

In this paper, we are to generalize a better lower bound technique for subsequence matching under time warping distance. Based on the proposed approach, an R-tree can be used to index the subsequences. Hence, the space overhead will be much smaller than that of the suffix tree approach.

The rest of the paper is organized as follows. Section 2 provides the background of Dynamic Time Warping. We will define the problem of subsequence matching under the time warping metric and describe its difficulties in Section 3. In Section 4, we will present the strategies that we used to handle these difficulties. Based on the strategies, we will show our algorithm in Section 5. Section 6 presents the experimental results. Finally in Section 7, our works are summarized and some extensions are suggested.

2. Preliminaries

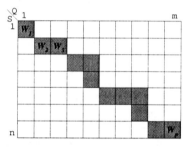

Figure 1. A warping path in an m-by-n grid

The idea of *dynamic time warping* is as follows. Given two sequences S and Q of lengths n and m respectively, where:

$$S = < s_1, s_2, \ldots, s_{n-1}, s_n >$$
$$Q = < q_1, q_2, \ldots, q_{m-1}, q_m >$$

we can develop an m-by-n grid, as illustrated in Figure 1. Each grid element, (i, j), represents an alignment between points s_i and q_j. A *warping path* W is a sequence of grid elements that define an alignment between S and Q.

$$W = (i_1, j_1), (i_2, j_2), \ldots, (i_p, j_p)$$
$$max(n, m) \leq p < m + n - 1 \quad (2)$$

,where (i_k, j_k) corresponds to the kth grid element in the warping path. For example, (i_3, j_3) in Figure 1 represents the grid element $(2, 3)$, which implies that s_2 is aligned with q_3. For practical reasons, several types of constraints, which concern the warping path, are introduced in prevalent research works [16, 3, 21]

End point constraints The warping path should start at (1,1) and end at (n,m).

Monotonicity and Continuity Given two grid elements in a warping path, (i_k, j_k) and (i_{k+1}, j_{k+1}), then $1 \geq i_{k+1} - i_k \geq 0$ and $1 \geq j_{k+1} - j_k \geq 0$. This restricts the allowable transitions of a node to adjacent elements, which located at either east, south, or south-east with respect to Figure 1.

Global Path Constraint The global path constraint defines the region of grid elements that are searched for the optimal warping path. The warping path is limited within the warping window [3], which is known as Sakoe-Chiba Band. For example, the grey area in Figure 2 refers to such a band. The constraint can be defined as follows:

$$\forall (i_k, j_k) \in W, \quad i_k - r \leq j_k \leq i_k + r, \quad (3)$$

where r is width of the warping window. For example, in Figure 2, $r = 2$.

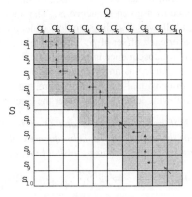

Figure 2. The warping path is restricted in the grey area (the warping window)

After aligning the sequences S and Q, their similarity can be measured by the cumulative distance of the warping path between them. Each element in the warping path is associated with a distance, i.e. $d(i_k, j_k) = |s_{i_k} - q_{j_k}|$. The cumulative distance of a warping path, e.g. $W = (i_1, j_1), (i_2, j_2), \ldots, (i_p, j_p)$, is defined as follows:

$$D_c(W) = \sum_{k=1}^{p} d(i_k, j_k) \quad (4)$$

There are possibly many warping paths. Among all the potential warping paths, we can always choose an *optimal warping path* such that its cumulative distance, D_c, is minimum. The corresponding distance is defined as the *time warping distance*, D_{tw}.

$$D_{tw}(S, Q) = \min_{\forall W} \{D_c(W)\} \quad (5)$$

As there are many warping paths, searching through all of them is computational expensive. Therefore, dynamic programming approach [2, 16] is proposed to find the *optimal warping path*. The approach is based on the following recurrence formula that defines the cumulative distance, $\gamma(i, j)$, for each grid element.

$$\gamma(i, j) = d(i, j) +$$
$$\min\{\gamma(i-1, j), \gamma(i, i-1), \gamma(i-1, j-1)\} \quad (6)$$

S \ Q	0	3	6	0	6	0
2	2	3	7	9	13	15
5	7	4	4	9	10	15
2	9	5	8	6	10	12
5	14	7	6	11	7	12
2	16	8	10	8	11	9

Figure 3. A cumulative distance matrix for sequences Q and S

By applying the dynamic programming algorithm, we can construct a cumulative distance matrix as shown in Figure 3, which demonstrates such an algorithm by sequences $Q = <0, 3, 6, 0, 6, 0>$ and $S = <2, 5, 2, 5, 2>$. Each value in the cell represents the cumulative distance of that cell. The cumulative distance of a cell is the sum of the distance associated with it and the minimum of the cumulative distances of its neighboring cells. For example:

$$\gamma(3, 4) = d(3, 4) + \min\{\gamma(2, 4), \gamma(3, 3), \gamma(2, 3)\} = 6$$

After filling up the table, the optimal warping path can be found by tracing backward from the lower right corner, $(5, 6)$, towards the upper left corner, $(1, 1)$. At each cell, we can choose the previous neighboring cell with minimum cumulative distance.

3. Subsequence Matching Under DTW

In this section, we introduce the problem of subsequence matching. The main symbols used in this paper and their definitions are summarized in Table 1. The problem is formally defined as follows:

(1) Given a set of time series $\{S_1, S_2, \ldots, Sn\}$ of arbitrary lengths.

(2) A query sequence Q together with a threshold ε are given.

Symbol	Definition
Q	A query sequences.
S_i	The i-th data sequence
$S[i:j]$	Subsequence of S, begin at position i and end at j.
$Len(S)$	The length of a sequence S.
l	The width of the sliding window.
r	The width of the warping window.
$D_{tw}(S,Q)$	The time warping distance between sequences S and Q.
$D_{tw-lb}(S,Q)$	The lower bound distance between sequences S and Q.

Table 1. Summary of Symbols and Definitions

(3) Find all the subsequences $S_k[i:j]$, for a given global path constraint, such that $D_{tw}(S_k[i:j],Q) \leq \varepsilon$, where $S_k[i:j]$ and Q may have different lengths.

3.1 Sequential Search

The most straightforward method is sequential search, by which, all the possible subsequences of every sequence will be examined. Consider the following example:

Given a sequence $S = <1,2,5,2,5,3,10>$ and a query $Q = <0,3,6,0,6>$, we want to find all the subsequences, $S[i:j]$, of S such that $D_{tw}(S[i:j],Q) \leq 8$. In particular, let's consider the subsequence started at the 2nd offset of S, i.e. $S[2:7] = <2,5,2,5,3,10>$. By using the dynamic programming approach, we can construct the matrix as shown in Table 2.

$S \setminus Q$	0	3	6	0	6
2	2	3	7	9	**13**
5	7	4	4	9	**10**
2	9	5	8	6	**10**
5	14	7	6	11	**7**
3	17	7	9	9	**10**
10	27	14	11	19	**13**

Table 2. An example of subsequence matching

From the last column of Table 2, we know that $D_{tw}(S[2:2],Q) = 13$, $D_{tw}(S[2:3],Q) = 10$, $D_{tw}(S[2:4],Q) = 10$, $D_{tw}(S[2:5],Q) = 7$, $D_{tw}(S[2:6],Q) = 10$, $D_{tw}(S[2:7],Q) = 13$. Therefore, the subsequence $S[2:5]$ satisfies our requirement and will be included in the answer set. The same procedure has to be used to examine each subsequence at every offset

in order to find all the qualifying answers. We call this method as "Sequential Search".

However, there are two major problems concerning sequential search:

- The I/O cost of examining all the possible subsequences is very high.

- The process of dynamic programming is computational costly($O(m*n)$, where n and m are the lengths of the sequences).

3.2. Indexing Scheme

Before introducing the indexing scheme of subsequence matching under DTW, we need to review the scheme under the Euclidean distance metric first.

Under the Euclidean metric, the sliding window approach [4] can be used to avoid examining each possible subsequence of a given sequence S. The approach is described as follows. A sliding window of length l is placed and slid over each offset of S. Then a prefix of length l of each possible subsequence is extracted. Each extracted prefix can be regarded as an l-dimensional point and indexed in a multidimensional indexing structure, e.g. R-tree. Note that the following lemma holds under the Euclidean metric.

Lemma 1 *If two sequences S and Q of length n agree within threshold ϵ, then the subsequences $S[i:j]$ and $Q[i:j]$ agree within the same threshold too, i.e.*

$$D(S,Q) \leq \epsilon \Rightarrow D(S[i:j],Q[i:j]) \leq \epsilon \quad (7)$$

From Lemma 1, the distance between the prefix of S and the corresponding prefix of Q is a lower bound of that between the whole sequences. Therefore, we can search for all prefixes, which match $Q[1:l]$ within ϵ, in the indexing structure. The results are the prefixes of the subsequences that will potentially match sequence Q within threshold ϵ. Then, the candidate set can be filtered by postprocessing to get the final answers.

Unfortunately, under the time warping metric, Lemma 1 does not hold. Let's consider the example in Section 3.1. If the length of the sliding window is 4, the prefix of length 4 of each possible subsequence of S will be extracted and indexed. $Q[1:4]$ will be used to perform searching. Consider the subsequence at the 2nd offset of S again. From Table 2,

$$D_{tw}(S[2:5],Q[1:4]) = 11$$
$$D_{tw}(S[2:6],Q[1:5]) = 10$$

Therefore, $D_{tw}(S[2:5],Q[1:4]) > D_{tw}(S[2:6],Q[1:5])$, and Lemma 1 does not hold. It is clear that we extract a "wrong" prefix of Q to compare with $S[2:5]$. If we use $Q[1:4]$ to perform index searching, it will cause false dismissal. Instead, from Table 2, we have the following example:

$$D_{tw}(S[2:5], Q[1:5]) = 7$$
$$D_{tw}(S[2:6], Q[1:5]) = 10$$
$$D_{tw}(S[2:5], Q[1:5]) < D_{tw}(S[2:6], Q[1:5])$$

Hence, $Q[1:5]$ is the "correct" prefix to be used. The remaining problems are:

- We need to find the "correct" prefix of Q to perform searching.

- Time warping distance does not satisfy triangle inequality, so that we cannot perform searching in a spatial index.

- The time complexity for the computation of dynamic programming is high.

To overcome these problems, lower bound technique [18, 10, 2] is used. We first discuss some existing lower bound techniques for whole "sequence matching". Then we will extend the idea for subsequence searching in the rest of the paper.

4. Lower Bound Technique

The computation process of dynamic programming has very high complexity. Performing such process on each data sequence in the database can be slow. Therefore, the lower bound technique is introduced [18, 10, 2]. A new distance measure, D_{tw-lb}, is defined, which is lower-bounding the actually DTW distance. Algorithm 1 describes how range query can be performed using D_{tw-lb}. Note that Al-

---

Algorithm 1 lower-bound-search

1: $C := \{\}$
2: **for** each possible subsequence S' in S **do**
3:    **if** $D_{tw-lb}(S', Q) \leq \epsilon$ **then**
4:       $C \leftarrow S'$
5:    **end if**
6: **end for**
7: **for** each S' in C **do**
8:    **if** $D_{tw}(S', Q) \leq \epsilon$ **then**
9:       $return(S')$
10:    **end if**
11: **end for**

---

gorithm 1 does not reduce the number of subsequences to be scanned. Instead, the speed up is contributed by the distance calculation. Therefore, a lower-bound function should have the following properties:

Property 1 *(Correctness) It must return all the qualifying subsequences, but may cause false alarms, which can be discarded afterwards using post-processing, i.e.*

$$D_{tw}(S, Q) \leq \varepsilon \Rightarrow D_{tw-lb}(S, Q) \leq \varepsilon \qquad (8)$$

Property 2 *(Efficiency) The time complexity for the computation should be low, e.g. O(n).*

Property 3 *(Tightness) With a relative tight lower bound, the number of candidate results for post-processing can be greatly reduced.*

Moreover, if the lower bound function satisfies triangle inequality, it can be further used as the filtering function in indexing search.

4.1. Existing Lower Bound Functions

To our best knowledge, two lower bound functions, which guarantee no false dismissals, have been proposed to handle "whole sequence" matching.

In [18], the authors proposed to extract a 4-tuple feature vector, $\langle$ First(S), Last(S), Greatest(S), Smallest(S) $\rangle$, from each sequence S. The features are the first, last, greatest and smallest elements of S respectively. Given two sequences S and Q, their lower bound function, D_{lb-kim}, is defined as follows:

$$D_{lb-kim} = \max \begin{cases} |First(S) - First(Q)| \\ |Last(S) - Last(Q)| \\ |Greatest(S) - Greatest(Q)| \\ |Smallest(S) - Smallest(Q)| \end{cases} \qquad (9)$$

Another lower bound function is proposed in [10], in which the indexing method is called an "exact indexing" of DTW. For any two sequences S and Q *of the same length n*, for any global path constraints of the form $i - r \leq j \leq i + r$, the lower bound function, $D_{lb-keogh}$, is defined as follows:

$$U_i = \max\{q_{i-r} \ldots q_{i+r}\}$$
$$L_i = \min\{q_{i-r} \ldots q_{i+r}\}$$
$$D_{lb-keogh} = \sqrt{\sum_{i=1}^{n} \begin{cases} (s_i - U_i)^2 & if s_i > U_i \\ (s_i - L_i)^2 & if s_i < L_i \\ 0 & otherwise \end{cases}} \qquad (10)$$

4.2. Lower Bound Technique for subsequences matching

Here, we want to utilize the lower bound function proposed in [10], which is designed for "whole sequence" matching, to handle subsequence matching. By the following deduction and observations, we utilize the lower bound function in the sliding window approach. Our deduction and observations are as follows:

An example: Given two sequences $S =<\ 2,5,2,5,3,7,1,8,4,10\ >$ and $Q =<\ 7,0,3,6,0,6,5,8,4\ >$, we can construct two matrixes as shown in Figure 4. The first matrix is the same as the grid illustrated in Figure 1 and each value in (i,j) represents the distance between points s_i and q_j, e.g. $d(1,5) = |s_1 - q_5| = |2 - 0| = 2$. The second matrix is the cumulative distance matrix, which is constructed by dynamic programming. There is an optimal warping path $\{(1,1),(2,1),(3,2),(4,3),(5,3),(6,4),(7,5),(8,6),(8,7),(8,8),(9,9)\}$, such that the time warping distance is 18.

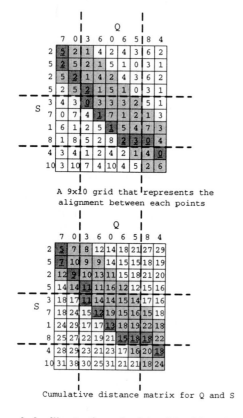

A 9x10 grid that represents the alignment between each points

Cumulative distance matrix for Q and S

Figure 4. An illustration of a 9-by-10 grid and a cumulative distance matrix for Q and S. The warping path is underlined and it is restricted in a warping window with width 2(grey area)

Let's consider the subsequence of S, $S[5 : 8]$. From Figure 4, $S[5 : 8]$ must align with one of the subsequences of Q within $Q[3 : 9]$ and the warping window, i.e. $Q[3 : 6]$, $Q[3 : 7]$, $Q[3 : 8]$, $Q[3 : 9]$, $Q[4 : 6]$, $Q[4 : 7]$, $Q[4 : 8]$, $Q[4 : 9]$, $Q[5 : 6]$ ...etc.

According to the above observation, we have the following Lemma.

Lemma 2 *If the time warping distance, for any global path constraints, between two sequences S and Q is within threshold ϵ, then for any given subsequence $S[i : j]$ of length l, there must exist at least one subsequence $Q[x : y]$, where $i - r \leq x \leq i + r$ and $j - r \leq y \leq j + r$, whose time warping distance with $S[i : j]$ agree within the same threshold ϵ.*

$$D_{tw}(S,Q) \leq \epsilon \Rightarrow \exists_{i,j,x,y}(D_{tw}(S[i:j],Q[x:y]) \leq \epsilon)$$
$$where \quad i - r \leq x \leq i + r \quad and \quad j - r \leq y \leq j + r \ (11)$$

In other words, if none of the potential subsequences of Q matches $S[i : j]$ within threshold ϵ, then S must not agree with Q within threshold ϵ. If there exist a subsequence of Q such that it matches $S[i : j]$ within threshold ϵ, then S may possibly agree with Q within threshold ϵ. In this example, $S[5 : 8]$ is aligned with $Q[3 : 7]$. The time warping distance between them is:

$$D_{tw}(S[5 : 8], Q[3 : 7]) = d(5,3) + d(6,4) + d(7,5) \\ + d(8,6) + d(8,7)$$

If we remove the duplicated elements (i.e. $(i,x),(i,y),(i,z)$ ...) in every row, e.g. $(8,6)$, we have:

$$D_{tw}(S[5 : 8], Q[3 : 7]) \geq d(5,3) + d(6,4) + d(7,5) \\ + d(8,7)$$

We define this operation as F_{rd}, i.e.

$$D_{tw}(S[i : j], Q[x : y]) \geq F_{rd}(D_{tw}(S[i : j], Q[x : y])) \ (12)$$

Furthermore, from (3), we have the following relation for each element of the warping path. Each s_u must align with one q_v, where $q_v \in \{q_{max(u-r,x)} \cdots q_{min(u+r,y)}\}$. For example, each element of $S[5 : 8]$ must align with at least one element of $Q[3 : 7]$ within the warping window, i.e. s_7 must align with q_5 or q_6 or q_7. By introducing this relation, we have the following inequality.

$$d(u,v) \geq \min\{d(u, max(u-r,x)) \ldots d(u, min(u+r,y))\}$$
$$\geq \min\{|s_u - q_{max(u-r,x)}| \ldots |s_u - q_{min(u+r,y)}|\}$$
$$\geq \begin{cases} |s_u - \max\{q_{max(u-r,x)} \cdots q_{min(u+r,y)}\}|, \\ \quad if\, s_u > \max\{q_{max(u-r,x)} \cdots q_{min(u+r,y)}\} \\ |s_u - \min\{q_{max(u-r,x)} \cdots q_{min(u+r,y)}\}|, \\ \quad if\, s_u < \min\{q_{max(u-r,x)} \cdots q_{min(u+r,y)}\} \\ 0 \quad otherwise \end{cases}$$
$$\equiv d_{lb}(u,v) \ \ (13)$$

We define the lower bound for each element as $d_{lb}(u,v)$. From (12) and (13), we have the following inequality:

$$D_{tw}(S[i : j], Q[x : y]) \geq F_{rd}(\sum_{u=i}^{j} d_{lb}(u,v)) \ \ (14)$$

Then, we construct a bounding rectangle for subsequences of Q based on the above observations. Given two subsequences $S[i:j]$ and $Q[x:y]$, where $l = Len(S[i:j])$ and $i-r \leq x \leq i+r$ and $j-r \leq y \leq j+r$, we regard $S[i:j]$ as an l-dimensional point. For any global path constraints, a query bounding hyper-rectangle(QBR) of l-dimension is defined by two endpoints, BL and BH, of its major diagonal, where $BL = (bl_1, bl_2, \ldots, bl_l)$ and $BH = (bh_1, bh_2, \ldots, bh_l)$ and $bl_i < bh_i$ for $1 < i < l$. An example of QBR is illustrated in Figure 5.

$$bl_{u-i+1} = \min\{q_{max(u-r,x)} \cdots q_{min(u+r,y)}\} \atop bh_{u-i+1} = \max\{q_{max(u-r,x)} \cdots q_{min(u+r,y)}\} \Big\}$$
$$for \quad u = i \ldots j \qquad (15)$$

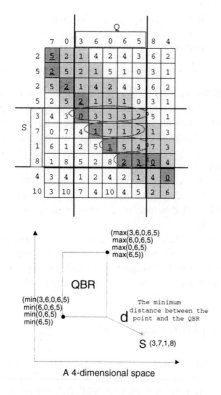

Figure 5. An example of the QBR.

Given a QBR, the ϵ-enlargement of the QBR, denoted by ϵ-QBR, is a QBR defined by $BL = (bl_1 - \epsilon, bl_2 - \epsilon, \ldots, bl_l - \epsilon)$ and $BH = (bh_1 + \epsilon, bh_2 + \epsilon, \ldots, bh_l + \epsilon)$. Then we have the following theorem:

Theroem 1 *Given two subsequences $S[i:j]$ and $Q[x:y]$, where $l = Len(S[i:j])$ and $i-r \leq x \leq i+r$ and $j-r \leq y \leq j+r$, if $S[i:j]$ is not contained in the ϵ-QBR of a QBR, then $D_{tw}(S[i:j], Q[x,y]) > \epsilon$.*

Proof: By contradiction,
Assume $S[i:j]$ is not contained in ϵ-QBR. If $D_{tw}(S[i:j], Q[x,y]) \leq \epsilon$, then from equation (14) we have,

$$F_{rd}(\sum_{u=i}^{j} d_{lb}(u,v)) \leq \epsilon \qquad (16)$$

By assumption, there exist a s_u such that,

$$\Rightarrow \begin{cases} s_u < \min\{q_{max(u-r,x)} \cdots q_{min(u+r,y)}\} - \epsilon \\ s_u > \max\{q_{max(u-r,x)} \cdots q_{min(u+r,y)}\} + \epsilon \end{cases}$$
$$\Rightarrow \begin{cases} |s_u - \min\{q_{max(u-r,x)} \cdots q_{min(u+r,y)}\}| > \epsilon \\ |s_u - \max\{q_{max(u-r,x)} \cdots q_{min(u+r,y)}\}| > \epsilon \end{cases}$$
$$\Rightarrow d_{lb}(u,v) > \epsilon$$

which contradicts with inequality (16), so that the proof is completed.

4.3. Merging all QBRs

By completing the above deduction, we can search for any subsequences that agree with the given query subsequence within the threshold. However, according to Lemma 2, we should perform searching for all possible query subsequences. One straightforward method is to traverse the index for every possible ϵ-QBR, but it is not efficient. To reduce the number of indexing searching, we can merge all the $QBRs$ into one single QBR. That is to define a minimum bounding box, which contains all the $QBRs$. Consider (15), as $i-r \leq x \leq i+r$ and $j-r \leq y \leq j+r$, we have:

$$u - r = \min \begin{cases} \max\{u-r, i-r\} \\ \max\{u-r, i+1-r\} \\ \vdots \\ \max\{u-r, i+r\} \end{cases} \qquad (17)$$

$$u + r = \max \begin{cases} \min\{u+r, j-r\} \\ \min\{u+r, j+1-r\} \\ \vdots \\ \min\{u+r, j+r\} \end{cases} \qquad (18)$$

Therefore, the large QBR is defined as follows:

$$bl_{u-i+1} = \min\{q_{u-r} \cdots q_{u+r}\} \atop bh_{u-i+1} = \max\{q_{u-r} \cdots q_{u+r}\} \Big\} for \quad u = i \ldots j \quad (19)$$

Figure 6 depicts this idea. By deducing this large QBR and Lemma 2. We generalize the "exact indexing" method [10], to handle subsequence queries of varying lengths as described in the following section.

5. Algorithm

In this section, we describe a subsequence searching method that is fast, guarantees no false dismissal and can handle query sequences of arbitrary lengths.

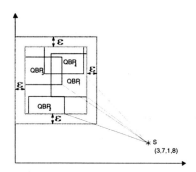

Figure 6. An illustration of merging all the QBRs

5.1. Index Construction

Given a set of data sequences $S = S_1, S_2, \ldots, S_l$ of different lengths, a sliding window of length l is placed and slid over each offset of each data sequence $S_i \in S$. Thus, a set of prefixes of length l of each possible subsequence will be extracted. The total number of subsequences is $\Sigma(Len(S_i) - l + 1)$. Every prefix with length l will be regarded as an l-dimensional point. To index a set of multi-dimensional points, we can use any spatial indexing technique, such as the R-tree [6], and the R*-tree [11]. In the following, we sketch the idea of indexing by R-tree, which uses hyper-rectangles as its minimum bounding volume. We choose R-tree because it is widely used and its behavior is well understood in the database community. A non-leaf node of R-tree contains entries of the form $< MBR_i, PTR_i >$, where MBR_i is the minimum bounding rectangle of the ith child node and PTR_i is the pointer pointing to the ith child node. A leaf node contains entries of the form $< SID'_i, S'_i >$, where S'_i is one of the prefixes of sequence S_i and the corresponding identity is SID'_i. Each MBR is represented by two end points, L and H, of its major diagonal, where $L = (l_1, l_2, \ldots, l_n)$ and $H = (h_1, h_2, \ldots, h_n)$ and $l_i < h_i$ for $1 \le i \le n$.

5.2. Searching subsequences of arbitrary lengths

Here we show how to search for subsequences that match the query sequence Q within threshold ϵ. We call this method 'IDTW-SSM'. If the length of the sliding window is l, the minimum query length is $l - r$. The proof is as follows:

Proof: Assume that we have a query Q, such that $Len(Q) < l - r$. If there exist a subsequence that matches

Q within threshold ϵ. By Lemma 2, we have:

$$D_{tw}(S, Q) \le \epsilon \quad \Rightarrow \quad (D_{tw}(S[1:l], Q[1:y]) \le \epsilon)$$
$$where \quad l - r \le \quad y \quad \le l + r$$

which contradicts the assumption that $y < l - r$.

Algorithm 2 RangeQuery(T,ϵ-QBR)

1: C := {}
2: **if** T is not a leaf node **then**
3:    **for** each child node of T **do**
4:       **if** $IsOverlap(MBR_i, \epsilon\text{-}QBR)$ **then**
5:          RangeQuery(PTR_i,ϵ-QBR)
6:       **end if**
7:    **end for**
8: **else**
9:    **if** $IsContain(S'_i, \epsilon\text{-}QBR)$ **then**
10:       $C \leftarrow SID'_i$
11:    **end if**
12: **end if**

If the input query is longer than $l - r$, then by Lemma 2, we can extract a set of subsequences of Q, which are used to perform searching. A large ϵ-QBR can be constructed from these subsequences of Q. We can use the ϵ-QBR to carry out range query as stated in Algorithm 2. $IsOverlap$ is used to determine if MBR_i overlaps with the ϵ-QBR. If it is true, searching will continue on that MBR_i. $IsContain$ is used to determine if the point S'_i is contained in the ϵ-QBR. If it is true, SID'_i will be included in the candidate set.

The candidate set will then be used for post-processing. For each SID'_i in the candidate set, we will retrieve the corresponding subsequences (which have prefix S'_i) from the database, e.g. $S_i[j:k]$. If $D_{tw}(S_i[j:k], Q) \le \epsilon$, then $S_i[j:k]$ is a qualified answer.

6. Experimental Results

In this section, we present the experimental results of our proposed method. The data in our experiments are from the historical data of S&P 500 stocks, which were extracted from http://kumo.swcp.com/stocks/. We used the close price of 537 stock sequences with average length of 231. The system is written in 'C' and an R-tree with 16 dimensions is used to store the data points. We performed the experiments on Sun Ultra 5/360 with 256MB of main memory.

We carried out experiments to measure the performance of 'IDTW-SSM'. For each experiment, the query sequences were generated by selecting random subsequences from the database. For each query sequence, a threshold ϵ was given and searching was performed with that threshold. In each experiment, 10 queries were performed. We evaluate our method in different aspects:

1. Compare our proposed method 'IDTW-SSM' with sequential search.

2. Measure the indexing size by increasing the number of data sequences.

3. Evaluate the average CPU time by varying the size of warping window and threshold value.

6.1. Comparison with sequential search

We evaluated the average CPU time by increasing the number of data sequences from 2×10^4 to 11×10^4. The query length is 16 and ϵ is 16. Figure 7 depicts the results. It can be observed that the 'IDTW-SSM' outperforms the sequential search. For sequential search, the query sequence needs to compare with all data sequences, so the CPU time increases as the number of data sequences increases. For our proposed method, the CPU time also increases as the number of data sequences increases. This is because more branches of the R-tree are needed to be traversed as the number of data points increases.

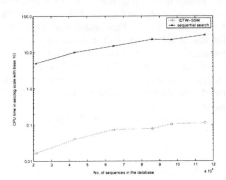

Figure 7. CPU time vs Number of data sequences

6.2. Index size vs Data size

Figure 8 shows the size of the index by increasing the number of data sequences. The size of the index increases from about 1MB to 4.5MB. The increasing rate of the indexing size is linear with respect to the number of data sequences. It is only about 320KB per 10000 data sequences.

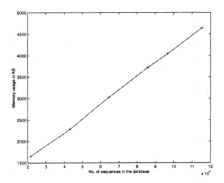

Figure 8. Index size vs Number of data sequences

6.3. Effects of warping window and threshold

We examined our method with different widths of warping window and threshold values. The query length is 16 and we use the full data set(537 stock) to perform our experiments. Figure 9 shows the CPU time of our method by varying the width of the warping window. The wider the warping window, the longer the CPU time is required. The similar behavior is observed in Figure 10, which delineates the CPU time by varying the threshold. The larger the threshold value, the longer the CPU time is required. This is because the query region depends on both the threshold and the volume of the QBR, which in turn depends on the width of the warping window.

7. Conclusions

Dynamic time warping is a more robust distance measure than Euclidean distance, but it does not satisfy the triangular inequality, so that it cannot be speeded up by indexing. Dozens of work proposed to use a lower bound function to facilitate the indexing structure. In this paper, we generalize the proposed method in [10], which is used to handle "whole sequence" matching under DTW. Our algorithm can handle subsequence matching of arbitrary length under DTW. We suggest an efficient approach, which guarantees no false dismissal and uses small space overhead. Our approach is based on the sliding window and the warping window constraints. Based on the sliding window approach, each prefix of all possible subsequences is indexed. For the query process, a set of potential subsequences are extracted from the query and a query bounding rectangle is formed to perform range query. Each answer in the candidate set will be examined by DTW to get the final answer. We show by experiment that our proposed method outperforms the traditional sequential search and uses small storage overhead.

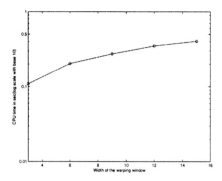

Figure 9. CPU time vs Width of warping window ($\epsilon = 16$)

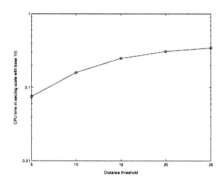

Figure 10. CPU time vs Distance threshold (width of warping window = 9)

From the experiments, we notice that the performance of the query process depends on the threshold and the volume of bounding rectangle(QBR). Therefore, we can further extend this work in these two directions. One of the ideas is to adopt the concept of 'MultiPiece' searching [4], which can reduce the threshold of each sub-query to $\epsilon/\sqrt{p}$. Furthermore, the QBR is very similar to the MBR. Thus we may try to form the $MBRs$ based on the warping window constraint for each possible subsequences. Then, the leaf nodes of the R-tree will contain $MBRs$ instead of points. Hence, the query sequence can be used directly as a multi-dimensional point in place of forming a bounding rectangle.

References

[1] R. Agrawal, K.-I. Lin, H. S. Sawhney, and K. Shim. Fast similarity search in the presence of noise, scaling and translation in time-series databases. *Proceedings of the 21st VLDB Conference*, pages 490–501, 1995.

[2] C. F. B. Yi, H. V. Jagadish. Efficient retrieval od similar sequences under time warping. *IEEE ICDE*, pages 201–208, 1998.

[3] J. Berndt, D. & Clifford. Using dynamic time warping to find patterns in time series. *AAAI-94 Workshop on Knowledge Discovery in Database*, pages 229–248, 1994.

[4] M. R. C. Faloutsos and Y. Manolopoulos. Fast subsequence matching in time-series database. *Proc. of the ACM SIGMOD Conference on Management of Data*, pages 419–429, 1994.

[5] M. J. P. Eamonn J. Keogh. Scaling up dynamic time warping to massive datasets. *Proceedings of the 3rd European Conference on Principles and Practice of Knowledge Discovery in Databases*, pages 1–11, 1999.

[6] A. Guttman. R-tree: A dynamic index structure for spatial searching. *Proc. ACM SIGMOD Conference on Management of Data*, pages 47–57, 1984.

[7] A. F. K. P. Chan. Efficient time series matching by watching wavelets. *15th IEEE ICDE*, pages 126–133, 1999.

[8] M. K. W. Chu. Fast time-series searching with scaling and shifing. *PODS*, pages 237–248, 1999.

[9] E. Keogh, K. Chakrabarti, S. Mehrotra, and M. Pazzani. Locally adaptive dimensionality reduction for indexing large time series databases. *SIGMOD*, pages 151–162, 2001.

[10] E. J. Keogh. Exact indexing of dynamic time warping. *VLDB*, 2002.

[11] R. S. N. Beckmann, H.-P. Kriegel and B. Seeger. The r*-tree: An efficient and robust access method for points and rectangles. *Proc. of the ACM SIGMOD COnference on Management of Data*, pages 322–331, 1990.

[12] M. H. W. P. Wan. Efficient and robust feature extraction and pattern matching of time series by a lattice structure. *Proceedings of the 2001 ACM CIKM*, pages 271–278, 2001.

[13] S. Park, W. W. Chu, J. Yoon, and C. Hsu. Efficient searches for similar subsequences of different lengths in sequence databases. *Proc.IEEE ICDE*, pages 23–32, 2000.

[14] S. Park, S.-W. Kim, J.-S. Cho, and S. Padmanabhan. Prefix-querying: An approach for effective subsequence matching under time warping in sequence databases. *CIKM 2001*, pages 255–262, 2001.

[15] C. F. R. Agrawal and A. Swami. Efficient similarity search in sequence databases. *Proc. of the Fourth Intl. Conf. On Foundations of Data Organization and Algorithm*, pages 69–84, 1993.

[16] L. Rabiner and B.-H. Juang. *Fundamentals of Speech Recognition*. Prentice Hall, 1993.

[17] D. Rafiei and A. Menedelzon. Similarity-based queries for time series data. *In Proc. ACM SIGMOD*, pages 13–24, 1997.

[18] W. W. C. S.-K. Kim, S. Park. An index-based approach for similarity search supporting time warping in large sequence databases. *IEEE ICDE*, pages 607–614, 2001.

[19] M. H. W. S. K. Lam. A fast project algorithm for sequence data seraching. *DKE 28(3)*, pages 321–339, 1998.

[20] W. W. C. S. Park, D. Lee. Fast retrieval of similar subsequences in long sequence databases. *Proc. IEEE KDEX Workshop*, 1999.

[21] S. Theodoridis and K. Koutroumbas. Pattern recognition. *San Diego : Academic Press*, 1999.

Neighborhood Signatures for Searching P2P Networks

Mei Li   Wang-Chien Lee   Anand Sivasubramaniam
Department of Computer Science and Engineering
Pennsylvania State University
University Park, PA 16802
E-Mail: {meli, wlee, anand}@cse.psu.edu

Abstract

Overlay networks have received a lot of attention due to the recent wide-spread use of peer-to-peer (P2P) applications such as SETI, Napster, Gnutella, and Morpheus. Through replications at numerous peers, digital content can be distributed or exchanged with high resilience and availability. However, existing P2P applications incur excessive overhead on network traffic. For example, Gnutella, which broadcasts queries to search shared content, suffers from an overwhelming volume of query and reply messages. In this paper, we investigate the issues of trading-off storage space at peers to reduce network overhead. We propose to use signatures for directing searches along selected network paths, and introduce three schemes, namely complete-neighborhood signature (CN), partial-neighborhood super-imposed signature (PN-S), and partial-neighborhood appended signature (PN-A), to facilitate efficient searching of shared content in P2P networks. Extensive simulations are conducted to evaluate the performance of our proposal with existing P2P content search methods, including Gnutella, Random Walk, and Local Index. Results show that PN-A gives much better performance at a small storage cost.

1 Introduction

The advent of facilities such as Napster [3] and Gnutella [1] has made the Internet a popular medium for the widespread exchange of resources and voluminous information between thousands of users. In contrast to traditional client-server computing models, these Peer-to-Peer (P2P) systems can employ the host nodes to themselves acting as servers for other nodes. Despite avoiding centralized server bottlenecks and single points of failure, the P2P systems present interesting challenges in locating data items among these numerous host nodes. The centralized server in Napster [3], which maintains a global index for all data items in the network, defeats the fundamental rationale of a P2P system.

One could control the placement of data among the nodes and/or exploit the topology of the P2P overlay network to perform certain kind of search ordering which can help in getting to the requested data items. CAN [11], Chord [13], Pastry [12], Tapestry [16] and P-Grid [4, 5] are examples of systems using such a strategy to control the number of hops that need to be traversed to get to the requested data items without flooding the network. However, the completely decentralized nature of P2P systems, which allow nodes and data items to come and go at will, makes the above techniques less suitable for these unstructured and dynamic environments, and are consequently not under consideration here.

There are two main strategies that have been proposed/explored for searching in decentralized and dynamic environments of P2P systems without relying on the network topology and data placement:

- **Strategy 1:** This strategy lets messages poll nodes, without having any idea of where the data may be held by the destination nodes, till the required items are found. Gnutella [1] and *random walk* [6, 10] use such a strategy. The down side of this strategy is the possible network overload due to a large number of generated search messages (Gnutella) or a long latency to satisfy a request (random walk).

- **Strategy 2:** This strategy maintains additional information in the network nodes (which Strategy 1 does not require) in order to reduce network traffic and/or the number of hop visits. Consequently, messages are directed specifically along paths that are expected to be more productive. The additional information is typically index over the data that are contained either within hierarchical clusters [2] or by nearby neighbors [7, 9, 14]. This indexing approach requires determining what attributes to index a priori and thus constraining the allowable search, in addition to the high space cost that is incurred in storing the index itself.

149

While Strategy 2 seems attractive in terms of message traffic, the downside is that the additional storage required can weigh on the actual implementation. In fact, one could argue that with infinite storage capacity, it is possible to replicate all availability information at every node, potentially leading to very efficient searches. While this is one extreme, at the other end are schemes in Strategy 1, which do not require any storage but incur high network costs for searches. Schemes which index neighborhood data in Strategy 2 fall in-between, trading off the storage requirements for the network overheads. We believe that this trade-off offers a rich space of mechanisms to explore, and we present/demonstrate a novel approach that uses *signature files* which can provide better message traffic behavior at a lower storage cost than index-based mechanisms within this space.

Signature methods have been used extensively for text retrieval, image database, multimedia database, and other conventional database systems. A signature is basically an abstraction of the information stored in a record or a file. By examining the signature only, we can estimate whether the record contains the desired information. Naturally, the signature technique is very suitable for filtering information stored in nodes of P2P systems. This paper presents three novel ways of using signatures, namely *complete neighborhood signature (CN), partial neighborhood superimposed signature (PN-S)* and *partial neighborhood appended signature (PN-A)*, to represent neighborhood data at network nodes for optimizing searches in P2P systems. Their merits in reducing network traffic are extensively evaluated for content search, node join, leave and update operations. These schemes are compared with the current state-of-the-art approaches, Gnutella [1] and Random Walk [6, 10] for strategy 1, and Local Index [14] for strategy 2. Our simulations show that the signature approaches are much better than these alternatives for most reasonable storage space availability assumptions on host nodes.

The rest of the paper is organized as follows. Next section presents the P2P system model and metrics. In Section 3, we presents details on our signature based search mechanisms. Section 4 gives the experimental setup for the evaluation and Section 5 details results from experiments under two different search criteria. Finally, Section 6 summarizes the contributions of this paper and outlines directions for future work.

2 Peer-to-Peer System Framework

A Peer-to-Peer (P2P) network[1] consists of numerous nodes (called *peers*) which connect to each other directly

[1]We use the terms, P2P systems, P2P networks and P2P applications, where appropriate. However, they are mostly interchangeable in the context of this paper.

or indirectly. The peers provide information resources to be shared with other peers. The shared information could be digital files such as music clips, images, pdf documents, or other forms of digital content. The P2P network is established by logical connections among the participating peers. Since the whole network is built through connections among the peers, its topology may change dynamically due to constant joins and leaves of the peers, namely *peer join* and *peer leave*, in the network. In addition, the shared information changes dynamically since the peers may update the digital content they offer, namely *peer update*.

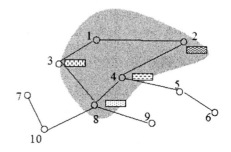

Figure 1. A partial snapshot of a P2P network.

Figure 1 shows a partial snapshot of a P2P network. In this figure, we use a vertex to represent a node (i.e., a peer) of the overlay P2P network and an edge to denote the connection between two peers. When a peer, A, has a direct connection with another peer, B, we call these two peers *neighbors*. In the network, a peer may reach another peer via one or a sequence of connections, called *paths*. The *path length* can be obtained by counting hops of connections. The *distance* between two peers is the minimal path length between them. For example, as illustrated in Figure 1, there are two paths of length 3 and 4, respectively, between node 1 and node 9. Thus, the distance between node 1 and node 9 is 3.

Traditionally, a peer knows its neighbors through direct connections. In this paper, we generalize the concept of neighbors to *neighborhood*, which includes all the peers reachable within a given distance. Following this definition, the *neighborhood radius* refers to the distance from a peer to the edge of its neighborhood. The shaded area shown in Figure 1 illustrates a neighborhood of radius 2 (consists of node 2, 3, 4, 8) for node 1.

2.1 Searches in P2P Networks

As mentioned above, P2P networks have been widely used for digital content sharing among the participating peers. Thus, efficient search of the shared content is one of the primary functions of the P2P networks. A user may initiate a search of digital content from any peer in the network. The search message is forwarded to all or a subset of its neighbors to extend the search. In order to prevent indefinite search in the P2P network, a stop condition is usually specified in the query. The following are two conditions that are typically used to stop excessive spreading of a search:

- **Maximum search depth**: This stop condition is used in Gnutella [1]. A preset time-to-live value (TTL) is included in the search message to keep track of maximum remaining search depth. Each time a search message is forwarded to a neighbor, its TTL is decreased by 1. Once the TTL reaches 0, a search message is dropped.

- **Minimum number of results**: This stop condition is used in random walk [6, 10]. Different from the first case, the total number of results (TNR) found so far is included in the search message. Each time a result is found, the TNR is increased by 1. The search is stopped when the total number of results reaches a system defined value.

2.2 Metrics

Since the primary issue investigated in this paper is the trading-off of storage space for reducing network traffic, we use the following metric to evaluate various P2P search techniques discussed in this paper:

- **Total message volume:** For signature schemes (as well as index schemes), besides the traffic incurred for search, additional traffic is incurred as construction/maintenance cost of auxiliary information at peers. In order to have fair comparison among different approaches, we use *total message volume*, the product of total number of messages and the size of different messages (including search messages and messages incurred for signature maintenance during peer join/leave/update), as the performance metric.

3. Neighborhood Signatures

In this section, we first provide some preliminary background on the signature method and then extend it for search in P2P networks. We propose three neighborhood signature schemes, *CN, PN-S*, and *PN-A*, to index the content offered within the neighborhood of a peer. This helps direct the search to a subset of the nodes, which are probabilistically more productive, while not requiring as much storage as index approaches. We describe the formation of the signatures for each scheme and then provide detailed algorithms for search and signature maintenance under various scenarios (i.e., peer join, peer leave, and peer update).

3.1 Preliminaries

Signature techniques have been widely used in information retrieval. A signature of a digital document, called *data signature*, is basically a bit vector generated by first hashing the attribute values and/or content of the document into bit strings and then superimposing them together[2]. Figure 2 depicts the signature generation and comparison processes of a digital file and some searches.

MP3 File: Title: Heartbreak Hotel, Artist: Elvis Presley

Heartbreak	001 000 110 010
Hotel	000 010 101 001
Elvis	000 100 011 110
Presley	101 000 100 001
Data Signature (V)	101 110 111 111

Search	Search Signatures	Results
Eagles	000 101 001 101	No Match
Elvis	000 100 011 110	True Match
Beatles	100 100 011 100	False Positive

Figure 2. Illustration of Signature Generation and Comparisons.

As illustrated in the figure, to facilitate search, a *search signature* is generated in a similar way as a data signature based on the search criteria (e.g., keywords) specified by a user. This search signature is matched against data signatures by performing a bitwise *AND* operation. When the result is not a match (i.e., for some bit set in the search signature, the corresponding bit in the data signature is NOT set), the corresponding document can be ignored. Otherwise, there are two possible cases. First for every bit set in the search signature, the corresponding bit in the data signature is also set, and the document is indeed what the search is looking for. This case is called a *true match*. In the second case, even though the bits may match, the document itself does not match the search criteria. This case, which occurs due to certain combinations of bit strings generated from various attribute values, keywords, or document content, is called *false positive*. The space devoted to the signature can influence the probability of false positives. Obviously the matched documents still need to be checked against the search criteria to distinguish a true match from a false positive.

3.2. Proposed Signature Schemes for P2P System

Before proceeding to introduce the proposed signature schemes, we first assume that a *local signature* is created at each peer of a P2P network to index the local content available at the peer. By doing this, search over the local content of a peer is processed efficiently. Furthermore, A peer

---

[2]In this paper, we use the term, *superimposing* to denote a bitwise *OR* of the bitstrings.

may collect and maintain auxiliary information regarding digital content available within a specific network distance (i.e., its neighborhood). Therefore, a peer can filter unsatisfiable search requests before forwarding them to a neighbor. Based on this idea, we propose three signature schemes classified as follows:

- **Complete Neighborhood (CN):** One intuitive approach is to index all the content available within the neighborhood of a peer. Thus, a *complete neighborhood (CN) signature* is generated by superimposing all the local signatures located within the neighborhood of a peer. Figure 1 shows a partial snapshot of a P2P network with the local signatures of peer 2, 3, 4, and 8 represented by rectangles with different filling patterns. Figure 3(a) shows an example of a complete neighborhood signature for peer 1, which indexes all the content available at peers 2, 3, 4, and 8. By holding a complete neighborhood signature, a peer can determine whether the search should be extended in its neighborhood or simply forwarded to some peers outside of its neighborhood.

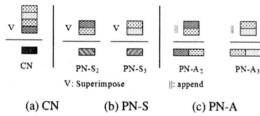

(a) CN (b) PN-S (c) PN-A

Figure 3. Illustration of neighborhood signature generation: (a) CN; (b) PN-S; (c) PN-A

- **Partial Neighborhood (PN):** While the CN scheme has the advantage of jumping out of a neighborhood when the search and neighborhood signatures do not match, it has to forward the search to all of its neighbors when there is a match between the neighborhood signature and search signature. Thus, instead of indexing the complete neighborhood, a signature can be generated to index a *partial neighborhood* branching from one of the neighbors directly connected to a peer. A *partial neighborhood signature* is generated for each of the neighbors. The search will only be extended to the neighbors whose associated partial neighborhood signatures have a match with the search signature. There are two alternatives for generating partial neighborhood signatures:

  - **Superimpose (PN-S):** In this approach, we use the traditional superimposing technique. Thus, all of the local signatures located within a neighborhood branch are compressed into one signature, called *PN-S signature*. Figure 3(b) shows

that peer 1 has 2 PN-S signatures, where $PN\text{-}S_2$, the neighborhood signature for branch 2, indexes all the contents available at peer 2 and 4 and $PN\text{-}S_3$, the neighborhood signature for branch 3, indexes the contents available at peer 3 and 8.

  - **Append (PN-A):** The superimposing technique has been shown to be effective in compressing a large amount of index information while supporting efficient information filtering function. However, this compression comes at the cost of losing some information, i.e. when the PN-S signature at a node matches, it does not give a clue of which peers should be visited, resulting in searching all of these peers. An alternative that we propose, called *PN-A Signature*, is to append (concatenate) all of the local signatures within a branch of the neighborhood into a partial neighborhood signature[3]. When a search signature matches with some sub-signatures within a PN-A signature, the search message will only be forwarded to these peers associated with the matched sub-signatures. Figure 3(c) shows that peer 1 has 2 PN-A signatures, where $PN\text{-}A_2$ indexes all the contents available at peer 2 and 4 and $PN\text{-}A_3$ indexes the contents available at peer 3 and 8.

3.3. Search Algorithms

The neighborhood signature schemes are generic mechanisms that can adapt to different search philosophies and protocols. As explained in Section 2, the Gnutella flooding approach uses the maximum search depth while the random walk uses the minimum number of results as the criteria for limiting message propagation. In order to compare the signature schemes with local index in Strategy 2, and Gnutella (which uses flooding) as well as random walk (which visits randomly chosen nodes one after another) in Strategy 1, we discuss the signature based search algorithms for the following two philosophies: flooding/maximum-depth and single-path/minimum-result. For clarity of our presentation, we use x to denote the radius of a neighborhood.

3.3.1 Flooding Search

In this section, we describe how a peer utilizes neighborhood signatures to perform searches based on maximum search depth as the stop condition. Since the search algorithms for the three proposed signature schemes are similar, we use Algorithm 1 to detail the flooding search at a peer

---

[3]An append-based CN signature can be generated by simply appending all of the partial neighborhood signatures, and is thus not proposed as a separate method.

based on CN signatures and point out the differences for the PN signatures afterwards.

This algorithm is invoked when a search message is initiated or received at a peer node of a P2P network. This search message comes with a time-to-live (*TTL*) counter which was preset to the maximum search depth that this message may be forwarded. The peer first computes a search signature to compare with the local signature. If there is a match, the content at this peer node is examined to determine whether this is a a true match or a false positive. If this is a true match, a pointer to the result is returned back to the peer from which this node got the request. Next, the peer checks the *TTL* to see whether the edge of the search neighborhood has been reached (i.e. *TTL* = 0), and if so, the search message is dropped. Otherwise, the search signature is compared with the neighborhood signature. If there is a match, the search is extended to all of the neighbors by forwarding the message with *TTL* decreased by 1. If the search signature does not match with the neighborhood signature, the peers located within x hops away (the neighborhood) need not be checked. As a result, the search message is dropped when $TTL \le x$. In this case, the search should be processed only at the peers x + 1 hops away. Here we assume that a peer has the knowledge of its peers at x + 1 hops away so that it may forward the search messages directly.

The flooding search algorithms for the two partial neighborhood (PN) signature schemes are only slightly different from the one discussed above (refer to line 14-19).

When a search signature matches with a PN-S signature, the search message is forwarded to the associated neighbor. Otherwise, the message is forward to the peers x + 1 hops away, located right outside of the partial neighborhood corresponding to the compared neighborhood signature.

The comparison of a search signature with a PN-A signature is performed by matching all of the included local signatures. For every matched local signature, a search message is directly forwarded to the corresponding peer node. If the search signature does not match with a PN-A signature, similar to PN-S, the search message is forward to the peers x + 1 hops away, located right outside of the partial neighborhood corresponding to this neighborhood signature.

3.3.2 Single-Path Search

In this section, we describe how a peer utilizes neighborhood signatures to perform single-path search based on the minimum number of results as the stop condition (for comparison with random walk). Due to space constraints, we omit the detailed algorithm here. The main difference between single-path search and flooding search is that if all of the neighborhood signatures do not match with the search signature, a peer located x + 1 hops away is randomly selected to extend the search. A system parameter *TNR* indicating total number of results found so far has the similar role as *TTL* in flooding search.

For CN signature, if the neighborhood signature matches with the search signature, all neighbors are possible candidates for true matches. In order to determine whether the match is a true match or not and how many results are there in the neighborhood, the search should be extended in the neighborhood for checking (called *neighborhood checking*). The difference among the single-path search algorithms for CN, PN-S and PN-A is similar to what we observed for flooding search. If there are signature matches, the neighborhood checking messages are only forwarded to the neighbors with matched neighborhood signatures in PN-S, or directly to the peers with matched local signatures in PN-A.

3.4 Signature Construction and Maintenance

After describing how the search is performed with neighborhood signatures, we next move on to discuss the construction and maintenance of these signatures. Basically, neighborhood signature(s) are constructed at a peer node when the peer newly joins a network. The neighborhood signatures of a peer will need re-constructions or updates when some peers join/leave its neighborhood or when some peers in its neighborhood (including itself) update their content. Thus, we describe the actions to be taken at peer join, peer leave, and peer update.

- **Peer join:**

  A new peer informs its arrival by sending a join message including its local signature to the peers in the neighborhood. When a node receives such a join message, it first adds (either superimposes or appends) the local signature in the join message to the corresponding neighborhood signature, then sends back its own local signature to the new peer so that the new peer can construct its neighborhood signatures. Besides this, some peers that were not in the neighborhood earlier, may be brought into this neighborhood through the connections of the newly joined node (when the new node joins the network through multiple connections and the neighborhood radius is greater than one). In this case, these peers also need to exchange signatures via the newly joined node to maintain the accuracy of their neighborhood signatures.

- **Peer leave:** When a peer leaves the network, it informs the neighbors by sending out a leave message. For PN-A, the leave message contains the node identifier of the leaving peer. The update on neighborhood signatures for PN-A only requires removing the signature of the leaving peer from the neighborhood signatures. For CN or PN-S, this step is more complicated. Since there is no simple way to remove the local signature of the leaving peer from the CN and PN-S signatures which are generated by superimposing, the affected peers in the neighborhood have to re-construct their neighborhood signatures from scratch. In order to construct a new CN neighborhood signature, the affected peer asks for individual signatures from the peers in the neighborhood. Slightly different from CN, for PN-S, the affected peers only need to ask for individual local signatures from the peers on the affected branch.

- **Peer update:** When a peer updates its data content, the local signature is updated accordingly. The procedure for updating the neighborhood signatures for CN and PN-S is the same as peer leave since new neighborhood signatures need to be constructed. For PN-A, the affected peers only need to update the relative sub-signatures in their neighborhood signatures.

4. Simulation Parameters

Simulation based experiments have been conducted to evaluate the performance of our proposed approaches with existing P2P search techniques such as Gnutella, random walk, and local index. We consider two different network topologies, *uniform* and *power-law*, which have been studied in related work as well [10, 14]. Based on [8], we set the power-law topology using an exponential efficiency of 1.4.

For both network environments, we consider two different data distribution patterns, uniform and nonuniform data distribution. Under uniform data distribution, each node holds the same number of data items. Under nonuniform data distribution, 80% data items are distributed among 20% of the nodes, called as *popular peers*, and the remaining 20% data are distributed among the remaining 80% nodes, called as *unpopular peers*. In addition, by assuming that there are 1000 peers pre-existing in a P2P network, the simulations are initialized by generating signatures for these initial 1000 peers. Then, we inject a large number of operations - a randomized mix of search, peer join, peer leave, and peer update - into the P2P network in each experiment. The relative proportion of these operations has also been considered.

We vary several system parameters, such as neighborhood radius, storage size, key attribute size, number of data items at a peer, relative proportion of different operations, and the average number of replicas per data in the network. In subsequent discussions, *search/update ratio* indicates the proportion of search operations to the other operations that require signature maintenance (i.e., peer join, peer leave and peer update), and *replication ratio* is defined as the number of replicas per data divided by the total number of peers in the network.

Now we present the parameters and their values used in the simulations with the justification for these choices.

- **System parameter settings:** The average number of shared files per peer has been observed to be around 340 in [14], and so we set number of data items per peer to 400. *Key attributes*, which contain the key value(s) of data items in various forms, e.g., binary music clip, keywords, integers, etc, are used for evaluation of search criteria. Since the size of data items itself is not a significant factor in differentiating the schemes under investigation, we use *size of key attribute* as an important parameter to characterize data items. In most of our experiments, we use 4 bytes as a default for the size of key attribute (i.e., we assume a single value attribute unless specified). We also ran experiments by increasing the size of key attribute (i.e., to represent a multi-key composite attribute or a complex attribute with binary data such as music clip) and the number of data items per peer in order to observe their impacts on different search approaches. To simulate a generic environment in P2P systems, we use synthesized key attributes generated by a random number generator in the simulation. The average number of neighbors is set to 4, which is consistent with the average node degree in Gnutella [15]. In P2P network, if a message traveling through an edge reaches a peer that has seen the same message before, this edge closes a cycle and we call this kind of edges *redundancy edges*. On the average about 30% of the searches are dropped due to cycles in the network, so we set the ratio of redundant edges to 30%.

- **Stop condition settings:** The maximum search depth is set to 7 in Gnutella. However, some detailed studies on Gnutella networks concluded that the network diameter is about 4 [8]. So we set the maximum search depth to 4 for power-law networks. We ran some preliminary experiments and found out that in order to achieve the same coverage for searching in both network topologies, the maximum search depth should be set to 5 in uniform network. While the replication ratios are varied in the single-path search, we set the minimum number of results to 1 in these experiments.

5. Simulation Results

In this section, simulation results for flooding and single-path search are presented. For each of these search methodologies, we present results with power-law network topology under uniform data distribution as well as nonuniform data distribution. We have also conducted simulation based on uniform network topology. The general trend observed from the results with uniform topology are similar to the one with power-law topology, so we omit it due to space constrains.

In the flooding experiments, we compare our signature mechanisms with Gnutella and local index, while in the single-path search we compare with random walk and local index. Total message volume, as discussed in Section 2.2, is used as the primary performance metric in our simulation.

5.1. Flooding

In the following experiments, we first vary the neighborhood radius and storage size to compare the performance of the proposed signature methods and to determine the best settings of those two parameters for the signature schemes. Then, we show the impacts of the other parameters as mentioned in Section 4 on performance of Gnutella, local index, and our signature methods. In the experiments, unless explicitly specified, search/update ratio is set at 10. We first present the results under uniform data distribution and then compare with the results under nonuniform data distribution.

Optimal neighborhood radius: Table 1 shows the values of neighborhood radius that give the lowest message volume for the given storage size (referred to as optimal radius). For CN and PN-S, the optimal radius is 1 for all considered sizes as shown in Table 1. The reason is that when the signature size is small, join/leave/update cost is small and query cost dominates the total message volume (figures are omitted due to space constraints). A small neighborhood radius forces less information superimposed together

and results in low false positive probability, thereby incurring lower total message volume. When the storage size increases, the cost of join/leave/update dominates the total cost and a smaller neighborhood radius results in lower join/leave/update message volume, providing the best results again. The latter effect (overhead of join/leave/update) is less significant for PN-A, making a larger neighborhood radius more preferable in this scheme when storage size is large, as shown in Table 1.

Table 1. Flooding: optimal neighborhood radius that generates the minimum total message volume for different storage sizes.

Storage size	0.064	0.256	1	6.4	25.6	83.2	256
CN	1	1	1	1	1	1	1
PN-S	1	1	1	1	1	1	1
PN-A	1	1	1	2	3	3	2

Size of Key Attribute: Figure 4 shows the total message volume with different sizes of key attribute. The y-axis is on a logarithmic scale for readability. In this simulation, we use increased attribute sizes to represent the situations where the (logical) key attribute consists of multiple keys or contains binary data (e.g., music clip). The values shown here uses a given storage size (i.e., 6.4KB) and a fixed number of data items per node (i.e., 400). Thus, by increasing the size of key attribute at a data item from 4 bytes to 1.6KB, the storage/total-attribute-size ratios at a peer for the chosen points in the figure are decreased from $400\%, 100\%, 50\%, 10\%, 5\%$, down to 1%[4]. It can be observed from the figure that the signature approaches outperforms Gnutella and local index significantly as the attribute size becomes large (i.e., the storage/total-attribute-size ratio becomes small). For instance, when the attribute size for each data item is 1.6KB (i.e., storage/total-attribute-size ratio is 1%), the total message volume for PN-A is merely 14% compared to Gnutella and local index. The total message volume for Gnutella increases as the size of key attribute increases, because the search message contains the attribute value(s). Local index performs well when the attribute size is small. However, as the attribute size increases, the given storage size is not sufficient to index all data items[5]. Therefore, local index's performance is the same as Gnutella approach for larger attribute size.

Number of Data Items: Figure 5 shows the total message volume as we allow the number of data items

---

[4]The storage/total-attribute-size ratio can be interpreted as the storage overhead normalized according to the total size of the key attributes of data items.

[5]The minimum storage overhead for local index is 6.4KB, 25.6KB, 51.2KB, 256KB, 512KB and 2560KB, respectively, for each of the points in Figure 4.

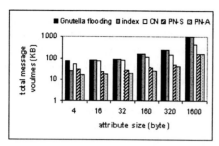

Figure 4. Flooding: effect of key attribute size on signature approaches. The y-axis is on logarithmic scale for readability.

per peer to increase from 100 to 160000. With a fixed storage of 6.4KB at each peer, the storage/total-attribute-size ratios for the chosen data points in Figure 5 are 1600%, 400%, 100%, 50%, 10%, 5%, 1%, respectively. As shown in the figure, local index outperforms PN-A only when each peer has merely 100 data items (i.e., the storage/total-attribute-size ratio is 1600%). On the other hand, the partial neighborhood signatures performs extremely well as the number of data items per peer increases rapidly. However, when the number of data items is overwhelmed, (e.g., > 16000), extra storage size should be allocated for signatures to reduce their false positive probability and the total message volume. Different from the previous figure, the total message volume for Gnutella remains as a constant since the attribute size for each data item is fixed.

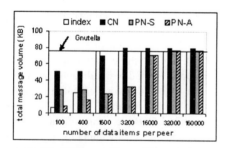

Figure 5. Flooding: effect of number of data items per peer on signature approaches. The total message volume of Gnutella is shown by the horizontal line.

Observed from the above two figures, it is obvious that the partial neighborhood signatures are much more storage efficient and flexible than local index. With very little storage overhead, the partial neighborhood signatures can facilitate focused search effectively while local index has some minimal storage requirement.

Search/Update Ratio: Figure 6 shows the optimal total message volume of PN-A (CN and PN-S exhibit similar behavior) with different search/update ratios. We can see that when the storage size is small, the differences are in-

significant. However, when the storage size becomes large, the total message volume with lower search/update ratios is significantly higher than that with high search/update ratios due to the high cost of join/leave/update operations at these sizes.

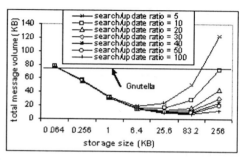

Figure 6. Flooding: effect of search/update ratio on signature approaches. Total message volume of Gnutella is shown by the horizontal line.

Message Volume and Storage Tradeoff: Figure 7 compares the performance of the three signature schemes with the index based approach, along with the Gnutella shown as a solid horizontal line, by increasing storage size. From the figure, we can observe that with storage size as small as 256 bytes, the signature schemes can reduce message traffic by over 25% compared to the Gnutella flooding approach. With a higher storage capability, PN-S and PN-A produce even further savings. On the other hand, the local index approach starts outperforming Gnutella only beyond 1KB. At this point, while traffic incurred by index is comparable to Gnutella, CN, PN-S and PN-A incur only 77%, 45% and 42% of the Gnutella traffic. With a storage size of 6.4KB, all three signature schemas provide further savings, and so does the local index. However, the message volume of PN-A is only 67% of local index's traffic at this point. As the storage space gets larger, index/signature construction and updates become more expensive (due to join/leave/update operations), causing their message volume to increase again. Even when the storage size keeps increasing, the performance of PN-A is similar to local index. These results demonstrate that the signature approaches (particularly PN-A) can have better performance than the local index with a much smaller storage space requirement.

Data Distribution: Figure 8 compares the performance of Gnutella flooding, local index and three signature schemas under uniform and nonuniform data distributions (as specified in Section 4). In this comparison, storage size for index and signatures are set to be 6.4KB. For both Gnutella flooding and index approach, there is no performance difference under these two different data distributions. For the signature schemas, the total message volume

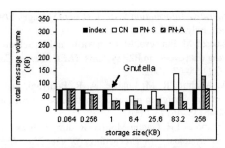

Figure 7. Flooding: total message volume comparison among local index, CN, PN-S and PN-A. Total message volume of Gnutella is shown by the horizontal line.

under nonuniform data distribution is increased a little bit. This can be explained by the increased false positive probability of the neighborhood signatures which are contributed by *popular peers*. One important observation from Figure 8 is that the performance of PN-A is better than local index under both uniform and nonuniform data distributions.

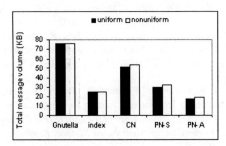

Figure 8. Flooding: effect of data distributions on Gnutella flooding, index and signature approaches.

5.2. Single-Path

In addition to the five parameters (neighborhood radius, storage size, key attribute size, number of data items, and search/update ratio) investigated in flooding search, we include one more parameter - replication ratio - in single-path search since the performance of search with minimum number of results as search stop condition can rely heavily on the number of replicas in the system. Similar to flooding where we compared the schemes with Gnutella and local index, we compare the performance of the proposed signature approaches with random walk and local index. The results are similar to that observed for flooding. Due to space constrains, we only present the comparison among random walk, index and signature schemas when the storage size and replication ratio increases, respectively.

Message Volume and Storage Tradeoff: Figure 9 shows the total message volume comparison between ran-

dom walk, local index, CN, PN-S and PN-A. Once again, we find the signature schemes (PN-A in particular) are able to incur lower message traffic in retrieving the required number of data items at a much lower storage cost than local index.

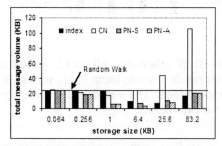

Figure 9. Single-path: total message volume comparison among local index, CN, PN-S and PN-A. Total message volume of random walk is shown by the horizontal line.

Replication Ratio: Figure 10 compares random walk, local index and PN-A for different degrees of replication of data items in the network. The y-axis is on a logarithmic scale for readability. In these experiments, both local index and PN-A are run with a storage size of 6.4KB (local index only starts to provide reasonable performance with storage size 6.4KB). At high degrees of replication, as expected, random walk can perform rather well, since there is a higher likelihood of finding the requested data items even when randomly traversing the network (without incurring any join/leave/update overheads). However, at lower degrees of replication it does much worse than the signature or index approaches which can direct searches in a more productive manner. Of these two approaches, we find that PN-A is more effective at reducing traffic even at very small degrees of replication. PN-A incurs an order of magnitude lower message traffic with respect to random walk under a replication ratio of 0.1% and only 17% of random walk traffic under a replication ratio of 0.5%. Compared to local index, PN-A incurs 29% of index traffic under a replication ratio 0.1% and 43% of index traffic under a replication ratio 0.5%.

6. Concluding Remarks and Future Work

Peer-to-Peer (P2P) applications such as Napster and Gnutella have made the Internet a popular medium for resource and information exchange between thousands of participating users. A primary consideration in the design of such applications is the high network traffic that they generate when searching for resources/information. We have proposed three new mechanisms based on signature files to facilitates search in p2p systems.

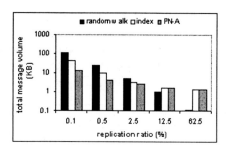

Figure 10. Single-path: effect of replication ratio on random walk, local index and signature approaches. The y-axis is on logarithmic scale for readability.

The schemes have been extensively evaluated and we uniformly find PN-A giving good savings in message volume over Gnutella, random walk and local index approaches at a small storage cost. In addition to the performance and storage savings with signatures, there are a couple of other advantages that they exhibit compared to index-based approaches: (a) Signature approaches can search across multiple attributes by appropriately encoding all the attributes when composing them, instead of being restricted to one or a small number of attributes which needs to be predetermined as in index approach. This facilitates keyword and content based search, etc. (b) It takes a certain minimum amount (threshold) of storage to compute (and store) an index. With storage size less than this threshold, index approach can not be used and we have to resort to broadcasts/flooding. On the other hand, signatures do not impose any such restrictions and can work with any amount of space allotted to them (though when the space gets too small the ability to focus the search diminishes, and in the worst case false positives can lead to flooding). All these observations lead us to believe that PN-A is an extremely popular mechanism for implementing resource and information lookup operations in P2P networks.

Our ongoing work is looking into reducing false positive effects in signatures by exploiting real data patterns. We are also looking into improving peer join/leave/update overheads, together with incorporating with other optimizations such as intermediate node caching and peer clustering. Finally, we are investigating P2P applications overlayed on wireless networks.

References

[1] Gnutella website. http://gnutella.wego.com.

[2] Morpheus website. http://www.musiccity.com.

[3] Napster website. http://www.napster.com.

[4] K. Aberer. P-Grid: a self-organizing access structure for P2P information systems. In *Sixth International Conference on Cooperative Information Systems (CoopIS)*, pages 179–194, Trento, Italy, 2001.

[5] K. Aberer, M. Punceva, M. Hauswirth, and R. Schmidt. Improving data access in P2P systems. *IEEE Internet Computing*, 6(1):58–67, 2002.

[6] L. A. Adamic, R. M. Lukose, A. R. Puniyani, and B. A. Huberman. Search in power-law networks. *Physics Review E*, 64:46135–46143, 2001.

[7] A. Crespo and H. Garcia-Molina. Routing indices for peer-to-peer systems. In *Proceedings of the 22nd IEEE International Conference on Distributed Computing Systems (ICDCS)*, pages 23–34, July 2002.

[8] M. A. Jovanovic, F. S. Annexstein, and K. A. Berman. Modeling peer-to-peer network topologies through "small-world" models and power laws. In *Telecommunications Forum (TELFOR)*, November 2001.

[9] J. Kubiatowicz et al. Oceanstore: An architecture for global-scale persistent storage. In *Proceedings of the 9th International Conference on Architectural Support for Programming Languages and Operating Systems (ASPLOS)*, pages 190–201, November 2000.

[10] Q. Lv, P. Cao, E. Cohen, K. Li, and S. Shenker. Search and replication in unstructured peer-to-peer networks. In *Proceedings of the 16th ACM International Conference on Supercomputing*, pages 84–95, June 2002.

[11] S. Ratnasamy, P. Francis, M. Handley, R. M. Karp, and S. Schenker. A scalable content-addressable network. In *Proceedings of ACM SIGCOMM*, pages 161–172, August 2001.

[12] A. I. T. Rowstron and P. Druschel. Pastry: Scalable, distributed object location and routing for large-scale peer-to-peer systems. In *Proceedings of the 18th IFIP/ACM International Conference on Distributed Systems Platforms (Middleware 2001)*, pages 329–350, November 2001.

[13] I. Stoica, R. Morris, D. Karger, M. F. Kaashoek, and H. Balakrishnan. Chord: A scalable peer-to-peer lookup service for Internet applications. In *Proceedings of ACM SIGCOMM*, pages 149–160, August 2001.

[14] B. Yang and H. Garcia-Molina. Improving search in peer-to-peer networks. In *Proceedings of the 22nd IEEE International Conference on Distributed Computing Systems (ICDCS)*, pages 5–14, July 2002.

[15] B. Yang and H. Garcia-Molina. Designing a super-peer network. In *Proceedings of the 19th International Conference on Data Engineering (ICDE)*, March 2003.

[16] B. Y. Zhao, J. D. Kubiatowicz, and A. D. Joseph. Tapestry: an infrastructure for fault-tolerant wide-area location and routing. Technical Report UCS/CSD-01-1141, Computer Science Division, U. C. Berkeley, April 2001.

Advanced Database
Techniques II

Implementing Views for light-weight Web Ontologies

Raphael Volz, Daniel Oberle, Rudi Studer

Institute AIFB
University of Karlsruhe (TH)
D-76128 Karlsruhe
Germany
email: {volz,oberle,studer}@aifb.uni-karlsruhe.de

Abstract

The Semantic Web aims at easy integration and usage of content by building on a semi-structured data model where data semantics are explicitly specified through ontologies. The use of ontologies in real-world applications such as community portals has shown that a new level of data independence is required for ontology-based applications. For example, the customization of information towards the needs of specific user communities is often need. This paper extends previous work [22, 21] on this issue and presents a view language for the fundamental data models of the Semantic Web, viz. RDF and RDFS, and how it can be implemented. The basic novelty of the view language is the semantically appropriate classification of views into inheritance taxonomies based on query semantics. Additionally, the underlying distinction between unary predicates (classes) and binary predicates (properties) taken in RDF/S is maintained in the view language. So-called external ontologies allow the integration of multiple source databases, offer control over the publishing of data and enable the generation of views spanning across databases.

1. Introduction

The vision of the Semantic Web incorporates distributed content that is machine understandable by relying on an explicit conceptual level. It builds on RDF [13], which is a semi-structured data model that allows the definition of directed labelled graphs. The required conceptual level is not given by a fixed schema, but rather by an ontology that specifies the formal semantics of content. For this purpose, RDF Schema (RDFS) has been devised as a particular vocabulary within RDF. It introduces a property-centric approach and allows to partition data into classes without expressing strict typing. Additionally, inheritance hierarchies on both classes and properties are provided.

The use of ontologies in real-world applications such as community portals has shown that they can enhance interoperability between heterogeneous information resources and systems on a semantic level. However, what has also become clear is that ontologies and thereby ontology-based applications themselves suffer from heterogeneity. This leads to difficulties when several communities try to establish a way of communication while using diverse ontologies. On the one hand, not all information that is accessible within one community (e.g. a department) might be intended to be accessible to other communities. On the other hand, overlapping content might be represented in different ways.

Therefore a new level of data independence is required to allow customization of information towards the needs of other agents, which can be achieved by exploiting database view principles.

Contribution of the paper In this paper we show how a view language that picks up the unique situation of data in the Semantic Web and allows easy selection, customization and integration of Semantic Web content can be implemented.

The central objective of this implementation is to acknowledge the underlying intention of the Semantic Web, i.e. adding explicit formal semantics to Web content. Therefore the implementation must ensure that views are classified to the semantically appropriate location in RDFS inheritance hierarchies.

Second, we maintain the underlying distinction between classes and properties taken in the ontology representation. This leads to a distinction of views on classes and views on properties. Hence, views can be composed and used within queries.

Third, our approach supports the construction of external ontologies by grouping views and base entities into new data sets to allow customization and integration of multiple databases towards application demands or other user communities.

Our approach facilitates data integration and usage and paves the way to Semantic Web information systems that nourish from various data sources and feed back into many different data sinks - like our SEmantic portAL (SEAL) [14]. Such a view mechanism for ontology-based semistructured data will be a crucial cornerstone to achieve many different exciting objectives. Examples for such objectives will be personalized access to metadata bases, authorization and the improved integration of ontologically disparate information sources - to name but a few.

The paper is structured as follows. Section 2 introduces the associated data model and ontology representation language proposed for the Semantic Web and discusses the query language that is used in our approach. In Section 3 the underlying design decision for an apt view language is presented. Then, Section 4 provides a brief look at the proposed view language and presents some example views. Section 5 introduces the notion of external ontologies that support the aggregation and integration of distributed data. Section 6 sketches the implementation issues before we talk about related work in section 7 and conclude.

2. The Semantic Web

2.1. RDF - A semi-structured data model

The underlying data model of the Semantic Web is the Resource Description Framework (RDF) [13]. It is a semistructured data model that was initially intended to enable the encoding, exchange and reuse of structured metadata describing Web-accessible resources. Data is encoded using so-called resource-property-value triples, which are also called statements.

Individual information objects are represented in RDF using a set of statements describing the same resource. Object identity is given via the uniform resource identifier (URI) that labels the resource [1]. This object identifier is globally unique.

A set of statements constitutes a partially labelled directed pseudograph[2] and is commonly called an RDF model. The fact that properties can have multiple values, e.g. 'x:email'[3] for the resource 'x:Rudi' in Figure 1, allows

---

[1]This can also be omitted creating so-called anonymous resources, e.g. the resource pointed to by 'x:name' in Figure 1

[2]We can speak of pseudographs since multiple edges between (possibly identical) nodes are allowed.

[3]For the sake of brevity, we use "x" to abbreviate a uniform resource identifier (URI) using XML namespaces. In a real world scenario, the "x"es would be replaced by URIs.

to combine statements from different RDF models very easily.

The data model distinguishes between two types of values. A value can either be another resource leading to object associations or may be a literal establishing object attributes. For example, in Figure 1 'x:Raphael' is a resource, whereas the name 'Volz' is a literal.

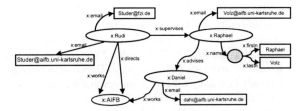

Figure 1. A simple, exemplary RDF model

2.2. RDFS – Light-weight ontologies

Ontologies provide a formal and shared conceptualization of a particular domain of interest. In the Semantic Web a light-weight (in comparison to classical knowledge representation languages) approach is currently in use. Ontologies are constructed from classes and properties. Both are embedded in a class and a property inheritance hierarchy. One of the proposed standards for the Semantic Web is RDF Schema (RDFS)[9][4]

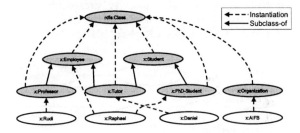

Figure 2. Class hierarchy in RDFS for a simple ontology

RDFS incorporates a unique notion of object orientation. It introduces classes and a subsumption hierarchy on classes (compare Figure 2). In RDFS subsumption allows for multiple inheritance and has set-inclusion semantics. As the subsumption establishes a partial order, class equivalence can be expressed via a cyclic class hierarchy. The extension of a class is defined by explicit assignment of resources to classes. A given resource can belong to several class extensions since multiple instantiation is allowed.

---

[4]A more expressive language in style of description logics is currently finalized by another W3C working group.

Attributes and associations are not defined with the class specification itself. Instead, such class properties are defined as first-class primitives, so-called properties, which exist on their own. Thereby classes do not specify types. Instances may have further (unspecified) properties and may also not use properties that were specified to be valid for their particular classes.

The definition of a property may include the specification of (multiple) domains and ranges. This defines the context, i.e. the class instances, in which a property may be validly used in an RDF statement. Multiple assignments have to be understood conjunctively. Therefore, a property can only be validly used on resources that are instances of all classes simultaneously. For example, in Figure 3 the property 'x:advises' has two domain classes: 'x:Employee' and 'x:PhD-Student', thus 'x:advises' is correctly instantiated in Figure 1 on 'x:Raphael' in Figure 1 (also cf. Figure 2 for class membership). The consistency of the constraints is maintained by entailing the appropriate class membership for resources when they are used in a property instantiation [12].

If the domain or range of a property is not defined, no entailments are made for the resource-value pair, e.g. this applies to 'x:responsible_for' in Figure 3. Properties may be placed into a subsumption hierarchy as well, e.g. in Figure 3 the property 'x:advises' is a specialization of the property 'x:responsible_for'. Property subsumption establishes a partial-order and has set-inclusion semantics as well. A query to the extension of the property 'x:responsible_for' to the data set of Figure 1 would therefore yield the two tuples (('x:Rudi','x:Raphael'), ('x:Raphael','x:Daniel')).

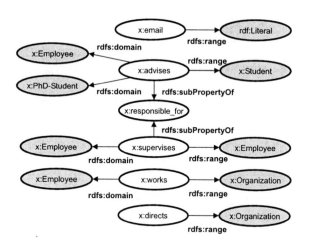

Figure 3. Properties in RDFS for a simple ontology

2.3. Query Language

We chose to extend RQL [3] with view primitives. RQL is the only RDF query language that takes the semantics of RDFS ontologies into account. The need to be aware of these semantics is the main reason why query languages operating on the syntactic XML-serialization (e.g. XQuery) also fail to meet our goals[5].

Due to lack of space, we can only give a short introduction to RQL in this section. The interested reader may refer to [3] for a more in-depth description.

RQL is a typed language following a functional approach (in style of OQL) and aims at querying RDF at the semantic level. Its basic building blocks are generalized path expressions which offer navigation in the RDF graph. The graph itself is viewed as a collection of elements which can be accessed in such path expressions. For example the following query would return the collection of all pairs of nodes which are related via the property email:

```
SELECT X,Y FROM {X}x:email{Y}
```

RQL queries follow the basic select-from-where construct known from SQL. The construct {X}x:email{Y} is called a basic data path expression and is the atom of all path expressions. The variables X and Y are bound to the resources and values of those RDF statements that use the property x:email. The {} notation is used in path expressions to introduce variables.

RQL permits the interpretation of the superimposed semantic descriptions offered by one or more ontologies. For instance, the inheritance hierarchy is considered when accessing class extents. Also path expressions can be concatenated by a ".", which is just a syntactic shortcut for an implicit join condition. The following query shows these features:

```
SELECT Y FROM Student{X}.x:advises{Y}
```

This query returns the identifiers of all students advised by other students. Since the class PhD-Student is a subclass of Student the above query would return "x:Daniel" for the RDF model depicted in Figure 1.

Furthermore, RQL supports set operators, such as union, intersection and difference. Boolean operations like $=$, $<$, $>$ can be used for selection in where-clauses.

3. Design of a view language

Views provide a new level of data independence and allow the required selection, customization and integration of data that is required for many Semantic Web applications.

---

[5]Additionally one would have to take care of the multiple syntactic variants that exist to represent the same data due to the RDF specification.

From the perspective of classical databases it is natural to consider views as arbitrary stored queries. Users should not be able to make a distinction between views and base data and should be able to state other queries or views on top of them. This mandates that the structure of views corresponds to the structure of base data.

However, in classical approaches to views (independent of the particular data model), no conceptual description of views are provided. Hence, the semantics of the view remain unclear to the agent. Since the Semantic Web builds on this very semantics, the semantics of the views must be described by an ontology and views must be embedded in the appropriate location of the inheritance hierarchies. This imposes the following requirements on a view language for ontology-based RDF data:

1. The structure of views must correspond to the structure of data. This results in the distinction between views on classes and views on properties. Hence, views can only involve queries which return either unary (views on classes) or binary (views on properties) tuples. RQL queries that return n-ary relations are therefore not allowed in view definitions.

2. The semantics of views have to be specified by an ontology and should be embedded in the respective inheritance hierarchies according to their semantics by classification. This classification must be part of every view definition.

3.1. Classification of views

Views have to be embedded into the inheritance hierarchies by explicit assignment. This imposes further work on the user. Therefore this burden should be taken from the user by deducing the appropriate classification from analysis of the query.

Unfortunately, this information cannot be deduced in all cases due to the undecidability of the general problem [17, 4]. However, the classification can be deduced automatically for many important queries. In our approach the required (and undecidable) analysis whether a particular query belongs to one of those special cases is avoided by introducing a special convenience syntax for each case. If these syntaxes are used the appropriate classification is automatically generated for the user.

Figure 4 provides an overview about the classification which is semantically correct for each algebraic operator. The illustrated classifications are motivated by the set-inclusion semantics of inheritance.

Selection always reduces the initial set and creates subsets. Therefore the class or property which is subject of the selection subsumes the view.

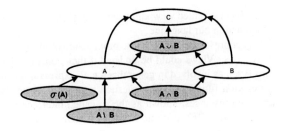

Figure 4. Placement of views in the hierarchy

Difference can always be rewritten into an equivalent selection (involving negation) on the minuend. Therefore the minuend subsumes the view.

Union unifies the extensions of classes or properties. Hence, the unified classes or properties are subsets of the view. Consequently, the view subsumes the unified classes or properties. The view itself is subsumed by the least common element in the respective inheritance hierarchy of all unified elements.

Intersection is a subset of the extents of all intersected classes or properties. Therefore every intersected class or property subsumes the view based on the intersection operation.

Join, negation and cross product do not introduce sub- or supersets wrt. to the interconnected classes or properties. Hence, the semantics have to be stated manually by the user. One exception are views on classes, where queries have to return unary results. Here, the join operator decomposes to selection[6]. The cross product operator does not have any effect wrt. the row that provides the unary result of the query[7]. Nevertheless the user has to stated even in this case which class or property is subject of the selection.

3.2. View Population and updates

Views that are created via this automatic classification are also updatable, since updates can be delegated to the involved classes or properties.

Since RDF uses object identifiers in form of URIs, updates on views could be propagated to base data. This requires that objects are preserved. Hence, views must be populated with base data. The generation of objects together with new instance identifiers, which is chosen in

---

[6]Since joins can be rewritten to a selection on the cartesian product. As we can only regard one row of the relation the results of the cartesian product vanish leaving the selection behind.

[7]Since duplicates are irrelevant with respect to the interpretation of the result since we regard the result as a set of instances

many object-oriented view languages (e.g. [5]), is therefore not applied in our language.

Object preservation allows the propagation of updates in many cases. Views could be updated if they don't involve joins (such as involved in generalized path expressions), or aggregation functions. The question where to put newly generated instances, known as the so-called interface resolution conflict [8], does not arise with RDFS ontologies since multiple instantiation is allowed.

For views based on the above-mentioned operations all updates are therefore propagated to the involved base classes or properties (cf. Figure 5). For example, if object x is deleted from $\cup(A, B)$ then x is deleted from both A and B. Any updates through a view are ultimately visible for views based on the union and intersection operations, since they automatically meet the query conditions afterwards. The latter is not necessarily true for selection-based views, since the updated data may not meet the query conditions anymore.

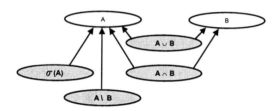

Figure 5. Update propagation

Updates are generally not permitted against elements of the ontology itself. Modifying or deleting classes and subclass relationships may invalidate view definitions, e.g. if a class is deleted. Inserts do not necessarily impose problems since they do not alter existing information. However, for union-based views, where the least common subsuming element is sought, a reclassification could be necessary. The same kind of problems arise with updates on property definitions. This problem is germane to schema evolution and not specific to the Semantic Web.

4. View Language

In this section we will describe the language constructs for creating class and property views as well as for external ontologies.

4.1. Views on classes

The definition of views on classes involves two components: First, users have to define an arbitrary RQL query. This query must return a set of resources, viz. unary tuples. This set of resources constitutes the instances that are in the

extent of the view. Second, the view must be properly classified in the class hierarchy. This enables the understandability of the view by using the semantics of the subclass relationship. The basic syntax for the definition of class views (cf. [22]) therefore involves these two components. For example, one could characterize the class of all "Wis. Mitarbeiter" consisting of PhD-Students that are employed and advise students at the same time:

```
CREATE CLASS VIEW x:WisMitarbeiter
   SUBCLASSOF x:Employee
   SUBCLASSOF x:PhD-Student
   USE
   (SELECT X FROM x:Employee{X})
   INTERSECT
   (SELECT X FROM
   x:PhD-Student{X},
   {Y} x:advises {Z}
   WHERE X = Y)
```

The fact that users can use arbitrary unary RQL queries within this syntax has two main consequences.

1. *Restricted Updatability* as it is impossible to decide where to propagate updates.

2. *Manual Classification* As users can combine arbitrary algebraic operations in the view[8] the semantic characterization of the view cannot be given automatically since this problem is undecidable [17, 4].

The latter fact leads to the introduction of additional possibilities to define views on classes conveniently where the classification can automatically be determined from query semantics. Consequently, the view language features convenience syntaxes which allow to define views via selection and set operations (i.e. union, intersection and difference). Multiple convenience syntaxes for selection are available, viz. rename, arbitrary selection and difference[9].

Convenience syntaxes are normalized into the above mentioned general syntax. The classification of the view, i.e. the creation of necessary subclassof statements, is automatically generated during the transformation. Besides, the appropriate RQL-query is created. Views which are defined in this way are additionally subject to the previously discussed updatability.

For example a class view "x:Scientist" which consists of professors as well as PhD-Students is created by the following definition:

```
CREATE CLASS VIEW x:Scientist
ON x:Professor UNION x:PhDStudent
```

---

[8]except for the default projection that fixes the arity

[9]As already mentioned, the difference operator can always be rewritten into an equivalent selection.

The translation of this definition into the standard form involves the computation of the least common super class of the unified classes.

With respect to our ontology example in Figure 2 no common superclass of "x:Professor" and "x:PhD-Student" can be found. Therefore the view has no super class and the subclassof statement is omitted in the translation. The generation of the RQL query which is used in the translated definition is straightforward:

```
CREATE CLASS VIEW x:Scientist USE
(SELECT X FROM x:Professor{X})
UNION
(SELECT X FROM x:PhD-Student{X})
```

The remaining convenience syntaxes can be found in [22].

4.2. Views on Properties

The declaration of views on properties involves the following:

1. an arbitrary, binary query[10]

2. the definition of the views' domains and ranges

3. embedding of the view into the property hierarchy

The following definition creates a new property view which relates all PhD-Students with the email addresses of advised students.

```
CREATE PROPERTY VIEW x:mails_of_advised
   SET DOMAIN x:PhD-Student
   SET RANGE rdf:Literal
   SUBPROPERTYOF x:email
   USE
   SELECT DOMAIN, RANGE
   FROM x:PhD-Student{DOMAIN}.
   x:advises{Y}.x:email{RANGE}
```

The updatability of views based on arbitrary queries cannot be automatically ensured. Furthermore, the consistency of the view definition with respect to constraints and property inheritance must be ensured at compile time (cf. section 6.4).

As the definition of property views involves quite a lot of information from the user, several convenience syntaxes are supported by our system, simplifying the construction of property views. Similar to views on classes, these short hand notations support automatic classification of the view

---

[10]Each tuple must be either (resource × resource) or (resource × literal) to reflect that literals cannot be in the domain of RDF properties

into the hierarchy. Additionally, appropriate domain and range constraints are generated.

For example, the following definition refines the property "x:email" from Figure 1 to carry only email addresses of Students.

```
CREATE PROPERTY VIEW x:student-mail
SET DOMAIN x:Student ON x:email
```

This can be automatically translated to the following standard property view definition:

```
CREATE PROPERTY VIEW x:student-mail
SET DOMAIN x:Student
SUBPROPERTYOF x:email
USE
SELECT DOMAIN, RANGE
FROM {DOMAIN} x:email {RANGE}
WHERE DOMAIN IN
(SELECT M FROM x:Student{M})
```

5. External ontologies

5.1. Motivation

Many typical Semantic Web applications such as community portals are characterized by the fact that they rely on more than one information source and collect information from many distributed sources in the web. Distributed information can be aggregated and combined easily due to the characteristics of the RDF model. The integrated information can be understood if all information providers have used the same ontology to mark up their data. Hence, information that is not presented according to the ontology of the consumer cannot be understood. This mandates a means to transform data such as provided by database views.

Accordingly, views should not only be applied on one data source, but on the integrated data of several data sources instead. This requires the ability to integrate information from several sources. A set of view definitions can then transform data outside of a particular data source.

The aggregated and transformed data is often intended to be republished as a new information artefact. Therefore it is necessary to be able to control which elements should be republished. This requires the adoption of the ontology. For example, the ontology should only talk about the aspects of the data that are visible, e.g. for security reasons.

5.2. Primitives

Figure 6 depicts the features offered by external ontologies. First, users can import classes and properties from multiple RDF databases and other external ontologies. Second, users may state new views on top of the integrated data

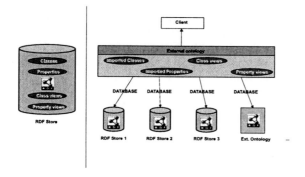

Figure 6. Classical and external ontologies approach

sources. View queries have access to all data not only the imported classes and properties. This allows to transform data without making the (raw) data itself visible to users.

One the one hand, this provides *external schemata* in the sense of the ANSI SPARC three-level architecture for databases, where applications or users can access a database through a specified subschema, e.g. to issue queries. On the other hand, this differs from the ANSI SPARC approach since external ontologies are hosted and specified completely outside of the data sources.

5.3. Example

The following example provides an external ontology that captures an administration perspective for a scientific department. This includes all information about people who actually receive payments. The view x:WorkingStudents grasps that students might employed by another faculty than the one they are enrolled in. The latter information would not be possible within an isolated faculty database.

```
CREATE EXTERNAL ONTOLOGY
x:HumanResources
DATABASE x:Faculty_1
DATABASE x:Faculty_2
IMPORT CLASS x:Scientist
IMPORT PROPERTY x:email
IMPORT PROPERTY x:supervises

CREATE CLASS VIEW x:WorkingStudents
ON x:Student INTERSECT x:Employee
```

The interested reader may refer to the normative syntax defined in [21].

6. Implementation

6.1. Storage of RDF

We use a standard relational database to store the physical RDF data. For each class, a separate unary relation is created, in which the particular instances of the class are stored. Furthermore, separate binary relations are created for each property, all triples[11] are then sorted on a per property basis and stored as (resource, value) pairs in these relations.

Please note, that this approach also creates six dedicated relations that store the ontology. Two of them are unary relations which store all class and property definitions. Besides, there are four binary relations storing the class and property hierarchies as well as the constraints for properties.

In our experience this physical representation outperforms the naive storage of RDF on a per triple basis within a single ternary relation with respect to read access. If updates are dominant for a RDF system the ternary representation is faster since it does not involve the generation and deletion of physical tables in the database.

Additionally the storage of data on a per class and property basis simplifies the integration of RDF data with legacy data. The latter can be done via the definition of unary and binary relational SQL views on top of existing database content. To realize this data access has to be realized via a catalogue component which determines the correct physical relation where property and class data is actually stored.

6.2. Realization of RDF Semantics

In order to speed up query processing all entailments supported by the RDF semantics specification [12] are materialized. This involves primarily the computation of transitive closure of the class and property hierarchies. All implicit members of classes and properties (e.g. instances of subclasses and subproperties) are stored in separate physical relations. The same is done for other entailments, e.g. for domain and range of properties.

This materialization of implicit information has to be maintained in case of updates. Insertions are easy to handle and simply require to compute the new closure resulting from the addition. Modifications and deletions are harder to handle. Trivially, we could simply recompute the whole materialization. More elaborate mechanisms such as implemented in the Sesame system [7] keep track of all the dependencies between statements (statement B was derived from statement A, etc.) and use this knowledge of the dependencies to determine which set of statements have to be

---

[11]except for those creating the class instance relationship, i.e. (x, rdf:type, <class>)

166

removed together. Naturally, this makes adding new statements slightly slower (since dependencies have to be computed and stored), but removing statements is a lot quicker.

6.3. Interpretation of queries

The implementation of the query language is straightforward because operations can be mapped easily to those offered by the relational algebra of the underlying database. Hence, operations are pushed down to the database. Consider the following query as an example. It returns all students working at AIFB, who are advised or supervised by someone:

```
SELECT Y
FROM {x} x:responsible_for
{y : Student}.works {z}
WHERE z = "x:AIFB"
```

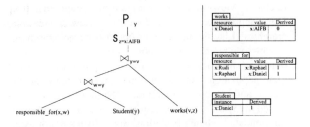

Figure 7. Query graph and involved physical db relations

First, the parser analyzes the syntax of the query, then the semantics of the query are captured via graph constructions. Figure 7 depicts the query graph of the above query. Then, this graph is translated into corresponding SQL queries, which are sent to the database engine:

```
SELECT responsible_for.value
FROM responsible_for, student, works
WHERE responsible_for.value =
student.instance AND
responsible_for.value =
works.resource AND
works.value = "x:AIFB"
```

During graph construction, the various shortcuts of RQL are expanded and variable dependencies are determined. The computation of the extents of classes and properties would involve the expensive computation of the transitive closure of the respective inheritance hierarchies. To avoid this and speed up read access, the transitive closure is computed with each update and materialized as mentioned before.

6.4. Realization of views

Views are created in a straightforward manner. First the provided convenience syntaxes are normalized into the general forms, creating the appropriate query, classification and constraints. Then the adequate tuples in the subclass-of and subproperty-of relations are created, respectively. For views on properties, additional tuples are created in the appropriate tables that store property constraints. Then, a relational view is created for each view whose query is the SQL query which was translated from the RQL query. Alternatively, we could store the normalized query in a dedicated relation and expand the queries issued by users with view queries in style of [20].

For views on properties additional consistency checks have to ensure that the returned tuples are actually instances of the specified domain and range constraints and that these constraints are compatible with respect to the constraints of super properties. While the latter is checked at compile time (cf. [16]), the first is implemented via a kind of type casting. It ensures that the domain and range can only take values that are in the extent of the specified classes. Hence, the RQL expressions of the following form are appended to the WHERE-clause of the RQL query for all specified domain and range constraints[12] before it is compiled into SQL:

```
AND DOMAIN IN (SELECT M FROM
CONSTRAINT_URI_i{M} )
```

6.5. Realization of External Ontologies

Since many user queries can only be answered by the integrated data, a materialized approach is chosen. Hence, all imported data is replicated and views are materialized. User queries are then processed in the normal manner.

The inheritance hierarchies of the external ontology have to be adopted to those classes and properties and views that are visible to the users. This is done by Algorithm 1 for the class hierarchy[13]. Following Figure 8, all inheritance information and is gathered from all sources and augmented with the information about the classification of views in the first step. Then, the full transitive closure of this merged inheritance hierarchy is computed. In the final, third step only the links that connect visible nodes remain.

The property hierarchy is computed in a similar fashion. Furthermore, the domain and range constraints for properties must be adopted to the visible classes, cf. [16] for the proposed solution.

---

[12]with the exception of literal ranges

[13]This algorithm is simplified, since the implementation can avoid unnecessary computation of the transitive close and has only to consider all upwards links from visible nodes, hence the algorithm can bring visible nodes into a topological order and do an incremental computation (unlike the presented algorithm)

Algorithm 1 Computation of the class hierarchy

Require: IC set of imported classes, CV set of class views, S set of RDF sources

$subclassof = \{\}$
for all $s \in S$ **do**
   $subclassof = subclassof \cup s.subclassof$
end for
for all $v \in CV$ **do**
   $subclassof = subclassof \cup v.subclassof$
end for
$subclassof = subclassof^*$
$newsubclassof = \{\}$
for all $c_1 \in (IC \cup CV)$ **do**
   for all $c_2 \in (IC \cup CV)$ **do**
      if $(c_1, c_2) \in subclassof$ **then**
         $newsubclassof = newsubclassof \cup (c_1, c_2)$
      end if
   end for
end for
Ensure: new class hierarchy ($newsubclassof$)

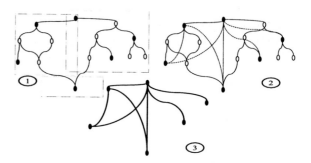

Figure 8. Steps in the computation of the class hierarchy. (1) merging all subclassof statements from all source databases, (2) computation of the transitive closure, (3) Keeping only links between visible classes

6.6. System Environment

The view language is currently implemented as an extension of the open-source RQL database system Sesame [7]. PostgreSQL is chosen as the relational database. Several technical details like the employed indexing techniques and translation of class and property URIs to the physically used names for tables have not been presented here.

A first implementation, described in [16] provides an in-memory variant of an earlier version of the view language and has been realized with the SiLRI F-Logic engine [10].

7. Related Work

There is a large body of work on views for the relational data model. These results are already incorporated in many database textbooks. Our approach differs substantially from the approach to views taken for the relational data model.

Also, we cannot rely on previous work about views for other semi-structured data models. The views of [23] consist of object collections only. Associations between objects - which are fundamental to RDF - are not considered. [2] do consider such edges, but do not provide semantic descriptions for views. Nevertheless our proposal is the only one that takes a superimposed conceptual model into account, viz. the ontology. Besides, consistency constraints such as situated by the RDF(S) data model are not considered in those approaches.

There is a large amount of work done on views for object-oriented data (e.g. [5, 1, 17, 18]). We have combined many aspects presented there. The proposition of external

ontologies and the terminology is similar to [8]. The idea to classify views in the hierarchy was first proposed in [18]. Other approaches, e.g. [5], do not mix view and class hierarchies. Like the majority of object-oriented approaches to views we mainly support object-preserving views. Many object-oriented approaches allow to support other forms of view population such as set-tuples (akin to the relational world) and of object-generation. The latter was first presented in [5] which present arguments such as its usefulness for simulated schema evolution. Some formation of external schemata was also proposed in [1, 18]. However, views can only be introduced in this context and not alternatively be added to the base database.

Generally those approaches do not fit an open world such as the Semantic Web. This is mainly due to the explicit typing of classes and local assignment of properties to classes taken in object-oriented databases. Web criteria such as the ability to base views on multiple data sources are not met either. Also property hierarchies are unknown to object-oriented models.

8. Discussion

We have presented a view mechanism that picks up the unique situation of data in the Semantic Web and implementation issues surrounding this mechanism. Our approach acknowledges the underlying intention of the Semantic Web - to add explicit formal semantics to Web content - and exploits the semantics of view definitions as far as possible to classify views into the semantically appropriate position in the entity hierarchies provided by RDFS. This allows agents to understand the semantics of the views autonomously. If the vocabulary of another ontology is used in the view definitions otherwise disparate ontologies are integrated by establishing is-a links between the classes and properties of both vocabularies leading to a proper articulation of both ontologies [15].

From our perspective, a view mechanism is an important step in putting the idea of the Semantic Web into practice. Based on our own experiences with building Semantic Web based community portals [14, 19] and knowledge management frameworks [6] we devise that view mechanisms for ontology-based semi-structured data will be a crucial cornerstone to achieve many different, exciting objectives.

Examples for such objectives will be personalized access to metadata bases in community portals, authorization and the improved integration of ontologically disparate information sources — to name but a few.

For the future much remains to be done. Currently, we are extending our view language towards a more expressive Web ontology language, DLP [11], which represents the intersection of Datalog and Description Logics. Additionally, we are investigating how updates can be consistently integrated for this extended Web ontology language. Furthermore, the materialization of views is of great importance in Web scenarios where read access to data is dominant, we are therefore also investigating how such materialized views can be incrementally maintained in presence of updates. We also plan to adapt the implicit classification approach to allow full description-logic style subsumption which might have benefits for using views in query rewriting.

Acknowledgements We thank Steffen Staab for discussion and work on previous versions of the paper. This work was funded by the EU in the WonderWeb project (IST-2001-33052).

References

[1] S. Abiteboul and A. Bonner. Objects and Views. In *Proc. Intl. Conf. on Management of Data*, pages 238–247. ACM SIGMOD, May 1991.

[2] S. Abiteboul, R. Goldman, J. McHugh, V. Vassalos, and Y. Zhuge. Views for semistructured data. In *Proc. of the Workshop on Management of Semistructured Data, Tucson, Arizona*, May 1997.

[3] S. Alexaki, V. Christophides, G. Karvounarakis, D. Plexousakis, K. Tolle, B. Amann, I. Fundulaki, M. Scholl, and A.-M. Vercoustre. Managing RDF metadata for community webs. In *(WCM'00), Salt Lake City, Utah*, pages 140–151, October 2000.

[4] C. Beeri. Formal Models for object oriented databases. In *Proc. 1st Intl. Conf. on Deductive and object-oriented databases*, pages 370–396, 1989.

[5] E. Bertino. A View Mechanism for Object-Oriented Databases. In *Proc. of Intl. Conf. on Extending Database Technology (EDBT)*, pages 136–151, March 1992.

[6] E. Bozsak and al. Kaon — towards a large scale semantic web. In *Proc. of 3rd Int'l Conference on Electronic*

[7] J. Broekstra, A. Kampman, and Frank van Harmelen. Sesame: A Generic Architecture for Storing and Querying RDF and RDF Schema. In *Proc. of 1st Int. Conf. on the Semantic Web (ISWC)*, Sardinia, Italy, 2002.

[8] C. D. C. S. Dos Santos and S. Abiteboul. Virtual schemas and bases. In *Proc. Extending Database Technology (EDBT)*, 1994.

[9] Dan Brickley and R. V. Guha. Resource description framework (RDF) schema specification 1.0. http://www.w3.org/TR/2000/CR-rdf-schema-20000372/, 2000.

[10] S. Decker, D. Brickley, J. Saarela, and J. Angele. A query and inference service for RDF. In *QL98 - Query Languages Workshop*, December 1998.

[11] B. Grosof, I. Horrocks, R. Volz, and S. Decker. Description Logic Programs: Combining Logic Programs with Description Logics. In *Proc. of WWW-2003*, Budapest, Hungary, 05 2003.

[12] P. Hayes. RDF Semantics. http://www.w3.org/TR/rdf-mt/, January 2003.

[13] O. Lassila and R. Swick. Resource description framework (RDF) model and syntax specification. http://www.w3.org/TR/REC-rdf-syntax/, 1999.

[14] A. Maedche, S. Staab, R. Studer, Y. Sure, and R. Volz. Seal tying up information integration and web site management by ontologies. In *IEEE Data Engineering Bulletin*, volume 25, March 2002.

[15] P. Mitra, G. Wiederhold, and M. L. Kersten. A graph-oriented model for articulation of ontology interdependencies. In *Proc. of Extending Database Technology (EDBT) 2000*, pages 86–100, 2000.

[16] D. Oberle and R. Volz. Implementation of a view mechanism for ontology-based metadata. Technical Report 422, University of Karlsruhe (TH), 2002. http://www.aifb.uni-karlsruhe.de/WBS/dob/pubs/KAON-Views.pdf.

[17] E. A. Rundensteiner. MultiView: A Methodology for Supporting Multiple Views in Object-Oriented Databases. In *Proc. 18th Intl. Conf. on Very Large Data Bases (VLDB)*, pages 187–198, Vancouver, Canada, 1992. ACM SIGMOD.

[18] M. H. Scholl, C. Laasch, and M. Tresch. Views in Object-Oriented Databases. In *Proc. 2nd Workshop on Foundations of Models and Languages of Data and Objects*, pages 37–58, Sept. 1990.

[19] S. Staab, J. Angele, S. Decker, M. Erdmann, A. Hotho, A. Maedche, H.-P. Schnurr, R. Studer, and Y. Sure. Semantic community web portals. In *WWW9 - Proc. of the 9th International World Wide Web Conference, Amsterdam, The Netherlands, May, 15-19, 2000*. Elsevier, 2000.

[20] M. Stonebraker. Implementation of integrity constraints and views by query modification. In *Proc. of Int. Conf. on Management of Data (SIGMOD)*, pages 65–78. ACM, 1975.

[21] R. Volz. External ontologies in the semantic web. In *Proc. of the 20th British National Conference on Databases (BNCOD)*, Coventry, UK, July 2003.

[22] R. Volz, D. Oberle, and R. Studer. Views for light-weight web ontologies. In *Proc. of ACM Symposium of Applied Computing (SAC)*, Melbourne, Florida, USA, 03 2003.

[23] Y. Zhuge and H. Garcia-Molina. Graph structured views and their incremental maintenance. In *Proc. 14th Int. Conf. on Data Engineering*, 1998.

Pushing Quality of Service Information and Requirements into Global Query Optimization*

Haiwei Ye
Université de Montréal
ye@iro.umontreal.ca

Brigitte Kerhervé
Université du Québec à Montréal
Kerherve.Brigitte@uqam.ca

Gregor v. Bochmann
University of Ottawa
bochmann@site.uottawa.ca

Vincent Oria
New Jersey Institute of Technology
oria@homer.njit.edu

Abstract

In recent years, a lot of research effort has been dedicated to the management of Quality of Service (QoS), mainly in the fields of telecommunication networks and multimedia systems. Emerging applications such as electronic commerce, health-care applications, digital publishing or data mining also have requirements regarding the quality of the service, the cost of the service, the quality of data to be delivered, the accuracy, and the precision of the retrieved data. These examples show the need to consider the concept of QoS from a broader perspective, requiring the collaboration of all the distributed system components involved. In this paper, we propose an approach to integrate user-defined QoS requirements, together with the dynamic properties of the system components involved, into a distributed query processing environment. We then propose a query optimization strategy in which multiple goals may be considered with separate cost models. Furthermore, we discuss some experiment results confirming the effectiveness of our approach.

1. Introduction

Quality of Service (QoS) management has attracted a lot of research in the last decade, mainly in the fields of telecommunication networks and multimedia systems. To support QoS activities, mechanisms have been provided mainly for individual components such as operating systems, transport systems, or multimedia storage servers and integrated into QoS architectures for end-to-end QoS provisions[1]. None of these proposals take database systems into consideration although database systems are an important component of present distributed systems.

Traditional database optimizers aim at minimizing the query response time and/or the number of disk I/O. Consideration of QoS within query processing means the inclusion of other dimensions such as the cost of the query, the data quality, or the throughput of the database systems. Single optimization goal strategies deployed in the traditional database optimizers cannot satisfy such QoS requirements. We argue that query optimization should take into account user-defined quality of service constraints[2]. In an electronic commerce application for example, a user could specify QoS requirements such as: "*I want the most up-to-date information even if it takes time. However, if the response time is longer than 3 minutes, I will accept less recent information, but only if it is less than 10 hours old*". Based on the specified QoS requirements and using the QoS metadata, in this example the query optimizer has to choose the most up-to-date information from the catalogs.

In our approach, the treatment of QoS requirements is reflected in the aspects of integrating multiple optimization goals and how to select a query access plan that is overall optimal. The related issues consist of identifying the possible optimization goal, the selection of cost models, the way to obtain the user's priority between different optimization goals, and how to obtain an overall optimal goal according to the user's preference.

In this paper, we propose an approach to integrate user-defined QoS requirements, in addition to the dynamic properties of the system components involved, into a distributed query processing environment. We then propose a query optimization strategy in which multiple goals may be considered with several cost models. Furthermore, we discuss some experimental results confirming the effectiveness of our approach.

The rest of the paper is organized as follows. The next section describes our QoS-based distributed query

*This work was supported by a grant from the Canadian Institute for Telecommunication Research (CITR), under the Network of Center for Excellence Program of the Canadian Government, a collaborative research and development grant from NSERC no CRD-226962-99, by a student fellowship from IBM and an individual research grant from NSERC no RGPIN138210.

processing. Section 3 presents the results of our experimentation. Section 4 discusses related work. Section 5 concludes and suggests future work.

2. QoS-based query processing

To support QoS in database systems, we propose to enrich query processing with some QoS features. We consider factors like user requirements, dynamic network performance, and dynamic server load in the procedure of global query processing. By global query processing, we mean that we position our work on top of existing database systems. The QoS features are plugged into the query processor that deals with inter-database operations. Therefore, our method does not require the modification of local database query processors. The main objective is to provide a flexible QoS model for multidatabase management systems and to offer differentiated services.

We base our work on classes of users, cost models for distributed query processing, and utility functions to describe system or user satisfaction for different optimization goals. Usually the utility function maps the value of one QoS dimension to a real number, which corresponds to a satisfaction level. For example, the following formulas give the utility functions for the response time and the service charge:

$$u_t(t) = 1 / t$$
$$u_s(x) = 1 / x$$

where t is the response time for a query plan and x is the corresponding service charge for that plan. Utility functions are used in our cost model to achieve an overall optimization since it is used to compare the quality of the access plans. It also provides an important link between the quality of a query plan and the user satisfaction. A user class is a generalization of a number of users sharing common characteristics. Classification of the users may be based on different policies and criteria[3]. For example, different users may exhibit various patterns of navigation through an e-commerce site, therefore based on the user's *navigation behavior*, we may segregate users into two classes: *buyer* and *browser*. We propose a new approach to the problem of evaluating the cost of a query plan in a multidatabase system. Our cost models are adaptive in the sense that first, they combine multiple optimization criteria (for example response time and money cost, into a simple cost model) and second they can give a more precise response time estimation based on the information captured by QoS monitoring of the network and the server.

2.1. Query processing and optimization revisited

When designing the QoS-based query processor we are guided by two main goals: 1) recognition of individual user requirements, and 2) consideration of the dynamic nature of the underlying system. A logical architecture is proposed in Figure 1 to show the relationships between QoS management and query processing.

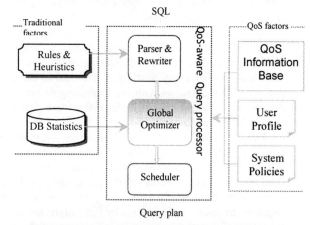

Figure 1. A big picture for QoS-aware distributed query processor

In this framework, we include the typical components introduced in [4]. The user's query is sent to the *Parser* to be syntactically analyzed and validated against the database schema. The output of the parser is transformed by a set of rewriting rules in the *rewriter*. These rules correspond to heuristics that transform the query into a semantically equivalent form that may be processed more efficiently.

The main tasks of the *Global Optimizer* are 1) choose an execution plan which satisfies the optimization objectives and 2) send it to the scheduler who coordinates the execution of the plan among the participating component DBMSs. We keep the traditional factors[4] considered in the query processor. These typical factors include table statistics, column statistics, and index statistics. In addition, we include the QoS factors, which are information from the *QoS Information Base (QoSIB)*, the *User Profile*, and the *System Policies*.

Adding QoS factors into a distributed query processing environment has several impacts and requires:

- to provide new optimization goals;
- to modify the corresponding cost models; and
- to propose a new algorithm for query optimization.

2.2. User profiles, QoS monitoring information and system policies

Pushing QoS into a distributed query processing environment requires the description of the information related to the user's requirements, the QoS level provided by the different system components and the objectives of the system in terms of resource allocation.

User profiles. A user profile is built to store the user's QoS expectation for a particular service. The QoS expectation is expressed according to different QoS dimensions[5]. For example, a good quality of service level may be expressed by the dimensions of response time and dollar cost. The user profile allows users to specify their QoS requirements by defining utility functions for each dimension. As mentioned previously, a utility function translates the values of an attribute into "utility" units. We consider decreasing utility functions since this type of utility function is practical in the case that the utility decreases with the increasing of one QoS dimension. Examples of such dimensions are response time and service charge.

The user profile is also useful to derive the trade-off between QoS dimensions, which is represented by the weight assigned to each dimension. In our approach, the Analytic Hierarchy Process (AHP) [6] is used to derive the weights from user's preference. This method only requires the user to provide his or her judgments about the relative importance of each criterion over another one (pairwise comparison of goals) and then specify a preference index. Based on these preference indexes, the output of the AHP is a prioritized ranking indicating the overall weights for each of the alternative decisions. In short, the utility functions and weights are then used to guide the optimizer for selecting a query access plan.

QoS information base. The QoS information base (QoSIB) stores some information about the service level offered by the different system components. Since we are working in the context of Internet-like networks, the performance of the TCP protocol is our key consideration when talking about network performance. Among all the performance factors, *TCP throughput* and *TCP delay* are two key parameters considered in our distributed query processor.

For the server performance category, the parameters of interest include availability and server load (CPU usage, memory usage, and the frequency of disk I/O). The availability is the fundamental measurement of a server. It includes the availability of hardware as well as the software. In our research, we refer to the availability of the database services. In our prototype, QoS information is stored as XML files.

System policies. We believe that many future applications, especially e-commerce systems, will be able to provide different levels of service to different classes of users[7]. In the simplest sense, the policy consists of one or more rules that describe the action(s) to occur when specific condition(s) exist[8]. In our study, the system policies determine the constraints under which the system resources can be used for providing services to the users. Usually, a policy is a formal set of statements that define the levels of services to be provided to particular

classes of users. If written in a natural language, policy statements may take the following forms:

"Give the *VIP* users the best service"

"Give the *normal* users the resource-effective service"

Different policies may be enforced to different classes of users. Policy statements are stored in *System Policies*. The parameters that make up a system policy include the optimization goals defined (as presented in Table 1), user class information, and the weighting factors associated with each goal.

Table 1 Example of optimization goals

Optimization category	Optimization goal
Performance oriented	- Minimize response time - Maximize DB throughput
Money oriented	- Minimize the cost of a service - Maximize the benefit of the database system
Data quality	- Multimedia vs. Plain text - Recency of data
System oriented	- Minimize resource utilization

When various optimization goals exist along multiple QoS dimensions, we should find an *optimal* solution that satisfies all of them, optimal either from the user perspective or the system perspective, or both. One way of combining various optimization objectives is to use *weighted combination* (for example, a weighted sum) of different goals. A weighted combination can express the overall satisfaction of all the optimization goals. The user must be presented with enough options that his or her desires can be adequately expressed and they can then be mapped to weighting factors associated with the different objectives.

All this information is later integrated into the QoS-aware distributed query processing for access plan selection. Different optimization goals may lead to different cost models or query processing strategies. In the performance category, the cost factors comprise the measures of local processing time, the communication time as well as some overhead due to parallelism. There are two types of query parallelism: *inter*-query parallelism (which enables the parallel execution of multiple queries) and *intra*-query optimization (which makes the parallel execution of multiple operations possible within the same query). For the optimization goals related to the monetary, the cost measures include information on the resource usage and the pricing scheme.

2.3. Global Query Optimization

Global query optimization is generally implemented in three steps[4]. After parsing, a global query is first decomposed into query units (subqueries) such that the data needed by each subquery is available from a single local database. Second, an optimized query plan is generated based on the decomposition results. Finally, each subquery of the query plan is dispatched to the related local database server to be executed and the result for each subquery is collected to compute the final answer.

In our study, we focus on the first two steps and map them to the problems of *global query decomposition*, *inter-site join ordering* and *join site selection*[10]. Before describing these three steps, we give an explanation about the evaluation of the cost of query plans.

2.3.1. Evaluating the cost of query plans.

We propose a new approach to the problem of evaluating the cost of a query plan in a multidatabase system. Our approach relies on the information from QoS monitor user profiles. The novelty of our approach lies in the consideration of user requirements, user classes as well as the way to deal with dynamic network performance.

In our work, three levels of cost models are used. The first level is the global cost model, which is used to calculate the overall utility of a query access plan. The second level is used to calculate the cost for each node in a query access plan. The last level is the local cost model, which is used to estimate the cost of an operator locally.

Global cost model. As discussed earlier, multiple optimization goals over different QoS dimensions are considered in our query optimizer. Consequently, the global cost model should reflect them. For our cost model, we adopt the method proposed for multi-criteria optimization in Operations Research area. Accordingly, the general cost model for one user is

$$ max \left\{ \sum_{i=1}^{n} \omega_i \cdot u_i(C_i) \right\} $$

where u_i is the utility function for cost component C_i (based on one of the QoS dimensions i); ω_i is the weighting factor assigned to the cost component C_i. Note that we want to maximize the utility for a given user; therefore this model could also be called a utility model. The range of ω_i is [0,1] and $\Sigma \omega_i = 1$.

Plan cost model. A query access plan is represented by a binary tree. Each internal node is an inter-site join operation and each leaf node is the subquery executed at one database server. Since we consider several cost components, the cost of each node is also expressed according to multiple dimensions. For example, if we select the response time, the service charge and the availability as our cost components, then the cost information recorded in each node will include three parts: time, dollar, and availability. The cost information for leaf nodes is based on the local cost model and the QoS Information Base (e.g. availability). The cost information for the internal node is calculated as a combination of the cost information of its left and right child nodes. The cost formula for each QoS dimension is

different. Table 2 lists the cost functions for time, dollar, and availability. The join time for each node is determined by the load of the server and the current TCP performance. The formula for each join is:

$$ T_{join} = local\ (site, query) + net\ (site_i, site_j) $$

where local (*site*, *query*) represents the local execution time for the *query* at *site*, net (site$_i$, site$_j$) represents the data transfer time spent over the network.

Table 2 Cost functions for each cost component

Cost Component	Cost function	Brief Description
Response time	Join-time + max (left.respose_time, right.response_time)	The join time is the response time to perform the join between the left and the right child.
Service Charge	Join-charge + left.charge + right.charge	The join charge is the money cost to perform the join between the left and the right child.
Availability	Left.availability * right.availability	The probability that both servers are available.

Figure 2 shows an example query plan marked with cost information for each node. We use a vector (time, money, availability) to record the cost information for each node in the plan tree. By using this representation, the cost information for the root node of the tree is the plan cost. Each item in the vector associated with that node is computed using the formula given in Table 2.

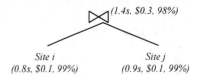

(1.4s, $0.3, 98%)

Site i   *Site j*
(0.8s, $0.1, 99%)   *(0.9s, $0.1, 99%)*

Figure 2. Cost calculation for a join node

Local cost model. As mentioned earlier, the local cost information relies on the estimation of the execution of a query at a local server, the pricing policy applied by the local server for a service charge and the server availability. Each local database server must report the price and the availability. However, the execution strategy, and therefore the execution time, of a query is hard to obtain since local database systems do not report the needed statistical information. To estimate the local database cost, we adopt the sampling method[9], where multiple regression models are used to guess the local cost structure (in terms of time). The idea of the query sampling method can be characterized by the following steps: 1) queries are classified according to a number of criteria; 2) sample queries from each class are selected and issued to run against the local database; and 3) the response time is then measured to derive the local cost model by multiple regression analysis. Such a cost formula includes a set of variables that affect the costs of queries and a number of coefficients that reflect the performance behaviour of the underlying DBMS. Due to space limitation, we will not give detailed information here. A complete discussion can be found in[11].

2.3.2. Global query processing. In our work, global query processing is implemented by three steps: global query decomposition, join ordering, and join site selection.

Global query decomposition. The main task of the global query decomposition is to break down a global query into several subqueries so that the tables involved in each subquery target one location. This is an NP-Complete problem[12]. Therefore, this step is usually guided by heuristics. Two goals used in our algorithm are to simplify the optimization at the global level and to reduce the data transmission among different sites. Therefore, the heuristic used is to decompose a global query into the largest possible subqueries.

The cost model used for this step mainly depends on the local information, based on the optimization goal selected. For example, if the optimization goal is the response time, the cost model could be the response time for each subqueries under various server loads. We do not consider data transfer in this step; therefore communication cost is not involved. The QoS factor considered is mainly the system performance information from QoS information base.

Join ordering. The global query decomposition phase generates a set of subqueries with location information. In the following join ordering step, the optimizer tries to come up with a good ordering of how to combine these joins between subqueries. The join ordering can be represented as a binary tree, where leaf nodes are the sub-queries and internal nodes are inter-site join operations. Because we want to utilize the distributed nature of the multidatabase system, we try to make this tree as low as possible, which means we hope the join can be done in parallel as much as possible.

A typical way is to generate a linear tree first and then balance this linear tree to a bushy tree [10][12]. Following the same method, we first build a left-deep tree using dynamic programming. The next step in the join ordering is to transform the left deep join tree into a more balanced bushy join tree. A feasible approach is to apply a sequence of basic transformations that can be easily identified and performed[11].

The cost models used in this step consist of both global cost model and local cost model. In this step all the QoS factors introduced in Section 3.2 are included in the decision.

Join site selection. In case of data duplication, one subquery might have several potential locations, thus the optimizer should decide at which location this subquery will be executed. Like the join ordering problem, all the QoS metrics are taken into account.

The key issue in the site selection is to decide which site is the best (depending on how the user defines his or her optimization goal) for each binary operator. Traditionally, the possible site to perform the join or the union is chosen from one of the operand sites, i.e. the site where one of its operands is located. However, there may be circumstances when shipping the two operand tables to a third site is a better solution, in terms of response time. We call the join site to be a *third* site if the selected site is neither of the operand sites.

For a binary operator node such as join or union, the selection process becomes complicated when several *third* sites are capable of handling the operator node.

After we decide which candidate set to choose for the "third site", the procedure of join site selection can be regarded as deciding (based on the cost model) the site for each internal node (which is usually the inter-site join operation) in the query access tree. This process may be done in a bottom-up fashion. In our algorithm, we use post order tree traversal to visit the internal nodes of the tree[11].

2.4. Prototype implementation

In order to validate our approach, we implemented a prototype where we concentrated on those aspects that are representative for the QoS-based distributed query processing we propose. For simplicity, we only integrate two QoS dimensions in the prototype. However, the implementation is not limited to these two dimensions, the modules implementing other dimensions can be easily plugged into our prototype. Highlights of the implementations are given below.

1) User classes: In order to show the differentiated services in our prototype, we have adopted the priority-based user classification and considered two user classes, namely *VIP user* and *normal user*.

2) QoS consideration. The dynamic characteristics of the underlying systems for our QoS consideration are *network performance*, *server load*, and *availability*. For the network performance, TCP performance is our main concern. Accordingly the QoS dimensions we considered are *available bandwidth* and *delay*. For the consideration of server load, we categorize the load into four levels: *no load*, *low*, *medium*, and *high*. They are used to show different levels of resource contention. In addition, a server is also characterized by its availability (*yes* or *no*).

3) Optimization goal. For our prototype implementation, we focus on two optimization goals: minimize the response time and/or the service charge. Basically, we want to demonstrate the integration of the criteria of *time* and *money* into our prototype. Accordingly the

overall optimization goal is calculated by the following formula:

$$\text{Min } \{ \omega_t\, u_t\, (\text{response\_time}) + \omega_S\, u_S\, (\text{service\_charge}) \}$$

where ω_t and ω_S are the weights specified by the users for the response time and service charge, respectively; u_t and u_S are utility functions used for the response time and service charge respectively. For the purpose of simplicity, we assume the utility function for the response time and the service charge are the utility functions given at the beginning of Section 2.

4) Global cost models. The global cost model (as explained in Section 2.3.1) contains two cost components: response time and service charge. Depending on the optimization goals, three cost models can be selected:
   i. C_{time} = response_time;
   ii. C_{dollar} = service_charge;
   iii. $C_{overall} = W_{time} * u_t(\text{response\_time}) +$
        $W_{dollar} * u_S(\text{service\_charge})$

The detailed cost model information can be found in [13]. The calculation of the response time is straightforward. The total response time of a query plan (represented as a tree structure) is the sum of the response time on each node along the critical path in the query access tree.

For the service charge, we are dealing with a pricing issue. Typically, two types of charging schemes are popular today. They are *flat-rate* and *usage-based* [14]. We adopt the usage-based pricing policy for our prototype implementation. We concentrate on network bandwidth utilization. A complete pricing schema, however, should consider all the resources including both the network and the server. The reason for only considering the network resource is not only because we want to simplify the implementation, but also because there have already been many studies for the pricing for the Internet. We assume the service charge of a query plan is proportional to the network resource consumed. Accordingly, this second optimization goal is eventually simplified as the problem of minimizing the network bandwidth utilization.

Prototype architecture. The functional modules of the prototype include the *user interface* part for SQL input and QoS schema selection, the *optimization part* based on the algorithms proposed, the *visualization part* for the query plan and QoS information and the *result display* part. Our prototype offers a simplified GUI for SQL input. This component allows a user to specify a query by selecting the desired attributes and tables as well as join and restriction predicates.

The user can also choose to view the XML representation of the specified query that will be forwarded to the optimizer by clicking the "show query (XML)" button. The other component integrated with the

SQL Input GUI is the User Preference manager, shown in the lower part in Figure 4. In this part, the user can select his trade-off between the response time and the service charge. The sliding bars are used for this purpose and this ratio is further integrated in the optimizer to derive the overall optimization goal.

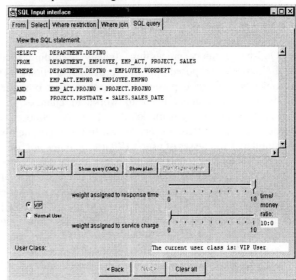

Figure 4 An example of SQL input interface and selection of query preference

When an SQL query and the QoS preferences are specified by the user, he/she can see the generated query access plan. For the query specified as in Figure 4, the query plan shown to the user will look like the one shown in Figure 5.

In short, through the implementation of the prototype, we have demonstrated the following points:

• Different user classes are provided in the prototype. Users are classified based on priority and a system policy is made for each user class;

• Two optimization goals are supported in the current prototype, according to two QoS dimensions: response time and service charge. The overall optimization goal is achieved by using the weighted sum of the resulting utility functions applied for different goals;

• Different query access plans can be generated for different user classes;

• Dynamic QoS conditions for systems may affect the decision. The system parameters include both the network information and server characteristics.

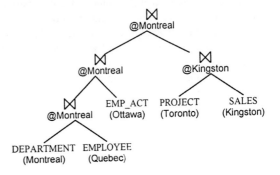

Figure 5 An example of generated query access plan

3. Experimentation

In this section, we evaluate the performance of our QoS-based query processing strategy according to the framework proposed in the previous sections. The objective of our experiment is to show that our query optimizer can adapt itself to workload changes (both server load and network load) and always chooses the best plan for different user classes. In the experiment we simulate two classes of users: *VIP* user and *normal* user.

The specific goals of the experimentation are two-fold: (i) how our estimated plan cost (in terms of response time) is close to the real execution cost; and (ii) what are the quality of service for VIP user and normal user under different workloads (we focus on response time in the experiment). Corresponding to these goals, two sets of experiments were set up. Two types of system loads are used for our measurement, one for network and the other for server load. For network load, we mainly focus on the available bandwidth as the indication of network congestion level. For server load, we concentrate on the CPU utilization as the indication of server load.

In the first experiment, named *estimated vs. executed*, we take the query plan generated by the prototype and execute under different server loads. The network bandwidth used for the plan estimation is 5Mbps since this is the most representative maximum bandwidth during the daytime according to our observation between University of Montreal and University of Ottawa.

The second experiment, named *VIP vs. normal* is designed to measure the response times for VIP users and normal users under different server loads and network congestion levels. The 3-way join with different resulting cardinalities is used for the second experiment.

3.1. Experimental setup and assumptions

All tests were performed under Windows NT 4.0 (SP 6) on a single Pentium III CPU and 192MB RAM. The tables used in this experiment are based on the SAMPLE database provided by the DB2 Universal Database [15]. The size of the database is about 7.5KB.

All the reported execution times of our experiments represent the average of executing the query 20 times. The purpose of this averaging is to avoid the influence of disk I/O to our result. In the measurement of the data transfer times, we have not included the disk I/O time for retrieving a table into memory in order to send it over the network. To simplify the discussion and highlight the points of interest, we disregard the disk I/O.

We mentioned in the previous section that the network congestion level and various server loads are two major system dynamics for our experiment. To study their influence in our prototype, we usually fix one and change the other to collect the performance numbers. It should be noted that as an experimental prototype, our execution engine was designed for ease of implementation and has not been tuned for performance. The main purpose is to demonstrate the feasibility of our ideas in practice.

3.2. Workload classification

The workload in the experiment includes both server load and network load. Concerning the server load, in our experiments we degrade the performance of one server by loading it with additional processes. Each process simply eats up CPU and competes with the database system for CPU utilization. Additional load is quantified by the number of these processes spawned on a server. The reason we concentrate on the CPU is that the buffer pool size for the SAMPLE database is about 1MB (250 pages, with size of 4KB for each page), which is more than enough to hold the whole database. Therefore, the number of disk I/Os does not affect our experiment result very much. As discussed before, we categorized the server load into 4 levels: *no load, low load, medium load,* and *high load.*

As for the network load, we consider the TCP congestion level. In our global database schema, we assume the data are distributed among different cities in Canada. Because performing experiments directly on the Internet would not provide repeatable results, we instead modeled the behavior of the network using trace data that could be easily relayed. Therefore we need to have knowledge about the available TCP throughput between two cities. We choose Montreal and Ottawa as our experimental base. For this purpose, we observed the TCP traffic using IPERF[16] between UdeM (University of Montreal) and UO (University of Ottawa).

The measurements were made in the morning, in the afternoon and at night each day, and statistics were collected. Based on the observation, we find the maximum bandwidth ranging from 0.2Mbps to 10 Mbps depending on the time of the day. Within this range, 5Mbps is the normal throughput during daytime and 8Mbps is the normal throughput at night. When the network is congested, 2Mbps is the throughput we saw around 4pm to 6pm. Very occasionally, we got 0.1 to 0.2 Mbps. These data are used to define our congestion level. The corresponding congestion level is defined in Table 3. A throughput of 8Mbps is regarded as no congestion.

Table 3 Measured network congestion levels

Network bandwidth	0.1Mbps	0.2Mbps	1Mbps	2Mbps	5Mbps	8Mbps
Congestion level	5	4	3	2	1	0

3.3. Result

We conducted a number of experiments and performance data are collected for the two sets of experiments identified previously.

Estimated versus execution time. In the first set of experiments, *estimated vs. executed*, we first varied the workload of the server. Then under different loads, a plan is generated with an estimated time. This plan is then executed and the observed execution time is recorded for the purpose of comparison. The network congestion level for all links is 1, that is 5Mbps. Figure 6 gives the plots for the comparison of two times under different server loads.

In Figure 6, the estimated times are given in dotted line and the collected times are given in solid line. As it can been seen from the figure, the two curves for each load are very close. We also analyze the result statistically by constructing a linear regression model of these two times. The regression results (detailed in [11]) indicate that the estimated times can explain about 95% of the real execution times.

We compare the execution times for VIP users and normal users under different server loads in Figure 7. The curves marked with square and triangle signs represent the performance for normal users and VIP users, respectively. As we can see from the figure, under no load, all the users will get the same performance (the lowest curve in Figure 6). With the increasing load, the VIP user always stays at the same curve (the same performance), while the normal user will get higher response time (the curves marked with square sign). And the advantage of performance for VIP users increases with increasing server load. In short, Figure 7 shows that the VIP users always get best performance while the normal user will suffer the slow response when the load increases.

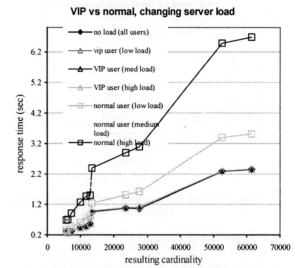

Figure 6. Estimated versus execution time, with various server loads

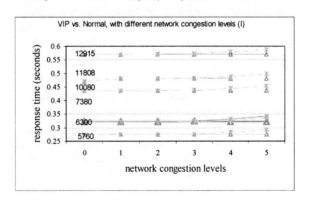

Figure 7. VIP vs. normal user with various server loads

Figure 8 depicts the effect of network congestion on the performance. In this set of tests, we assume that the links among the nodes involved in the join are congested while other links have the normal throughput (5Mbps). In addition, there is no load of the server during the experimental periods. Again, estimated times are used for the comparison of this experiment. Each of the curves in Figure 8 has six data points, which correspond to the six congestion levels. The curves marked with a triangle sign represent the VIP user. The curves marked with a square sign represent the normal user. We observe the same trend as in the load test, whenever the links are congested to a certain level (usually at level 3), the plan for the VIP user can choose another smooth route for data transformation and maintain the fast response time. Since doing so may incur extra data transmission, and this is regarded as "expensive" for normal users, the normal user will experience a slower query response in these cases.

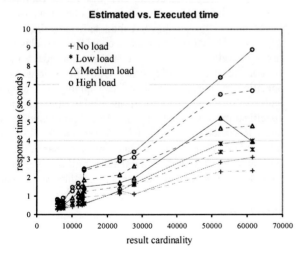

Estimated vs. Executed time

(a)

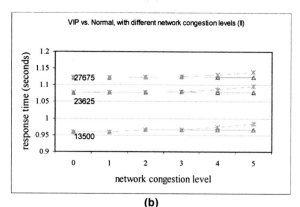

(b)

Figure 8. VIP vs. normal user, with various network congestion levels

3.4. Experiment summary

In the experiment discussed in this section, we first evaluated how close the estimated query execution time comes to the real execution time. The results shown in Figure 6 illustrates that under various server loads, the observed response time is very close to the estimated time. We then demonstrate, through the second set of experiments, that under all the circumstance the VIP user will get fast response time, or in general the better service.

Using the same experimental setup, we can also compare our algorithm for join site selection (which considers a third candidate site) with the traditional one (which always ships the small table to the large table site). The results in [11] also show the superiority of our algorithm over the traditional algorithm under different system loads. The experiment described in this section attempts to demonstrate the feasibility of the integration of QoS into distributed query processing, which means different treatments for different classes of users. Although our initial experimental result is a very first attempt and is subject to future refinement, this first attempt gives a fairly clear picture showing the capability of delivering QoS differentiation in query processing.

4. Related work

In the last decade, several approaches have been proposed for decomposition and optimization of queries across different data sources. They can be classified into two categories: 1) strategies for providing universal access over multiple information sources and 2) dynamic and adaptive query optimization strategies. Proposals for the first category are based on mediator architectures, where different data sources are described and integrated.

Different query capabilities are taken into account during the query optimization. Such approaches include Garlic[17], IRO-DB[18] and Mariposa [19]. The query optimizer implemented in Garlic uses enumeration rules for describing query capabilities and uses dynamic programming to find a good plan. IRO-DB provides federation of object-oriented and relational database systems through the ODMG model and the OQL query language. The global query processor uses services of local cost tuners and their corresponding calibrating procedure to derive the local cost parameters. The originality of the approach proposed in Mariposa is its economic model in the query optimization phase. The bidding mechanism allows sites to observe their environment from query to query, and autonomously restate their costs of operation for subsequent queries.

The approaches proposed in the second category generally provide techniques for dealing with delays in data processing and transfer at remote sites [20][21] and dynamic query processing [22][23]. Our approach falls into the second category and we propose to use QoS monitoring tools to push dynamic properties of the systems into global query optimization. The novelty of our approach lies in the fact that we take the user QoS requirements and the system policies into consideration to support several optimization goals.

5. Conclusion and future work

In this paper, we have proposed a general framework for integrating QoS requirements in a distributed query processing environment. This framework is based on user classes, cost models, utility functions, and policy-based management. Our approach allows to offer differentiated services to different classes of users according to their expectations in terms of QoS. We have presented our QoS-based distributed query processing strategy where we push QoS requirements and information into the different steps of global query optimization: global query decomposition, join ordering and join site selection. We presented the prototype we have developed as well as experimentation we have conducted to validate our approach. The current prototype considers two classes of users as well as two different optimization goals. In the future, we will consider other QoS dimensions to be specified by the user, such as data quality or freshness and will work on rewriting rules to transform specifications on these dimensions into optimization goals and corresponding cost models. To test the feasibility of our method, we designed a very simple scenario. To test our algorithm in a more general case, further experiments should be conducted on a larger and real database system.

References

[1] C. Aurrecoechea, A. Campbell, and, L Hauw, A Survey of QoS Architectures. ACM Multimedia Journal, 6, May 1998, pp. 138-151

[2] H. Ye, B. Kerhervé, G. v. Bochmann, QoS-aware distributed query processing, DEXA Workshop on Query Processing in Multimedia Information Systems (QPMIDS), Florence, Italy, 1-3 September, 1999

[3] D.A. Menasce, V. A.F. Almeida, Scaling for E-Business Technologies, Models, Performance, and Capacity Planning, Prentice Hall Canada, 2000

[4] D. Kossmann, The state of the art in distributed query processing, ACM Computing Surveys (CSUR), Volume 32, Issue 4, December 2000, pp 422 – 469

[5] Frolund, S., & Koistinen, J., Quality-of-Service Specification in Distributed Object Systems. Distributed Systems Engineering Journal (December 1998), vol 5 no 4, pp 179-202.

[6] T. Saaty. Multicriteria Decision Making - The Analytic Hierarchy Process. Technical report, University of Pittsburgh, RWS Publications, 1992

[7] G.v. Bochmann, B. Kerhervé, H. Lutfiyya, M. M. Salem, H. Ye, Introducing QoS to Electronic Commerce Applications, Second International Symposium, ISEC 2001 Hong Kong, China, April 26-28, 2001, pp 138-147

[8] A. Westerinen, J. Schnizlein, J. Strassner, M. Scherling, B. Quinn, S. Herzog, A. Huynh, M. Carlson, J. Perry, S. Waldbusser Terminology for Policy-Based Management, November 2001

[9] Q. Zhu, Y. Sun and S. Motheramgari, Developing Cost Models with Qualitative Variables for Dynamic Multidatabase Environment, Proceedings of IEEE Int'l Conf. On Data Eng. (ICDE2000), San Diego, Feb 29-March 3, 2000, pp 413-424

[10] W. Du, M.-C. Shan, U. Dayal, Reducing Multidatabase Query Response Time by Tree Balancing. SIGMOD Conference 1995, pp 293-303

[11] H. Ye, Integrating Quality of Service Information and Requirements in a Distributed Query Processing Environment, Ph.D thesis (preliminary draft), University of Montreal, 2002

[12] C. Evrendilek, A. Dogac, S. Nural, and F. Ozcan, Multidatabase Query Optimization, Distributed and Parallel Databases, Volume 5, 1997, pp 1-39

[13] H. Ye, G.v. Bochmann, B. Kerhervé, An adaptive cost model for distributed query processing, UQAM Technical Report 2000-06, May 2000

[14] A.M. Odlyzko, Internet pricing and the history of communications, *Computer Networks* 36 (2001), pp. 493-517

[15] DB2 UDB Administration Guide V7.2, http://www-4.ibm.com

[16] National Laboratory for Applied Network Research, http://www.nlanr.net/

[17] Hass, L., Kossmann, D., Wimmers, E., Yang, J. Optimizing queries across diverse data sources in Proceedings of tthe Conference on Very Large Data Bases (VLDB), Greece, Aug. 1997, pp276-285

[18] G. Gardarin, F. Sha, and Z. Tang, Calibrating the Query Optimizer Cost Model of IRO-DB, an Object-Oriented Federated Database System, Proceedings of the 22nd VLDB, Mumbai (Bombay), India, 1996, pp 378-389

[19] Stonebraker, M. and al. Mariposa: A Wide-Area Distributed Database System, VLDB Journal, 5,1 (January 1996) pp48-63

[20] Z. Ives, D. Florescu, M. Friedman, A. Levy, D. Weld, An Adaptive Query Execution Engine for Data Integration Proc. of ACM SIGMOD Conf. on Management of Data 1999

[21] J. Hellerstein, M. Franklin, S. Chandrasekaran, A. Deshpande, K. Madden, S. Hildrum, V. Raman, M. Shah, Adaptive Query Processing: Technology in Evolution. In IEEE Bulletin on Data Engineering, vol 23, no 2, 2000, pp 7-18

[22] R. Cole, G. Graefe, Optimization of Dynamic Query Evaluation Plans. SIGMOD Conference 1994, pp 150-160

[23] T. Urhan, M.J. Franklin, and L. Amsaleg, Cost-based Query Scrambling for Initial Delays, SIGMOD'98, Volume 27, Number 2, Seattle, June 1998

Dynamic Data Management for Location Based Services in Mobile Environments

Shiow-yang Wu   Kun-Ta Wu
Department of Computer Science and Information Engineering
National Dong Hwa University
Hualien, Taiwan, R. O. C.

Abstract

We characterize the dynamic data management problem for location based services(LBS) in mobile environments and devise a cost model for servicing both location independent and location dependent data. The cost analysis leads to a set of dynamic data management strategies that employs judicious caching, proactive server pushing and neighborhood replication to reduce service cost and improve response time under changing user mobility and access patterns. Simulation results suggest that different strategies are effective for different types of data in response to different patterns of movement and information access.

1 Introduction

The advances in portable devices and wireless communication technologies enables a new form of services named *location based services(LBS)* which deliver location dependent and context sensitive information to mobile users. Typical examples of such services include local maps, local weather, traffic condition, tour guide, and shopping guide, etc. A key characteristic of LBS is that the same service request may need to be answered with complete different results as the user changes his/her location or the targets move. Because of the highly dynamic nature of the problem, traditional information management techniques are not well suited for LBS. Developing proper infrastructure, location management, as well as data management strategies for LBS has been a major challenge to both wireless service providers and application developers. To answer this challenge, we first analyzed the nature of the problem and proposed a classification of potential application domains. Based on the analysis, we characterized the *dynamic data management* problem for LBS and devised a general service architecture flexible enough to provide dynamic access to both location dependent and location independent data. We further devised a cost model to analyze the dynamic behavior of the system as well as the service cost. The cost analysis leads to a set of dynamic data management strategies that employs judicious caching, proactive server pushing and neighborhood replication to improve service response time under changing user mobility and access patterns. Simulation results suggest that different strategies are effective for different types of data in response to different patterns of user movement and information access.

The rest of the paper is organized as follows. Section 2 provides a survey of related issues and research work. Section 3 presents our framework for problem analysis, application characterization and domain classification which leads to the challenging dynamic data management problem. In Section 4, we proposed a system architecture for location-based information services to answer the challenge. Based on the service architecture, we devised a cost model in Section 5 to facilitate the design of a set of dynamic data management strategies as well as the analysis of the system behavior. Simulation results presented in Section 6 demonstrate the feasibility and performance of our framework toward the construction of highly responsive systems for location-based mobile information services. Section 7 concludes the paper.

2 Related Work

Data management in mobile computing environments is especially challenging for the need to process information on the move, to cope with resource limitation, and to deal with heterogeneity. Among the applications of mobile data management, LBS have been identified as one of the most promising area of research and development [1]. The problem has also been studied under various terms such as location-aware, context-aware, or adaptive information systems [8, 9]. Many of the previous work on LBS treated location as an additional attribute of the data tables[4, 10]. LBS queries can be processed like ordinary queries except with additional constraints on the location attribute. Caching techniques specially tailored for LBS or mobile computing environments in general have also been a major research area [2, 4]. Semantic caching techniques employed semantic descriptions of cached items to facilitate better cache admission and replacement decisions that are responsive to the user movement[3, 6]. Research effort on moving objects database are also related to our work in the need to process data in a highly dynamic environment [5, 7, 11]. Our work differs from the previous works in that we consider the problem from a global point of view. Our strategies take into account both location dependent and location independent queries to information from centralized broadcasting channel such as the stock pro or world news, as well as localized services such as the nearby restaurants or local weather. The dynamic nature of our approach also facilitates timely responses to rapid changes in access and/or mobility patterns.

3 Mobile Information Service Characterization and Classification

Based on the characteristics of data and their typical usage patterns, we classify information service applications in mobile environments along four dimensions.

- Source of data : *central* vs. *local*
  The data can be from a *central* broadcasting channel such as the CNN world news, or from a *local* service station such as area map or tourist attractions.

- Period of validity : *static* vs. *dynamic*
  The period of validity of the data can be relatively *static* such as various kinds of traffic timetables, or *dynamic* such as the current traffic condition.

- Target audience : *public* vs. *personal*
  The intended target audience of the data can be to the general *public* such as a public announcement, or to a particular *person* such as email or personalized news.

- Location dependency : *location independent* vs. *location dependent*
  The nature of the queries and results can be *location independent* such as the stock pro, or *location dependent* such as the nearby restraints within a given range.

In Table 1, we give several examples of the mobile information services along these four dimensions. Note that some services may appear in more than one places. Area news, for example, may be provided by a central news agency or by a local station. The classification helps us in designing a general service architecture that can be easily adapted to incorporate different data management strategies to fit the characteristics of different application domains. For example, information having the properties of central, public, static, and location independent are good candidates for traditional techniques such as keeping cached copies at the client devices or local servers. On the other hand, the data of local, personal, dynamic, and location dependent applications are best handled with dynamic strategies that can quickly respond to the changes in user location or data status. In general, central data sources call for proper dissemination infrastructure while local data need good caching

mechanism. Static data can be efficiently served with proper replication schemes while the processing of dynamic data may consider prefetching or semantic caching techniques. The access patterns to public data are often predictable and therefore amenable to proactive dissemination techniques such as pushing hot data closer to the clients. Personalized data, however, may need to be processed with dynamic profiling and data migration techniques. The location dependency of data raises a new issue of answering *range queries* such as the nearby motels within 5 miles of the current location. Supporting such services requires neighboring base stations(local servers) to exchange information on target objects. Some optimization techniques can be adopted such as the prefetching and caching of popular range query targets.

As a summary, the challenge is to design a flexible service architecture and dynamic data management strategies to provide highly responsive and location dependent information access in resource constrained and rapidly changing environments for the application domains discussed above. We call it the *dynamic data management* problem for location based services in mobile environments. The dynamic nature of the problem is strongly emphasized in here since both the clients and targets may change locations at any time.

4 Location-Based Service Architecture

Based on the application classification and service characterization, we devised a general system architecture as the basis for our cost modelling and strategy design. Our system were designed with several criteria in minds. First of all, the architecture must reflect the current and foreseeable future status of the wireless networking technologies. The system must also be flexible enough to allow the installment of different data management strategies on different classes of applications. Finally, since we want to serve both location dependent as well as location independent data, the architecture must take the source characteristics into consideration. Figure 1 depicted our architectural design consisting of the central server, local server, and the client device.

The central server is used to model a service site for centralized data such as the New York Stock Exchange. In addition to a central information database, a push unit is included to facilitate server-initiated pushing strategies that proactively send selected data items toward the clients. Since the downlink bandwidth is usually much larger and cheaper than uplink connection, pushing techniques turn out to be efficient and valuable tools with little extra cost.

The local server is the data manager and wireless information server for a single cell. Each cell is assumed to have a unique local server which provides wireless access for all the clients in its cell and acts as a bridge between the central server and the client devices at the same time. It is the

		Location Independent		Location Dependent	
		Static	Dynamic	Static	Dynamic
Central	Public	global public announcement, traffic timetable, ...	news, stock pro, mobile banking, ...	area transportation info, area map, tourist attractions, ...	area news, area weather, traffic condition, ...
	Personal	email, medical record, personal note, student grade, ...	personalized news, investment guide, chat messages, ...	personalized tour arrangement, route planning, ...	personalized area news, exhibition guide, ...
Local	Public	local public announcement, service directory, ...	area news, area weather, area broadcasting, ...	nearby hotels and restaurants, local transportation info, ...	local news, local traffic, ...
	Personal	personal information (schedule, to do list, shopping list), ...	personalized area news, push services, advertising, ...	nearby specified targets, personalized local attractions, ...	current location, route, nearby moving targets, ...

Table 1: Mobile information service classification

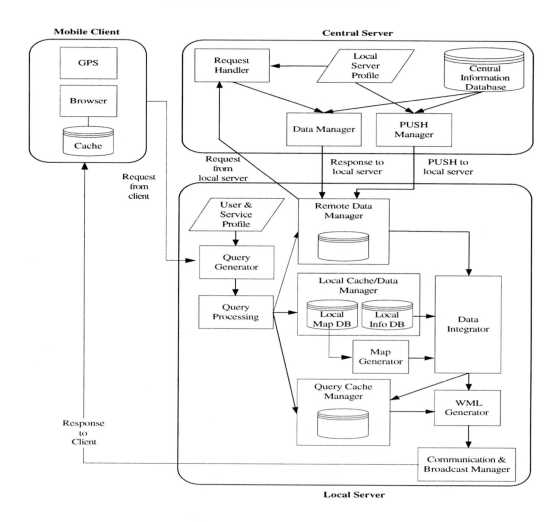

Figure 1: LBS System Architecture.

center for managing local information as well as the key player to provide location based services. All local servers are connected to the Internet via fixed network and therefore can send information to each others with almost negligible delay in comparison with wireless access. This is an important factor since neighboring local servers must work closely together to provide efficient location-based services. The cache and data manager is responsible for maintaining the information received from the central server as well as other local servers. A local server is also equipped with a map database for answering location dependent map queries.

The client is any end user device that is capable of wireless communication as well as user interface services. This is probably the branch of the wireless technologies that evolves with the fastest pace. Therefore we do not presume the computing power and storage capacity of a client device. We only assume that it can send out information requests via a wireless link, can do some local processing if required, and has a client cache for keeping frequently accessed data items. The most distinctive feature of a client is that it moves. A client can change its position at will, in and out of a cell, from one cell to another, without the obligation to notify any server in advance. Since a client can issue a query at any time any where, this is especially challenging for information service providers. In our architectural design, a client always sends requests to the local server of the cell where the client resides. The target objects may be available right at the client cache, at the local server of the same cell, from the local servers of other cells, or from central servers.

To make our design general and flexible, we assume an object-based service environment. The information requests are categorized into three types of queries:

- *Object queries* : that target specified objects.

- *Range queries* : that target objects located within a range restriction and satisfy certain constraints.

- *Map queries* : for area map information.

The service of map queries is out of the scope of this paper. We will discuss only object and range queries. Object queries are like traditional type of queries that are issued by explicitly naming the target objects or by giving the object classes and the constraints that must be satisfied. Range queries are location dependent queries to locate the desired type(s) of object(s) within a specified distance around the client. "List all the restaurants within 5 miles of my current location." for example, is a typical range query. "Give me the hotel reservation phone number of the Pleasant Plaza." on the other hand, is an object query since the target object is directly specified. We note that if the target object(s) is(are) located within the same cell as the client, the local server of the cell can answer the query without consulting other servers. If, however, the target objects reside in other cells

or in a central server, the local server must request the desired objects from other servers and pass them to the client when the objects arrive. Since the client can move at will, a target that can be accessed from within the same cell may have to be accessed from other cell for the next request. This is also true for the range queries since any target object can be in and out of range as the client moves. Static query processing strategies have little use in such environments. Dynamic data management strategies that can effectively locate the desired objects as well as quickly respond to the location changes are in order.

5 Cost Model and Dynamic Data Management Strategies

To facilitate the design of dynamic data management strategies for location based services, we devise a simple yet effective cost model that abstract away nonessential details of the wireless environment and characterize only the key players and dominant cost factors. As depicted in Figure 2, a location based service environment is modelled as consisting of four major types of abstract entities:

C The client device.

L The local server of the cell where the client resides.

L' The neighboring servers, i.e. the local servers of the neighboring cells.

S The central information server.

The client access the network through a wireless connection to the local server while all other connections between servers (local and/or central) are through wired links. As the current technology stands, the cost of a wireless link is much higher than that of a wired link. The connection cost between neighboring servers is relatively lower than the cost of accessing from a remote central server. We therefore classify the communication cost into three categories:

d The wireless communication cost between a client and its local server.

l The communication cost between neighboring local servers.

r The cost of accessing information from a remote central server to the local server.

Based on the abstraction and characterization, we proposed three sets of dynamic data management strategies, namely *judicious caching*, *proactive pushing*, as well as *neighborhood replication* to improve service response time and reduce communication cost. The first two sets of strategies are designed for object queries that target information

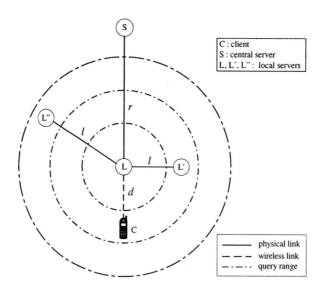

C : client	
S : central server	
L, L`, L" : local servers	

————	physical link
— — —	wireless link
—·—·—	query range

Figure 2: LBS cost model — Central, location dependent, and range services

largely from central data services while the third set is for location based range queries. We then conducted detail cost analysis to understand the exact situations for these strategies to be cost effective. This help us in determining when to apply and adjust the strategies for better services.

Judicious Caching

As discussed in section 4, both local servers and clients have caches to retain downloaded information. If certain types of objects published by a particular central server were accessed frequently by the clients of a cell, a simple idea is to maintain cache copies of all such objects at the local server and keep them always up to date. In this way, the clients in the cell can always access fresh copies of the objects directly from the local server without further delay. We termed this *judicious caching* since the target objects to be cached can range from the entire central server to certain categories or to a particular class of objects. However, any caching strategies bring about maintenance cost as well. To keep the cached copies up to date, a local server must spend the extra cost of getting new copies from the central server whenever updates occur. The question is then how to determine when to apply such a strategy to what types of data objects? Our proposed solution is to first partition the data at the central server according to their publishing characteristics. Data objects that are closely related and updated at the same or similar rate are grouped together. Then for each group of target objects, we perform a detail analysis of the potential benefit of caching those objects in a particular local server based on a set of dynamically maintained access statistics listed as follows.

R The total number of requests to the target objects issued by the clients in the cell.

U The total number of updates to the target objects.

c The average hit rate of the client cache.

h The average hit rate of the local server cache.

The caching of the target objects is beneficial if the sum of the access cost and the update maintenance cost is lower than conventional on-demand caching. That is,

$$Rc + R(1-c)d + Ur \quad < \quad Rc + R(1-c)hd + \\ R(1-c)(1-h)(d+r)$$

With simple algebraic manipulation, we have

$$U \quad < \quad R(1-c)(1-h)$$

Since $R(1-c)(1-h)$ is the number of requests actually received by the central server to the target objects, the equation above means that as long as the update rate to a particular class of objects is smaller than the request rate experienced on the central server, then it is beneficial to cache that class of objects at the local server and keep them always up to date. This is a reasonable decision to make since if the requests to the same class of objects are much higher than the update rate, the cache maintenance cost can easily be covered by the saving on access cost. Therefore, the judicious caching strategy is to maintain a class of objects at the local server cache and keep them up to date if the update and request rates satisfy the condition above. When the request rate drops at latter time, or the update increases such that the condition no longer holds, the local server can stop requesting further maintenance update from the central server.

Proactive Pushing

A natural alternative to the judicious caching strategy is to push a certain percentage of "hot" data to the local server in an attempt to minimize the access cost and response time experienced by the clients. We call this *proactive pushing* since it is the central server that proactively pushes selected objects to the local server. Similar to judicious caching, we need to determine exactly when and how to push the data. With two additional parameters, a detail analysis of the access cost with respective to conventional on-demand caching reveals the condition for applying the strategy.

p The percentage of the "most frequently requested" data to be proactively pushed to the local server.

q The percentage of update to the proactively pushed data with respective to the total number of updates U.

In other words, among the requests received by the local server, p percentage of which can be responded locally since they have been pushed from the central server to the local server. We also pay the maintenance cost for q percentage of the total update since we must keep them up to date. Similar to judicious caching, we must have a lower cost than conventional on-demand caching for such a strategy to be effective. We therefore have the following cost formula.

$$Rc + R(1 - c)pd + R(1 - c)(1 - p)(d + r) + Uqr$$
$$< Rc + R(1 - c)hd + R(1 - c)(1 - h)(d + r)$$

With simple algebraic manipulation, we obtain the formula

$$Uq < R(1 - c)(p - h)$$

which means that if the extra number of maintenance updates due to proactive pushing is less than the additional number of requests that can be satisfied locally, then it is worthy of the cost. We note that whenever p increases, q also increases. When the update cost overwhelms the request saving, further pushing can do more harm than good. Therefore in the proactive pushing strategy, the central server selects an initial p and maintains the statistics discussed above. When the requests to the "hot" data increase, p can be increased accordingly. If the update rate to the pushed data becomes higher, then the central server can reduce the pushing percentage.

So far, we have assumed that all objects at the central server are considered together. There is no reason why we can't partition the data in a similar way as judicious caching and maintain a separate p for each data group. In such case, judicious caching becomes a special case of proactive pushing with p equals 100%.

Neighborhood Replication

For range queries, the target objects are no longer from central servers but from the local servers of the current and neighboring cells within the specified range. Data management strategies must be tailored accordingly. In general, different range queries may overlap with each others. If similar range queries were repeatedly issues by the clients, then it would be beneficial to replicate the data objects of the most frequently accessed neighboring cells at the local server. We name this *neighborhood replication*. The set of replicated cells is called the *replication range* of the strategy. To maintain the cost effectiveness of such a strategy, we need to record a different set of access parameters as follows.

R The total number of range requests issued by the clients in the cell.

G The total number of updates to the location dependent data objects.

c The average hit rate of the client cache.

m The number of neighboring servers to replicate.

n The average number of servers within the query ranges but not replicated.

k The number of neighboring servers to be added to ($k > 0$) or excluded from ($k < 0$) the replication range.

n' After adjusting the replication range, the average number of servers within the query ranges but not replicated.

The idea is to maintain replica of location dependent data from selected neighboring cells and keep them up to date. On each evaluation period, we try to evaluate the potential benefit of adding k additional neighboring servers into the replication range. Naturally, the inclusion of more replica is beneficial if the expected cost is less than the cost without them. This can be expressed by the following formula.

$$Rc + R(1 - c)d + R(1 - c)n'l + G(m + k)l$$
$$< Rc + R(1 - c)d + R(1 - c)nl + Gml$$

The formula can be simplified as

$$G < R(1 - c)(n - n')/k \quad \text{if } k > 0 \text{ and } n - n' > 0$$
$$G > R(1 - c)(n - n')/k \quad \text{if } k < 0 \text{ and } n - n' < 0$$

We note that when adding more servers into the replication range (i.e. $k > 0$ and thus $n - n' > 0$), $R(1 - c)(n - n')$ is the number of requests to the neighboring servers that can be saved due to replication. Therefore, the first formula states that if the number of updates to the location dependent data is less than the average number of neighboring requests that can be saved, then we can go ahead replicate those neighboring servers. On the other hand, if we were to remove some servers from the replication range (i.e. $k < 0$ and thus $n - n' < 0$), $R(1-c)(|n-n'|)$ becomes the additional number of requests that can no longer be satisfied by the cache and must be sent to the neighboring servers. Therefore, the second formula states that if the number of updates is greater than the average increase in requests to the neighboring servers, then we should shrink the replication range.

The neighborhood replication strategy can be summarized as follows. Each local server determines an initial replication range on startup and replicates the location dependent objects from the neighboring servers. On each evaluation period, a local server determines whether to grow or shrink the replication range according to the decision equations. We note that a local server does not need to actually replicate the additional k neighbors in order to obtain n' and G. Since we know where each objects came from. After servicing the client requests, we can always make the assumption of any desirable replication configuration and derive the values of these access statistics whenever we need them.

As a summary, all three types of strategies are designed to dynamically respond to the rapid changes in access contexts and request/update patterns. By carefully analyzing the relative benefits of caching and/or replication, we can determine exactly when to apply and how to adjust the strategies to facilitate highly responsive location based services.

6 Simulation and Evaluation

We have designed and implemented a simulation system (Figure 3) consisting of an environment generator, a request/update generator, as well as a simulation engine. On each experiment, we first select appropriate values for the set of cost model parameters (i.e., d, l, and r) and the set of environment parameters (such as the number of cells, clients, data objects, requests, and updates). The former is for cost accumulation while the latter is for generating a request file. Then a set of server side parameters (such as the cache size, push percentage, and initial replication range) is supplied to initialize the simulation engine. The simulation proceeds through a specified number of rounds. During each round, we simulate the execution of the requests/updates and maintain the statistics needed for each data management strategy accordingly. The changes in access statistics may trigger the dynamic adaptation of the strategy which may in turn affect the access statistics thereafter. In addition to the execution simulation and strategy application, we also keep records of the access cost of each request based on the cost model parameters and write to the result file.

Figure 4 represents the results of performance comparison between conventional on-demand caching and judicious caching with varying cache sizes as well as request/update ratios. The size of the cache is the capacity measured in terms of the percentage of data objects received from the central server. We can see very clearly that the judicious caching strategy is superior in all cache sizes especially when the number of requests are higher than the updates. When the updates are much higher than the request rate, two strategies coincide since caching provides little benefit in such a scenario.

Figure 5 demonstrates the combined effect of request/update ratio and cache size on judicious caching. Due to the judicious nature, our strategy can effectively explore cache resource and take advantages of the situations when the requests are higher than the updates.

In order to understand the responsiveness of judicious caching in reaction to the rapid change of access patterns, we have conducted an experiment of 100 simulation rounds with request/update ratio set to 20/80 for the first 50 rounds and rapidly changed to 80/20 for the rest 50 rounds. The result shown in Figure 6 not only demonstrates the performance advantage of judicious caching over conventional on-demand caching but also the adaptation capability of our approach.

For evaluating the proactive pushing strategy, we fixed the cache size and varied the push percentage to obtain the result presented in Figure 7. Contrary to our expectation, while proactive pushing performs consistently superior than conventional on-demand caching, higher push percentage does not provide significant advantage. After careful examination of the data set, we found that this may be due to the random generation of request patterns which tends to access data evenly without hot spot. In such case, proactive pushing does not provide significant advantage since no data are "really" hot.

A rather interesting result was obtained from the response time comparison between conventional on-demand caching and neighborhood replication on range queries. Figure 8 shows that both strategies are relatively independent of the request/update ratio. This is because the clients are constantly moving which results in the cache being of little use. We can also see that neighborhood replication consistently outperforms on-demand caching by a large gap. This is due to the dynamic nature of our strategy. When the request/update ratio is high, the strategy can take advantage of the situation by increasing the number of neighbors into the replication scope. On the other hand, when the reverse is true, the strategy can automatically decrease the number of replication sites to save the replica maintenance cost.

As a summary, dynamic data management is essential for location based services. Even for location independent data, dynamic strategies are still required since the clients can move from one place to another. By characterizing the data sources and access trends, we have designed effective strategies that successfully balanced between the saving in access cost and the increase in maintenance cost.

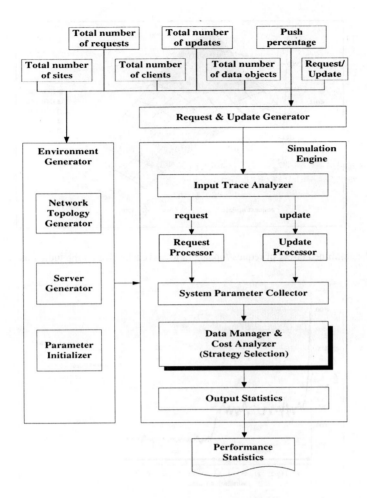

Figure 3: Simulation system architecture.

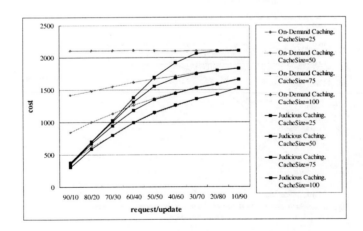

Figure 4: Performance comparison of the judicious caching strategy with on-demand caching.

187

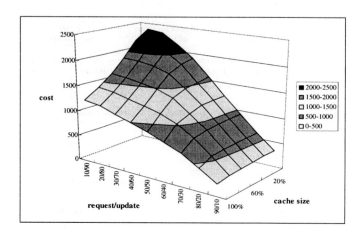

Figure 5: The combined effect of request/update ratio and cache size on the judicious caching strategy.

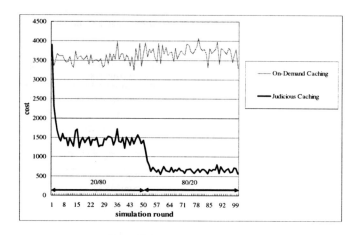

Figure 6: The adaptation capability of the judicious caching strategy in response to the change on request/update pattern.

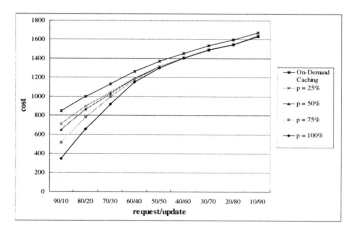

Figure 7: Execution cost of the proactive pushing strategy with varying push rate.

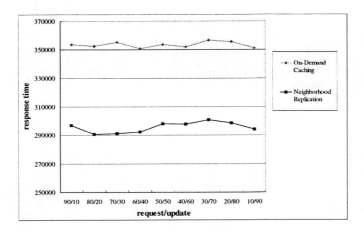

Figure 8: Response time comparison of the neighborhood replication strategy against on-demand caching on range queries.

7 Conclusions and Future Work

We have proposed a service framework, system architecture, simple but effective cost models and dynamic data management strategies for location based services in mobile computing environments. Analytical and simulation results successfully demonstrate not only the feasibility but also the effectiveness of our approach. The most distinctive features of the proposed strategies are their capability to dynamically respond to changes in the mobility and/or access patterns. We plan to further extend our system framework and cost model to handle information services on moving data sources, not just moving clients. We are also evaluating the potential of employing mobile agent technologies to support continuous location based service queries.

References

[1] Daniel Barbara. Mobile computing and databases - a survey. *IEEE Transaction on Knowledge and Data Engineering*, 11(1):108–117, January/February 1999.

[2] B. Y. Chan, A. Si, and H. V. Leong. Cache management for mobile databases: Design and evaluation. In *Proceedings of 14th ICDE*, pages 54–63, 1998.

[3] Shaul Dar, Michael J. Franklin, B. Jonsson, Divesh Srivastava, and Michael Tan. Semantic data caching and replacement. In *Proceedings of VLDB*, pages 330–341, 1996.

[4] M. H. Dunham and V. Kumar. Location dependent data and its management in mobile databases. In *Proceedings of DEXA Workshop*, pages 414–419, August 1998.

[5] R. H. Guting, M. Erwig M. H. Bohlen, C. S. Jensen, N. A. Lorentzos, M. Schneider, and M. Vazirgiannis. A foundation for representing and querying moving objects. *ACM Transactions on Database Systems*, 25(1):1–42, March 2000.

[6] Qun Ren and Margaret H. Dunham. Using semantic caching to manage location dependent data in mobile computing. In *MobiCom'00: The Sixth Annual International Conference on Mobile Computing and Networking*, pages 210–221, August 2000.

[7] Simonas Saltenis and Christian S. Jensen. Indexing mobing objects for location-based services. In *Proc. 18th International Conference on Data Engineering*, pages 463–472, 2002.

[8] M. Satyanarayanan, B. Noble, P. Kumar, and M. Price. Application-aware adaptation for mobile computing. *Operating System Review*, 29, January 1995.

[9] B. Schilit, N. Adams, and R. Want. Context-aware mobile applications. In *IEEE Workshop on Mobile Computing Systems and Applications*, Santa Cruz, CA, U.S., December 1994.

[10] Ayse Y. Seydim, Margaret H. Dunham, and Vijay Kumar. Location dependent query processing. In *MobiDE'01: 2nd ACM International Workshop on Data Engineering for Mobile and Wireless Access*, pages 47–53, 2001.

[11] Ouri Wolfson, Bo Xu, Sam Chamberlain, and Liqin Jiang. Moving objects databases: Issues and solutions. In *Proceedings of the 10th International Conference on Statistical and Scientific Database Management*, pages 111–122, Capri, Italy, 1998.

Imprecise and Temporal Databases

Specification and Management of QoS in Imprecise Real-Time Databases*

Mehdi Amirijoo, Jörgen Hansson
Dept. of Computer and Information Science
Linköping University, Sweden
{meham,jorha}@ida.liu.se

Sang H. Son
Dept. of Computer Science
University of Virginia, Virginia, USA
son@cs.virginia.edu

Abstract

Real-time applications such as e-commerce, flight control, chemical and nuclear control, and telecommunication are becoming increasingly sophisticated in their data needs, resulting in greater demands for real-time data services. Since the workload of real-time databases (RTDBs), providing real-time data services, cannot be precisely predicted, they can become overloaded and thereby cause temporal violations, resulting in a damage or even a catastrophe. Imprecise computation techniques address this problem and allow graceful degradation during overloads. In this paper, we present a framework consisting of a model for expressing QoS requirements in terms of data and transaction preciseness, an architecture based on feedback control scheduling, and a set of algorithms implementing different policies and behaviors. Our approach gives a robust and controlled behavior of RTDBs, even for transient overloads and with inaccurate run-time estimates of the transactions. Further, performance experiments show that the proposed algorithms outperform a set of baseline algorithms, including FCS-EDF that schedules the transactions using EDF and feedback control.

1 Introduction

Lately the demand for real-time data services has increased and applications used in manufacturing, web-servers, e-commerce etc. are becoming increasingly sophisticated in their data needs. The data normally spans from low-level control data, typically acquired from sensors, to high-level management and business data. In these applications it is desirable to process user requests within their deadlines using fresh data. In systems, such as web-servers and sensor networks with non-uniform access patterns, the workload of the databases cannot be precisely pre-dicted and, hence, the databases can become overloaded. As a result, deadline misses and freshness violations may occur during the transient overloads. To address this problem we propose a quality of service (QoS) sensitive approach to guarantee a set of requirements on the behavior of the database, even in the presence of unpredictable workloads. Further, for some applications (e.g. web service) it is desirable that the quality of service does not vary significantly from one transaction to another. Here, it is emphasized that individual QoS needs requested by clients and trans-actions are enforced, and hence, any deviations from the QoS needs should be uniformly distributed among clients to ensure QoS fairness.

In earlier work [2, 3] we presented the algorithms FCS-IC-1, FCS-IC-2, FCS-HEF, and FCS-HEDF for managing QoS using imprecise computation [9] and feedback control scheduling [10, 11]. An important feature of this class of algorithms is their ability to adapt to various workloads and tolerate inaccurate estimates of execution times, and still conform to a given QoS specification. In this paper we give an overview of FCS-IC-1 and FCS-IC-2. These algorithms control the preciseness of the results, given by transactions, by monitoring the system deadline miss percentage and adapt the system such that a QoS specification in terms of miss percentage and data preciseness is satisfied. Furthermore, we present a more complex model of transaction preciseness by presenting the notion of transaction error, together with FCS-HEF and FCS-HEDF. These two algorithms support QoS specifications given in terms of transaction error and also address QoS fairness, i.e., they are designed to minimize the deviation in QoS among admitted transactions. In this paper we unify our earlier work into a common framework consisting of a model for expressing QoS requirements in terms of data and transaction preciseness, an architecture based on feedback control scheduling, and a set of algorithms implementing different policies and behaviors. Furthermore, we report new experimental results that show that the proposed algorithms also adapt to various QoS specifications and transaction sets showing different transaction error characteristics.

*This work was funded, in part by CUGS (the National Graduate School in Computer Science, Sweden), CENIIT (Center for Industrial Information Technology) under contract 01.07, and NSF grant IIS-0208758.

We have carried out a set of experiments to evaluate the performance of the proposed algorithms. The studies show that the suggested algorithms give a robust and controlled behavior of RTDBs, in terms of transaction and data preciseness, even for transient overloads and with inaccurate execution time estimates of the transactions.

The rest of this paper is organized as follows. The detailed problem formulation is given in Section 2. In Section 3, the database model is given. In Section 4 we present our approach, and in Section 5, the results of performance evaluations are presented. In Section 6 we give an overview on related work, followed by Section 7, where conclusions and future work are discussed.

2 Problem Formulation

In our database model, data objects in a RTDB are updated by update transactions, e.g. sensor values, while user transactions represent user requests, e.g. complex read-write operations. The notion of imprecision may be applied at data object and/or user transaction level. The data quality increases as the imprecision of the data objects decreases. Similarly, the quality of user transactions (for brevity referred to as transaction quality) increases as the imprecision of the results produced by user transactions decreases. In this work we model transaction quality and data quality as orthogonal entities.

Starting with data impreciseness, for a data object stored in the RTDB and representing a real-world variable, we can allow a certain degree of deviation compared to the real-world value. If such deviation can be tolerated, arriving updates may be discarded during transient overloads. In order to measure data quality we introduce the notion of data error (denoted DE_i), which indicates how much the value of a data object d_i stored in the RTDB deviates from the corresponding real-world value, which is given by the latest arrived transaction updating d_i.[1]

The quality of user transactions is adjusted by managing the data error, which is done by considering an upper bound for the data error given by the maximum data error (denoted MDE). An update transaction T_j is discarded if the data error of the data object d_i to be updated by T_j is less or equal to MDE (i.e. $DE_i \leq MDE$). If MDE increases, more update transactions are discarded, degrading the quality of data. Similarly, if MDE decreases, fewer update transactions are discarded, resulting in improved data quality.

The goal of our work is to derive algorithms for adjusting data error such that the data quality and the transaction quality satisfy a given QoS specification and the deviation

---

[1] Note that the latest arrived transaction updating d_i may have been discarded and, hence, d_i may hold the value of an earlier update transaction.

of transaction quality among admitted transactions is minimized (i.e. QoS fairness is enforced). A major issue is how to compute MDE, depending on the user transaction quality.

3 Data and Transaction Model

We consider a main memory database model where there is one CPU as the main processing element. In our data model, data objects can be classified into two classes, temporal and non-temporal [12]. For temporal data we only consider base data, i.e., data that holds the view of the real-world and are updated by sensors. A base data object d_i is considered temporally inconsistent or stale if the current time is later than the timestamp of d_i followed by the length of the absolute validity interval of d_i (denoted AVI_i), i.e. $CurrentTime > TimeStamp_i + AVI_i$. For a data object d_i, let data error, $DE_i = 100 \times \frac{|CurrentValue_i - V_j|}{|CurrentValue_i|} (\%)$, where V_j is the value of the latest arrived transaction updating d_i and $CurrentValue_i$ the current value of d_i.

Transactions are classified either as update transactions or user transactions. Update transactions arrive periodically and may only write to base data objects. User transactions arrive aperiodically and may read temporal and read-/write non-temporal data. User and update transactions (T_i) are assumed to be composed of one mandatory subtransaction (denoted M_i) and $\#O_i$ optional subtransactions (denoted $O_{i,j}$, where $O_{i,j}$ is the jth optional subtransaction of T_i). For the remainder of the paper, we let $t_i \in \{M_i, O_{i,1}, \ldots, O_{i,\#O_i}\}$ denote a subtransaction of T_i. We use the milestone approach [9] to transaction impreciseness. Thus, we have divided transactions into subtransactions according to milestones. A mandatory subtransaction completes when it successfully finishes. The mandatory subtransaction is necessary for an acceptable result and it must be computed to completion before the transaction deadline. Optional subtransactions are processed if there is enough time or resources available. While it is assumed that all subtransactions of a transaction T_i arrive at the same time, the first optional subtransaction, i.e. $O_{i,1}$, becomes ready for execution when the mandatory subtransaction is completed. In general, an optional subtransaction $O_{i,j}$ becomes ready for execution when $O_{i,j-1}$ ($2 \leq j \leq \#O_i$) completes. Hence, there is a precedence relation among the subtransactions as given by $M_i \prec O_{i,1} \prec O_{i,2} \prec \ldots \prec O_{i,\#O_i}$.

We set the deadline of all subtransactions t_i to the deadline of T_i. A subtransaction is terminated if it is completed or has missed its deadline. A transaction is terminated when its last optional subtransaction completes or one of its subtransactions misses its deadline. In the latter case, all subtransactions that are not yet completed are terminated as well.

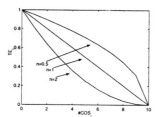

Figure 1. Contribution of $\#COS_i$ to TE_i.

For update transactions we assume that there are no optional subtransactions (i.e. $\#O_i = 0$). Each update transaction consists only of a single mandatory subtransaction, since updates do not use complex logical or numerical operations and, hence, normally have lower execution times than user transactions.

In some applications it is possible to formally model the preciseness of the answers given by transactions through the use of error functions (e.g., closed systems where the set of transactions that are processed are known in advance). For a transaction T_i, we use an error function to approximate its corresponding transaction error given by, $TE_i(\#COS_i) = \left(1 - \frac{\#COS_i}{\#O_i}\right)^{n_i}$, where n_i is the order of the error function and $\#COS_i$ denotes the number of completed optional subtransactions. This error function is similar to the one presented in [4]. By choosing n_i we can model and support multiple classes of transactions showing different error characteristics (see Figure 1).

4 Approach

Next we describe our approach for managing the performance of a RTDB in terms of transaction and data quality. First, we start by defining performance metrics and QoS. An overview of the feedback control scheduling architecture is given, followed by issues related to modeling of the architecture and the design of controllers. Finally, we present the algorithms FCS-IC-1, FCS-IC-2, FCS-HEF, and FCS-HEDF.

4.1 Performance Metrics

In this work we adapt both steady-state and transient-state performance metrics [10]. We adapt the following notation of describing discrete variables in the time domain: $A(k)$ refers to the value of the variable A during the time window $[(k-1)W, kW]$, where W is the sampling period and k is the sampling instant.[2] Let $|Terminated(k)|$ be the number of terminated transactions, whereas $|Terminated^M(k)|$ and $|Terminated^O(k)|$ are the number of terminated mandatory and optional subtransactions,

<hr/>

[2]For the rest of this paper, we sometimes drop k where the notion of time is not of primary interest.

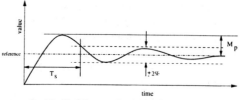

Figure 2. Definition of settling time (T_s) and overshoot (M_p)

respectively. The number of transactions that have missed their deadline is denoted by $|DeadlineMiss(k)|$, and the number mandatory and optional subtransactions that have missed their deadlines is given by $|DeadlineMiss^M(k)|$ and $|DeadlineMiss^O(k)|$, respectively. We exclusively consider transactions admitted to the system.

User Transaction Quality Metrics:

- Deadline miss percentage of mandatory user subtransactions is defined as,
  $$M^M(k) = 100 \times \frac{|DeadlineMiss^M(k)|}{|Terminated^M(k)|}(\%).$$

- Deadline miss percentage of optional user subtransactions is defined as,
  $$M^O(k) = 100 \times \frac{|DeadlineMiss^O(k)|}{|Terminated^O(k)|}(\%).$$

- Average transaction error gives the preciseness of the results of user transactions, and it is defined as,
  $$ATE(k) = 100 \times \frac{\sum_{i \in Terminated(k)} TE_i}{|Terminated(k)|}(\%).$$

Data Quality Metric. Maximum data error ($MDE(k)$) is used as a metric for data quality (see section 2).

QoS Fairness Metric. Standard deviation of transaction error ($SDTE$) gives a measure of how much the transaction error of terminated transactions deviates from the average transaction error, and it is defined as, $SDTE(k) = \sqrt{\frac{1}{|Terminated(k)|-1} \sum_{i \in Terminated(k)} (TE_i - ATE(k))^2}$.

System Utilization. We measure system utilization (U) in order to acquire a better understanding of the performance of the algorithms.

Transient-State Performance Metrics. We consider the following transient-state performance metrics (see Figure 2) applied on user transaction quality and data quality performance metrics.

- Overshoot (M_p) is the worst-case system performance in the transient system state and it is given in percentage.

- Settling time (T_s) is the time for the transient overshoot to decay and reach the steady state performance, given by $100\% \pm 2\%$ of the performance reference. Hence, this is a measure of how fast the system converges towards the desired performance.

4.2 QoS Specification

The QoS specification is given in terms of steady-state and transient-state performance metrics as described in Section 4.1. For each performance metric y we specify its steady-state by a reference y_r, meaning that we want y to stay at y_r at all times, and apply overshoot and settling time to specify its transient-state performance. Quality of data (QoD) is defined in terms of MDE. An increase in QoD refers to a decrease in MDE. In contrast a decrease in QoD refers to an increase in MDE. We consider the following ways of defining QoS.

QoS Specification A. We define quality of transaction (QoT) in terms of deadline miss percentage of optional subtransactions (M^O). QoT decreases as M^O increases (similarly, QoT increases as M^O decreases). The DBA can specify steady-state and transient-state behavior for M^M, M^O, and MDE. A QoS requirement can be specified as the following: $M_r^M = 1\%$ (i.e. reference M^M), $M_r^O = 10\%$, $MDE_r = 2\%$, $U \geq U_l = 80\%$, $T_s \leq 60s$, and $M_p \leq 30\%$. This gives the following transient-state performance specifications: $M^M \leq M_r^M \times (M_p + 100) = 1.3\%$, $M^O \leq 13\%$ and $MDE \leq 2.6\%$. A lower utilization value is given by U_l, meaning that U must be greater or equal to U_l at all times.

QoS Specification B. We define QoT in terms of average transaction error (ATE). QoT decreases as ATE increases (similarly, QoT increases as ATE decreases). The DBA can specify steady-state and transient-state behavior for ATE and MDE. A QoS requirement can be specified as the following: $ATE_r = 20\%$ (i.e. reference ATE), $MDE_r = 5\%$, $T_s \leq 60s$, and $M_p \leq 30\%$. This gives the following transient-state performance specifications: $ATE \leq ATE_r \times (M_p + 100) = 26\%$, and $MDE \leq MDE_r \times (M_p + 100) = 6.5\%$.

4.3 Feedback Control Scheduling Architecture

We employ feedback control scheduling [10, 11] to manage the quality of the service provided by the RTDB. The goal is to control the performance, defined by a set of controlled variables, such that the controlled variables satisfy a given QoS specification. The general outline of the feedback control scheduling architecture is given in Figure 3. Admitted transactions are placed in the ready queue. The transaction handler manages the execution of the transactions. We choose M^M and M^O as controlled variables when the QoS is specified according to QoS specification A, while ATE is the controlled variable when QoS specification B applies. At each sampling instant, the controlled variable(s) is monitored and fed into the QoS controller, which compares the performance reference(s), i.e. M_r^M and M_r^O, or ATE_r, with the controlled variable(s) to get

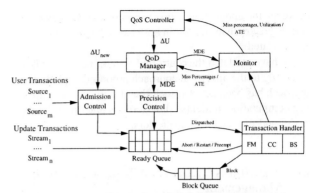

Figure 3. Feedback Control Scheduling Architecture

the current performance error. Based on this the controller computes a change, denoted ΔU, to the total estimated requested utilization. We refer to ΔU as the manipulated variable. Based on ΔU, the QoD manager changes the total estimated requested utilization by adapting the QoD (i.e. adjusting MDE). The precision controller then schedules the update transactions based on MDE. The portion of ΔU not accommodated by the QoD manager, denoted ΔU_{new}, is returned to the admission controller, which enforces the remaining utilization adjustment.

The transaction handler provides a platform for managing transactions. It consists of a freshness manager (FM), a unit managing the concurrency control (CC), and a basic scheduler (BS). The FM checks the freshness before accessing a data object, using the timestamp and the absolute validity interval of the data. We employ two-phase locking with highest priority (2PL-HP) [1] for concurrency control. 2PL-HP is chosen since it is free from priority inversion and has well-known behavior. We use three different scheduling algorithms as basic schedulers: (i) Earliest Deadline First (EDF), where transactions are processed in the order determined by increasing absolute deadlines (ii) Highest Error First (HEF), where transactions are processed in the order determined by decreasing transaction error, and (iii) Highest Error Density First (HEDF), where transactions are processed in the order determined by decreasing transaction error density given by, $TED_i = \frac{TE_i}{AT_i + D_i - CurrentTime}$, where AT_i and D_i denote the arrival time and relative deadline of the transaction T_i, respectively.[3] For all three basic schedulers (EDF, HEF, and HEDF) the mandatory subtransactions have higher priority than the optional subtransactions and, hence, scheduled before them.

The precision controller discards an update transaction writing to a data object (d_i) having an error less or equal to the maximum data error allowed, i.e. $DE_i \leq MDE$.

---

[3]Note that HEF and HEDF cannot be used in the case when error functions for transactions are not available, as they are error-cognizant and require knowledge of transaction error for each transaction.

However, the update transaction is executed if the data error of d_i is greater than MDE. In both cases the time-stamp of d_i is updated.

We have modeled the controlled system, i.e. the RTDB, according to the analytical approach proposed in [10]. The approach has been adapted such that it supports the imprecise computation model [9]. For deriving and tuning of the model and the feedback controllers, we refer to [2, 3] for details.

4.4 Algorithms for Data and Transaction Quality Management

The algorithms FCS-IC-1 and FCS-IC-2 control QoT by monitoring M^M, M^O, and U, adjusting MDE such that a given QoS specification, according to QoS specification A, is satisfied. Here, we use EDF as a basic scheduler, i.e., transactions are scheduled according to EDF. FCS-HEF and FCS-HEDF are error-cognizant and control QoT by monitoring ATE and adjusting MDE, such that a QoS specification in terms of QoS specification B is satisfied. Furthermore, FCS-HEF and FCS-HEDF are designed to enhance QoS fairness among transactions. We use the same feedback control policy for FCS-HEF and FCS-HEDF, but use different basic schedulers, i.e., FCS-HEF schedules the transactions using HEF and FCS-HEDF schedules the transactions using HEDF.

Given a certain $\Delta U(k)$, we need to set $MDE(k+1)$ such that the change in utilization due to discarding update transactions corresponds to $\Delta U(k)$. Remember that setting $MDE(k+1)$ greater than $MDE(k)$ results in more discarded update transactions and, hence, an increase in gained utilization. In order to compute $MDE(k+1)$ given a certain $\Delta U(k)$, we use a function $f(\Delta U(k))$ that returns, based on $\Delta U(k)$, the corresponding $MDE(k+1)$. The function f holds the following property. If $\Delta U(k)$ is less than zero, then $MDE(k+1)$ is set such that $MDE(k+1)$ is greater than $MDE(k)$ (i.e. QoD is degraded). Similarly, if $\Delta U(k)$ is greater than zero, then $MDE(k+1)$ is set such that $MDE(k+1)$ is less than $MDE(k)$ (i.e. QoD is upgraded). Due to space limitation we refer to [2, 3] for the derivation of f.

4.4.1 FCS-IC-1.

FCS-IC-1 employs one utilization and two miss percentage controllers, i.e., one controller to adjust the utilization U according to a lower bound U_l, and two controllers to adjust M^M and M^O. Initially, U is set to a U_l. As long as M^M and M^O are below their references, U is increased by a certain step. As soon as M^M or M^O (or both) are above their references, U is reduced exponentially. This is to prevent a potential deadline miss percentage overshoot due to a too

```
Monitor M^M(k), M^O(k), and U(k)
Compute ΔU(k)
if (ΔU(k) > 0 and MDE(k) > 0) then
    Upgrade QoD according to MDE(k + 1) := f(ΔU(k))
    Inform AC about the portion of ΔU(k) not accommodated by
    QoD upgrade
else if (ΔU(k) < 0 and MDE(k) < MDE_r × (M_p + 100))
then
    Downgrade QoD according to MDE(k + 1) := f(ΔU(k))
    Inform AC about the portion of ΔU(k) not accommodated by
    QoD downgrade
else if (ΔU(k) < 0 and MDE(k) = MDE_r × (M_p + 100))
then
    Reject any incoming transactions
else
    Inform the AC of ΔU(k)
end if
```

Figure 4. FCS-IC-1

optimistic utilization reference. In addition to this, FCS-IC-1 performs the following.

The system monitors the deadline miss percentages and the CPU utilization. At each sampling instant, the CPU utilization adjustment, $\Delta U(k)$, is derived. Based on $\Delta U(k)$ we perform one of the following. If $\Delta U(k)$ is greater than zero, upgrade QoD as much as $\Delta U(k)$ allows. However, when $\Delta U(k)$ is less than zero, degrade QoD according to ΔU, but not greater than the highest allowed MDE (i.e. $MDE_r \times (M_p + 100)$). Degrading the data further would violate the upper limit of MDE given by the QoS specification. In the case when $\Delta U(k)$ is less than zero and MDE equals $MDE_r \times (M_p + 100)$, no QoD adjustment can be issued and, hence, the system has to wait until some of the currently running transactions terminate. An outline of FCS-IC-1 is given in Figure 4.

4.4.2 FCS-IC-2.

In FCS-IC-2, two miss percentage control loops, one for M^M and one for M^O, are used. In the case of FCS-IC-1, the miss percentages may stay lower than their references, since the utilization exponentially decreases every time one of the miss percentages overshoots its reference. Consequently, the specified miss percentage references (i.e. M_r^M and M_r^O) may not be satisfied. In FCS-IC-2, the utilization controller is removed to keep the miss percentages at the specified references.

One of the characteristics of the miss percentage controller is that as long as M^O is below its reference (i.e. $M^O \leq M_r^O$), the controller output ΔU stays positive.[4] Due to the characteristics of f (i.e. $\Delta U(k) > 0 \Rightarrow$

---

[4]If we have transient oscillations, ΔU, may temporaly stay positive (negative) even though the M^O has changed from being below (above) the reference to be above (below) the reference value. This is due to the integral operation, i.e., due to earlier summation of errors, causing a delay before a change to the utilization is requested and has effect.

$MDE(k + 1) < MDE(k))$, a positive ΔU is interpreted as a QoD upgrade. Consequently, even if M^O is just below its reference, QoD remains high. We would rather that M^O, which corresponds to QoT, increases and decreases together with QoD given by MDE. For this reason, MDE is set considering both ΔU and M^O. When ΔU is less than zero (i.e. M^O overshoot), MDE is set according to f. However, when ΔU is greater or equal to zero, MDE is set according to the moving average of M^O, computed by $M_{MA}^O(k) = \alpha M^O(k) + (1 - \alpha)M_{MA}^O(k - 1)$, where α ($0 \leq \alpha \leq 1$) is the forgetting factor. Setting α close to 1 results in a fast adaptation, but also captures the high-frequency changes of M^O, whereas setting α close to 0 results in a slow but smooth adaptation. The outline of FCS-IC-2 is given in Figure 5.

```
Monitor M^M(k) and M^O(k)
Compute ΔU(k)
if (ΔU(k) ≥ 0) then
    MDE(k + 1) :=
          min( (M^O_MA(k)/M^O_r) MDE_r , MDE_r × (M_p + 100))
    if (MDE(k) < MDE(k + 1)) then
        Add the utilization gained after QoD degrade to ΔU(k)
    else
        Subtract the utilization lost after QoD upgrade from ΔU(k)
    end if
    Inform AC of the new ΔU(k)
else if (ΔU(k) < 0 and MDE(k) < MDE_r × (M_p + 100))
then
    Downgrade QoD according to MDE(k + 1) := f(ΔU(k))
    Inform AC about the portion of ΔU(k) not accommodated by
    QoD downgrade
else if (ΔU(k) < 0 and MDE(k) = MDE_r × (M_p + 100))
then
    Reject any incoming transactions
else
    Inform the AC of ΔU(k)
end if
```

Figure 5. FCS-IC-2

4.4.3 FCS-HEF and FCS-HEDF

FCS-HEF and FCS-HEDF are extensions to FCS-IC-2, but where QoT is measured in terms of ATE, instead of M^O. Hence, we replace the miss percentage control loops for a single average transaction error control loop. Here, MDE is adjusted based on the control signal ΔU and the moving average of ATE, given by $ATE_{MA}(k) = \alpha ATE(k) + (1 - \alpha)ATE_{MA}(k - 1)$. Due to space limitation we do not provide full algorithm descriptions for FCS-HEF and FCS-HEDF but refer instead to Figure 5 where M_{MA}^O is replaced with ATE_{MA}.

5 Performance Evaluation

5.1 Experimental Goals

The main objective of the experiments is to determine if the presented algorithms can provide QoS guarantees according to a QoS specification. We have for this reason studied and evaluated the behavior of the algorithms by varying a set of parameters:

- Execution time estimation error ($EstErr$). Often exact execution time estimates of transactions are not known. To study how runtime error affects the algorithms we measure the performance considering different execution time estimation errors.

- QoS specifications. It is important that an algorithm can manage different QoS specifications. Here we compare the results of the presented algorithms with regards to different QoS specifications.

- Transaction error functions. The characteristics of the error functions depend on the actual application. For this reason, we evaluate the performance of the algorithms with regard to different transaction sets showing different transaction error characteristics.

5.2 Simulation Setup

The simulated workload consists of update and user transactions, which access data and perform virtual arithmetic/logical operations on the data. Update transactions occupy approximately 50% of the workload. In our experiments, one simulation run lasts for 10 minutes of simulated time. For all the performance data, we have taken the average of 10 simulation runs and derived 95% confidence intervals. The workload model of the update and user transactions are described as follows. We use the following notation where the attribute X_i refers to transaction T_i, and $X_i[t_i]$ is associated with subtransaction t_i (where $t_i \in \{M_i, O_{i,1}, \ldots, O_{i,\#O_i}\}$). We analyze $ATE(k)$, $MDE(k)$, $SDTE$, and CPU Utilization (below referred to as utilization) U.

Data and Update Transactions. The DB holds 1000 temporal data objects (d_i) where each data object is updated by a stream ($Stream_i$, $1 \leq i \leq 1000$). The period of update transactions (P_i) is uniformly distributed in the range (100ms,50s) (i.e. $U : (100ms, 50s)$) and estimated execution time (EET_i) is given by $U : (1ms, 8ms)$. The average update value (AV_i) of each $Stream_i$ is given by $U : (0, 100)$. Upon a periodic generation of an update, $Stream_i$ gives the update an actual execution time given by the normal distribution $N : (EET_i, \sqrt{EET_i})$ and a value (V_i) according to $N : (AV_i, AV_i \times VarFactor)$, where $VarFactor$ is uniformly distributed in (0,1). The deadline is set to $ArrivalTime_i + P_i$.

User Transactions. Each $Source_i$ generates a transaction T_i, consisting of one mandatory subtransaction, M_i, and $\#O_i$ ($1 \leq \#O_i \leq 10$) optional subtransaction(s), $O_{i,j}$ ($1 \leq j \leq \#O_i$). $\#O_i$ is uniformly distributed between 1 and 10. The estimated (average) execution times of mandatory and optional ($EET_i[t_i]$) subtransactions are given by $U : (5ms, 15ms)$. The estimation error $EstErr$ is used to introduce an execution time estimation error in the average execution time given by $AET_i[t_i] = (1 + EstErr) \times EET_i[t_i]$. Further, upon generation of a transaction, $Source_i$ associates an actual execution time to each subtransaction t_i, which is given by $N : (AET_i[t_i], \sqrt{AET_i[t_i]})$. The deadline of a transaction is set to $ArrivalTime_i + EET_i \times SlackFactor$. The slack factor is uniformly distributed according to $U : (20, 40)$. The inter-arrival time is exponentially distributed with the mean inter-arrival time set to $EET_i \times SlackFactor$.

We have considered two different transaction sets having different transaction error characteristics. In the first set, referred to as $TSet1$, transactions are evenly distributed in four classes representing error function orders of 0.5, 1, 2, and 5 (e.g. 25% of the transactions have an error order of 1). In the second set, referred to as $TSet2$, 50% of the transactions have an error order of 0.5, 30% have error order of 1, 15% have error order 2, and 5% have error order 5.

In our experiments we use the following QoS specification: $QoSSpecA = \{M_r^M = 1\%, M_r^O = 10\%, MDE_r = 2.5\%, T_s \leq 60s, M_p \leq 30\%, U_l = 80\%\}$, $QoSSpecB_1 = \{ATE_r = 20\%, MDE_r = 5\%, T_s \leq 60s, M_p \leq 30\%\}$, $QoSSpecB_2 = \{ATE_r = 10\%, MDE_r = 10\%, T_s \leq 60s, M_p \leq 30\%\}$.

5.3 Baselines

To the best of our knowledge, there has been no earlier work on techniques for managing data impreciseness and transaction impreciseness, satisfying QoS or QoD requirements. For this reason, we have developed three baseline algorithms, FCS-EDF, Baseline-1, and Baseline-2, to study the impact of the workload on the system. We compare the behavior of FCS-HEF and FCS-HEDF with FCS-EDF, which is similar to FCS-HEF and FCS-HEDF, but where EDF is used as a basic scheduler. We choose EDF since it is optimal (in minimizing deadline misses) and has well-known behavior. The algorithm outline of Baseline-1 and Baseline-2 is given below. Depending on the given QoS specification, let Υ be either M^O or ATE.

Baseline-1. If Υ (i.e. M^O or ATE) is greater than its reference, the utilization has to be lowered, which is achieved by discarding more update transactions, i.e. increasing MDE. MDE is set according to $MDE(k+1) = \min(\frac{\Upsilon(k)}{\Upsilon_r} MDE_r, MDE_r \times (M_p + 100))$. A simple AC is applied, where a transaction (T_i) is admitted if the estimated

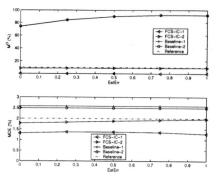

Figure 6. Average Performance: $Load = 200\%$, $QoSSpecA$

utilization of admitted subtransactions and EET_i is less or equal to 80%.

Baseline-2. To prevent a potential overshoot, we increase MDE as soon as Υ is greater than zero. If $\Upsilon(k)$ is greater than zero, $MDE(k)$ increases stepwise until $MDE_r \times (M_p + 100)$ is reached (i.e. $MDE(k+1) = \min(MDE(k) + MDE_{step}, MDE_r \times (M_p + 100))$). If $\Upsilon(k)$ is equal to zero, $MDE(k)$ decreases stepwise until zero is reached (i.e. $MDE(k+1) = \max(MDE(k) - MDE_{step}, 0)$). The same AC as in Baseline-1 is used.

5.4 Experiment 1: Results of Varying EstErr

The setup of the experiment is given below, followed by the presentation of the results.

Experimental setup. We apply 200% load and measure M^O, ATE, $SDTE$, MDE, and U. The execution time estimation error is varied according to $EstErr = 0.00$, 0.25, 0.50, 0.75, and 1.00. For FCS-IC-1 and FCS-IC-2 we use QoS specification $QoSSpecA$, while for FCS-HEF and FCS-HEDF QoS specification $QoSSpecB_1$ and transaction set $TSet1$ holds. Figure 6 shows the performance of FCS-IC-1 and FCS-IC-2, and Figure 7 shows the performance of FCS-HEF, FCS-HEDF, and FCS-EDF. Dash-dotted lines indicate references.

Results. For all algorithms the confidence intervals are within $\pm 3.5\%$ for M^O, ATE, and $SDTE$, and within 0.3% for MDE. For all algorithms and baselines the utilization has been observed to be above 95%. As we can see for Baseline-1 and Baseline-2, the controlled variables (i.e. M^O and ATE) and MDE change for varying $EstErr$. However, FCS-IC-1, FCS-IC-2, FCS-HEF, and FCS-HEDF provide a robust control of the performance as M^O, ATE, and MDE do not change considerably for varying execution time estimation errors. Further, we see that FCS-HEF provides a lower $SDTE$ than the other algorithms. Note that FCS-IC-1 provides a much lower M^O than M_r^O. This is due to the properties of the utilization controller, where

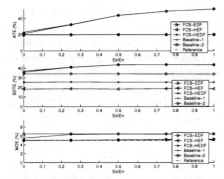

Figure 7. Average Performance: $Load = 200\%$, $QoSSpecB_1, TSet1$

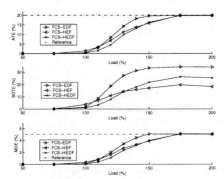

Figure 8. Average performance: $EstErr = 0$, $QoSSpecB_1, TSet1$

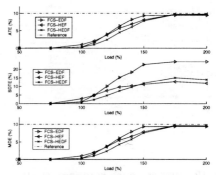

Figure 9. Average performance: $EstErr = 0, QoSSpecB_2, TSet1$

the utilization decreases exponentially every time M^O overshoots its reference, yielding an overall lower utilization, and consequently, a lower M^O compared to M_r^O. From above we can conclude that FCS-IC-1, FCS-IC-2, FCS-HEF, and FCS-HEDF are insensitive to changes to execution time estimation and, hence, they can easily adapt when accurate run-time estimates are not known.

5.5 Experiment 2: Varying QoS Specification

The setup of the experiment is given below, followed by the presentation of the results.

Experimental setup. We apply loads from 50% to 200% and measure ATE, $SDTE$, and MDE. The execution time estimation error is set to zero (i.e. $EstErr = 0$). Transaction set $TSet1$ is used. Figure 8 shows the performance of FCS-HEF, FCS-HEDF, and FCS-EDF given $QoSSpecB_1$, while Figure 9 shows the performance of the algorithms under $QoSSpecB_2$. Dash-dotted lines indicate references.

Results. For all algorithms, the confidence intervals of ATE and $SDTE$ are within ±1.9%, while the same figure for MDE is ±0.8%. As we can see, ATE and MDE grow

towards their references as the applied load increases, consequently satisfying the QoS specifications. Thus, we have shown that the proposed algorithms can support different QoS specifications.[5]

It can be observed that the difference in $SDTE$ between FCS-HEF and FCS-HEDF is smaller for $QoSSpecB_2$ than $QoSSpecB_1$. We notice that when ATE is lower than approximately 10%, FCS-HEDF performs better than FCS-HEF with regard to lowering $SDTE$. For $QoSSpecB_2$, the reference ATE_r is set to 10%, resulting in a lower ATE (compared to the ATE generated for $QoSSpecB_1$) and, hence, the difference in $SDTE$ becomes smaller.

5.6 Experiment 3: Effects of Varying Order of Transaction Error Functions

In experiment 2 we evaluate the algorithms using the transaction set $TSet1$. Below we compare the results obtained from experiment 2 using a different set of transactions, $TSet2$. This is to evaluate the performance of FCS-HEF and FCS-HEDF with regard to different sets of transactions having different transaction error characteristics.

Experimental setup. We apply loads from 50% to 200% and measure ATE, $SDTE$, and MDE. The execution time estimation error is set to zero (i.e. $EstErr = 0$). QoS specification $QoSSpecB_1$ and transaction set $TSet2$ are used. Figure 10 shows the performance of FCS-HEF, FCS-HEDF, and FCS-EDF. Dash-dotted lines indicate references.

Results. The confidence intervals of ATE and $SDTE$ for all algorithms are within ±1.7%, while for MDE the same figure is ±0.4%. For FCS-EDF, FCS-HEF, and FCS-HEDF we can see that ATE and MDE satisfy the given QoS specification as they are consistent with the references during high applied loads.

Comparing to Figure 8, it can be observed that ATE for

---

[5]We do not present the results of the Baseline-1 and Baseline-2, since they have showed poor results in earlier experiments.

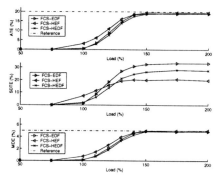

Figure 10. Average performance: $EstErr = 0$, $QoSSpecB_1$, $TSet2$

FCS-HEF is higher than the other algorithms. Given a set transactions where the error order of each transaction is less than one (i.e. $n < 1$), ATE is lower under EDF scheduling than under HEF scheduling. Consider two transactions, T_1 and T_2, that have error functions with $n = 0.5$ (see Figure 1) and where the difference in deadlines is very small (imagine that the difference is infinitely small). Assume that it takes one time unit to complete an optional subtransaction and that there are 10 time units to the deadline of both transactions, hence, we can only execute and complete 10 subtransactions before their deadline. The question is how to schedule the subtransactions such that the average transaction error is minimized. In the case of HEF, we assign 5 time units to each transaction (i.e. completing 5 optional subtransactions), giving an average transaction error of approximately 0.75. In the case of EDF we assign 10 time units to the transaction with the earlier deadline and zero time units to the second, giving an average error of 0.5. Thus the average error becomes lower under EDF scheduling. Studying $TSet2$, we see that about 50% of the transactions have error functions with orders less than 1 (i.e. $n < 1$), hence, here ATE becomes lower under EDF scheduling than under HEF scheduling.

Further, for loads less than 110% we can see that FCS-HEF produces higher $SDTE$ than the other algorithms. This is due to the high ATE during the same load interval. However, $SDTE$ for FCS-HEF is lower for the other algorithms for loads above 130% as the difference in ATE becomes smaller between the algorithms.

Comparing the performance of the algorithms given in Figure 8 and Figure 10, we conclude that FCS-HEF and FCS-HEDF are robust against varying applied load and varying transaction error characteristics.

5.7 Summary of Results and Discussion

Our experiments show that FCS-IC-1, FCS-IC-2, FCS-HEF, and FCS-HEDF are robust against inaccurate execu-

tion time estimations as M^O, ATE, and MDE remain unaffected for varying execution time estimation errors. Also, FCS-HEF and FCS-HEDF can adapt to different QoS specifications and various transaction sets showing different transaction error characteristics. The proposed algorithms outperform the baseline algorithms and FCS-EDF and they can manage a given QoS specifications well. We have carried out other types of experiments [2, 3] for the algorithms given in this paper, where we evaluate the performance of the algorithms with regard to transient-state behavior, i.e., overshoot and settling time. The results of the additional experiments show that the FCS-IC-1, FCS-IC-2, FCS-HEF, and FCS-HEDF are able to handle transient overloads and control the magnitude and settling time of the overshoots. In particular, we have observed that FCS-IC-1 and FCS-HEF efficiently suppress overshoots and, hence, perform better during transient-states than FCS-IC-2, FCS-HEDF, and FCS-EDF.

FCS-IC-1 can manage to provide near zero M^O and it is able to efficiently suppress potential overshoots, but does not fully satisfy the QoS specification with regard to the reference. FCS-IC-2, on the other hand, provides an M^O near its reference, M_r^O. Thus FCS-IC-1 should be applied to RTDBs where overshoots cannot be tolerated, but where consistency between the controlled variables and their references is relaxed, i.e., we do not require the system to produce the desired miss percentages and MDE. The experiments show that FCS-IC-2 is particularly useful when consistency between the controlled variables and their references is emphasized, but where overshoots are accepted.

Moreover, it was showed that FCS-HEF in general provides a lower $SDTE$ than FCS-HEDF and the baselines. We conclude that FCS-HEF should be used in applications where QoS fairness among transactions is important, but also where the performance of the RTDB during transient-state must not violate given QoS specifications.

6 Related Work

There has been several algorithms proposed addressing imprecise scheduling problems [9, 5, 4]. These algorithms require the knowledge of accurate processing times of the tasks, which is often not available in RTDBs. Further, they focus on maximizing or minimizing a performance metric (e.g. total error). These optimization problems cannot be applied to our problem, since in our case we want to control a set of performance metrics such that they converge towards a set of references given by a QoS specification.

Lu et al. have presented a feedback control scheduling framework where they propose three algorithms for managing the miss percentage and/or utilization [10]. However they do not address the problem of maximizing QoS fairness among admitted tasks. In the work by Parekh et al., the length of a queue of remote procedure calls (RPCs) arriving at a server is controlled [11] using automatic control.

Labrinidis et al. introduced the notion of QoD in the context of web-servers [8]. Their proposed update scheduling policy of cached web pages can significantly improve data freshness compared to FIFO scheduling. Kang et al. used a feedback control scheduling architecture to balance the load of user and update transactions [7]. In our previous work, we presented a set of algorithms for managing QoS based on feedback control scheduling and imprecise computation [2, 3], where QoS was defined in terms of transaction and data preciseness.

The correctness of answers to databases queries can be traded off to enhance timeliness. The database query processors, APPROXIMATE [13] and CASE-DB [6] are examples of such databases where approximate answers to queries can be produced within certain deadlines.

7 Conclusions and Future Work

In this paper we have argued for the need of increased adaptability of applications providing real-time data services. To address this problem we have proposed a QoS-sensitive approach based on feedback control scheduling and imprecise computation applied on transactions and data objects. Imprecise computation techniques have shown to be useful in many areas where timely processing of tasks or services is emphasized. In this work we combine the advantages from feedback control scheduling and imprecise computation techniques, forming a framework consisting of a model for expressing QoS requirements, an architecture, and a set of algorithms. The expressive power of our approach allows a DBA to specify the desired QoS with regard to steady-state and transient-state, capturing the dynamics of a RTDB. FCS-IC-1 and FCS-IC-2 address QoS specifications given in terms of deadline miss percentage of optional subtransactions, while FCS-HEF and FCS-HEDF address specifications based on the notion of transaction error. Given a QoS specification, the four algorithms FCS-IC-1, FCS-IC-2, FCS-HEF, and FCS-HEDF give a robust and controlled behavior of RTDBs in terms of transaction and data preciseness, even for transient overloads and with inaccurate run-time estimates of the transactions. The proposed algorithms outperform the baseline algorithms and FCS-EDF, where transactions are scheduled with EDF and feedback control, and can manage the given QoS specifications well. This is a significant improvement over current techniques for specifying and satisfying QoS requirements.

For our future work, we will model the relationship between data error and transactions error, expressing transaction error in terms of completed optional subtransactions and the data error of the data objects accessed by a transaction. Further, we also intend to extend our work to manage the notion of service differentiation and derived data management.

References

[1] R. Abbott and H. Garcia-Molina. Scheduling real-time transactions: A performance evaluation. *ACM Transactions on Database System*, 17:513–560, 1992.

[2] M. Amirijoo, J. Hansson, and S. H. Son. Algorithms for managing QoS for real-time data services using imprecise computation. In *Proceedings of the 9th International Conference on Real-Time and Embedded Computing Systems and Applications (RTCSA)*, 2003.

[3] M. Amirijoo, J. Hansson, and S. H. Son. Error-driven QoS management in imprecise real-time databases. In *Proceedings of the 15th Euromicro Conference on Real-Time Systems (ECRTS)*, July 2003.

[4] J. Chung and J. W. S. Liu. Algorithms for scheduling periodic jobs to minimize average error. In *Real-Time Systems Symposium (RTSS)*, pages 142–151, 1988.

[5] J. Hansson, M. Thuresson, and S. H. Son. Imprecise task scheduling and overload managment using OR-ULD. In *Proceedings of the 7th Conference in Real-Time Computing Systems and Applications (RTCSA)*, pages 307–314. IEEE Computer Press, 2000.

[6] W. Hou, G. Ozsoyoglu, and B. K. Taneja. Processing aggregate relational queries with hard time constraints. In *Proceedings of the 1989 ACM SIGMOD International Conference on Management of Data*, pages 68–77. ACM Press, 1989.

[7] K. Kang, S. H. Son, J. A. Stankovic, and T. F. Abdelzaher. A QoS-sensitive approach for timeliness and freshness guarantees in real-time databases. 14th Euromicro Conference on Real-time Systems (ECRTS), June 19-21 2002.

[8] A. Labrinidis and N. Roussopoulos. Update propagation strategies for improving the quality of data on the web. *The VLDB Journal*, pages 391–400, 2001.

[9] J. W. S. Liu, K. Lin, W. Shin, and A. C.-S. Yu. Algorithms for scheduling imprecise computations. *IEEE Computer*, 24(5), May 1991.

[10] C. Lu, J. A. Stankovic, G. Tao, and S. H. Son. Feedback control real-time scheduling: Framework, modeling and algorithms. *Journal of Real-time Systems*, 23(1/2), July/September 2002. Special Issue on Control-Theoretical Approaches to Real-Time Computing.

[11] S. Parekh, N. Gandhi, J. Hellerstein, D. Tilbury, T. Jayram, and J. Bigus. Using control theory to achieve service level objectives in performance managment. *Journal of Real-time Systems*, 23(1/2), July/September 2002. Special Issue on Control-Theoretical Approaches to Real-Time Computing.

[12] K. Ramamritham. Real-time databases. *International Journal of Distributed and Parallel Databases*, (1), 1993.

[13] S. V. Vrbsky and J. W. S. Liu. APPROXIMATE - a query processor that produces monotonically improving approximate answers. *IEEE Transactions on Knowledge and Data Engineering*, 5(6):1056–1068, December 1993.

Preferred Repairs for Inconsistent Databases*

S. Greco, C. Sirangelo, I. Trubitsyna and E. Zumpano

DEIS – Università della Calabria

87030 Rende, Italy

{greco, sirangelo, irina, zumpano}@si.deis.unical.it

Abstract

The objective of this paper is to investigate the problems related to the extensional integration of information sources. In particular, we propose an approach for managing inconsistent databases, i.e. databases violating integrity constraints. The presence of inconsistent data can be resolved by "repairing" the database, i.e. by providing a computational mechanism that ensures obtaining consistent "scenarios" of the information or by consistently answer to queries posed on an inconsistent set of data. In this paper we consider preferences among repairs and possible answers by introducing a partial order among them on the base of some preference criteria. More specifically, preferences are expressed by considering polynomial functions applied to repairs and returning real numbers. The goodness of a repair is measured by estimating how much it violates the desiderata conditions and a repair is preferred if it minimizes the value of the polynomial function used to express the preference criteria. The main contribution of this work consists in the proposal of a logic approach for querying and repairing inconsistent databases that extends previous works by aallowing to express and manage preference criteria. The approach here proposed allows to express reliability on the information sources and is also suitable for expressing decision and optimization problems. The introduction of preference criteria strongly reduces the number of feasible repairs and answers; for special classes of constraints and functions it gives a unique repair and answer.

---

*Work partially supported by a MURST grants under the projects "D2I" and "Sistemi informatici Integrati a supporto di bench-marking di progetti ed interventi ad innovazione tecnologica in campo agro-alimentare". The first author is also supported by ICAR-CNR.

1 Introduction

The problem of dealing with inconsistent information has recently assumed additional relevance as it plays a key role in all the areas in which duplicate information or conflicting information is likely to occur [2, 6, 7, 16, 18, 23, 27]. In this paper we address the problem of managing inconsistent databases, i.e. databases violating integrity constraints. The fact that a database may be inconsistent with respect to a set of integrity constraints is not surprising if it is obtained as the result of an integration process over a set of knowledge bases.

The following example shows a typical case of inconsistency.

Example 1 Consider the database consisting of the three binary relations *Teaches(Professor, Course)*, *Faculty(Professor, Faculty)* and *Course(Course, Faculty)* with the integrity constraint

$$\forall (P, C, F)[Teaches(P, C) \wedge Faculty(P, F) \supset Course(C, F)]$$

stating that if a professor P teaches a course C and P is in the faculty F, then the course C must belong to the faculty F. Assume there are two different sources of the databases: $D_1 = \{Teaches(t_1, c_1), Teaches(t_2, c_2), Faculty(t_1, f_1), Course(c_1, f_1)\}$ and $D_2 = \{Teaches(t_1, c_1), Faculty(t_2, f_1), Course(c_2, f_2)\}$. The two instances satisfy the constraint, but from their union we derive a relation which does not satisfy the constraint. □

The presence of inconsistent data can be resolved by "repairing" the database, i.e. by providing a computational mechanism that ensures to obtain consistent "scenarios" of the information (repairs) in an inconsistent environment or to consistently answer to queries posed on an inconsistent set of data. Informally, a repair for a possibly inconsistent database is a minimal set of insert and delete operations which makes the database consistent, whereas a consistent answer is a set of tuples derived from the database, satisfying all integrity constraints [3, 4, 12, 13, 25].

Thus the integration of, possibly inconsistent, databases must consider the possibility of constructing an integrated consistent database by replacing inconsistent tuples. For instance, for the integrated relation of the above example, it is possible to obtain a consistent database by i) deleting the tuple $Teaches(t_2, c_2)$, ii) deleting the tuple $Faculty(t_2, f_1)$, or iii) adding the tuple $Course(c_2, f_1)$. These three update operations are repairs that make the database consistent, but one should prefer a repair with respect to an alternative one. For instance, one could prefer a repair which minimize the number of deletion and insertion of tuples in the relation $Teaches$ and, in such a case, the second and third repair are preferred to the first one, or one should prefer repairs minimizing the set of deletions and in such a case the third repair is preferred to the first two repairs.

Example 2 Consider the relation $Teaches$ $(Name, Faculty, Course)$ with the functional dependency $Name \rightarrow Faculty$. Assume to have three different sources for the relation $Teaches$ containing, respectively, the tuples $Teaches(john, science, databases)$, $Teaches(john, engineering, algorithms)$ and $Teaches(john, science, operating\_systems)$. The three different source relations satisfy the functional dependencies, but from their integration we derive the inconsistent relation $D = \{(john, engineering, algorithms), (john, science, operating\_systems), (john, science, databases)\}$.

The integrated relation can be repaired by applying a minimal set of update operations. In particular it admits two repairs: R_1 obtained by deleting the tuple $(john, engineering, algorithms)$ and R_2 obtained by deleting the two tuples $(john, science, databases)$ and $(john, science, operating\_systems)$. □

In the presence of an alternative set of repairs one could express preferences on them, for instance, if, in the above example, preferred repairs are those minimizing the number of deletion and insertion of tuples then the repair R_1 preferred to the repair R_2.

In this paper we introduce a flexible mechanism that allows specifying preference criteria so that selecting among a set of feasible repairs the preferable ones, i.e. those better conforming to the specified criteria. Preference criteria introduce desiderata on how to update the inconsistent database in order to make it consistent and are expressed by means of a polynomial function, named *evaluation function*. The evaluation function "measures" the repairs with respect to the database and allows defining a partial order both among repairs and possible answers, so that allowing the selection of the feasible repairs which result preferred w.r.t. the evaluation function: the preferred repairs. Informally a preferred repair is a repair that better satisfies preferences, i.e. it minimizes the value of the evaluation function.

In the integration of two conflicting databases a simple way to remove inconsistencies consists in the definition of preference criteria such as a partial order on the source information, or in the use of the majority criteria [19], which in the presence of conflicts gives more credit to the information present in the majority of the knowledge bases.

Observe that the selection of the element which occurs a maximum number of times in the integrated knowledge bases is easily obtained by specializing the evaluation function to compute the cardinality of the deleted atoms, since a consistent scenario, obtained by performing the minimum number of delete operation, surely maintains the majority of the information which overlaps among the knowledge bases.

The application of the majority criteria [19] in the integration phase of the above example, eliminates the tuple $(john, engineering, algorithms)$; this corresponds to give preference to the repair R_1 with respect to the repair R_2, i.e. we express preference for the repaired databases which need a lesser number of updates to be consistent or equivalently we give credit to the information which occurs a greater number of times.

Note that, while integrity constraints can be considered as a query which must always be true after a modification of the database, the conditions expressed by the evaluation function can be considered as a set of desiderata which are satisfied if possible by a generic repair. The goodness of a repair is measured by estimating how much the updates to be performed on the inconsistent database respect the preference criteria or in other words how much the repaired database violates them.

The main contribution of this work consists in the definition of a logic approach for querying and repairing inconsistent databases that extends previous works by also considering techniques to express and manage preference criteria. The approach here proposed allows to express reliability on the information sources and moreover is also suitable for expressing decision and optimization problems. Obviously the introduction of preference criteria reduces the number of feasible repairs and answers, moreover for special cases of constraints it gives a unique repair and answer.

The rest of the paper is organized as follows. In Section 2 we present basic definitions on logic languages (Datalog, disjunctive Datalog and classical negation). In Section 3 we recall standard definitions on repairs and consistent answers and introduce preference criteria on repairs and answers. In Section 4 we present the rewriting of integrity constraints into disjunctive rules and show how preferred repairs and answers are computed. Finally, in Section 5, we present our conclusions.

2 Basic Definitions and Datalog Extensions

In this section we introduce preliminaries on deductive databases and integrity constraints. Integrity constraints define restrictions on the instance of relational databases. Deductive databases are defined by logical rules which are used to derive new knowledge starting from a given (relational) database. We present first the language Datalog and next two extensions: Disjunctive Datalog and Datalog with aggregates.

2.1 Datalog

We assume the existence of finite domains of constants, variables and predicate symbols. A term is either a variable or a constant. An atom is of the form $p(t_1, ..., t_n)$ where p is a predicate symbol and $t_1, ..., t_n$ are terms. A literal is either an atom A or its negation $not\ A$. A *Datalog program* (or, simply, a *program*) P is a finite set of rules. Each *rule*

of P has the form $A \leftarrow A_1, ..., A_m$, where A is an atom (the *head* of the rule) and $A_1, ..., A_m$ are literals (the *body* of the rule). A ground rule with an empty body is called a *fact*.

Given a Datalog program P, the Herbrand universe for P, denoted H_P, is the set of all constants occurring in P; the Herbrand Base of P, denoted B_P, is the set of all possible ground atoms whose predicate symbols occur in P and whose arguments are elements from the Herbrand universe. A *ground instance* of a rule r in P is a rule obtained from r by replacing every variable X in r by a ground term in H_P. The set of ground instances of r is denoted by $ground(r)$; accordingly, $ground(P)$ denotes $\bigcup_{r \in P} ground(r)$. An interpretation I of P is a subset of B_P. A ground positive literal A (resp. negative literal $\neg A$) is true w.r.t. an interpretation I if $A \in I$ (resp. $A \notin I$). A conjunction of literals is true in an interpretation I if all literals are true in I. A ground rule is true in I if either the body conjunction is false or the head is true in I. A *(Herbrand) model* M of P is an interpretation that makes each ground instance of each rule in P true. A model M for P is minimal if there is no model N for P such that $N \subset M$.

Let I be an interpretation for a program P. The *immediate consequence operator* $T_P(I)$ is defined as the set containing the heads of each rule $r \in ground(P)$ s.t. the body of r is true in I. The semantics of a *positive* (i.e. negation-free) logic program P is given by the unique minimal model; this minimum model coincides with the least fixpoint $T_P^\infty(\emptyset)$ of T_P [20]. Generally, the semantics of logic programs with negation can be given in terms of total stable model semantics [9] which we now briefly recall.

Given a program P and an interpretation M, M is a *(total) stable model* of P if it is the minimum model of the positive program P^M defined as follows: P^M is obtained from $ground(P)$ by (i) deleting all rules which have some negative literal $\neg b$ in their body with $b \in M$, and (ii) removing all negative literals in the remaining rules. Logic programs may have zero, one or several stable models. Positive programs have a unique stable model which coincides with the minimum model [9].

Given a program P and two predicate symbols p and q, we write $p \rightarrow q$ if there exists a rule where q occurs in the head and p in the body or there exists a predicate s such that $p \rightarrow s$ and $s \rightarrow q$. A program is *stratified* if there exists no rule where a predicate p occurs in a negative literal in the body, q occurs in the head and $q \to p$ i.e. there is no recursion through negation [1]. Stratified programs have a unique stable model which coincides with the *stratified model*, obtained by partitioning the program into an ordered number of suitable subprograms (called 'strata') and computing the fixpoints of every stratum from the lowest one up [1].

Queries

Predicate symbols are partitioned into two distinct sets: *base predicates* (also called EDB predicates) and *derived predicates* (also called IDB predicates). Base predicates correspond to database relations defined over a given domain and they do not appear in the head of any rule whereas derived predicates are defined by means of rules. Given a database D, a predicate symbol r and a program $\mathcal{P}$, $D(r)$ denotes the set of r-tuples in D whereas $\mathcal{P}_D$ denotes the program derived from the union of $\mathcal{P}$ with the tuples in D, i.e. $\mathcal{P}_D = \mathcal{P} \cup \{r(t) \leftarrow \mid t \in D(r)\}$. In the following a tuple t of a relation r will also be denoted as a fact $r(t)$. The semantics of $\mathcal{P}_D$ is given by the set of its stable models by considering either their union (*possible semantics* or *brave reasoning*) or their intersection (*certain semantics* or *cautious reasoning*). A *query* Q is a pair $(g, \mathcal{P})$ where g is a predicate symbol, called the *query goal*, and $\mathcal{P}$ is a program. The answer to a query $Q = (g, \mathcal{P})$ over a database D, under the possible (resp. certain) semantics is given by $D'(g)$ where $D' = \bigcup_{M \in SM(\mathcal{P}_D)} M$ (resp. $D' = \bigcap_{M \in SM(\mathcal{P}_D)} M$).

2.2 Disjunctive Datalog

A *(disjunctive Datalog) rule* r is a clause of the form

$$A_1 \vee \cdots \vee A_k \leftarrow B_1, \ldots, B_m, not\ B_{m+1}, \ldots, not\ B_n$$

where $k + m + n > 0$ and $A_1, \ldots, A_k, B_1, \ldots, B_n$ are atoms. The disjunction $A_1 \vee \cdots \vee A_k$ is the *head* of r, while the conjunction $B_1, \ldots, B_m, not\ B_{m+1}, \ldots, not\ B_n$ is the *body* of r. We also assume the existence of the binary built-in predicate symbols (comparison operators) which can only be used in the body of rules.

The (model-theoretic) semantics for positive programs $\mathcal{P}$ assigns to $\mathcal{P}$ the set of its *minimal models* $\mathcal{MM}(\mathcal{P})$ [21]. The more general *disjunctive stable model semantics* also applies to programs with (unstratified) negation [10, 8]. Disjunctive stable model semantics generalizes stable model semantics, previously defined for normal pro-

grams [9]. For any interpretation M, denote with $\mathcal{P}^M$ the ground positive program derived from $ground(\mathcal{P})$ by 1) removing all rules that contain a negative literal $not\ a$ in the body and $a \in M$, and 2) removing all negative literals from the remaining rules. An interpretation M is a (disjunctive) stable model of $\mathcal{P}$ if and only if $M \in \mathcal{MM}(\mathcal{P}^M)$. For general $\mathcal{P}$, the stable model semantics assigns to $\mathcal{P}$ the set $\mathcal{SM}(\mathcal{P})$ of its *stable models*. It is well known that stable models are minimal models (i.e. $\mathcal{SM}(\mathcal{P}) \subseteq \mathcal{MM}(\mathcal{P})$) and that for negation free programs minimal and stable model semantics coincide (i.e. $\mathcal{SM}(\mathcal{P}) = \mathcal{MM}(\mathcal{P})$). Observe that stable models are minimal models which are 'supported', i.e. their atoms can be derived from the program.

Extended disjunctive databases

Extended Datalog programs extend standard Datalog programs with a different form of negation, known as *classical* or *strong negation*, which can also appear in the head of rules [10, 17, 11]. An extended atom is either an atom, say A or its negation $\neg A$. An extended Datalog program is a set of rules of the form

$$A_1 \vee \cdots \vee A_k \leftarrow B_1, \ldots, B_m, not\ B_{m+1}, \ldots, not\ B_n \quad k + n > 0$$

where $A_1, \ldots, A_k, B_1, \ldots, B_n$ are extended atoms. A (2-valued) interpretation I for an extended program $\mathcal{P}$ is a pair $\langle T, F \rangle$ where T and F define a partition of $\mathcal{B}_\mathcal{P} \cup \neg \mathcal{B}_\mathcal{P}$ and $\neg \mathcal{B}_\mathcal{P} = \{\neg A \mid A \in \mathcal{B}_\mathcal{P}\}$. An interpretation $I = \langle T, F \rangle$ is *consistent* if there is no atom A such that $A \in T$ and $\neg A \in T$. The semantics of an extended program $\mathcal{P}$ is defined by considering each negated predicate symbol, say $\neg p$, as a new symbol syntactically different from p and by adding to the program, for each predicate symbol p with arity n the constraint $\leftarrow p(X_1, \ldots, X_n), \neg p(X_1, \ldots, X_n)$[1]. In the following, for the sake of simplicity, we shall also use rules whose bodies may contain disjunctions. Such rules, called generalized (extended) disjunctive rules, are used as shorthands for multiple standard disjunctive rules. More specifically, a generalized disjunctive rule of the form

$$A_1 \vee \ldots \vee A_k \leftarrow (B_{1,1} \vee \ldots \vee B_{1,m_1}), \ldots, (B_{n,1} \vee \ldots \vee B_{n,m_n})$$

denotes the set of standard rules

$$A_1 \vee \cdots \vee A_k \leftarrow B_{1,i_1}, \ldots, B_{n,i_n} \quad \forall j, i : 1 \leq j \leq n \text{ and } 1 \leq i_j \leq m_j$$

---

[1] A rule with empty head is a constraint is satisfied only if its body is false.

2.3 Integrity constraints

Database schemata contain the knowledge on the structure of data, i.e. they define constraints on the form the data must have. Integrity constraints express semantic information on data, that is relationships that must hold among data in the theory and they are mainly used to validate database manipulations. Integrity constraints represent the interaction among data and define properties which are supposed to be explicitly satisfied by all instances over a given database schema. They are usually defined by first order rules or by means of special notations for particular classes such as keys and functional dependencies.

Definition 1 *An* integrity constraint *(or* embedded dependency*) is a formula of the first order predicate calculus of the form:*

$$(\forall X) \, [\, \Phi(X) \supset (\exists Z)\Psi(Y) \,]$$

where X, Y and Z are sets of variables, Φ and Ψ are two conjunctions of literals such that X and Y are the distinct set of variables appearing in Φ and Ψ respectively, $Z = X - Y$ is the set of variables existentially quantified. □

In the definition above, the conjunction Φ is called the *body* and the conjunction Ψ the *head* of the integrity constraint. The semantics of the above constraints is that for every value of X which makes the formula $\Phi(X)$ true there must be an instance of Z which makes $\Psi(Y)$ true. Most of the dependencies developed in database theory are restricted cases of some of the above classes [15].

In this paper we consider *full* (or *universal*) *single-head* constraints, where Ψ is a literal or a conjunction of built-in literals (i.e. comparison operators). Therefore, an integrity constraint is a formula of the form: $(\forall X) \, [\, B_1 \wedge \cdots \wedge B_n \wedge not \, A_1 \wedge \cdots \wedge not \, A_m \wedge \phi \supset A_0 \,]$ where $A_1, ..., A_m, B_1, ..., B_n$ are base positive literals, ϕ is a conjunction of built-in literals, A_0 is a base positive atom or a conjunction of built-in atoms, X denotes the list of all variables appearing in $B_1, ..., B_n$; moreover the variables appearing in $A_0, ..., A_m$ and ϕ, also appear in $B_1, ..., B_n$.

Often we shall write our constraints in a different format by moving literals from the head to the body and vice versa. For instance, the above constraint could be rewritten as $(\forall X) \, [\, B_1 \wedge \cdots \wedge B_n \wedge \phi \supset A_0 \vee \cdots \vee A_m \,]$ or in the form of rule with empty head, called *denial*:

$(\forall X) \, [\, B_1 \wedge \cdots \wedge B_n \wedge not \, A_0 \wedge \cdots \wedge not \, A_m \wedge \phi \supset \,]$ which is satisfied only if the body is false. Moreover, in some case we shall write the above constraint as

$$(\forall X) \, [\, B_1 \wedge \cdots \wedge B_n \wedge not \, A_0 \wedge \cdots \wedge not \, A_m \supset not(\varphi) \,]$$

Example 3 *The integrity constraint $(\forall X) \, [\, p(X) \supset q(X) \vee r(X) \,]$ states that the relation p must be contained in the union of the relations q and r. It could be rewritten as $(\forall X) \, [\, p(X) \wedge not \, q(X) \supset r(X) \,]$ or as $(\forall X) \, [\, p(X) \wedge not \, q(X) \wedge not \, r(X) \supset \,]$.* □

3 Preferred repairs and answers

In this section we recall the formal definition of consistent database and repair; we present a computational mechanism that ensures selecting preferred repairs and preferred answers for inconsistent database.

3.1 Preferred repairs for inconsistent databases

In this section we introduce a polynomial function through which expressing preferences criteria. The function introduces a partial order among repairs, so that allowing the evaluation of the goodness of a repair for an inconsistent database. Moreover we define preferred repairs as feasible repairs that are minimal with respect to the partial order.

Let us first recall the formal definition of consistent database and repair.

Definition 2 Given a database D and a set of integrity constraint $\mathcal{IC}$ on D, we say that D is *consistent* if $D \models \mathcal{IC}$, i.e. if all integrity constraints in $\mathcal{IC}$ are satisfied by D, otherwise it is *inconsistent*. □

Definition 3 Given a (possibly inconsistent) database D, a *repair* for D is a pair of sets of atoms (R^+, R^-) such that 1) $R^+ \cap R^- = \emptyset$, 2) $D \cup R^+ - R^- \models \mathcal{IC}$ and 3) there is no pair $(S^+, S^-) \neq (R^+, R^-)$ such that $S^+ \subseteq R^+, S^- \subseteq R^-$ and $D \cup S^+ - S^- \models \mathcal{IC}$. The database $D \cup R^+ - R^-$ will be called the *repaired database*. □

Thus, repaired databases are consistent databases which are derived from the source database by means of a minimal set of insertion and deletion of tuples. Given a repair R, R^+ denotes the set of tuples which will be added to the database, whereas R^- denotes the set of tuples of D which will be deleted. In the following, for a given repair R and a database D, $R(D) = D \cup R^+ - R^-$ denotes the application of R to D. Moreover, given a database schema DS, we denote with $\mathbf{D}$ the set of all possible database instance over DS.

Example 4 Assume we are given a database $D = \{p(a), p(b), q(a),\ q(c)\}$ with the *inclusion dependency* $(\forall X)\,[\,p(X) \supset q(X)\,]$. D is inconsistent since $p(b) \supset q(b)$ is not satisfied. The repairs for D are $R_1 = (\{q(b)\}, \emptyset)$ and $R_2 = (\emptyset, \{p(b)\})$ producing, respectively, the repaired databases $R_1(D) = \{p(a), p(b), q(a), q(c), q(b)\}$ and $R_2(D) = \{p(a), q(a), q(c)\}$. $\square$

Definition 4 Given a (possibly inconsistent) database D over a fixed schema $\mathcal{DS}$, and a polynomial function $f : (\mathbf{D}, \mathbf{D}) \times \mathbf{D} \to \Re$. A repair R_1 is preferable to a repair R_2, w.r.t. the function f, written $R_1 \ll_f R_2$, if $f(R_1, D) \le f(R_2, D)$. A repair R for D is said to be *preferred* w.r.t. the function f if there is no repair R' for D such that $R' \ll_f R$. A repaired database $D' = D \cup R^+ - R^-$ is said to be a *preferred database* if $R = (R^+, R^-)$ is a preferred repair. $\square$

The above function f will be called *(repair) evaluation function* as it is used to evaluate a repair R with respect to a database D. A preferred database minimizes the value of the evaluation function f applied to the source database and repairs. Observe that, in the above definition, $\mathbf{D}$ denotes the domain of all possible database instances whereas $(\mathbf{D}, \mathbf{D})$ denotes the domain of all possible database updates. This means that the evaluation function f can be used to measure any possible modification of the input databases and not only to measure repairs, i.e. modification which make the database consistent. In the following, for the sake of simplicity, we only consider function which minimize the cardinality of a set.

Example 5 Consider the database $D = \{Teaches(t_1, c_1), Teaches(t_2, c_2),\quad Faculty(t_1, f_1), Faculty(t_2, f_1), Course(c_1, f_1), Course(c_2, f_2)\}$ derived from the union of the databases D_1 and D_2 of Example 1 and the integrity constraint

$\forall(P, C, F)[Teaches(P, C) \wedge Faculty(P, F) \supset Course(C, F)]$

Let R be a repair for the database D, possible evaluation functions are:

- $f_1(R, D) = |R^+|$ computing the number of inserted atoms,

- $f_2(R, D) = |R^-|$ computing the number of deleted atoms,

- $f_3(R, D) = |R^-| + |R^+|$ computing the number of deleted and inserted atoms.

As seen in Example 1, there are three repairs for D: $R_1 = (\emptyset, \{Teaches(t_2, c_2)\})$, $R_2 = (\emptyset, \{Faculty(t_2, f_1)\})$ and $R_3 = (\{Course(c_2, f_1)\}, \emptyset)$. With respect to the above evaluation functions we have the following relations:

1. $R_1 \ll_{f_1} R_3$ and $R_2 \ll_{f_1} R_3$

2. $R_3 \ll_{f_2} R_1$ and $R_3 \ll_{f_2} R_2$

Thus, considering the minimization of the above evaluation functions we have that under the function f_2, R_3 is the unique preferred repair, under the function f_1, we have two preferred repairs: R_1 and R_2, and under the function f_3 all repairs are preferred. $\square$

Given a database D, a set of integrity constraints $\mathcal{IC}$ and an evaluation function f, we denote with $\mathbf{R}(D, \mathcal{IC}, f)$ the set of preferred repairs for D. In the above example $\mathbf{R}(D, \mathcal{IC}, f_1) = \{R_1, R_2\}$, whereas $\mathbf{R}(D, \mathcal{IC}, f_2) = \{R_3\}$.

Moreover, we denote with f_0 any constant evaluation function (e.g. $f_0(R, D) = 0$, the function returning the value 0). $\mathbf{R}(D, \mathcal{IC}, f_0)$ denotes the set of all feasible repairs for D as no preference is introduced.

3.2 Preferred answers for queries over inconsistent databases

A (relational) query over a database defines a function from the database to a relation. It can be expressed by means of alternative equivalent languages such as relational algebra, 'safe' relational calculus or 'safe' non recursive Datalog [24]. In the following we shall use Datalog. Thus, a query is a pair $(g, \mathcal{P})$ where $\mathcal{P}$ is a safe non-recursive Datalog program and g is a predicate symbol specifying the output (derived) relation. Observe that relational queries define a restricted case of disjunctive queries. The reason for considering relational and disjunctive queries is that, as we shall show next, relational queries over databases with constraints can be rewritten into extended disjunctive queries over databases without constraints.

Definition 5 Given a database D, a set of integrity constraints $\mathcal{IC}$, and an evaluation function f, an atom A is *true* (resp. *false*) with respect to $\mathcal{IC}$ and f, if A belongs to all preferred repaired databases (resp. there is no preferred repaired database containing A). The atoms which are neither true nor false are *undefined*. □

Thus, true atoms appear in all preferred repaired databases whereas undefined atoms appear in a proper subset of preferred repaired databases. Given a database D, a set of integrity constraints $\mathcal{IC}$ and an evaluation function f, the application of $\mathcal{IC}$ to D (under f), denoted by $\mathcal{IC}_f(D)$, defines three distinct sets of atoms: the set of true atoms $\mathcal{IC}_f(D)^+$, the set of undefined atoms $\mathcal{IC}_f(D)^u$ and the set of false atoms $\mathcal{IC}_f(D)^-$.

Given a database D, a set of integrity constraint $\mathcal{IC}$, an evaluation function f and a query $Q = (g, \mathcal{P})$, the application of the query Q to the database D with constraint $\mathcal{IC}$ under the function f is denoted by $Q(D, \mathcal{IC}, f)$.

Definition 6 The answer to a query $Q(D, \mathcal{IC}, f)$ consists of three sets, denoted as $Q(D, \mathcal{IC}, f)^+$, $Q(D, \mathcal{IC}, f)^-$ and $Q(D, \mathcal{IC}, f)^u$, containing, respectively, the sets of g-tuples which are *true* (i.e. belonging to $Q(D')$ for all preferred repaired databases D'), *false* (i.e. not belonging to $Q(D')$ for all preferred repaired databases D') and *undefined* (i.e. set of tuples which are neither true nor false). □

Example 6 Consider the integrated databases of Example 2, the query $Q = (q, P)$ where P consists of the following rule: $q(Y) \leftarrow Teaches(john, Y, Z)$ and the evaluation function f measuring the cardinality of the repairs. The preferred answer to the query Q over the inconsistent databases (w.r.t. the constraint defined by the functional dependency), gives the unique result $\{science\}$. □

Theorem 1 *Given a database D, a set of integrity constraint $\mathcal{IC}$, an evaluation function f and a query $Q = (g, \mathcal{P})$, then*

1. $R(D, \mathcal{IC}, f) \subseteq R(D, \mathcal{IC}, f_0)$
2. $Q(D, \mathcal{IC}, f_0) \subseteq Q(D, \mathcal{IC}, f)$ □

The above theorem states that the introduction of preference criteria reduces the number of repairs and enlarges the answer (i.e. reduces the set of undefined elements of the answer).

4 Managing Inconsistent Databases

We present a technique which permits us to compute repairs and consistent answers for possibly inconsistent databases. The technique is based on the generation of a disjunctive program $\mathcal{DP}(\mathcal{IC})$ derived from the set of integrity constraints $\mathcal{IC}$. The repairs for the database can be generated from the stable models of $\mathcal{DP}(\mathcal{IC})$ whereas the computation of the consistent answers of a query $(g, \mathcal{P})$ can be derived by considering the stable models of the program $\mathcal{P} \cup \mathcal{DP}(\mathcal{IC})$ over the database D.

Integrity constraints express semantic information over data, i.e. relationships that must hold among data in the theory and they are mainly used to validate database transactions. Integrity constraints represent the interaction among data and define properties which are supposed to be satisfied by all instances over a given database schema explicitly. They are usually defined by first order rules or by means of special notations for particular classes such as keys and functional dependencies. Generally, a database D has associated a schema $\mathcal{DS} = \langle Rs, \mathcal{IC} \rangle$ which defines the intentional properties of D: Rs denotes the structure of the relations whereas $\mathcal{IC}$ contains the set of integrity constraints.

Definition 7 Let c be a universally quantified constraint of the form

$$(\forall X)[B_1 \wedge \ldots \wedge B_n \wedge \varphi \supset A_1 \vee \cdots \vee A_m]$$

where $B_1, ..., B_n, A_1, ..., A_n$ are positive atoms and φ is a conjunction of built-in atoms. Then, $dj(c)$ denotes the extended disjunctive rule

$$\neg B_1' \vee \ldots \vee \neg B_n' \vee A_1' \vee \ldots \vee A_m' \leftarrow$$
$$(B_1 \vee B_1'), ..., (B_n \vee B_n'), \varphi,$$
$$(not\ A_1 \vee \neg A_1'), ..., (not\ A_m \vee \neg A_m')$$

where C_i' denotes the atom derived from C_i by replacing the predicate symbol p with the new symbol p_d. □

Example 7 Consider the following integrity constraints:

1. $(\forall X)[p(X) \supset s(X) \vee q(X)]$
2. $(\forall X)[q(X) \supset r(X)]$

and the database D containing the facts $p(a), p(b), s(a)$ and $q(a)$. The derived generalized extended disjunctive program is defined as follows:

$$\neg p_d(X) \vee s_d(X) \vee q_d(X) \leftarrow (p(X) \vee p_d(X)),$$
$$(not\ s(X) \vee \neg s_d(X)), (not\ q(X) \vee \neg q_d(X))$$
$$\neg q_d(X) \vee r_d(X) \leftarrow (q(X) \vee q_d(X)), (not\ r(X) \vee \neg r_d(X))$$

The above rules can be now rewritten in standard form by eliminating body disjunctions. Let $\mathcal{P}$ be the corresponding extended disjunctive Datalog program, the computation of the program $\mathcal{P}_D$, derived from the union of $\mathcal{P}$ with the facts in D, gives the following stable models:

$$M_1 = D \cup \{\neg p_d(b), \neg q_d(a)\},$$
$$M_2 = D \cup \{\neg p_d(b), r_d(a)\},$$
$$M_3 = D \cup \{\neg q_d(a), s_d(b)\},$$
$$M_4 = D \cup \{r_d(a), s_d(b)\},$$
$$M_5 = D \cup \{q_d(b), \neg q_d(a), r_d(b)\},$$
$$M_6 = D \cup \{q_d(b), r_d(a), r_d(b)\}.$$

$\square$

Thus, $\mathcal{DP}(\mathcal{IC})$ denotes the set of generalized disjunctive rules derived from the rewriting of $\mathcal{IC}$, $\mathcal{DP}(\mathcal{IC})_D$ denotes the program derived from the union of the rules in $\mathcal{DP}(\mathcal{IC})$ with the facts in D and $\mathcal{SM}(\mathcal{DP}(\mathcal{IC})_D)$ (resp. $\mathcal{MM}(\mathcal{DP}(\mathcal{IC})_D)$) denotes the set of stable (resp. minimal) models of $\mathcal{DP}(\mathcal{IC})_D$. Recall that every stable model is consistent, according to the definition of consistent set given in Section 2, since it cannot contain two atoms of the form A and $\neg A$.

A *functional dependency* $X \rightarrow Y$ over a relation p can be expressed by a formula of the form

$$(\forall(X, Y, Z, U, V))[\, p(X, Y, U) \wedge p(X, Z, V) \supset Y = Z \,]$$

where X, Y, Z, U, V are lists of variables and X, Y, Z may be empty lists. An *inclusion dependency* is of the form

$$(\forall(X, Y))[\, p_1(X_1) \wedge ... \wedge p_n(X_n) \supset q(Y) \,]$$

where $X_1, ..., X_n$ and Y are lists of variables and $Y \subseteq X_1 \cup ... \cup X_n$.

4.1 Computing preferred database repairs

Every stable model can be used to define a possible repair for the database by interpreting new derived atoms (denoted by the subscript "d") as insertions and deletions of tuples. Thus, if a stable model M contains two atoms $\neg p_d(t)$ (derived atom) and $p(t)$ (base atom) we deduce that the atom $p(t)$ violates some constraint and, therefore, it must be deleted. Analogously, if M contains the derived atoms $p_d(t)$ and does not contain $p(t)$ (i.e. $p(t)$ is not in the database) we deduce that the atom $p(t)$ should be inserted in the database. We now formalize the definition of repaired database.

Definition 8 Given a database D and a set of integrity constraint $\mathcal{IC}$ over D and letting M be a stable model of $\mathcal{DP}(\mathcal{IC})_D$, then, $\mathcal{R}(M) = (\, \{p(t) \mid p_d(t) \in M \wedge p(t) \notin D\}, \{p(t) \mid \neg p_d(t) \in M \wedge p(t) \in D\} \,)$. $\square$

Theorem 2 *[12]*
Given a database D and a set of integrity constraints $\mathcal{IC}$ on D, then

1. *(Soundness) for every stable model M of $\mathcal{DP}(\mathcal{IC})_D$, $\mathcal{R}(M)$ is a repair for D;*

2. *(Completeness) for every database repair S for D there exists a stable model M for $\mathcal{DP}(\mathcal{IC})_D$ such that $S = \mathcal{R}(M)$.* $\square$

Example 8 Consider the database of Example 4. The rewriting of the integrity constraint $(\forall X)[\, p(X) \supset q(X) \,]$ produces the disjunctive rule

$$r : \neg p_d(X) \vee q_d(X) \;\leftarrow\; (p(X) \vee p_d(X)),$$
$$(not \; q(X) \vee \neg q_d(X)).$$

which can be rewritten in the simpler form

$$r' : \neg p_d(X) \vee q_d(X) \;\leftarrow\; p(X), not \; q_d(X).$$

since the predicates p_d and $\neg q_d$ do not appear in the head of any rule. The program P_D, where P is the program consisting of the disjunctive rule r' and D is the input database, has two stable models $M_1 = D \cup \{\, \neg p_d(b)\}$ and $M_2 = D \cup \{\, q_d(b)\}$. The derived repairs are $\mathcal{R}(M_1) = (\{q(b)\}, \emptyset)$ and $\mathcal{R}(M_2) = (\emptyset, \{p(b)\})$ corresponding, respectively, to the insertion of $q(b)$ and the deletion of $p(b)$.

Theorem 3
Let D be a database, $\mathcal{IC}$ a set of functional dependencies and f an evaluation function measuring the cardinality of repairs. Then,

1. *(Soundness) for every stable model M of $\mathcal{DP}(\mathcal{IC})_D$ with minimum cardinality, $\mathcal{R}(M)$ is a preferred repair (w.r.t. f) for D;*

2. *(Completeness) for every preferred database repair S for D there exists a stable model M for $\mathcal{DP}(\mathcal{IC})_D$ with minimal cardinality such that $\mathcal{R}(M) = S$.*

3. *$\mathcal{R}(M)$ can be computed in polynomial time.* $\square$

Theorem 4

Let D be a database, $\mathcal{IC}$ a set of full inclusion dependencies and f an evaluation function measuring the number of insertions (resp. deletions). Then

1. *there is a unique preferred (w.r.t. f) repair S and there exists a unique stable model M such that $\mathcal{R}(M) = S$;*

2. *$M^+ = \emptyset$ (resp. $M^- = \emptyset$);*

3. *$\mathcal{R}(M)$ can be computed in polynomial time.* $\square$

4.2 Computing preferred answers

We now consider the problem of computing a preferred (consistent) answers without modifying the (possibly inconsistent) database. We assume that tuples, contained in the database or implied by the constraints, may be *true*, *false* or *undefined*.

Let D be a database, $\mathcal{IC}$ a set of integrity constraints and f an evaluation function, then we denote with $\mathcal{PSM}_f(\mathcal{DP}(\mathcal{IC})_D)$ the set of preferred stable models of $\mathcal{DP}(\mathcal{IC})_D$ with respect to the function $f(\mathcal{R}(M), D)$.

From the results of Section 3.1 we derive

$\mathcal{IC}_f(D)^+ =$
$\{ p(t) \in D \mid \nexists M \in \mathcal{PSM}_f(\mathcal{LP}(\mathcal{IC})_D) \text{ s.t. } \neg p_d(t) \in M \} \cup$
$\{ p(t) \notin D \mid \forall M \in \mathcal{PSM}_f(\mathcal{LP}(\mathcal{IC})_D) \text{ s.t. } p_d(t) \in M \}$,

$\mathcal{IC}_f(D)^- =$
$\{ p(t) \notin D \mid \nexists M \in \mathcal{PSM}_f(\mathcal{LP}(\mathcal{IC})_D) \text{ s.t. } p_d(t) \in M \} \cup$
$\{ p(t) \in D \mid \forall M \in \mathcal{PSM}_f(\mathcal{LP}(\mathcal{IC})_D) \text{ s.t. } \neg p_d(t) \in M \}$,

$\mathcal{IC}_f(D)^u =$
$\{p(t) \in D \mid \exists M_1, M_2 \in \mathcal{PSM}_f(\mathcal{LP}(\mathcal{IC})_D) \text{ s.t. }$
$\quad \neg p_d(t) \in M_1, \neg p_d(t) \notin M_2 \} \cup$
$\{p(t) \notin D \mid \exists M_1, M_2 \in \mathcal{PSM}_f(\mathcal{LP}(\mathcal{IC})_D) \text{ s.t. }$
$\quad p_d(t) \in M_1, p_d(t) \notin M_2 \}$.

Observe that the sets $\mathcal{IC}_f(D)^+, \mathcal{IC}_f(D)^-$ and $\mathcal{IC}_f(D)^u$ are disjoint and that $\mathcal{IC}_f(D)^+ \cup \mathcal{IC}(fD)^-$ defines a set of consistent atoms. We are now in the position to introduce the computation of (preferred) consistent answer.

The preferred consistent answer for the query $Q = (g, \mathcal{P})$ over the database D under constraints $\mathcal{IC}$ is as follows:

$Q(D, \mathcal{IC}, f)^+ =$
$\{g(t) \in D \mid \nexists M \in \mathcal{PSM}_f((\mathcal{P} \cup \mathcal{LP}(\mathcal{IC}))_D) \text{ s.t.} \neg g_d(t) \in M \} \cup$
$\{g(t) \notin D \mid \forall M \in \mathcal{PSM}_f((\mathcal{P} \cup \mathcal{LP}(\mathcal{IC}))_D) \text{ s.t. } g_d(t) \in M \}$,

$Q(D, \mathcal{IC}, f)^u =$
$\{ g(t) \in D \mid \exists M_1, M_2 \in \mathcal{PSM}_f((\mathcal{P} \cup \mathcal{LP}(\mathcal{IC}))_D) \text{ s.t. }$
$\quad \neg g_d(t) \in M_1, \neg g_d(t) \notin M_2 \} \cup$
$\{ g(t) \notin D \mid \exists M_1, M_2 \in \mathcal{PSM}_f((\mathcal{P} \cup \mathcal{LP}(\mathcal{IC}))_D) \text{ s.t. }$
$\quad g_d(t) \in M_1, g_d(t) \notin M_2 \}$.

whereas the set of atoms which are neither true nor undefined can be assumed to be false.

Theorem 5

Let D be a database, $Q = (g, \mathcal{P})$ a query, f a polynomial evaluation function and D' a repaired database preferred (w.r.t. f). Then

1. *each atom $A \in Q(D, \mathcal{IC}, f)^+$ belongs to the stable model of $\mathcal{P}_{D'}$ (soundness)*

2. *each atom $A \in Q(D, \mathcal{IC}, f)^-$ does not belong to the stable model of $\mathcal{P}_{D'}$ (completeness).* $\square$

Example 9 Consider the database of Example 5, the integrity constraint:

$$\forall (P, C, F)[Teaches(P, C) \wedge Faculty(P, F) \supset Course(C, F)]$$

and the evaluation functions $f_1(R, D) = |R^+|$ and $f_2(R, D) = |R^-|$ computing respectively the number of inserted and deleted atoms. The program P_D has three stable models: $M_1 = D \cup \{\neg Teaches_d(t_2, c_2)\}$, $M_2 = D \cup \{\neg Faculty_d(t_2, f_1)\}$ and $M_3 = D \cup \{Course_d(c_2, f_1)\}$. Considering the evaluation function $f_1(R, D) = |R^+|$ the set of preferred models consists of M_1 and M_2; therefore, the atoms which are true and undefined are: $\mathcal{IC}_{f_1}(D)^+ = \{Teaches(t_1, c_1), Faculty(t_1, f_1), Course(c_1, f_1), Course(c_2, f_2)\}$ and $\mathcal{IC}_{f_1}(D)^u = \{Teaches(t_2, c_2), Faculty(t_2, f_1)\}$. Considering the evaluation function $f_2(R, D) = |R^-|$, M_3 is the unique preferred model; thus, the set of undefined atoms is empty, whereas the set of true atoms is $\mathcal{IC}_{f_2}(D)^+ = \{Teaches(t_1, c_1), Teaches(t_2, c_2), Faculty(t_1, f_1), Faculty(t_2, f_1), Course(c_1, f_1), Course(c_2, f_2), Course(c_2, f_1)\}$. The answer to the query $(Teaches, \emptyset)$ is $\{(t_1, c_1)\}$ under the evaluation function f_1 and $\{(t_1, c_1), (t_2, c_2)\}$ under the evaluation function f_2. The answer to the query $(Course, \emptyset)$ is $\{(c_1, f_1), (c_2, f_2)\}$, under the function f_1 and $\{ (c_1, f_1), (c_2, f_2), (c_2, f_1) \}$ under the function f_2. □

5 Conclusions

In this paper we have proposed a logic programming based framework for managing possibly inconsistent databases. The main contribution of this work consists in the definition of a logic approach for querying and repairing inconsistent databases that extends previous works by also considering techniques to express and manage preferences among repairs and possible answers. Preference criteria can be introduced to specify desiderata on how to update the inconsistent database in order to make it consistent and are expressed by means of *evaluation functions*, i.e. polynomial functions that are applied to repairs and return real numbers. The evaluation function defines a partial order both among repairs and possible answer, thus it represents a flexible mechanism for selecting among a set of feasible repairs those better conforming to the specified criteria. The goodness of a repair is measured by estimating how much it violates the desiderata conditions and a repair is "preferred" if it minimizes the value of the polynomial function used to express the preference criteria. A further important characteristic related to the introduction of preference criteria is the reduction of feasible repairs and answers, which let, for special cases of constraints, to unique repair and answer.

References

[1] Abiteboul S., Hull R., Vianu V. *Foundations of Databases*. Addison-Wesley, 1994.

[2] Argaval, S., Keller, A. M., Wiederhold, G., Saraswat, K., Flexible Relation: an Approach for Integrating Data from Multiple, Possibly Inconsistent Databases. *ICDE*, 1995.

[3] Arenas, M., Bertossi, L., Chomicki, J., Consistent query Answers in inconsistent databases. *PODS*, pp. 68–79, 1999.

[4] Arenas, M., Bertossi, L., Chomicki, J., Specifying and Querying Database repairs using Logic Programs with Exceptions. *FQAS*, pp. 27-41, 2000.

[5] Baral, C., Kraus, S., Minker, J., Combining Multiple Knowledge Bases. *TKDE*, 3(2), pp. 208-220, 1991.

[6] Bry, F., Query Answering in Information System with Integrity Constraints, *IFIP WG 11.5 Working Conf. on Integrity and Control in Inform. System*, 1997.

[7] Dung, P. M., Integrating Data from Possibly Inconsistent Databases. *CoopIS*, pp. 58-65, 1996.

[8] Eiter, T., Gottlob, G., Mannila, H., Disjunctive Datalog. *TODS*, 22(3), pp. 364–418, 1997.

[9] Gelfond, M., Lifschitz, V. The Stable Model Semantics for Logic Programming, *ICLP*, pp. 1070–1080, 1988.

[10] Gelfond, M., Lifschitz, V., Classical Negation in Logic Programs and Disjunctive Databases, *NGC*, No. 9, pp. 365–385, 1991.

[11] Greco, S., Saccà, D., Negative Logic Programs. *NACLP*, pp. 480-497, 1990.

[12] Greco, S., Zumpano, E., Querying Inconsistent Database *LPAR*, pp. 308-325, 2000.

[13] Greco, G., Greco, S., Zumpano, E., A Logic Programming Approach to the Integration, Repairing and Querying of Inconsistent Databases. *ICLP*, 2001.

[14] Grant, J., Subrahmanian, V. S., Reasoning in Inconsistent Knowledge Bases, *TKDE*, 7(1), pp. 177-189, 1995.

[15] Kanellakis, P. C., Elements of Relational Database Theory. *Handbook of Theoretical Computer Science*, Vol. 2, J. van Leewen (ed.), North-Holland, 1991.

[16] Kifer, M., Li, A., On the Semantics of Rule-Based Expert Systems with Uncertainty. *Int. Conf. on Database Theory* pp. 102-11, 1988.

[17] Kowalski, R. A., Sadri, F., Logic Programs with Exceptions. *NGC*, 9(3/4), pp. 387-400, 1991.

[18] Lin, J., A Semantics for Reasoning Consistently in the Presence of Inconsistency. *AI*, 86(1), pp. 75-95, 1996.

[19] Lin, J., and Mendelzon, A. O., Knowledge Base Merging by Majority, in *Dynamic Worlds: From the Frame Problem to Knowledge Management*, R. Pareschi and B. Fronhoefer (eds.), Kluwer, 1999.

[20] Lloyd, J., *Foundation of Logic Programming*. Spinger-Verlag, 1987.

[21] Minker, J., On Indefinite Data Bases and the Closed World Assumption, *6-th Conf. on Automated Deduction*, pp. 292–308, 1982.

[22] Sakama, C., Inoue, K., Priorized logic programming and its application to commonsense reasoning. *AI*, No. 123, pp. 185-222, 2000.

[23] Subrahmanian, V. S., Amalgamating Knowledge Bases. *ACM ToDS*, 19(2), pp. 291-331, 1994.

[24] Ullman, J. K., *Principles of Database and Knowledge-Base Systems*, Vol. 1, Computer Science Press, 1988.

[25] Wijsen, J., Condensed representation of database repairs for consistent query answering, *ICDT*, pp. 378-393, 2003.

[26] Wang, X, You, J. H., Yuan, L. Y., Nonmonotonic reasoning by monotonic inferences with priority conditions. *Proc. Int. Workshop on Nonmonotonic Extensions of Logic Programming*. pp. 91-109, 1996.

[27] Yan, L.L., Ozsu, M.T., Conflict Tolerant Queries in Aurora. *CoopIS*, 1999; pp. 279–290.

[28] Zang, Y., Foo, N., Answer sets for prioritized logic programs. *(ILPS*, pp. 69-83, 1997.

V2: A Database Approach to Temporal Document Management

Kjetil Nørvåg
Department of Computer and Information Science
Norwegian University of Science and Technology
7491 Trondheim, Norway

E-mail: Kjetil.Norvag@idi.ntnu.no

Abstract

Temporal document databases are interesting in a number of contexts, in general document databases as well as more specialized applications like temporal XML/Web warehouses. In order to efficiently manage temporal document versions, a temporal document database system should be employed. In this paper, we describe the V2 temporal document database system, which supports storage, retrieval, and querying of temporal documents. We also give some performance results from a mini-benchmark run on the V2 prototype.

1 Introduction

In order to efficiently manage temporal document versions, a temporal document database system should be employed. In this paper, we describe an approach to temporal document storage, which we have implemented in the V2 temporal document database system. Important topics include temporal document query processing, and control over what is temporal, how many versions, vacuuming etc., something that is necessary for practical use.

We have in a previous project studied the realization of a temporal XML database using a *stratum* approach, in which a layer converts temporal query language statements into conventional statements, executed by an underlying commercial object-relational database system. That project demonstrated the usefulness of a temporal XML databases in general, and gave us experience from actual use of such systems. The next step is using an *integrated* approach, in which the internal modules of a database management system are modified or extended to support time-varying data. This is the topic of this paper, which describes V2, a temporal document database system. In V2, previous versions of documents are kept, and it is possible to search in the historical (old) versions, retrieve documents that was valid at a

certain time, query changes to documents, etc.

Although we believe temporal databases should be based on the integrated approach, we do not think using special-purpose temporal databases is the solution. Rather, we want the temporal features integrated into existing general database systems. In order to make this possible, the techniques used to support temporal features should be compatible with existing architectures. As a result, we put emphasis on techniques that can easily be integrated into existing architectures, preferably using existing index structures[1] as well as a query processing philosophy compatible with existing architectures.

The organization of the rest of this paper is as follows. In Section 2 we give an overview of related work. In Section 3 we describe an example application that originally motivated the work of this project. In Section 4 we give an overview of our approach and our assumptions. In Section 5 we describe the operations supported by V2. In Section 6 we describe the architecture for management of temporal documents used in V2. In Section 7 we describe the architecture and implementation of V2. In Section 8 we give some performance results. Finally, in Section 9, we conclude the paper and outlines issues for further work.

2 Related work

In order to realize an efficient temporal XML database system, several issues have to be solved, including efficient storage of versioned XML documents, efficient indexing of temporal XML documents, and temporal XML query processing. Storage of versioned documents is studied by Marian et al. [7] and Chien et al. [3, 4, 5]. Chien et al. also considered access to previous versions, but only snapshot retrievals. Temporal query processing is discussed in [8].

---

[1]History tells us that even though a large amount of "exotic" index structures have been proposed for various purposes, database companies are very reluctant to make their systems more complicated by incorporating these into their systems, and still mostly support the "traditional" structures, like B-trees, hash files, etc.

An approach that is orthogonal, but related to the work presented in this paper, is to introduce valid time features into XML documents, as presented by Grandi and Mandreoli [6].

Another approach to temporal document databases is the work by Aramburu et al. [2]. Based on their data model TOODOR, they focus on static document with associated time information, but with no versioning of documents. Queries can also be applied to metadata, which is represented by temporal schemas. The implementation is a stratum approach, built on top of Oracle 8.

3 Example application

In order to motivate the subsequent description of the V2 approach, we first describe an example application that motivated the initial work on V2: *a temporal XML/Web warehouse* (Web-DW). This was inspired by the work in the Xyleme project [12]: Xyleme supported monitoring of changes between a new retrieved version of a page, and the previous version of the page, but no support for actually maintaining and querying temporal documents.

In our work, we wanted to be able to maintain a temporal Web-DW, storing the history of a set of selected web pages or web sites. By regularly retrieving these pages and storing them in the warehouse, and at the same time keeping the old versions, we should be able to: 1) retrieve the sites/pages valid at a particular time t, 2) retrieve all pages that contained one or more particular word at a particular point in time t, and 3) ask for changes, for example retrieve all pages that did not contain "Bin Laden" before September 11. 2001, but contained these words afterwards.

It should be noted that a temporal Web-DW based on remote Web data poses a lot of new challenges, for example 1) consistency issues resulting from the fact that it is not possible to retrieve a whole site of related pages at one instant, and 2) versions missing due to the fact that pages might have been updated more than once between each time we retrieve them from the Web.

4 General overview and assumptions

In previous work on temporal database, including temporal XML documents [7, 8], it has been assumed that it is not feasible to store complete versions of all documents. The proposed answer to the problem has been to store delta documents (the changes between two documents) instead. However, in order to access an historical document version, a number of delta documents have to be read in order to reconstruct the historical versions. Even in the unlikely case that these delta versions are stored clustered, the reconstruction process can be expensive, in terms of disk accesses cost

as well as CPU cost. As a result, temporal queries can be very expensive, and not very applicable in practice. We take another approach to the problem, based on the observation that during the last years storage capacity has increases at a high rate, and at the same time, storage cost has decreased at a comparable rate. Thus, it is now feasible to store the complete versions of the documents. Several aspects make this assumption reasonable:

- In many cases, the difference in size between a complete version and a delta version is not large enough to justify storage of delta versions instead of complete document version. For example, deltas are stored in a format that simplifies reconstruction and extracting change-oriented information, a typical delta can in fact be larger than a complete document version [7]. Even a simpler algorithm for creating deltas of document can generate relatively large deltas for typical document. The main reason for this, is that changes between document versions can be more complex than typical changes between fixed-size objects or tuples. For example, sections in a document can be moved, truncated, etc.

- Even though many documents on the web are very dynamic, and for example change once a day, it is also the case that in many application areas, documents are relatively static. When large changes occur, this is often during site reorganization, and new document names are employed.

Instead of storing delta documents, we will rely on other techniques to keep the storage requirements at a reasonable level: 1) compression, 2) granularity reduction [10], and vacuuming.

Although we argue strongly for not using the delta approach in general, we also realize that in some application areas, there will be a large number of versions of particular document with only small changes between them, and at the same time a small amount of queries that require reconstruction of a large number of versions. For this reason, we will in the next version of V2 also provide diff-based deltas as an option for these areas.

Document names and document version identifiers. A document is identified by its *document name*, i.e., every time a document with a given name is inserted, and there is already stored a document with the same name, the new document is considered a new version of the stored document.

A document version stored in V2 is uniquely identified by a *version identifier* (VID). The VID of a version is persistent and never reused, similar to a logical object identifier (OID) used in object databases.

Time model and timestamps. The aspect of time in V2 is *transaction time*, i.e., a document is stored in the database at some point in time, and after it is stored, it is *current* until logically deleted or updated. We call the non-current versions *historical versions*.

The time model in V2 is a linear time model (time advances from the past to the future in an ordered step by step fashion). However, in contrast to most other transaction-time database systems, V2 does support reincarnation, i.e., a (logically) deleted version can be updated, thus creating a non-contiguous lifespan, with possibility of more than one tombstone (a tombstone is written to denote a logical delete operation) for each document.

5 Supported operations

In this section we summarize the most important user operations supported by V2 through the V2 API. A more detailed description of the operations can be found in [9].

Document insert, update, and delete. V2 is a general document database system, and in some of our application areas exact round-trip[2] of documents is required. As a result, we use a *FileBuffer* as the basic access structure, which is the intermediate place between the outside world (remote web page or local file), and the document version in the database. Thus, a document can be inserted into the File-Buffer from an external source, inserted into the version database from the FileBuffer, inserted into the FileBuffer from the version database, or written back to an external destination, for example a file.

Retrieving document versions. In order to retrieve a particular version into the FileBuffer from the version database, operations for retrieving the current version as well as the version valid at time t exist. These operations will be sufficient for many applications. However, in order to support query processing a number of operators will be needed. Included are operators for temporal text-containment queries (i.e., queries for document versions containing a particular word or set of words), the Allen operators [1] (i.e.: `before`, `after`, `meets`, `overlaps`, etc.) and operators for granularity reduction, vacuuming, compression, and deletion.

6 An architecture for management of temporal documents

In order to support the operations in the previous section, careful management of data and access structures is important. In this section, we present the architecture for management of temporal documents as implemented in V2.

As a starting point for the discussion, it is possible to store the document versions directly in a B-tree, using *document name* and *time* as the search key. Obviously, this solution has many shortcomings, for example, a query like "list the names of all documents stored in the database" or "list the names of all documents with a certain prefix stored in the database" will be very expensive. One step further, and the approach we base our system on, is to use 1) one tree-based index to do the mapping from name and time to VID, and 2) store the document versions themselves separately, using VID as the search key.

6.1 Document name index

A document is identified by a *document name*, which can be a filename in the local case, or URL in the more general case. It is very useful to be able to query all documents with a certain prefix, for example `http://www.idi.ntnu.no/grupper/db/*`. In order to support such queries efficiently, the document name should be stored in an index structure supporting prefix queries, for example a tree-structured index.

Conceptually, the document name index has for each document name some metadata related to all versions of the document, followed by specific information for each particular version. For each document, the document name and whether the document is temporal or not is stored (i.e., whether previous versions should be kept when a new version of the document is inserted into the database.)

For each document version, some metadata is stored in structures called *version descriptors*. This includes the timestamp and whether the actual version is compressed or not.

In order to keep the size of the document name index as small as possible, we do not store the size of the document version in the index, because this size can efficiently be determined by reading the document version's meta-chunk (a special header containing information about the document version) from the version database.[3]

6.1.1 Managing many versions

For some documents, the number of versions can be very high. In a query we often only want to query versions valid at a particular time. In order to avoid having to first retrieve the document metadata, and then read a very large number of version descriptors spread over possibly a large number of leaf nodes until we find the descriptor for the

---

[2]Exact round-trip means that a document retrieved from the database is exactly the same as it was when it was stored.

[3]We assume that queries for the size of a document are only moderately frequent. If this assumption should turn out to be wrong, the size can easily be included in the version descriptor in the document name index.

particular version, document information is partitioned into chunks. Each chunk contains a number of descriptors, valid in a particular time range, and each chunk can be retrieved separately. In this way, it is possible to retrieve only the descriptors that are necessary to satisfy the query. The chunks can be of variable size, and because transaction time is monotonously increasing they will be append-only, and only the last chunk for a document will be added to. When a chunk reaches a certain size, a new chunk is created, and new entries will be inserted into this new chunk.

The key for each chunk is the document name and *the smallest timestamp of an entry in* the next chunk *minus one time unit*. The reason for this can be explained as follows:

1. One version is valid from the time of its timestamp until (but not including) the time of the timestamp of the next version. Thus, a chunk covers the time from the timestamp of its first version descriptor until the timestamp of the first version descriptor in the next chunk.

2. In the B-tree library we base our system on, the data item (chunk) with the smallest key larger than or equal to the search key is returned.

The document metadata is replicated in each chunk in order to avoid having to read some other chunk in order to retrieve the metadata. In the current version of V2, the only relevant replicated metadata is the information on whether the document is temporal or not.

6.1.2   One vs. two indexes

When designing a temporal index structure, we have to start with one design decision, namely choosing between 1) one temporal index that indexes both current and historical versions, or 2) two indexes, where one index only indexes current or recent versions, and the other indexes historical versions.

The important advantage of using two indexes is higher locality on non-temporal index accesses. We believe that support for temporal data should not significantly affect efficiency of queries for current versions, and therefore either a one-index approach with sub-indexes or a two-index approach should be employed. One of our goals is to a largest possible extent using structures that can easily be integrated into existing systems, and based on this we have a two-index approach as the preferred solution. An important advantage of using two indexes is that the current version index can be assumed to be small enough to always fit in main memory, making accesses to this index very cheap.

The disadvantage of using one index that indexes only current document versions, and one index that only indexes historical versions is potential high update costs: when a temporal document is updated, both indexes have to be updated. This could be a bottleneck. To avoid this, we use a more flexible approach, using one index that indexes the most recent n document versions, and one index that indexes the older historical versions. Every time a document is updated and the threshold of n version descriptors in the current version index is reached, all but the most recent version descriptors are moved to the historical version index. This is an efficient operation, effectively removing one chunk from the current version index, and rewriting it to the historical version index.

When keeping recent versions in the current version index, we trade off lookup efficiency with increased update efficiency. However, it should be noted that this should in most cases not affect the efficiency of access to non-temporal documents: We expect that defining documents as non-temporal or temporal in general will be done for collections of documents rather than individual documents. This will typically also be documents with a common prefix. These will only have a current version descriptor in the index, and the leaf nodes containing the descriptors will have the entries for many documents, and should in many cases achieve high locality in accesses.

6.1.3   Lookup operations on the document name index

In a temporal document database, a typical operation is to retrieve the current version of a particular document, or the version valid at a particular time. Using the architecture described in this section, this will involve a lookup in the document name index in order to find the VID of the document version, followed by the actual retrieval of the document version from the version database.

Retrieving the current version simply involves a search in the current version document name index. When retrieving the version valid at time t, the version descriptor can be in either the 1) historical or 2) current version index. In which index to start the search, depends on whether we expect that most such retrievals are to recent (current version index) or older (historical version index) versions. The best strategy also depends on the number of versions of most documents. In V2 it is possible for the user to give hints about this when requesting the search. When query processing is added to the system, this decision can be made by the query optimizer. One simple strategy that should work in many cases is simply to 1) maintain statistics for hit rates in the indexes versus the age of the requested document, and 2) use this statistics to start searching in the historical version index if the time searched for is less than current time minus a value t. Note that even if there is no entry for the document in the current version index, it is possible that it exists in the historical version index. The reason for this is that information about temporal documents that have been (logically) deleted is moved to the historical version index even if the chunk is not full (because we want the current version index only to contain information about non-deleted documents).

6.2 Version database

The document versions are stored in the version database. In order to support retrieval of parts of documents, the documents are stored as a number of chunks (this is done transparently to the user/application) in a tree structure, where the concatenated VID and chunk number is used as the search key.

The most significant part of the version key is the VID. The VID is essentially a counter, and given the fact that each new version to be inserted is given a higher VID than the previous versions, the document version tree index is append-only. This is interesting, because is makes it easy to retrieve all versions inserted during a certain VID interval (which can be mapped from a time interval). One interesting use of this feature is reconnect/synchronization of mobile databases, which can retrieve all versions inserted into the database after a certain VID (last time the mobile unit was connected).

In some situations, for example during execution of some queries, we get VIDs as results. In this way, we are able to retrieve the actual document versions. However, often information about the documents is requested at the same time, for example the document name. For this reason, some metadata is stored in a separate header, or *meta-chunk*. In this way, it is easy to do the reverse mapping from VID to document name. Currently we also store the timestamp in the meta-chunk, because we decide the timestamp at an early stage anyway. However, if we later should use another approach for timestamp management, this can be changed. The meta-chunk also contains the size of the document version.

As described previously, V2 has a document-name index that is divided in a current (or rather *recent*) and historical part. This approach, as has been proposed in the context of traditional temporal databases, could also be used for the version database. However, for several reasons we do not think this is appropriate:

- First of all, considering the typical document size which is much larger than tuples/objects in traditional temporal databases, the locality aspect is less important.

- Second, it would involve more work during update, because we would not only write a new version, but also read and rewrite the previous version (move from current to historical version database). It is also possible to achieve the same in a more flexible and less costly way by actually creating two separate databases, and regularly move old versions to the historical database,

for example as a result of vacuuming or granularity reduction processing.

6.2.1 Non-temporal documents

For some documents, we do not want to store their history. When such a *non-temporal* document is updated, the previous version of the document becomes invalid. However, instead of updating the document in-place, we append the new version to the end of the version database. The previous version can be immediately removed from the version database, but a more efficient approach is to regularly sweep through the version database and physically delete old versions, compacting pages (moving contents from two or more almost-empty database pages into a new page), and at the same time vacuum old temporal documents.

There is also another reason for doing updates this way: documents do not have a fixed size, and quite often new versions will be larger than the previous versions. In that case, in-place updating would often result in 1) splitting of pages, 2) writing to overflow pages, or 3) wasted space if space is reserved for larger future versions. All these three approaches are expensive and should be avoided.

6.3 Full-text index

A text-index module based on variants of inverted lists is used in order to efficiently support text-containment queries.

In our context, we consider it necessary to support dynamic updates of the full-text index, so that all updates from a transaction are persistent as well as immediately available. This contrasts to many other systems that base the text indexing on bulk updates at regular intervals, in order to keep the average update cost lower. In cases where the additional cost incurred by the dynamic updates is not acceptable, it is possible to disable text-indexing and re-enable it at a later time. When re-enabled, all documents stored or updated since text indexing was disabled will be text-indexed. The total cost of the bulk-updating of the text-index will in general be cheaper than sum of the cost of the individual updates.

As mentioned previously, one of our goals is that it should be possible to use existing structures and indexes in systems, in order to realize the V2 structures. This also applies to the text-indexing module. The text-index module actually provides three different text-index variants suitable for being implemented inside ordinary B-trees. Each variant have different update cost, query cost, and disk size characteristics:

Naive text-index: This index uses one index record for every posting, i.e., a (*word,VID*) tuple in the index for each document version containing *word* (although the word is in practice only stored once in the index). The advantage of this index structure is easy implementation, and easy insertion and deletion of postings. The disadvantage is of course the size: in our experiments the disk space of naive text-indexes was close to the size of the indexed text itself.

Chunk-based text index: This index uses one or more chunks for each word. Each chunk contains the index word, and a number of VIDs. For each VID inserted into the chunk, the size increases, until it reaches its maximum size (typically in the order of 0.5-2 KB, but should always fit in one index page). At that time, a new chunk is created for new entries (i.e., we will in general have a number of chunks for each indexed word). The size of this text-index variant will be much lower than the previous variant, because the number of records in the index will be much low, meaning less overhead information. The disadvantage is higher CPU cost because more data has to be copied in memory for each entry added (this is the reason for the chunk size/insert cost tradeoff, giving chunk sizes relatively smaller than maximum size constrained by the index page size). However, the text-index size is much lower than the previous approach. In order to support zig-zag joins, each chunk uses the VID in addition to the index words as the chunk key.

Improved chunk-based text index: Traditionally the size of text-indexes is reduced by using some kind of compression. The compression techniques usually exploit the fact that documents can be identified by a document number, making them ordered, and that in this way each document number d_i can be replaced by the distance $d = d_i - d_{i-1}$. This distance usually requires a lower number of bits for its representation. Given the size of the moderate size of our chunks and the desire to keep complexity and CPU cost down, we use a simpler approach, where we use a constant-size small integer in order to represent the distance between two VIDs. Each chunk contains the ordinary-sized VID for the first version in the chunk, but the rest of the VIDs are represented as distances, using short 16-bit integers. In the case when the distance is larger than what can be represented using 16 bit, a new chunk is started. It should be noted that this will in practice happen infrequently. When using the improved chunk-based text index, we have in our experiments experienced a typical text-index size of less than 7% of the indexed text. This size can be further reduced if the text-index is compacted (the typical fill-factor of the index in the dynamic case is 67%, but this can be increased to close to 100% with reorganization). This can be useful if the document database is static most of the time, and dynamic only in periods.

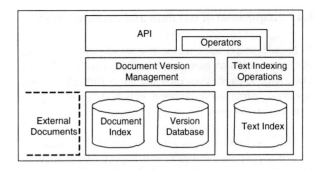

Figure 1. The V2 prototype architecture.

7 Implementation of the V2 prototype

The current prototype is essentially a library, where accesses to a database are performed through a V2 object, using an API supporting the operations and operators described previously in this paper.

In the current prototype, the bottom layers are built upon the Berkeley DB database toolkit [11], which we employ to provide persistent storage using B-trees. However, we will later consider to use a XML-optimized/native XML storage engine instead. An XML extension to Berkeley DB will be released later this year, and would be our preferred choice sine this will reduce the transition cost. Other alternatives include commercial products, for example Tamino, eXcelon, or Natix. Using a native XML storage should result in much better performance for many kinds of queries, in particular those only accessing subelements of documents, and also facilitate our extension for temporal XML operators. The main parts of the architecture of V2 are illustrated in Figure 1.

8 Performance

The performance of a system can be compared in a number of ways. For example, benchmarks are useful both to get an idea of the performance of a system as well as comparing the system with similar systems. However, to our knowledge there exists no benchmarks suitable for temporal document databases. An alternative technique that can be used to measure performance, is the use of actual execution traces. However, again we do not know of any available execution traces (this should come as no surprise, considering that this is relatively new research area). In order to do some measurements of our system, we have created a execution trace, based on the temporal web warehouse as described in Section 3.

8.1 Acquisition of test data and execution trace

In order to get some reasonable amount of test data for our experiments, we have used data from a set of web sites. The available pages from each site are downloaded once a day, by crawling the site starting with the site's main page. This essentially provides an insert/update/delete trace for our temporal document database.

The initial set of pages was of a size of approximately 91 MB (approximately 10000 web pages). An average of 510 web pages were updated each day, 320 web pages were removed (all pages that were successfully retrieved on day d_i but not available at day d_{i+1} were considered deleted), and 335 web new pages were inserted. It should be noted that the update/insert rate is relatively high because many of the web sites were web-newspapers/magazines that were updated daily. The average size of the updated pages was relatively high (37.5 KB), resulting in an average increase of 45 MB for each set of pages loaded into the database (with 90% fill factor, this equals 40 MB of new text into the database).

We kept the temporal snapshots from the web sites locally, so that insertion to the database is essentially loading from a local disk. In this way, we isolate the performance of the database system, excluding external factors as communication delays etc.

For our experiments, we used a computer with a 1.4 GHz AMD Athlon CPU, 1 GB RAM, and 3 Seagate Cheetah 36es 18.4 GB disks. One disk was used for program/OS, one for storing database files, and one for storing the test data files (the web pages). The version database and the text index has separate buffers, and the size of these are explicitly set to 100 MB and 200 MB, respectively. The rest of the memory is utilized by the operating system, mostly as disk page buffers. The database page size is set to 8 KB.

8.2 Measurements

We now describe the various measurements we have done. All have been performed both using the naive and chunk-based text indexes, and both with and without compression of versions. In order to see how different choices for system parameter values like chunk sizes and cache sizes affects performance, we have also run the tests with different document/version/text-index chunk sizes and different cache size for the version database and the text index.

Loading and updating. The first part of the tests is loading data into the system. Loading data into a document database is a heavy operation, mainly because of the text indexing. Our text indexes are dynamic, i.e., are updated immediately. This implies that frequent commit operations will result in a very low total update rate. However, for our intended application areas we expect much data to be loaded in bulk in each transaction. For example, for the web warehouse application we assume commit is only done between each loaded site, or even set of sites. We load all the updates for one day of data in one transaction. In the first transaction, the database is empty, so that approximately 10000 pages are inserted into the system. For each of the following transactions, on average of 510 web pages/documents are inserted, 320 documents logically deleted, and 335 documents inserted, as described above. Note that in order to find out whether a web page has changed or not, the new page with the same name has to be compared to the existing version. Thus, even if only 510+335 document versions are actually inserted, approximately 10000 documents in total actually have to be retrieved from the database and compared with the new document with the same URL during each transaction. For each parameter set, we measure the time of a number of operations. The most important measurements which will discuss below is:

- The update time for the last transaction, when the last set of documents are applied to the system.

- After the initial updates based on test data, we also insert a total of 10000 new pages with documents names not previously found in the database, in order to study the cost of inserting into a database of a certain size, compared to updates (when inserting, no comparison with the previous version is necessary).

- In order to study the cost of inserts of individual documents, when only one document is inserted during one transactions, we also insert a number of documents at different sizes from 800 B to 30 KB, using a separate transaction for each. As a measure of this cost, we use the average time of the insert of these documents. Because we have not enabled logging, every insert result in every disk page changed during the transaction to be forced to disk (this is obviously a relatively costly operation).

Query and retrieval: After loading the database, we do some simple test to measure the basic query performance. The operations are text lookup of a set of words, and with some additional time operations as described below. When searching, we have used three categories of words:

- Frequently occurring words, which typically occurs in more than 10% of the documents. In our database, all entries for one frequently occurring word typically occupies in the order of 10 disk pages.

- Medium frequently occurring words, which occurs in approximately 0.5% of the documents). In our

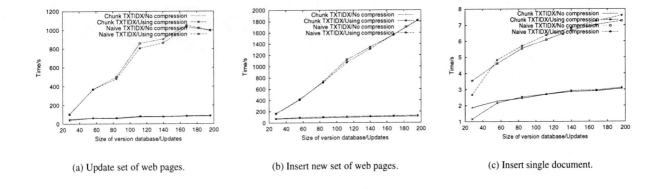

| (a) Update set of web pages. | (b) Insert new set of web pages. | (c) Insert single document. |

Figure 2. Load and update performance. The size is given as number of update transactions, each typically increasing the database size with 40-50 MB.

database, all entries for a medium frequently occurring word fit in one disk page (but are not necessarily stored in one disk page, because the chunks can be in two different pages).

For each query we used different words, and for each query type we used several of the words and use the average query time as the result. In practice, a set of such basic operations will be used, and only the resulting documents are to be retrieved. Thus, for each query we do not retrieve the documents, we are satisfied when we have the actual VIDs available (the retrieval of the actual versions is orthogonal to the issue we study here). The query types presented in this paper were:

- AllVer: All document versions that contain a particular word.

- TSelMid: All document versions valid at time t that contained a particular word. As the value for time t we used the time when half of the update transactions have been performed. We denote this time $t = t_{Mid}$.

For all text-containment queries involving time, the meta-chunk of the actual versions have to be retrieved when we have no additional time indexes.

8.3   Results

We now summarize some of the measurement results. The size given on the graph is the number of update transactions. As described, the first one loads 10000 documents, giving a total database size of 91 MB, and each of the following increase the size with between 40 and 50 MB. The final size of the version database is 9.7 GB (1.9 GB when

compression is enabled). Based on measurements with different chunk size, we found that a chunk size of 400 B was a suitable choice for both the version database and the text index (a tradeoff between overhead and CPU/memory-bandwidth usage).

8.3.1   Load and update cost

The initial loading of the document into the database was most time consuming, as every document is new and have to be text indexed The loading time of the first set of documents (inserting 10000 documents) was 56 s without compression, and 71 s with compression enabled. At subsequent updates, only updated or newly created documents have to be indexed. In this process, the previous versions have to be retrieved in order to determine if the document has changed. If it has not changed, it is not inserted. Figure 2a shows this cost for different database sizes. The size is given as number of update transactions. After the initial load, 91 MB of text is stored in the database, and each transaction increases the amount with approximately 45 MB of text, up to a total of 9.7 GB. The cost of updating/inserting a set of web documents increases with increasing database size because of a decreasing buffer hit rate for disk pages containing the previous document version and pages where postings have to be inserted. From the graph we see that the increase in cost using the improved chunk-based text index is much lower than when using the naive text index. One of the main reasons is that more disk pages have to be written back in the case of the naive text index. Also note the last point (at 196) on the graph for naive text index/no compression in Figure 2a. The cost at this point is lower than the cost at the previous point (at 168). This might seem like an error, but the reason is actually that the documents loaded at this point resulted in less updated documents than at the previ-

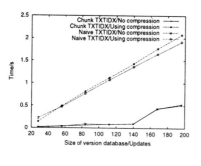

(a) Frequent words.

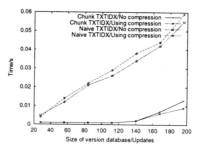

(b) Medium frequent words.

Figure 3. Text containment, all versions.

ous point.

If a document does not already exist in the database (the name is not found in the document name index), there is no previous version that has to be retrieved. However, it is guaranteed that the document has to be inserted and indexed. This is more expensive on average. This is illustrated in Figure 2b, which shows the cost of inserting a set of new documents into the database as described previously.

Figure 2c illustrates the average cost of inserting a single document into the database, in one transaction. The cost increases with increasing database size because pages in the text index where postings have to be inserted are not found in the buffer. It also illustrates well that inserting single documents into a document database is expensive, and that bulk loading, with a number of documents in one transaction, should be used when possible.

As can be seen from the graphs in Figure 2, the use of compression only marginally improves performance, and in some cases also reduces the performance in the case of insert/update. However, the retrieving the actual documents, and in particular large documents, the cost will be significant. It is also likely that when using larger databases than the one used in this study, but with the same amount of main memory, the gain from using compression will increase because of the increased hit rate (when using compression, the database will in total occupy a smaller number of pages, thus increasing the hit ratio). However, the main advantage of using compression is the fact that it reduces the size of the version database down to 20% of the original size. This is important: even though disk is cheap, a reduction of this order can mean the difference between a project that is feasible and one that is not.

8.3.2 Query cost

Figure 3 illustrates the cost of retrieving the VIDs of all document version containing a particular word. As ex-

pected, the costs increases with increasing database size. The main reason for the cost increase with smaller database sizes is a higher number of versions containing the actual word, resulting in an increasing number of VIDs to be retrieved. When the database reaches a certain size, only parts of the text index can be kept in main memory, and the result is reduced buffer hit probability (as is evident by the sharp increase after 140 update transactions, which equals a database size of 6.8 GB).

Figure 4 illustrates the average cost of retrieving the VIDs of all document versions valid at time $t = t_{Mid}$ that contained a particular word. For more details on other kind of queries, as well as disk space usage, we refer to [9].

9 Conclusions and further work

We have in this paper described the V2 temporal document database system, which supports storage, retrieval, and querying of temporal documents. We have described functionality and operations/operators to be supported by such systems, and more specifically we described the architecture for management of temporal documents used in the V2 prototype. We also provided a basis for query processing in temporal document databases, including some additional query operators that are useful in a temporal document database. All of what has been described previously in this paper is implemented and supported by the current prototype. This is also what we believe to be one of the most important contributions of this paper; to actually integrate existing aspects of various areas in temporal database management into a working system, capable of managing temporal documents.

We have studied the performance of V2, using a benchmark based on a real-world temporal document collection. The temporal document collection is created by regularly retrieving the contents of a selected set of Web sites. We

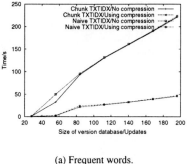 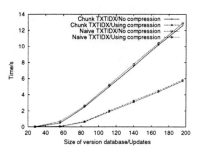

| (a) Frequent words. | (b) Medium frequent words. |

Figure 4. Temporal text containment, time selection at time $t = t_{Mid}$.

have studied document load/update time, as well as query performance using the operators described previously. As we expected, the performance results indicate good performance in the case of large transactions (essentially bulk-loading of data), where an amount of 155 text files/1.7 MB of text is indexed per second.

One of the main reasons for developing this prototype was to identify performance bottlenecks in temporal document databases, as well as have a toolbox to work with in our ongoing work on temporal XML databases. Future work include a temporal browser, which should make it possible in a user-friendly way to ask for a page valid at a particular time, and in the case of Web documents, automatically retrieve and display the page valid at that time when following a link. Such a browser could also make it easier to see changes between versions valid at particular times.

Acknowledgments

Many of the basic ideas of this paper were developed during the 9 months the author spent as an ERCIM fellow in the Verso group at INRIA, France, in 2001. The main part was done when the author visited Athens University of Economics and Business in 2002, supported by grant #145196/432 from the Norwegian Research Council.

References

[1] J. F. Allen. Maintaining knowledge about temporal intervals. *Communications of the ACM*, 26(11), 1983.

[2] M. J. Aramburu-Cabo and R. B. Llavori. A temporal object-oriented model for digital libraries of documents. *Concurrency and Computation: Practice and Experience*, 13(11), 2001.

[3] S.-Y. Chien, V. J. Tsotras, and C. Zaniolo. A comparative study of version management schemes for XML documents (short version published at WebDB 2000). Technical Report TR-51, TimeCenter, 2000.

[4] S.-Y. Chien, V. J. Tsotras, and C. Zaniolo. Efficient management of multiversion documents by object referencing. In *Proceedings of VLDB 2001*, 2001.

[5] S.-Y. Chien, V. J. Tsotras, and C. Zaniolo. Version management of XML documents: Copy-based versus edit-based schemes. In *Proceedings of the 11th International Workshop on Research Issues on Data Engineering: Document management for data intensive business and scientific applications (RIDE-DM'2001)*, 2001.

[6] F. Grandi and F. Mandreoli. The valid web: An XML/XSL infrastructure for temporal management of web documents. In *Proceedings of Advances in Information Systems, First International Conference, ADVIS 2000*, 2000.

[7] A. Marian, S. Abiteboul, G. Cobena, and L. Mignet. Change-centric management of versions in an XML warehouse. In *Proceedings of VLDB 2001*, 2001.

[8] K. Nørvåg. Algorithms for temporal query operators in XML databases. In *Proceedings of Workshop on XML-Based Data Management (XMLDM) (in conjunction with EDBT'2002)*, 2002.

[9] K. Nørvåg. The design, implementation and performance evaluation of the V2 temporal document database system. Technical Report IDI 10/2002, Norwegian University of Science and Technology, 2002. Available from http://www.idi.ntnu.no/grupper/DB-grp/.

[10] K. Nørvåg. Algorithms for granularity reduction in temporal document databases. Technical Report IDI 1/2003, Norwegian University of Science and Technology, 2003. Available from http://www.idi.ntnu.no/grupper/DB-grp/.

[11] M. A. Olson, K. Bostic, and M. Seltzer. Berkeley DB. In *Proceedings of the FREENIX Track: 1999 USENIX Annual Technical Conference*, 1999.

[12] L. Xyleme. A dynamic warehouse for XML data of the web. *IEEE Data Engineering Bulletin*, 24(2), 2001.

Querying XML Data and Web Issues

Abstract

Evaluating Nested Queries on XML Data

Carlo Sartiani

Dipartimento di Informatica

Università di Pisa

Via Buonarroti 2, Pisa, Italy

e-mail: sartiani@di.unipi.it

Abstract

In the past few years, much attention has been paid to the study of semistructured *data, i.e., data with irregular, possibly unstable, and rapidly changing structure, and, in particular, to the study of their best-known incarnation: XML. The growing interest toward XML leaded to the definition of many querying and manipulating tools, such as the standard query language XQuery [3].*

Unlike SQL, XQuery poses no restriction on query nesting (a XQuery query can be nested wherever a well-formed XML document is expected), and lacks explicit clauses for performing group-by *operations. As a result, nested queries play an important role in the context of XQuery.*

This paper shows the techniques used in the Xtasy system for processing and evaluating nested queries on XML data. These techniques applies to the physical level only, and they are based on the massive use of node sharing, *with the aim of decreasing as much as possible the use of secondary storage. The proposed solutions are general enough to be applied, with a few modifications, to more structured contexts.*

1. Introduction

In the past few years, much attention has been paid to the study of *semistructured* data, i.e., data with irregular, possibly unstable, and rapidly changing structure, and, in particular, to the study of their best-known incarnation: XML. XML is a universal data representation format that can be used to describe any kind of information, from highly structured data (e.g., relational databases) to loosely structured documents (e.g., bibliographic documents) as well as unstructured documents (e.g., texts); given its flexibility in data representation and its *auto-descriptiveness*, XML became the *de-facto* standard representation format for semistructured data.

While the prevalent use of XML is data interchange between applications, for the purpose of interoperability and/or integration [4] [2], XML allows one to naturally represent and manipulate particular kinds of data that would not fit well a highly structured context: genetic data, paleobiological data, movies [12], etc. The growing interest toward XML leaded to the definition of many querying and manipulating tools, and, in particular, to the standard query language XQuery [3].

XQuery is a functional, *strongly typed*, Turing-complete query language designed by W3C as an evolution of past object-oriented and semistructured query languages. Unlike SQL, XQuery poses no restriction on query nesting (a XQuery query can be nested wherever a well-formed XML document is expected), and, at the time we write this paper, it lacks explicit clauses for performing *group-by* operations. As a result, nested queries play an important role in the context of XQuery. Despite this importance, little attention has been devoted to the problem of efficiently processing and evaluating nested queries in XQuery. While techniques developed for relational and OO databases can be partially adapted to this context, only a small fraction of nested queries can be *unnested* at compile time; moreover, the ordered, tree-structured shape of XML data makes the processing of nested queries much more complex than in the relational case (as shown in [13], the same happens for recursive query optimization and evaluation), so there is the need for techniques for efficiently processing nested queries on XML data.

Our Contribution This paper shows the techniques used in Xtasy [1] for processing and evaluating nested queries on XML data. These techniques applies to the physical level only, hence they are used for *unnestable* queries only (logical rewriting rules for nested queries on XML data are described in [14]); they are based on the massive use of *node sharing*, with the aim of decreasing as much as possible the use of secondary storage, and of producing a good degree of scalability. The proposed solutions are general enough to be applied, with a few modifications, to more structured contexts.

Paper Outline The paper is structured as follows. Sections 2 and 3 briefly describe the storage scheme of Xtasy, as well as its main physical operators. Section 4, then, illustrates the techniques adopted for processing nested queries. In Sections 5 and 6, finally, we comment on some related works, and draw our conclusions.

2. Storage scheme

Xtasy storage scheme was designed with the aim of supporting XML updates; hence, sophisticated *IR-like* data structures [7] were discarded in favor of simpler and more easily *updatable* data structures. The result is a storage scheme that allows the system to access data relatively fast, and to support good update rates.

Xtasy storage scheme is based on the clustering of elements and attributes according to their tags and names; node clustering is combined with the use of *parent/child* pointers, hence making this scheme a combination of relational and object-oriented storage schemes (see [17] for a taxonomy of storage schemes for XML data). Element and attribute clustering is combined with the use of an external index (the Structural Index) for storing the parent/child relationship. As a consequence, XML nodes can be accessed by scanning the correspondent cluster, or by looking up the index.

2.1. Node clustering and representation

Given a XML tree $\mathcal{T} = (\mathcal{N}, \mathcal{E})$, each node $n \in N$ is endowed with a pair of integer numbers $(pos, endpos)$, denoting respectively its position in a preorder visit and the position of its last descendant (the rightmost one); given a node n_e, $pos(n_e)$ may also be regarded as the position of the node in the tag (respectively, attribute name) opening partial order.

From the definition of pos and $endpos$, it follows that, given two nodes x and y, x is ancestor of y if and only if $pos(x) < pos(y)$ and $endpos(x) \geqslant endpos(y)$. This relation is very important for efficiently evaluating $//$ operations, since it allows the system to quickly check for the ancestor/descendant relationship.

Given a XML tree $\mathcal{T}$, its nodes are distributed in heapfiles according to their *types*. Specifically, the system creates:

- one heapfile per tag name, e.g., the heapfile `*book*` for book elements;

- one heapfile per attribute name, e.g., the heapfile `**class**` for class attributes;

- one heapfile for storing values, e.g., the heapfile `***value***`.

The system associates a unique fileID to each heapfile (for obvious reasons); this, together with the encapsulation of tag and attribute names into heapfile names, allows the system to use integers in place of tag and attribute names, hence introducing a very modest form of data compression.

Element and attributes are represented as fixed-length record containing the following fields: a), the position and the end position of the node, and b), the pointer to the father node.

Node pointers are represented by EIDs (Element IDs), where the EID of a node n is a pair containing the fileID of the heapfile enclosing n and the record identifier of n; each XML node, hence, has its own unique EID, which can be used for directly accessing the node and for inspecting its *type* (element, attribute, or value): in particular, EIDs of element and attribute nodes denote also their tags or names, thus filtering a list of EIDs according to a given tag or name requires no persistent storage access.

Value nodes are, instead, represented as variable-length records containing: a), the position of the node (the end position of the node is equal to its position); b), the father EID; and c), the string representation of the value itself.

The choice of keeping values separate from their enclosing elements and attributes allows an easy representation of *mixed content* element.

2.2. The Structural Index

Even though the only use of back pointers is sufficient to reconstruct the structure of the whole tree, evaluating path expressions with the only aid of back pointers is a nightmare. For this purpose, Xtasy stores the parent/child relationship in the Structural Index, which is just a $B^+ - tree$ associating each element EID with the EIDs of its children nodes.

The use of a $B^+ - tree$ instead of more complex index structures has a threefold motivation. First of all, the $B^+ - tree$ is a simple and well-known data structure that can be easily managed; second, the $B^+ - tree$ allows a better handling of updates than IR-like data structures, and it can be easily adapted to support XML update languages [16]; finally, the $B^+ - tree$ allows a relatively easy dynamic indexing of synthetic elements created during nested query evaluation, which is a *must* in the case of free nesting languages as XQuery. These advantages are counterbalanced by a significant space overhead w.r.t. structures combining IR and compression techniques [7].

The main advantages of the storage scheme of Xtasy are the support for efficient execution of path operations such as $//$, the support for updates as well as the relatively easy management of nested queries; these *pros*, however, are counterbalanced by a significant space overhead (mostly due to the Structural Index), and by the need of dynamically reconstructing XML fragments during the execution of *return*-like operations.

3. Physical operators overview

Xtasy physical operators are based on the iterative execution model [9], where each operator works on a single *data granule* per time, hence decreasing the memory requirements and enhancing the scalability of the system.

Physical operators communicate through method invocation, and exchange a particular kind of data granule called *unboxed tuple*. Even if its name is a true non-sense, the unboxed tuple is designed for combining tuple-based and slot-based data granules, therefore eliminating the need for two different data granule kinds: indeed, path evaluation operators work on document and indexes, hence manipulating EIDs, while other operators work on variable binding tuples.

An unboxed tuple is composed by a vector of pairs $(var\_name, EID\ sequence)$, and by a slot for a single free EID.

The vector part is used for hosting variable bindings collected during query evaluation, and it is accessed by most physical operators; the free EID slot, instead, is used for carrying EIDs collected during path evaluation. In particular, these EIDs are produced by path evaluation operators, and consumed by path evaluation and binding operators.

Xtasy operators can be roughly divided into two categories: *unary* operators, which have at most one input operator, and *binary* operators, which have two input operators. Unary operator class contains operators such as XMLCut (projection without duplicate elimination), XMLDistinct (duplicate elimination), MergeSort (sorting operator), XMLSelection (predicate evaluation), XMLBinder (variable binding), XMLReturn (construction of query result), and XMLSeqPath (path evaluation). Binary operator class, instead, contains XMLUnion (set union without duplicate elimination), XMLExternalUnion (external union), XMLNestedLoopJoin (general purpose join operator), and XMLDependentJoin (dependent join operator). The operators directly involved in nested query evaluation are XMLReturn and XMLDependentJoin, so it is worth to take a deeper look inside them.

3.1. XMLReturn

XMLReturn is used for creating new XML fragments by filling a XML skeleton with variable values. XMLReturn comes in two versions. XMLFinalReturn produces the final result of a query, which can be serialized on screen or on disk. Therefore, XMLFinalReturn fills skeleton gaps with

the XML trees pointed by the EIDs extracted from tuples; these trees are reconstructed on the fly, which makes this operator quite expensive.

XMLNestedReturn, instead, produces the result of a nested query, and it is described in detail in Section 4.

3.2. XMLDependentJoin

This operator behaves as a standard join operator, with the only exception that tuples from the left input are passed to the right operand, and used for instantiating and evaluating the right input. Indeed, this operator can be used for performing d-joins, and it is introduced only during the compilation of nested queries.

4. Nested query evaluation

As previously noted, the system uses XMLNestedReturn for producing results of nested queries: this operator takes care of most of the issues regarding nested query processing.

Before describing our approach, and seeing how XMLNestedReturn works, it is necessary to briefly analyze what kind of results nested queries produce, as well as the main issues related to them. The following example shows a typical use of nested queries.

Example 4.1 Consider the bibliographic database previously illustrated and the following query, which returns, for each author, the list of her works.

```
for $a in input()/*/author
let $title_list :=
      for $b in input()/*,
          $t in $b/title
      where some $ba in $b/author
            satistfies ($ba is $a)
      return <pubtitle> data($t) </pubtitle>
return <ref> { $a, $title_list} </ref>
```

The inner query selects the titles of works published by any given author, and returns their values enclosed in the new tag pubtitle. As prescribed by XQuery Formal semantics [6], data($t) nodes have new object identifiers, and their positions should refer to the new enclosing context. ∎

This sample query shows that nested queries may return newly created XML nodes (e.g., pubtitle elements), as well as nodes directly copied from the existing database (e.g., data(t)). Hence, it is worth to classify XML nodes according to the way they are built; this taxonomy will greatly simplify the discussion.

Definition 4.2 *XML nodes (regardless of their type) can be classified as follows:*

- natural *nodes: nodes existing in the persistent database;*

- artificial *nodes: nodes existing in the persistent database and copied into the result of queries;*

- synthetic *nodes: newly created nodes by nested queries.*

Artificial nodes have different OIDs w.r.t. their natural versions, and assume new positional information (they are considered part and parcel of a new document). XMLNestedReturn, hence, have to generate synthetic and artificial nodes, to assign them new positional information, to refresh artificial node oids, as well as to generate new Structural Index fragments.

For the sake of simplicity, we will consider only element and attribute nodes, and we will not take into account reference semantics RETURN clauses.

4.1. Synthetic nodes and extended EIDs

For supporting synthetic nodes, the system must set them apart from natural nodes, since they do not survive the execution of the outer query. To this end, the use of simple EIDs, as shown in Section 2, is not sufficient, because they discriminate nodes by their name and not by their provenance; hence, we associate each query execution with a unique ID, which is then used for extending EIDs. QueryIDs uniquely identify query executions (the same nested query can be instantiated and invoked many times during outer query evaluation), and they are assigned both at compile time and at run time: during query parsing, the system creates a unique ID for each query block; at run time, then, each execution of the query generates a new dynamic ID (*invocation ID*). Hence, each query has associated a set of QueryIDs of the form $\{queryBlock.queryExec\}$.

QueryIDs are volatile, since they perish after outer query execution. The following example shows the assignment of QueryIDs.

Example 4.3 Consider the following query, returning book authors grouped with the titles of their books, and with their publisher.

```
for $a in input()/book/author
let $title_list :=
      for $b in input()/book,
          $t in $b/title
      where some $ba in $b/author
            satistfies ($ba is $a)
      return <pubtitle> data($t)
             </pubtitle>
```

```
let $p_list :=
      for $b in input()/book,
          $p in $b/publisher
      where some $ba in $b/author
            satistfies ($ba is $a)
      return <pubpublisher> data($p)
             </pubpublisher>
return <ref> { $a, $title_list, $p_list}
       </ref>
```

As the system parses the query, it assigns ID qid1 to the first query, and then assigns IDs qid2 and qid3 to the inner queries. During query execution, the system generates invocation IDs for the set of queries; as a result, assuming 10 execution for query block qid2 and 15 executions for query block qid3, the system generates the following list of QueryIDs:

$$
\begin{array}{lll}
qid1.1 & qid2.1 & qid3.1 \\
       & qid2.2 & qid3.2 \\
       & \ldots & \ldots \\
       & qid2.10 & qid3.10 \\
       &   & \ldots \\
       &   & qid3.15
\end{array}
$$

∎

QueryIDs are used for extending EIDs. An extended EID (ExtEID in the following) is a triple $< QueryID, fileID, Rid >$, where $QueryID$ is the ID of the originating query (0 for persistent elements), $fileID$ is the ID of the file containing the element representation, and Rid is the record id of the element representation. Extended attribute IDs can be defined in the same way.

Beyond uniquely identifying synthetic nodes and distinguishing them from natural nodes, it is necessary to store synthetic nodes in a way allowing the operators of the outer query plan to access and manipulate them. The simplest way to do so is to build for synthetic nodes exactly the same tabular representation as for natural nodes. Synthetic nodes, hence, are represented as records grouped by tag or attribute name, the hierarchical structure being captured by a new Structural Index fragment. Both the node records and the Structural Index fragment are stored in a reserved storage area, distinct from that of the natural nodes or other query nodes (they do not survive the execution of the outer query, so dirtying the representation of persistent nodes has no justification). As a further distinctive feature, synthetic node records are assigned negative fileIDs, obtained by complementing the fileID assigned to their natural counterparts: if book elements are stored in file $fileID1$, then synthetic book elements are stored in file $-fileID1$. For newly created tags or attribute names, new (negative) fileIDs are generated.

For improving the performance of the system during nested query execution, synthetic nodes (as well as their Structural Index fragment) are stored into *virtual* files: these files are allocated in main memory, and flushed to secondary storage only when their size exceeds the capacity of the allocated memory: this policy, similar to the storage policy of hybrid hash join, allows the system to reduce as much as possible the use of secondary storage during query execution.

4.2. Artificial nodes

While synthetic nodes are explicitly stored by the system, artificial nodes (i.e., persistent nodes copied in nested query results) are *shared*, i.e., no new records are created for them, and their EIDs are refreshed by using a special-purpose hash table; this hash table contains one entry for each artificial subtree root, and maps the original EID to the new full QueryID.

Artificial nodes are shared primarily for performance and scalability reasons; without node sharing, artificial nodes should be "duplicated", hence leading to potential unpleasant consequences (e.g., copying the whole database).

Example 4.4 Consider the following simple query:

```
for $b in input()/book
let $ops := for $c in input()/book
            where $b isnot $c
            return $c
return <oddPair> {$b,$ops} </oddPair>
```

This query returns each book in the database, as well as the list of all non-matching book. Without node sharing, executing the inner query would bring to the materialization of nearly the whole database. ∎

4.3. Updating positional information

Both synthetic and artificial nodes have their own positions in the nested query result document order. Synthetic node positions are computed in a way close to the position assignment during database creation and indexing, while artificial nodes require a slightly more complex procedure. Since artificial nodes are kept un-materialized, their new positions are obtained by using an offset as shown in Figure 1.

Since each artificial tree has its own offset, the correspondence between tree root EIDs and offsets is kept in a hash table stored in secondary storage (in most case it will be used only during the MergeSort phase, so there is no need to waste precious main memory space). For queries executed under the UNORDERED keyword, artificial and synthetic node positions are ignored and not computed.

Since in both cases accessing the positions of artificial nodes is not so cheap (or possible), nested query results can be accessed by using the XMLForwardSeqPath operator only (it uses the Structural Index only); this choice affects only the performance of query execution when inner results are too large to be kept in main memory, so the *trade off* is fully justified.

5. Related works

Most of the work on nested queries is devoted to their logical treatment and manipulation. In [10] author introduced the first algorithm for nested query rewriting in relational databases, along with a classification of such queries. This algorithm was then found incorrect, and alternative algorithms were proposed in [8] and many others.

In [5], authors study the problem of nested query rewriting in object databases. First, they extend Kim's taxonomy of relational nested queries by defining three classification criteria: the *kind of nesting*, i.e., queries of type A, N, J, JA; the *nesting location*, i.e., the presence of nested queries into the *select*, *from*, or *where* clause of OQL queries; the *kind of dependency*, i.e., the location of references to external variables. Relying on this taxonomy, authors then describe algebraic rewriting rules for most query types.

In [15] author further extends Cluet's approach for supporting a wider range of nested query types.

Rewriting rules for nested queries on XML data, derived from object database rules, are described in [14].

6. Conclusions

This paper describes techniques for efficiently processing and evaluating nested queries on XML data. These techniques, implemented in the Xtasy system, are based on the massive use of node sharing, with the purpose of minimizing the need for intermediate result materialization.

Much work has still to be done: in particular, techniques for correlating results produced by different invocation of the same nested query must be found, in order to reduce evaluation time for queries working on significants fragment of the database.

References

[1] http://www.di.unipi.it/sartiani/projects/xtasy
[2] C. K. Baru, V. Chu, A. Gupta, B. Ludäscher, R. Marciano, Y. Papakonstantinou, and P. Velikhov. Xml-based information mediation for digital libraries. In *Proceedings of the Fourth ACM conference on Digital Libraries, August 11-14, 1999, Berkeley, CA, USA*, pages 214–215. ACM, 1999.
[3] S. Boag, D. Chamberlin, M. F. Fernandez, D. Florescu, J. Robie, and J. Siméon. XQuery 1.0: An XML Query

---

Input: a XML tree $\mathcal{T}$, a node creation operation label[$v], an outer node n
Output: a hash table Position Offsets

---

begin
  if $\$v = t$ then $offset(t) = startpos(n) + 1 - startpos(t)$ fi
  if $\$v = t_1, \ldots, t_n$ then
            begin
                $offset(t_1) = startpos(n) + 1 - startpos(t)$
                $offset(t_2) = endpos(t_1) + 1 - startpos(t_2)$
                $\ldots$
                $offset(t_n) = endpos(t_{n-1}) + 1 - startpos(t_n)$
            end
  fi
end

Figure 1. Position update algorithm

Language. Technical report, World Wide Web Consortium, November 2002. W3C Working Draft.

[4] S. Cluet, C. Delobel, J. Siméon, and K. Smaga. Your mediators need data conversion! In *Proceedings of the ACM SIGMOD International Conference on Management of Data (SIGMOD-98)*, volume 27,2 of *ACM SIGMOD Record*, pages 177–188, New York, June 1998. ACM Press.

[5] S. Cluet and G. Moerkotte. Classification and optimization of nested queries in object bases. Technical report, University of Karlsruhe, 1994.

[6] D. Draper, P. Fankhauser, M. Fernandez, A. Malhotra, K. Rose, M. Rys, J. Siméon, and P. Wadler. XQuery 1.0 and XPath 2.0 Formal Semantics. Technical report, World Wide Web Consortium, November 2002. W3C Working Draft.

[7] P. Ferragina, N. Koudasa, S. Muthukrishnan, and D. Srivastava. Two-dimensional substring indexing. In *Proceedings of the Twenteenth ACM SIGACT-SIGMOD-SIGART Symposium on Principles of Database Systems, May 21-23, 2001, Santa Barbara, California, USA*, 2001.

[8] R. A. Ganski and H. K. T. Wong. Optimization of nested sql queries revisited. In U. Dayal and I. L. Traiger, editors, *Proceedings of the Association for Computing Machinery Special Interest Group on Management of Data 1987 Annual Conference, San Francisco, California, May 27-29, 1987*, pages 23–33. ACM Press, 1987.

[9] G. Graefe. Query evaluation techniques for large databases. *ACM Computing Surveys*, 25(2):73–170, 1993.

[10] W. Kim. On optimizing an sql-like nested query. *TODS*, 7(3):443–469, 1982.

[11] A. Malhotra, J. Melton, J. Robie, and N. Walsh. XQuery 1.0 and XPath 2.0 Functions and Operators. Technical report, World Wide Web Consortium, Nov. 2002. W3C Working Draft.

[12] J. M. Martinez. Overview of the mpeg-7 standard (version 5.0). Technical report, International Organisation for Standardisation, 2001.

[13] G. Moerkotte. Incorporating XSL Processing into Database Engines. In *VLDB 2002, Proceedings of 28th International Conference on Very Large Data Bases, August 20-23, 2002, Hong Kong, China*, 2002.

[14] C. Sartiani and A. Albano. Yet Another Query Algebra For XML Data. In M. A. Nascimento, M. T. Özsu, and O. Zaïane, editors, *Proceedings of the 6th International Database Engineering and Applications Symposium (IDEAS 2002), Edmonton, Canada, July 17-19, 2002*, 2002.

[15] H. Steenhagen. *Optimization of Object Query Languages*. PhD thesis, University of Twente, 1995.

[16] I. Tatarinov, Z. G. Ives, A. Y. Halevy, and D. S. Weld. Updating xml. In *SIGMOD 2001*, 2001.

[17] F. Tian, D. J. DeWitt, J. Chen, and C. Zhang. The design and performance evaluation of alternative xml storage strategies. *SIGMOD Record*, 31(1):5–10, May/June 2002.

Effective Schema-Based XML Query Optimization Techniques

Guoren Wang and Mengchi Liu
School of Computer Science
Carleton University, Canada
{wanggr, mengchi}@scs.carleton.ca

Jeffrey Xu Yu
Department of SEEM
CUHK, Hong Kong, China
yu@se.cuhk.edu.hk

Bing Sun, Ge Yu, and Jianhua Lv
Department of Computer Science
Northeastern University, China
{sunbing,yuge,dbgroup}@mail.neu.edu.cn

Hongjun Lu
Department of Computer Science
HKUST, Hong Kong, China
luhj@cs.ust.hk

Abstract

Use of path expressions is a common feature in most XML query languages, and many evaluation methods for path expression queries have been proposed recently. However, there are few researches on the issue of optimizing regular path expression queries. In this paper, two kinds of path expression optimization principles are proposed, named path shortening *and* path complementing, *respectively. The* path shortening *principle reduces the querying cost by shortening the path expressions with the knowledge of XML schema. While the* path complementing *principle substitutes the user queries with the equivalent lower-cost path expressions. The experimental results show that these two techniques can largely improve the performance of path expression query processing.*

1 Introduction

Although XML is usually used as an information exchange standard, storing, indexing and querying XML data are still important issues and recently have become research hotspots in the database community. To retrieve XML data from databases, many query languages have been proposed, such as *XQuery* [4], *XPath* [2], *XML-QL* [3], XML-RL [7], and *Lorel* [1]. Because the use of regular path expressions (RPE) is a common feature of these languages, query rewriting and optimization for RPE is becoming a research hotspot and a few research results have been published recently [9, 12].

Most implemented XML systems are based on relational DBs. In the relational way [5, 12], XML data is mapped into tables of a relational/object-relational database system and queries on XML data are translated into SQL statements.

One of the ways to evaluate RPE in relational XML management systems is rewriting an RPE to some SPEs (Simple Path Expression) according to the schema information and statistic information on XML documents, and then computing the SPEs respectively by translating the SPEs into SQL statements and executing them. Take *VXMLR*[12] for example, RPE queries containing '//' and '*' are rewritten to SPEs, which will be translated into SQL statements for a later processing in accordance with relational database schema. In the *Lore* system[1], there are three strategies to compute SPE queries: *top-down*, *bottom-up* and *hybrid*. In the *top-down* way, an XML document tree (DOM tree) is navigated from its root to get proper results; and in the *bottom-up* way, an XML document tree is traversed from its leaves to the root with the help of value indices; finally, in the *hybrid* way, a long path is divided into several short paths, each of which can be evaluated in either the *top-down* way or the *bottom-up* way, and then the results of these short paths are joined together to get proper results.

As an improvement of the *hybrid* way, the *extent join* algorithm [9] has been paid a lot of attention recently. This paper introduces two optimization strategies based on the *extent join* algorithm: *path shortening* Strategy and *path complementing* Strategy. These strategies can also be used for other path evaluation algorithms besides the *extent join* algorithm. The *path shortening* Strategy shortens the path to reduce the number of join operations so that the query performance can be improved. The *path complementing* Strategy computes the original path expression query through some other low-cost path expressions.

2 Background

An XML document can be represented as a rooted tree, $T_d = (V_d, E_d, L_d)$, called an XML data tree, where V_d

is a set of nodes, each of which represents either an *element* or an *attribute*; L_d is a set of node labels representing *tags* of the nodes, each of which is associated with a label; E_d is a set of edges, each of which represents either a parent-child relationship between two element nodes or an element-attribute relationship between an element and an attribute. In the following, we use r_d to represent the root of an XML data tree.

Figure 1 shows an XML data tree for an XML document in the XML benchmark project, *XMark*. Here, an *ellipse* represents an element node, whereas a *triangle* represents an attribute node. The numbers with prefix "&" marked on the nodes are the node identifers. Note, &1 is the root node of the XML data tree whose label is `site`.

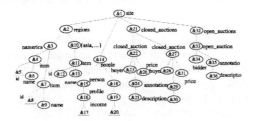

Figure 1. An XML Data Tree

An XML data tree is a set of *paths*. Given a node, a *data path* is a sequence of node identifers from the root to the node, and a *label path* is a sequence of labels from the root to the node. For example, &1.&2.&3.&4.&6 and &1.&21.&22.&24.&25 are two data paths from the root to the nodes &6 and &25. The corresponding label paths are `/site/regions/namerica/item/name` and `/site/close_auctions/close_auction/annotation/description`, respectively.

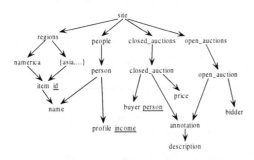

Figure 2. An XML Schema Graph

An XML schema graph is a rooted directed graph, $G_t = (V_t, E_t)$, where V_t is a set of labelled nodes and E_t is a set of edges. We use r_t to denote the root of the XML schema graph. It is important to note that an XML schema graph specifes the possible structures of XML data trees. The label structure of an XML data tree shall be a subgraph of the corresponding XML schema graph. In other words, the label paths imposed by the XML schema graph put restrictions on the possible label paths in the corresponding XML data trees. Figure 2 shows the XML schema graph for the XML data tree in Figure 1. In Figure 2, the root node is the node with a label `site`. The node labels with underline, such as <u>income</u> are for attributes.

Given an XML schema graph and an XML database consisting of XML data trees that conform to the XML schema graph, let p be a label path of an XML schema graph $p = /l_1/l_2/\cdots/l_k$, where l_1 is the label of the root node of the XML schema graph, and l_k the ending label of the label path. An extent of the label path p, denoted $ext(p)$, is a set of nodes (or node identifers) of any data path $/\&n_1/\&n_2/\cdots/\&n_k$ in an XML data tree such that their corresponding label path matches p. In addition, an extent of a label, l_j, denoted $\overline{ext}(l_j)$, is a set of nodes (or node identifers) that have label l.

Consider a label path of the XML schema graph in Figure 2 $p = $ `/site/regions/namerica/item/name`. The extent of p, $ext(p)$, includes &6 in the XML data tree in Figure 1, because there is a data path &1.&2.&3.&4.&6 such that the corresponding label path of the data path matches p. On the other hand, $\overline{ext}($name$) = \{\&6, \&9, \&13\}$.

```
PathExpression ::= CONNECTOR PathSteps
              | PathSteps CONNECTOR PathSteps
PathSteps ::= Label
          | Label '|' PathSteps
          | (PathSteps)
          | '*'
CONNECTOR ::= '/' | '//'
```

Figure 3. BNF Defnition of Path Expression

Figure 3 shows the BNF defnition of path expressions, as a simplifed version of XPath. In Figure 3, *Label* represents node labels. A symbol '*' is introduced as a wildcard for an arbitrary node label in the XML schema graph. The *CONNECTOR* represents the connector of paths. We mainly discuss two widely used connectors: '/' and '//', where the former represents a parent-child relationship, and the latter represents an ancestor-descendant. Given an XML schema graph, G_t, and an XML database consisting of XML data trees that conform to the XML schema. A path expression query, Q, is a path expression (Figure 3). A path expression query, Q, is valid if it at least match a label path, $p = l_1/l_2/\cdots/l_k$, in G_t. A directed query graph $G_q = (V_q, E_q)$ is defned as a rooted subgraph of G_t such that G_q only includes the label paths of G_t that the query Q matches. The root of G_q is the root of G_t and the no-child nodes are the nodes with label l_k. The result of the query,

Q, denoted $ext(Q)$, is $\cup_i \, ext(p_i)$ where p_i is a label path from the root to the no-child node with label l_k in G_q.

3 Simple but Effective Optimization Techniques: Path Shortening and Path Complementing

The path shortening technique is based on the following observation.

Observation 1. *Given an XML schema graph G_t, and let $Q_i = //l_k$ be a valid path expression query, where l_k is a label in the XML schema graph. Then, $ext(Q_i) = \overline{ext}(l_k)$.*

As shown in Figure 1, given a path expression query, `//closed_auction`, $ext(//\texttt{closed\_auction})$ is equal to $\overline{ext}(\texttt{closed\_auction})$ which includes $\{\&22, \&27\}$. It is because that all appearances of the label `closed_auction`, that appear in the XML schema graph (Figure 2), are all included in the corresponding query graph for the query `//closed_auction`. Observation 1 leads to the utilization of an XML indexing mechanism, called XML extent index [9], which indexes all nodes that have the same label, l, e.g., $\overline{ext}(l)$.

Technique 1. (Simple Path Shortening) *Given an XML schema graph G_t and a path expression query $Q = \cdots /l_k$, a corresponding query graph G_q can be constructed ($G_q \subseteq G_t$). All no-child nodes in G_q are labeled with l_k. This query Q can be processed using $\overline{ext}(l_k)$, if and only if l_k does not appear in $G_t - G_q$, that is, l_k only appears in the intersection of two graphs, G_t and G_q.*

As shown in Figure 1, given a path expression query $Q_1 = /\texttt{site/closed\_auctions/closed\_auction}$, $ext(Q_1)$ is equal to $\overline{ext}(\texttt{closed\_auction})$ which includes $\{\&22, \&27\}$. Technique 1 utilizes the XML extent index. As another example, consider the path expression query $Q_2 = /\texttt{site/closed\_auctions/closed\_auction/annotation/description}$, to access the XML data tree in Figure 1 that conforms to the XML schema graph in Figure 2. The result of Q_2 shall include all nodes that have `description` as theirs label along the label path as specified in Q_2, $ext(Q_2) = \{\&25, \&30\}$. As noted, in this case, $ext(Q_2) \neq \overline{ext}(\texttt{description})$ because $\overline{ext}(\texttt{description}) = \{\&25, \&30, \&36\}$. The reason is that the label `description` does not only appear in the corresponding query graph. There exists a label path in the XML schema graph, `/site/open_auctions/open_auction/annotation/description`, which leads to the label `description` and is not included in the corresponding query graph. In order to fully utilize the XML extent index, we propose an effective path shortening technique.

Technique 2. (Effective Path Shortening) *Let G_t be an XML schema graph and $Q = \cdots /l_k$ be an arbitrary valid path expression query. A corresponding query graph G_q can be constructed ($G_q \subseteq G_t$) as follows. Let Q_u be a set of labels, l_u, that such that, (i) l_u only appears in G_q and does not appear in $G_t - G_q$, (ii) all data paths, that satisfy the query Q, must traverse at least one node with label l_u, and (iii) the label path $l_1 / \cdots /l_u$ is unique. We call those labels unique labels. The effective path shortening technique logically divides a given query, Q, into two parts, Q_1/Q_2, where the end label in Q_1 is a unique label, say l_u. Therefore, Q_1 can be processed using the XML extent index, for $\overline{ext}(l_u)$, followed by extent join to process the second part of path Q_2. If multiple unique labels appear in Q, then the last unique label shall be used as the end label of Q_1.*

Reconsider $Q_2 = /\texttt{site/closed\_auctions/closed\_auction/annotation/description}$, which cannot be processed using the simple path shortening technique. In this case, we find that there exist three unique labels: `site`, `closed_auctions` and `closed_auction`. The `closed_auction` is the last in the path. Here, Q_2 can be rewritten as two parts Q_{2_a}/Q_{2_b}, where $Q_{2_a} = /\texttt{site/closed\_auctions/closed\_auction}$ and $Q_{2_b} = \texttt{annotation/description}$. The path of Q_{2_a} can be processed using the XML extent index, because $ext(Q_{2_a}) = \overline{ext}(\texttt{closed\_auction})$.

The effective path shortening technique is a generalization of the simple path shortening technique. The effective path shortening technique improves the query performance by optimizing the path expression. Next, we introduce the *path complementing* technique, which rewrites a complex and high cost path expression, and produces an equivalent simple and low cost path expression. The technique is based on the following observation.

Observation 2. *Given the XML schema graph, G_t, (Figure 2), and a valid path expression query, $Q_3 = /\texttt{site/regions/*/item/name}$. This query cannot be processed using simple path shortening technique, because there exits a label path in G_t, /\texttt{site/people/person/name}. The query can be processed as $\overline{ext}(\texttt{name}) - ext(/\texttt{site/people/person/name})$.*

Technique 3. (Path Complementing) *Let G_t be an XML schema graph and $Q = \cdots /l_k$ be an arbitrary valid path expression query. A corresponding query graph G_q can be constructed ($G_q \subseteq G_t$) as follows. Let G_q' be a query graph including paths $/l_d / \cdots /l_k$ that are not included in G_q, where l_d is the label of the root node of G_t. Then, $ext(Q) = \overline{ext}(l_k) - ext(Q')$, where Q' represents the query that corresponds to G_q'.*

For a given path expression query, Q, there are many choices to process Q using either the effective path shortening technique, or the path complementing technique, or both. For instance, reconsider $Q_3 = $ /site/ regions/*/item/name using the XML schema graph (Figure 2). Using the path complement technique, Q can be processed using $\overline{ext}$(name) - ext(/site/ people/person/name). Furthermore, the path expression /site/people/person/name can be further processed using the effective path shortening technique, because person is a unique label. That is, we can process /site/people/person using the XML extent index followed by an extent join.

Now we show how to use these two RPE optimization techniques in query processing procedure. The selectivity of path expression and cost estimation are not the focuses of this paper, so the details of these issues are ignored. The general steps of querying and optimizing path expression queries are shown as follows.

(1) Rewriting path step '*'. With the XML schema graph, label paths containing path step '*' are rewritten to the unions of all possible label paths only containing connectors '/' and '//'. (2) Rewriting connector '//'. With the XML schema graph, label paths containing connector '//' are rewritten to the unions of all possible label paths only containing connects '/'. (3) Complementary path selection. With the XML schema graph, the complementary paths of each label path are found and their costs are estimated. Check if the cost of complementary paths is lower than that of the original path. If does, the complementary approach is chosen. Otherwise, the original path is chosen. (4) *Path shortening*. With the given XML schema information, every label path is shorten by techniques 1 and 2 described before. (5) Index selection and query execution plan generation. Select correct indexes and transform the path expressions into query execution plans. (6) Query plan execution. Executing the query plan including indexes and joins.

4 Performance Evaluation

The hardware platform of the benchmark is a PC with a 993MHz CPU and 386MB memory, and the software platform is XBase system [8]. The entire benchmark program is written in C++ and Inada 2.0 (an object oriented persistent programming language), and it is compiled using MS VC++ 6.0. All the benchmarks are based on four data sets: two benchmark data sets (XMark and XMach-1) and two real dataset (Shakes and DBLP).

The partial schema of XMark [11] is shown in Figure 2. It has 20 queries that cover a lot of operations such as exact match, ordered access, casting, regular path expressions etc. The data scale factor used in our experiments is 1.0, and the

size of the document is about 100M bytes. XMach-1 [10] is used to simulate applications on the web. The data set contains many documents having different DTDs. A special document is designed in the benchmark used as a directory to record the information of the documents. There are 8 query operations and 3 update operations in XMach-1. This paper does not analyze the performance of update operations. DBLP is a real data set, the XML document set of DBLP web site. The feature of this data set is that the number of the documents is very large, while the size of each of them is very small. The data set can be gotten on Internet at ftp://ftp.informatic.uni-trier.de/ pub/users/Ley/bib/records.tar.gz. 8 queries are defned on the *DBLP* data set [6]. Shakes is another real data set, s a set of XML documents of operas of Shakespear marked by Bosak. There are 8 queries [6]. This data set can be gotten on Internet at http://metalab.unc.edu/ bosak/xml/eg/shakes200.zip.

Figures 4, 5, 6 and 7 show the performance improvement of the *path shortening* strategy on benchmark data sets XMark, XMach-1, DBLP and Shakes, respectively, comparing to the *extent join* algorithm. Obviously, *path shortening* has better performance than *extent join* in all queries. It seems that the performance improvement on XMark is not very much. This is because the queries in XMark is XQuery queries other than path expression queries, there thus are time-consuming post-processing operations to do after path expression computing. Even through, *path shortening* do a much better job than *extent join*. Unlike real data sets, simulation data sets specially designed for XML database benchmarks have more complete types of queries, so the query performances on XMark and XMach-1 are studied £rst. Because of different query features, the performance improvement of *path shortening* is different.

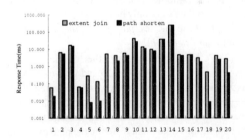

Figure 4. Path Shortening Query Performance (XMark)

(1) Performance of some queries is greatly improved, such as Q5, Q6, Q7, Q18 and Q20 in XMark and Q2, Q3, Q4, Q5, Q6 and Q7 in XMach-1. Path expressions of these queries can be shortened to very short paths, even to one

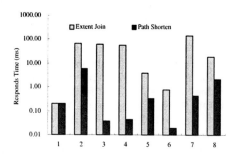

Figure 5. Path Shortening Query Performance (XMach-1)

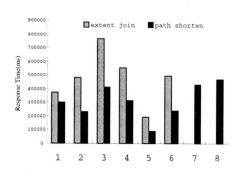

Figure 6. Path Shortening Query Performance (DBLP)

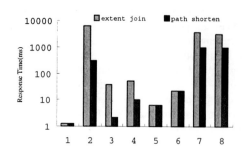

Figure 7. Path Shortening Query Performance (Shakes)

step paths. Another feature of these queries is that they have no predicates or only have predicates at the end of their paths. In these queries, *path shortening* is 10 to 200 times faster than *extent join*.

(2) Performance of some other queries is slightly improved, such as Q13, Q14, Q15 and Q16 in XMark and Q1 in XMach-1. In these queries, the performance improvement of *path shortening* is 0.3% to 8%. There are various reasons. Some queries consume much time to compute special operations other than compute the path expressions. For example, in XMark, Q13 has a complicated reconstruction operation and Q14 has a full-text search operation. Some path expressions are very long themselves but parts that can be cut off are very limited. For example, Q15 and Q16 can only be cut off 3 steps respectively while their original lengths are 12 and 14. Some other path expressions can hardly be shortened any more, such as Q1 in XMach-1.

(3) Performance improvement of the remainder queries is between the above two cases. For example, Q1, Q2, Q3,

Q4, Q8, Q9, Q10, Q11, Q12 and Q17 in XMark and Q8 in XMach-1. Their path expressions can be slightly shortened or also have some high-cost operations such joins on values, ordered access, dereference etc, the performance improvement is not clearly seen. Most queries belongs to this type, and their performance that can be promoted by *path shortening* ranges from 10% to 400%.

The performance of queries on DBLP and Shakes are shown in Figures 6 and 7, respectively, in which Q7 and Q8 of DBLP using *extent join* cost too much time and cannot get the results. Except for a few queries such as Q1, Q5 and Q6 in Shakes, most queries can benefit from *path shortening*, some of which are improved greatly. These queries can also be divided into the types above. Unlike the simulation data sets, the real data sets are not very complicated, so they are more suitable to use the *path shortening* strategy.

Another valuable conclusion is that the data sets containing large quantity of small documents such as XMach-1, DBLP and Shakes benefit more from the *path shortening* strategy than one large document data set XMark. This is because, in the data set with numerous small documents, the set of joins is very large and even one step path may contain a lot of joins, the performance would be greatly improved when the paths are shortened even by only one step. Since the queries of the benchmark are all path expression queries, according to Observation 1, all the queries can be shortened at least by one step using the *path shortening* strategy.

Because cost evaluation is necessary for the *path complementing* strategy, whether or not this strategy can be used for a query depends not only on path expressions and XML schemas but also on the statistic information of XML documents. Thus, only some queries can be computed use their equivalent complementary paths. We use three queries based on XMark shown in Table 1. Figure 8 gives the average performance of the *path complementing* strategy. In some queries, the *path complementing* strategy can improve the performance by more than 20% to 200% on the basis of

234

Table 1. Path Complementing Queries

Query	Original Path Expression	Complementary Expression
Q1	/site/regions/(asia|africa|europe |australia|samerica)/item	/site/regions/namerica/item
Q2	/site/regions/(asia|africa|europe |australia|samerica|namerica)/item/name	/site/people/profile/name
Q3	/site/(closed_auctions/closed_auctions|open_auctions /open_auction)/annotation/description	/site/category/description

the *path shortening* strategy.

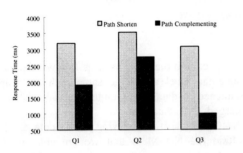

Figure 8. Path Complementing Query Performance

5 Conclusion

This paper proposed two optimizing strategies to improve the performance of path expressions: the *path shortening* strategy and the *path complementing* strategy. The *path shortening* strategy shortens path expression to reduce the cost of the query, while the *path complementing* strategy uses equivalent path expression with the least cost to compute the original path expression. The experimental results of simulation data and real data show that these two strategies are efficient and effective, and they can greatly improve the performance of path expression queries. The performance of 80 percent of the queries in the four benchmarks can be improved by 20% to 400%.

Acknowledgement. Guoren Wang's research is partially supported by the Teaching and Research Award Programme for Outstanding Young Teachers in Post-Secondary Institutions by the Ministry of Education, China (TRAPOYT) and National Natural Science Foundation of China under grant No. 60273079. Mengchi Liu's research is partially supported by National Science and Engineering Research Council of Canada.

References

[1] S. Abiteboul, D. Quass, J. McHugh, J. Widom, and J. Wiener. The lorel query language for semistructured data. *Int'l Journal on Digital Libraries*, 1(1):68–88, 1997.

[2] J. Cark and S. DeRose. Xml path language (xpath), ver. 1.0. tech. report rec-xpath-19991116, w3c. Technical report, November 1999.

[3] A. Deutsch, M. Fernandez, D. Florescu, A. Levy, and D. Suciu. A query language for xml. In *Proceedings of the Eighth International World Wide Web Conference*, Toronto, Canada, May 1999.

[4] P. Fankhauser. Xquery formal semantics: State and challenges. *SIGMOD Record*, 30(3):14–19, 2001.

[5] D. Florescu and D. Kossmann. Storing and querying xml data using an rdmbs. *IEEE Data Engineering Bulletin*, 22(1):27–34, 1999.

[6] H. Jiang, H. Lu, W. Wang, and J. Yu. Path materialization revisited: An efficient storage model for xml data. In *Proceedings of Thirteenth Australasian Database Conference*, Melbourne, Victoria, 2002.

[7] M. Liu and T. Ling. Towards declarative xml querying. In *Proceedings of The 3rd International Conference on Web Information Systems Engineering(WISE'02)*, Singapore, December 2002.

[8] H. Lu, G. Wang, G. Yu, Y. Bao, J. Lv, and Y. Yu. Xbase: Making your gigabyte disk queriable. In *Proc. of the 2002 ACM SIGMOD Conference*, Wisconsin, USA, 2002.

[9] J. Lv, G. Wang, J. X. Yu, G. Yu, H. Lu, and B. Sun. Performance evaluation of a dom-based xml database: Storage, indexing and query optimization. In *Proceedings of the 3rd International Conference On Web-Age Information Management(WAIM2002)*, pages 13–24, Beijing, China, August 2002.

[10] E. Rahm and T. Bohme. Xmach-1: A multi-user benchmark for xml data management. In *Proc. of 1st VLDB Workshop on Efficiency and Effectiveness of XML Tools, and Techniques (EEXTT2002)*, Hong Kong, China, 2002.

[11] A. Schmidt, F. Waas, M. L. Kersten, M. J. Carey, I. Manolescu, and R. Busse. Xmark: A benchmark for xml data management. In *Proceedings of the 28th International Conference on Very Large Data Bases*, Hong Kong, China, 2002.

[12] A. Zhou, H. Lu, S. Zheng, Y. Liang, L. Zhang, W. Ji, and Z. Tian. Vxmlr: A visual xml-relational database system. In *Proceedings of the 27th International Conference on Very Large Data Bases (VLDB2001)*, pages 719–720, Roma, Italy, September 2001.

Querying XML Data by the
Nested Relational Sequence Database System

Ho Lam, Lau and Wilfred Ng
Department of Computer Science
The Hong Kong University of Science and Technology
{lauhl, wilfred}@cs.ust.hk

Abstract

In this concise paper, we present the Nested Relational Sequence Model (NRSM), which is an extension of the Nested Relational Data Model in order to handle XML data. We also introduce a set of algebraic operations pertaining to the Nested Relational Sequence Model, which is an extension of the Nested Relational Data Model in order to handle XML data, to manipulate XML documents via NRS relations. We demonstrate NRS operations by examples and illustrate how XML queries can be formulated within the NRSM. We also introduce the ongoing work of translating XQuery into NRS operations.

1. Introduction

XML [12] is becoming a standard format for representing and exchanging data on the World-Wide-Web. With the growth of electronic commerce, the quantity of XML documents on the Web has rapidly increased. To cope with the large amount of XML documents, we need an XML DataBase Management System (DBMS) that is efficient enough to handle storage, management and retrieval of XML documents. This depends on establishing an effective data model in a formal manner, which serves as a foundation for the development of future XML DBMS.

We propose the Nested Relational Sequence Model (NRSM) [5, 6, 7], which is an extension of the well-established Nested Relational Data Model (NRDM) [4, 10, 11] in order to cater for the nesting structure and node ordering of XML documents. Like the NRDM, the NRSM is capable of supporting composite and multi-valued attributes, which are essential for representing hierarchically structured information such as XML data. In addition, the NRSM extends the NRDM to support ordering of XML data by allowing nested tuple sequences in a *nested sequence relation* (or a NRS relation). An important feature in our model is that XML data can be

collapsed into the same node as follows: data that has the same tag label along the same path are mapped to a sequence of data nodes under the same label node in a merged XML data tree.

One benefit of viewing XML data as nested data within the NRSM is that we are able to eliminate a substantial amount of redundancy in XML documents. Another benefit is that based on the NRSM we are able to preserve the original structure of XML documents, that means, in general XML documents can be retrieved from NRS relations in our system without loss of information. Descriptive information such as "comments" and "processing instructions" can also be stored in an NRS relation. The proposed method for mapping between XML documents and NRS relations is straightforward enough to implement on top of most common DBMSs such as Oracle. Comparing with other approaches in XML modeling [2, 8, 9], our approach requires extra efforts on grouping those data that shares the same tag labels. We also find that the preparation time for loading an XML document into the NRSD System is longer than other proposed data models such as the *attribute inlining* approach proposed in [3]. In addition, we need to consume extra resources to reconstruct the original XML documents from the NRSD System.

Figure 1 presents our main idea of the mapping between an XML document and an NRS relation. We model the document as a *merged data tree* (or simply a *data tree*), where the leaf nodes are *sequences of data values,* called the *data nodes,* and the non-leaf nodes are the labels of XML tags and attributes, called the *label nodes.* Figure 2 illustrates a data tree which incorporates three types of order as follows: (1) the *data order* resulting from the sequence of data elements in a data node; (2) the *sibling order* resulting from the left to right sides for label nodes which share the same parent; and (3) the *ancestor order* resulting from different levels of the label nodes in the data tree.

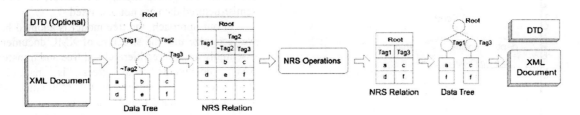

Figure 1. Mapping an XML document to an NRS relation and retrieving under NRS operations

Table 1. Brief description of NRS operations

Type	Name	Description
Nesting Operations	NEST (η)	Create a new structure of the selected attributes (tags) into a sequence of nested tuple.
	UNNEST (μ)	The reverse operation of η, which flattens an (or a subset of) NRS relation into a sequence of flat tuples.
Ordering Operations	ORDERBY (ω)	Reorder the tuple in value order by sorting the selected column(s). The default sorting direction is ascending.
	REARRANGE (κ)	Reorder all the children of the selected tags with the given arrangement.
	SWAP (χ)	Exchange the position of two columns and changing their sibling order.
	GROUPBY (φ)	Group the NRS relation by a selected tag.
Unary Operations	PROJECT (π)	Return the selected columns in the NRS relation.
	SELECE (σ)	Return a sequence of tuples from an NRS relation according to some selection conditions.
Structural Operations	NEW ($\otimes$)	Create a new NRS relation by stating the schema of the new relation.
	INSERT ($\oplus$)	Insert new columns/values into an NRS relation before or after a specify location. (Insert at the end by default.)
	DELETE ($\varnothing$)	Delete selected columns/tuple values in the NRS relation.
Aggregate Operations	COUNT (ς)	Count the number of tuples that satisfy some conditions.
	SUM (Σ)	Return the total of the selected locations of cells, where the data in given columns is numeric.
	AVG (α)	Return the average of the selected locations of cells, where the data in given columns is numeric.
	MIN ($\top$)	Return the smallest of the selected locations of cells.
	MAX ($\bot$)	Return the largest of the selected locations of cells.
Binary Operations	UNION ($\cup$)	Return a sequence of tuples in either the first NRS relation or second NRS relation over the same NRS schema.
	DIFFERENCE ($-$)	Return a sequence of tuples in the first NRS relation but not in the second NRS relation over the same NRS schema.
	PRODUCT ($\times$)	Concatenate the second NR relation onto the selected group of the first NRS relation.

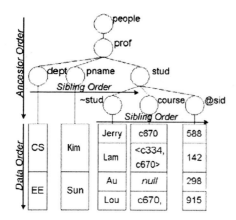

Figure 2. A data tree showing the three types of order

The XML semantics and the order of the document structure are preserved in an NRS relation and the mapping between a data tree and an NRS relation is reversible. After mapping XML documents into NRS relations, we are able to apply a sequence of NRS operations on the relations to formulate useful queries. A brief description of the NRS operations is shown in Table 1. The output of a sequence of NRS operations is always an "order-preserving" NRS relation, which preserves three types of orderings of XML data: data, sibling and ancestor orders. An NRS relation can be naturally converted back to XML data. Our suggested method of conversion is also applicable to usual flat relations, since they can be regarded as a special case of NRS relations having an imposed sibling order on tuples.

2. Related Work

The *Nested Relational Data Model* (NRDM) is one of the NF^2 relational data models proposed in 1979. In the NRDM, data is modelled as a collection of tables, named *Nested Tables* (NTs), which can have nested columns. Under the NRDM, a variety of form-based documents can be formally and uniformly handled as NTs within database systems.

The closest research with the NRSM is the QSByE [1]. QSByE represents semistructured data using nested tables with structural variants, they objective is to reduce the complexity in typical query languages for semistructured data. It allows distinct rows to contain object with distinct structures. Similar to our approach, it extends the nested relational operators to implement a QBE-like query language. QSByE represents semistructured data as an OEM tree, each tag is represent as a distinct subtree and each subtree is composed of distinct atomic components. However, if the document contains many tags with the same label,

the OEM tree grows rapidly. Moreover, the orders of semistructured data are not discussed.

In our approach, the tree model is adopted because we recognize that the structure of XML documents are essentially an ordered hierarchical tree and transforming XML documents into trees is natural and straightforward. We observe that if information with the same tag is grouped together and the values are stored under the same node, we can save much space and remove the unwanted redundancy. Therefore, we propose a tree representation called the *merged data tree* (or simply *data tree*), in which XML data has the same label along the same path is collapsed into the same node and the XML data are mapped to a sequence of data nodes as shown in Figure 2.

3. NRS Operations and Running Examples

We define a set of algebraic operations on the NRSM, which is employed to formulate a query over an NRS relation. These operations enable users to retrieve XML information from NRS relations. The output result of these operations is an NRS relation, taking one or more NRS relations as input. These operations have been briefly introduced in Table 1. We now demonstrate some examples to show how to perform queries by using NRS operations. The first example highlights the fact that the most common kind of queries can be expressed as NRS operations in the NRSM. In this section, the example queries are operating the NRS relaton R as shown in Figure 3, which is built from the XML document "sample.xml" as shown in Figure 4.

R				
people				
prof+				
^(dept, pname)		stud*		
dept	pname	~stud	course*	@sid
CS	Kim	Jerry	c670	588
		Lam	<c334, c670>	142
EE	Sun	Au	-	298
		Lou	c670	915
		Ray	<c630, c334>	611

Figure 3. The corresponding NRS Relation *R* of sample.xml

```
<people>
    <prof>
        <dept>CS</dept>
        <pname>Kim</pname>
        <stud sid="588">Jerry
            <course>c670</course>
        </stud>
        <stud sid="142">Lam
            <course>c334</course>
            <course>c670</course>
        </stud>
    </prof>
    <prof>
        <dept>EE</dept>
        <pname>Sun</pname>
        <stud sid="298">Au
        </stud>
        <stud sid="915">Lou
            <course>c670</course>
        </stud>
        <stud sid="611">Ray
            <course>c630</course>
            <course>c334</course>
        </stud>
    </prof>
</people>
```

Figure 4. The sample XML (sample.xml)

We now illustrate NRS operations by the following queries.

(Q₁) List the names of the students who are taking the course "c670".

The query Q_1 can be expressed in XQuery [14] as follows:

FOR $s IN
    document("sample.xml")//people/prof/stud
WHERE $s/course = "c670"
RETURN $s/text()

We first transform the XML document "*sample.xml*" and its DTD into the corresponding NRS relation, *R*, which is shown in Figure 3. Then we perform the following sequence of operations:

1. $S \leftarrow \pi_{(people\ prof\ stud)}(R)$
2. $T \leftarrow \sigma_{(stud\ course="c670")}(S)$
3. $R_{result} \leftarrow \pi_{(stud\ \sim stud)}(T)$

For the sake of clarity, we use the temporary NRS relations, *S* and *T*, for storing the intermediate results in each step of processing. In the first step, we project on "*people/prof/stud*" over *R*. Then we perform the selection according to the condition "*/stud/course = "c670""* over *S*. Finally, we project on "*/stud/~stud*" over *T*, which generates the required results R_{result}. The

temporary NRS relations *S*, *T* and R_{result} for this query are shown in Figure 5.

stud*		
~stud	course*	@sid
Jerry	c670	588
Lam	c334	142
	c670	
Au	-	298
Lou	c670	915
Ray	c630	611
	c334	

S

stud*		
~stud	course*	@sid
Jerry	c670	588
Lam	c334	142
	c670	
Lou	c670	915

T

stud*
~stud
Jerry
Lam
Lou

R_{result}

Figure 5. Generated NRS relations for answering the query Q₁

Then we transform the resulting NRS relation by using its corresponding DTD. The conformed XML document is represented as follows:

<!ELEMENT stud(#PCDATA)>
<stud>Jerry</stud>
<stud>Lam</stud>
<stud>Lou</stud>

(Q₂) Create a new XML document with the format given below, where *X* is the number of professors, *Y* is the number of students in the department and *Z* is the name of the department:

<university>
    <dept numP="X" numS="Y"> Z</dept>
</university>

First, we create a new NRS relation named "*university*" with the given schema "*university (dept (~dept, @numP, @numS))*" using the operation "*New*". Then we insert the value of "*dept*" corresponding to the "*dept*" of *R*. Each "*dept*" has two attributes, "*numP*" and "*numS*". Thus, we use the aggregate function "*Count*" to find out the number of professors and students in the "*dept*". The operations are shown below and the corresponding NRS relations are shown in Figure 6.

$1.$ $S \leftarrow New_{(university(dept(\sim dept, @numP, @numS))};$

$2.$ $T \leftarrow Insert_{(university \, dept \, \sim dept \, = \, R \, people \, prof \, dept)}(S);$

For each data value under "university/dept/":

$R_{result} \leftarrow Insert_{(university \, dept \, @numP \, =}$
$\qquad {}_{Count(\, people \, prof \, pname)(U)),}$
$3.$ $\qquad {}_{university \, dept \, @numS \, =}$
$\qquad {}_{Count(\, people \, prof \, stud \, \sim stud)(U))}(T);$

where $U = \sigma_{(R \, people \, prof \, dept = \, university \, dept)}(R).$

University		
Dept		
~dept	@numP	@numS

S

university		
dept		
~dept	@numP	@numS
CS		
EE		

T

university		
dept		
~dept	@numP	@numS
CS	1	2
EE	1	3

R_{result}

Figure 6. Generated NRS relations for the query Q_2.

The resulting NRS relation and its corresponding DTD and XML document is represented as follows:
<university>
  <dept numP="1" numS="2">CS</dept>
  <dept numP="1" numS="3">EE</dept>
</university>

4. Translating XQuery into NRS Operations

In this section, we introduce the undergoing research on translating Xquery [14] into expressions of NRS operations. We show how to translate the XQuery expression *"FOR-WHERE-RETURN"*, which is the most basic and the most common form of XQuery, into sequences of NRS operations:

FOR $b IN path1,
  $c IN path2, ...
WHERE condition1, condition2,...
RETURN
<tag1>

{
  <tag2>
    $b/path3
  </tag2>
  <tag3>
    $c/path4
  </tag3>
  ...
}
</tag1>

Before we translate the XQuery expressions into sequences of NRS operations, we map the XML documents into NRS relations, $\{R_1, R_2, ...\}$. Since a query may involve several XML documents, we need to map them into NRS relations before we apply NRS operations. After the mapping, the following sequence of NRS operations is performed:

1. $S_1 \leftarrow \pi_{(path1)}(R_1), S_2 \leftarrow \pi_{(path2)}(R_2), ...$
2. $T_1 \leftarrow \sigma_{(condition1)}(S_i), T_2 \leftarrow \sigma_{(condition2)}(S_i), ...$
3. $U \leftarrow \otimes_{(tag1(tag2, tag3))}$
4. $R_{result} \leftarrow \oplus_{(tag2 \, - \, T1 \, path3, tag3 \, - \, T2 \, path4, \, ...)}(U)$

First, we translate the XQuery expressions *"FOR $x IN pathx"* into a sequence of project operations (π) and store the result into intermediate NRS relations S_1, S_2, ... Second, basing on the conditions stated in the XQuery expression *"WHERE condition1, condition2,..."*, we perform the select operations (σ) on the involved intermediate NRS relations, S_i. For example, if *"conditionx"* in the XQuery expression is equal to *"$b/name = "abc" "*, we know that S_i is involved and we perform the select operation on S_i. Now, we obtain the required data in the intermediate NRS relation $T_1, T_2, ...$ .The third step is to return the results in the specified format stated in the *"RETURN"* expression. To achieve this, we perform the new operation ($\otimes$) to create a new NRS relation with the schema corresponding to the one stated in the XQuery *"RETURN"* expression. Finally, we perform the insert operations ($\oplus$) to insert the corresponding results into the new NRS relation. Since the mechanism of handling the hierarchical structure of the returned format is very complex, in the current stage of our translating algorithm, we can only handle the structure of at most two nested levels.

5. Conclusions

In this paper, we have introduced the Nested Relation Sequence Model (NRSM). The NRSM is desirable for managing XML since technologies developed for the existing DBMSs can be naturally adapted to our system. We believe that the NRSM is a simple and natural database model for handling the storage and querying for XML documents, since it allows us to address the important features of multi-valued nesting and different kinds of ordering in XML data.

We have also presented a set of NRS operators, which is a combination of a refined version of existing relation algebra for nested relations [10] and some newly defined operations such as the rearrange and the swap operations [6]. The set of NRS operators provides us a basis for manipulating NRS relations in an optimized way, in which the nesting and ordering operations are useful in transforming and restructuring the XML relations to other forms. We have also demonstrated with examples how to formulate XML queries in terms of NRS operations and showed that querying using NRS operations are compatible with XQuery. Currently, we are able to translate the XQuery of the form "FOR-WHERE-RETURN" by using the NRS operations. Finally, we have discussed the ongoing research on translating XQuery expressions into sequences of NRS operations. We are going to compare the efficiency of the NRSM with other data model and perform experiments on the efficiency of the NRS operations.

References

[1] A.S. da Silva, I.M.E. Filha, A.H.F. Laender, and D.W. Embley, "Representing and Querying Semistructured Web Data Using Nested Tables with Structural Variants", *Proceedings of ER*, 2002

[2] D. Beech, A. Malhotra and M. Rys. "A Formal Data Model and Algebra for XML", *Communication to the W3C*, 1999.

[3] D. Florescu and D. Kossmann. "A Performance Evaluation of Alternative Mapping Schemes for Storing XML Data in a Relational Database", *Technical Report 3680*, INRIA Rocquencourt, France, 1999.

[4] H. Kitagawa and T. L. Kunii. *The Unnormalized Relational Data Model, For Office Form Processor Design*, Springer-Verlag, 1989.

[5] H. L. Lau and W. Ng, "Querying XML Data Based on Nested Relational Sequence Model", *Proceedings of Poster Track of WWW*, Honolulu, 2002.

[6] H. L. Lau and W. Ng, "The Development of Nested Relational Sequence Model to Support XML Databases", *Proceedings of the International Conference on Information and Knowledge Engineering (IKE'02)*, Las Vegas, USA, 2002, pp. 374-380.

[7] H. L. Lau and W. Ng, *The Development of the Nested Relational Sequence Model to support XML Databases*, Master Thesis of the Department of Computer Science, HKUST, 2002.

[8] I.M.E. Filha, A.S. da Silva, A.H.F. Laender, and D.W. Embley, "Using Nested Tables for Representing and Querying Semistructured Web Data", *The Fourteenth International Conference on Advanced Information Systems Engineering* Toronto, Canada, 2002.

[9] M. Fernandez, J. Simeon and P. Wadler. "An Algebra for XML Query.", *In Foundations of Software Technology and Theoretical Computer Science, number 1974, 2000*.

[10] M. Levene. *The Nested UniversityRelation Database Model*, Springer-Verlag, 1992.

[11] P. Atzeni and V. De Antonellis. *Relational Database Model Theory*, The Benjamin / Cummings Publishing Company, INC., 1993.

[12] T. Bray, J. Paoli, C. M. Sperberg-McQueen and E. Maler, "Extensible Markup Language (XML) 1.0 (Second Edition)", *W3C Recommendation*, 2000.

[13] W. Ng. "Maintaining Consistency of Integrated XML Trees", *International Conference on Web-Age Information Management WAIM'2002*. LNCS Vol. 2419, Beijing, China, 2002, pp 145 -157.

[14] World Wide Web Consortium. "XQuery 1.0 and XPath 2.0 Data Model", In: http://www.w3.org/TR/query-datamodel/, 2002.

E-Learning as a Web Service
(Extended Abstract)

Gottfried Vossen, Peter Westerkamp
University of Münster
D-48149 Münster, Germany
{vossen|pewe}@wi.uni-muenster.de

1 Introduction

E-learning has been a topic of increasing interest in recent years. It is often perceived as a group effort, where content authors, instructional designers, multimedia technicians, teachers, trainers, database administrators, and people from various other areas of expertise come together in order to serve a community of learners [1]. In a typical e-learning scenario, many of the activities can be perceived and modeled as processes [16] and consequently be executed as workflows [19, 17]; there are even prototypical system developments that are experimenting with this approach [8, 11, 16]. On the other hand, there are increasingly many activities which aim at providing services of any kind on the Web [9]; these can occur as business-to-business or as business-to-consumer services and are generally subsumed under the term *Web services*. In this paper we suggest to combine the areas of e-learning and Web services, by providing electronic learning offerings as (individual or collections of) Web services as well. We elaborate on this by showing how content providers and content consumers (i.e., learners) can communicate appropriately through a Web service platform with its common description, publication, and retrieval functionalities. Finally, we indicate how a corresponding system can be realized.

A common agreement seems to exist on the decomposition of a learning system from a functional perspective into a *learning management system* (LMS) that stores and manages content, an *authoring system* that helps creating content, and a *run-time system* that interacts with learners. We have shown in [16] how to perceive the central activities occurring in these components uniformly as processes or workflows which interact with *resources* (including people such as *learners, administrators, trainers*, and *authors*, and also including learning content), with one another (so that, for example, a learning workflow may trigger the execution of an authoring workflow or vice versa), and with the *outside world* (such as existing software systems) in predefined ways. In this paper we take these ideas one step fur-

ther and show what the implications of this perception can be as soon as suitable languages are chosen for a description of the components and activities involved, and appropriate platforms are used for an implementation and enactment. In particular, we will show how to realize a logical organization as a collection of *Web services*, where learners can search for suitable content offerings and, if successful, configure an appropriate delivery, learners can additionally arrange for a suitable observation of their progress and achievements, and authors can adhere to content production services that can be called upon depending on the subject at hand. Generally, we try to design such learning services using tools and languages that are common in this area as far as possible. To this end, we will rely upon established Web service standards, since they appear sufficient for our purposes.

In Section 2, we collect preliminaries relevant to our proposal from the e-learning field as well as from the area of Web services. In Section 3 we combine the two, and show how service providers and service consumers can be brought together in such a way that e-learning needs can be serviced via an appropriate platform. In Section 4 we discuss realization aspects which we are investigating in the context of our prototypical LearnServe system, and in Section 5 we offer some conclusions and directions for future study. This paper is an extended abstract of [18], where further explanations and details of the approach can be found.

2 Preliminaries

Some Background on E-Learning

A general agreement seems to exist regarding roles played by people in a learning environment as well as regarding the core functionality of modern e-learning platforms; see [1, 3, 4]. The main players in these systems are the *learners* and the *authors*; others include trainers and administrators. Authors (which may be teachers or instructional designers) create content, which is stored under the control of a learning management system (LMS) and typically in a database [3, 14]. Existing content can be updated, and it can also be exchanged with other systems. A learning management system (LMS) is under the control of an administrator, and it interacts with a run-time environment which is addressed by learners, who in turn may be coached by a trainer. Importantly, these three components of an e-learning system can be logically and physically distributed, i.e., installed on distinct machines, and provided by different vendors or content suppliers. In order to make such a distribution feasible, standards such as IMS and SCORM try to ensure plug-and-play compatibility [5].

E-learning systems often do not address just a special kind of learner, but may rather be implemented in such a way that a customization of features and appearance to a particular learner's needs is supported. Learners vary significantly in their prerequisites, their abilities, their goals for approaching a learning system, their pace of learning, their way of learning, and the time (and money) they are able to spend on learning. Thus, the target group of learners is typically very heterogeneous; a system is ideally able to provide and present content for all (or at least several of) these groups, in order to be suitable, for example, for a student who wants to learn about database concepts or for a company employee who wants to become familiar with company-internal processes and their execution. To fulfill the needs of a flexible system as sketched, a learning platform has to meet a number of requirements, including the integration of a variety of materials, the potential deviation from predetermined sequences of actions [2], personalization and adaptation, and the verifiability of work and accomplishments [16].

Content consumed by learners and created by authors is commonly handled, stored, and exchanged in units of *learning objects* (LOs). Basically, LOs are units of study, exercise, or practice that can be consumed in a single session, and they represent reusable granules that can be authored independently of the delivery medium and be accessed dynamically, e.g., over the Web [14]. Ideally, LOs can be exchanged between different LMS and plugged together to build classes that are intended to serve a particular purpose or goal. To this end, LOs need to be *context-free* in the sense that they have to carry around useful description information on the type and context in which they may be used. For example, a LO on the basics of SQL can be used in classes on software engineering, database administration, and data modeling.

As the number of objects and authors grows, meta-data on the objects becomes a critical factor; indeed, meta-data is needed for an appropriate description of learning objects so that plug-and-play configuration of classes and courses is enabled. To this end, several standardization efforts have been launched, including IEEEs *Learning Object Metadata*

(LOM) and the already mentioned *Sharable Content Object Reference Model* (SCORM), which is a collection of specifications adapted from multiple sources to provide a comprehensive suite of e-learning capabilities that enable interoperability, accessibility, and reusability of Web-based learning content. We remark that the descriptions of learning content that can be formed by following one or more of these standardization proposals resemble those of electronic services found in e-commerce that are prepared using the UDDI framework.

Learning objects can be stored in a relational or an object-relational database and are typically broken down into a collection of attributes, some of which are mandatory, and some of which are optional; a more concrete proposal appears in [14]. In a similar way, other information relevant to a learning system (e.g., learner personal data, learner profiles, course maps, LO sequencing or presentation information, general user data, etc.) can be mapped to common database structures. This does not only make interoperability feasible, but also allows for a process support inside an e-learning system that can interact with the underlying database appropriately [8, 13, 16]. Indeed, the area of e-learning consists of a multiplicity of complex activities such as content authoring or learner tracking and administration which interact with resources (including people such as learners and authors), with one another (some activities trigger others), and with the outside world (such as existing software systems) in a predefined way. As has been shown in the references just cited, these activities can be modeled as processes or workflows and can be attributed to and associated with the various components of a learning platform. If a system then uses a workflow management system to control these activities, it is possible, for example, to track the work and performance of a learner automatically, and it can also deliver content or process feedback. This idea can be taken to higher levels as well; for example, one can think of a college degree program that is fully supervised by an electronic system.

If a process view or even workflow management is accepted as fundamental modeling and enactment paradigm, it is a straightforward task to turn this kind of learning, at least for certain situations and applications, into a Web service of content and course offerings, as will be discussed next.

Web Service Basics

As we are aiming at a provision of e-learning features and components as a collection of Web services, we need to collect several preliminaries from that area. A *Web service* is essentially a stand-alone software component that has a unique URI (the Uniform Resource Identifier is a unique address), and that operates over the Internet and especially the

Web. The basic premise is that Web services have a provider and (hopefully) users or subscribers. The provider needs to implement the service, but also to write a specification and to make this specification available to potential customers through publication in a directory. The service directory can be queried so that services can be found by potential users. Service clients or users will typically search through such a directory, in order to find a single service that suits their needs, or a collection of services that can be composed appropriately.

Clearly, Web services need to be interoperable. Moreover, they have to be independent of the operating system they are running on, they should be usable on every Web service engine regardless of their programming language, and they should be able to interact with each other. To achieve these goals, Web services are commonly based on standards; currently most used are the XML-based specifications SOAP (Simple Object Access Protocol), UDDI (Universal Description, Discovery and Integration), and WSDL (Web Services Description Language), yet this picture is under constant evolution (see below). The basic steps to publish and use an implemented software component as a Web service are as follows:

The provider of a Web service registers his service at a UDDI directory, which acts as a global repository of metadata for all registered services and stores information about a service, but it does not store the service itself. This meta information includes, for example, the author, the category of service, and technical specifications. UDDI further defines a query language, an authoring authorization, and a replication strategy, since UDDI data is typically stored on several distributed servers. This ensures that a service can efficiently be found in response to a request; a request is answered by delivering information on how to use and call the service at the server of the provider. The communication rules for client and Web service are described in a WSDL file, which is not part of the UDDI directory; it is instead referenced by the information a client obtains from the UDDI directory upon his request. This document describes the conditions for the input and output data and the protocol for the communication. The WSDL document is used to generate a proxy to communicate with the actual Web service via SOAP messages [6, 9].

In [18], the reader can find a simplified WSDL file which describes a Web service to search for a specific learning object. The Web service gets a topic to search for LOs that are classified to this topic. The result of the search is an information set of the author, the date of creation, the price, the reference and a description of the content. Besides WSDL, there are other specification languages such as Microsoft's XLANG or IBM's WSFL (*Web Services Flow Language*), which has so far made a linkage of different Web services into a single business process difficult. To remedy these

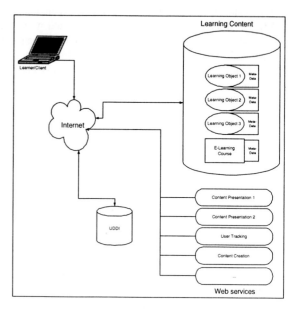

Figure 1. E-learning as a Web Service.

difficulties, a recent standardization effort has started to merge WSFL and XLANG into the Business Process Execution Language for Web Services (BPEL4WS); it may be expected that this is not the end of the story. BPEL combines the preferences of WSFL (e.g., the support of graph-oriented processes) and XLANG (e.g., the structural constructs for processes).

Up to now Web services have mostly been studied and realized in connection with business applications, such as B2B electronic commerce. For the future, a reasonable expectation, supported by the host of service platforms recently set up by major vendors, is that more and more service scenarios will be implemented in the form of Web services. In the remainder of this paper, we argue that one such scenario could be electronic learning.

3 Towards E-Learning Web Services

In this section, we describe the basic assumptions and ideas behind our prototypical *LearnServe* system. Essentially, there are the learner (or client) side as well as the provider side. The latter includes the roles of a learning system other than learners. We discuss each side individually in the following subsections.

In an e-learning system, a variety of aspects, features, and components can be perceived and realized as a Web service, including content authoring, content configuration into classes or courses, LO management, content updating, learner registration and management, content adaptation, learner profiling and tracking, testing of acquired knowledge, tutoring, virtual classroom setups, organization of chat rooms and the search for and presentation of content itself. Thus, we imagine that the entire functionality of a learning system is decomposed into individual activities which can be modeled as processes and provided as services, in such a way that the originally functionality can be reconstructed through suitable service compositions. In such a deviation from traditional learning platforms, all LOs, classes, and courses, which may be stored on different servers, register their offerings in a central directory with additional information on the content of the learning material. An individual LO is not stored in this directory.

A second type of Web service that is registered in the directory can be called directly by the platform to use its functionality. To this end, Figure 1 shows the service subsystems that we will describe in detail below; we mention that the choice of subsystems we discuss here is not exhaustive, and that various additions may be feasible. We also mention that this architecture allows for a variety of implementation choices, i.e., which part of the system is implemented in the central platform that is used by the client and what parts just call upon Web services.

Provider Side

The provider side of an e-learning Web service is split into different sections that can be handled by individual services. There are authors who create LOs, authors who build courses or classes composed of existing LOs, and trainers or teachers who communicate with learners. Authors creating content do this for a special group of people or just for an anonymous circle of learners. The first step in building learning material is to create individual LOs which may afterwards be configured into classes and courses. The author decides which attributes are important to be used in the context of a particular LO and which are not necessary. The easiest way to create an LO is to provide a number of forms depending on the attribute structure. Content can also be created from scratch, can be imported from foreign sources or even be generated on the basis of another system. We assume that authoring tools are made available as appropriate Web services, so that an author can choose between different services to select the one which is best suited for his content. At the end of a content creation session, an author has to register the new content in a service directory; in addition, the LOs that have been produced are stored on a selected server.

Figure 2 shows the process of content creation using a Petri net notation (see [10] for an introduction to Petri nets). After the author has locally prepared what he wants to do, he can choose a service for content creation by searching

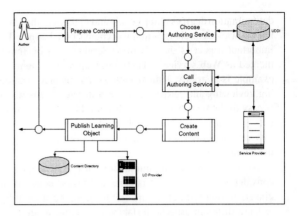

Figure 2. Process of creating a learning object.

through a UDDI directory; this service may comprise a commercial authoring system that can be used on a per-session basis. The system calls the service found, and the author can create the content using the chosen module. Upon finishing the creation of the learning material, the author has to register the new LO to the central content directory and store it on a server. In the end, the author can choose to create another LO or to perform a different task like creating classes from existing LOs. Even this process can be divided into two sub-processes, namely the creation of the LO and the publication of the LO. Both actions can be implemented as atomic Web service.

The creation of classes and courses can even be done by persons who are not themselves authors. To do so, they use existing LOs from other suppliers and combine them into a class or course. This creates a kind of added value by plugging the LOs together and cutting development time. New classes are also stored on a server and registered in the central directory as new services, without storing the LOs again, because the latter are reused from the publisher. Even the action of publishing may be handled by the same Web service as the publication of the LO as described before. The provider side also has to offer Web services to deliver and represent the content to the learner. The presentation of the material depends on the technical requirements of the LO and is not discussed in detail here.

Special services, also on the provider side, need to be available for handling trustworthy actions, like the collection of payment from a content user and the transfer of royalties to the respective content author, the certification of classes for special exams, or the storage of user profiles. Even special tests and the tracking of a user during his work can be handled by corresponding services. A tracking service is designed to check for completions of assignments, determination degrees if applicable and updates to the learning allowances or charges in the account of the learner. The important aspect is that all these services can be implemented as Web services. The certification of content, for example is a strictly defined process that includes searching, reviewing and certifying of the material. That is why it is easy to define a Web service that handles all these activities in a unique way, which can even be composed of Web services that only execute one of the actions necessary for the whole process.

As an example of the interactions at the provider side, consider an online class to become a database certified engineer. In order to obtain this certification, the student has to learn different aspects of database systems, as included in classes on database administration, database tuning, or database application development. These classes and an examination are now combined into a course called *database certified engineer*. The authors of each class can be members of different educational institutions. Even each class can be comprised of several LOs from potentially different authors, e.g., the database tuning is composed of an LO for query tuning, an LO for schema tuning, an LO for storage tuning etc. The LOs, classes, and the course are made by using authoring services; the database course itself is certified by a certification organization. Before a learner can use the content of a course, he has to pay for the program, which is handled by a casher service. The tracking and examination information of the user arising during the learning process are handled by a tracking and a testing service, resp., and are stored in an independent database. If the user passes the exam, he will become a database certified engineer, and be sent a diploma through a graduation service.

Learner Side

As already mentioned, different kinds of learners will want to access to an e-learning system and use e-learning with various motivations and perspectives. In a Web-based system the learner ideally just needs a Web browser to use the system, and he or she does not have to bother about what part of the platform is part of the server system and what part is just an included Web service. A personal login ensures that a profile can be created for each user, in order to adapt the system to a users preferences.

A learner usually logs into the system with a clear intension of what to learn. Often a learner has already been assigned to a course and can start working on the respective material right away. In our vision of future learning scenarios, the learner searches a content directory and orders LOs, classes, or courses that match his or her needs. The search depends on several conditions, including prerequisites, budget, meta-data, client hardware and software, preferences, age of material, author/provider, or profile. Upon presentation of search results, a learner can choose and book the content he or she wants to use. If the learner does not want to book an entire course, he might combine several topics into his own one. Suppose the choice is a class which is generally composed of several LOs that will be presented one after the other to the learner. The learner just uses the presented material as it would be in a centralized runtime system of common LMS. In fact, each presentation of material is a search in the content directory, a call of the LO, and a call of the corresponding Web service to present the material to the learner.

During the work on an LO the executing platform has to decide whether or not a learner has passed the learning section (assuming that LOs come with test sections which decide about successful passing). This leads to the problem of choosing the next LO for the user. If he fails, the system has to decide if he has to work on a different but similar LO or if he has to repeat the LO. The selection of a similar object can be done by a Web service based on the content, the learners preferences and the authors prerequisites as mentioned above. If he passed the LO, the platform has to call the next LO to go further in the course.

Learners normally need help during their work on the material. Help can be provided in an e-learning system using asynchronous techniques like email or message boards or by using synchronous techniques like chat with a tutor or video conferencing with virtual classmates. Clearly, all these functionalities can be included in an e-learning environment by calling respective Web services of special vendors; details are omitted.

To return to our previous example, the learner logs into the system to become a database certified engineer. He starts a search for a corresponding course, and the system returns a result set which is already reduced to his special dependencies, e.g., an affordable price of the course, his prerequisites etc. He chooses a course and uses a payment service to get the allowance to use the material. A presentation and delivery Web service then starts displaying the material, and the class eventually ends with a certification. The tracking service involved automatically notices the completion of all requirements.

4 Towards the LearnServe Realization

Building an e-learning system on the basis of a collection of Web services basically needs to compose a variety of services, in order to enable and provide the functionality of common e-learning applications. From a technical perspective, complex Web services composed of atomic ones call each other by using the URI of a follow-up service the moment that service is needed; if a Web service is not reachable or available at the moment of the call, the entire process fails. Since this is unacceptable, we are interested in

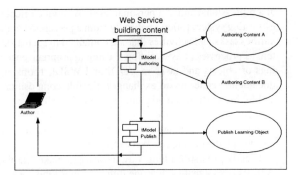

Figure 3. A dynamic call of a Web service.

a dynamic form of service selection where services are not called directly, but a technical description of the required service is requested first. The underlying service platform needs to select the appropriate services by using the available UDDI directory. To this end, we are currently considering the use of *tModels* [6], which can be used in a UDDI environment both as a technical fingerprint of a service and as a name space identifier.

Figure 3 shows a sample dynamic service call of the authoring process described above in Figure 2. The author calls service building content, which only consists of two activities here to simplify matters: the authoring of the content itself and the publication of the content thereafter. Both activities are themselves implemented as Web services. UDDI uses the same tModel for services with the same semantics; as a result, services Authoring Content A and Authoring Content B are assigned to the same tModel Authoring. Web service building content just calls tModel Authoring, and the service platform calls the assigned Web services to build up content. Upon completion, the author selects an authoring service and has to publish the newly created content. This is done by calling tModel Publish from Web service building content. Since there is only one publishing service registered, only that one can be used in this case to publish the LO.

The dynamic selection of services has several advantages over a static one. Indeed, the availability of composed services no longer depends on the availability of each single service in the chain of services. A dynamic choice enables the system to call the accessible services and call only these, independently of crashed services. Notice that not only the call of the described actions can be made more flexible, but even the usage of LOs can become dynamic. Traditional systems have to import learning objects to their own data pool in order to use them. This prevents the underlying system from the problem that LOs might not be available, but makes it difficult to reuse data from authors not being

in their community, since nobody may be aware that content from a specific author already exists. Using a central content directory enables authors to reduce the workload of creating courses by reusing content from other authors. Because this content is stored on distributed servers we have to transfer the dynamic call of Web services to the call of learning objects.

Recall our example of the database system certification. The learner registers for the course and starts the first LO. The system knows how to assemble LOs of a special type thanks to the authors class (and course) definition. Lets have a closer look at an LO for "schema tuning". The platform triggers the call of the LO by using the definitions the author has made while building up the class. In fact, the author has defined different LOs for "schema tuning" to be possibly used in the class. Depending on the preferences of the user and on the allowance of the author, the system selects that LO for the users that fits the learners needs and profile best. Hence different learners can receive different LOs working on the same class depending on their personal data and preferences. Let us now assume the system has chosen an object to be submitted to the student. Based on the meta-data of the object, a Web service is called that performs the presentation of the material to the learner. This is not a static call either, but a dynamic one using the tModel for the presentation of the object. Restrictions and preferences of learner, author, and client trigger the choice of the Web service to present the material.

Building a system of dynamic selection of LO has the advantage of an increased flexibility and adaptability. The learner does not need to notice the exchange of LO to adapt the course material to his needs and even does not recognize an exchange of content in case of an LO being off-line. Critical, however, is the authoring of content in that the reuse of LOs and the storage of data about LOs in a central content directory implies the use of standards. Today, many e-learning systems do not even care about standards and use their own way of handling content, what makes this material difficult to reuse for a system based on Web services. This lack of interchangeability can be solved by using Web services to create the content, which are implemented carefully to use standards. On the other hand, the dynamic call and flexible exchange of LOs leads to the problem of being able to evaluate and compare LOs. To use different LOs on schema tuning in a database course, the LOs must have a comparable and similar content to ensure that all learners can learn the same topics but in different ways. This problem can only be solved by the choice of an author of a course or by a special instance that certifies LOs. The latter has the advantage that certified content can be used to confer degrees after passing an (online) exam.

Realizing an e-learning platform as a collection of Web services can basically use an existing service platform and development tools, such as HP Web Services Platform, Microsoft .NET, Sun ONE, BEA WebLogic Enterprise Platform, or IBM WebSphere, to name just some of the major players. However, for the moment we are experimenting with a prototypical implementation called LearnServe, see Figure 4, that grew out of our experience in building the XLX learning platform described in [3] as well as out of the e-learning workflow studies reported in [14, 15, 16]. The idea behind LearnServe is to take the functionality of an e-learning system apart and specify its major components and activities through processes that can be executed as workflows. These processes, of which a small sample was shown in Figure 2, are grouped into atomic and complex Web services, for which UDDI as well as WSDL documents are prepared next. The prototypical implementation outside a commercial platform, which is discussed next, renders it possible to study various aspects specific to learning environments and scenarios.

As mentioned, the LearnServe system is based on our Web-based platform XLX [3], which has already been used by several German universities to train graduate level students in various scientific courses. XLX is implemented using the typical three-tier architecture of information systems (client-layer, application-layer, data-layer). To build up a platform with some of the functionality of LearnServe, we have decided to enhance XLX for Web services. In particular, the Web server now has to decide if it has to call a Web service or to use one of the functions already existing in the system. Two different kinds of Web services are possible, internal and external ones. External Web services are provided by other authors and are stored on remote systems. They are registered in a UDDI directory, which provides all necessary information to use the functionality of the remote service in our XLX platform. Internal Web services are provided by the LearnServe system itself and can be used via the existing XLX server. They are also registered in the UDDI directory for use by other systems and come with corresponding WSDL files. If one of these internal Web services is called, the listener module recognizes this and executes the service. Upon execution, the services are able to communicate with different data sources to read or write the information as needed to (e.g., LOs or data of a user profile). We plan to have a first version of LearnServe up later this year.

5 Conclusions

In this paper we have tried to advocate the idea of composing e-learning systems as collections of Web services. This has been motivated on the one hand by the inflexibility of many custom e-learning platforms we have been looking at recently, and on the other hand by the fact that Internet-based Web services are becoming ubiquitous, both at a professional and at a personal level. A service-oriented e-learning system follows naturally from a perception of the various tasks and activities that are contained in such a system as processes or as workflows; using appropriate encodings of objects and tasks in UDDI and WSDL forms and documents render broad exchanges, flexible compositions, and highly customized adaptations possible. This even allows for a reuse of services already offered on the Web, such as payment and cashing services, chat rooms, or conferencing (via platforms such as Webex).

Clearly, it is still a long way in order to make learning Web services a reality. For one thing, various kinds of supporting tools and services need to be provided, including authoring tools, testing and examination services, certification and accreditation, simulation environments, etc. On top of this, search and selection of learning service offerings must be made as easy as surfing the Web, which requires, for example, the development of ontologies or markup languages (such as the ones described in [7, 12]) through which learning content can be adequately classified, grouped, annotated, and registered. Another challenge arising in a distributed e-learning system as the one sketched in the previous section concerns the presentation of the learning material on the client: To ensure the usage of various presentation styles, the presentation of an LO might need to execute an application on the client. This might induce security problems, since the creation of content is not controlled by some security agency in order to ensure that an LO does not comprise an attack on the client. To meet this challenge, we are also considering the design of specific transactional guarantees for learning sessions. We plan to report on these developments in a forthcoming paper.

References

[1] Adelsberger, H.H., B. Collis, J.M. Pawlowski, eds. (2002). Handbook on Information Technologies for Education and Training. Springer-Verlag, Berlin.

[2] Casati, F., U. Dayal, eds. (2002). Special Issue on Web Services. IEEE Bulletin of the Technical Committee on Data Engineering, 25 (4), December 2002.

[3] Hüsemann, B., J. Lechtenbörger, G. Vossen, P. Westerkamp. XLX - A Platform for Graduate-Level Exercises; in Proc. Int. Conf. on Computers in Education, Auckland, Newzealand, December 2002, pp. 1262-1266.

[4] IEEE Standards Department (2002). Draft Standard for Learning Object Metadata. IEEE Publication P1484.12.1/D6.4, March 2002.

[5] IMS Global Learning Consortium, Inc. (2001). IMS Content Packaging Best Practice Guide, Version 1.1.2. August 2001.

[6] Keidl, M., Kreutz, A., Kemper, A., Kossmann, D. (2002). A Publish & Subscribe Architecture for Distributed Metadata

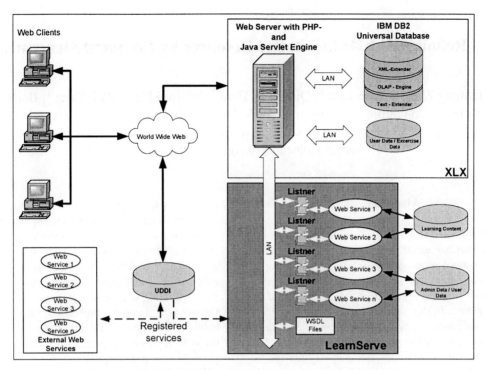

Figure 4. Architecture of the LearnServe prototype.

Management. In Proc. 18th IEEE Int. Conf. on Data Engineering (ICDE), San Jose, CA, February 2002. IEEE Computer Society, pp. 309–320.

[7] Kooper, R. (2001). Modeling units of study from a pedagogical perspective the pedagogical meta-model behind EML. Open University of the Netherlands, Heerlen, June 2001.

[8] Lin, J., C. Ho, W. Sadiq, M.E. Orlowska (2001). On Workflow Enabled e-Learning Services. In Proc. IEEE Int. Conf. on Advanced Learning Technology (ICALT), Madison, WI, August 2001. IEEE Computer Society, pp. 349–352.

[9] Pilioura, T., A. Tsalgatidou (2001). E-Services: Current Technology and Open Issues. In Proc. 2nd Int. Workshop on Technologies for E-Services, Rome, Springer-Verlag, Berlin, pp. 1–15.

[10] Reisig, W. (1985). Petri Nets, An Introduction. EATCS, Monographs on Theoretical Computer Science, W.Brauer, G. Rozenberg, A. Salomaa (Eds.), Springer Verlag, Berlin.

[11] Sadiq, W., M.E. Orlowska (2001). Flex-eL - Managing e-Learning through Workflows. SAP Research and Applications Congress, February 2001, San Diego, USA.

[12] S, C., B. Freitag (2001). Learning Material Markup Language LMML. IFIS-Report 2001/03, University of Passau, Germany.

[13] Vantroys, T., Y. Peter (2001). A WMF-based workflow for e-learning. In Proc. European Research Seminar on Advances in Distributed Systems (ERSADS), Bertinoro, Italy, May 2001.

[14] Vossen, G., P. Jaeschke (2002). Towards a Uniform and Flexible Data Model for Learning Objects; In Proc. 30th Annual Conf. of the Int. Bus. School Computing Assoc. (IBSCA), Savannah, Georgia, July 2002, pp. 99–129.

[15] Vossen, G., P. Jaeschke (2003): Learning Objects as a Uniform Foundation for E-Learning Platforms; these proceedings.

[16] Vossen, G., Jaeschke P., Oberweis A. (2002). Flexible Workflow Management as a Central E-Learning Support Paradigm, in Proc. 1st European Conf. on E-Learning, Uxbridge, UK, Nov. 2002, pp. 253–267.

[17] Vossen, G., M. Weske (1998). The WASA Approach to Workflow Management for Scientific Applications; in: A. Dogac, L. Kalinichenko, T. Ozsu, A. Sheth, eds., *Workflow Management Systems and Interoperability*, NATO ASI Series F, Vol. 164, Springer-Verlag, Berlin, pp. 145–164.

[18] Vossen, G., P. Westerkamp (2003). *E-Learning as a Web Service*; Technical Report No. 92, Department of Information Systems, University of Münster, January 2003

[19] Weske, M., G. Vossen (1998). Workflow Languages; in: P. Bernus, K. Mertins, G. Schmidt (eds.): Handbook on Architectures of Information Systems; Springer-Verlag, Berlin, pp. 359–379.

Refining Web Authoritative Resource by Frequent Structures *

Haofeng Zhou [1], Yubo Lou [1], Qingqing Yuan [1], Wilfred Ng [2], Wei Wang [1], Baile Shi [1]
[1] Dept. of Computing and Information Technology, Fudan University, Shanghai, China
[2] Dept. of Computer Science, Hong Kong University of Science & Technology
[1] haofzhou@eastday.com, [2] wilfred@cs.ust.uk

Abstract

The web resource is a rich collection of the dynamic information that are useful in various disciplines. There has also been much research work related to improving the quality of information searching in the web. However, most of the work is still inadequate to satisfy a diversified demand from users. In this paper, we exploit the hyperlinks in the web and propose a new approach called SFP in order to improve the quality of research results obtain from search engines. The SFP algorithm evolves from the frequent pattern mining technique which is a common data mining technique for conventional databases. The essential idea of our approach is to mine the frequent structures of links from a given web topology. By using the SFP algorithm, we extract the authoritative pages and communities from the complex web topology. We demonstrate our approach by running several experiments and show that the performance and functionalities of using the SFP in managing search results are better than other known methods such as HITS.

1 Introduction

The World Wide Web (WWW) serves as a huge, widely distributed, global information service center for different kinds of information services. It is important to note that the authoritative resources on the web, which are not explicit in the structure of web links, are able to serve as a reference to facilitate much better navigation. When a web designer/adminstrator includes a hyperlink referencing to another web site in his/her own page, he/she actually uses a hyperlink to represent a semantic relationship between the linked pages.

The work related to mining the web's link structures to recognize authoritative web pages has been known in the community for several years [6, 15]. Some algorithms were also proposed for this purpose [5, 14]. Most of them are applied in the search engines over the Web. But there are still some limitations in these methods, for example the *recall* and it precision, which indicate the quality of the search result, are not satisfactory. The previous work on frequent pattern mining, such as the well-known Apriori [2] and FP-Growth [10], faces the problem of finding the relationship between the relations of items. It is also well perceived that the web structure can be described in the form of directed-graph in a natural way, where vertices represent pages with URLs as their labels, and directed-edges for hyperlinks [8].

In this paper, we apply our earlier proposed method, called the SFP algorithm, for improving the precision of web search. The SFP algorithm has been applied in the context of simple semi-structured data [22], which shares the similar spirit of the conventional frequent pattern mining technique [2]. Using several experiments concerning keyword searching, we show that our proposed method is effective to refine the results obtained from a search engine.

The rest of this paper is organized as follows. In Section 2, some related work is reviewed and the problem of our work is stated. Then, our proposed method, SFP, is introduced in Section 3. In Section 4, a set of experiments is presented to illustrate the process of refinement in our method. Finally, the conclusion is given in Section 5.

2 Related Work

There has been much work on both the structure analysis and frequent pattern mining [2, 5, 6, 8, 10, 14, 15].

The idea of determining the importance of a document using its corresponding link information was proposed as early as the emergence of the WWW. However, the link structure of web pages has some special features which are detailed as follows: (1) many links on the web, for example those links for advertising or navigation, do not denote the authority preference; and (2) some links may be authoritative to some specific part but have no relationship with other links in the same page. Hence, some research work

---
*This paper was supported by the Key Program of National Natural Science Foundation of China (No. 69933010) and China National 863 High-Tech Projects (No. 2002AA4Z3430 and 2002AA231041)

has been done to study the authority of a web page, among which HITS of Kleinberg [14] is a typical web information retrieval algorithm which perform link analysis to improve the quality of search result. In [9, 16], HITS algorithm is further employed to find communities over the web. The concept of community is important, since it represents a group of authoritative web pages. However, we find that there are some drawbacks of HITS algorithm. First, HITS either treats internal links within the same site as the external ones or just ignores them completely. These two ways of handling internal links are not satisfactory in our opinions. In fact in [11], this problem has been noted and thus HITS-SW is then proposed to improve HITS algorithm. HITS-SW assigns similarity weights to all the links in a collection of web pages, and runs a connectivity-analysis considering both the links and the content of the document. Second, HITS (including HITS-SW) needs to perform iteration until reaching a convergent state and as a result the process is inefficient. Comparing to HITS, our proposed SFP algorithm, which will be introduced later on, do not need to perform iteration when generating authoritative pages.

There has also been other related work such as [20] which calculates web communities by using links. However, this class of work does not consider the features of the communities in detail, such as the mutual influence of communities, e.g, the weight or the number being linked.

Frequent pattern mining plays an important role in the field of data mining [1, 2, 4, 10, 19]. Most of them do not assume any association between basic data items. In the case of a web structure, if the links are considered as the basic items for mining, they are apparently associated. Therefore, it is necessary to provide an algorithm to deal with the mining problem on these inherently associated data items.

Recently, some research work has been done on mining structured data [3, 7, 21, 23]. In addition, [12, 17, 18] also did research on mining frequent sub-graphs. However these methods have paid too much attention on the isomorphism problem, which both considers the structrual and label mapping. But it will not happen in the a web structure graph, where URLs serve as unique labeling on each vertex. So the mentioned methods are not efficient enough for mining frequent patterns in a web structure . Besides, most of these methods are based on the well-known Apriori algorithm, in which the generation of a large number of candidate itemsets is the bottleneck. We remark that, in [22] we has proposed a new algorithm SFP for mining graph structures, which will be applied in this paper.

3 SFP: Mining the Frequent Structure from the Web

In this section, we first introduce the basic terminology and the SFP algorithm (or simply SFP). Then, we describe the modification of SFP in order to adapt it to the context of web mining.

3.1 Terms and Concepts

In SFP algorithm, all the graphs are assumed to be *simple unique labeled graphs*, which means that in such graphs, there is no loop, no multiple edges, and no two vertices assigned the same label. SFP only applies to connected graphs. In the sequel we assume all original graphs G consist the graph dataset GD. The result of running SFP on G is a frequent connected structure represesed as the connected subgraph, which is only a connected part of the original graph. As a frequent pattern mining algorithm, SFP also has the similar definitions with the original ones, such as support and minimum support. A new term here is "rank" of G, which is defined as the total number of edges in a given graph. As a special case, 0-rank graph is a graph G having only one vertex.

Therefore, a web page is authoritative if it is a 0-rank frequent sub-graph, and an authoritative community demonstrates the close relationship among authoritative pages. It is one co-op consists of linked authoritative pages.

3.2 Adapting SFP for Web Mining Case

SFP extracts frequent subgraphs from a given set of simple unique labeled graphs. The idea is similar to the well-known FP-Growth, but we consider the relationship between edge items rather than the vertices. For more details about SFP, please refer to [22].

In order to adapt the SFP in the context of web structure, two parts of works are to be considered. One is related to the mapping from a web structure to a graph, and another is related to how to handle the connectivity in a directed graph.

The solution for the first part of work is straightforward. We simply use the directed-graph to represent the web structure, where the vertex denotes the web page, its label is the URL of this page, and directed edge represents the hyperlink from the one page to another. In the web structure, we should remove all the hyperlinks pointing to the pages that contain themselves, which means that there is no loop in the directed graph.

Next, in SFP, the edge is denoted as the form $l_i l_j$, where the l_i and l_j are the labels on the two vertices related to the edge. Since the edge is undirected, it forces the edge in the form of $l_i l_j$ with $l_i < l_j$ in the lexical order, which may need some transformation between the original data and the data used in SFP. One subtle point is that the $l_i l_j$ and the $l_j l_i$ are the same in SFP. But in a directed graph, this way of handling of links will lose the direction of the edge. The $l_i l_j$ and the $l_j l_i$ are regarded as two different edges in the graph.

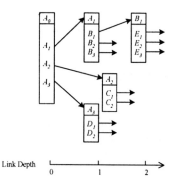

Figure 1. Mapping from Web to a SFP graph

Therefore, we need to deal with them separately. The $l_i l_j$ and the $l_j l_i$ will be two elements in the SFP, each of them has its own support or frequency.

For the second part of work, in SFP, we still need the bi-direction links which preserve the information about the connectivity of the original data. However, we should mark a tag on the bi-direction which indicates its real direction. This mark is used only for the purpose to restore the subgraphs in the results, and nothing else.

The final remark is the issue of connectivity. We adopt the definition of weak connectivity, which require that there exists a undirected path between any two vertices. The idea is also used for the SFP in [22].

The graph used in SFP is generated from the result of search engine. In this paper, we use a root page to denote each result page returned by the search engine (e.g. in Figure 1, A_0 is one result page of a certain search, and it is a root page). If we start from the root page, separate out the links contained in the page content iteratively, we can finally obtain a tree-like directed graph (Strictly speaking, this graph is not a tree because it may have cycles). Then, according to a certain search order (breadth first), we simply put all these links into a set for SFP.

For convenience, we use *Level*, *MaxPages* and *MaxLinks*, respectively, to represent the level of linked pages (or page depth), maximum page number and maximum link number. For each page and within the limit of *MaxPages*, we analyze its content and separate out the links. The *Level* of root page is set to be zero. Starting from the root page, we are able to obtain a directed connected graph by traversing and analyzing the link structure based on the method and constraints above, which we call such a graph a Generated Graph. Obviously, each root page has a corresponding Generated Graph and all the Generated Graphs consist the dataset *GD*

4 Experiment of Using SFP for Search Results

The experiments were running on a desktop PC with PentiumII 433MHz CPU, 384MB RAM and Windows 2000 Advanced Server. All the algorithms such as SFP, HITS, and a tool named pageSnagger are coded in C++.

Algorithm HITS is implemented by referencing [13]. The data is from the first 200 entries of the search results, the filter threshold is set to be 5, and the iterating turn is set to be 20. The domains which have the same name are regarded as the same domain.

The pageSnagger was used to get corresponding link structure within a certain depth between pages induced from each separate result of search engine. In pageSnagger, we can set the previously mentioned parameters: *Level*, *MaxPages* and *MaxLinks*. In our experiment, we set page depth to be 2, since the memory resource in our system is not able to handle the number of pages and links if using higher page depth.

As Google has adopted the methods of PageRank, anchor text, and proximity information to improve search quality, which is a common search engine adopted by users. Therefore, we use Google's search result as a reference to justify our algorithm.

4.1 Searching Authoritative Web Pages

4.1.1 Search key = "search engine" (input in Chinese)

After running the query having the search key "Search Engine"(input in Chinese), we obtain the result in Figure 2(a). But it is far from the list of authoritative sites that we expect. The well-known search engine in China - Sohu only appears as a news page which has little similarity with the search key. Moreover, it ranks even behind some less common search engines, e.g. http://www.beijixing.com.cn/. Other important search engines like Lycos, Google, AltaVista are not listed in Figure 2(a). We find that Lycos ranks 35, and that AltaVista and Google, unfortunately, are not in the top 200. It indicates that current search engines, even the popular one like Google, still have shortcomings in this case. As to the HITS, shown in Figure 2(b), it seems that it has been trapped by the pages from the site fm365.com, which is clearly an unsatisfactory result.

We now discuss the testing result of SFP algorithm. According to the frequency of each page, we show the top 10 URLs in Figure 2(c). This result is much better than that in Figure 2(a). It is because the result in Figure 2(a). are all famous search engines and most of them are the front page of the search engines. One unexpected result is that Google does not appear in the top 10 of the list. The underlying reason is that our authority mining algorithm is based

	URL
1	http://www.126.com/
2	http://search.sina.com. cn/
3	http://search.sina.com. cn/wap/pc/
4	http://search.163.com/
5	http://search.163.com/help/search box/searchbox.html
6	http://cn.yahoo.com/
7	http://www.yahoo.com/
8	http://www.beijixing.com.cn/
9	http://search.focus.com.cn/
10	http://news.sohu.com/

(a) Google's result of "Search Engine"

	URL	Auth
1	http://search.fm365.com/	0.289
2	http://www.fm365.com/	0.289
3	http://news.fm365.com/	0.289
4	http://stock.fm365.com/	0.289
5	http://mail.fm365.com/	0.289
6	http://people.fm365.com/	0.289
7	http://searchnews.fm365.com/	0.289
8	http://dir.fm365.com/	0.289
9	http://bbs.fm365.com/	0.289
10	http://card.fm365.com/	0.289

(b) HIT's result of "Search Engine"

	URL	F
1	http://www.sohu.com/	17
2	http://www.yahoo.com/	16
3	http://www.21cn.com/	14
4	http://www.163.com/	13
5	http://www.baidu.com/	12
6	http://www.lycos.com/	11
7	http://cn.yahoo.com/	11
8	http://www.goyoyo.com/	11
9	http://service.21cn.com/weather/index.html	11
10	http://www.altavista.com/	10

(c) SFP's result of "Search Engine"

	URL	F
1	http://www.w3.org/	45
2	http://www.w3.org/xml/	35
3	http://www.xml.com/	31
4	http://www.oasis-open.org/	25
5	http://www.w3.org/tr/rec-xml	22
6	http://www.w3.org/dom/	22
7	http://www.w3.org/style/css/	21
8	http://www.w3.org/tr/	20
9	http://www.w3.org/xml/query	19
10	http://www.xml.org/	19

(d) SFP's result of "XML"

	URL	F
1	http://www.w3.org/	45
2	http://www.xml.com/	31
3	http://www.oasis-open.org/	25
4	http://www.xml.org/	19
5	http://www.ucc.ie/xml/	17
6	http://validator.w3.org/	16
7	http://xml.apache.org/	15
8	http://www.oreilly.com/	15
9	http://www.oreillynet.com/	14
10	http://www.internet.com/sections/webdev.html	14

(e) SFP's result of "XML" on site grouping

	URL	Auth
1	http://www.w3.org/	0.128
2	http://www.textuality.com/	0.110
3	http://www.jclark.com/	0.110
4	http://www.ucc.ie/	0.106
5	http://www.xml.com/	0.104
6	http://www.microsoft.com/	0.101
7	http://www.arbortext.com/	0.098
8	http://java.sun.com/	0.091
9	http://xml.coverpages.org/	0.091
10	http://www.idealliance.org/	0.091

(f) HIT's result of "XML"

	URL	F
1	http://java.sun.com/	45
2	http://www.earthweb.com/	35
3	http://www.internet.com/sections/webdev.html	31
4	http://www.sun.com/	25
5	http://java.sun.com/docs/books/tutorial/	22
6	http://javaboutique.internet.com/	22
7	http://www.gamelan.com/	21
8	http://developer.apple.com/java/	20
9	http://www.jars.com/	19
10	http://www.javaworld.com/	19

(g) SFP's result of "Java"

	URL
1	http://java.sun.com/
2	http://java.sun.com/docs/books/tutorial/
3	http://javaboutique.internet.com/
4	http://softwaredev.earthweb.com/java
5	http://www.javaworld.com/
6	http://www.javaworld.com/columns/jw-tips-index.shtml
7	http://www.apple.com/java/
8	http://www.javalobby.org/
9	http://developer.java.sun.com/developer/
10	http://developer.java.sun.com/developer/onlineTraining/new2java/

(h) Google's result of "Java"

	URL	Auth
1	http://java.sun.com/	0.0920
2	http://www.jars.com/	0.0784
3	http://www.cs.cmu.edu/	0.0781
4	http://www.javaworld.com/	0.0773
5	http://www.developer.com/	0.0769
6	http://www.sun.com/	0.0767
7	http://www.amazon.com/	0.0760
8	http://www.javasoft.com/	0.0753
9	http://www.ibm.com/	0.0750
10	http://developer.java.sun.com/	0.0747

(i) HIT's result of "Java"

Figure 2. Figures of the Experiment result

on Generated Graphs of the search results, a search engine is authoritative only if it is contained by many Generated Graphs, i.e. it is linked by many search results. As Google is a brand new search engine for ordinary people (especially to Chinese due to the impact of the language and the range), it is inevitably lower in the list using our approach. Moreover, using a search key in Chinese in this test also implies that Chinese web sites are considered to be more important in the returned result. In fact, Google has many specific search pages, with respect to different languages and different search methods. For example,

http://www.google.com/dirhp?hl=en,

http://www.google.com/,

http://www.google.com/en,

http://www.google.com/imghp?hl=zh-cn,

http://www.google.com/advanced_search?hl=en,

http://www.google.com/grp-hp?hl=zh-cn,

http://www.google.com/grphp?hl=en,

http://www.google.com/intl/zh-cn/.

The total frequency of all these pages will be 36, which is much greater than 17 or Sohu. In fact, this is a common happening for multilingual search engines, e.g. Yahoo!.

We note that when the search key is in English input, Google performs well. Therefore, SFP is useful to improve the quality of the search results when a search engine suffers from the poor interpretation of Chinese search keywords.

4.1.2 Search key = "XML"

XML has been greatly promoted by the research community and industry. Many XML related standards have been established. W3C (World Wide Web Consortium, http://www.w3c.org) is commonly regarded as the authority of the language standard. In this experiment, we set the parameters to the same values as the previous one and we obtain the top 200 Generated Graphs. The result we obtain for searching "XML" is as follows: 4932 pages, 160.4MB page content, 18,581 links, and 127,110 edges. Figure 2(d) shows the top 10 results obtained by running SFP algorithm. Figure 2(e) lists the result by grouping the pages in the same site. As expected, XML standard pages from W3C occupy most of the positions. The result is much better than that obtained from HITS, which is shown in Figure 2(f). Herein, http://www.xml.com/ and http://www.xml.org are listed the third, fourth and fifth, sixth respectively in Google result. http://www.oasis-open.org is an international nonprofit consortium that designs and develops industry specifications for interoperability based on XML. The ninth and tenth result of Google are linked to this site.

4.1.3 Other Search Results

Java is a new object-oriented language in recent years, since the feature of platform-independence makes it a favorite tool for programmers. In this experiment we set $MaxPages = 100$, $MaxLinks = 100$, $Level = 2$ and key="java", by applying SFP to analyze the first 110 entries of the Google search result. After running SFP algorithm ($minfreq = 7$), the site being ranked first is http://java.sun.com/. Again, this result demonstrates the accuracy of our algorithm. We achieve the result in Figure 2(g), which is not in the shade of those in Google and HITS shown in Figure 2(h) and Figure 2(i), respectively.

In the algorithms based on matrix iteration, many navigation and advertisement links will have illegal weights due to the spread of weights. However, in our algorithm, these kinds of links do not possess high frequency and eventually they are filtered out.

Topic	Search Engine	XML	JAVA
Num. of Graphs	198	200	110
Num. of Edges	65983	127110	85287
Num. of Vertices	16375	18581	7527
SFP time (ms)	12	13	8
HITS time (ms)	313	350	331

Figure 3. Performance Comparison of SFP and HITS on some topics

As shown in Fig. 3, when we analyze the first 200 entries in the google search results, HITS is relatively stable but much higher in processing time, no matter which query topic is chosen. SFP avoids the iterating calculation, which is used by HITS, by counting the frequency of hyperlinks, which shortens the processing time considerably. Clearly,

Labels	URL
2	http://www.w3.org/style/xsl/
3	http://www.w3.org/xml/query
48	http://www.w3.org/dom/
102	http://www.w3.org/xml/linking
150	http://www.w3.org/
151	http://www.w3.org/rdf/
159	http://www.w3.org/style/css/
166	http://www.w3.org/xml/
174	http://www.w3.org/xml/schema
15	http://www.oreilly.com/
63	http://www.xmlhack.com/
439	http://www.oreillynet.com/
512	http://www.xml.com/
551	http://www.ixiasoft.com/?from=xml.com

Figure 4. XML Authoritative Community

SFP performs much better than HITS, as shown in this experiment.

4.2 Authoritative Communities

We observe that a common feature of many web sites share resources through collaboration in order to strengthen the content for each others, which lead to the concept of *community* in the web. We view a web page as a member unit of a community and aim at finding out authoritative community and important information within a web site. In this respect, SFP is able to find both the single pages (0-rank sub-graphs) and higher rank frequent sub-graphs. Thus, our approach is effective in detecting authoritative communities in the web, since SFP provides a more explicit understanding of the structure of the web through related to authoritative communities.

For example, in the "XML"experiment in Section 4.1.2, there are seven out of top ten which are from the same web site http://www.w3c.org. They are linked to the XML related standards. It shows that multiple authoritative pages can occur within the same web site. If we set 13 to be the minimum frequency, we are able to obtain the two most important authoritative communities in Figure 4.

In the "java" experiment, it can easily find that the authoritative community led by http://java.sun.com/. When illustrating these search results, we can simply show all of them with an extensible tree rooted by http://java.sun.com/, which will be helpful for users to find the important pages and their relationships. Furthermore, this is also helpful for advertisers to decide which page is the best place for advertisement. We believe that authoritative community deserves a further study to discover the potential in real applications.

5 Conclusions

In this paper, we take into account the link structure in the Web and adapt our early proposed SFP algorithm in the context of web mining, which is able to refine authoritative pages and communities based on their frequency of users' accessing.

From the experiments we discussed in Section 4, we observe the following desirable features in our result: (1) SFP is subject-sensitive, (2) SFP reflects user expected authoritative pages, and (3) SFP is able to discover authoritative communities. Overall, SFP alleviates the problem that a user needs to consume too much time to filter out those poor results returned from a search engine. Our method performs relatively better in terms of the quality of search result and the processing time for organizing and filtering the search results. We notice that there are some shortcomings in mining authoritative communities, e.g., some community members deviate from the subject. We are still researching on how to calculate the authority of multi-version pages more effectively.

Acknowledgement

Here we want to give our many thanks to Jian Ma for the initial literal work of this paper.

References

[1] R. Agrawal, et al. Mining association rules between sets of items in large databases. In *Proc. of SIGMOD'93*, pp. 207–216.

[2] R. Agrawal, et al. Fast algorithms for mining association rules in large databases. In *Proc. of VLDB'94*, pp. 487–499.

[3] T. Asai, et al. Efficient substructure discovery from large semi-structured data. In *Proc. of SDM'02*, pp. 158–174.

[4] S. Brin, et al. Dynamic itemset counting and implication rules for market basket data. In *Proc. of SIGMOD'97*, pp. 255–264.

[5] S. Brin, et al. The anatomy of a large-scale hypertextual web search engine. In *Proc. of WWW'98, Computer Networks*, vol. 30, no. 1-7.

[6] S. Chakrabarti, et al. Mining the web's link structure. *IEEE Computer*, 32(8):60–67, 1999.

[7] L. Dehaspe, et al. Finding frequent substructures in chemical compounds. In *Proc. of KDD'98*, pp. 30–36.

[8] D. Florescu, et al. Database techniques for the world-wide web: a survey. *ACM SIGMOD Record*, 27(3):59–74, 1998.

[9] D. Gibson, et al. Inferring web communities from link topology. In *Proc. of the 9th ACM conference on Hypertext and hypermedia*, pp. 225–234.

[10] J. Han, et al. Mining frequent patterns without candidate generation. In *Proc. of SIGMOD'00*, pp. 1–12.

[11] J.D. Herbach. Improving authoritative sources in a hyperlinked environment via similarity weighting. BSE Thesis, Dept. of Computer Science, Princeton University, 2001.

[12] A. Inokuchi, et al. An apriori-based algorithm for mining frequent substructures from graph data. In *Proc. of PKDD'2000, LNCS*, vol. 1910, pp. 13–23.

[13] J. Kleinberg. Authoritative sources in a hyperlinked environment. In *Proc. of SODA'98*, pp. 668–677.

[14] J. Kleinberg. Authoritative sources in a hyperlinked environment. *Journal of the ACM*, 46(5):604–632, 1999.

[15] J. Kleinberg et al. Applications of linear algebra in information retrieval and hypertext analysis. In *Proc. of PODS'99*, pp. 185–193.

[16] R. Kumar, et al. Trawling the web for emerging cyber-communities. In *Proc. of WWW'99, Computer Networks*, vol. 31, no. 11-16.

[17] M. Kuramochi,et al. Frequent subgraph discovery. In *Proc. of ICDM'01*, pp. 313–320.

[18] T. Matsuda, et al. Extension of graph-based induction for general graph structured data. In *Proc. of PAKDD'2000, LNCS*, vol. 1805, pp. 420–431.

[19] J.Park, et al. An effective hash based algorithm for mining association rules. In *Proc. of SIGMOD'95*, pp. 175–186.

[20] P. Reddy, et al. Inferring web communities through relaxed-cocitation and power-laws. In *Proc. of the 12th Data Engineering Workshop*.

[21] K.Wang, et al. Discovering typical structures of documents: A road map approach. In *Proc. of SIGIR'98*, pp. 146–154.

[22] Q. Yuan, et al. Extract frequent pattern from simple graph data. In *Proc. of WAIM'2002, LNCS*, vol. 2419, pp. 158–169.

[23] M. Zaki. Efficiently mining frequent trees in a forest. In *Proc. of SIGKDD'02*.

Database Applications I

Persistent Applications via Automatic Recovery

Roger Barga, David Lomet
Microsoft Research
{barga, lomet}@microsoft.com

Stelios Paparizos
University of Michigan
spapariz@umich.edu

Haifeng Yu
Duke University
yhf@cs.duke.edu

Sirish Chandrasekaran
UC Berkeley
Sirish@cs.berkeley.edu

Abstract

Building highly available enterprise applications using web-oriented middleware is hard. Runtime implementations frequently do not address the problems of application state persistence and fault-tolerance, placing the burden of managing session state and, in particular, handling system failures on application programmers. This paper describes Phoenix/APP, a runtime service based on the notion of recovery guarantees. Phoenix/APP transparently masks failures and automatically recovers component-based applications. This both increases application availability and simplifies application development. We demonstrate the feasibility of this approach by describing the design and implementation of Phoenix/APP in Microsoft's .NET runtime and present results on the cost of persisting and recovering component-based applications.

1. Introduction

Application developers, unless instructed otherwise, tend to write stateful applications, retaining information necessary for correct and successful execution across interaction and transaction boundaries. However, stateful applications risk losing state when the system on which they execute crashes. This can create a "semantic mess" that may require human intervention to repair or restart the application, resulting in long service outages. The classic response to this is to insist that an application be "stateless", where stateless means "no meaningful information is retained across transactions". Unfortunately, stateless applications force a rather unnatural form of workflow programming. The application must, within a transaction, first read its state from, e.g., a transactional queue, execute its logic, and then commit the step by writing its state back to a queue for the next step. This programming model also has a potential performance problem due to the need for two phase commit (2PC).

Consider an enterprise middle tier application. It is typically made up of one or more server components that implement business logic and expose a set of interfaces. A handful of the components in the application may access persistent data, typically stored in a relational database. Many components perform a specific task

(calculation, data formatting, etc) on behalf of server components, possibly modifying data and returning a result but they retain no state. Finally, there are a small number of critical components which maintain state for the application during the session.

A classic example is a middle tier e-commerce system for shopping and price comparison. A client session begins when a customer logs in and customer information is read from a database into a component. As the customer shops, purchases are recorded in the stateful component representing the market basket. When the customer checks out, items in the basket are written to databases (e.g., orders and billing) and the customer database is updated to reflect recent activity.

If a failure occurs during the session, all volatile state is lost and the session must be restarted. This can result in lost revenues and frustrated customers. Depending on the application and point of failure, updates may have to be manually backed out to restore consistency to the system. To avoid this, middle tier systems have been designed as stateless applications. This unnatural programming style increases development costs and may reduce system throughput.

1.1 Phoenix/APP for Improved Availability

In this paper we describe Phoenix/APP, a runtime service that provides transparent state persistence and automatic recovery for component-based applications. Phoenix/APP is based on the recovery guarantees framework [7], the techniques and protocol of which offers several distinct advantages:

- Exactly-once execution semantics;
- Protocols to reduce logging cost, especially log force, enabling efficient log management;
- Recovery independence, allowing components to recover independently;

The Phoenix/APP prototype is implemented as a runtime service in Microsoft's .NET framework and supports any component based application. The Phoenix/APP approach could also be adapted to CORBA [23] or EJB [9]. All that is required is a middleware framework that supports message interception between components so the appropriate logging can occur.

Phoenix/APP is so named because it persists application state across system failures. An earlier prototype, Phoenix/ODBC [4] persisted database session state across system failures. Both efforts have the intent to permit applications to survive system failures and, as such, are part of a movement in systems research to turn focus away from its performance-oriented agenda to other important aspects of computing, such as availability and maintainability. Phoenix/APP offers a unique perspective on how to achieve high availability for enterprise applications that requires very little effort from the application developers to deploy.

To achieve fault-tolerance using Phoenix/APP simply requires a programmer to identify stateful components and declare them as persistent or transactional. Components not so declared are by default external. Application code is written without the need to consider possible system failures. Thus it can be focused entirely on business logic. Phoenix/APP transparently logs component interactions and, if a failure occurs, automatically recovers all components marked persistent up to the last logged interaction1. Components that interact with a (transactional) database are marked transactional. These are recovered up to the last successfully completed transaction – in-flight transactions will be aborted by the database. Applications must be written to deal with (e.g., retry) aborted transactions, which is required in any case since transactions can fail for many reasons. External components are outside of the boundary of the system, and cannot be recovered. However, we limit our dependence upon them by prompt logging of interactions with them. Thus, the application can continue execution across system failures without loss of state (market basket, orders, etc) and need not take any special actions to ensure its persistence.

Phoenix/APP hence provides two major advantages for building enterprise applications:

- It enables an application to be written naturally as a stateful program. No special measures need to be taken to persist application state. Application developers do not have to format state so it can be saved to disk, nor do they have to provide code to read and write their state. Instead, they are free to focus on writing application business logic.
- It masks and recovers from failures, which improves overall system availability. High availability is crucial to the success of businesses engaged in e-commerce. Unfortunately, system and application failures do occur. Most application failures are recoverable by

Phoenix/APP because problems giving rise to most failures are "heisenbugs"2. [Database recovery works well for the same reason.] If an application or process crashes, Phoenix/APP intercepts errors from the failure and initiates recovery on the failed components. The recovery is transparent from the application's point of view, except for response time delay as components are recovered.

1.2 Other Enterprise Attributes

Phoenix/APP captures component state by logging interactions between components, forming an event history. This history is on the log and is used to recover, i.e. make persistent, a component's state up to the last logged interaction. This captures the execution state of a component while it is active. Hence it is possible to interrupt execution at arbitrary points and capture the state. Capturing active application state provides other benefits to enterprise applications.

- **Scalability**: Scalability requires the reuse of resources drawn from a pool of anonymous inactive resources. The middle tier wants to multiplex resources used by stateful components, keeping these resources at work. Phoenix/APP, because it captures application state at arbitrary points, allows stateful components to be passivated and the physical resources they held, e.g. process or thread, to be reused by another application at any time.
- **Load Balancing**: With a clustered server, Phoenix/APP enables stateful components to transparently failover from one machine to another, again at arbitrary execution points. So, if stateful components are running on machine A, the state for these components can be captured in the log on a shared disk. If the system or an administrator notices that machine A is overloaded, some stateful components on A can be passivated and then failover to machine B. That is, their state is recovered and the runtime updated to redirect subsequent calls for these components to Machine B.
- **Debugging**: Phoenix/APP uses a log to capture component state by recording the sequence of events that produce the state. Hence, when a system fails, the log contains the precise set of events leading to the failure. If there is a hard failure caused by the component, the failed state can be re-created. This facilitates debugging, which has been notoriously difficult in distributed systems. Even when the failure is soft (a heisenbug), the log can offer clues as to what went wrong.

---

1 For middle tier applications, the majority of response time is interactions with remote components, or resource managers. During recovery, Phoenix/APP replaces these interactions with their logged effects. Hence replay is much faster than original execution, further enhancing system availability.

---

2 A Gartner Group study reports that 60% of unplanned downtime in commercial systems is due to application failure [14], and 90% of errors leading to failure in production-quality code were transient "heisenbugs".

- **Programmatic response to transaction failures**: Stateless applications are not easily able to respond to transaction aborts. By definition, they have no interesting state between transactions. So reporting and responding to transaction aborts has been cumbersome. Because Phoenix/APP enables the persistence of stateful applications, such applications can respond to transaction aborts in a straightforward way, e.g., re-executing them, executing alternative logic, or reporting the error.

2. Background

2.1 Computational Model

A middle tier application is composed of a collection of components. We require that each component be piecewise deterministic (PWD), i.e., its computation is deterministic between successive messages from other components. This enables the deterministic replay of the component from an earlier saved state when the original messages are fed to it, resending the same messages to other components as were sent in the original execution, and producing the same end state.

A component can be made PWD by eliminating non-determinism from its execution. We identify and remove three types of non-determinism:

1. A multi-threaded component may access shared data in a non-deterministic order. We assume components are single-threaded and that multiple components access common data only in a data server, where non-determinism is removed by the server logging the interleaved accesses to the data.
2. A component may depend on non-repeatable events such as asynchronous messages, system clock or external interrupts. These are recorded on the log to guarantee deterministic replay.
3. A recovered component usually exploits different system elements, e.g. threads, message ids, etc. than in its original execution. To cope with this, we "virtualize" underlying resources, introducing logical ids for messages, component instances, etc., and log the mapping to the physical elements.

Phoenix/APP logs asynchronous events and the logical to physical mapping of system elements. And we require data access in middle tier applications to be via a data server. These restrictions ensure that our components are PWD.

We further assume that failures are (i) soft, i.e., no damage to stable storage so that logged records are available after a failure, (ii) fail-stop [24] so that only correct information is logged and erroneous output does not reach users or persistent databases, and (iii) the fault is caused by a Heisenbug [13]), to avoid recreation of a failure producing state.

2.2 Components, Interactions and Guarantees

Phoenix/APP transparently provides the recovery contracts of [7] to make components persistent. We describe these contracts here. However, a multi-tier application is rarely composed solely of persistent components. So, we also describe contracts for other components in their interactions with persistent components.

An interaction contract specifies the joint behavior of two interacting components in the presence of failures of one or both components. It requires each component to make guarantees, the exact form of which depend on the nature of the contract and the roles of the components. Interaction contract guarantees pertain to a mutual state transition resulting from the interaction.

Interaction contracts between component pairs are combined into a system-wide recovery constitution that provides guarantees to external users. Our recovery constitution allows arbitrary asynchronous interactions between persistent components. However, we require that external components only interact with persistent components, and transactional components only reply to persistent components.

Inability to mask failures can occur only with a failure during an external interaction. This is unavoidable without special hardware support, e.g., if an ATM for dispensing cash with a mechanical counter that records when money is dispensed, then output messages (e.g., cash) are guaranteed to be delivered exactly once.

2.3 Interaction Types

There are different contract types, depending on the type of components involved.

2.3.1 Persistent-Persistent Interactions When persistent components interact with each other, they must ensure the persistence of both state and message. A committed interaction contract is used and is fundamental to making applications persistent and masking failures.

A committed interaction contract ensures that an interaction, once it occurs, will become part of the history of both the sender and receiver of a message. It requires the sender repeatedly send the message until it knows the receiver has received it, and that the receiver eliminate any duplicate sent messages. Further, both components guarantee that their state will persist across a system failure. Finally they must agree as to how each component deals with the message being exchanged and how the obligation to resend the message is released. The exact specification of this contract is given in [7].

The sender exposes its current state and doesn't know the implications on other components or, ultimately, external users, that could (transitively) result from subsequent receiver execution. Thus the sender must ensure that its state transition is persistent when it initiates the interaction, by forced logging if there is nondeterminism that needs to be captured. Only when the receiver later becomes a sender does it need to ensure the persistence of the effects of the received message on its state. Before this, receiver forced logging is not required. When a receiver releases the sender from its contract, the sender can discard the interaction data while still guaranteeing the persistence of its own state as of interaction time.

With a committed interaction, forced logging is needed only if there are non-deterministic events not yet on the stable log of a component. If not, then forcing is not required to make the interaction persistent via replay.

2.3.2 Persistent-External Interactions External components are, by definition, outside of the part of the system in which we provide our service. Our intent is to come as close as possible to providing immediately committed interactions with external components, including users. This leads us to external interaction contracts.

An external interaction contract is between a persistent component that subscribes to the rules for an immediately committed interaction, and an external component, which does not. The persistent component must immediately log input received from an external component. And when it sends a message to an external component, it must be prepared to resend until it receives an indication the external component has received it. Because a persistent component can crash during this interaction, it may be necessary for:

- External component to resend an input message, but such a resend cannot be guaranteed.
- Persistent component to resend an output message, since it may not be sure the message arrived. But the external component is not guaranteed to eliminate duplicate messages.

Thus, a failure during an interaction may not be masked. However, in the absence of a failure during the interaction, the result is like a committed interaction, masking failures from external components.

2.3.3 Persistent-Transactional Interactions Interactions with a transactional component, e.g. a data server, are solely request/reply interactions, and they are not guaranteed to complete. A transactional component might abort and forget the transaction. There is also a risk that a transactional data server's final reply might not be delivered even though the transaction commits.

We require more. Our requirements are described in a transactional interaction contract between a persistent component and a transactional component. A transactional interaction contract requires a transactional component to guarantee an atomic state transition (either committing or aborting) and a faithful and persistent message describing a commit outcome. An abort can be reported with either an explicit message or with the transactional component indicating "no memory" of the transaction, which the persistent component interprets as an abort.

With this background for our work in place, we present our design and implementation of Phoenix/APP in the following section.

3. Phoenix/APP Implementation

Our Phoenix/APP prototype implements the recovery guarantees of [7]. It is built as a runtime service on Microsoft's .NET infrastructure. In this section we first present an overview of the architectural setting for a persistent stateful application. This is followed by a description of .NET runtime services. Then we describe how a Phoenix/APP enabled application operates, both during normal execution and failure recovery to illustrate the end-to-end persistence story.

3.1 Persistent Application Architecture

Each stateful component of an application lives in a context. Contexts define a boundary at which calls for component creation and all subsequent method calls and associated responses can be intercepted. There are four main elements to providing persistent components in Phoenix/APP:

1. Interception at the context boundary is handled by the .NET interceptor, which captures all events and method calls crossing the context. Depending on the event type, the interceptor passes the call to the appropriate Phoenix/APP module, described below, before processing.
2. Logging is handled by the Log Manager (LM);
3. Error detection and masking is handled by the Error Handler (EH);
4. Component recovery and runtime update is handled by the Recovery Manager (RM);

Figure 1 illustrates the relationship of these elements to an application running on .NET using Phoenix/APP. We illustrate the client and server in different processes, which can be on the same or different machine. The highlighted boxes in Fig 1 are code modules we supply to implement Phoenix/APP, specifically one Error Handler (EH) module, one Recovery Manager (RM) module, and one Log Manager (LM) module per process.

When the runtime intercepts an event it calls the appropriate Phoenix/APP module for method call logging or error handling, as detailed in following sections.

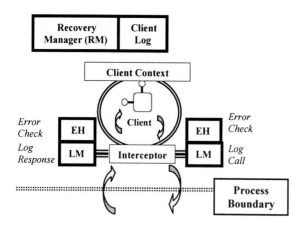

Figure 1 – Simplified overview of Phoenix/APP

3.2 Runtime Services in .NET

.NET is a runtime infrastructure for component-based software. It provides a set of runtime services to make building scalable distributed systems easier [18][3]. .NET stores the information it needs to provide runtime services in each component's context. A context is a set of properties, maintained by the .NET runtime, that describe what is required for the correct operation of a component. If a class requires a service, .NET makes sure that class instances reside in a context that provides the service. For example, if a class requires a transaction for method calls, .NET puts each class instance in a context that will provide a transaction for the component.

.NET provides services to components at runtime via interception. At component creation, .NET creates an interceptor that wraps the component's interface and contains the .NET "property" logic to provide services at runtime. When a component in one context calls a component in another context, the interceptor captures the call and processes it through a series of message sinks (see Figure 2) allowing the runtime to execute any attached property logic before forwarding the call. Runtime services like transaction management, just-in-time activation, security, object pooling, etc., are implemented as properties attached to message sinks to be called by the interceptor.

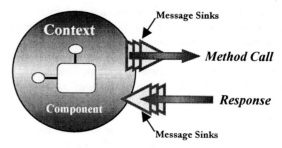

Figure 2 – Contexts and Interception

A developer specifies a runtime service by setting a declarative attribute on a class. Each service defines one or more declarative attributes that are used to control its behavior. When an object of the class is instantiated, the component creation interceptor examines the service requirements, as expressed by the class's declarative attribute values and ensures that the new component is created in a context that provides the specified runtime services. Subsequently, interceptors examine calls and provide the appropriate services for the component. The same general process applies to all services in .NET. There are no new APIs to learn, no complex code to obscure application logic, just attributes to select. Application programmers write business logic; the runtime provides the services.

3.3 Phoenix/APP as a Runtime Service

To describe our implementation of Phoenix/APP as a .NET runtime service we describe the creation of a component and follow a request from client (caller) to server (callee) and back, including error handling and recovery actions that would take place if a failure were to occur. Although we refer to clients and servers, any component can be a client, a server, or both.

Component Creation: Each stateful component lives it its own context. To make a component persistent, a developer simply declares its class as PERSISTENT, as illustrated in Figure 3. The class MarketBasket is specified to be persistent – all instances of MarketBasket will be created in contexts that provide persistence functionality.

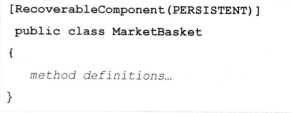

```
[RecoverableComponent(PERSISTENT)]

public class MarketBasket

{

    method definitions...

}
```

Figure 3 – Attribute declaring a class PERSISTENT.

---

[3] .NET runtime services were previously referred to as COM⁺ services.

The creation call (ConstructionCallMessage) for any component specified to be PERSISTENT is intercepted. The PERSISTENT property construction code called by the interceptor generates a logical identifier (LogicalID) for the instance and calls the log manager to log the creation information. The logical identifier is a string that uniquely identifies the component and encodes information useful for locating it. Component creation need not be force logged, as the component has not yet "committed" its state.

The constructor for PERSISTENT components adds a client message sink and server message sink to the context. The client message sink intercepts messages when the component acts as a client; the server message sink intercepts messages when the component acts as a server. All calls go through this chain of message sinks when they enter or exit a context and we attach our code to this chain. Our property code will extract information from each message, log it, and check for exceptions indicating component failure. The client message sink also generates a unique request id for each method call of the component and attaches the LogicalID of the component to the message so the server knows with whom it is talking.

Client sends request: During a method call the client property code will log all information pertaining to the call, including the client identity (LogicalID), server identity (LogicalID), method identity, along with the method arguments. Each method call is stamped with a new request identifier (requestID). The client identity and method identity are passed to the server side property using a call buffer, which is an out-of-band way of passing information between components.

Server receives request: Upon receiving a method call, the server property first checks if the call is a duplicate request and, if not, it records the call and passes it on for normal processing. The server property code maintains an in-memory list of the last call from every client and the response (if any) that was returned precisely to enable checking for duplicates.

Server sends response: The server property code intercepts the return and records the message in the in-memory list, force logging the response before passing the result on to the client. This makes the last call list persistent, i.e. changes to the list are logged and reconstructed when recovery takes place. When a server receives a method call after a failure, it can detect if the call is a duplicate and act appropriately.

Client receives response: The client property code intercepts the response to the original method call and logs the response before passing on the result message to the application.

Error detection and interception: Phoenix/APP detects errors resulting from component failure, masks the error from the application and initiates recovery. An error handler (EH) stub is built into the runtime and is called by the interceptor whenever an error is detected on an attempted method call or response delivery. Our EH code first determines if the error is the result of component failure, and if so it collects all information pertaining to the failed component and calls a local Recovery Manager (RM) to initiate recovery. If recovery is successful the RM returns a new reference for the recovered component to the EH. The EH updates the runtime so that subsequent calls to the failed component are redirected to the recovered instance. The EH then returns control to the runtime for normal method processing.

Automatic component recovery: At a high level, the recovery manager (RM) is given a component's LogicalID and returns a reincarnated version of that component. The RM creates a new instance of the failed component based on the log record containing ConstructionCallMessage and replays the creation call. The RM then reinstalls state into the recreated component by scanning the log and replaying method calls associated with the failed component. The RM intercepts all actions involving method invocation and response, or other non-deterministic events; the relevant information is reconstructed from the corresponding log entry and fed to the component instead of re-executing the event. Outgoing messages that the recipient is known to have successfully and stably received prior to failure are suppressed. However, if this cannot be determined (e.g. the message is the last one and a reply has not been received), the message is re-sent, and the receiver must test for duplicates. Recovery completion brings the component state up to the point of the last logged interaction (i.e. right before the failure occurred).

The RM is optimized to support concurrent recovery for multiple components. The LM will first perform a log scan for all records pertaining to the failed component and return an in-memory structure to the RM, without blocking read/write access to the log. Upon receiving the in-memory structure of log records the RM will initiate redo-recovery playback using thread safe code, enabling other concurrent threads to perform recovery for other failed components. The RM maintains a list of components (by logical ID) currently being recovered to avoid servicing multiple requests to recover a failed component.

Retransmission of messages: Because Phoenix/APP retransmits messages across crashes, and because the information needed for the recipient to eliminate duplicate messages is persistent, Phoenix/APP provides persistent exactly-once message delivery.

Unmasking Errors: An error resulting from a failure is unmasked when the error handler determines that a failed component cannot be successfully recovered. This should be rare, but in the event a component repeatedly fails without making forward progress (i.e., a Bohr bug) or the Recovery Manager is unable to recreate the component (i.e., system on which the component resides is dead), the error handler unmasks the error by propagating a message to the application.

Recovery Service: All applications running on .NET are "hosted", which means to execute an application the systems administrator must submit a start string containing the .DLL or .EXE to execute, along with a port number for communications and associated URI (universal resource identifier). The .NET execution manager will load the .DLL or .EXE, then listen for requests (method calls) for the given URI over the specified port number.

In addition to a recovery manager, our implementation of Phoenix/APP includes a recovery service that monitors hosted applications which contain recoverable components. When a hosted application creates a persistent component, Phoenix/APP will send a message to the recovery service to register the application for monitoring and record its restart string, consisting of the .EXE or .DLL, port number and URI. The recovery service will monitor Windows events and if it detects the process running the application has terminated abnormally it will automatically restart the application using the restart string and issue a request to the recovery manager to initiate recovery on all stateful components. As a Windows runtime service, the recovery service is automatically started when the system reboots so if the system itself failed the recovery service will be restarted at reboot and initiate recovery all active applications.

4. Phoenix/APP Performance

We had two objectives in our performance evaluation of Phoenix/APP:

(i) to measure the overhead to persist stateful component interactions and its impact on application response time;
(ii) to measure how fast Phoenix/APP can recover the persistent components of a stateful application after a failure and reestablish normal application operation.

To conduct this evaluation we implemented a test program and designed controlled experiments.

4.1 Micro-benchmarks

We performed our measurements using a simple distributed application that sends book order requests of varying sizes to a middle tier server and receives responses back from the server. This application is illustrated below in Figure 4. The middle tier server maintains a shopping basket of orders for the client and communicates with two backend servers which maintain

inventory and order requests. We used two versions of this distributed application.

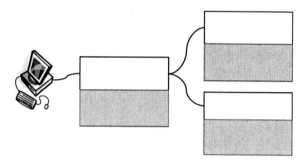

Figure 4 – Illustration of the book buyer application used in the performance evaluation of Phoenix/APP.

Our baseline system is a non-recoverable implementation of this application with volatile state. If a failure occurs in any process during a session then messages, data and state are lost as a result of the crash. In particular, the shopping basket maintained at the middle tier is lost, as are orders placed at backend bookstore servers. We compared this baseline system with a fully persistent and recoverable implementation, built using the Phoenix/APP runtime service by simply declaring selected classes as "persistent".

Both versions of the application are implemented using Microsoft's .NET platform and components are linked to .NET runtime services (i.e. inherit from the class "managed component"). Hence, by comparing round-trip request/response times between client and middle tier, we get an accurate picture of the latency caused by making an application persistent using Phoenix/APP.

4.2 Environment

We ran our benchmark on two Intel-based PC's, each a 795 MHz Pentium III CPU with 256 Megabytes of memory. The systems are connected via a switched 100 Base-T network, using an Intel Express 10/100 Fast Ethernet Switch. The client and middle tier (price shopper) processes run on separate machines.

Because the client and server are located on the same local area network (LAN), the relative overheads we present greatly overstate what a typical client would experience in a real deployment of Phoenix/APP. In a more conventional setting, where client and server connect over a wide area network, the latency for a request/response would be orders of magnitude higher, resulting in lower relative latency impact for Phoenix/APP. However, this experimental set-up still gives us an indication of logging overheads at the server and the time required to recover a stateful session, which is the focus for this discussion.

4.3   Results

Table 1 shows the results of our benchmark runs measuring the request/response cycle for each of our two test systems, averaged over 1000 trials. Each request message is roughly 240 bytes after marshalling for transfer. For reference, we also show the round-trip time to send a remote procedure call of the same size from the client to the middle tier server and back.

Table 1: Elapsed time (msecs) to process request (book order) and response between client and server.

A. Elapsed Time for Native Implementation	**3.34 msecs**
B. Elapsed Time for Phoenix/APP	**7.39 msecs**
C. Elapsed Time for RPC	**2.42 msecs**
D. Difference (B-A)	**4.05 msecs**

Table 1 shows that the Phoenix/APP based implementation of the application requires approximately four additional milliseconds to complete the request/response cycle over the non-recoverable implementation. This overhead is due largely to the time required to force write records to the log. The latency introduced by the logging is approximately half the rotation time of our 7200 rpm disk. While that latency is significant relative to LAN latencies, in a wide area network implementation where network latencies are closer to 200 milliseconds than the 2.42 milliseconds measured on our LAN, this latency is a small fraction (about 2%) of the request/response round trip time.

Next, we measured the time required to recover the persistent components of the middle tier application that manage the shopping basket. To conduct this experiment we submitted book order requests from the client to the middle tier to the server. We "crashed" the "Price Shopper" application by issuing the command "end task" from the Windows Task Manager, terminating the process running the middle tier. We then issued a request from the client to display the contents of the shopping basket. At this point the client application is left waiting for the middle tier server to respond to this request. The Phoenix/APP runtime service on the client intercepted the error message resulting from the failed RPC and initiated recovery of the middle tier application running on the server. We measured the time required for Phoenix/APP to recover the stateful components in the session and respond to the outstanding client request.

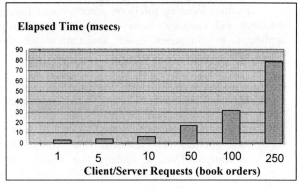

Time to Recover Middle Tier Price Shopper Shopping Basket Component

Figure 5: Elapsed time to recover a component.

Figure 5 presents results of the experiment to recover the middle tier application for a varying number of logged request/response messages. When the recovery request is received by the server, the Phoenix/APP runtime recreates the stateful components and replays all logged method calls against these components to reinstall application state. When only one order was received prior to failure, it required 3.16 milliseconds to recover the application and respond to the outstanding client request. An examination of this base case revealed that 2.41 milliseconds were spent sending the recovery request from the client machine to the server and the remaining 0.7 milliseconds were spent recreating components representing the market basket and replaying the logged method call. Since each method is replayed as an intraprocess function call, avoiding the cost of a RPC and cross process call, component state recovery is quite fast. As expected, as the number of logged method calls increases the time required to recover the application and respond to the outstanding client request increases. However, the average cost per logged interaction declines, approaching .3 milliseconds. This reflects high sequential read performance from our log disk and very small computational load for recovery.

6. Related Work

Recoverability for communicating processes has been studied in the fault-tolerance community (e.g., [1,10,11]), but the main focus has been long-running computations (e.g., scientific applications). The goal has been to avoid a failure losing too much work and failures have usually not been masked from users. Masking failures has required "pessimistic logging" (see, e.g., [16]), with log forcing for both sender and receiver upon every message exchange. Earlier, process checkpointing (i.e., copying process state to disk) upon every interaction, was used in the pioneering fault-tolerant systems of the early eighties [2, 8, 17].

Techniques focusing solely on process-based failure detection and recovery, however, are not necessarily applicable to component-based applications for the following reasons:

- *Overly coarse granularity:* A process may contain several active components. If individual components fail, e.g., due to a crash or abnormal termination, a process may not terminate. More importantly, it may not be possible to resurrect the components independently. Thus, a strategy that detects only process failures cannot deal with redeployment of the finer-grained components.

- *Inability to restore component relationships:* Components communicate with other components and identify them via component identifiers. When a failed component is recovered, identifiers for the failed component held by other components must be remapped to the recovered component. Restoring these "relationships" is unique to distributed component middleware and is not handled well by process-based recovery strategies.

- *Restriction on process checkpointing and recovery:* Components often maintain state that must be checkpointed periodically to survive crash failures. Process checkpointing may incur excessive overhead or be unable to checkpoint the state for individual components. Thus, a finer granularity for persisting state is needed to permit components in a process to checkpoint their state independently of each other, and at arbitrary times.

Hence, it is necessary to have strategies specifically tuned to component-based distributed applications. The most successful prior approach uses queued transactions and in OLTP [15, 3], supported by most TP monitors, e.g., MQ Series, Tuxedo, MTS. This is the stateless application paradigm that requires transactions to enqueue a client request on a queue; to dequeue it, process and enqueue the reply; and to dequeue the reply at the client. This incurs forced-logging for three commits. It requires significant effort to implement applications in this stateless paradigm.

Some work on failure masking for stateful applications exists, but is limited in the architectures that it can support [20].

Fault tolerance is being discussed for component middleware like CORBA [23] and EJB, but that focus is also on service availability for stateless applications (i.e., restarting re-initialized application server processes). Products (e.g., BEA WebLogic, or Sun's J2EE suite) support failover techniques that do not relieve the application programmer from having to either code

failure handling logic or structure his application as "stateless", and are not geared for masking process or message failures to users. More recently, failover techniques for web servers have been presented [21], based on application-transparent replication and redirection of http requests.

The need for execution guarantees for e-services has been raised by a number of researchers (e.g., [25, 22]), but they have been concerned with specific applications such as payment protocols or mobile data exchange and do not specifically address system-wide failure masking in general multi-tier architectures. Closest to our approach in terms of objectives is the work in [12] that presents a multi-tier protocol for exactly-once transaction execution based on asynchronous message replication and a distributed consensus protocol. However, this work focuses on stateless application servers and does not address the autonomy requirements of components and logging optimization.

Prior work on user-transparent database application recovery was restricted to applications embedded in the data server such as stored procedures [19] and two-tier client-server systems [20, 4, 5]. A key difference between a client and an application server is that clients are trivially piecewise deterministic, while application servers typically are multi-threaded and asynchronously receive messages. It is not obvious how to extend client-server protocols. Our interaction contract is the key for the generalization to multi-tier systems.

The recovery guarantees framework [7] upon which Phoenix/APP is based improves the state of the art in a number of ways. Compared to traditional techniques based on pessimistic logging or frequent process state saving, these protocols reduce logging and state saving costs while providing very fast recovery. Our approach can handle stateful applications, removing the burden to the application programmer of making his application stateless. It can be extended to deal with clients interacting with browsers [6], enabling browser state persistence.

7. Summary

Writing distributed component-based applications that reliably manage persistent state requires application programmers to address a host of difficult issues, such as carefully logging application state, masking errors resulting from the failure, ensuring consistent recovery for various component types, ensuring exactly once-message delivery, etc.

Phoenix/APP automatically recovers component-based applications, without requiring any special modifications to the application. This increases application availability by avoiding the extended down-time that failures can produce when manual intervention is needed to correct failed application state and restart the application.

Because Phoenix/APP transparently handles stateful applications, it removes the burden on the application programmer of making his application stateless. This substantially improves application programmer productivity and reduces the complexity of the resulting program, a side effect of which should be to reduce the number of programming errors.

In this paper we presented the design, implementation and evaluation of Phoenix/APP, our runtime service based on the notion of recovery guarantees. Our prototype is built on the .NET middleware framework that supports extensible interception, which we use to insert our logging, error handling and recovery extensions. We confirmed the feasibility of Phoenix/APP by presenting performance results on the cost to persist component state and recover from failures.

While our implementation is built on the .NET platform, the techniques described are more widely relevant. For example, the approach has been extended to deal with clients interacting with internet browsers [6], enabling browser state persistence. Moreover, functionality similar to .NET is available in both J2EE and CORBA [23] runtime environments. Thus, our general approach should be widely relevant.

8. References

[1] L. Alvisi, K. Marzullo: Message Logging: Pessimistic, Optimistic, and Causal. Int'l Conf. on Distributed Computing Systems, 1995.

[2] J.F. Bartlett: A NonStop Kernel. SOSP 1981.

[3] P. Bernstein, M. Hsu, B. Mann: Implementing Recoverable Requests Using Queues. SIGMOD 1990.

[4] R. Barga, D. Lomet, S. Agrawal: Persistent Client-Server Database Sessions. EDBT 2000.

[5] R. Barga, D. Lomet: Measuring and Optimizing a System for Persistent Database Sessions. ICDE 2001.

[6] R. Barga, D. Lomet, G. Shegalov G. Weikum: Recovery Guarantees for Internet Applications. Submitted for publication (2003).

[7] R. Barga, D. Lomet, and G. Weikum, Recovery Guarantees for General Multi-Tier Applications. ICDE 2002.

[8] A. Borg, W. Blau, W. Graetsch, F. Herrmann, W. Oberle: Fault Tolerance under UNIX. ACM TOCS, 7(1), 1989.

[9] Enterprise JavaBeans Technology, http://java.sun.com/products/ejb/.

[10] E.N. Elnozahy, D.B. Johnson, Y.M. Wang: A Survey of Rollback-Recovery Protocols in Message-Passing Systems. Technical Report, Carnegie-Mellon University, 1996.

[11] J. C. Freytag, F. Cristian, B. Kähler: Masking System Crashes in Database Application Programs, in the proceedings of VLDB 1987.

[12] S. Frolund and R. Guerraoui: Implementing E-transactions with Asynchronous Replication, in the proceedings of Int'l Conf. on Dependable Systems and Networks, 2000.

[13] J. Gray, Why Do Computers Fail and What Can We Do About It. 5th Symposium on Reliability in Distributed Software and Database Systems, 1986.

[14] Gartner Group Publication: The Zero Latency Enterprise. Roy Schulte, VP of Applications Systems and Middleware, 1999.

[15] J. Gray, A. Reuter: Transaction Processing: Concepts and Techniques. Morgan Kaufmann, 1993.

[16] Y. Huang, Y-M. Wang: Why Optimistic Message Logging Has Not Been Used In Telecommunications Systems. FTCS 1995.

[17] W. Kim: Highly Available Systems for Database Applications. ACM Computing Surveys, 16(1), 1984.

[18] M. Kirtland: Object-Oriented Software Development Made Simple with COM+ Runtime Services. *Microsoft Systems Journal*, 12, Nov. 1997.

[19] D. Lomet: Persistent Applications Using Generalized Redo Recovery. ICDE 1998.

[20] D. Lomet, G. Weikum: Efficient Transparent Application Recovery in Client-Server Information Systems. SIGMOD 1998.

[21] M.-Y. Luo, C.-S. Yang: Constructing Zero-Loss Web Services. IEEE International Conference on Computer Communications (INFOCOM) 2001.

[22] C.P. Martin, K. Ramamritham: Guaranteeing Recoverability in Electronic Commerce, 3rd Int'l Workshop on Advanced issues of E-Commerce and Web-Based Information Systems, 2001.

[23] Object Management Group: Fault Tolerant CORBA, http://cgi.omg.org/cgi-bin/doc?ptc/00-04-04/

[24] F. Schneider. Byzantine Generals in Action: Implementing Fail-Stop Processors. ACM TOCS, 2(2), May 1984.

[25] J. D. Tygar: Atomicity versus Anonymity – Distributed Transactions for Electronic Commerce, in the proceedings of VLDB 1998.

Implementation Issues of a Deterministic Transformation System for Structured Document Query Optimization

Dunren Che
Department of Computer Science
Southern Illinois University
Carbondale, IL 62901, USA
dche@cs.siu.edu

Abstract

As the popularity of XML keeps growing rapidly, XML compliant structured document management becomes an interesting and compelling research area. Query optimization for structured documents stands out as a very challenging issue because of the much enlarged optimization (search) space, which is a consequence of the intrinsic complexity of the underlying data model of structured documents. We therefore propose to apply deterministic transformations on query expressions to most aggressively control the search space and fast achieve a sufficiently improved alternative (if not the optimal) for each incoming query expression. This idea is not just exciting but practically attainable. This paper first provides an overview of our optimization strategy, and then focuses on the implementation issues of our transformation system for structured document query optimization.

1. Introduction

Because of the rapidly growing popularity of XML, the management of structured documents, especially XML compliant structured documents, is now a very interesting and practical research issue. XML data is essentially semistructured and distinct from conventional data, e.g., relational data and object-oriented data, which gained successful management functionality from RDBMS and OODBMS. It has been strongly believed that XML document/data should benefit from the same type of management functionalities as conventional data benefits from RDBMS/OODBMS.

In recent years, almost all kinds of storage schemes have been proposed, e.g., mapping XML data to relational [13, 14, 31, 4] or object-relational models [19, 33], using special-purpose databases such as semistructured databases

[23], or even native XML databases. Query processing is yet another, probably more challenging issue because of the much enlarged optimization space. With regard to query processing for structured documents, a lot of work has been done on developing efficient processing algorithms [12, 23, 16, 22, 18, 10, 32] and appropriate indexing schemes [22, 5, 25, 17, 6]. Relatively, only a little work has been reported that focuses on specialized techniques for structured-document query optimization.

In [8], we proposed to use equivalence-based algebraic transformations on XML query optimization. We have identified a large number of equivalences and transformation rules [8, 9] exploiting the DTD constraints, the structural properties of XML documents, and potential indices. One striking feature of our approach is *deterministic* transformation, which in our setting is not just an exciting idea but practically attainable. Our goal is to quickly obtain a much improved alternative (if not the optimal) for each input query expression. This idea fits well with the dynamic nature of web-hooked applications, which are the major applications now asking for highly efficient document management and querying functionalities. This paper mainly focuses on the implementation issues of our deterministic transformation strategy for query optimization in a structured document database environment.

Related work. With regard to structured document database management, a lot of work has been done focusing on storage modeling, e.g., [1, 29, 28, 20, 34, 11, 7, 26, 27, 15, 13, 14, 31, 4, 19, 33], indexing [22, 5, 25, 17, 6], and algorithms [12, 23, 16, 22, 18, 10, 32] for supporting regular path processing. To the best of our knowledge, there is no reported work that is really closely related with ours, i.e., focuses on algebraic transformation for query optimization by exploiting DTD knowledge, structural properties of documents, and other heuristics. In the following, we briefly review some work that might be conceived as generally related.

Lore [23, 24] is a DBMS originally designed for semistructured data and later migrated to XML-based data model. Lore has a fully-implemented cost-based query optimizer that transforms a query into a logical query plan, and then explores the (exponential) space of possible physical plans looking for the one with least estimated cost. Lore is well known by its DataGuide path index that together with stored statistics describing the "shape" of the database provides the structural knowledge about the data to help Lore's optimizer prune its search space for a better plan. In this sense, Lore is related to our work, but we capture the structural knowledge of document data mainly from its DTD and apply this knowledge to conduct exclusively deterministic transformations on query expressions.

We are aware of another piece of work reported that deals with query optimization by using the document type definition knowledge. In [11], Consens and Milo replace a query-algebra operator with a cheaper one whenever the DTD allows that. The DTDs considered in that study are simpler than the ones of SGML/XML, and in contrast to our work the authors do not look at the different grammar constructors. The optimization in [11] also makes use of a special cost model and the results are thus not directly transferable to our application scenario. In contrast, the contribution of our work is the independence of a specific data model and of a specific cost model. Our approach is strongly heuristics-based.

In [12] a comparable strategy for exploiting a grammar specification for optimizing queries on semistructured data is studied in a similar setting – where efforts were made on how to make complete use of the available grammar to expand a given query. Our focus is different. We identify transformations that introduce improvements on query expressions in a very goal-oriented manner. Other generally related work includes [28, 20, 34, 11, 7, 26, 27].

The remainder of this paper is organized as follows. Section 2 provides preliminaries and sets context for subsequent discussion. Section 3 addresses the major implementation issues and presents corresponding algorithms adopted in our system. Section 4 shows a little flavor of our deterministic transformation by giving a few transformation examples. Section 5 concludes the discussion of this paper.

2. Preliminaries

This paper addresses the implementation issues of our structured document query optimizer. To make this paper self-contained, we provide this section for introducing background knowledge, including notions about DTD, our optimization algebra - the PAT algebra, an overview of our deterministic optimization strategy, and the six key semantic transformation rules.

2.1. DTD notions

The documents we target at in our system are SGML/XML compliant structured documents. For a given class of documents, the legal markup tags (i.e., entity or element types) are defined in document type definition (DTD). Thus a DTD is the grammar for a class of documents. The content model of each entity describes the composition structure of that entity and is normally defined using the following production:

$$c \rightarrow \; <\text{etn}> \; | \; c_1, c_2 \; | \; c_1 | c_2 \; | \; c_1 \& c_2 \; | \; c_1? \; | \; c_1^* \; | \; c_1^+ \; | \; (c_1)$$

etn stands for element-type-name. Using SGML terminology, the comma is the sequence connector (SEQ) or a SEQ-node if the term is seen as a tree; "|" is the OR-connector (OR) or an OR-node; "?" is the optional occurrence indicator; "*" is the optional-and-repeatable occurrence indicator.

A DTD is usually a graph structure, which plays an import role in our implementation. So, we give a more formal definition of it below.

Definition 2.1 (DTD graph) *The DTD graph of a specific DTD is a directed graph $G = (V, K)$. Its vertices are the names of the element types from the DTD, and each etn occurs only once. An edge (ET_i, ET_j) in K indicates that ET_j occurs in the content model of ET_i. $RT \in V$ is the root element type of the DTD.*

If element type ET_j occurs in the content model of ET_i, we may say that ET_j is *internal* to ET_i and ET_i is *external* to ET_j. The *internal* and *external* terminologies here introduced understandably extend to the instance level of the element types as well.

By means of a *DTD graph*, we can visualize some important relationships induced by a DTD, such as the *contained-in/contains* relationships among document elements. The general containment relationship (either directly or indirectly) between document elements is actually determined by the content models of the corresponding element types in the DTD.

A path in a DTD graph is another important notion used in our system, and is defined as below.

Definition 2.2 (Path in a DTD graph) *A path in a DTD graph G, is a sequence of element types $(ET_i, ..., ET_j)$ s.t. ET_k directly contains ET_{k+1}, $i \leq k < j$. The reverse of this sequence is called a reverse path with regard to the original one.*

In the sequel, when not necessary we may not need to differentiate a reverse path from an ordinary path and refer to either one between two element types E1 and E2 as $path(E1, E2)$.

2.2. The PAT algebra

Our optimization strategy is based on the PAT algebra, which is originally designed as an algebra for searching structured documents [30]. We adopted it as our optimization algebra and extended it according to the features of SGML/XML compliant documents. The PAT algebra is *set* oriented, in the sense that each PAT algebra operator and each PAT expression evaluate to a *set* of document elements. A complete version of the extended PAT algebra has been described in [2]. Herein we focus on only a restricted version, which is sufficient to serve the purpose of this paper.

A query expression conforming to the PAT algebra is generated according to the following grammar:

$$E ::= etn \mid E1 \cup E2 \mid E1 \cap E2 \mid E1 - E2 \mid \sigma_r(E)$$
$$\mid \sigma_{A,r}(E) \mid E1 \subset E2 \mid E1 \supset E2 \mid (E)$$

"E" (as well "E1" and "E2") generally stands for a PAT expression, etn introduces a document element type name, "r" is a regular expression representing a matching condition on the textual content of the document elements, and "A" designates an attribute of the document elements.

$\cup$, $\cap$ and $-$ are the standard set operators, union, intersection and difference. $\sigma_r(E)$ takes a set of elements and returns those whose content matches the regular expression r, while $\sigma_{A,r}(E)$ takes a set of elements and returns those whose value of attribute A matches the regular expression r. Operator $\subset$ returns all elements of the first argument that are contained in an element of the second argument, while $\supset$ returns all elements of the first argument that contain an element of the second argument.

In the remainder of this paper, we will not intentionally distinguish an element type from an element type name when confusion is not anticipated. Furthermore, we may simply use etn to refer to an element type name for compactness.

More precisely, the semantics of the PAT algebra can be given by using two (partial) functions, $type : \mathcal{P} \rightarrow ETN$ and $ext : \mathcal{P} \rightarrow \mathcal{E}$, where $\mathcal{P}$ is the set of PAT expressions, ETN is the set of element types names (and thus element types) in a document database, and $\mathcal{E}$ is the set of all elements in the document database.

The following corollary holds for our PAT algebra:

Corollary 2.1 *Each expression, say E, evaluates to a set of document elements of a single type, namely $type(E)$.*

Consequently, we will refer to the result type of a PAT expression, e.g., E, by $type(E)$.

2.3. Stategy overview

In this subsection we provide a brief overview of our optimization strategy, which is detailed in [8, 9].

Ever since the beginning of this research, we envisioned a typical scenario of the use of our query optimizer – as a backend support for large document servers hooked on the web. Therefore, the *efficiency* of the query optimizer itself is of extreme importance. Furthermore, because the intrinsic data model of structured documents is complex, the underlying optimization algebra contains many operators as compared with the relational algebra. This complexity means that we have to crawl in a much enlarged search space for optimal plans when we apply a transformation-based approach to the query optimization. Traditional heuristics-based and cost-based approaches are inappropriate in this scenario simply because we cannot afford the time needed by these time-consuming approaches when confronted with a very big search space. Therefore, we proposed to pursue the heuristics-based approach at its extreme by applying exclusively *deterministic* transformations. In other words, our optimizer does not produce and evaluate different alternatives, but runs after only convinced improvement stepwise on input query expressions via each transformation performed.

We have identified totally 46 generic equivalences, including set-oriented algebraic equivalences and document-structure based semantic equivalences. These equivalences are *generic* because we introduced generic operation symbols for compactness of description, e.g., $\supsetneq$ stands for either $\subset$ or $\supset$. Equivalences are not directly useful according to our strategy because we do not evaluate different alternatives. However, based upon these equivalences we derived 62 *generic* deterministic transformation rules, which translate into 98 instantiated transformation rules.

To efficiently direct deterministic transformation, the whole optimization process in our system is organized as three transformation phases: *normalization, semantic transformation* (mainly to enable index application or shorten navigation paths), and *cleaning-up* (or simplification).

Most of the implementation issues we are going to address in the remainder of this paper are related to either enabling an application of a structure index[1] that is superficially inapplicable or to shorten a navigation path involved in a query expression. Most of this type of rules are based on exploitation of document structure knowledge that is captured in our system through DTD graph analysis. A DTD normally covers a class of documents and is much smaller and more stable than the database itself. The time spent on DTD graph analysis for gathering the structure knowledge is easily paid off through amortization by repeated database querying.

Now we introduce three important notions regarding

---

[1] Although structure indices in our system are sophisticated, but for understanding of the subsequent discussion, suffice it to know that a structure index between two element types simply provides a short-cut between the elements of the two types so that a (long) path navigation can be avoided.

DTD graph, *exclusivity*, *obligation*, and *entrance locations* between element types, which bear potential for query optimization.

Definition 2.3 (Exclusivity) *Element type ET_j is exclusively contained in element type ET_i if each path $(e_j, \ldots, e_k)$ with e_j being an element of type ET_j and e_k being the document root contains an element of type ET_i. Conversely, element type ET_i exclusively contains ET_j if the condition holds.*

If $type(E1)$ is exclusively contained in $type(E2)$, the containment selection predicate imposed by the expression $E1 \subset E2$ is exempt for examination, hence $E1 \subset E2$ can be simply rewritten as $E1$.

Definition 2.4 (Obligation) *Element type ET_i obligatorily contains element type ET_j if each element of type ET_i has to contain in any document complying with the DTD an element of type ET_j. Conversely, we say that ET_j is obligatorily contained in ET_i.*

The concept of obligation justifies the rewrite of $E1 \supset E2$ as $E1$ if E1 obligatorily contains E2.

Definition 2.5 (Entrance location) *Element type EL is an entrance location for $type(E1)$ and $type(E2)$ if in any document complying with the given DTD, all paths from an element e1 of $type(E1)$ to an element e2 of $type(E2)$ pass through an element el of type EL.*

As special cases, $type(E1)$ and $type(E2)$ themselves are entrance locations for $type(E1)$ and $type(E2)$. The notion of *entrance location* gives rise to the following equivalences. $E1 \subset E2 \iff E1 \subset (E3 \subset E2)$ if $type(E3)$ is an entrance location for $type(E1)$ and $type(E2)$.

The primary use of above properties regarding DTD structure is to equivalently transform a query expression to a different form so that a potential structure index can be used, which otherwise is impossible. Another usage of these notions is to help shorten the navigation paths involved in a query expression in case of no beneficial structure index available.

Five different cases concerning exploitation of structure indices for query optimization have been identified as illustrated in Figure 1.

In case (1), the structure index is straightforwardly applied.

Case (2) corresponds to rule $\mathcal{R}55$ in our generic rule system, where input expression $E1 \subset E2$ is rewritten as $E1 \subset E3$ for enabling the application of a structure index between E1 and E3 (which is otherwise inapplicable) provided that the newly introduced element type E3 is an entrance location for E1 and E2 and is exclusively contained in E2.

Case (3) corresponds to rule $\mathcal{R}56$ in our generic rule system, where input expression $E1 \supset E2$ is rewritten as $E1 \supset E3$ for enabling the application of a structure index between E1 and E3 provided that element type E3 is an entrance location for E1 and E2 and obligatorily contains E1.

Case (4) corresponds to rule $\mathcal{R}57$ in our generic rule system, where input expression $E1 \subset E2$ is rewritten as $E1 \subset E3$ for enabling the application of a structure index between E1 and E3 provided that E2 is an entrance location for E1 and the newly introduced element type E3 and is exclusively contained in E3.

Case (5) corresponds to rule $\mathcal{R}58$ in our generic rule system, where input expression $E1 \supset E2$ is rewritten as $E1 \supset E3$ for enabling the application of a structure index between E1 and E3 provided that E2 is an entrance location for E1 and E3 and obligatorily contains E3.

For case (2) and (3), even if a potential structure index is not available, the transformation is still beneficial because it helps shorten the original navigation path, supposing $path(E1, E3)$ is sufficiently shorter than the original $path(E1, E2)$. The two cases under this situation account for the other two rules, $\mathcal{R}59$ and $\mathcal{R}60$, in our system, respectively.

The above mentioned six semantic rules, i.e., $\mathcal{R}55$ through $\mathcal{R}60$, are furnished to this paper as appendix.

3. Algorithms

Now we are ready to address the interesting implementation issues of our deterministic transformation system. One major goal of query transformation is to identify potential structure indices of XML documents and enable the application of these indices to input query expressions. The majority of these index-related rules come with a complex condition, which is based on the availability of relevant indices and special knowledge about the structure of the source documents such as those indicated by the notion of exclusivity, obligation, and entrance location. The condition of a rule and the pattern of a given query expression collaboratively determine the applicability of the rule to the given input query. In the following, we describe the algorithms that accomplish deterministic transformations and the algorithms that support these transformations in our system – identifying the exclusivity and obligation knowledge, and the entrance locations for element types related by a containment relation.

3.1. Transformation algorithms

As pointed out in Subsection 2.3, our strategy divides the whole transformation process for the optimization of a query as three phases. We use a switch mechanism to control the applicability of rules with regard to a specific

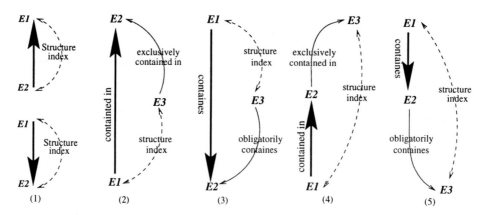

Figure 1. Combining entrance locations and structure Indices for optimal transformation

transformation phase for a given query expression. Another major characteristic of our strategy is the deterministic nature of our transformations, which makes our transformation process simplified and highly efficient. In other words, we don't concern multiple alternatives at each transformation step - we always keep a single optimal alternative. A high level description of our transformation is given below.

```
optimize(input) := {
    return type: PAT_expression;
    enable all normalization rules
        (but disable all other rules);
    normalized = transform(input);
    enable all DTD semantic rules
        (but disable all other rules);
    improved = transform(normalized);
    enable all simplification rules
        (but disable all other rules);
    optimized = transform(improved);
    return optimized
}

transform(expr) := {
    return type: PAT_expression;
    for each argument arg of expr
        arg = transform(arg);
    while there are applicable rules in
        the currently enabled rule set
    {
        let r be the first of such rules;
        generate a new expression new_e
        by applying r to expr;
        result = transform(new_e);
    }
    /* if no more applicable rule */
    return result;
}
```

In our implementation, the switching mechanism of rules is obtained by a separate Boolean array. The *enable* and

disable are the two operations needed for turning on and off the switch of a rule. At each specific transformation phase, only the rules in "on" state will be considered. This is a simple but effective mechanism for putting the rule system under well control to achieve better performance.

The order of the rules in the rule system is of significance because in case of multiple applicable rules we always choose the first one to pursue our *deterministic transformation*. The first applicable rule in our system is believed to be the most beneficial one of all the applicable rules - this order arrangement is made based on relevant heuristics. The last alternative that our *transform* algorithm obtained through a stepwise transformation chain is the optimal one. At this point, there are no more applicable "on" rules can be applied to that expression; otherwise the while loop in the transform algorithm would continue.

3.2. Identifying exclusivity and obligation properties

In Subsection 2.3, we gave the definitions of the three important notions about the structural properties of documents at the DTD level. These properties imply the corresponding relationships among element instances, but are practically identifiable through a given DTD. This saves significantly physical database accesses during the evaluation phase of queries.

Based on its definition, our algorithm for examining the exclusivity property between two given element types, e.g., whether B is exclusively contained in A, is simply to check the paths between B and the DTD's root type: if none is found without the occurrence of A then the property holds.

In order to identify all cases of obligation, a deeper look at the content model of element types is indispensable. Otherwise, we cannot distinguish whether an element requires or just optionally contains a sub-element. Thus, as a first step we eliminate all optional occurrence indicators from the content models.

Definition 3.1 (Reduced version of a DTD) *Let D be a DTD. By taking all content models and removing all subexpressions whose root has an optional occurrence indicator (?) or an optional-and-repeatable occurrence indicator (*), we obtain a reduced DTD D'.*

The following proposition holds [3]:

Lemma 3.1 *The obligation properties within a DTD and its reduced version are identical.*

For examining the obligation property between element type A and B ($A \supset B$), we next flatten the content model of A so that the obligatory occurrence of B in A's content model eventually become obvious, and the result is called A's **extended content model** for B, which is achieved through the following algorithm:

```
extend_content_model(A,B) := {
  return type:  content model;
  let c_A be the content model of A;
  while (c_A contains non-terminal
      element types different from B)
  {
    let o be the occurrence of such an
      element type and let C be the
      element type;
    replace o in c_A with the content
      model of C;
  }
  return c_A;
}
```

Base on the *extended content model* notion, we produce a **normalized form** for the content model of element type A by performing the following steps, which were specified in detail in [3]:

1. Recursively inline all child SEQ-nodes into their parent SEQ-nodes;

2. Recursively inline all child OR-nodes into their parent OR-nodes;

3. If any OR-node is not root, transform the content model so that the OR-node is relocated to the root;

These steps do not alter the content represented by a content tree but leads to a normal form that possesses the following properties:

- the root is an OR-node,

- the children of the root are SEQ-nodes,

- the children of SEQ-nodes are leaves, i.e., element types.

In the context of our work, content model normalization is important for revealing implicit obligation property, which is otherwise easily not to be identified [3, 9].

Finally, based on the normalized content model of A for B, we can conveniently identify the existence of the obligation property between A and B by examining obvious occurrences of B in A's content model.

As a summary, our algorithm for examining the obligation property between element type A and B is specified at a high level as below:

```
obligatorily_contains(A,B) := {
  return type: Boolean;
  step 1. Produce a reduced version of
          the DTD;
  step 2. Extend the content model of A
          for B;
  step 3. Generate normalized form for
          the content model of A;
  step 4. Search for occurrence of B
          in each SEQ-node of A's
          content model;
          Return true if found,
          otherwise false;
}
```

3.3. Identifying relevant entrance locations

The essential six, i.e., $\mathcal{R}55$ to $\mathcal{R}60$, of 10 generic semantic rules ($\mathcal{R}51$ to $\mathcal{R}60$) in our system all rely on the *entrance location* notion. In addition, simplification rules $\mathcal{R}31$ through $\mathcal{R}34$ are based on availability of entrance locations. Thus how to find all *relevant* entrance locations to satisfy the conditions of and to enable these rules becomes an important implementation issue at this point.

As is depicted in Figure 1, the notion, "entrance location", as a requisite condition, is mainly used for enabling profitable transformations in two different manners: introduce a new element type $E3$ that is an *entrance location* for $E1$ and $E2$ (corresponding to case (2) and (3) in Figure 1), or $E2$ itself becomes an entrance location for the newly introduced element type $E3$ and the existing type $E1$ (corresponding to case (4) and (5) in Figure 1), and then replace $E2$ with the new type $E3$.

For terminological uniformity, we generalize our *entrance location* concept so that, when the term is generally used, it covers both the situations above.

Definition 3.2 (Entrance location generalization) *If $E3$ is an entrance location for $E1$ and $E2$ as defined in Definition 2.5, we call $E3$ an inset entrance location for $E1$*

and E2, and call E1 (or E2) an outside entrance location for E3 and E2 (or E1).

Therefore, in the remainder of this paper, the general notion "entrance location" may refer to either an *inset entrance location*, applying to case (2) and (3) of Figure 1, or an *outside entrance location*, applying to case (4) and (5) of Figure 1.

The algorithm identifying inset entrance locations between a pair of element types heavily relies on exploring the element type graph. For the sake of efficiency, we suppose (precompute) that each element type ET maintains all the paths that diverge from the element type down to the leaves of the DTD-graph considered and call it $down\_paths(ET)$. The algorithm identifying inset entrance locations is described as follows:

```
identify_ELs(ET1, ET2) := {
  return type: set of <ent>;
  return identify_ELs(ET2, ET1) if ET2
     is external to ET1;
  for each path maintained in
     down_paths(ET1),
    mark up those containing vertex ET2;
  let s_path be the shortest path among
     the marked-up ones w.r.t. the
     length from vertex "ET1" to "ET2";
  for each intermediate vertex ET
     contained in s path,
    if it is also contained in all other
       paths marked up,
    collect it into the entrance
       location set el_set;
  return el_set;
}
```

This algorithm identifies all inset entrance locations for element type E1 and E2. It is evident from the algorithm that an entrance lactation EL is *relevant* for type E1 and E2 if it falls on the shortest path between the type $type(E1)$ and $type(E2)$.

With regard to identifying the outside entrance locations for element type E1 and E2, our algorithm is relatively simple because we have a much focused area to investigate for this case – only the types that are related to either E1 or E2 via a structure index need to be examined. For example, if EL is related to E1 by a structure index, we would just examine whether E2 is an inset entrance location for E1 and EL. In other words, we simply check every path from E1 to EL to see if it contains a solid occurrence of E2 on the path. We use the *outside entrance location* notion solely to enable the application of a superficially unrelated structure index (outside entrance locations do not contribute to the shortening of any navigation path).

3.4. Determine optimal entrance locations

For a given expression of form $E1 \supsetneq E2$, algorithm $identify\_ELs(ET1, ET2)$ identifies relevant inset entrance locations for E1 and E2. The purpose for us to identify these entrance locations is to apply one of the semantic rules $\mathcal{R}55$ to $\mathcal{R}60$ to an (sub-)expression of form $E1 \supsetneq E2$. But if the additional conditions of the rules regarding structure indices and exclusivity or obligation of a containment relation do not hold for the identified entrance locations, these entrance locations are not interesting. So we need to further identify those interesting entrances from all identified relevant ones. After that, if multiple interesting entrance locations exist, we still need to choose the most profitable one, i.e., the optimal one, to activate a corresponding rule of the set $\mathcal{R}55$ through $\mathcal{R}60$ because our deterministic transformation strategy asks us to always apply the most beneficial rule to a query expression whenever multiple are applicable. Therefore, we need certain criteria to determine which one is the optimal entrance location for a given (sub-)expression of form $E1 \supsetneq E2$.

Definition 3.3 (Optimal entrance location) *If multiple relevant entrance locations, of which each may cause a separate application of one of the rules $\mathcal{R}55$ through $\mathcal{R}60$ to an expression of form $E1 \supsetneq E2$, exist, then the optimal entrance location is determined according to the following criteria:*

(1). When a structure index can be exploited (this case corresponding to $\mathcal{R}55$ through $\mathcal{R}58$), the optimal entrance location is the one that has the smallest cardinality of extension[2].

(2). When using a structure index is not possible (this case corresponds to $\mathcal{R}59$ and $\mathcal{R}60$), the optimal is the one that results in the shortest navigation path, i.e., the path from $E1$ to the entrance location in the DTD graph.

Now we give the steps that are needed by our algorithm to determine the optimal entrance location for a given query (sub-)expression of form $E1 \supsetneq E2$.

```
identify_optimal_EL(E1,E2) := {
  return type: element type name;
  Step 1. Find relevant inset entrance
     locations;
  Step 2. Collect all interesting
     entrance locations;
  Step 3. Determine the optimal entrance
     location and return it;
}
```

---

[2]The extension of an element type is the set of all the element instances conforming to that type.

The details of each of the steps are addressed below:

Step 1: Find entrance locations

All relevant inset entrance locations for element type E1 and E2 are found (if exist) by calling $identify\_ELs\text{-}(E1, E2)$; the result is annotated as $rELs(E1, E2)$, which is a set of element type names; all relevant outside entrance locations can be decided accordingly as discussed in the last paragraph of Subsection 3.3.

Step 2: Collect interesting entrance locations

Assume, beside the diverging paths, each element type t maintains two transitive closures, say, $excl\_C^*(t)$ and $obli\_C^*(t)$, which are the transitive closure of the relationship "*exclusively contained in*" and the relationship "*obligatorily contains*" on this type t, respectively. The closures can be computed by the methods given earlier in this section. In addition, each element type t maintains a set of interesting etn's, annotated as $indices(t)$, which relate to the type t through an available structure index.

For identifying interesting entrance locations, the following two cases are treated separately:

(Case 1: for $\mathcal{R}55$, $\mathcal{R}56$, $\mathcal{R}59$, $\mathcal{R}60$) check each inset entrance location for E1 and E2 obtained from last step to see if it, say E3, is contained in $excl\_C^*(E2)$ or in $obli\_C^*(E2)$. Next, check whether E3 is a member of $indices(E1)$. If yes, mark it as "structure index defined". For instance, the output of this step for Rule $\mathcal{R}55$ is $rELs(E1, E2) \cap excl\_C^*(E2) \cap indices(E1)$, for Rule $\mathcal{R}56$ is $rELs(E1, E2) \cap obli\_C^*(E2) \cap indices(E1)$, for Rule $\mathcal{R}59$ is $rELs(E1, E2) \cap excl\_C^*(E2)$, and for Rule $\mathcal{R}60$ is $rELs(E1, E3) \cap obli\_C^*(E2)$.

(Case 2: for $\mathcal{R}57$ and $\mathcal{R}58$) if $indices(E1)$ is not empty, for each $E3 \in indices(E1)$ check whether $E3$ is an outside entrance location for E1 and E2 (in other words, E2 is an inset entrance location for E1 and E3), and whether $E2$ belongs to $excl\_C^*(E3)$ or $E2$ belongs to $obli\_C^*(E3)$. Mark the element types that satisfy these conditions as "structure index defined", then output.

Step 3: Determine the optimal entrance location

This step differentiate the output of last step as either "structure index defined" (thus will be applied) or "no structure index defined" (will be used only for shortening the navigation paths):

(Case 1) For the entrance locations output by Step 2 and marked as "structure index defined", choose and output the one that holds the smallest extension cardinality. If none is found, continue with (Case 2).

(Case 2) For the entrance locations output by Step 2 and not marked as "structure index defined", select the one that produces the shortest navigation path for reaching $type(E1)$ in the element type graph.

The last step of the above algorithm output the optimal entrance location that actually helps decide which of the six essential semantic rules is the most profitable one and thus should be chosen next for conducting transformation on the incoming (sub-)expression of form $E1 \; {}_{\overleftarrow{c}} \; E2$.

4. Transformation examples

In the following we give three transformation examples using our deterministic transformation rules. Our transformations explore the following indices: content index $I_{\sigma_r}(Surname)$ and structure indexes $I_{Article}(Name)$, $I_{Paragraph}(Article)$, and $I_{Paragraph}(ShortPaper)$. For structure indices, the subscript of the index operator indicates the result type of the index operation. Since we did not introduce all the transformation rules used in the fowllowing examples beforehand due to the space limitation and the purpose of this paper, we do not expect a sharp understanding of the details of the examples from the readers but just to give them a tast of the flavors of our deterministic transformation system for query optimization.

Example 1. Find the paragraphs of the "Introduction" section of each article that has the words "Data Warehousing" in its title.

$(Paragraph \subset (\sigma_{A=Title, r='Introduction'}(Section)$
$\subset (Article \supset \sigma_{r='Datawarehousing'}(Title))))$
$\implies$ (by 1st step of $\mathcal{R}54$, i.e., associativity)
$((Paragraph \subset \sigma_{A=Title, r='Introduction'}(Section))$
$\subset (Article \supset \sigma_{r="Datawarehousing"}(Title)))$
$\implies$ (by 2nd step of $\mathcal{R}54$, i.e., commutativity)
$((Paragraph \subset (Article \supset$
$\sigma_{r='Datawarehousing'}(Title))) \subset$
$\sigma_{A=Title, r='Introduction'}(Section))$
$\implies$ (by 3rd step of $\mathcal{R}54$, i.e., index introduction)
$((I_{Paragraph}(Article \supset$
$\sigma_{r='Datawarehousing'}(Title)) \cap Paragraph)$
$\subset \sigma_{A=Title, r='Introduction'}(Section))$
$\implies$ (by $\mathcal{R}61$: $\cap$ deletion)
$((I_{Paragraph}(Article$
$\supset \sigma_{r='Datawarehousing'}(Title)))$
$\subset \sigma_{A=Title, r='Introduction'}(Section))$

Example 2. Find all articles in which the surname of an author contains the value "Aberer".

$(Article \supset \sigma_{r='Aberer'}(Surname))$
$\implies$ (by $\mathcal{R}50$, suppose index $I_{\sigma_r}(Surname)$ is ailable)
$(Article \supset I_{\sigma_{r='Aberer'}}(Surname))$

Notice that $\mathcal{R}57$ is unfortunately not applicable for using the index between *Name* and *Article* since the *free expression* condition does not hold for $\sigma_{r='Aberer'}(Surname)$.

Example 3. Find all "Summary" paragraphs of all sections (if any).

$$(\sigma_{A=Title,r='Summary'}(Paragraph) \subset Section)$$
$$\Longrightarrow (\text{by } \mathcal{R}57)$$
$$(\sigma_{A=Title,r='Summary'}(Paragraph) \subset Article)$$
$$\Longrightarrow (\text{by } \mathcal{R}53)$$
$$(I_{Paragraph}(Article) \cap$$
$$\sigma_{A=Title,r='Summary'}(Paragraph))$$
$$\Longrightarrow (\text{by } \mathcal{R}62)$$
$$(\sigma_{A=Title,r='Summary'}(I_{Paragraph}(Article)))$$

5. Summary

Query optimization is a critical and challenging issue for structured document management, especially for efficient query processing. Being driven by the high efficiency request by the web-hooked applications for structured document query processing, our approach applies exclusively deterministic transformations on structured document queries to achieve the best possible optimization efficiency. Our strategy is based on heuristics about DTD knowledge and structural properties of XML documents, with the main purpose for fast exploring potential structure indices to speed up query processing in a database environment. In this paper, we addressed mainly the implementation issues of our deterministic query transformation strategy. Our work is original as we did not notice really closely related work being done so far to the best of our knowledge.

Acknowledgement. The author would like to show great appreciation to his former colleagues at Fraunhofer-IPSI (formerly known as GMD-IPSI), Germany. This continuing research at the author's current affiliation was initiated at GMD-IPSI in close collaboration with Prof. Karl Aberer, Dr. Klemens BÖehm, and Prof. M. Tamer Özsu (during his visit to GMD-IPSI on his sabbatical leave).

References

[1] Serge Abiteboul, Sophie Cluet, Vassilis Christophides, et al. *Querying Documents in Object Databases.* Digital Libraries. No. 1, pp5-19, 1997.

[2] Klemens Böhm, Karl Aberer, Erich J. Neuhold, and Xiaoya Yang. *Structured Document Storage and Refined Declarative and Navigational Access Mechanisms in HyperStorM.* The VLDB Journal, Vol. 6, No. 4, pp296-311, November 1997.

[3] Klemens Böhm, Karl Aberer, M. Tamer Özsu, and Kathrin Gayer. *Query Optimization for Structured Documents Based on Knowledge on the Document Type Definition.* Proc. of IEEE International Forum on Research and Technology Advances in Digital Libraries (ADL'98), pp196-205, Santa Barbara, California, April 22-24, 1998.

[4] P. Bohannon, J. Freire, P. Roy, J. Simon. From XML Schema To Relations: A Cost-Based Approach to XML Storage. Proc. of the 18th International Conference on Data Engineering (ICDE'02).

[5] C.Y. Chan, P. Felber, M. Garofalakis, and R. Rastogi, "Efficient Filtering of XML Documents with XPath Expressions", Proc. of Intl' Conference on Data Engineering, pp235-244, San Jose, California, February 2002.

[6] Chee Yong Chan, Minos N. Garofalakis, Rajeev Rastogi: RE-Tree: An Efficient Index Structure for Regular Expressions. Proc. of VLDB 2002.

[7] Surajit Chaudhuri and Luis Gravano. *Optimizing Queries over Multimedia Repositories.* Proc. of SIGMOD'96, pp91-102, Montreal, Canada, June 1996.

[8] Dunren Che and and Karl Aberer. *A Heuristics-Based Approach to Query Optimization in Structured Document Databases.* Proc. of 1999 International Database Engineering & Application Symposium, pp24-33, Montreal, Canada, August 2-4, 1999, IEEE Computer Society.

[9] Dunren Che, Karl Aberer, M. Tamer Özsu, and Klemens Böhm. *Query Processing and Optimization in Structured Document Database Systems.* Manuscript in preparation for publication on The VLDB Journal.

[10] Shu-Yao Chien, Zografoula Vagena, Donghui Zhang, Vassilis J. Tsotras, Carlo Zaniolo. *Efficient Structural Joins on Indexed XML Documents.* Proc. of VLDB 2002, Hong Kong.

[11] Mariano Consens and Tova Milo. *Optimizing Queries on Files.* Proc. of the 1994 ACM SIGMOD International Conference on Management of Data, pp301-312, Vol. 23, ACM Press, May 1994, Minneapolis, Minnesota.

[12] Mary F. Fernandez and Dan Suciu. *Optimizing Regular Path Expressions Using Graph Schemas.* Proc. of the Fourteenth International Conference on Data Engineering, pp14-23, February 23-27, 1998, Orlando, Florida, USA, 1998.

[13] M. Fernandez, W. Tan, D. Suciu. SilkRoute: Trading between Relations and XML. 9th Int. World Wide Web Conf. (WWW), Amsterdam, May, 2000

[14] D. Florescu, and D. Kossmann. Storing and Querying XML Data Using an RDMBS. IEEE Data Engineering Bulletin 22(3), pp. 27-34, 1999.

[15] G.H. Gonnet, R.A. Baeza-Yates, and T. Snider. *Information Retrieval–Data Structures and Algorithms.* New Indices for Text: PAT trees and PAT arrays, Prentice hall, 1992.

[16] Georg Gottlob, Christoph Koch, Reinhard Pichler. *Efficient Algorithms for Processing XPath Queries.* Proc. of VLDB 2002.

[17] Torsten Grust: Accelerating XPath location steps. Proc. of SIGMOD Conference 2002: 109-120.

[18] Sudipto Guha, H. V. Jagadish, Nick Koudas, Divesh Srivastava and Ting Yu. *Approximate XML joins.* Proc. of the ACM SIGMOD Conference on Management of Data, 2002

[19] M. Klettke, H. Meyer. XML and Object-Relational Database Systems - Enhancing Structural Mappings Based on Statistics. Proc. of Int. Workshop on the Web and Databases (WebDB), Dallas, May, 2000

[20] Kyuchul Lee, Yong Kyu Lee and P. Bruce Berra. *Management of Multi-Structured Hypermedia Documents: A Data Model, Query Language, and Indexing Scheme.* Multimedia Tools and Applications, Vol. 4, No. 2, pp199-224, march 1997.

[21] Wen-Syan Li, Junho Shim, K. Selcuk Candan and Yoshinori Hara. *WebDB: A Web Query System and its Modeling, Language, and Implementation.* Proc. of IEEE International Forum on Research and Technology Advances in Digital Libraries (ADL'98), pp216-225, Santa Barbara, California, Aprill 22-24, 1998.

[22] Q. Li and B. Moon. Indexing and Querying XML Data for Regular Path Expressions, Proc. of the 27th International Conference on Very Large Databases (VLDB'2001), pp361-370, Rome, Italy, September 2001.

[23] J. McHugh, S. Abiteboul, R. Goldman, D. Quass, and J. Widom. *Lore: A Database Management System for Semistructured Data.* SIGMOD Record, 26(3), pp54-66, September 1997.

[24] J. McHugh and J. Widom. *Query Optimization for XML.* Proc. of the Twenty-Fifth International Conference on Very Large Data Bases, pp315-326, Edinburgh, Scotland, September 1999.

[25] Tova Milo, Dan Suciu: Index Structures for Path Expressions. Proc. of ICDT 1999: 277-295.

[26] Atsuyuki Morishima and Hiroyuki Kitagawa. *A Data Modeling and Query Processing Scheme for Integration of Structured Document Repositories and Relational Databases.* Proc. of the Fifth International Conference on Database Systems for Advanced Applications, Melbourne, Australia, April 1-4, 1997.

[27] Atsuyuki Morishima and Hiroyuki Kitagawa. *A Data Modeling Approach to the Seamless Information Exchange among Structured Documents and Databases.* Proc. of 1997 ACM System on Applied Computing, San Jose, Feb. 1997.

[28] Gonzalo Navarro and Ricarrdo Baeza-Yates. *Proximal Nodes: A Model to Query Document Databases by Content and Structure.* ACM Transaction on Information Systems, Vol. 15, No. 4, pp400-435, October 1997.

[29] M. T. Özsu, P. Iglinski, D. Szafron, S. El-Medani, M. Junghanns. *An Object-Oriented SGML/HiTime Compliant Multimedia Database Management System.* Proc. of Fifth ACM International Multimedia Conference (ACM Multimedia'97), pp239-249, Seattle, WA, November 1997.

[30] A. Salminen and F. W. Tompa. *PAT Expressions: an Algebra for Text Search* Acta Linguistica Hungarica 41 (1994), no.1, pp277-306.

[31] J. Shanmugasundaram, K. Tufte, G. He, C. Zhang, D. DeWitt, and J. Naughton. Relational Databases for Querying XML Documents: Limitations and Opportunities. Proc. of VLSB, pp. 302-314, 1999.

[32] D. Srivastava, S. Al-Khalifa, H. V. Jagadish, N. Koudas, J. M. Patel, Y. Wu. Structural Joins: A Primitive for Efficient XML Query Pattern Matching. Proc. of ICDE02.

[33] B. Surjanto, N. Ritter, H. Loeser. XML Content Management based on Object-Relational Database Technology. Proc. Of the 1st Int. Conf. On Web Information Systems Engineering (WISE), Hongkong, June 2000.

[34] Tak W. Yan and Jurgen Annevelink. *Integrating a Structured-Text Retrieval System with an Object-Oriented Database System.* Proc. of the 20th VLDB Conference, pp740-749, Santiago, Chile, 1994.

Appendix

$\mathcal{R}55.$ $(E1 \subset E2) \implies (E1 \subset E3)$ *if* $type(E3)$ is an entrance location for $type(E1)$ and $type(E2)$, and is exclusively contained in $type(E2)$, and $free(E2)$ holds, in addition, a structure index between $type(E3)$ and $type(E1)$ is available.

$\mathcal{R}56.$ $(E1 \supset E2) \implies (E1 \supset E3)$ *if* $type(E3)$ is an entrance location for $type(E1)$ and $type(E2)$, and obligatorily contains $type(E2)$, and $free(E2)$ holds, in addition, a structure index between $type(E3)$ and $type(E1)$ is available.

$\mathcal{R}57.$ $(E1 \subset E2) \implies (E1 \subset E3)$ *if* $type(E2)$ is an entrance location for $type(E1)$ and $type(E3)$, and is exclusively contained in $type(E3)$, and $free(E2)$ holds, in addition, a structure index between $type(E3)$ and $type(E1)$ is available.

$\mathcal{R}58.$ $(E1 \supset E2) \implies (E1 \supset E3)$ *if* $type(E2)$ is an entrance location for $type(E1)$ and $type(E3)$, and obligatorily contains $type(E3)$, and $free(E2)$ holds, in addition, a structure index between $type(E3)$ and $type(E1)$ is available.

$\mathcal{R}59.$ $(E1 \subset E2) \implies (E1 \subset E3)$ *if* $type(E3)$ is an entrance location for $type(E1)$ and $type(E2)$, and is exclusively contained in $type(E2)$, and $free(E2)$ holds.

$\mathcal{R}60.$ $(E1 \supset E2) \implies (E1 \supset E3)$ *if* $type(E3)$ is an entrance location for $type(E1)$ and $type(E2)$, and obligatorily contains $type(E2)$, and $free(E2)$ holds.

Note. In the above rules, the condition $free(E_i)$ requests that the evaluation of the E_i returns the full extent of the element type of E_i, i.e., all elements of the type in the database. One typical example of such an E_i is an expression comprising just an etn, meaning all elements of the type are to be returned.

$\mathcal{R}59$ has almost the same condition as $\mathcal{R}55$ except for an available structure index. $\mathcal{R}55$ is assigned a higher priority (with less ID#) and is tried first during query optimization for enabling a potential structure index. Analogously for $\mathcal{R}56$ and $\mathcal{R}60$.

Learning Objects as a Uniform Foundation for E- Learning Platforms*

Gottfried Vossen
University of Münster
D-48149 Münster, Germany
vossen@wi.uni-muenster.de

Peter Jaeschke
Credit Suisse Group
CH-8070 Zurich, Switzerland

Abstract

Learning objects are under discussion in the context of electronic and in particular Web-based learning. Intuitively, they represent reusable units of learning content that can be consumed or studied within a single learning session, and that can be sequenced into larger units such as classes and courses if necessary or desired. To achieve these goals, making learning objects amenable to the technical support of a database system appears appropriate. Once this view is in place, learning objects can be used as the central and uniform foundation of an e-learning platform that, for example, is capable of tracking users or of adapting content to users, and that can simultaneously handle a companys knowledge management. It is shown in this paper how the latter can be achieved through a common exploitation of (and interaction between) database objects and suitably designed processes.

1 Introduction

Learning objects are under discussion in the context of electronic and in particular Web-based learning [1]. Intuitively, they represent reusable units of learning content that can be consumed or studied within a single learning session or within a predefined, finite amount of time, and that can be sequenced into larger units such as classes and courses if necessary or desired. These goals have previously been made precise by various people, including [5, 7] and others. In [16], we have described the initial version of an object model which makes learning objects amenable to the technical support of a database system. Beyond this, we will show in this paper that learning objects can be used as the central and uniform foundation of an e-learning platform. Indeed, they can form the basis, for example, of *tracking*

*This work was done while both authors were affiliated with PROMA-TIS in Germany.

users or of *adapting* content to users, and they can simultaneously become a link into a companys knowledge management system. We show how this central role of learning objects can be accomplished by a suitably chosen interaction of database learning objects and processes that use and manipulate these objects.

Various communities have recently entered into a discussion of learning objects, and an agreement on what a learning object is *about* seems in sight. Indeed, according to Eduworks (see www.eduworks.com/LOTT/tutorial/), "learning objects are the core concept in an approach to learning content in which content is broken down into bite size chunks. These chunks can be reused, independently created and maintained, and pulled apart and stuck together like so many legos." Similar definitions are given by other people; see, for example, [2, 5, 7]. Moreover, researchers and developers of e-learning platforms seem to have come to a general agreement that learning objects are the piece of information that has to be handled by a *learning management system* (LMS). On the other hand, what exactly constitutes a learning object in practice is not clear at all; even standardization bodies such as IEEE, IMS, and SCORM remain vague on what really constitutes the *inside* of a learning object and delve more into general aspects such as who authored it or what are relevant keywords, and into the packaging of several such objects from potentially distinct sources into larger units of learning.

We have tried to lay the foundations for a more technical view of learning objects in [16]. Our view is derived from the way objects are handled in a database. If learning objects are stored in relational tables or in object-oriented class extensions, they need a *schema* as well as *attributes* which have (simple or complex) *types*. A schema specifies the content structure of an object that is stored in the underlying database, and hence serves as a time-invariant conceptual description of what a database object is comprised of. Besides being mandatory from a storage point of view, viewing learning objects as database objects brings

278

along several advantages, among them that we can now exploit database techniques for handling learning objects; in particular, SQL can be used for querying, updating, and managing them. Second, it is easy to devise interfaces for authoring learning objects, since transporting data into and out of a (potentially even Web-based) form can be realized as database insertion or retrieval, resp. Third, databases nicely interact with other systems, an experience we have confirmed when developing our XLX e-learning system for doing exercises over the Web [10]. For example, data stored in a, say, relational database can easily be published in XML format, where the particular XML documents produced can follow a generic structuring (i.e., one driven by the table constituents in the database) or they can be created according to an XML Schema (that in turn may be derived from the underlying database schema). The relevance of this aspect stems from the fact that XML is generally accepted as a data exchange format these days, and XML is also employed by the standards bodies mentioned above for learning object exchanges.

Once such a database-oriented notion of a learning object has been established, the various expectations an LMS developer or deployer may have about learning objects can be materialized. Indeed, learning objects taken from a database can easily form the units underlying a content authoring system. Moreover, as individual learning objects get combined into larger units such as classes, maps can be attached to the larger granules that enable content adaptation at the level of individual objects. Finally, user tracking (in a positive as well as in a negative sense) can be based on learning objects, thereby retaining an appropriate level of tracking detail. Other uses can be designed for learning objects, thereby making them the central construct underlying a learning platform.

These ideas are worked out in the rest of this paper, which is organized as follows: In Section 2, we sketch the database model of learning objects we have developed and briefly describe other object model components (e.g., learners and their profiles) relevant for what follows; we also discuss the authoring of learning objects. In Section 3 we elaborate on the access to and management of learning objects, which is described using Petri nets as process specification formalism. In Section 4 we present some conclusions and directions for future work.

2 A Database Model for Learning Objects

Learning objects are essentially units of content to be studied by people through an electronic platform. We assume that, in the context of such a platform, *learners* are the "customers" who consume the content, and that *authors* are those who produce the learning objects; other roles (such as *teachers*, *trainers*, or *administrators*) are not relevant

for the purposes of this paper. Regarding content, training and learning offerings are supposed to come in reusable granules that can be authored independently of a delivery medium and accessed dynamically, e.g., over the Web. To this end, it is crucial to design and develop learning objects in such a way that a certain validity period or lifetime as well as (re-) usability in a variety of contexts are achieved. This section presents our learning object and learner model.

Overview

The model of learning objects whose initial version we have described in [16] is intended to accommodate a variety of learning object instances whose content can vary considerably in size, volume, and presentation, i.e., from the short note that informs about a product update in written form, to the comprehensive lecture that introduces the learner to a, say, technical topic in a self-contained way. Our model is based on the following design decisions:

1. We derive structural aspects of a learning object (i.e., its attributes) from an analysis of typical classes or courses as well as from the content of our prime learning targets, and from the notion of an object commonly used in object-relational databases.

2. We make the resulting object model amenable to knowledge management (by introducing knowledge objects as *generalizations* of learning objects).

3. Besides this, administrative information is gathered in such a way that various learning object exploitations become possible (as described below).

In addition to the above, learning objects should conform to relevant standards; we are using portions of the *Learning Object Metadata* (LOM) recommendation from IEEE as described in [11] as well as meta attributes as suggested in *Dublin Core* (see Figure 1; here the intention is that a learning object comes with either set of meta-attributes, not necessarily with both sets). Moreover, we have cast the result into a class diagram which is straightforwardly amenable to a database (or XML) schema representation. We emphasize that we are not looking into presentation aspects of a learning object here (i.e., questions such as which parts of a learning object get animated and what media are appropriate for that purpose), but only into structural aspects.

The object model we have designed for learning objects is shown in Figure 1. A learning object has an *orientation* section in the beginning, followed by a *learning* section where the actual content is conveyed to the learners, and concluded by a *resources* section which comprises hints for further study. The center portion of this decomposition has again an inner structure: Learning some material or content

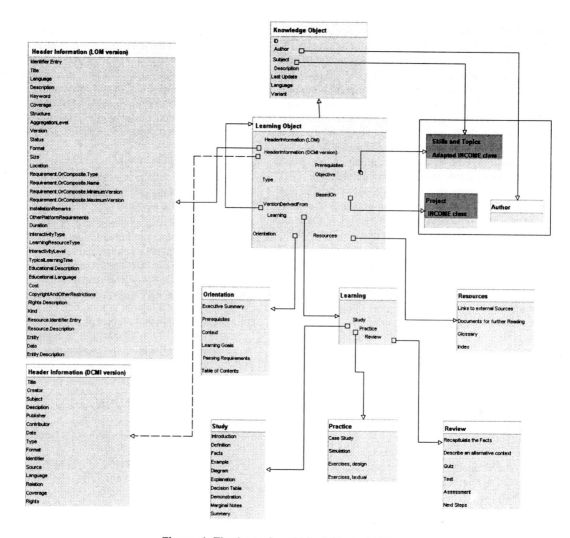

Figure 1. The Learning Object Class Lattice.

is typically a combination of *study*, *practice*, and undergoing a *review*. In more detail, an orientation section comprises an *executive summary*, *prerequisites* stating what the learner is expected to know prior to "entering" this learning object, a description of the *context* in which this particular learning object occurs or should be used, *learning goals* that are associated with this learning object, *passing requirements* that state what the learner has to do to get credit for studying this learning object, and a *table of contents*. In a similar way, a study section has components such as *introduction, definition, facts, example, diagram, explanation*, or *summary*; a practice section can comprise a *case study, simulation*, or *exercises*; and a review section may contain a *recapitulation, quiz, test, assessment*, or *next steps*. Finally, a resources section contains *links, documents*, a *glossary*,

and an *index*.

As shown in Figure 1, a decomposition like this can directly be transferred to a class diagram, where the various content pieces are represented as attributes. Technically, these attributes will have types such as text or image so that content can adequately be represented. Figure 1 also shows the LOM and the DCMI attributes that we consider part of the head of a learning object. Finally, a learning object may further be characterized by global information, such as prerequisites, i.e., a brief statement of is expected from the learner when studying this object, or an objective of what the learner is supposed to learn here.

As a consequence of this way of modeling learning objects, there is considerable flexibility in their inner structure, which can be exploited to model a large variety of learning items and learning situations, e.g., the object that resembles a lecture in class, consisting of definitions, examples, scenario explanations, and summarizing comments; the object that explains a certain process model (in one of several forms: through an animated slide show or a movie showing a simulation, through a textual explanation of the various activities and object stores occurring in the model); the situation where a sales person needs to read a short note or be instructed about a special offer of his company; the object comprising a strategy exposition for a company; the object containing a legal text or regulation that needs to be brought to an employees attention.

Figure 1 also indicates how we are trying to come across an integration of knowledge management and learning: A learning object is perceived as a *specialization* of a knowledge object. The idea behind this is that any user of the learning system at large could easily create a knowledge object (and other users can contribute to a knowledge object already created); in order to motivate people to do this, creation should be vastly unrestricted (e.g., not confined to editing certain attributes). However, it could happen after a while that such an object has accumulated so much or so important content that it is turned (specialized) into a learning object. Therefore, a knowledge object references an "author," i.e., the person responsible for its content; this person ideally retains this role even after a specialization has occurred. Clearly, this may be considered preliminary, yet it should be seen as an attempt to integrate knowledge management and learning at a technical level.

Usage of Learning Objects

Regarding the usage of learning objects, we imagine that they are consumed by learners (individually or in chunks called classes) and that they are created by authors, both under the supervision of some management system. When learning objects are grouped together and sequenced to form a *class*, this class will have an associated *class map* the learner can use as a navigation aid; in particular, a class map constitutes a partial order among the learning objects involved. Additionally, we use a *person* class as a generalization of the roles of a *learner* as well as of an *author* (and possibly others). A specific feature of a learner is the associated *profile* as well as the *learning allowance*. The profile, among other things, is intended to keep track of a learning history, i.e., what a learner has been doing. Finally, the learning allowance records the time a class has consumed and counts backwards in order to determine when a "time account" is used up; notice that a learning allowance resembles the (monetary or time) accounts under discussion for learning in various countries at the moment. We will return to this issue in Section 3 (cf. Figure 2).

As mentioned, the map associated with a class can be thought of as a partial order (or directed acyclic graph) of the learning objects making up that class; in particular, there is a starting point, i.e., a learning object that has to be accessed first, and thereafter there may be parallel branches within the class content for which the exact order in which a learner works through the respective objects is immaterial. Finally, there are no loops in a class map, so what a learner actually will have done in the end is to have consumed a topological sort of the class map, i.e., one of possibly several linear orders of learning objects derived from the class map. Clearly, the underlying system should allow a learner to redo individual learning objects on such a map if necessary. Class maps give rise to a straightforward navigation mechanism: Since individual learning objects may occur in more than one class a learner has to attend, we can avoid that he or she has to do the same object over and over by deriving an *active* class map from the generic one associated with a class; the active class map is personalized towards the learner and takes his learning history (recorded in the profile) into account.

Now that we have established a basic technical understanding of learning objects as used in this paper, we can look at their various exploitations in the context of a learning system. We devote the remainder of this section to the "easy" part of authoring learning objects.

Authoring Learning Objects

Learning objects as introduced above will typically form the basis of a variety of learning assignments; for the latter, we see at least three relevant types:

- *Individual* learning objects should be appropriate, for example, for individual topics that can be extracted from a larger context (e.g., basics of Entity-Relationship modeling), and for which it can be specified precisely where their usage would be appropriate.

- A *class* could be comprised of a collection or sequence of learning objects according to a class map, and would roughly correspond to a class in a university that extends over several sessions or class meetings (appropriate, for example, for the novice learner).

- Finally, a *course program* comprised of several classes (such as one offered in a virtual university) would need a larger collection of learning objects, potentially from a variety of sources and grouped into several classes.

Clearly, the task of authoring content is simplified if a certain structuring of the target learning object has been prescribed. To this end, a learning object structured as shown in Figure 1 is easily cast into a number of forms an author can fill out. Indeed, for a particular learning object under design, the first decision to be made is which attribute is needed and which is not. For the ones that are left, content can be either created from scratch, imported from a foreign source, or even generated on the basis of another system. We mention that we are developing a prototypical system that makes use of the latter approach; our system is intended to support an easy creation of learning objects that teach process models (as well as various other subjects).

We also mention that we consider learning objects as being *versioned*, i.e., updates to an existing learning object are not made in place, but lead to another version. In this way, the participation of a learning object (or different versions of it) in distinct classes becomes manageable. We are even considering to attach a lifetime to a learning object so that it can no longer be used once its *lifetime* has expired.

Finally, we note again that, according to Figure 1, learning objects are *specializations* of knowledge objects in our approach. Since we let knowledge objects be simpler in structure than learning objects (actually freely chosen by its creator), it is easier to create a knowledge object than a learning object, a fact that should motivate users to participate in knowledge creation and conservation. Moreover, as more and more content gets accumulated in a knowledge object, a course designer may decide that it is now appropriate to derive a learning object from that particular knowledge object. In that case, that way to accomplish this would be to create a corresponding specialization and then enter into an authoring process.

3 Accessing and Managing Learning Objects

In this section, we look at learning objects from two other perspectives, that of a *learner* who is the consumer of such objects and that of an *administrator* (or a teacher or even the underlying LMS) responsible for information derivation and management pertinent to learning objects. To this end, we particularly look into the aspect of *user profiling* as well as *tracking*, which we perceive as processes that are modeled using the Petri net formalism.

Profiling Learners

A user profile is typically established and maintained by an LMS for several purposes, including content adaptation, content presentation, and progress monitoring. Indeed, content to be worked on by a learner is ideally adapted by an LMS to the learners prior knowledge, his or her preferences, standing, learning style and speed, as well as to the overall study program he or she has been assigned or chosen [4, 6, 9]. For example, a learner may take several classes on a similar subject of increasing difficulty (e.g.,"Introduction to Process Modeling," "Advanced Process Modeling," etc.); it may then happen that initial parts of both classes overlap, so that the learner may get bored if the classes are taken

shortly after one another and the learner can indeed experience the redundancy involved. If the class is properly organized into learning objects, user adaptation could make sure that if such an object occurs in either class, the learner can skip over it when the object is encountered the second time, provided he or she has successfully mastered it in the first place.

From the content perspective, we are able to provide this using class maps as described earlier. From the learner perspective, we take such considerations into account by associating a *learner profile* with every learner as shown in Figure 2. This figure shows an excerpt from the learner data model we have designed (and also references the learning object class explained above as a class specified elsewhere). A learner profile comprises goals, a learning history, information about a learner's performance, and preferences that drive content selection and presentation. Importantly, a learning history is given by the learning objects he or she has successfully completed. Since learning objects may be repeated throughout various courses, it makes sense to associate them to a profile. The profile is continuously updated as a learner works through various assignments.

The learner profile contains an attribute called *Learning Allowance* (already mentioned in Section 2) which represents an amount of hours a learner has available to spend freely on learning material. It has to be set to an initial value as part of the initialization of a learner profile, and it is updated whenever a class is completed. Updating means that the current allowance is *reduced* by the class duration. Three aspects are worth noting here:

- The allowance is currently connected to classes only, not to course programs, and also not to individual learning objects. In a more refined scheme, this could be extended.

- The current approach is to recalculate an allowance based on class *durations* only, which is an estimated time that simply adds up the durations of the learning objects comprising the class. Thus, a "slow" learner, taking more time than estimated, is treated fair by this approach, while the "fast" learner, taking less time than estimated, does not really benefit from it. This could also be changed in the future.

- The learning allowance could ultimately be transformed into a "pricing scheme" where a learner is charged for the delivery of an individual learning object or an entire class content (or for taking an exam) and, beyond that, become part of a business model for e-learning.

As a consequence, we consider awards a learner can earn for the successful completion of an assignment as having an

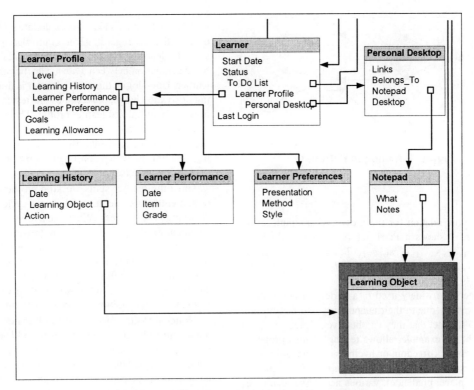

Figure 2. Excerpt from the Learner Data Model.

effect on a learners allowance, which is reflected, for example, in our approach to user tracking. The *Learning History* can technically be as simple as a table representing what a learner has been doing to a learning object, and when he or she has been doing it. From the values of the attributes included here it is possible to calculate the time a learner has needed to complete this class. The *Learner Performance* represents a possibility to record a learner's performance, not in terms of what he or she has been doing (that appears in the *Learner History*), but how he or she has been doing it. Thus, entries here carry grading information. An extension would be to enable the calculation of GPA (grade point average) values reflecting an average taken over the results of several assignments, or to calculate degrees resulting from the successful completion of a course program in combination with a certain grade.

Entries in the *Learner Preferences* class represent preferences a learner might have with respect to his or her learning style and the presentation of learning material (see above). For example, some learners prefer written text (to be read) over spoken text (to be listened to), or still images over animated ones. Clearly, an appropriate selection of attributes (and their allowed values) must be guided by expertise from

learning theories, which goes beyond the scope of this paper.

Petri Nets

For describing our next exploitations of learning objects, we need a model to describe processes. To this end, we use this modeling approach for the specification of relevant processes. For the sake of completeness, we briefly recall some Petri net basics next; further details can be found, for example, in [14]. Petri nets are a graphical formalism for the description of processes and allow for a specification of sequential or concurrent activities that may or may not exclude each other. The crucial feature is that only two graphical constructs are needed: *Circles* are used to represent static aspects, e.g., states, documents, object stores; *rectangles* are used to represent events or activities. Moreover, circles and rectangles are connected by arcs in such way that the resulting graph is *bipartite*, i.e., states and activities occur in a strictly alternating manner.

More formally, a net is a triple $N = (S, T, F)$ s.t. S ("states") and T ("transitions") are non-empty, disjoint, and finite sets, and $F \subseteq (S \times T) \cup (T \times S)$ repre-

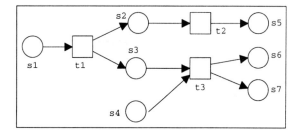

Figure 3. A sample Petri net.

sents the flow relation (or the arcs). As a simple example, Figure 3 shows a Petri net $N = (S, T, F)$ where $S = \{s_1, s_2, s_3, s_4, s_5, s_6, s_7\}$, $T = \{t_1, t_2, t_3\}$, and $F = \{(s_1, t_1), (t_1, s_2), (t_1, s_3), (s_2, t_2), (t_2, s_5), (s_3, t_3), (s_4, t_3), (t_3, s_6), (t_3, s_7)\}$.

Petri nets are widely used in a variety of applications, which is mainly due to their adaptability and flexibility as well as to the fact that they can be given a precise semantics which, for example, allows testing various properties such as deadlock-freedom or liveliness. Depending on the particular interpretation given to the circles (e.g., channel, condition, place, predicate), various net classes can be established with distinct expressive power. This aspect together with the fact that they can be refined in a top-down fashion (where rectangles are replaced by entire "sub-nets") and that they can be described in a strictly mathematical fashion (using techniques from linear algebra) makes them amenable to process modeling, as has been described, for example, in [15, 13].

In the context of process modeling, Petri nets informally come with the interpretation that rectangles are activities occurring in a process, and circles are object stores that provide input to an activity, get manipulated by the activity, and also represent output created by an activity. Clearly, in order to make this amenable to the modeling of processes representing workflows, a variety of additional aspects need to be covered. For example, each activity needs to be associated with one or more roles that are played by available resources and beyond that maybe with costs, times, or ratings, while each object store has associated object types or classes representing the entities that are relevant in the particular context. To make the latter precise, an underlying object model is needed which captures, at a conceptual level, the ingredients and properties of objects that are relevant to the process being modeled.

Using Petri Nets to Describe Learning Sessions

We now give several examples of how to describe processes relevant to e-learning using Petri nets; various other exam-

ples can be found in [17]. One exploitation of what has been described above regarding learner profiles appears in our vision of a learning session as shown in Figure 4. There is a basic distinction between a *novice* learner and an *advanced* learner. Upon login, the novice learner is first tested regarding prior knowledge; the result of this test is recorded in the previously initialized learner profile. The advanced learner is a person with prior learning experience, and for which the initial test is not necessary. Both types of learners get learning assignments which consist of course programs, classes, or learning objects.

Once the learner starts working on the assignment, he or she enters a cycle and within that cycle essentially the "learning" sub-process. When the learner considers the assignment finished, he or she has to provide feedback on the assignment itself. Finally, the learner profile is updated in order to record what has been done and what the result was. Notice that the result itself is obtained inside the learning sub-process (which is not shown here), as each learning object has a review section that may eventually contain a test.

Notice that the object of study ultimately is the individual learning object, several of which could be accessed consecutively within one session. Moreover, the profile of a learner is updated upon completion of a learning assignment and the subsequent test, and keeps track of the learner's abilities and knowledge, yet all this information is broken down to the granularity of the individual learning object.

Tracking Learners

When a new tracking record is created and sent to the LMS, the system tests whether a class or a learning assignment is now successfully finished; this and further details of learner tracking are shown in Figure 5. If no assignment is complete, the learner simply continues, and the system continues to monitor her or him. However, if the former is the case, the system will check the degree obtained for the assignment against a predefined skill map. The point is that a new tracking record is created every time a learner starts working on a new learning object, and that record is updated once the learner finishes the learning object.

We mention that if the assignment under consideration has been a course program, the test just described will be made every time a class from that program is finished. If the learning assignment just completed has been a class, the first thing to do is update the learning allowance, i.e., to subtract the class duration from the learning allowance associated with a learner in his or her profile. The next goal is to automatically match the degree earned as a result of completing an assignment; after that it can be tested whether the degree obtained matches a skill. For the time being, this test is simple, as a class is considered as a sequence of learning objects, and it is easy to see from the tracking records col-

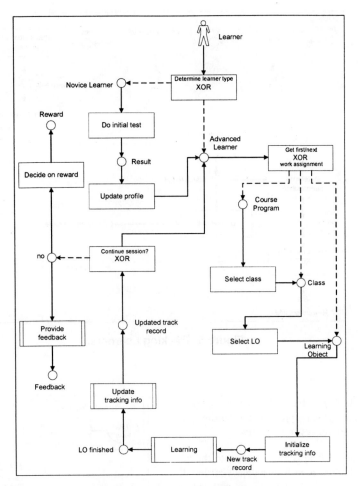

Figure 4. A Learning Session.

lected whether or not that sequence is complete. Similarly, a course program is a sequence of classes, and again it is easily tested whether that sequence is now complete. Notice that the situation is more complicated (although computationally not much harder) when classes are partial orders of learning objects, and course programs are partial orders of classes.

We conclude this section by mentioning that content selection and presentation is also based on user profiles and on the fact that the core granularity is that of a learning object. Indeed, we plan to give users an ability to subscribe to certain content based on their personal interests. Moreover, presentations are created for individual learning objects and are driven by the preferences, styles and standing recorded in a learners profile.

Putting the Pieces Together

We now put the various pieces we have designed together. To this end, Figure 6 summarizes the various aspects we have been considering and for which learning objects are the fundamental paradigm:

- *Content creation* is done based on (knowledge objects and on) learning objects, where the former can be turned into the latter, and where the latter are essentially based on predefined "patterns" that drive their authoring. Learning objects can be sequenced into classes, where the ordering can be a total or a partial one.

- *Content consumption* (learning) is done based on course programs consisting of classes, which in turn consist of learning objects, so the ultimate study item

285

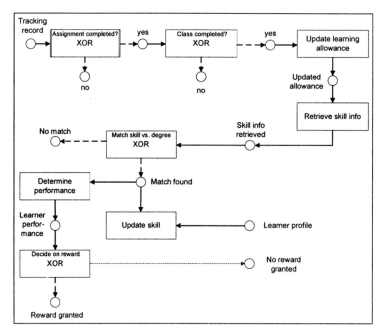

Figure 5. Tracking Learners.

is the individual learning object. For the purposes of learning, objects are given a presentation tailored towards a learners preferences and abilities.

- *User profiling and tracking* is also attached to the individual learning object, as each such object carries all the information relevant to a user profile, including test results and learning times.

Clearly, learning objects and the system that manages them also need to be interfaced with systems or sources from which it is possible to derive or import content.

4 Conclusions and Future Work

In this paper we have tried to advocate the role of learning objects as a central and fundamental paradigm underlying an e-learning system. We have started out from a database perspective of learning objects, which materializes in a well-defined structure with mandatory and optional attributes that leads to a class-based, object-model representation of what has for a long time already been called a learning object. We have then indicated how to surround this object model with other database objects representing further LMS ingredients, in particular learners and their profiles. Finally, we have shown how various LMS activities, both of learning nature and of administrative nature, can be

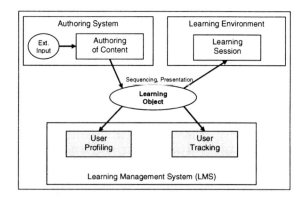

Figure 6. Overview of Learning Object Exploitations.

founded upon this object-based approach. On the side, we have indicated how learning objects can also be related to knowledge objects, by considering the former a specialization of the latter.

Future work could be pursued along a variety of lines, some of which are indicated next:

Course evaluation: As is common nowadays for every course offering, be it related to learning or not, an evaluation cycle may be a reasonable issue to be added. Up to now we foresee the collection of feedback from learners in our system, and the use of collected feedback when learning objects are updated, yet there is no special evaluation mechanism that looks, for example, for issues such as the following: How well was a particular learning object or class received? How well are the authors currently involved in content creation? What are good external sources? How does learner performance relate to the evaluation learners have given a course?

Learner evaluation: Once a learner has finished an assignment, he or she could undergo a critical performance evaluation. For example, from the learning history the sequence of learning objects worked upon can be derived, and it could be tested whether the route taken through these objects is indeed conformant to the (active) class map for the class under consideration. Moreover, the learning speed could be calculated, and from route and speed a classification of the learner could be derived.

Calendaring: The environment presented to a learner could integrate a calendaring system through which a learner can arrange his or her assigned learning objects over time, and then be reminded of an upcoming learning session.

Personalization: A learning environment could be personalized to some extent, and the learner could be given some freedom in that respect. So far it has only been specified that a learner should be able to create and manipulate a personal desktop including a "notepad," but clearly much more could be done in terms of personalization. To this end, user profiling techniques as used in Web site management for the personalization of content may be useful for a learning system [3, 8]. By the same token, recommender systems which select items that could be of interest to a particular user could be employed for learning situations; see [12] for an evaluation of corresponding algorithms.

We mention that we are investigating in a separate project to what extend the processes and components of an e-learning system can be perceived and be made available as Web services; details can be found in [18].

References

[1] Adelsberger, H.H., B. Collis, J.M. Pawlowski, eds. (2002). Handbook on Information Technologies for Education and Training. Springer-Verlag, Berlin.

[2] Barritt, C. (2001). CISCO Systems Reusable Learning Object Strategy Designing Information and Learning Objects Through Concept, Fact, Procedure, Process, and Principle Templates, Version 4.0. White Paper, CISCO Systems, Inc., November 2001.

[3] Bradley, K., Rafter, R., Smyth, B.: Case-Based User Profiling for Content Personalisation. Proc. International Conference on Adaptive Hypermedia and Adaptive Web-based Systems, Trento, Italy, 2000.

[4] De Bra, P., Calvi, L.: AHA! An open Adaptive Hypermedia Architecture. The New Review of Hypermedia and Multimedia 4, Taylor Graham Publishers, 1998, pp. 115-119.

[5] Downes, S.: Learning Objects: Resources for Distances Education Worldwide. International Review of Research in Open and Distance Learning 2 (1) 2000.

[6] El Saddik, A., Fischer, S., Steinmetz, R.: Reusability and Adaptability of Interactive Resources in Web-Based Educational Systems. ACM Journal of Educational Resources in Computing 1 (1) 2001.

[7] Fischer, S. (2001). Course and Exercise Sequencing Using Metadata in Adaptive Hypermedia Learning Systems. ACM Journal of Educational Resources in Computing, 1(1), Spring 2001.

[8] Fink, J., Kobsa, A.: A Review and Analysis of Commercial User Modeling Servers for Personalization on the World Wide Web. User Modeling and User-Adapted Interaction 10, 2000, pp. 209-249.

[9] Henze, N., Nejdl, W.: Adaptivity in the KBS Hyperbook System. Proc. 2nd Workshop on Adaptive Systems and User Modeling on the WWW 1999.

[10] Hüsemann, B., Lechtenbörger, J., Vossen, G., Westerkamp, P.: XLX - A Platform for Graduate-Level Exercises. Proc. International Conference on Computers in Education, Auckland, New Zealand, December 2002, pp. 1262-1266.

[11] IEEE: Draft Standard for Learning Object Metadata. IEEE Standards Department Publication P1484.12.1/D6.4, March 2002.

[12] Karypis, G.: Evaluation of Item-Based Top-N Recommendation Algorithms. Proc. 10th ACM International Conference on Information and Knowledge Management (CIKM) 2001.

[13] Oberweis, A., Sander, P., Stucky, W.: Petri net based modelling of procedures in complex object database applications, Proc. 17th IEEE Annual International Computer Software and Applications Conference (COMPSAC), Phoenix/Arizona 1993, pp. 138-144.

[14] Reisig, W.: Petri Nets, An Introduction. EATCS, Monographs on Theoretical Computer Science, W. Brauer, G. Rozenberg, A. Salomaa (Eds.), Springer Verlag, Berlin, 1985.

[15] Van der Aalst, W., Desel, J., Oberweis, A., eds.: Business Process Management - Models, Techniques and Empirical Studies, Lecture Notes in Computer Science Vol. 1806, Springer-Verlag, Berlin, 2000.

[16] Vossen, G., Jaeschke, P.: Towards a Uniform and Flexible Data Model for Learning Objects. Proc. 30th Annual Conference of the International Business School Computing Association (IBSCA), Savannah, Georgia, 2002, pp. 99-129.

[17] Vossen, G., Jaeschke, P., Oberweis, A.: Flexible Workflow Management as a Central E-Learning Support Paradigm. Proc. 1st European Conference on E-Learning (ECEL), Uxbridge, UK, 2002, pp. 253-267.

[18] Vossen, G., Westerkamp, P.: E-Learning as a Web Service (Extended Abstract). these proceedings.

Database Applications II

Applying Bulk Insertion Techniques for Dynamic Reverse Nearest Neighbor Problems

King-Ip Lin, Michael Nolen, Congjun Yang
Division of Computer Science,
The University of Memphis,
Dunn Hall 373,
Memphis, TN 38152, U.S.A.
linki@msci.memphis.edu, mnolen@memphis.edu, yangc@msci.memphis.edu

Abstract

Reverse Nearest Neighbors queries has emerged as an important class of queries for spatial and other types of databases. The Rdnn-tree is an R-tree based structure that has been shown to perform outstandingly for such kind of queries. However, one practical problem facing it (as well as other type of indexes) is how to effective construct the index from stretch In this case, the cost of constructing and maintaining a Rdnn-Tree is about twice the cost of an R-Tree. Normal insertion into a Rdnn-Tree is performed one point at a time, known as single point insertion. The question arises, can insertion be improved there by reducing the construction and maintenance cost. In this paper we propose a bulk-loading technique, which is capable of significantly, improve the performance of constructing the index from stretch, as well as insert a large amount of data. Experiments shows that our method outperform the single point insertion significantly.

1. Introduction

Indexing is an important aspect of any efficient database system. Indexes enable queries to look at only a small portion of data, thus avoiding costly sequential scan operations on databases. Thus new kinds of indexes have been developed to speed-up execution of many different kinds of queries. Nowadays indexes come in various shape and size: B+-tree (which handle single-dimensional data); R-trees and its variants [2, 10, 16] (which handles spatial data well); indices designed for high dimensional data, like the TV-tree [15] and X-trees [6]; and indexes that work under any metric space, like the MVP-tree [5] and M-tree [9]. Most index structures are tree-based, and in this paper we focus on such type of indexes.

Traditionally, indexes deal with simple queries like exact match and range queries. Nowadays indexes are called to speed up various kinds of queries, like joins, nearest neighbor queries and reverse nearest neighbor queries. Of special interest to us is the reverse nearest neighbor query, which has a wide range of applications from Geographic Information Systems to E-commerce. Korn and Muthurksirhnan [13] provided more applications for the query.

One area that has recently received more attention is bulk loading of indexes. This means creating an index from scratch based on data we already have on-hand. In many cases, the amount of data can be huge. The need for bulk loading arises in many situations. For instance, the decision to build an index may come long after the database is populated. In addition, one may decide to completely reorganize an index for improved performance. In any case, effective bulk loading is an important part of index operations. A related operation is bulk insertion. While bulk loading focused on building the index from scratch, bulk insertion aims at inserting a significant amount of new data into an index, without dumping the original one.

While every index structure has a standard insertion algorithm for inserting a single data item, it is not a good idea to apply this algorithm repeatedly for bulk loading/inserting data. This approach leads to wasted effort. For instance, multiple data items may end up being inserted into the same leaf node, leading to the same nodes being updated repeatedly, thus wasting effort. Moreover, bulk loading/insertion implies that we already have all the data in front of us, thus we can make use of that fact to speed up the process.

In this paper, we present a bulk loading/insertion algorithm for the Rdnn-tree [19], an indexing structure devised to efficiently answer nearest neighbor and reverse nearest neighbor queries. The algorithm utilizes the notion of in-memory organization of the data to efficiently insert multiple data objects. This algorithm has many advantages: it does not require the input data to be ordered in any way –

the same cannot be said of many bulk insertion algorithms; the algorithm is orthogonal to the buffer management that is used; it is applicable to both bulk loading from scratch and bulk insertion.

The rest of the paper is organized as follows. Section 2 provides a brief outline of the reverse nearest neighbor problem, and the Rdnn-tree index structure. Section 3 surveys some related bulk loading/insertion algorithms. We provide an in-depth description of our method in section 4. Experimental results are presented in section 5. Finally, future directions – especially how our method can generalize to other index structures, are outlined in section 6.

2.   Reverse Nearest Neighbor and the Rdnn-tree

We illustrate the reverse nearest neighbor problem by an example. Suppose the business of a grocery store is most affected by the store that is closest to it. Now if a grocery chain is going to open a new store, it may want to find all the stores that have the new store as its closest neighbor. Also one may want to contact potential customers. Assuming customers tend to visit the store that is closest to them, one would need to find customers who have the new store as its closest store.

In both cases, we are given a query object (the new store), instead of finding the stores that are closest to it (its nearest neighbor), we are actually looking for stores (or customers) that take the new store as their nearest neighbors. We call these stores/customers the *reverse nearest neighbor* of the query object. Formally we have the following:

Definition (Reverse Nearest Neighbor)

Given a set *S* of points in some *d* dimensional space and a query point *q*, the *Reverse Nearest Neighbor* of *q* (denoted RNN$_S$(q)) is a subset of *S* defined as

$$RNN_S(q) = \{r \in S \mid \forall p \in S : D(q,r) \leq D(r,p)\}$$

where *D(p,q)* denote the distance between point *p* and *q*

Figure 1 shows an example for reverse nearest neighbors. Notice that in contrast to the nearest neighbor, a point *q* does not necessary have reverse nearest neighbors – or it can have multiple reverse nearest neighbors. For instance, in 2-d Euclidean space, a point may have up to six reverse nearest neighbors.

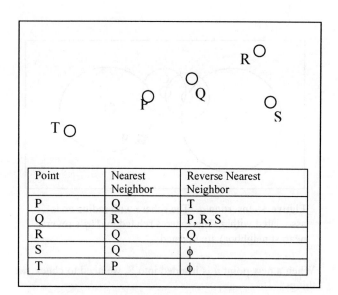

Point	Nearest Neighbor	Reverse Nearest Neighbor
P	Q	T
Q	R	P, R, S
R	Q	Q
S	Q	φ
T	P	φ

Figure 1. Illustration of Reverse Nearest Neighbors

A good method to find reverse nearest neighbors efficiently is proposed by Korn and Muthukrishnan [13]. They preprocess the data set S by finding the nearest neighbor of every point of S and store them. Then when a query point *q* arrives, if it is closer to the nearest neighbor of a point *p* in the data set then *p* itself, than *p* is a reverse neighbor of *q*. This implies that we need to keep track of the current nearest neighbor of each point in S. This can be represented by a set of hyperspheres, one for each point, with radius equal to the nearest neighbor distance. If S is static, any multi-dimensional index structure suffices. However, when S is dynamic, we need to update the nearest neighbor of the points in S dynamically. The case of insertion is illustrated below in figures 2 and 3.

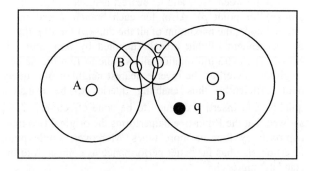

Figure 2.   Illustrates nearest neighbor distances before insertion of point *q*.

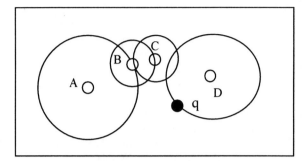

Figure 3. Inserting q. The sphere with radius qc is associated with q. The spheres related to d (q's reverse nearest neighbor) are updated.

When a new point u is inserted into S, we need to check two things:

- Find the nearest neighbor of u in S and store it
- Find all points in S whose nearest neighbor is u – that is, the reverse nearest neighbor of u, and update them

Thus one needs an efficient index structure to find both the nearest neighbor as well as the reverse nearest neighbor of u in S. In the original paper, one needs two separate indexes to do the job. This leads to duplicate effort and inefficiency. Thus, we are motivated by this to develop the Rdnn-tree (R-tree with distance to nearest neighbor). Here we only provide a brief outline of the tree structure and algorithms. The interested reader is referred to the paper by Yang and Lin [19].

The Rdnn-tree is based on the R-tree, the major addition is that for each data point, we also store the current distance between itself and its nearest neighbor (denoted by $dnn_S(p)$ for point p). Also, for each branch stored in an internal node, the maximum of all the $dnn_S(p)$ for all p that is the descendent of that branch (denoted by *max_dnn*) is stored. The extra information allows one to find the nearest neighbor as well as the reverse nearest neighbor of a query point efficiently, thus enabling queries to be executed quickly, and insertion/deletion to be done effectively. [19] showed that the Rdnn-tree outperforms the original two trees approach by four or more times. Moreover, single point insertion also has far better performance as compared to the standard approach.

Interested readers are directed to the following papers [3] [17] [18] for a discussion of other algorithms for reverse nearest neighbors.

3.   Related work in bulk loading/inserting indexes

The problem of bulk loading arises in indexes for multi-dimensional data. In one-dimensional indexes like B-tree, one can first sort the data to be loaded, and then group the data into leaf nodes based on the ordering, and then build the tree bottom up. With higher-dimensional data, there is no natural ordering of the data that preserve proximity of the data, making this solution less applicable. Still, quite a few methods adopt a sorting-based technique for bulk loading indexes like R-tree. For instance, Faloutsos and Kamel [12] suggested using the Hilbert-values to order the data for bulk-inserting the R-tree; while Hjaltason and Samet [11] used z-ordering for bulk-insertion in quadtrees; and Leutenegger et al. [14] suggests a method that requires multiple sorts.

A different approach of bulk loading is to partition the data to be loaded, build a tree for each partition, and then combine the trees together. Care must be taken in how to partition the data; otherwise, significant reorganization is needed during the combination process. In the method for bulk loading M-tree [8], samples are drawn from the data set, and each data point is assigned to the sample that is closest to it. In this case, reorganization is still necessary. A similar concept is applied in the case of bulk insertion. For instance, [7] proposed to bulk insert points into an R-tree by using clustering to partition the points to be inserted into spatially-close clusters, and then build a small R-tree for each partition and then graft it into the original R-tree.

A third approach of building the index is via buffering the points to be inserted. For example, [1] proposed a method where the internal nodes have buffers attached to it. When an insertion occurs, rather then traversing down the whole path, the insertion stops at a certain level, and the points to be inserted is stored in the buffer. When enough points are accumulated, they are pushed down to the next level.

Recent work of bulk loading includes that of Bercken and Seeger [4], which proposes a generalized recursive partition based bulk-loading algorithm.

4.   Bulk loading/inserting the Rdnn-tree

In section 2, we briefly outlined the Rdnn-tree and the query and insertion algorithms. We have seen that with the slight addition of extra information, one can efficiently answer the reverse nearest neighbor query. Moreover, the single index enables insertion to be done quickly.

However, inserting data points one at a time still is a very poor option for bulk loading and inserting. Our tests shows that, for a 2,000,000-point data set, inserting one point at a time requires 17 page requests per insertion on average. Our goal is to significantly lower this by designing a better bulk-loading algorithm.

For the Rdnn-tree, we incorporate bulk loading and bulk insertion into one algorithm. Bulk loading is done by first reading a set of points into main memory and preprocessing them, and then inserting those points into an existing Rdnn-tree. This enables us to treat both bulk loading and bulk insertion uniformly. Moreover, the algorithm is flexible enough to deal with variable size of main memory.

The goal of the preprocessing is to enable multiple points to be inserted into the tree without duplicating effort. The most intuitive way is to organize the points such that we can determine which points are going to be in the same node, or traverse a very similar path during insertion. Then multiple points can be inserted only via one transversal of the tree, saving a significant amount of page access.

An additional point to consider for the Rdnn-tree is that inserting a point not only requires finding the correct leaf node, but also finding its nearest neighbor (so to store the nearest neighbor distance), as well as its reverse nearest neighbors (so that those points can update their nearest neighbor distances). This has two implications. Firstly, it makes the grouping of points even more important. One can see that points that are to be inserted into the same node are likely to be close together, thus likely to share the same nearest neighbors. Thus inserting them at the same time will save effort in finding nearest neighbors. Moreover, the points may share the same reverse nearest neighbors. This implies that inserting them together can reduce the number of updates of nearest neighbor distances. This is illustrated by the following example:

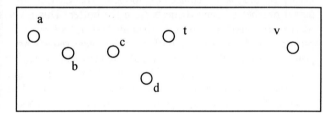

Figure 4 Illustration of wasted effort in single point insertion. *v* is *t*'s original nearest neighbor. Insertion of *a, b, c, d* in that order will cause successive updates of *t*'s nearest neighbors.

In figure 4, assume point *t* is a point that is already in the Rdnn-tree. Point *a, b, c, d* are points to be inserted. Notice that if we insert the points individually in that order, *t* is going to be the reverse nearest neighbor of all four points at the instance when each of the points is inserted. Thus, we need to update the nearest neighbor distance of *t* four times. This can lead to a large amount of wasted effort if *t* is actually in a different node then the other four points. However, if we can insert all four points at once, then *t*'s nearest neighbor distance only needs to be updated once, thus saving a lot of disk access.

A second implication of the extra work needed is that we cannot directly apply the standard bulk

loading/insertion algorithms that is in the literature, thus we need to propose a new method.

All of the discussion above directs us to the idea of organizing the points such that we insert the closest points together. However, one needs to be cautious. As we mentioned, during insertion one need to find the nearest neighbors as well as the reverse nearest neighbors of the point to be inserted. However, in the case of bulk insert, the nearest neighbor/reverse nearest neighbor of a point to be inserted may actually be some other point that are to be inserted. This implies that one has to be careful about determining those values.

Putting everything into consideration, we propose building an in-memory Rdnn-tree for the points that are to be bulk loaded/inserted. This essentially kills two birds with one stone: the Rdnn-tree automatically clusters the data points, so that one can determine which points can be inserted simultaneously; also the in-memory Rdnn-tree provides the nearest neighbor distance of the points to be inserted (relative to other points in the input set). This can help speed up finding the real nearest neighbors and reverse nearest neighbors of the points to be inserted. Once the in-memory tree is built, we pick up each leaf node and insert the points together. If there are too many points to be loaded/inserted, then we first read a portion of the data points to be inserted. After that, we insert all the points in the in-memory tree, and then we build a new in-memory tree for the next portion of points. The overall pseudo-code is listed below.

Algorithm 1: Bulk Insertion/Loading an Rdnn-tree

BulkInsert (Rdnn-tree T, PointSet S)

While not all points inserted do
    Read the next portion of S and build an in-memory Rdnn-tree T'
    For each leaf node lnode in T' do
        BulkInsertNode(T, lnode)
    End
End

The *BulkInsertNode* procedure takes a leaf node (denoted as *lnode*) of the in-memory Rdnn-tree and inserts the points in into the main Rdnn-tree. The insertion procedure is the same as the original tree: first, the nearest neighbors and reverse nearest neighbors of the points to be inserted are located ([19] shows that these two search usually travel down the same path, so they can be performed in one traversal). After that the nearest neighbor distance of the reverse nearest neighbors are updated. Finally, the points in *lnode* are inserted by traversing the tree again. Since there is a possibility that the points in *lnode* will eventually reside in different leaf nodes in the main Rdnn-tree, for the last traversal we apply a depth first traversal (as multiple branches of the tree may have to be traversed). Depth first search has an advantage of a fixed upper bound on the memory required. The pseudo code is listed below.

Algorithm 2: Bulk Insert Individual node

BulkInsertNode (Rdnn-tree *T*, LeafNode *N*)

1. Let *P* = the set of points in *N* (For each point p, there is a *dnn(p)* denoting the current distance from its nearest neighbor)
2. Apply *Batch-NN-Search* [19] to find the nearest neighbor for each point in *P* (call this set NN$_P$)
3. Update dnn(p) for each point in P if necessary
4. *BatchUpdateCurrentTree(T, P)*
5. *BatchInsertPoints(T, N, NN$_P$)*

BatchUpdateCurrentTree(Node *N*, set\<Points\> *P*)

If *N* is not a leaf
    For each branch *B*
  1. Let *R* be the bounding rectangle for *B*, and *max_dnn* as described in section 2
  2. Find the set *P'* ∈ *P* such that ∀ *p* ∈ *P'*, *dist(p' R)* < *max_dnn*
  3. *BatchUpdateCurrentTree(B.child, P')*
else
    For each point q in Node
      If ∃ p' in P' s.t. Dist(p', q) < dnn(q).
          Find the minimum of such distance and update dnn(q)

We omit details of *BatchInsertPoints()*. It is basically the depth first traversal of the tree while input each point in P in the appropriate node, and apply the R*-tree insert procedure accordingly. One thing to notice that, since each set be inserted cannot contain too many points, so there is no danger of, say, a single node over flowing into 3 or more nodes. Thus the standard R*-tree algorithms can be applied directly.

5. Experimental Results

In this section, we present our experimental results. Here we measured two things: whether the bulk load/insert algorithm perform better than the single point insertion; and whether the index generated by the bulk loading/insertion algorithm build an index of equal or better quality then that produced by single point insertions.

We ran tests using both synthetic data and real world data. For the synthetic data five different test sets of one million 2D non-clustered points were randomly generated, as are five different test sets of one million 2D clustered points. Also to see how the algorithm handles higher dimensional data we generated 5 sets of 4D non-clustered data. We compare the two methods of bulk loading the index. We first apply individual point insertion to bulk load the index. Then we apply our algorithm, varying the number of points in the in-memory Rdnn-tree (denoted by *Rsize*) from 1,000 to 10,000. For each value of *Rsize* we apply the 5 different test sets. For the real world data, a single test set was retrieved from the US government web site: http://mapping.usgs.gov/www/gnis/. This test set contained 288,000 points (represented by latitude and longitude) for interesting location in the southeastern United States. Using the real world data an additional 11 tests were run. All testes where run on a Pentium III with 128MB main memory.

5.1 Bulk Loading/Insertion Results

Here we present comparison of the cost of building the index. We measure the cost in two ways. First we measure the number of read and write requests made. This gives us an overview of the cost. However, in case of bulk operations, buffering is an important aspect, as the same pages may be read and written repeatedly. Thus, we maintain a buffer with 1,000 4K pages (4K is the size of a tree node in our experiment), with LRU (Least Resently Used) as the page replacement policy. We measure the actual number of page requests from the buffer. This gives us realistic numbers. Space limitation does not allow us to present results with other buffer size or page replacement policies. As mentioned, we run multiple tests and we report the average values. It should be noted that each graph presented both single point and multiple point cost. The single point cost is always the left most point, and is denoted on the x-axis as *Single Point*, where as the multiple point cost is denoted by increasing *Rsize* in increments of a 1,000.

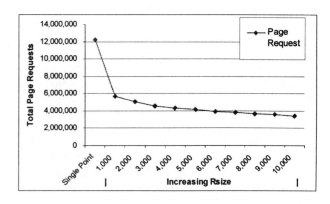

Figure 5. Total page requests for 2D Non-clustered data showing both single point and multiple point insertion.

2D Non-clustered Random Data Figure 5 shows the results for page request, while Figure 6 shows the results for read and write requests.

The results clearly show that as *Rsize* increases there is a reduction in the number of page request, as compared to single point insertion. There is n immediate reduction in page request when *Rsize* = 1,000 and a continued improvement as it approaches 10,000. Figure 6 show the change in pages read and write for the same set of test.

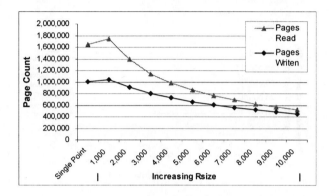

Figure 6. Read/Write page counts for 2D Non-clustered data showing both single point and multiple point insertion.

Figure 6 shows that the number of read requests is more than halved while the number of write request is also closed to being halved. Thus we can see our method provide inherit advantage regardless of the buffering algorithm One other thing to note is that small *Rsize* actually put the bulk insertion algorithm at a disadvantage. This is because it is less likely to locate points in the in-memory Rdnn-tree that are actually close together and will benefit from bulk insertion. However, this situation is quickly remedied even with a modest *Rsize*.

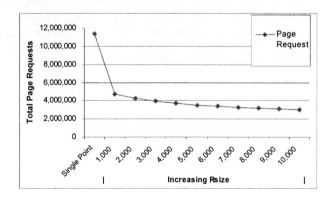

Figure 7. Total page requests for 2D clustered data showing both single point and multiple point insertion.

2D Clustered Data Identical experiments are run again but this time with the data being clustered. Figure 7 shows the results.

Just as with the non-clustered data figure 7 clearly shows that as *Rsize* increases the number of page request decreases, as compared to single point insertion. The improvement is as much as 4 times. Figure 8 show the change in pages reads and writes.

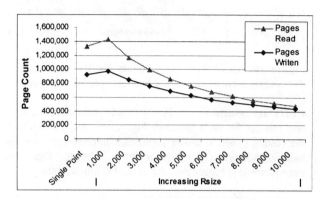

Figure 8. Read/Write page counts for 2D clustered data showing both single point and multiple point insertion.

4D Non-clustered Random Data Figure 9 shows the results for page request, while Figure 10 shows the results for read and write requests.

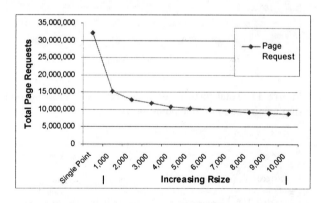

Figure 9. Total page requests for 4D Non-clustered data showing both single point and multiple point insertion.

From the figures, we can see improvement in performance for 4D data also. For instance, figure 9 denotes 3-fold improvement in terms of number of page requests. Figure 10 show the change in pages reads and writes. These two figures show that at higher dimensional data (at least 4D) the algorithm still achieves good results.

295

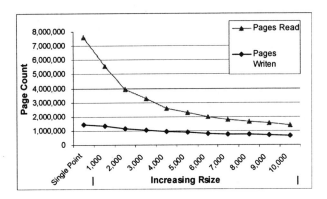

Figure 10. Read/Write page counts for 4D Non-clustered data showing both single point and multiple point insertion.

Real Data results For the real world data we have one test set for each instance. Figures 11 and 12 highlight the results – which shows significant improvement for the bulk loading/insertion algorithms. Notice that the improvement is bigger than the case of synthetic data.

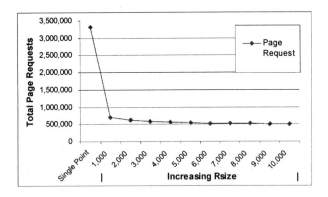

Figure 11. Total page requests for real data showing both single point and multiple point insertion.

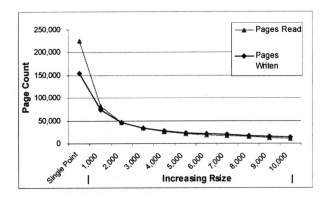

Figure 12. Read/Write page counts for real data showing both single point and multiple point insertion.

Robustness One concern for this algorithm is that whether the performance of the bulk insertion will degenerate when the database size becomes large. That is, whether the performance of the bulk insertion algorithm will degrade when more points are inserted. To test this, we keep the running average of the page request for every 10,000 points inserted. From figure 13, we can see that the number of insertions grows at a slow pace. Moreover, the growth rate for the bulk insert is similar to that of single point insert. Thus we can see that the bulk insert algorithm is as robust as single point insertion.

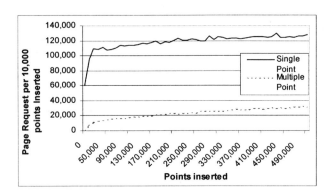

Figure 13. Comparison of average page request and leaf request for indexes created with both single point and multiple point insertion.

5.2 Index quality

As we mentioned, we need to check whether the index created by our bulk loading algorithm has similar quality then the one using single point insertion. To verify this, we execute a series of 100 reverse nearest neighbor queries for each of the indexes produced from the same test data set. The same queries are posed to all indexes. We measure the cost of the query by the average number of nodes visited as well as the average number of leaves visited – as in some cases, all but the leaf nodes of an index are stored in main memory. Figure 14 shows the results of these tests. We can see that as *Rsize* varies, the average page request remains stable. This shows that the index build by bulk insertion is of good quality.

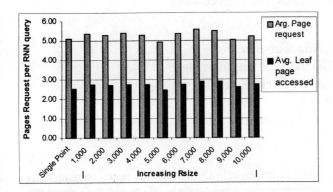

Figure 14. Comparison of page request per 10,000 points inserted for both single point and multiple point insertion.

6. Conclusion and future work

In this paper, we presented a bulk loading/insertion algorithm for the Rdnn-tree, an index structure designed for efficient nearest neighbor and reverse nearest neighbor queries. The algorithm takes advantage of the Rdnn-tree structure to enable a tree to be built quickly. Moreover, the algorithm can also be used for bulk insertion purposes. Experiments show that the algorithm outperforms single point insertion significantly, while maintaining the index's query performance.

Our goal in the future is to generalize the method to other indexes. While the Rdnn-tree has unique properties (need to update nearest neighbor distance) that leads to this bulk insertion algorithm, the algorithm's principle can be applied to other tree-based indices: building a smaller in-memory structure, and then insert the data points in groups. We plan to extend it to other index structures. We believe that can provide excellent results.

7. References

1. Arge, L., et al. *Efficient bulk operations on dynamic R-trees.* in *1st Workshop on Algorithm Engineering and Experimentation.* 1999. Baltimore, MD.
2. Beckmann, N., et al. *The R*-tree: An efficient and robust access method for points and rectangles.* in *ACM-SIGMOD Conference on Management of Data.* 1990. Atlantic City, NJ.
3. Benetis, R., et al. *Nearest Neighbor and Reverse Nearest Neighbor Queries for Moving Objects.* in *7th International Database Engineering and Application Symposium.* 2002. Edmonton, Canada.
4. Bercken, J.v.d. and B. Seeger. *An Evaluation of Generic Bulk Loading Techniques.* in *27th Internation Conference of Very Large Databases.* 2001. Rome, Italy.
5. Bozkaya, T. and M. Ozsoyoglu. *Distance-based indexing for high-dimensional metric spaces.* in *ACM SIGMOD International Conference on Management of Data.* 1997. Tucson, Arizona.
6. Brechtold, S., D.A. Keim, and H.-P. Kriegel. *The X-tree: An index structure for high-dimensional data.* in *The 22nd International Conference of Very Large Databases.* 1996. Mumbai, India.
7. Choubey, R., L. Chen, and E.A. Rundensteiner. *GBI: A Generalized R-Tree Bulk-Insertion Strategy.* in *6th International Symposium on Large Spatial Databases.* 1999. Hong Kong.
8. Ciaccia, P. and M. Patella. *Bulk loading the M-tree.* in *9th Australasian Database Conference.* 1998. Perth, Australia.
9. Ciaccia, P., M. Patella, and P. Zezula. *M-tree: an Efficient Access Method for Similarity Search in Metric Spaces.* in *23rd International Conference on Very Large Databases.* 1997. Athens, Greece.
10. Guttman, A. *R-trees: A dynamic index structure for spatial searching.* in *ACM-SIGMOD Conference on Management of Data.* 1984: Boston, MA.
11. Hjaltason, G. and H. Samet. *Improved Bulk-Loading Algorithms for Quadtrees.* in *7th ACM Symposium on Advances in Geographic Information Systems.* 1999. Kansas City, MO.
12. Kamel, I. and C. Faloutsos. *On Packing R-trees.* in *2nd International Conference on Information and Knowledge Management.* 1993. Arlighton, VA.
13. Korn, F. and S. Muthurksirhnan. *Influence sets based on reverse nearest neighbor queries.* in *ACM SIGMOD International Conference on Management of Data.* 2000. Dallas, USA.
14. Leutenegger, S.T., J.M. Edgington, and M.A. Lopez. *STR: A simple and efficient algorithm for R-tree packing.* in *The 13th International Conference on Data Engineering.* 1997. Birmingham, England.
15. Lin, K.I., H.V. Jagadish, and C. Falooutsos, *The TV-tree: an index structure for high-dimensional data.* VLDB Journal, 1994. **3**(4): p. 517-549.
16. Sellis, T.K., N. Roussopoulos, and C. Faloutsos. *The R+-Tree: A Dynamic Index for Multi-dimensional Objects.* in *The 13th international conference in Very Large Databases.* 1987.
17. Stanoi, I., D. Agrawal, and A. El Abbadi. *Reverse Nearest Neighbor Queries for Dynamic Databases.* in *ACM SIGMOD Workshop on Research Issues in Data Mining and Knowledge Discovery.* 2000.
18. Stanoi, I., et al. *Discovery of Influence Sets in Frequently Updated Databases.* in *Proceedings of the International Conference on Very Large Databases.* 2001.
19. Yang, C. and K.I. Lin. *An index structure for efficient reverse nearest neighbor queries.* in *IEEE International Conference on Data Engineering.* 2001. Heidelberg, Germany.

Enhancements on Local Outlier Detection

Anny Lai-mei Chiu, Ada Wai-chee Fu
Department of Computer Science and Engineering
The Chinese University of Hong Kong
Hong Kong
{lmchiu, adafu}@cse.cuhk.edu.hk

Abstract

Outliers, or commonly referred to as exceptional cases, exist in many real-world databases. Detection of such outliers is important for many applications. In this paper, we focus on the density-based notion that discovers local outliers by means of the Local Outlier Factor (LOF) formulation. Three enhancement schemes over LOF are introduced, namely LOF', LOF'' and GridLOF. Thorough explanation and analysis is given to demonstrate the abilities of LOF' in providing simpler and more intuitive meaning of local outlier-ness; LOF'' in handling cases where LOF fails to work appropriately; and GridLOF in improving the efficiency and accuracy.

Keywords: *outlier detection, outlier-ness, density*

1. Introduction

In contrast to most KDD tasks, such as clustering and classification, outlier detection aims to find the small portion of data which are deviating from common patterns in the database. Studying the extraordinary behavior of outliers helps uncovering the valuable knowledge hidden behind them. The hidden knowledge obtained can be useful in the detection of criminal activities in E-commerce, telecom and credit card frauds, video surveillance, pharmaceutical research, loan approval and intrusion detection.

A well-quoted definition of outliers is the Hawkin-Outlier which first appeared in [10]. This definition states that *an outlier is an observation that deviates so much from other observations as to arouse suspicion that it was generated by a different mechanism.* Hawkin-Outlier is defined in an intuitive manner.

With increasing awareness on outlier detection in both statistical and database literatures, more concrete meanings of outliers are defined for solving problems in specific domains. Nonetheless, each of these definitions follows the

spirit of the Hawkin-Outlier. In this paper, we emphasize the scheme of density-based outliers and the corresponding Local Outlier Factor (LOF) formulation, which is used to indicate the local outlier-ness of objects in databases. Strength and weakness of the LOF formulation will be considered.

Our contributions in this paper are three enhancement schemes which address the weaknesses of LOF accordingly, they are (1) LOF', (2) LOF'' and (3) GridLOF. The first two schemes are variants of the original LOF formulation. LOF' provides simpler and more intuitive meaning of local outlier-ness, while LOF'' can handle cases which LOF fails to work appropriately. The third enhancement, GridLOF, is an efficient and adaptive algorithm in calculating LOF value of each data objects in the databases, GridLOF can also increase accuracy since it avoids some false identifications that can occur with LOF.

1.1. Related Work in Outlier Detections

Early schemes that consider outlier detection as the primary objective are in the field of statistics [5]. The distribution-based approach works by fitting suitable statistical models on the data. Another approach used in statistics is based on a depth notion (e.g. [13]) but this method is unscalable with the dataset dimensionality.

In order to perform effective clustering, most clustering algorithms are able to handle noise in the datasets. We refer to the returned noisy data as clustering-based outliers. Example clustering algorithms which also handle outliers are BIRCH [19], CLARANS [15], DBSCAN [9], GDB-SCAN [17], OPTICS [4] and PROCLUS [1]. However, the outliers are identified as by-products and are highly dependent on the algorithms used. In outlier analysis, we want to focus our efforts on outlier detections. In this case, finding outliers without the need of clustering operations is desirable.

A distance-based outlier is a data point having a far distance to the other data points in the data space [14] [16]. The density-based notion of local outliers overcomes the problem that distance-based approaches fail to handle clusters of different densities [8]. A degree of outlier-ness is given by the Local Outlier Factor (LOF) in [8]. Local outliers are points having considerable density difference from their neighboring points, they have high LOF values.

Despite the fact that the concept of LOF is a useful one, the computation of LOF value of each data object requires a lot of k-nearest neighbors queries. This makes each calculation of LOF a costly operation. Based on the assumption that most data objects are unlikely to be outliers and users are only interested in getting the information of the strongest n local outliers in a large database of size N, an algorithm is proposed in [12] which let users decide the number of strongest outliers they would like the algorithm to return. As such, a lot of the LOF computations are avoided (assuming $n << N$) which results in higher efficiency for the algorithm.

2. LOF Revisited

Based on the same theoretical foundation as DB-SCAN [9] and OPTICS-OF [7], LOF [8], a method identifying density-based local outliers, computes the local outliers of a dataset, by assigning an outlier factor to each object, based on the outlying property relative to their surrounding space.

Definition 1 $(k\text{-}dist(p))$
Given any positive integer k and dataset D, the k-distance of an object p, denoted as $k\text{-}dist(p)$, is defined as the distance $dist(p, o)$ between p and an object $o \in D$ satisfying:

1. *at least k objects $q \in D \setminus \{q\}$ having $dist(p, q) \leq dist(p, o)$, and*

2. *at most $(k-1)$ objects $q \in D \setminus \{q\}$ having $dist(p, q) < dist(p, o)$.*

Definition 2 $(N_{k\text{-}dist(p)}(p))$
Given $k\text{-}dist(p)$, $N_{k\text{-}dist(p)}(p)$ denotes the k-distance neighborhood of p which is the set of objects q whose distance from p is at most $k\text{-}dist(p)$. More formally, $N_{k\text{-}dist(p)}(p) = \{q \mid q \in D \setminus \{p\}, dist(p, q) \leq k\text{-}dist(p)\}$ with q being the k-nearest neighbors of p.

Figure 1 is a example which shows the meaning of k-distance for $k = 5$. In this example, the k-distance of object o is the radius of the dashed circle, while the k-distance neighborhood of o are the five points inside this circle except for o.

Definition 3 $(reach\text{-}dist_k(p, o))$
For a given positive integer k and an object p, reachability distance of p w.r.t. object o is defined as $reach\text{-}dist_k(p, o) = \max\{k\text{-}dist(o), dist(p, o)\}$.

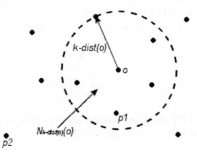

Figure 1. $k\text{-}dist(o)$ and $N_{k\text{-}dist(o)}(o)$ **for** $k = 5$

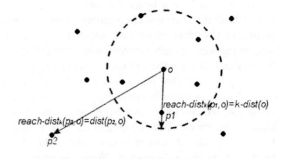

Figure 2. $reach\text{-}dist_k(p_1, o)$ **and** $reach\text{-}dist_k(p_2, o)$ **for** $k=5$.

Figure 2 is a example which demonstrates the concept of reachability distance when $k=5$. The k-distance of object o is the radius of the dashed circle. For object p_1, since its distance to object o is less than the k-distance of o, the reachability distance of it w.r.t. o equals to the d-distance of o. For object p_2, the distance between the object and object o is greater than o's k-distance, so the reachability of p_2 w.r.t. o is the distance between p_2 and o.

In order to detect density-based outliers, the density of the neighborhood of each object p is determined. A parameter $MinPts$, which is a positive integer, is kept to specify the minimum number of points that resides in p's neighborhood. Let $o \in N_{MinPts\text{-}dist(p)}(p)$, the reachability distance $reach\text{-}dist_{MinPts}(p, o)$ regarding this $MinPts$ is used as a measure of volume of p's neighborhood.

Definition 4 $(lrd_{MinPts}(p))$
The local reachability density of object p is defined as

$$lrd_{MinPts}(p) = 1 \left/ \frac{\sum_{o \in N_{MinPts\text{-}dist(p)}} reach\text{-}dist_{MinPts}(p, o)}{|N_{MinPts\text{-}dist(p)}(p)|} \right.$$

The local reachability density of object p is the inverse of the average reachability distance of the $MinPts$-distance neighborhood of p. Finally, the Local Outlier Factor (LOF) is defined as below.

Definition 5 ($LOF_{MinPts}(p)$)
The local outlier factor of object p is defined as

$$LOF_{MinPts}(p) = \frac{\sum_{o \in N_{MinPts\text{-}dist(p)}} \frac{lrd_{MinPts}(o)}{lrd_{MinPts}(p)}}{|N_{MinPts\text{-}dist(p)}(p)|}.$$

The LOF of object p is the average ratio of local reachability density of it and its $MinPts$-distance neighborhood.

2.1. LOF′: A Simpler Formula

We propose here a better formulation compared with LOF. Unlike the method of connectivity-based outlier factor (COF) in [18] which focuses on outlier detections for low density patterns, our enhancement scheme improves the efficiency and effectiveness of LOF for general datasets.

It can be seen that the notion of LOF is quite complex. Three components including $MinPts$-dist, reachability distance and local reachability density are to be understood before the understanding of the LOF formulation. Local reachability density is an indication of the density of the region around a data point. We argue that $MinPts$-dist already captures this notion: a large $MinPts$-dist corresponds to a sparse region, a small $MinPts$-dist corresponds to a dense region. In view of this, LOF′ is defined as a simpler formula for ease of understanding, and also simpler computation. This variant of LOF bears more intuitive meaning and exhibits similar properties as LOF.

Definition 6 (LOF′)

$$LOF'_{MinPts}(p) = \frac{\sum_{o \in N_{MinPts\text{-}dist(p)}(p)} \frac{MinPts\text{-}dist(p)}{MinPts\text{-}dist(o)}}{|N_{MinPts-dist(p)}(p)|}$$

LOF′ defined here is the average ratio of $MinPts$-dist of an object and that of its neighbors within $MinPts$-dist. We reason that $MinPts$-dist is already an indicator of the local density of a data point. A large $MinPts$-dist means that the density is low since the distance to the nearest $MinPts$ neighbors is large. With this new definition, the components reachability distance and local reachability density needed in the LOF formula are not required anymore. LOF′ captures the degree of outlier-ness in a similar way as LOF but provides a clear and simple way of formulation.

Resembling the formula of LOF, LOF′ value increases as the degree of outlier-ness increases for an object. We can derive a lemma that is similar to the one exhibited in [8] for LOF to show the correctness of LOF′ for clustered points. Similar to [8], we assume inside the cluster, the maximum distance between neighbors and minimum distance between neighbors are very close in values. Then objects deep inside clusters have LOF′ values approximately equal to 1:

Lemma 1
Let C be a set of objects forming a cluster,
$minDist = \min\{MinPts\text{-}dist(o) \mid o \in C\}$,
$maxDist = \max\{MinPts\text{-}dist(o) \mid o \in C\}$, *and*
$\varphi = \frac{maxDist}{minDist}$.
Assume φ is close to 1. Let $p \in C$ be an object embedded inside the cluster. Then $LOF'(p)$ is approximately 1.

Proof:
Within the specific cluster C, since $LOF'(p)$ is the average ratio of $MinPts\text{-}distance(p)$ to $MinPts\text{-}distance(q)$, for some q also in C, therefore $\frac{minDist}{maxDist} \leq LOF'(p) \leq \frac{maxDist}{minDist}$. Hence, $1/\varphi \leq LOF'(p) \leq \varphi$. If C is a tight cluster such that $maxDist$ is nearly the same as $minDist$, then φ is quite close to 1 and thus $LOF'(p)$ is approximately 1.

∎

Another advantage of the simplicity is that to compute LOF′ is more efficient than computing LOF since one pass over the data is saved by eliminating the reachability distance and local reachability density in the definition. For very large databases, each scan through the data is a costly operation, so saving a pass is a nice feature.

2.2. LOF″ for Detecting Small Groups of Outliers

Sometimes outlying objects may be quite close to each other in the data space, forming small groups of outlying objects. An example illustrating this phenomenon is shown in Figure 3(a). Since $MinPts$ reveals the minimum number of points to be considered as a cluster, if the $MinPts$ is set too low, the groups of outlying objects will be wrongly identified as clusters. On the other hand, $MinPts$ is also used to compute the density of each point, so if $MinPts$ is set too high, some outliers near dense clusters may be misidentified as clustering points.

We notice there are in fact two different neighborhoods: (1) neighbors in computing the density and (2) neighbors in comparing the densities. In LOF, these two neighborhoods are identical. Here we suggest that they can be different, so we have two $MinPts$ values. For example, consider Figure 3(a). If we use a small neighborhood ($MinPts_1$) for computing the density, o' (see the labeled point at the lower right corner) in Figure 3(a) will be uncovered. If we compare the density of a point to a large neighborhood of points ($MinPts_2$), G (the group of points in the upper right corner of Figure 3(a)) will be identified as outliers. The new notion of LOF″ is given below:

Definition 7 (LOF″)

$$LOF''_{MinPts_1, MinPts_2} = \frac{\sum_{o \in N_{MinPts_1\text{-}dist(p)}} \frac{lrd_{MinPts_2}(o)}{lrd_{MinPts_2}(p)}}{|N_{MinPts_1\text{-}dist(p)}(p)|}$$

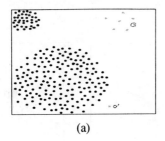

(a)

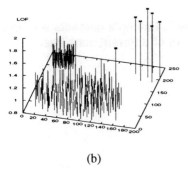

(b)

Figure 3. (a) Sample dataset $DB2$. (b) LOF″ result of $DB2$.

One can put a relatively small value as $MinPts_2$ compared with $MinPts_1$. With this simple amendment, LOF″ is able to capture local outliers under different general circumstances. In the example in Figure 3(a), if we choose $MinPts_1 = 10$, and $MinPts_2 = 5$, we can identify both o' and G as shown in Figure 3(b). If we use only a single $MinPts$ value as in LOF, then we show in Figure 8 that no value of $MinPts$ can uncover all outliers exactly.

When $MinPts_2 = MinPts_1$, the formula of LOF″ is reduced to that of LOF. It can be said that LOF″ is a generalization of LOF. LOF″ exhibits the similar property as LOF and LOF′ that points deep inside a cluster have LOF″ values close to 1:

Lemma 2
Let C be a set of objects forming a cluster,
$$minDist'' = \max\{reach\text{-}dist(a,b)|a,b \in C\},$$
$$maxDist'' = \min\{reach\text{-}dist(a,b)|a,b \in C\}, \text{ and}$$
$$\varphi'' = \frac{maxDist''}{minDist''}.$$
Assume that φ'' is close to 1. Let $p \in C$ be an object embedded inside the cluster. Then $LOF''(p)$ is approximately 1 for p.

Proof:
Within the specific cluster C, since $LOF'(p)$ is the average ratio of $MinPts\text{-}distance(p)$ to $MinPts\text{-}distance(q)$,

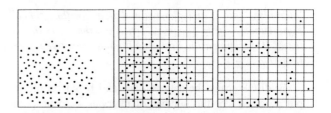

Figure 4. Example illustrating the idea of GridLOF algorithm.

for some q in C, therefore $\frac{minDist}{maxDist} \leq LOF'(p) \leq \frac{maxDist}{minDist}$. Hence, $1/\varphi \leq LOF'(p) \leq \varphi$. If C is a tight cluster such that $maxDist$ is nearly the same as $minDist$, then φ is quite close to 1 and thus $LOF'(p)$ is approximately 1.

∎

2.3. GridLOF for Pruning Reasonable Portions from Datasets

In common situations, the number of outliers in any dataset is expected to be extremely small. It is highly inefficient for the LOF algorithm in [8] to compute the LOF values for all points inside a dataset. According to this observation, we introduce an adaptive algorithm called GridLOF (Grid-based LOF) algorithm which prunes away the portion of dataset known to be non-outliers, LOF of the remaining points are then calculated. Hence the overall cost for computing LOF can be reduced.

GridLOF utilizes a simple grid-based method as the pruning heuristic. At first, each dimension of the data space is quantized into equi-width intervals, resulting in a grid-based structure. Then for each non empty grid cell c, the neighboring grid cells are examined, c is labeled as a boundary cell once a neighboring grid cell with less than or equal to the pre-defined threshold (σ) number of points residing in it is found. σ is a relatively small number. In the extreme case, σ can be set to zero. (In our experiments, we found that $\sigma = 0$ gives pretty good results.) Finally, only the LOF values of points inside boundary cells are calculated. This heuristic works if the interval value used in partitioning the data space is appropriate. Figure 4 illustrates the idea of GridLOF algorithm.

Instead of keeping all the grids explicitly, GridLOF uses a method similar to the coding function for grid cells in [11]. To do this, $signature$ is defined (Definition 8) to play the role as the coding function and serves as the identity number of each grid cell.

Definition 8 (sig)
Given a dataset D with dimensionality l and the number of

intervals ω. sig is an l-dimensional array for the grid cell signatures. sig = $[s_1][s_2]\ldots[s_l]$ such that s_i is the interval ID for dimension i ranging from any positive integer from 0 to ω − 1.

GridLOF scans the dataset once and based on the input parameter of the number of intervals ω to be partitioned in each dimension, it determines the grid cell that each point belongs to and determine the *signature* of that grid cell. In this case, the data space is partitioned logically and GridLOF only remembers non empty grid cells which containing points. This method prevents the exponential growth of number of grid cells as dimensionality increases, since the number of distinct grid cells obtained is at most N (N is the size of the dataset), which is independent of the dimensionality when each point is residing in a different grid cell. The data structure used to store the set of unique grid cell signatures should guarantee efficient retrieval of the signatures, thus we choose hashing as the data structure for signatures storage. For each distinct grid cell signature in the hash table, GridLOF determines its *1-cell thick neighboring grid cells* $Nsig$ as in Definition 9. Once GridLOF finds that there is an empty cell in $Nsig$, the grid cell with the current signature can be identified as a **boundary grid cell**.

Definition 9 ($Nsig(sig_i)$)
For a given signature of a grid cell, $sig_i = [s_1][s_2]\ldots[s_l]$, $Nsig(sig_i)$ is a set of signatures for the 1-cell thick neighboring grid cells of this grid cell.

$$Nsig(sig_i) = \{[n_1][n_2]\ldots[n_l] \mid n_i = s_i \pm 1, 0 \leq n_i \leq \omega - 1\}$$

Up to this step, a preprocessing for LOF computation is done. The resulting set of points R residing in boundary grid cells is used in the later steps, where their LOF values are computed as for the original LOF. For typical situations, most points from the dataset D are pruned, so $|R| \ll |N|$. GridLOF scans through R and obtain the $MinPts$-dist and $MinPts$ nearest neighborhood of each point. Then the reachability distance and local reachability density are computed in a second pass over R. Finally a pass through R is needed to compute the LOF value for each of the points in R.

Aside from improving efficiency, GridLOF can handle datasets with overlapping clusters with different densities for which LOF algorithm fails to work appropriately. Two example datasets are shown in Figure 5. For these examples, since the LOF value of an object is the measure of the relative degree of isolation of that object with respect to its surrounding neighborhood, points of the less dense cluster that are close to the border points of the denser cluster will be wrongly regarded as local outliers.

GridLOF does not have this misidentification problem. By partitioning with reasonable equi-width intervals, the

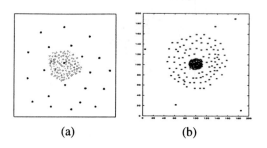

(a)   (b)

Figure 5. Example datasets with overlapping clusters of different densities.

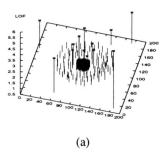

(a)

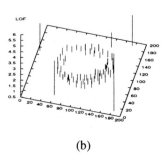

(b)

Figure 6. Example showing the ability of GridLOF to correctly identify outliers.

whole dense cluster and the layer of points in less dense cluster surrounding the dense one are pruned. As a consequence, only the outer boundary points of the less dense clusters are examined and this solves the problem.

Figure 6(a) is the LOF result obtained for the dataset in Figure 5(b). The original LOF algorithm finds the LOF values of every point in the dataset. The top 5% of points with the largest LOF values are indicated by crosses in Figure 6(a). The five outliers have high LOF values, however we find that some points of the less dense cluster which are near the denser cluster have even higher LOF values, and they are misidentified as outliers. This problem is solved by GridLOF algorithm. In Figure 6(b), the result obtained by using GridLOF is shown. Since points of the denser cluster are pruned and most of the points inside the less dense cluster are pruned too, it is easy to distinguish the five outliers from the unpruned points in the dataset and avoid the problem of misidentification of clustering points as outliers.

Selection of w: The correctness of GridLOF method depends on the choice of w. An error will occur if there is an outlier in a grid cell x, and all the neighboring grid cells are non-empty. This can happen if the grid size is large, or w is small.

When an outlier exists in a grid cell x where all neighboring grid cells are occupied, there are two possible cases when considering any two of such neighboring grid cells: either they belong to the same cluster, or they belong to two different clusters. In one possible scenario, a grid cell x with an outlier is inside a cluster, meaning there is a hollow or concave area of a cluster where the outlier is located. Suppose a cluster has a boundary surface. We consider hyper-rectangles defined by ranges of values on each dimension of the data space. Let us define a hollow hyper-rectangle inside a cluster as a hyper-rectangle which is within the boundary of the cluster, containing no cluster points, and with an edge length much greater than the average distances between neighboring points in the cluster. (That is, we do not want to consider any empty spaces in between cluster points as a hollow hyper-rectangle.) For any cluster C, suppose we are given a lower bound e on the edge length of any hollow hyper-rectangle. Then if we set the grid cell edge length to be at most 1/3 of e, an outlier that may exist inside such a hollow can be detected, or it will not be pruned. This can be easily shown by contradiction.

We may consider a second case where a grid cell x with an outlier is surrounded by neighbor grid cells containing points in different clusters. For two clusters A and B, there will be at least one dimension d where the closest points from the two clusters are the furthest apart. Let us call the distance between the closest points at such a dimension the cluster distance for A and B. If we also have a lower bound on the cluster distance for any two clusters, we can set the

grid cell edge length to be smaller than one third of this lower bound. Then we shall have an empty neighboring grid cell for a cell containing an outlier even if the outlier is at the narrowest strait between two close clusters.

3. Time Complexity

Mining local outliers by LOF typically requires three passes over the data. A first pass for finding every objects' $MinPts$-dist and $MinPts$-nearest neighborhoods. Then a second pass to compute the reachability distance and local reachability density of each object. Finally LOF value of all objects in the database is calculated in the third pass. For LOF' computation, the second pass described above is eliminated since the reachability distance and local reachability density are not needed. As a consequence, only two passes over the data is needed. Also note that the second pass that is saved is more complex than the first pass, since for each data point, it requires the collection of information for the neigborhood of a data point.

The algorithm for finding LOF'' is nearly the same as that of LOF except for the first pass. No extra pass is required since the $MinPts_2$-distance neighborhood can be obtained directly from $MinPts_1$-distance neighborhood.

For LOF, LOF' and LOF'', suppose that objects in a database D of size N is being examined, totally there are N $MinPts$-nearest neighbors queries in the first pass. The complexity ranges from $O(N \log N)$ to $O(N^2)$ depending on the use of indexing structure and dimensionality of data.

Although the runtime complexity of GridLOF also depends on the number of $MinPts$-nearest neighbors queries, because most of the points residing deep inside clusters are pruned, the total number of $MinPts$-nearest neighbors queries is much less than N. It can be observed from analysis and from experiments that the runtime of the preprocessing step of partitioning and data pruning is being dominated by the querying step.

4. Experiments

Several programs were written in C++ language to calculate LOF, LOF' and LOF'' by the original LOF algorithm as stated in [8]. In addition, the GridLOF algorithm is implemented in a C++ program. Experiments on these programs are made under the computing environment of a Sun Enterprise E4500 running Solaris 7 with 12 UltraSPARC-II 400MHz and 8 GB RAM.

For all the formulations, an X-tree [6] indexing structure is provided for speeding up the $MinPts$-nearest neighbors queries. X-tree is chosen because it is an index structure for efficient query processing of high-dimensional data and building time of the X-tree index structure is considerably small.

There are two types of data used in the experiments. The first type of data is a set of 2-dimensional datasets created especially to verify the correctness and to demonstrate the idea of our enhancement schemes. 2-dimensional datasets are also used for better visualization.

The second type is a set of data generated by the synthetic data generator which generates data following the synthetic data generation suggested in [3] with some modifications, so that clusters are associated with the whole data space, instead of associating with a subspace. The generated clusters have arbitrary orientation regarding the whole data space and data objects in each cluster follow the normal distribution with small variance. Variances used are randomly drawn from an exponential distribution. Outliers are generated by restricting the distances between outliers and each cluster to be greater than five standard deviation in all dimensions. The number of outliers generated is set to be 0.5 percent of the size of the datasets.

LOF': In order to verify the correctness of the newly proposed LOF' formulation, a sample 2-dimensional dataset $DB1$ is used for better visualization. $DB1$ is a 2-D dataset with 640 points within. The original datasets is illustrated in Figure 7(a). In Figure 7(b), the corresponding LOF' and LOF values for $MinPts = 5$ are plotted in the same figure for ease of comparison. The LOF' values are indicated by the impulse lines while the LOF values of the corresponding points are indicated by a square point on the impulse lines. By investigating the plotted graph in detail, it can be observed that the proposed LOF' formulation captures the same degree of local outlier-ness as the original LOF formulation does. For points whose LOF values are high, they also possess high LOF' values, and vice versa. For different $MinPts$ values used, similar experimental results are obtained. To further investigate the accuracy of our LOF' formulation, the LOF' and LOF values for the different sets of synthetic data are studied, with different dimensionality, dataset size, and the value of k. It is found that the results are always very close and in most cases, they are identical.

Based on the fact that LOF' requires one pass over the data less than LOF, it is computationally more efficient when compared to LOF. In Table 1, experimental results in counting the total number of page access required for different datasets in traversing all data points in the index (we use X-tree) once is shown. Since we have saved a pass of the data that requires more than a simple scan of data, the actual page access improvements would be more than what is shown in the table.

LOF'': In order to verify the ability of LOF'' in capturing small groups of outliers, a set of 2-dimensional data called $DB2$ is generated to illustrate the scenario as in Figure 3(a). $DB2$ is a 2-D dataset with 250 points, there is a local outlier o' at the bottom right hand corner and a small group of

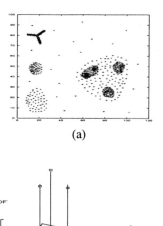

(a)

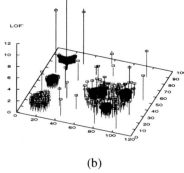

(b)

Figure 7. (a) Sample dataset $DB1$. (b) LOF' and LOF results of $DB1$.

outliers G at the top right hand corner of the graph. Original LOF plots with different $MinPts$ values used are shown in Figure 8. From the plots, it can be seen that LOF is inadequate to capture the set of outliers G and the local outlier o' at the same time. In Figure 8(a), $MinPts$ is set to 5. In this case LOF successfully point out the local outlier-ness of o', however all points in the outlier group G have LOF values approximately equal to 1, that means G is determined as a small cluster instead of outliers.

By increasing the $MinPts$ value used as in Figure 8(b), Figure 8(c) and Figure 8(d), LOF is capable to uncover G as outliers. However, this lowers the degree of outlier-ness of some local outliers, which are relatively close to some cluster. This problem can be solved by using two $MinPts$ values as stated if LOF''. In the dataset $DB2$, $MinPts_2$ and $MinPts_1$ values used are 5 and 10 respectively. The corresponding LOF'' results are plotted in Figure 3(b) which correctly identifies all the outliers.

GridLOF: The GridLOF algorithm is developed to perform pruning upon the dataset. Two datasets $DB1$ and $DB3$ are used to illustrate the pruning performed by GridLOF. Two sample 2-dimensional datasets are used for ease of visualization and understanding. $DB1$ is the aforementioned dataset used in the LOF' experiment, and is illustrated in Figure 7(a). $DB3$ is a more complex dataset with overlap-

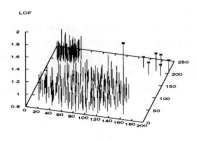

(a) $MinPts = 5$

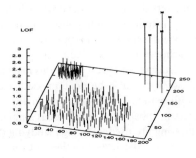

(b) $MinPts = 10$

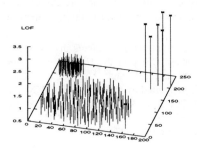

(c) $MinPts = 15$

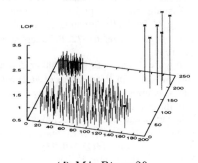

(d) $MinPts = 20$

Figure 8. LOF plot of $DB2$ with different $MinPts$.

Size of database (10^3)	Number of page access (10^3) for		
	1 pass	LOF$'$	LOF
60	66.6	188.0	254.6
80	88.9	262.2	351.1
100	111.0	338	449.0
120	133.2	416.2	549.4
140	155.4	496.0	651.4
200	222.0	742.9	964.9
500	554.9	2077.7	2632.6

Table 1. Page access of indexes for databases with different size.

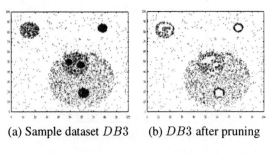

(a) Sample dataset $DB3$ (b) $DB3$ after pruning

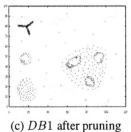

(c) $DB1$ after pruning

Figure 9. Datasets after the pruning step in GridLOF.

ping clusters of different densities showing a hierarchical structure. $DB3$ is shown in Figure 9(a) which is a dataset with 5000 points. Figure 9(b) is the resulting $DB3$ after being pruned by GridLOF. The LOF values of this set of remaining points are to be computed in the later steps in GridLOF. From this figure, it can be seen that GridLOF succeeds in pruning noisy dataset with highly complex structure. In $DB3$, the range of points are $0 < 100$ for both dimensions. By partitioning each dimension into 100 equi-width intervals and applying the pruning, 2079 points are pruned as stated in Figure 9(b).

The resulting $DB1$ after the pruning step in GridLOF is given in Figure 9(c). The range of points are $0 < 100$ for both dimensions in $DB1$ and each dimension is partitioned into 50 equi-width intervals. This yields a set of 483 points

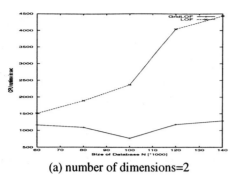

(a) number of dimensions=2

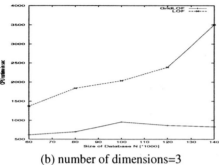

(b) number of dimensions=3

Figure 10. CPU runtime of GridLOF and LOF for datasest.

in Figure 9(c) for further LOF computation.

Experiments were performed to examine the runtime complexity difference between GridLOF and LOF on a set of synthetic data with size (N) ranging from 60000 to 140000. Each CPU runtime obtained is the average time required for five experimental runs on the datasets. With different setting of dimensionalities, number of clusters and $MinPts$ values, we find that GridLOF can reduce the computation time in all cases. It works best for dimensionality less than 6 and is very good for 2 dimensional and 3 dimensional datasets. In Figure 10, the CPU runtimes for 2 dimensional and 3 dimensional datasets with 8 clusters of varying dataset size (N) are shown.

5. Conclusion

Recently, the topic of outlier detection in data mining arouses attention because of their potential usage in many applications. In this paper, the LOF formulation and algorithm for grading the degree of outlier-ness for local outlier detection is examined. Three enhancements aiming to address different problems of LOF are introduced, with two new definitions for the degree of outlier-ness, LOF' and LOF'', and an algorithm GridLOF which adds a pruning step before the original LOF algorithm. By formal analysis and experimental results, the three enhancement techniques are shown to work effectively with advantages over LOF in different aspects.

Our future work can include the following. In this paper, we have separately considered three proposed methods and compared with original LOF method, this will let us identify their individual effects. In the future, we can combine the techniques and hopefully that would combine their different strengths.

In our GridLOF algorithm, a parameter indicating the number of intervals to be partitioned in each dimension is needed. In our further work, we hope to include in our GridLOF algorithm the ability to self determine the appropriate interval values. For example, GridLOF can starts to use a small interval number to partition each dimension and further fine partition some intervals based on certain judgement. This yields an uneven partitioning on the data space which can achieve more effective pruning and can be more adaptive to datasets with great variations in density.

Further work can also be done on outlier detection of datasets with extremely high dimensionality and datasets with clusters in subspaces. In [2], ideas similar to the projected clustering are used. Through studying the behavior of projections from the dataset, outliers are identified. Combining the projection technique with the use of evolutionary algorithm, density-based outliers are found with the corresponding subspace dimensions that these outliers showing their most deviating behavior. We can examine similar issues in the future for the outlier detection problem.

ACKNOWLEDGEMENT The authors thanks Mr. M. M. Breunig of the Database Group of the University of Munich in providing two datasets ($DB1$ and $DB3$) for experimental use. This research is supported by the Hong Kong RGC Earmarked Grant UGC REF.CUHK 4179/01E. This research is also supported by the Chinese University of Hong Kong RGC Research Grant Direct Allocation, Proj ID 2050279.

References

[1] C. C. Aggarwal, C. Procopiuc, J. L. Wolf, P. S. Yu, and J. S. Park. Fast algorithms for projected clustering. In *Proceedings of ACM SIGMOD International Conference on Management of Data*, pages 61–72, Philadephia, Pennsylvania, U.S.A., 1999.

[2] C. C. Aggarwal and P. S. Yu. Outlier detection for high dimensional data. In *Proceedings of ACM SIGMOD International Conference on Management of Data*, pages 37–46, Santa Barbara, California, U.S.A., 2001.

[3] C. C. Aggarwal and P. S. Yu. Redefining clustering for high-dimensional applications. *IEEE Transactions on Knowledge and Data Engineering*, 14(2):210–255, 2002.

[4] M. Ankerst, M. M. Breunig, H.-P.Kriegel, and J. Sander. OPTICS: Ordering points to identify the clustering structure. In

Proceedings of ACM SIGMOD International Conference on Management of Data, pages 49–60, Philadephia, Pennsylvania, U.S.A., 1999.

[5] V. Barnet and T.Lewis. *Outliers in Statistical Data*. John Wiley, 1994.

[6] S. Berchtold, D. A. Keim, and H.-P. Kreigel. The X-tree: An index structure for high-dimensional data. In *Proceedings of 22nd International Conference on Very Large Data Bases*, pages 28–39, Bombay, India, 1996.

[7] M. M. Breunig, H.-P. Kriegel, R. T. Ng, and J. Sander. OPTICS-OF: Identifying local outliers. In *Proceedings of 3rd European Conference on Principles of Data Mining and Knowledge Discovery*, pages 262–270, Prague, Czech Republic, 1999.

[8] M. M. Breunig, H.-P. Kriegel, R. T. Ng, and J. Sander. LOF: Identifying density-based local outliers. In *Proceedings of ACM SIGMOD International Conference on Management of Data*, pages 93–104, Dallas, Texas, U.S.A., 2000.

[9] M. Ester, H. Kriegel, J. Sander, and X. Xu. A density-based algorithm for discovering clusters in large spatial databases with noise. In *Proceedings of 2nd International Conference on Knowledge Discovery and Data Mining (KDD-96)*, pages 226–231, Portland, Oregon, 1996.

[10] D. Hawkins. *Identification of Outliers*. Chapman and Hall, London, 1980.

[11] A. Hinneburg and D. A. Keim. Optimal grid-clustering: Towards breaking the curse of dimensionality in high-dimensional clustering. In *Proceedings of 25th International Conference on Very Large Data Bases*, pages 506–517, Edinburgh, Scotland, U.K., 1999.

[12] W. Jin, A. K. H. Tung, and J. Han. Mining top-n local outliers in large databases. In *Proceedings of 7th ACM SIGKDD International Conference on Knowledge Discovery and Data Mining*, pages 293–298, San Francisco, California, U.S.A., 2001.

[13] T. Johnson, I. Kwok, and R. T. Ng. Fast computation of 2-dimensional depth contours. In *Proceedings of 4th International Conference on Knowledge Discovery and Data Mining (KDD-98)*, pages 224–228, New York City, New York, U.S.A., 1998.

[14] E. M. Knorr and R. T. Ng. Algorithms for mining distance-based outliers in large datasets. In *Proceedings of 24th International Conference on Very Large Data Bases*, pages 392–403, New York City, New York, U.S.A., 1998.

[15] R. T. Ng and J. Han. Efficient and effective clustering methods for spatial data mining. In *Proceedings of 20th International Conference on Very Large Data Bases*, pages 144–155, Santiago de Chile, Chile, 1994.

[16] S. Ramaswamy, R. Rastogi, and K. Shim. Efficient algorithms for mining outliers from large data sets. In *Proceedings of ACM SIGMOD International Conference on Management of Data*, pages 427–438, Dallas, Texas, U.S.A., 2000.

[17] J. Sander, M. Ester, H.-P. Kriegel, and X. Xu. Density-based clustering in spatial databases: the algorithm GDBSCAN and its applications. *Data Mining and Knowledge Discovery*, 2(2):169–194, 1998.

[18] J. Tang, Z. Chen, A. Fu, and D. Cheung. Enhancing effectiveness of outlier detections for low density patterns. In *Proceedings of Advances in Knowledge Discovery and Data Mining 6th Pacific-Asia Conference (PAKDD 2002)*, pages 535–548, Taipei, Taiwan, 2002.

[19] T. Zhang, R. Ramakrishnan, and M. Livny. BIRCH: an efficient data clustering method for very large databases. In *Proceedings of 1996 ACM SIGMOD International Conference on Management of Data*, pages 103–114, Montreal, Quebec, Canada, 1996.

AUTOMATED EJB CLIENT CODE GENERATION SING DATABASE QUERY REWRITING

Jianguo Lu
School of Computer Science
University of Windsor
jlu@cs.uwindsor.ca

John Mylopoulos
Department of Computer Science
University of Toronto
jm@cs.toronto.edu

Abstract

Enterprise JavaBean (hereafter EJB) technology has been widely adopted in software industry to develop web information systems. However, most of EJB applications are reengineered from legacy database applications. This means that legacy SQL statements need to be translated into EJB client code. Since many methods in Enterprise Beans can be regarded as view definitions of the underlying database, the EJB client code generation can be mapped to the problem of query rewriting using views. This paper addresses the automatic generation of EJB client code using query rewriting.

Keywords: Object-relational mapping, Enterprise JavaBean, query rewriting, software reengineering

1   Introduction

There has been a great divide in Information Technology between the object world and the relational world. Both techniques are successful in mainstream industrial practice, one for programming and the other for data management. In many cases these two worlds cohabitate peacefully, not interfering with each other. Unfortunately, many large applications, especially multi-tier e-commerce ones, need to use objects as the programming interface and use relations to manage their data. Current common practice in combining the two worlds is to embed SQL expressions inside classes. This close coupling of the objects and relations runs against many software engineering principles, such as modularity, information encapsulation, usability, maintainability, etc.

One of the objectives of the Enterprise JavaBean (EJB) [32] technology is to address gracefully this object-relation interface. Among other things, EJBs provide an object view of relational databases. With EJBs, databases are transparent to application developers.

However, EJB-based applications are seldom developed from scratch. In most cases they are reengineered from existing systems, especially multi-tier applications that use relational databases as their back-ends. In particular, such legacy applications include large number of SQL queries imbedded in various programming or scripting languages such as C++, or proprietary languages such as PL/SQL [15] and Net.Data [12]. While reengineering such systems to EJB-based architectures, we need to translate the legacy queries to the EJB client code that access the enterprise beans.

By viewing EJBs as wrappers that represent object views for an underlying relational database, the translation of a query to the EJB client code can be formulated as a query rewriting problem, a problem that has been widely studied in the Databases literature [25][24].

In this paper, we propose an SQL-EJB mediator that generates EJB client code given an SQL query. The mediator uses descriptions of the query-answering capabilities of available enterprise beans in order to translate the input query into equivalent EJB client code.

This paper focuses on the automated generation of EJB client code from legacy queries. An outline of the problem and the generation of EJB itself are presented in [19]. For ease of discussion, we are assuming the database table names and column names have a one-to-one correspondence with the names of enterprise beans and the attribute names in the bean, respectively. Also, we only consider conjunctive queries and views. SQL statements other than select statements (e.g., insertions and updates) are not discussed. Other migration tasks, such as data migration and the translation of legacy presentation code to JSP [22], are not covered in this paper either.

The rest of the paper is organized as follows. Section 2 introduces background terminology and knowledge on EJB, Object-relational mapping and query rewriting. Section 3 describes the transformation of SQL expressions to EJB client code, assuming that an EJB architecture already exists. Section 4 discusses related and future work.

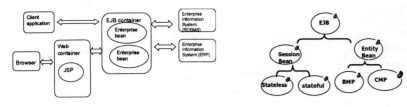

Figure 1: EJB architecture   Figure 2: Kinds of enterprise beans

2   Background

2.1   *Motivating Example*

Our research is motivated by a reengineering project that aims to develop tools that support the transition from the Net.Commerce 5-year-old e-commerce framework to the new Websphere Commerce Suite architecture that uses EJB technology.

Both Net.Commerce and Websphere Commerce Suite (hereafter WCS) are frameworks for building e-commerce websites. They provide templates for realizing functionalities such as product catalog browsing, payment processing, product promotion, auction, and other web-based services. Both frameworks are multi-tier applications that use browsers at the client side, web-servers in the middle, and relational DBMS at the backend to manage data.

Although there are similarities, these two frameworks are actually quite different. WCS is a successor of Net.Commerce. It is redesigned without much consideration for backward compatibility. Most notably, WCS uses EJB technology. Table 1 highlights the differences between the two systems.

For a presentation language, Net.Commerce uses Net.Data, an IBM proprietary product for dynamic HTML. WCS, on the other hand, uses JSP (the Java Server Page) that is widely accepted for dynamic web pages. For business logic, Net.Commerce uses SQL in many cases within C++ and Net.Data code, while WCS uses EJB. For a programming language, Net.Commerce uses C++, while WCS uses Java. For a programming model, Net.Commerce is rather ad hoc, while WCS adopts a clean MVC (Model, View and Control) design pattern.

Given the huge size and complexity of the two frameworks, there are many reengineering tasks. We found that the most challenging task is the migration of legacy queries to EJB client code in JSP.

2.2   *An EJB Architecture*

EJB is a distributed component framework that provides services for transactions, specifically security and persistence in a distributed multi-tier environment [32]. EJB is intended to separate business logic from low-level details, so that developers can concentrate on a business solution. With the growing popularity of the EJB framework, more and more legacy systems and old web-based systems are being migrated into an EJB architecture. Typically, in the legacy systems there are large amount of SQL queries. On the other hand, in EJB-based applications, these queries are wrapped inside the EJBs by adopting the popular model-view-control design pattern. Figure 1 shows a typical EJB-based application .

In the figure, the EJB container manages a set of enterprise beans. The beans connect with the backend systems, typically a relational database. The web container typically uses JSP to access the EJB, and serves the JSP to the browser. EJB client applications other than JSP, such as Java applets or any other systems, can also access the enterprise beans.

The enterprise beans in the middle tier function as wrappers over various systems, especially relational databases. There are two kinds of enterprise beans, i.e., *entity beans* and *session beans*. Roughly speaking, session beans are business process objects that implement business logic, business rules, and workflow (e.g., placeOrderSessionBean) and entity beans represent persistent objects that are part of durable storage such as database (e.g., `employeeBean`, `managerBean`). In a simple scenario, each entity bean corresponds to a row in a (relational) table. The selection of certain rows of the table corresponds to the selection of a group of beans satisfying a given predicate. The selection of beans is accomplished by the finder method, which can have embedded SQL statements. We are particularly interested in entity beans, especially CMP (Container Managed Persistence) [32] entity bean.

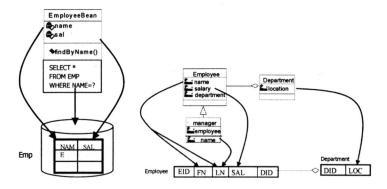

Figure 3: Simple mapping   Figure 4: Complex mapping

By using EJBs, application developers no longer need to learn the details of database structure. Also, changes in the database are shielded off by the beans, thus making the maintenance of JSP pages easier.

2.3   *Object-relational mappings in EJB*

Object-relational mappings refer to the transformation between object and relational models and between the applications that are built on top of these models. While such mappings between objects and relations have been extensively studied, the mappings between SQL expressions and object behaviours/methods have only been barely touched. With the introduction of EJB technology, there is a growing demand to support transformation between queries and object behaviours.

A simple object–relational mapping can be illustrated in *figure* 3. In this mapping, the table `Emp` maps to the class `EmployeeBean`, the columns `NAME` and `SAL` corresponds to the attributes `name` and `sal` in the class, respectively. For a query in a relational database such as finding all the employees by name, there is a corresponding method called `findByName` in the entity bean that has a SQL expression

embedded inside the method.

An object-relational mapping is often complicated in several ways. First, there may not a simple 1-1 mapping between classes and tables. The same applies for attribute-column mappings. Second, there are relationships between objects, such as associations, aggregations and inheritance. In the relational model there are also associations between tables defined by foreign keys. When mapping the relational model to the object model, we need to map those relationships as well. This situation is illustrated in *figure* 4.

2.4   *Query rewriting*

The *query rewriting problem* has been extensively studied in the areas of query optimization [7] and data integration [24]. Informally speaking, the problem can be formulated as follows: Given a query and a set of view definitions, compose an answer to the query using answers to the views.

Definition 2.1 (*Query containment and equivalence*) A query Q is contained in another query Q', denoted as $Q \subseteq Q'$,

	Net. Commerce	Websphere Commerce Suite
Presentation language	Net.Data	JSP
Business logic	SQL	EJB
Programming language	C++	Java
Programming model	Ad hoc	MVC

Table 1: Differences between the two frameworks.

if for any instance of the base relations, the set of tuples computed for Q is a subset of those computed for Q'. Two queries Q and Q' are equivalent (denoted as Q = Q') if Q ⊆ Q' and Q ⊇ Q'.

Definition 2.2 (*query rewriting*) Given a query Q and a set of views V, a *rewriting* of Q using V is a query Q' such that Q = Q', and Q' refers to one or more views in V.

In the following examples we will use the schema as follows:

```
MANAGER(MAN_ID, NAME, EMP_ID)
EMPLOYEE(EMP_ID, NAME, DEPT_ID, SAL)
DEPT(DEPT_ID, LOC).
```

Example 2.3 Given a query

```
Q: SELECT MANAGER.NAME, DEPT.LOC
   FROM MANAGER, EMPLOYEE, DEPT
   WHERE MANAGER.EMP_ID=EMPLOYEE.EMP_ID
      AND EMPLOYEE.DEPT_ID= DEPT.DEPT_ID
```

And views V1 and V2:

```
CREATE VIEW V1 AS
SELECT MANAGER.NAME, MANAGER.EMP_ID,
   EMPLOYEE.DEPT_ID
FROM MANAGER, EMPLOYEE
WHERE MANAGER.EMP_ID=EMPLOYEE.EMP_ID

CREATE VIEW V2 AS
SELECT EMPLOEE.EMP_ID, EMPLOYEE.DEPT_ID, DEPT.LOC
FROM EMPLOYEE, DEPT
WHERE EMPLOYEE.DEPT_ID=DEPT.DEPT_ID
```

One of the rewritings of Q using views V is

```
Q': SELECT NAME, LOC
    FROM V1, V2
    WHERE V1.EMP_ID=V2.EMP_ID AND
          V1.DEPT_ID=V2.DEPT_ID
```

We should note that rewritings do not always exist. As a simple example, the following query Q2, which is a slight modification of Q, won't have a rewriting. We may be tempted to have Q2' as its rewriting. However, EMPLOYEE.NAME does not appear in either of the views and it becomes a 'dangling' variable.

```
Q2: SELECT MANAGER.NAME, DEPT.LOC, EMPLOYEE.NAME
    FROM MANAGER, EMPLOYEE, DEPT
    WHERE MANAGER.EMP_ID=EMPLOYEE.EMP_ID
       AND EMPLOYEE.DEPT_ID= DEPT.DEPT_ID

Q2': SELECT MANAGER.NAME, DEPT.LOC, EMPLOYEE.NAME
     FROM V1, V2
     WHERE V1.EMP_ID=V2.EMP_ID
        AND V1.DEPT_ID=V2.DEPT_ID
```

2.5 Datalog notation

It is easier and a common practice to discuss query rewriting in terms of the Datalog notation [34]. Datalog is similar to Prolog, but does not allow functions in Horn clause expressions. In the following sections of this paper we will use this notation.

A conjunctive query has the form:

$$Q(X):-P_1(X_1),P_2(X_2),...,P_n(X_n),C_1(Y_1),C_2(Y_2),...,C_m(Y_m).$$

where Q, P_i (i=1,…, n), and C_j (j=1,…,m) are predicate names. X, X_1, …, X_n, Y_1, …, Y_m are vectors of variables and constants. $Q(X)$ is called the head of the query. P_i (i=1,…, n) refer to the relations in the database, and are called base predicates. C_j (j=1, …, m) are arithmetic comparison predicates.

Example 2.4 Reformulating the queries and views in example 2.4, we have the following Datalog expressions:

```
Q(NAME, LOC):-MANAGER(ID, NAME, EID),
   EMPLOYEE(EID,NAME', D_ID, S),
   DEPT(D_ID, LOC).

V1(NAME, EMP_ID, DEPT_ID):-
   MANAGER(NAME, EMP_ID, MAN_ID),
   EMPLOYEE(NAME0, SAL, DEPT_ID, EMP_ID).

V2(EMP_ID, DEPT_ID, LOC) :-
   EMPLOYEE(NAME, SAL, DEPT_ID, EMP_ID),
   DEPT(DEPT_ID, LOC).
```

A rewriting of Q is as follows:

```
Q'(NAME, LOC) :-
   V1(NAME, EMP_ID, DEPT_ID),
   V2(EMP_ID, DEPT_ID, LOC).
```

3   EJB-SQL mediator

Given a query in a legacy system, and a set of enterprise beans with SQL statements embedded in the finder methods of the EJB architecture, the task of the SQL-EJB mediator is to identify the enterprise beans, their relevant methods, and the way to combine those methods.

Obviously, several questions need to be answered before we can automate the reengineering of the SQL queries to the client Java code in the EJB architecture:

1. Is there a way to decide which finder method in EJB architecture is semantically equivalent to a query in the legacy system?

2. When there does not exist a single corresponding finder method, is there a way to find several finders that are semantically equivalent?

3. After we decompose the query into several sub-queries, how to combine them in the EJB client Java program?

In the following we use several examples to address these situations.

Table 2: Locate the same query in finder method

Query in legacy code	SELECT * FROM employee WHERE phone = $1
Query in finder	SELECT * FROM employee WHERE phone=?
Finder name	Collection FindByPhone(String p)
Bean Name	Employee Bean
Code generated	EmployeeBean employee; Enumeration result= employee.findByName(p);

Table 3: Locate logically equivalent queries in finder method

Query in legacy code	SELECT * FROM employee WHERE phone=$1 AND salary>$2
Query in finder	SELECT * FROM employee WHERE salary>? AND phone=?
Finder name	Collection FindByPhoneAndSal (String p, int s)
Bean Name	Employee Bean
Code generated	EmployeeBean employee; Enumeration result= employee=findByNameAndSal(p, s);

In Table 2, the SQL query and the finder method are the same and it is simple to generate the EJB client code. There are still minor differences such how to represent the parameters in SQL statements. In Table 3 the two queries are logically equivalent and we need to determine that the where conditions of the two queries are actually the same. This can be done by query containment testing. In Table 4 the legacy query has to be reproduced using two queries in different finder methods, and possibly in different beans. In this case, a query rewriting procedure is needed to produce the code that has the same functionality. The reader should note that the format of complex queries in finder methods may differ due to conventions imposed by EJB vendors. The format we followed in this paper is based on Websphere Version 3.5.

From the examples we can observe that if we regard the finders as view definitions of the database, the first question corresponds to the query containment test, the second corresponds to query rewriting using views [25].

The SQL-EJB mediator can be illustrated in *figure* 7, which resembles many of the information mediator systems [24]. The main difference is that we have enterprise beans instead of heterogeneous information sources, and we produce client Java code instead of actually running the queries. As with information sources, enterprise beans are wrappers of one or more databases and have limited query answering capabilities.

3.1 Representing the query answering capabilities of the enterprise bean

One factor that makes query rewriting systems different is how views are represented. Remember that views are the SQL queries in the finder methods of entity beans. Due to the EJB specification, there are several format requirements for the view definition:

Table 4: Using query rewriting

Query in legacy code	SELECT name, loc FROM emp, dept WHERE name=$(n) AND emp.dept_id=dept.dept_id	
Query in finder	Select * From emp Where name=?	SELECT * FROM Dept WHERE dept_id= any(SELECT dept_id FROM emp WHERE Emp.dept_id=?)
Finder name	Collection findByName(String n)	FindByEmpDeptID(String id)
Bean Name	EmpBean	DeptBean

Code skeleton generated	Set result;
	Vector row;
	Emp[] emps=empEjbHome.findByName(n);
	Row.add(n);
	For each emp in emps{
	   Dept_id=emp.getDeptID();
	   Dept[] depts=DeptEjbHome.findByEmpDeptID(dept_id);
	   For each dept in depts {
	      Loc=Dept.getLoc();
	      Row.add(loc);
	      Result.add(row);
	   }
	   return result;
	}	

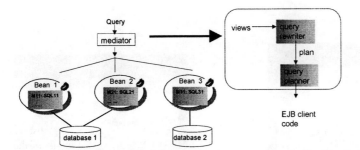

Figure 7: SQL-EJB mediator

- The finder method always returns one entity bean or a collection of beans. That means the head of the view definition will always have attributes from one particular bean. It will never be able to contain attributes from different beans. Also, views always select all the attributes from an entity bean.

- The finders have arguments. That means that the view definition has to be parameterized.

- The entity bean will have a getter for each attribute. That means by default there is a projection for every attribute in the base relation.

Using these observations, we can extract the view definitions from the EJB source code as described in [23].

3.2 Maximal query rewriting in SQL-EJB mediator

When designing a query rewriting system, there are two factors that need to be considered:

1. *What if there are multiple choices for the rewritings?* In the case of optimizing queries using rewriting [7], the best rewriting could be selected by comparing the cost of each candidate.

2. *What if there is no complete and equivalent rewriting of a query?* A complete rewriting is the one that contains view predicates only. In many cases, a complete and equivalent rewriting of a query using a set of views may not exist. When such a case occurs, there are two choices. One is to relax the completeness requirement and allow both view predicates and base predicates occur in the rewriting. The other is to compromise the equivalent requirement and make the rewriting not equivalent but the maximally-contained rewriting.

We have designed the rewriting system with the following considerations in mind:

1. When there are multiple complete rewritings, we select the one that has the fewest views. This is because each view amounts to a separate database access. Consequently, fewer views mean fewer database connections and travels. Also, there is less code needed at the client side to compose the final result of the query.

2. When there is not a complete rewriting, we sacrifice completeness and minimize the number of base predicates. This is necessary since we want to have an equivalent rewriting. Besides, the base predicates that can't be removed from the query will be suggested as new view definitions. Those new definitions will become the input of the EJB generator and will eventually be added as new finders in entity beans.

Given the above design desiderata, we present next an algorithm that satisfies both conditions.

Definition 4.1 (*Partial and complete rewriting*) For a rewriting Q' of a query Q using a set of views V, when the body of Q' contains view predicates from V as well as base predicates, it is called a *partial rewriting*. When the body of Q' contains view predicates only, it is called a *complete rewriting*.

Definition 4.2. (*Maximal rewriting*) Given two partial rewritings Q' and Q'' of Q using views V. Q' is greater than Q'' if the number of base predicates in Q' is less than that of Q''. A partial rewriting Q' is *maximal* if there is no other partial rewriting Q'' of Q using V such that Q'' is greater than Q'.

313

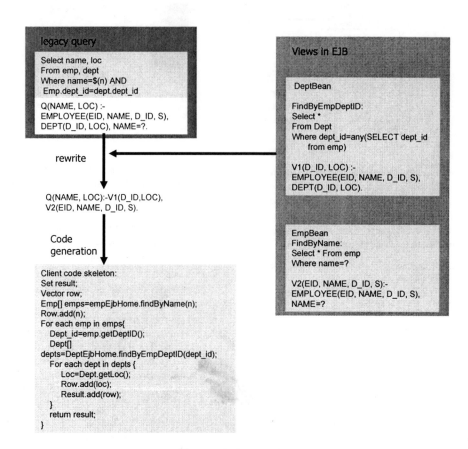

Figure 8: Code generation

Please note that the maximal rewriting we define here is different from the well known maximally-contained rewriting as described in [29].

Example 4.3. Given the query Q and views V_1 and V_2 in example 2.4. Q' in example 2.4 is the complete rewriting. One of the partial rewritings of Q using views

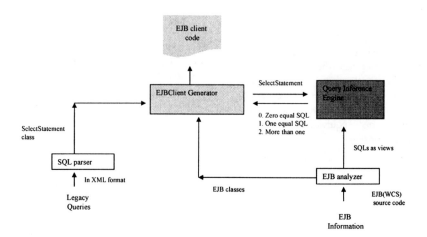

Figure 9: Overall System Architecture

V_1 and V_2 is

```
Q''(NAME,LOC):-
V1(NAME,EMP_ID,DEPT_ID),Dept(DEPT_ID,LOC).
```

On the other hand, if V_2 does not exist, Q'' is also the maximal rewriting of Q.

3.3 Extended bucket algorithm

There are two classes of rewriting algorithms. One is used in query optimization that guarantees the efficiency and sacrifices the completeness, such as join enumeration [25]. The other is used in data integration that guarantees the completeness and sacrifices the equivalence, such as the Bucket algorithm [25] and Inverse-rule algorithm [25]. Our approach is to extend the Bucket algorithm so that equivalence and the maximalarity as defined in previous section are ensured. Besides, we have other requirements that are specific in our particular application area.

3.4 Generate the EJB client code

Once a rewriting is obtained, we need to generate a plan for the query so that client Java code can be generated to actually execute the query. A query plan is a sequence of accesses to the EJB methods interspersed with local processing operations. Given a query Q of the form:

$$Q(X):-V_1(X_1),...,V_n(X_n).$$

A plan to answer it consists of a set of conjunctive plans. Conjunctive plans are like conjunctive queries except that each subgoal has input and output specification associated with it. For example, a plan for the above query could be

```
Q(X):-V₁(X₁)(In₁,Out₁),V₂(X₂)(In₂,Out₂),...,
      Vₙ(Xₙ)(Inₙ,Outₙ).
```
A plan is executable if the input of the i-th predicate appears in the output of the preceding predicates, i.e., $In_i \subseteq Out_1 \cup ... \cup Out_{i-1}$

Once we generated the execution plan, we can replace the view predicates with finder methods invocations, and provide the input parameters using input/output definitions.

Figure 8 presents a concrete example of how this algorithm works. The starting point is a SQL query Q and a set of enterprise Java beans like `EmpBean` and `DeptBean`. In those entity beans there are some finder methods like `findByName` and `findByEmpDeptId`, which have their corresponding SQL queries. When page designers want to access database, they will use the beans instead the queries. In this case, we need to decompose query Q into Q1 and Q2, which corresponds to `findByName` and `findByEmpDeptID`, respective. Then, according to the

logic of the decomposition, we need to insert Java code to combine the results of the two finder methods.

4   System implementation

The system implantation is being carried out on two fronts. One involves the query rewriting system, and the other the EJB client code generator.

The architecture of the query rewriting system is depicted in Figure 9. SQL4J is a SQL parser written in Java that parses a SQL statement into an abstract syntax tree. The Datalog translator is based on the SQL parser and can translate SQL queries into Datalog programs and vice versa.

The SQL parsing, Datalog translation, and query rewriting have been implemented and are being tested on hundreds of queries from the IBM Net.Commerce platform, along with hundreds of views from the IBM Websphere Commerce platform. The EJB client code generation is under construction and is going to be tested with the same data.

5   Related work and conclusions

There are tools and methods for migrating EJB applications from one platform to another (see, for example, WebLogic, Websphere and iPlanet [17] [33].) Our work differs from those approaches in that we are migrating the database applications to an EJB architecture, instead of moving EJB applications between different application servers. There are also tools for mapping database schemas or UML models to entity beans [15] [14]. However, these do not address SQL translation issues. Such tools are more relevant to the traditional object-relational mapping problem [1] [9].

Database reverse engineering and schema mapping [18] [35] are relevant to our work as well. Most database reverse engineering research attempts to map a relational schema to an object schema, or the transformation of relational queries to object-oriented queries [6] [9]. In our case, we translate SQL expressions from database application to object wrappers of the relational database.

Compared with work on query rewriting, we have several contributions as well. First, we proposed a new applications area for query rewriting which entails a different approach for query rewriting. We developed the notion of maximal rewriting and the extended bucket algorithm. The SQL-EJB mediator differs from other information mediators in several respects, such as the query capability representation in EJB and the query rewriting algorithm. More importantly, this is the first publicly available query rewriting system. Up to now, the largest query rewriting system we know of is described in [29], which experimented with queries and views that are randomly generated. In our case, thousands of queries and hundreds of views come from a real industry application. Thirdly, unlike other query rewriting system, we translate query plans to Java programs.

The research on object-relational mapping has been largely at the schema level, i.e., between object and relational models. There has been little work on the study of the mappings between the applications that are built on top of these models, and in particular, the mapping and translation between the SQLs and the methods in the objects. In the settings of EJB technology and software reengineering application area, this paper demonstrates the importance of such a mapping and presents methods for carrying it out. We should emphasize that our methods are applicable not only to the EJB reengineering problem, but also to other object persistent mechanism, such as JDO (Java Data Object).

From a reengineering point of view, we propose the reengineering of database applications using query rewriting technology.

This is an on going project. There are several issues need to be investigated further.

1. In this paper the EJB architecture is assumed to be very simple, with no instances of inheritance and associations [14]. Also, we are only considering CMP entity beans. BMP entity beans and session beans are not considered.

2. When rewriting a query the cost model is not used for selecting a good rewriting over a bad one.

3. All our algorithms are assuming SPJ queries. Further investigation is required to deal with disjunctive queries, groupings, etc.

4. In the new version of EJB specification EJB 2.0, a vendor-independent query language EJB-QL is defined. We need to expand our approach to accommodate EJB-QL, instead of SQL.

Acknowledgements

The author would like to thank Kenneth Cheung for his help in the implementation of the query rewriting system.

References

[1] R.S. Arnold, editor. *Software Reengineering*, Los Alamitos, CA, 1993. IEEE Computer Society Press.

[2] Andreas Behm and Andreas Geppert and Klaus R. Dittrich, *On the Migration of Relational Schemas and Data to Object-Oriented Database Systems*, in Proc. 5th International Conference on Re-Technologies for Information Systems, 13-33, 1997.

[3] S. Bergamaschi and A. Garuti and C. Sartori and A. Venuta, *The object wrapper: an object oriented interface for relational databases*, In Euromicro 1997.

[4] Kyle Brown, *Handling N-ary relationships in VisualAge for Java*, http://www.ibm.com/vadd, August 2000.

[5] Elliot Chikofsky and James Cross. *Reverse Engineering and Design Recovery: A Taxonomy*. IEEE Software, 7(1): 13-17, January 1990.

[6] Chang, Y., Raschid, L. and Dorr, B., *Transforming queries from a relational schema to an equivalent object schema: a prototype based on F-logic*, Proceedings of the International Symposium on Methodologies for Intelligent Systems, 1994.

[7] Surajit Chaudhuri, Ravi Krishnamurthy, Spyros Potamianos, Kyuseok Shim, *Optimizing Queries with materialized views*, ICDE 1995.

[8] Cohen, Y.; Feldman, Y.A., *Automatic high-quality reengineering of database programs by temporal abstraction*, Proceedings of the 1997 International Conference on Automated Software Engineering (ASE '97) (formerly: KBSE)

[9] Fong, J., *Converting Relational to Object-Oriented Databases*. SIGMOD Record, Vol.26, No. 1, March 1997.

[10] H. Gupta, I. S. Mumick, *Selection of views to materialize under a maintenance cost constraint*, in Proceedings of ICDT, pages 453-470, 1999.

[11] H. Gupta, *Selection of views to materialize in a data warehouse*, in Proceedings of ICDT, pages 98-112, 1997.

[12] IBM, *IBM Net.Data Reference*, Version 7, http://www4.ibm.com/software/data/net.data/, June 2001 Edition.

[13] IBM, *Websphere Commerce Suite Version 5.1: An introduction to the programming model*, IBM white paper, Feb 2001.

[14] IBM, *VisualAge for Java 3.5*, IBM, 2001.

[15] In2j, *Automated tool for migrating Oracle PL/SQL into Java*, www.in2j.com, April, 2001.

[16] Ivar Jacobson , Fredrik Lindström, *Reengineering of old systems to an object-oriented architecture*, OOPSLA 1991, ACM SIGPLAN Notices, Volume 26 Issue 11.

[17] IPlanet, *Migration Guide, iPlanet Application Server*, Version 6.0, www.iplanet.com, May 2000.

[18] J. Jahnke and W. Schafer and A. Zundorf, *A Design Environment for Migrating Relational to Object Oriented Database Systems*, In Proceedings of the International Conference on Software Maintenance, IEEE Computer Society Press, 163--170, 1996.

[19] Jianguo Lu, *Reengineering Database Applications to EJB based architecture*, CAiSE*02, 14th Conference on Advanced Information Systems Engineering, Toronto, May 27-31, 2002

[20] Yannis Kotidis, Nick Roussopoulos, *DynaMat: A Dynamic View Management System for Data Warehouses*, SIGMOD 99, June.

[21] Terry Lau, Jianguo Lu, Erik Hedges, Emily Xing, *Migrating E-commerce Database Applications to an Enterprise Java Environment*, CASCON'01.

[22] Terry Lau, Jianguo Lu, John Mylopoulos, Erik Hedges, Kostas Kontogiannis, Emily Xing, and Mark Crowley, *Net.Data to JSP Helper*, IBM alphaWorks, www.alphaworks.ibm.com/tech/netdatatojsp, 2001.

[23] Terry Lau, Jianguo Lu, John Mylopoulos, Kostas Kontogiannis, *Migrating E-commerce Database Applications to an Enterprise Java Environment*, Journal of Information Systems Frontiers, 2002..

[24] Alon Levy, Anand Rajaraman, Joann J. Ordille, *Querying heterogeneous information sources using source descriptions*. In proceedings of the international conference on Very Large Data Bases, Bombay, India, 1996.

[25] Alon Levy, *Answering queries using views: a survey*, VLDB Journal 2001.

[26] Chen Li, Mayank Bawa, Jeffrey D. Ullman, *Minimizing view sets without losing query-answering power*, ICDT'01.

[27] R. J. Miller, L. M. Haas and M. Hernández. *Schema Mapping as Query Discovery*. VLDB 2000.

[28] Wie Ming Lim and John Harrison, *An Integrated Database Reengineering Architecture - A Generic Approach*, Proceedings of the 1996 Australian Software Engineering Conference (ASWEC '96).

[29] Rachel Pottinger, Alon Y. Levy, *A Scalable Algorithm for Answering Queries Using Views*, VLDB 2000.

[30] William J. Premerlani, Michael R. Blaha, An approach for reverse engineering of relational databases, CACM, 1994 Vol 37(5).

[31] Chandrashekar Ramanathan, *Providing Object-Oriented Access To Existing Relational Databases*, PhD dissertation, Mississippi State University, 1997.

[32] Sun, *Enterprise JavaBeans 2.0 Specification*, www.java.sun.com, 2001.

[33] Tech Metrix, *Moving from IBM Websphere 3 to BEA WebLogic Server 5.1*, White Paper, TechMetrix Research, September 2000.

[34] Jeffrey D. Ullman, *Principles of Database and Knowledge-base Systems*, Volumes I, II, Computer Science Press, Rockville MD, 1989.

[35] M. W. W. Vermeer & P. M. G. Apers, *Reverse engineering of relational database applications*, in Proceedings Fourteenth International Conference on Object-Oriented and EntityRelationship Modeling (ER'95). LNCS 1021.

[36] L. Yan, R. J. Miller, L. M. Haas and R. Fagin. *Data-Driven Understanding and Refinement of Schema Mappings*, SIGMOD, May 2001.

Database Reliability/Stability and Security

Expressing Database Transactions as Atomic-operations

Andrew G. Fry

School of Computer Science and Information Technology,
RMIT University, GPO Box 2476V, Melbourne 3001, Australia.
andrewfry@acm.org

Abstract

DBMS are widely used and successfully applied to a huge range of applications. However the transaction paradigm that is, with variations like nested transactions and work-flow systems, the basis for durability and correctness is poorly suited to many modern applications. Transactions do not scale well and behave poorly at high concurrency levels and in distributed systems. The Atomic-operations model, which is proposed in this paper, is an alternative database paradigm based upon complete isolation between application and database and on explicit consistency management.

We describe this model and outline classes of applications for which atomic-operations might provide advantages such as better performance than transactions. We describe a graph-based approach that expresses database transactions consisting of four types of graph (operation, consistency, combined and atomic) and a transformation algebra (the operators $\oplus$, $\ominus$, $\bullet$, Φ and Ψ) to enable transactional applications to be rewritten into forms usable under the Atomic-operations model.

1. Introduction

Amongst database management systems, the 'transaction' concept is the almost universal model of durability and consistency control. Not all applications are suited to simple transactions, so extended or weakened transaction models have been applied to complex or long-term applications and problems of scale and distribution are under active investigation. Silberschatz et al [29] identifies a series technical barriers not addressed by existing DBMS, some can be addressed within existing DBMS models, others are fundamental to the transaction paradigm.

We see the 'transaction' paradigm as poorly suited to many applications; here we introduce the non-transactional Atomic-operations model and explore an alternate paradigm that addresses some fundamental issues.

Transactions (including queuing, nested, work-flow and object-oriented systems) are implicitly and tightly bound to an executing process; consistency is implicitly managed by the DBMS and concurrency control may require re-executing the application process.

In contrast, the Atomic-operations model enforces complete isolation between application processes and the database. An Atomic-operation is a mapping from one consistent database state to another, existing independently of the application. Consistency is managed explicitly by the application designers (using application semantics and atomic-operations mechanisms) and isolation provided by performing atomic-operations strictly serially.

Conventional DBMS design stresses overlapping I/O with processing and maximizing the number of concurrent transactions; this has discouraged non-concurrent DBMS but our previous work [18] demonstrates that even under conditions suited to a transactional DBMS, a strictly serial DBMS can perform similarly. Because the Atomic-operations model doesn't suffer from inter-transaction interference, under life-like conditions it can maintain high performance levels while a transactional DBMS system degrades under load.

This paper outlines the Atomic-operations model developed to suit asynchronous and distributed applications. We introduce graph-based representations of transactions—operation graphs describe the application; consistency graphs detail inter-attribute consistency relationships; combined graphs extend operation graphs to include inter-operation consistency relationships; and atomic graphs detail operation groups and inter-relationships. We describe a series of graph-based operators—together $\oplus$ and $\ominus$ relax consistency constraints; the $\bullet$ operator makes inter-operation consistency relationships explicit; Φ groups operations to ensure consistency; and Ψ produces operation groups conforming to the Atomic-operations model. Through these graphs and operations, we explore the equivalence of atomic-operations and transactional database models.

After discussing areas where the Atomic-operations

model displays advantages over transactional models and giving an example of an application suited to our model, sections 3 and 4 briefly outline the Atomic-operations model and detail our graph-based method of rewriting transactions into atomic-operations, leading to discussion of variations that can be produced from a given transaction, section 4.14.

1.1. Motivation

Many of the technical barriers that Silberschantz catalogued are fundamental to the nature of transactions. The atomic-operations paradigm differs significantly in some important areas.

Overhead Silberschantz et al discuss overhead requirements for hardware; expertise; planning; and systems management. For many realistic applications and interesting load-levels, atomic-operations produce better throughput than transactional systems.

Scale DBMS are not cost-effective in very small scale applications, where overhead is disproportionately high; nor are they suited to very large applications, due to problems of distribution and concurrency. Concurrent atomic-operations applications do not interfere—the model is well-suited to web-scale applications.

A priori schema DBMS force data to conform to a schema. Because atomic-operations are based on operations instead of data, there is no requirement for prior knowledge of the schema.

Security model Security is conventionally defined in terms of data elements rather than operations permitted by a user. The Atomic-operations model suits control defined in terms of operations.

Guaranteeing outcomes The transaction model links atomicity, isolation and persistence (durability); 'database centric' consistency management imposes barriers to WAN- and object-based systems. Durability, isolation and consistency management are fundamentally distinguished in the Atomic-operations model, which permits users to manage outcome guarantees.

Also, some conventional control mechanisms are unsuited to modern applications; throttling is a widely available mechanism used to prevent thrashing, however web-scale systems may require supporting very large numbers of slowly progressing transactions. Further, amongst the current range of DBMS, there is a paupacy of systems that providing timely, asynchronous processing [13]. Because atomic-operations are completely independent of the application, they are naturally asynchronous.

1.2. Example

Imagine the parts database of a large airliner manufacturer. Each of many thousand aircraft, is composed of perhaps a million parts; each part is tracked over the aircraft's lifetime. There are multiple parts warehouses worldwide and these parts are also tracked. Further, the corresponding engineering database records drawings and details replacement parts for each subsystem variant, this is accessed by maintenance engineers worldwide and updated regularly by designers. Naturally, the entire database operates on-line and to set service levels; strict legal constraints and liability issues require timely updates, consistent information, and 24×7 access.

Boeing [12] found that a database of this scale exceeds the capacity of existing systems, in particular lock contention on literally global tables effects response times but lazy replication systems provided insufficient consistency and/or timeliness.

This parts database is well suited to the Atomic-operations model: identifying information is largely non-volatile and well suited to building references (section 3.3) that permit atomic-operations to be fully asynchronous and to have guaranteed outcomes. As there is no lock contention, throughput is not affected by load or scale, and because atomic-operations are asynchronous, application response time can be independent of database throughput, an important factor when availability and usability are mandated. Finally, as Atomic-operations hide the underlying data organisation, structural changes to the database can be hidden from applications.

2. Related Work

Transactions guaranteeing the *ACID* properties are used almost universally for concurrency control and failure management in large-scale DBMS [9, 24].

Mutual exclusion, typically locking, is a favourite method of serialising transactions and various protocols have been devised to resolve problems and maximise performance [31]. Both lock- and restart-based protocols are prone to thrashing as load and transaction size increases [16, 30], they are not well suited to distributed environments; but optimistic [19] and multi-version protocols [26] are best suited to read-only environments.

Early approaches to reducing inter-transaction interference explicitly revealed its effects—Epsilon transactions [25] reveal the uncertainty of incomplete transactions, Escrow transactions [22] can 'reserve' a specified amount of certainty. Gray [19] explains many variations that perform better than simple 2PL, see Lynch [20, 21] and Climent [11] for more recent approaches, and Elmagaramid [14] for a catalogue of work-flow style models. Unlike transaction-based models, interference does not arise under the Atomic-operations model.

Some work has focused on splitting transactions because smaller transactions are known to interfere less [16]; Agrawal [1, 2] and Bernstein [7, 8], Shasha [28] examine various transaction decomposing approaches.

Object-oriented systems [4] have encouraged designers to reveal and use operation semantics, for example [3, 23, 27]. Similarly, knowledge of the application or data is used by [5, 6, 15], and work-flow models look to manual decomposition of long-running applications [10, 32]. The Atomic-operations model involves the user in consistency management and permits considerable gain from that involvement.

3. The Atomic-operations Model

This section briefly outlines the Atomic-operations model [17]. We distinguish between *transactions* and *atomic-operations* —transactions exist in a conventional DBMS; atomic-operations, but not transactions, exists in the Atomic-operations model.

In our model, an application is a conventional application process $\mathcal{A}$ (implementing the user interface) that invokes a series of atomic-operations $\mathcal{O}_i$. $\mathcal{A}$ has no direct access to the database, it cannot perform *read* or *write* operations.

$\mathcal{A}$'s only control over any atomic-operation $\mathcal{O}_i$ is to *invoke* it and perhaps accept whatever response it produces. Invocation is durable; the system guarantees to perform all invoked $\mathcal{O}_i$ once and exactly once, and ensures that any results produced by $\mathcal{O}_i$ will be available to $\mathcal{A}$.

3.1. Atomic-operations

An Atomic-operation $\mathcal{O}_i$ is a mapping from one consistent database state to another, $\mathcal{O}_i$ may return some result values. All $\mathcal{O}_i$ are entirely specified by their invocation parameters, that is they have no access to any executing process $\mathcal{A}$ nor to the non-database environment. One atomic-operation may invoke another using nested calls or two degraded forms, chaining and forking, see 4.12.

Each $\mathcal{O}_i$ exists in complete isolation from all other $\mathcal{O}$. Though isolation could be ensured by locking, previous results [18] have demonstrated advantages to simple serial execution.

3.2. Consistency

Under the Atomic-operations model, correctness is defined as the absence of violations of any database consistency constraints. A conventional DBMS requires that no transaction (in isolation) violates consistency constraints, the Atomic-operations model has similarly requirements on

$\mathcal{A}$ and $\mathcal{O}_i$. All $\mathcal{O}_i$ must be specified such that they can never produce an inconsistent database state. This can be accomplished largely using strict argument checking and *references*, see below.

No $\mathcal{A}$ or $\mathcal{O}_i$ may combine information which *could* have been produced by mutually inconsistent database states (e.g. from different $\mathcal{O}_i$ invocations, for any information which is related by consistency constraints.) This restriction forces potentially inconsistent updates to be performed within a single atomic-operation but is relaxed below.

3.3. References

To permit information to be passed between different $\mathcal{O}_i$ without violating the previous rule, information guaranteed consistent by some external means (e.g. application semantics) may be expressed using a *reference*.

A reference is the combinations of an object identifier, a set of attributes which will remain consistent for the life of the reference, and a reference-lifetime function. Because information obtained from references is guaranteed consistent, it is not subject to the restrictions of section 3.2. References have a long but not eternal lifetime, $\mathcal{A}$ may not invoke any $\mathcal{O}_i$ with stale reference arguments.

For example, a part-reference may identify a particular aircraft part if application semantics can guarantee that the part will continue to exist in the database for at least the reference lifetime. The part-reference can be used to access specified attributes of one specific part object. The lifetime of an aircraft part may be many years, so a part-reference might be assigned a lifetime of a week—vastly longer than the life of the reference instance. [17] discusses semantic mechanisms for ensuring reference integrity.

4. Rewriting

Rewriting produces an Atomic-operations application from a transactional application. This section describes graphs which express application transactions and a series of graph operators that produce atomic-operations and an invoking application. We prove that rewritten results are equivalent to the original transaction.

Rewriting begins with an *operation graph* expressing a transaction's operations and the attributes accessed, and a *consistency graph* showing the consistency relationships between database attributes. These can be combined by the $\bullet$ operator, producing a graph of transaction's operation interdependence. We define this graph's correctness in terms of equivalence to some (consistent) transaction, expressed by the $\mathbb{I}$ operator.

Rewriting involves several steps; to reduce the consistency constraints on an application, the $\oplus$ operator produces further operation graphs that make use of reference r. Each

$\oplus$ operator is paired with an $\ominus$ reducing the consistency graph to reflect the guarantees provided by r. We demonstrate that after any sequence of same-reference $\oplus$ and $\ominus$ operations, the combined graph is equivalent to the original transaction.

The second rewriting step uses the Φ operator that, from a combined graph, produces the maximal set of subgraphs conforming to isolation requirements. Each subgraph contains some portion of the original transaction; each is isolation from all other subgraphs; and the total effect of all subgraphs is equivalent to the original transaction. The Φ operator is defined in terms of the ϕ operator which produces the minimal subgraph containing any given node.

The third rewriting step involves Ψ operating on a set of combined graphs and producing a set of subgraphs that conform to the invocation requirements of the Atomic-operations model. Ψ is defined in terms of ψ, which produces a combined graph containing a given node.

Finally, we define the λ function that expresses the I/O requirements that our model imposes and informs us if the set of combined graphs are legal within the atomic-operations model.

4.1. Database

A *database* is the universal relation—the set of all possible object attributes where non-existence is expressed by the special value *nil*. The smallest uniquely addressable entity is an *attribute*, identified by an <object-id, attribute-name> pair, usually written 'object.attribute'.

The correctness of all database states is defined as the absence of violations of consistency rules (constraints), rules that may or may not be expressed formally. We assume the existence of some oracle function that informs us if a given database state is consistent.

4.2. References

A *reference* ρ on attribute set A is a value that can be used to consistently access any attribute $\alpha \in A$ across the lifetime of the reference. The correctness of references is guaranteed by the application semantics, so valid references may not be available for all attributes. References are produced by a special (*ref*) operation and used by de-referencing variations of the access operations (*readref* and *writeref*), they can be passed between distinct atomic-operations and reused without introducing inconsistency. References have a long (but not eternal) lifetime and incorporate a mechanism for deciding when they are stale. α^{REF} denotes the set of reference-values for attribute α. Conversely, ρ_{ATTR} is the set of attributes which can be accessed through reference ρ, without introducing inconsistency.

4.3. Value Dependency

Attributes inter-related by some consistency constraint are said to have a *value dependency*, expressed $\alpha \xrightarrow{v} \beta$, informally the value of α is used to 'produce' β. Formally $\alpha \xrightarrow{v} \beta$ is true if and only if there is some change to β which produces an inconsistent database and there is a corresponding change to α that produces a consistent database.

4.4. Transaction

A 'transaction' is the abstracted database operations produced by the execution of conventional database application $\mathcal{T}$, it relies on the ACID properties provided by the DBMS. We also consider the application producing the transaction, so we consider transaction $\mathcal{T}$ to be an ordered set of *operations* including 'read' and 'write' operations. We are only concerned with correct transactions which when executed serially produce consistent results.

4.5. Operations

Operations define both transactions and atomic-operations. An operation is completely described by a *code* tuple of <type, dstSet, srcSet>. Operation 'types' are listed in table 1; 'dstSet' is a set of unique identifiers of data destination 'variables'; and 'srcSet' elements are either constant values or identifiers that appear elsewhere in a dstSet.

The database attribute accessed by operation s is known as s_ω, for the operations given above, s_ω is either the empty set ϕ or a set containing one attribute.

The dataflow between a set S of operations is expressed $\Diamond(S)$, being a set of (graph) edges 'to' each operations' *source* operands 'from' the identically named *destination* operand.

4.6. Operation graphs

Operation graphs represent both transactions and atomic-operations, figure 1 shows an operation graph and the transaction from which it was produced. An operation graph is a directed graph $S = <\mathcal{S}_N, \mathcal{S}_E>$ being the sets of nodes $\mathcal{S}_N$ and edges $\mathcal{S}_E$. The nodes correspond to all operations and are labelled with each operation's code, as given in table 1. The edges $\mathcal{S}_E$ indicate dataflow between operations and are derived from the nodes by $\Diamond(\mathcal{S}_N)$.

Similarly to single operations, for graph S the set of attributes accessed by the operations $\mathcal{S}_N$, is known as $\mathcal{S}_\omega$ and defined as $\underset{a \in \mathcal{S}_N}{\cup}(a_\omega)$.

4.7. Consistency-graph

A consistency graph represents the value dependencies $\xrightarrow{v}$ between attributes. When a combined-graph is pro-

Type	Example	s_ω	Group
	Database access		
read	read $d \leftarrow o, a$	o	db
write	write $o, a \leftarrow s$	o	db
	External access		
input	input $d \leftarrow$		io
print	print $\leftarrow s$		io
	Reference		
ref	ref $r \leftarrow o, l$		db
readref	readref $d \leftarrow r, a$		db
writeref	write $r, a \leftarrow s$		db
	Control		
let	let $d \leftarrow f(s)$		
if	...		

Table 1. Transaction operations and operation-graph nodes are taken from the set of *operations* given here, using destination value d, source value s, source object id o, attribute specifier a, and constructing reference r to attribute-set l. Operations of different 'groups' do not appear together in a correct subgraph because *db* operations are restricted to atomic-operations and *io* operations are limited to application processes.

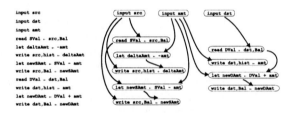

Figure 1. The operation-graph S, on the right, is simply derived from the operations executed by a transaction (example on the left) or an atomic-operation.

duced by applying • to a consistency graph and an operation graph, edges represent operation interdependencies and are used to control grouping of operations into consistent atomic-operations.

A consistency graph C is the set of nodes C_N and edges C_E. The nodes correspond to database attributes and are uniquely labelled with the attributes' name. An edge exists between all nodes and themselves (a, a) and between nodes (a, b) if and only if a is value dependent on b, that is $a \xrightarrow{v} b$.

4.8. The Combining Operator •

A *combined-graph* G, see figure 3, expresses both operations (actions performed) and the existence of consistency relationships between operations, they are produced by applying the combining (•) operator to an operation graph

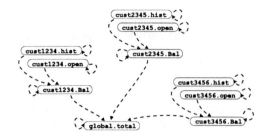

Figure 2. A consistency-graph C expresses the existence of value dependency relationships between database attributes; applying this information to an operation graph enables us to produce atomic-operations.

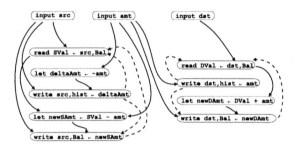

Figure 3. A combined-graph G expresses the transaction's or atomic-operations' operations and the consistency relationships between attributes accessed by those operations. 'Dataflow' edges are shown as solid lines, 'value-dependency' edges are dashed lines.

and a consistency-graph, they are used to decide which operations may be expressed in separate atomic-operations.

Where operation graph S and consistency graph C are —

$$S = <S_N, S_E>, \quad C = <C_N, C_E>$$

the graph G produced by $S \bullet C$ has the same nodes and edges as S, and additional edges $V(S)$ between nodes a and b when the attributes accessed by those operations have a value dependency edge in C—

$$<G_N, G_E> = <S_N, S_E> \bullet <C_N, C_E>$$

$$G_N = S_N, \quad G_E = S_E \cup V(S, C)$$

$$V(S, C) = \bigcup_{a, b} ([a, b]) :$$

$$\forall a \in S_N, \forall b \in S_N, [a_\omega, b_\omega] \in C_E$$

where $[a, b]$ indicates an edge from a to b.

4.9. The Consistently-equivalent Operator $\bar{\sqsubseteq}$

We use the $\bar{\sqsubseteq}$ operator to expresses the equivalence of two combined graphs proving that a rewriting step does not introduce the potential for inconsistent results.

Definition: Two combined graphs $\mathcal{G}$ and $\mathcal{H}$ are *consistently equivalent*, expressed $\mathcal{G} \bar{\sqsubseteq} \mathcal{H}$, if 1) the same attributes are updated, that is $\mathcal{G}_\omega = \mathcal{H}_\omega$, and 2) the value dependency relationships between attributes is retained (either the same dependency edges exist or the value dependency is otherwise guaranteed by references.)

Explanation: Only updates can *introduce* inconsistency; as $\mathcal{G}$ and $\mathcal{H}$ update the same attributes, inconsistency could only be introduced if the value dependencies between those objects was violated. As the same value dependency relations are retained, and the combined-graph expresses all consistency constraints between all pairs of attributes accessed, so consistency will not be introduced.

4.10. Reference Operators $\oplus$ and $\ominus$

The $\oplus$ operator adds reference usage to an operation graph, and the $\ominus$ operator removes value dependencies from consistency graphs. By 'adding' a reference to an operation graph and 'subtracting' from the corresponding consistency graph those dependencies that are guaranteed by the reference, we reduce the isolation required of the atomic-operation and permit the original transaction to be split into more feasible atomic-operations.

The *add* operator $\mathcal{S} \oplus r$ applies a reference r to operation graph $\mathcal{S}$, yielding an operation graph $\mathcal{S}'$. The resulting $\mathcal{S}'$ contains operation nodes that creates reference r and uses 'referenced' accesses instead of direct access for all of $a \in r_{ATTR}$.

Where r is a reference to attribute $\alpha \in r^{ATTR}$, we define $\mathcal{S}_r^{RW}$ as the set of nodes in $\mathcal{S}$ containing operations which 'read α' or 'write α.'

In a related vein, $\mathcal{S}_r^{RWR}$ is the same set of nodes as $\mathcal{S}_r^{RW}$ but replacing 'read' with 'readref', see table 2, and similarly 'write' with 'writeref'.

To initially obtain a reference, $\mathcal{S}_r^{REF}$ is a graph consisting of a single 'ref' node producing a reference value r.

Now $\mathcal{S}' = \mathcal{S} \oplus r$ is the original $\mathcal{S}$ graph, excluding direct read/write nodes, but including referenced-form read/write nodes and a reference constructing node—

$$< \mathcal{S}'_N, \mathcal{S}'_E > \ = \ < \mathcal{S}_N, \mathcal{S}_E > \oplus r$$

$$\mathcal{S}'_N \ = \ \mathcal{G}_N - \mathcal{G}_r^{RW} + \mathcal{G}_r^{RWR} + \mathcal{G}_r^{REF}$$

The graph's edges are the dataflow edges corresponding to these nodes—

$$\mathcal{S}'_E = \Diamond (\mathcal{S}')$$

Direct access	s_ω	Referenced access	s_ω
read $d \leftarrow o, a$	o	readref $d \leftarrow r, a$	
write $o, a \leftarrow s$	o	writeref $r, a \leftarrow s$	

Table 2. Alternate (referenced) forms of data access operations, using destination value d, source value s, source object id o, and attribute specifier a. As the alternate forms apply an object reference (r) instead of an object id o, consistency between multiple uses of r^{ATTR} is assured externally.

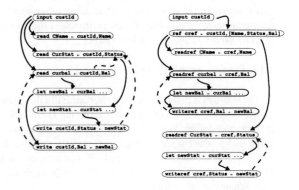

Figure 4. $\mathcal{G} \oplus r$. To the combined graph $\mathcal{G}$ on the left, we add reference r which references attributes $r^{ATTR} = [Name, Status, Bal]$. This yields another combined graph, shown on the right, but with reduced value dependencies.

$\oplus$ has produced an operation graph which doesn't access any of r's attributes directly but which obtains reference r and then uses de-referencing operations.

Removing references: The *subtract* operator $\mathcal{C} \ominus r$ removes a reference r from consistency graph $\mathcal{C}$, producing a reduced consistency graph $\mathcal{C}'$. $\ominus$ is always used paired with $\oplus$, so as value dependencies are removed from the consistency graph (permitting parts of the original transaction to become atomic-operations), supporting reference usage is added to the operation graph.

Where r is a reference to attributes α, that is $(r_{ATTR} = \alpha)$, then $\mathcal{G}_E^r$ is the value dependency edges in $\mathcal{G}$ going *to* some $a \in \alpha$.

$$\mathcal{G}_E^r = \bigcup_{a \in G_N} (\ [b, a] \ ),$$

$$\exists b \in G_N, \ \exists [b, a] \in G_E$$

Now $\mathcal{C} \ominus r$ is the graph excluding those edges,

$$< \mathcal{C}'_N, \mathcal{C}'_E > \ = \ (\mathcal{C} \ominus r)$$

325

$$\mathcal{C}'_N = \mathcal{C}_N, \quad \mathcal{C}'_E = \mathcal{G}_E - \mathcal{G}^r_E$$

Theorem 1 $\mathcal{C} \bullet \mathcal{S} \supset\!\subset (\mathcal{C} \ominus r) \bullet (\mathcal{S} \oplus r)$, *that a graph $\mathcal{G}'$ derived by applying a reference to $\mathcal{G}$ is consistently equivalent $\mathcal{G}$. Informally, that we do not introduce inconsistency when we apply the same reference to a pair of operation/consistency graphs.*

Proof 1 *Informally the proof is simple; all value dependency edges that are removed from $\mathcal{C}$ (by $\ominus$) have been replaced by reference usage (by $\oplus$.) The consistency of dereferenced attributes is guaranteed by some external mechanism (application semantics.) Thus some other mechanism guarantees consistency for those attributes that are no longer linked by value dependency edges.* □

4.11. Partial-graph Operators Φ and ϕ

The combined graphs produced after applying the $\oplus$ and $\ominus$ operators express an entire application that is equivalent to some transaction. We apply the Φ operator to a combined graph and produce a set of subgraphs, each of which is the smallest distinct subgraph necessary for consistency. Φ is defined in terms of ϕ, which produces the smallest subgraph that includes some given node.

Firstly, a *partial-graph* of $\mathcal{G}$ is a connected subgraph of $\mathcal{G}$, we represent isolated consistent operations using partial-graphs. Note that $[g, h]$ is the combined effect of performing two partial-graphs g and h in isolation from each other.

$\mathcal{G}\phi n$ is the minimal subgraph of $\mathcal{G}$ which includes all cycles for which node $n \in \mathcal{G}_N$ is a member. $\mathcal{G}\phi n$ can be performed in isolation without introducing inconsistency.

When $\Theta_\mathcal{G}$ is the set of all cyclic subgraphs of $\mathcal{G}$, then

$$\mathcal{G}\phi n = \bigcup_{n \in c_N} (\; <c_N, c_E>\;), \forall c \in \Theta_\mathcal{G}$$

Informally, this subgraph is the portion of graph $\mathcal{G}$ which includes all operations that are in some way dependent on operation n or on which n is dependent.

We specify by $(\mathcal{G}\phi n)_N$, the set of nodes which appear in graph $\mathcal{G}\phi n$; this is a set of operations that cannot be split without introducing the potential for inconsistency.

To obtain all $(\mathcal{G}\phi n)$, we define $\Phi\mathcal{G}$ as the set of $\mathcal{G}$'s distinct partial-graphs; for every node $n \in \mathcal{G}$ of some combined-graph, we take $(\mathcal{G}\phi n)$ (Note that the same partial-graph can be derived from several different nodes but $\Phi\mathcal{G}$ is the set of unique graphs.) So—

$$\Phi\mathcal{G} = \bigcup_{n \in \mathcal{G}_N} [(\mathcal{G}\phi n)_N]$$

Theorem 2 $[g - h, h] \supset\!\subset g$ *for all partial-graphs h of g, $h \in \Phi g$, informally that partial graphs of a transaction are equivalent to the original transaction.*

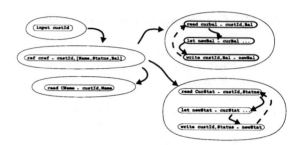

Figure 5. Each node of an *atomic-graph* represents a consistently complete partial-graph. Each edge represents an intra-partial-graph dataflow or value-dependency.

Proof 2 *Informally, if dataflow exists from any $n \in g$ to $m \in g$, $n \neq m$ (directly or indirectly) and dependency exists between m and n (directly or indirectly) then a cycle is formed and $[n, m] \in \mathcal{G}\phi n$. By definition $\mathcal{G}\phi n$ includes all cycles containing n, so there are no operations that are both dataflow connected to n and consistency related to n that are not included in $\mathcal{G}\phi n$; thus $\mathcal{G}\phi n$ is independent of the rest of $\mathcal{G}$.* □

4.12. Atomic-graph Operators Ψ and ψ

The previous section described partial-graphs $\Phi\mathcal{G}$, the set of which is consistently equivalent to the transaction from which they are derived. Being unstructured, partial graphs may contain dataflow which cannot be expressed in the atomic-operations model. The Ψ operator operates on *atomic graphs*, combining subgraphs such that they contain only acceptably structured dataflow.

Atomic-graphs: An atomic-graph $\mathcal{A}$, e.g. figure 5, is a graph of partial-graphs. Each node $n \in \mathcal{A}_N$ is an element of the set of partial (sub) graphs originally derived from $\mathcal{G}$ by Φ. The edges $e \in \mathcal{A}_E$ represent dataflow or value-dependency between some element within node $n \in \mathcal{A}_N$ and some element within another node $m \in \mathcal{A}_N$, $m \neq n$.

Within the atomic-operations model, independent atomic-operations may interact only in the three forms illustrated in figure 6.

Combining atomic-graphs: Similar to the way in which we defined the Φ and ϕ operators, we will use the Ψ operator to produce the set of consistent atomic-graphs. It is defined as the union of ψ over all nodes of $\mathcal{A}$;

$$\Psi\mathcal{G} = \bigcup_{n \in \mathcal{G}_N} [(\mathcal{G}\psi n)_N]$$

where ψ produces y, a consistent atomic-graph containing some given node and where the dataflow to and from y can be expressed in the acceptable forms of figure 6.

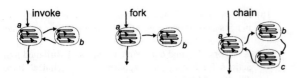

Figure 6. The basic form of atomic-operation interaction is the *invoke* operation (similar to call/return.) Two degraded forms are also permitted—*fork* (invoke/no-result) expresses naturally asynchronous operations and *chain* (invoke/deferred-result) expresses operations distributed in time or location.

Definition: $\mathcal{A}\psi n$ is defined as the minimal subgraph of $\mathcal{A}$ which includes node $n \in \mathcal{A}$ and in which all edges *from* $\mathcal{A}\psi n$ can be expressed in one of the forms shown in figure 6.

The definition of ψ is that there are no value dependency edges between any y_i and y_j produced by ψ from the same $\mathcal{A}$ and all (if any) dataflow edges can be expressed using acceptable mechanisms. This means that each y_i can be isolated from all others without introducing inconsistency.

Theorem 3 *That for atomic-graphs* p, $q \in \Psi(\mathcal{G})$, *the combined graph is consistently equivalent to the individual graphs* $p + q \asymp [p, q]$.

Proof 3 *Informally,* Ψ *operates on partial graphs which are known to be distinct and independently consistent. The result of* Ψ *is to combine subgraphs; a graph produced combining two subgraphs contains the same nodes as the subgraphs, so it will perform the same updates. As* $[p, q]$ *performs the same updates as* $p + q$, *if one form does not introduce inconsistency, neither will the other.* $\square$

4.13. Correct Atomic-graphs

Various subgraphs can be produced from transaction $\mathcal{T}$, depending on the order in which references are applied using $\oplus$ and $\ominus$ and on the order that Φ and Ψ are applied. Some, or all, subgraphs may violate atomic-operations I/O requirements—the λ function can be used to select acceptable subgraphs from the set of those that can be produced.

Correct atomic-graphs: $\lambda_{\mathcal{G}}$ is the set of atomic-graphs $\mathcal{A}_G$ for which all operation nodes that have non-nil type are of the same *type* (*db* or *io*), see table 1

As the atomic-operations model enforces isolation of *database* and *interactive* operations, a transaction can be expressed as an atomic-operation only if $\lambda_{\mathcal{G}} = \mathcal{A}_G$.

4.14. Optimisations

A range of different subgraphs can be produced by applying references (using the $\oplus$ and $\ominus$ operators) in various

orders. Similarly, different results might be produced depending on the order in which Φ and Ψ are applied.

For any given application, some set of references $\mathbb{R}$ are logically possible. Of these, R are made available by the application designers. Rewriting a given transaction's operation graph T is performed using references R. Concerning the order of reference application by the $\oplus$ and $\ominus$ operators; because $\oplus$ operates by repeatedly combining inter-dependent subgraphs, and all inter-dependent nodes are eventually combined into one subgraph, the order in which references are applied will not affect the final result.

Similarly, concerning the order of the Φ and Ψ operators; we've defined them such that they must be applied Φ and Ψ but the reverse could just as easily be the case, and the order in which these are applied could conceivably affect the outcome. However similarly to $\oplus$ and $\ominus$, because Φ and Ψ produce unions of inter-dependent node sets and all inter-dependent nodes are eventually combined into subgraphs, operator order does not affect the final outcome.

However, each reference that is applied effectively removes interdependencies between operations, so the largest set R will produce the smallest number of interdependencies and lead to the largest number of subgraphs. This maximises opportunities to use the 'fork' form and concurrent/asynchronous processing; or to use the 'chain' form, which maximises the potential to distribute processing by location or time.

5. Conclusion

We have outlined some technical issues that apply to transactional database systems and modern variations. The 'transaction' paradigm, the basis of consistency and durability, is based upon controlling the interaction of application process and database.

The Atomic-operations model is an alternative database paradigm based on completely isolating application from database and explicit consistency management. We outlined the Atomic-operations model and described ways in which it is better suited to certain modern applications.

We have given a graph-based representation of application transactions, inter-attribute consistency relationships, inter-operation consistency relationships, and operation grouping. We discussed a series of graph-based operators $\oplus$, $\ominus$, $\bullet$, Φ and Ψ that are applied to transaction graphs, culminating in the production of an Atomic-operations application equivalent to the original transaction. The Atomic-operations application displays increased asynchronism and for many applications will display better throughput and/or scalability than the original transaction based application. Finally we described how the order in which operations are applied does not affect the atomic-operations produced but increasing the set of references can produce better applications.

In future work, we intend to report on the practical aspects of the Atomic-operations model and to extend it into time- and location-distribution.

References

[1] D. Agrawal, A. E. Abbadi, and R. Jeffers. An approach to eliminate transaction blocking in locking protocols. In *Proc. ACM Principles of Database Systems*, pages 223–235, 1992.

[2] D. Agrawal, J. L. Bruno, A. E. Abbadi, and V. Krishnaswamy. Relative serializability: An approach for relaxing the atomicity of transactions. In *Proc. ACM SIGMOD Int. Conf. Management of Data*, pages 139–149, 1994.

[3] G. Alonso, D. Agrawal, and A. E. Abbadi. Reducing recovery constraints on locking based protocols. In *Proc. ACM Principles of Database Systems*, pages 129–138. ACM, 1994.

[4] P. Ammann and S. Jajodia. Semantics-based transaction processing: satisfying conflicting objectives. *IEEE Concurrency*, 5(2):8–10, April 1997.

[5] B. R. Badrinath and K. Ramanritham. Semantics-based concurrency control: Beyond commutativity. *ACM Trans. on Database Systems*, 17(1):163–199, March 1992.

[6] M. Benedikt, T. Griffin, and L. Libkin. Verifiable properties of database transactions. In *Proc. ACM Principles of Database Systems*, 117–127, 1996. ACM.

[7] A. J. Bernstein, D. S. Gerstl, P. M. Lewis, and S. Lu. Using transaction semantics to increase performance. In *High Performance Transaction Processing Workshop*, 1999. pre-publication copy.

[8] A. J. Bernstein and P. M. Lewis. Transaction decomposition using transaction semantics. *Distributed and Parallel Databases*, 4(1), 1996.

[9] P. A. Bernstein and E. Newcomer. *Principles of Transaction Processing*. Morgan Kaufmann, 1997.

[10] P. K. Chrysanthis and K. Ramamritham. ACTA: A framework for specifying and reasoning about transaction structure and behavior. In *Proc. ACM SIGMOD Int. Conf. Management of Data*, pages 194–203, 1990.

[11] A. Climent, M. Bertran, and M. Nicolau. Database concurrency control on a shared-nothing architecture using speculative lock modes. In *Advances in Database and Information Systems, Proc. 5th East European Conf.*, 2001.

[12] L. Do, P. Drew, W. Jin, V. Jumani, and D. V. Rossum. Issues in developing very large data warehouses. In *Proc. VLDB Conf.*, pages 633–636, 1998.

[13] L. S. Do and P. Ram. State of the art of asynchronous transaction management. Technical Report 98–016, The Boeing Company, 1998.

[14] A. K. Elmagarmid, editor. *Database Transaction Models for Advanced Applications*, volume 1. Morgan Kaufmann, 1995.

[15] A. A. Farrag and M. T. Özsu. Using semantic knowledge of transactions to increase concurrency. *ACM Trans. on Database Systems*, 14(4):503–525, December 1989.

[16] P. Franaszek and J. T. Robinson. Limitations of concurrency in transaction processing. *ACM Trans. on Database Systems*, 10(1):1–28, March 1985.

[17] A. G. Fry. Beyond concurrency control: Distributed transactions for E-commerce applications. Technical Report TR-01-4, RMIT University, Melbourne, Australia, October 2001.

[18] A. G. Fry. The atomic-operations transaction model—Advantages to simplifying DB access. Technical Report TR-02-6, RMIT University, Melbourne, Australia, 2002.

[19] J. Gray and A. Reuter. *Transaction Processing: Concepts and Techniques*. Morgan Kaufmann, 1993.

[20] N. Lynch, M. Merritt, W. Weihl, and A. Fekete. *Atomic Transactions*. Morgan Kaufmann, 1994.

[21] N. A. Lynch. Multilevel atomicity—a new correctness criterion for database concurrency control. *ACM Trans. on Database Systems*, 8(4):484–502, Dec 1983.

[22] P. E. ONeil. The Escrow transactional method. *ACM Trans. on Database Systems*, 11(4):405–430, December 1986.

[23] G. Pardon and G. Alonso. Cheetah: A lightweight transaction server for plug-and-play internet data management. In *Proc. VLDB Conf.*, pages 210–219, 2000.

[24] R. Ramakrishnan and J. Gehrke. *Database Management Systems*. McGraw-Hill, second edition, 2000.

[25] K. Ramamritham and C. Pu. A formal characterisation of Epsilon serializability. *IEEE Trans. Knowledge and Data Engineering*, 7(6):997–1007, December 1995.

[26] D. P. Reed. Naming and synchronization in a decentralized computer system. Tech. Report MIT/LCS/TR-205, MIT Laboratory for Computer Science, Cambridge, Massachusetts, 1978.

[27] R. F. Resende, D. Agrawal, and A. E. Abbadi. Semantic locking in object-oriented database systems. In *Proc. ACM OOPSLA Conf.*, pages 388–402, 1994.

[28] D. Shasha. Simple rational guidance for chopping up transactions. In *Proc. ACM SIGMOD Int. Conf. Management of Data*, pages 298–307. ACM, 1992.

[29] A. Silberschatz and S. Z. et al. Strategic directions in database systems–Breaking out of the box. *ACM Computing Surveys*, 28(4):764–778, Dec 1996.

[30] A. Thomasian. Two-phase locking performance and its thrashing behavior. *ACM Trans. on Database Systems*, 18(4):579–625, December 1993.

[31] A. Thomasian. Concurrency control: Methods, performance and analysis. *ACM Computing Surveys*, 30(1):70–119, March 1998.

[32] H. Wächter and A. Reuter. *The ConTract Model*, chapter 7, pages 219–264. Volume 1 of Elmagarmid [14], 1995.

Identification of Malicious Transactions in Database Systems[*]

Yi Hu
*Computer Science and Computer
Engineering Department
University of Arkansas
Fayetteville, AR 72701, USA
Email: yhu@uark.edu*

Brajendra Panda
*Computer Science and Computer
Engineering Department
University of Arkansas
Fayetteville, AR 72701, USA
Email: bpanda@uark.edu*

Abstract

Existing host-based intrusion detection systems (IDSs) use the operating system log or the application log to detect misuse or anomaly activities. These methods are not sufficient for detecting intrusion in database systems. In this paper, we describe a method for database intrusion detection by using data dependency relationships. Typically before a data item is updated in the database some other data items are read or written. And after the update other data items may also be written. These data items read or written in the course of updating one data item construct the read set, pre-write set, and the post-write set for this data item. The proposed method identifies malicious transactions by comparing these sets with data items read or written in user transactions. We have provided mechanisms for finding data dependency relationships among transactions and use Petri-Nets to model normal data update patterns at user task level. Using this method we ascertain more hidden anomalies in the database log.

1. Introduction

A secure information system has three important features: prevention, detection, and recovery [1]. Intrusion Detection is employed to detect the malicious activities in case the system prevention mechanism fails. Almost all current host-based anomaly detection approaches are based on the data generated by auditing mechanism of the operating system or application. But these data don't sufficiently reflect what special data items in the system are modified, e.g. what particular attributes in the database

are read or written, and whether it's legal to modify these data items at that time.

Our database intrusion detection system tries to find malicious database transactions submitted to the DBMS by an intruder masqueraded as a normal user. The malicious transactions identified in this work can be used later by damage evaluation and recovery procedures [15] [16]. In our approach, we concentrate on analyzing the *dependencies* among the data items in the database. By data dependency we refer to the data access correlations between two or more data items. That is, which data items must be read or written before a data item gets updated and which others are written after the update. By checking whether each update operation in the user transaction conforms to the data dependencies generalized, anomalous activities at the transaction level are detected. We also propose the method for finding anomalies at the user task level by using Petri-Nets to model normal data update sequences in user tasks. This method is especially useful for finding hidden malicious activities that consists of several transactions, each of which appears as a normal transaction.

The following section describes past efforts related to our research. Section 3 outlines the model. Static semantic analyzer is discussed in section 4. The notion of Data dependency at user task level is described in section 5 and an implementation approach using Petri-Nets is presented in section 6. Section 7 offers conclusions of this paper.

2. Related Work

Currently most research on intrusion detection concentrates on anomaly detection in computer systems. The method used by IDES [2] [11] tries to construct user profiles statistically based on different categories of system parameters. By comparing current user activities with the profiles created from history data, anomaly

---
[*] This work has been supported in part by US AFOSR under grant F49620-01-10346

activities could be found. Other techniques offered in [3] [7] attempt to profile normal program behavior. They try to find the normal system call sequences and save these sequences as normal program access patterns in the database. The method used in [4] creates normal user command sequence. It's based on the observation that users generally make use of fixed set of UNIX commands, and different users have different ways of using these commands. Artificial intelligence [8] and Data mining [9] [10] applications in intrusion detection are employed by some researchers to make the IDS more intelligent.

Very limited research has been conducted in the field of database intrusion detection. Lee et al. [5] have used time signatures in discovering database intrusions. Another method presented by Chung et al. [6] identifies data items frequently referenced together and saves this information for later comparison. If the system observes substantial incidents of data items that are referenced together, but not in normal patterns as established before, an anomaly is signaled.

3. The Model

The proposed model is designed to identify malicious transactions submitted to the DBMS by an intruder masquerading as a normal user. Here the normal user activity means a user accessing the data items through a DBMS by using database application program instead of by submitting transactions to the DBMS manually and these activities do not include system maintenance and administration activities.

3.1. Database Model

This work is based on the relational database model [14]. A transaction is a logical unit of database processing that includes one or more database access operations. Our model only considers transactions that do not contain conditional statements, i.e., *if...then...else* statements, to simplify the process of data dependency analysis. However if a transaction has conditional statements, such a transaction can be divided into multiple sub-transactions each of which only contains one sequential execution path and can be used for data dependency analysis. Our model requires that the database log not only records the database access operations in each transaction, but also keeps the identification information of the user submitting the transaction to the DBMS. We also require that timestamps associated with each transaction indicating the transaction start and end times are also kept in the database log.

The database log records not only the write operations but also the read operations of each transaction. In the case some log information hasn't been stored on the permanent storage devices before a transaction commits, our database intrusion detection system can still access the contents of the log for uncommitted transactions from the temporary log.

The user task in this research refers to a group of transactions that are always submitted to the DBMS together to achieve a certain goal. For example, in order to perform the account transfer in a banking application, several transactions may be submitted to the database consecutively to fulfill the task.

3.2. Assumptions

We assume that the intruder has no access to the database application program that a normal user has. So an intruder cannot submit malicious transactions to the DBMS through the database application program at the normal user site. This is the case when an intruder accesses the database from a remote site. It's possible, for example, when the intruder has obtained the password of a legitimate database user account, (s)he can submit transactions manually or through a different application.

The total number of transactions a normal user can use is limited. They are the transactions in a database application program. So in this case our database intrusion detection system will raise alarm when the database administrator does some legal modification to the database system that doesn't conform to the data dependencies observed. In this case database administrator is responsible for identifying whether the cause of the alarm is due to a normal database maintenance work or due to the intruder masquerading as the database administrator performing malicious activities.

4. Static Semantic Analyzer

The static semantic analyzers perform the analysis of the data dependencies among data items in the database. The following definitions help in understanding the concept.

4.1. Definition of Data Dependency

Read set, pre-write set, and post-write set define data dependencies among data items.

Definition 1: The *Read Set* for one data item is a set of different data item sets, each of which consists of zero or more ordered data items. Additionally, the transaction must read all data items in one data item set of the read set *before* the transaction updates this data item. The notation $rs(x)$ is used to denote the read set for data item x. The read set is used to calculate the new value of this data item for updating purposes. For example, consider the following update statement.

Update Table1 set x = a + b + c where ...

In this statement, before updating *x*, the value of *a*, *b*, and *c* must be read and added together to get the new value of *x*. So $\{a, b, c\} \in rs(x)$.

Since when constructing the read set for *x* we only consider the data items read and used for the purpose of calculating the new value of *x*, we don't need to consider the data items read in the *where* statements. That's why the part in the *where* statement is ignored.

Definition 2: The *Pre-Write Set* for one data item is the set of different data item sets, each of which consists of zero or more ordered data items. Furthermore, the transaction must write all data items in the specified order in one data item set of the pre-write set *before* the transaction updates this data item. The notation $ws0(x)$ is used to denote the pre-write set of data item *x*. The reason we define pre-write set is that sometimes a data item is updated in the database after other data items are updated. For example, we have three update statements in one transaction in the following sequence. Note that one SQL statement doesn't necessarily immediately follow the other; there can be other non-updating SQL statements between them.

Update Table1 set x = a + b + c where ...
Update Table1 set y = x + u where ...
Update Table1 set z = x + w + v where ...

It must be noted that when *x* is updated, *y* and *z* are updated subsequently. Because of the hard-coded sequence, the transaction always updates *y* before updating *z*. So considering data item *z*, we observe that $\{x, y\}$ belongs to its pre-write set, that is $\{x, y\} \in ws0(z)$.

Definition 3: The *Post-Write Set* for one data item is the set of different data item sets, each of which consists of zero or more ordered data items. Moreover, the transaction must write all data items in the specified order in one data item set of the post-write set *after* the transaction updates this data item. Using the above example, it can be noted that $\{y, z\}$ belongs to the post-write set of data item *x*, that is $\{y, z\} \in ws1(x)$, where *ws1* denote the post-write set.

4.2. Functionality of Static Semantic Analyzer

The static semantic analyzer is used to analyze the database application program statically to decide the read set, the pre-write set, and the post-write set. Here the word static is used to describe that our method is based on the transaction program, not based on the database log. First we want to find out all the possible transactions one user may use. These transactions can be identified by checking the database application program. Then the static semantic analyzer is used to check all statements that update data items in each transaction to find out the read, pre-write,

and post-write sets for each data item that is updated in the transaction. Other statements that are not for updating purpose are not checked.

The examples below show how to construct the read, pre-write, and post-write sets. Consider the following three SQL statements in the given sequence appearing in a transaction, say T_1.

Update Table1 set x = a + b + c where ...
Update Table1 set y = x + u where ...
Update Table1 set z = x + w + v where ...

In this example, *x*, *y*, *z* etc. are used to represent attributes in a table instead of explicitly listing the attribute names. The result of static semantic analysis is as shown in table 1.

Table 1. Result of static semantic analysis after T_1 is analyzed

	Read Set	Pre-Write Set	Post-Write Set
x	$\{\{a, b, c\}\}$	$\{\varnothing\}$	$\{\{y, z\}\}$
y	$\{\{x, u\}\}$	$\{\{x\}\}$	$\{\varnothing\}$
z	$\{\{x, w, v\}\}$	$\{\{x, y\}\}$	$\{\varnothing\}$

Suppose in another transaction, say T_2, the following statements are used to update *x* and *w* as follows:

Update Table1 set x = a + d where...
Update Table1 set w = x + c where ...

Then the static semantic analyzer updates Table 1 as follows.

Table 2. Result of static semantic analysis after T_2 is analyzed

	Read Set	Pre-write Set	Post-write Set
x	$\{\{a, b, c\}, \{a, d\}\}$	$\{\varnothing\}$	$\{\{y, z\}, \{w\}\}$
y	$\{\{x, u\}\}$	$\{\{x\}\}$	$\{\varnothing\}$
z	$\{\{x, w, v\}\}$	$\{\{x, y\}\}$	$\{\varnothing\}$
w	$\{\{x, c\}\}$	$\{\{x\}\}$	$\{\varnothing\}$

The table constructed by the static semantic analyzer is used to check the transactions in the database log to find out whether they conform to the data dependency represented by the read, pre-write, and post-write sets. Before a transaction updates a data item, all data items in at least one data item set of its read set must be read and all data items in at least one data item set of its pre-write set must be written by the same transaction. Then after a transaction updates a data item, all data items in at least one data item set of its post-write set also must be written by the same transaction. Please note that we also consider the sequence of the elements in the read, pre-write and post-write sets. By considering this kind of sequence imposed by the transaction program, it will be easier to detect intrusions in a stricter sense.

Now let's go through an example to illustrate the use of Table 2. Consider the following transaction T_i, and each data item updated in this transaction has the corresponding read, pre-write, and post-write sets as shown in Table 2.

T_i: $r[y]$, $r[a]$, $r[q]$, $r[b]$, $r[c]$, **$w[x]$**, $r[x]$, $r[w]$, $r[v]$, **$w[z]$**, $r[x]$, $r[u]$, **$w[y]$**, $r[c]$, $r[d]$, $r[e]$.

First the transaction is scanned to see which data items were updated, then the read set, pre-write, and post-write sets are checked. For data item x, the read set consists of two data item sets $\{a, b, c\}$ and $\{a, d\}$. By checking the transaction T_i it is found that before the operation $w[x]$ this transaction read data items $\{a, b, c\}$ but not $\{a, d\}$. As long as all data items in at least one data item set of the read set are read before updating one data item, the read set of this data item is satisfied. So in this case, the read set of x is satisfied. Then the pre-write set for x is checked. Since the pre-write set of x is $\{\varnothing\}$, there is no need to check whether any particular data item is updated before $w[x]$. Hence the pre-write set of x is also satisfied. However, the post-write set of x is not checked at this time, because to do that one must scan the log to the end of the transaction and it may take a long time if the transaction is large. Moreover, in order to do that one must wait until the transaction is committed; in that case, it is not possible to stop a malicious transaction before it's committed. So z, the next data item updated, is checked. The read set consists of one data item set $\{x, w, v\}$. Before the write operation $w[z]$ this transaction read data items $\{x, w, v\}$, therefore, the read set of z is satisfied. The pre-write set of z consists of one data item set $\{x, y\}$. It is found that before the operation $w[z]$, x is updated but y is not. So the pre-write set of z is not satisfied. After the transaction executes $w[z]$, our database IDS could detect an anomaly in this transaction and notify the site security officer. Thus, the malicious transaction can be stopped by rolling back the transaction; hence, no data are damaged.

It must be noted that our proposed method cannot detect the malicious transactions that are compliant to the data dependencies observed in normal user transactions. In the case that a malicious transaction updates a data item, which is independent of other data items, the data dependency model will not be able to detect the update.

5. Data Dependency at User Task Level

As we illustrated above, by checking the read, pre-write, and post-write sets for data items updated in one particular transaction, many anomalous activities performed by the transaction can be detected. But it's hard to find the anomalous activity carried out by a group of transactions, each of which individually satisfies the read, pre-write, and post-write sets for the data items updated in the course of the activities. We propose a method below to identify the anomaly based on data dependencies

observed among transactions. The idea is that when a user executes some part of the database application to fulfill the user task, generally not one but several transactions are submitted to the DBMS. For instance, when a customer transfers money from one account to another account, several transactions may have been involved. One transaction may be used for decreasing the balance of one account by some amount and increasing the balance of another account by the same amount. Another transaction may be utilized to update some internal accounts for the use of the bank, e.g., some accounts used for statistical or audit purpose. By using a training procedure, we try to find out what data items are updated and also determine their update sequence in a user task.

5.1. Methodology

Our method for deducing data dependency at user task level is as follows. In the training phase, a user task is executed extensively to make sure almost all different cases for this user task are performed. We collect data items updated in each training cases. Since these executions must also satisfy the read, pre-write, and post-write sets of data items updated, we check which data item set in the read, pre-write, and post-write sets is actually used in the training phase. Then we use the actual post-write set and read set for creating the data dependency among transactions. Based on the definition of post-write set, it's natural to use post-write set to construct the normal data update sequence. The reason we use the read set besides using the post-write set is as follows. Suppose data item x is updated and data item x, y, z should be updated consequently. And after data item y is updated, data item u and v also should be updated. The situation is x, y, z, u, and v are not necessarily updated in the same transaction. It's possible that x, y, and z are updated in one transaction, and then u and v are updated in another transaction. Even it is possible that x, y, and z are not updated in the same transaction. For example, the following transactions T_1 and T_2 are executed consecutively in a user task:

T_1: *update Table1 set $x = 120\% \, x$ where ...*
update Table2 set $y = x + a$ where ...
update Table3 set $z = x + b$ where...
T_2: *update Table4 set $u = y + c$ where...*
update Table5 set $v = y + d$ where...

The read, pre-write, and post-write sets constructed based on these two transactions are in Table 3. From Table 3, it can be seen that the post-write set for data item y is $\{\varnothing\}$; that means after updating y no other data items need to be updated by the same transaction. And since the pre-write set for u and v is $\{\varnothing\}$, before the transaction updates u and v, nothing needs to be written by the same transaction. However, since T_1 and T_2 always execute consecutively, after y is updated, u and v must be updated based on the new value of y. So at the higher level of the user task instead of the transaction, we can find some new data dependencies.

Table 3. Read, pre-write, and post-write sets of T_1

	Read set	Pre-write Set	Post-write Set
x	{{x}}	{∅}	{{y, z}}
y	{{x, a}}	{{x}}	{∅}
z	{{x, b}}	{{x, y}}	{∅}
u	{{y, c}}	{∅}	{∅}
v	{{y, d}}	{∅}	{∅}

5.2. Write-chain

To help understand the concept of write-chain, the notions of *active* and *passive* data items are defined first.

Definition 4: An *active* data item is the data item that when updated causes other data item(s) to be updated.

Definition 5: A *passive* data item is the data item that is updated as a result of other data item(s) being updated.

Based on above discussion, we define a term *write-chain* to capture this kind of data dependencies at the user task level. *Write-chain* is a sequence of data items that are always updated together and have complete order among these data items. The first data item of the write-chain is the active data item; other data items are passive data items. It's clear that some write-chains can be created directly from the post-write set of data items. For example, from table 3 we can have write-chain $wc1: x \rightarrow y \rightarrow z$ based on the post-write set of x. Other write-chains are deduced from the data dependencies among y, u, and v that are hidden in several transactions.

The method for constructing write-chains deduced from several transactions is as follows. Suppose there's a write operation $w[y]$ in one user task which includes several transactions. Check the $rs(y)$ to see if there is any data item x_i, $x_i \in$ any data item set in $rs(y)$, updated before $w[y]$ in this user task. And if there's anyone, create a write-chain $wc: x_i \rightarrow y$. Still using the above example, from T_2 we get $\{y, c\} \in rs(u)$. Moreover, y is updated in T_1 before write operation $w[u]$ in T_2. So the write-chain $y \rightarrow u$ can be deduced. Similarly, another write-chain $y \rightarrow v$ can also be obtained from the above example.

By considering the data update sequence in the transactions, we can combine several write-chains into one. For example, in transaction T_2, u is updated before v and both of them are updated because y is updated. So we can produce a combined write-chain $y \rightarrow u \rightarrow v$.

6. Petri-Net Implementation of the Data Dependency Model

Petri-Net is a modeling tool to specify systems that are concurrent, distributed, parallel, non-deterministic,

and asynchronous. A Petri-Net is a bipartite directed graph, which consists of two kinds of nodes, namely places and transitions. Places are represented by circles and transitions are represented by bars. The edges are between transitions and places, and they indicate the input or output to the transitions. Each place can hold tokens and only when the input places for a transition has required tokens, the transition can fire. Due to space constraint we do not provide detailed information about Petri-Nets other than what is needed for our implementation. Interested readers may refer to [13].

6.1. Petri-Net Implementation of User Task Level Data Dependency

In this work, we use Petri-Nets to profile data relationships. Some researchers have also used Petri-Nets for multi-source attacks detection [12]. However, our model is different from theirs as can be observed below. After constructing write-chains for one user task from the read set and post-write set, it may be observed that there are some common data elements among these write-chains. It will be useful to connect these write-chains to a graph-like structure to reflect the data dependency among transactions. Suppose we have the following 5 write-chains.

$wc1: x1 \rightarrow x2 \rightarrow x3 \rightarrow x4$
$wc2: x2 \rightarrow x5 \rightarrow x6$
$wc3: x5 \rightarrow x7$
$wc4: x3 \rightarrow x8$
$wc5: x6 \rightarrow x9 \rightarrow x10$

It is assumed that a data item is updated only once in a user task. This assumption will make it easier to find data dependencies among transactions. Although theoretically a user task may update a data item more than once, this case is rare in practice.

In Figure 1, each place represents the write operation on one data item. We use the name of the data item to represent each node. The transition represents the end of the input operations and beginning of output operations. We add an additional place, the name of which is "end" to identify the normal write sequence. Additionally, we use two colors for tokens, red and blue.

The tokens with different colors are used to guarantee that a transition occurs only when the write sequence in the database log is in the required sequence. This was different from the general transition rule of Petri-Nets. When a write operation is found in the database log, a blue token is added to the place identified by the name of the data item. When a transition fires, a red token is put to each output place of the transition. Suppose a place x_i is an output place of a transition t_j. If a place x_i holds a blue token, then a transition t_j fires which adds a red token to x_i, that causes misfire. The newly added red token is removed from x_i and the blue token(s) from the input place(s) of t_j are also removed. Whenever this happens, we can infer that a write operation corresponding to the place x_i is executed before the execution of write operation(s) that caused the transition t_j to fire. This indicates that this write sequence doesn't conform to normal update sequence.

Petri-Net is utilized to model the partial order in which data items are updated in a user task. Using the above example, if $x1$ is updated, all other data items must be updated in this user task. Furthermore, all these data items should be updated according to the partial order in this Petri-Net. Petri-Net profiles the normal data update sequence for a user task and can be used for detecting anomalous transactions in the database system.

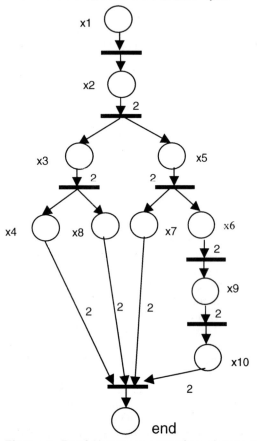

Figure 1: Petri-Net representation of data dependency

6.2. Modeling Time Pattern of Transaction Execution over the Petri-Net

A reasonable range in the database log needs to be decided to check the Petri-Net model. If we can find a method to group transactions in the database log that are used collectively to perform one user task, then that user task can be tested using the Petri-Net. The time pattern of transaction executions can be used for this purpose.

In order to facilitate our discussion, we define the term *gap*, which is used to describe the time difference between the two consecutive user tasks or two consecutive transactions submitted by the same user in the database log. The gap refers to time difference between the end of one task (transaction) and the beginning of another task (transaction). In the following discussion, the *gap between two user tasks* refers to the gap between two consecutive tasks submitted by the same user. Similarly, the *gap between two transactions* refers to the gap between two consecutive transactions submitted by the same user.

Generally the gap between two user tasks is much bigger than the gap between two transactions. For example, when an accountant in the bank serves customers, there's always a time interval from several seconds to several minutes between serving two different customers. This time interval is the gap between two user tasks. In the case the machine load is not very heavy, we can always assume this interval is bigger than the interval between executions of two transactions in a user task. By checking the distribution of the length of the gap between two transactions, grouping transactions in the database log into user tasks becomes simple. The timestamps indicating the end of one transaction and beginning of another can be used to calculate the length of the gap between the two transactions.

In Figure 2, we illustrate the gap between two transactions of the same task and the gap between two tasks. A threshold is used to decide the gap between two tasks. Whenever any two transactions' gap is larger than the threshold, we consider the end of the first transaction as the end of a user task. That means the next transaction after the gap does not belong to the same user task.

Gap between two tasks

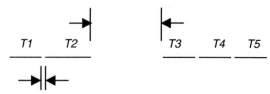

Gap between two transactions

Figure 2. Transaction and task gaps

By using the method described above, the gap between two user tasks can be determined. All transactions between two of these consecutive gaps can be grouped together and considered in the same user task. Although the purpose of the user task is unknown, the Petri-Net modeled normal updated sequence can be applied to this user task to check whether there are anomalies in the task.

To do so, the data items that are updated in the transactions of the user task are checked. The transactions of the user task are scanned and whenever a write operation is found, all Petri-Nets are checked to see if any of them has a place corresponding to the name of the data item updated. If there is one, a blue token is put into that place. It is possible that several Petri-Nets may have a place corresponding to the name of the data item updated. In that case a blue token is added to each of those places of those Petri-Nets. After the last write operation in the user task is checked the Petri-Nets are assessed to see if any of them have all the transitions fired and there's a red token in the "end" place. If there's at least one Petri-Net having a red token in the "end" place, this user task is considered to be a normal user task. Otherwise, the user task is considered anomalous indicating these transactions as malicious.

7. Conclusion

In this paper we have offered a database intrusion detection model that uses data dependency relationships observed in transactions or user tasks . Dependencies are determined by using the read, pre-write, and post-write sets of data items which are generated by the static semantic analyzer. User applications program can be analyzed to construct these sets. By finding the data dependencies hidden among transactions, we identify anomalies at the user task level. A Petri-Net based implementation concept has been offered to check these data correlations at user task level as opposed to the transaction level. Moreover, time pattern of transaction executions is used to identify the range of database log for verifying normal data update sequence in order to reduce false negatives.

Acknowledgment

We are thankful to Dr. Robert L. Herklotz for his support, which made this work possible.

References

[1] B. Panda and J. Giordano. Defensive Information Warfare. In *Communications of the ACM*, Vol. 42, No. 7, pages 31-32, July 1999.

[2] H. S. Javitz and A. Valdes. The SRI IDES Statistical Anomaly Detector. In *Proceedings of the IEEE Symposium on Security and Privacy*, May 1991.

[3] S. Forrest, S. A. Hofmeyr, A. Somayaji, and T. A. Longstaff. A Sense of Self for Unix Processes. In *Proceedings of the 1996 IEEE Symposium on Security and Privacy*, pages 120–128, IEEE Computer Society Press, 1996.

[4] T. Lane and C. E. Brodley. Sequence Matching and Learing in Anomaly Detection for Compute Security. In *Proceedings of the AAAI-97 Workshop on AI Approaches to Fraud Detection and Risk Management*, pages 43-49, 1997.

[5] V. C.S. Lee, J. A. Stankovic, S. H. Son. Intrusion Detection in Real-time Database Systems Via Time Signatures, In *Proceedings of the Sixth IEEE Real Time Technology and Applications Symposium*, 2000.

[6] C. Chung, M. Gertz, K. Levitt. DEMIDS: A Misuse Detection System for Database Systems. In *Third Annual IFIP TC-11 WG 11.5 Working Conference on Integrity and Internal Control in Information Systems*, Kluwer Academic Publishers, pages 159-178, November 1999.

[7] A.K. Ghosh, A. Schwartzbard and M. Schatz. Learning Program Behavior Profiles for Intrusion Detection. In *1st USENIX Workshop on Intrusion Detection and Network Monitoring*, 1999.

[8] J. Frank. Artificial Intelligence and Intrusion Detection: Current and Future Directions. In *Proceedings of the 17th National Computer Security Conference*, October 1994.

[9] W. Lee and S. Stolfo. Data Mining Approaches for Intrusion Detection. In *USENIX Security Symposium*, 1998.

[10] W. Lee, R.A. Nimbalkar, K.K. Yee, S.B. Patil, P.H. Desai, Tran T.T., and S.J. Stolfo. A Data Mining and CIDF Based Approach for Detecting Novel and Distributed Intrusions. In *Proceedings of 3rd International Workshop on the Recent Advances in Intrusion Detection*, October 2000.

[11] T. F. Lunt et al. *IDES: A Progress Report.* In Proceeding of 6th Annual Computer Security Applications Conference, December 1990.

[12] B. Panda, R. Yalamanchili. A Host Based Multi-Source Information Attack Detection Model Design and Implementation. In *Information: An International Journal*, Vol. 4, No. 4, October 2001.

[13] T. Murata. Petri-Nets: Properties, Analysis and Applications. In *Proceedings of the IEEE*, Vol. 77, No. 4, p. 541-580, April 1989.

[14] E. Codd. A Relational Model for Large Shared Data Banks. In *Communications of ACM*, June 1970.

[15] P. Liu, P.Ammann, and S. Jajodia. Rewriting Histories: Recovering from Malicious   Transactions. In *Distributed and Parallel Databases*, Vol. 18, No. 1, p. 7-40, January 2000.

[16] R. Sobhan and B. Panda. Reorganization of Database Log for Information Warfare Data Recovery. In *Proceedings of the 15th Annual IFIP WG 11.3 Working Conference on Database and Application Security*, July 2001.

Database Damage Assessment Using A Matrix Based Approach: An Intrusion Response System[!]

Brajendra Panda and Jing Zhou
Compuer Science and Computer Engineering Department
University of Arkansas, Fayetteville, AR 72701, USA
Email: {bpanda, jzhou}@uark.edu

Abstract

When an attacker or a malicious user updates a database, the resulting damage can spread to other parts of the database through valid users. A fast and accurate damage assessment must be performed as soon as such an attack is detected. In this paper, we have discussed two approaches for damage assessment in an affected dataabbase. While the first one uses transaction dependency relationships to determine affected transactions, the second approach considers data dependency relationships to identify affected data items for future recovery. These relationships are stored in a matrix format for faster manipulation.

1. Introduction

Database management systems have the ability of recovering from system, media, transaction and communication failures. But when a data item is modified by an attacker such that the modified value satisfies database constraints, the DBMS itself cannot identify the malicious activities and respond accordingly. An intrusion detection system can be employed to find the suspicious activities in the database system and spot any malicious transactions. Once a malicious transaction is identified, damage assessment and recovery can be carried out to restore the database to a safe state.

In this research, we focus on fast and precise damage assessment after the identification of a malicious committed transaction. We have presented two damage assessment models targeted at two different database recovery schemes. The first one uses dependency relationships among transactions to identify all affected transactions and then uses their updates to determine all affected data items. The second method considers the updates made by the attacker and all subsequent updates by valid transactions that either directly or indirectly use values of damaged data items to calculate values of other data items, thus, damaging them.

The rest of the paper is organized as follows. The next section presents necessary background and motivations for this work. Section 3 and 4 are the core of this paper and discuss our models based on transaction dependency and data dependency approaches respectively. Section 5 concludes the paper.

2. Background and Motivations

Defending data from illegal access is extremely important for any critical information system [5]. Since there are always loopholes in the prevention mechanisms of the system, the intrusion detection system is critical for discovering the misuse of the database system. Nowadays many signature based misuse detections and non-signature based anomaly detections [2, 3, 4] have been used to detect intrusion. Unfortunately, most of the detections are at the operating system level, detections at the DBMS level are limited and cannot guarantee the prompt detection of malicious database modification [1]. Once the attacking transaction commits, the database system will make the transaction's effect permanent and those data items will be available to other valid transactions. Thus, the damage will spread quickly through the database by legitimate users as they update other data items after reading any damaged data. So it is extremely important to perform fast damage assessment and recovery to stop the spreading and make the database system available as soon as possible. Ammann and Jajodia *et al.* presented an approach based on marking damage to maintain database consistency [1]. Liu *et al.* [6] reordered transactions for efficient recovery. But in all these approaches, log was accessed and significant I/Os were involved. Panda and Lala [9] eliminated the damage assessment time by saving the dependency relationship to avoid frequent log access. However, the shortcoming with that model was that data

[!] This work has been supported in part by US AFOSR under grant F49620-01-10346

items were not made available before the whole recovery work was completed.

The main goal of this research work is to provide a fast and accurate damage assessment model, which limits the amount of damage by hiding the affected data items from other transactions until recovery is complete, and at the same time, reduces denial-of-service by not withholding intact data items. Our model, unlike previous models, does not access the log during the damage assessment process. Rather it uses two pre-developed bit-matrices to identify transaction or data dependency relationships. It then processes the matrices using simple logic (AND and OR) operations to calculate the damage. This dramatically decreases the I/O overhead and accelerates the damage assessment procedure. Following damage assessment, the unaffected data items can be made available to legitimate users immediately and the recovery work can be carried out right away based on the damaged transaction/data list.

3. Transaction Dependency Based Model

Our model is based on the assumptions listed below: The malicious transaction has been identified; The scheduler produces a rigorous history; The database log can not be changed by users; Dependency relationships among transactions will not change during recovery.

Our proposed method is used to perform fast database damage assessment and recovery. In the damage assessment procedure, the affected transactions are identified and recorded. This will be used to facilitate the transaction dependency based recovery. In this transaction dependency based method, two data structures, called *Read_Matrix* and *Write_Matrix*, are generated from the database log. *Damaged_Data_Vector* keeps information on data items that have been damaged. *Damaged_Transaction_List* stores the transaction IDs of damaged transactions. All these additional data structures are utilized to facilitate damage assessment.

3.1. Data Structures

First we define some of the terms that are essential for this model. Definition 1 is taken from [8] and definition 2 is taken from [9].

Definition 1: A write operation $w_i[x]$ of a transaction T_i is dependent on a read operation $r_i[y]$ of T_i if $w_i[x]$ is computed using the value obtained from $r_i[y]$.

Definition 2: A write operation $w_i[x]$ of a transaction T_i is dependent on a set of data items I if $x = f(I)$ i.e., the values of data items in I are used in calculating the new value of x. There are the following three cases for the set of data items I. (*previous value of x* is the value before current operation)

Case1: $I = \varnothing$. This means that no data item is used in calculating the new value of x. We denote such an operation as a *fresh write*. If $w_j[x]$ is a fresh write and if the previous value of x is damaged, the value of x will be refreshed after this write operation.

Case2: $x \notin I$. Then $w_j[x]$ is called a *blind write*. If $w_j[x]$ is a blind write and if the previous value of x is damaged and none of the data items in I are damaged, then the value of x will be refreshed after this write operation.

Case3: $x \in I$. If the previous value of x is damaged, then x remains damaged. Otherwise, if any other item in I is damaged, x is damaged.

Definition 3: A transaction T_i is dependent on another transaction T_j if any of the data item(s) in T_i has been updated based on a data item that has been modified by T_j.

Definition 4: A *legitimate write* operation $w_i[x]$ of T_i is either a *fresh write* or a write operation that does not use any damaged data in its calculation.

Definition 5: The *legitimate write* that has refreshed the damaged data is called a *valid write.*

Read_Matrix: This matrix is created to store information on data items that all updating type committed transactions have read. The first column records transaction IDs and the other columns represent all data items in the database. Each row represents a transaction. The corresponding columns that represent the data items that have been read by the transaction are set to 1s, other columns that have not been read are set to 0s. If all the updates made by a transaction are *fresh writes*, then a 0-vector is stored in the corresponding row.

Write_Matrix: This matrix stores information on all the data items that updating type committed transactions have written. Like the read_matrix, the first column records the transaction IDs, while remaining columns represent all data items in the database, and each row represents a transaction. In a vector of a transaction, the bits corresponding to the data items written by the transaction are set to 1s, and the rest of the bits are set to 0s.

Damaged_Data_Vector: This vector, which is a zero-vector initially, represents all data items that have been marked as damaged during the damage assessment procedure. In this vector, if the value at the position of data item d_i is 1 then d_i has been identified as damaged; otherwise, d_i has a consistent value.

Damaged_Transaction_List: This list shows all transactions that have been marked as damaged.

3.2. Damage Assessment Procedure

The *Read_Matrix* and *Write_Matrix* are constructed by scanning the database log and extracting information on the committed transactions. The order of the transactions in the matrices must remain the same as the order of commit sequence of the transactions in the log. Upon identification of a malicious transaction, the damage assessment procedure begins. Our damage assessment method is based exclusively on *Read_Matrix* and *Write_Matrix* instead of database log. We will explain the damage assessment procedure using following example.

Example 1:

$H = r_1[B]\ r_1[D]\ r_1[E]\ r_3[E]\ w_1[C]\ r_1[D]\ w_1[D]\ c_1\ r_2[C]\ r_2[D]\ r_2[E]\ w_2[B]\ w_2[A]\ c_2\ w_3[A]\ w_3[B]\ c_3\ r_4[A]\ w_4[D]\ r_4[C]\ w_4[E]\ c_4.$

The transaction dependency relationship for *H* can be established based on the definition of transaction dependency (see *Definition 3*). A directed acyclic graph is used to represent the dependency as in Figure 1. (We assume that a data item will not be updated twice in one transaction.) A directed edge indicates the transaction that the arrow points to is dependent on the transaction where the edge starts. For example, transaction T_2 is dependent on transaction T_1, T_4 is dependent on both T_1 and T_3.

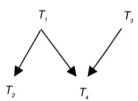

Figure 1. Transaction dependency graph

Construct *Read_Matrix* and *Write_Matrix* for *H* based on the commit sequence of the transactions. Mark the data items that a transaction have read or written as 1, the matrices for *H* are depicted in Table 1 and Table 2.

Table 1. Read_Matrix

ID	A	B	C	D	E
T_1	0	1	0	1	1
T_2	0	0	1	1	1
T_3	0	0	0	0	1
T_4	1	0	1	0	0

Table 2. Write_Matrix

ID	A	B	C	D	E
T_1	0	0	1	1	0
T_2	1	1	0	0	0
T_3	1	1	0	0	0
T_4	0	0	0	1	1

Following is the damage assessment procedure:
1) Identify the corresponding row in the *Write_Matrix* that represents the data items written by the malicious transaction. For example, suppose transaction T_1 is the malicious transaction. Add transaction T_1 to the *Damaged_Transaction_List*. Then locate the position of transaction T_1 in the matrix (say *m*).

2) Do the logical *OR* operation (*Damaged_Data_Vector OR Write_Matrix* [*m*]). Positions of 1-bits in the *Write_Matrix* indicate that the corresponding data items have been damaged. Initially the *Damaged_Data_Vector* is set to 0s, that is, nothing is identified as damaged. For the previous example, after the OR operation, the *Damaged_Data_Vector* becomes: 0 0 1 1 0 . This indicates that data items *C*, *D* are damaged.

3) To find out the transactions that have read the damaged data items, first increase *m* by 1. Then carry out the logical AND operation (*Read_Matrix* [*m*] AND *Damaged_Data_Vector*). If the resulting vector is not zero, then the corresponding transaction has read one or more damaged data and, thus, has been affected. Add the transaction to the *Damaged_Transaction_List*. Moreover, perform the operation (*Write_Matrix* [*m*] OR *Damaged_Data_Vector*) and store the result as the new *Damaged_Data_Vector*. Here we assume that once a transaction reads a damaged data, all data items written in this transaction are damaged. Since T_2 has read {*C, D, E*} and {*C, D*} ∈ *Damaged_Data_Vector*, the data items written by T_2, i.e. *A* and *B*, are damaged, too. The new *Damaged_Data_Vector* becomes: 1 1 1 1 0 .

If a transaction *valid_writes* any data item, those data items are removed from the *Damaged_Data_Vector*. For example, since T_3 has read {*E*} and *E* is not damaged by the malicious transaction, so what T_3 has written, {*A, B*} in this case, will be refreshed if they have been damaged before. The corresponding value for these data items in the *Damaged_Data_Vector* will become 0s.

4) Repeat step 3 until all the transactions in the *Read_Matrix* and *Write_Matrix* are processed. For the above example, it can be observed that transactions T_2, T_4 are all damaged, which is consistent with the transaction dependency relationship depicted in Figure 1. *Damaged_Data_Vector* shows that the damaged data items include {*C, D, E*}.

After damage assessment work is completed, the damaged transactions are located and damage data items are marked, undamaged data items can be available to the legitimate user right away. Consequently recovery work can be performed. We will not discuss the recovery algorithm in detail. Researchers have developed several models such as in [10] to perform recovery work. Next, a formal algorithm for damage assessment is given.

Algorithm 1: (Damage Assessment)
1. Set *Damaged_Transaction_List* = {};
2. Initialize elements of *Damaged_Data_Vector* to 0;
3. Initialize a variable, (say *Scan_Position*) to the position of the malicious transaction (say T_i) in the *Write_Matrix*;
4. For every corresponding column, do the logical operation (*Damaged_Data_Vector* OR *Write_Matrix*[*Scan_Position*]), the result will be the new value of *Damaged_Data_Vector*;

5. Add T_i to the *Damaged_Transaction_List;*
6. For every following transaction in the *Read_Matrix*
   6.1. Increment the value of *Scan_Position* by 1.
   6.2. Get the Transaction ID from the *Read_Matrix(* say T_j)
   6.3. If the value of every data item is 0
       6.3.1. For every corresponding column, do the logical operation (*Damaged_Data_Vector* AND NOT(*Write_Matrix*[*Scan_Position*])), the result will be the new value of *Damaged_Data_Vector*;   /* valid write */
   6.4. else if {For every corresponding column, after the logical operation (*Damaged_Data_Vector* AND *Read_Matrix*[*Scan_Position*]), the results are all 0s,}
                    /* valid write */
       6.4.1. do the logical operation (*Damaged_Data_Vector* AND NOT(*Write_Matrix*[*Scan_Position*])), the result will be the new value of *Damaged_Data_Vector*;
   6.5. else   /*damaged transaction */
       6.5.1. do the logical operation (*Damaged_Data_Vector* OR *Write_Matrix*[*Scan_Position*]), the result will be the new value of *Damaged_Data_Vector*;
       6.5.2. add current transaction T_j into the *Damaged_Transaction_List;*

Comments: Step 3,4,5 deals with the malicious transaction. Step 6 scans the transactions after the malicious transaction, Step 6.3.1 and Step 6.4.1 consider the situation of valid write to refresh the *Damaged_Data_Vector*. Step 6.4.2 checks if a transaction is damaged, then add it to the *Damaged_Transaction_List* and marked what it has written as damaged, too.

3.3. Compact Structure

The above approach would reduce the damage assessment time since it avoids accessing the database log, consequently, decreasing the page I/Os significantly. On the other hand, if we use this method in a considerable large database, it will be very space consuming to store the matrices. We propose to solve this problem by modifying the above mentioned data structures to a more compact format.

Compact_Read_List: This list contains *n* sublists each of which shows all the data items the transaction has read (*n* is the total number of transactions). Every sublist will keep the transaction ID as the first element, followed by the position that has been marked as 1. If there are continuous 1s, we will record only the start and the end

position, e.g., The *Compact_Read_List* for *Example 1* is $((T_1, (1), (3, 4))(T_2, (3, 5))(T_3, (5))(T_4, (1), (3)))$.

Compact_Write_List: This list contains *n* sublists each of which shows all the data items the transaction has written (*n* is the total number of transactions). The construction for the sublist is the same as the *Compact_Read_List*. The *Compact_Write_List* for *Example 1* is $((T_1, (3, 4))(T_2, (1, 2))(T_3, (1, 2))(T_4, (4, 5)))$.

For every transaction, we will use a list to hold only the data items that are marked as 1. For instance, in *example 1*, T_1's corresponding row in the *Compact_Read_List* is: $(T_1, (1), (3, 4))$. If there are two items between a pair of round brackets in the sub-list that represents all data items between these two data items are marked as 1s. For example (3, 4) means that all values from position 3 to position 4 are 1s. If there is only one item, then it is the position that is marked 1. If all the data items are 0s, we will record only the transaction ID. This way, we can reduce the storage space especially when the matrix is sparse. Also, when there is continuous 1s in the matrix, we can save space. We will use another list *Data_Position* to store the relationship between a data item and its position. For *example 1*, the list will be (A, B, C, D, E). So after we get the final position of the damaged data items, we can use this list to translate it to the actual data items that are affected.

The damage assessment procedure can be easily processed using Algorithm 1. The only change is that we will first use a function to translate the compact structure to the matrix structure form, and then the damage assessment work can be done using algorithm 1.

4. Data Dependency Based Model

In the Transaction Dependency Based Model, the result of the damage assessment procedure is not very accurate since it assumes that once a transaction reads a damaged data item, all data items written by the transaction are considered damaged. Consider the following situation. Suppose a transaction T_i reads data item *p* and writes *q*, then it reads *r* and updates *s*. If *r* is damaged, then obviously, *s* becomes damaged, but, *q* remains unaffected if it was before T_i accessing it. Using the transaction dependency approach, T_i will be considered affected and therefore all data items updated by it will be identified as affected. Then if another transaction T_j reads *q*, T_j will also be considered affected. This leads to the problem of superfluous rollback of many transactions and later re-execution of them during recovery. Consequently, more data items will be blocked unnecessarily during the process resulting in actual denial-of-service setback.

The data dependency based model would identify exactly what data items are damaged in the database by considering the position of read and write operations in the transaction. Using the above example, in case of T_i, only data item s will be considered damaged and will be added to the *Damaged_Data_Vector*. This way, the damage assessment work will be more precise and will limit denial-of-service. The model is based on same assumptions listed in section 3.

4.1. Data Structures

In this section, modified data structures are used to record the data dependency relations between operations. Without transaction semantics it is impossible to extract exact data dependency relationships. Semantic log [7] can be used to achieve precise data dependency relationship. For simplicity we use the following notions in determining data dependencies from the normal log file. The write operation in a transaction is dependent on all read operations that are performed by the same transaction and appear between the last write operation and current write operation. The first write operation is dependent on all prior read operations that are performed by the same transaction. If there is no read operation between current write operation and previous write operation then the write operation is identified as a *fresh write*.

Data_Dependency_Read_Matrix(DDRM): This matrix stores the data items that all committed transactions have read. The first column will record the transaction ID, the next column records the operation number, and the remaining columns represent all data items in the database. Each row represents part of a transaction's read operations (data items) on which the subsequent write operation depends on. A 1 bit denotes that the transaction has read the corresponding data item; 0-bit denotes otherwise.

Data_Dependency_Write_Matrix(DDWM): The structure of this matrix is similar to the DDRM except that a 1-bit in a row in this structure indicates that the corresponding transaction has updated that data item. All write operations in such a vector are dependent on the data items represented by the corresponding vector in the DDRM.

4.2. Damage Assessment Procedure

The procedure to do damage assessment is similar to that in the *Transaction Dependency Based Model*, except that we will deal with the operations here instead of transactions. We will illustrate the damage assessment procedure based on the same log history H as in *Example 1*. Table 3 and Table 4 show the DDRM and DDWM for *Example 1* respectively.

DDWM and DDWM are constructed by scanning the log. A row with the transaction ID number and operation number will be added every time a write operation is encountered, in the DDRM, the data items that have been read are marked as 1, in the DDWM, the data item that has been written is marked as 1.

Table 3. DDRM

ID	OP	A	B	C	D	E
T_1	1	0	1	0	1	1
T_1	2	0	0	0	1	0
T_2	1	0	0	1	1	1
T_2	2	0	0	0	0	0
T_3	1	0	0	0	0	1
T_3	2	0	0	0	0	0
T_4	1	1	0	0	0	0
T_4	2	0	0	1	0	0

Table 4. DDWM

ID	OP	A	B	C	D	E
T_1	1	0	0	1	0	0
T_1	2	0	0	0	1	0
T_2	1	0	1	0	0	0
T_2	2	1	0	0	0	0
T_3	1	1	0	0	0	0
T_3	2	0	1	0	0	0
T_4	1	0	0	0	1	0
T_4	2	0	0	0	0	1

During damage assessment procedure, the first operation of the malicious transaction is located first. Suppose transaction T_1 is the malicious transaction. Add transaction T_1 to *Damaged_Transaction_List*. Then find the position of transaction T_1 operation *1* in the matrix (say m).

Similar to the procedure in the *Transaction Dependency Based Model*, do the logical OR operation (*Damaged_Data_Vector* OR *DDWM* [m]) and the *Damaged_Data_Vector* becomes: 0 0 1 0 0. This indicates that data items C is damaged, repeat until all the operations in the malicious transaction have been processed. The current position m will increase by one after each operation, suppose it is n after all the operations in the malicious transaction are done.

To find out the operations that have read the damaged data items, first increase n by one. Then carry out the logical AND operation (*DDRM* [n] AND *Damaged_Data_Vector*). If the resulting vector is not zero, then the corresponding operation has read one or more damaged data and, thus, has been affected. Add the transaction to the *Damaged_Transaction_List* if this is the first damaged operation in the transaction. Moreover, perform the operation (*DDWM* [n] OR *Damaged_Data_Vector*) and store the result as the new *Damaged_Data_Vector*. Since *operation 1* in T_2 has read

$\{C, D, E\}$ and $\{C, D\} \in$ *Damaged_Data_Vector*, the data items written by this operation, i.e. *B* is damaged, too. The new *Damaged_Data_Vector* becomes: 0 1 1 1 0 . For *operation 2* in T_2, it *blind writes A*, so that A is refreshed. Keep on doing this until all the operations in the *DDRM* and *DDWM* are processed. Finally we get the damaged data items $\{C, E\}$. Compare to the *Transaction Dependency Based Model,* data item *D* can be refreshed to the legitimate user earlier.

Based on the observation that only one of the data item will be marked as one for every row of the *DDWM*, the compact structure as we described in *Transaction Dependency Based Model* will be more efficient when applied here. Using operations in the transaction instead of transaction itself, the same algorithm as described in *Transaction Dependency Based Model* can be used after minor change. We will not present the algorithm due to limited space. Interested reader can contact the author for the detail.

5. Conclusion

Database systems play a vital role in almost any organization's information system. Since it is extremely difficult to obtain foolproof protections for these systems, intrusion detection and subsequent damage assessment and recovery methods become essential to build dependable systems. In this paper, we have focused on damage assessment of an affected database. Two damage assessment methods have been presented that use pre-developed data structures to identify all affected transactions without requiring any log accesses. Since these data structures are built using bit-vectors and are manipulated using logical AND and OR operations, the damage assessment process can become extremely fast. After affected transactions are identified, undamaged data items can be available to legitimate users while recovery phase continues. Although the transaction dependency based model would work faster than the data dependency based model since the former approach accesses less number of bit-vectors requiring less processing, the latter can aid in precise damage assessment. As a future work, using simulation we wish to compare performance of these two models. Furthermore, we wish to extend the model to consider the case when the dependencies might change during the re-execution of transactions.

Acknowledgment:

We are thankful to Dr. Robert L. Herklotz for his support, which made this work possible.

References

[1] P. Ammann, S. Jajodia and C.D. McCollum, B.T. Blaustein, Surviving Information Warfare Attacks on Databases. In proceedings of the 1997 IEEE Symposium on Security and Privacy.

[2] W. Lee, R.A. Nimbalkar, K.K. Yee, S.B. Patil, P.H. Desai, T.T. Tran and S.J. Stolfo. A Data Mining and CIDF Based Approach for Detecting Novel and Distributed Intrusions. In Proceedings of 3rd International Workshop on the Recent Advances in Intrusion Detection, October 2000.

[3] A.K. Ghosh, A. Schwartzbard and M. Schatz. Learning Program Behavior Profiles for Intrusion Detection. In 1st USENIX Workshop on Intrusion Detection and Network Monitoring, 1999.

[4] V.C.S. Lee, J.A. Stankovic, S.H. Son. Intrusion Detection in Real-time Database Systems Via Time Signatures, In Proceedings of the Sixth IEEE Real Time Technology and Applications Symposium, 2000.

[5] Defending America's cyberspace: National plan for information system protection, version 1.0. The White House, Washington, DC, 2000.

[6] P. Liu, P. Ammann and S. Jajodia. Rewriting histories: recovering from malicious transactions. Distributed and Parallel Database, vol. 8, no.1, pp.7 – 40, Jan. 2000.

[7] R. Sobhan and B. Panda. Sequential Damage Assessment and Recovery Using Semantic Logging. In Proceedings of the 2002 IEEE Workshop on Information Assurance United States Military Academy, West Point, NY June 2002

[8] S. Patnaik and B. Panda. Dependency Based Logging for Database Survivability from hostile transactions. In Proc. of 12th International Conference Computer Application and Industry Engineering, Atlanta, GA, Nov. 1999.

[9] C. Lala and B. Panda. Evaluating Damage from Cyber Attacks: A Model and Analysis. IEEE Transactions on System, Man, and Cybernetics – Part A: Systems and Humans, Vol. 31, No. 4, July 2001.

[10] B. Panda and R. Yalamanchili. Transaction Fusion in the Wake of Information Warfare. In Proceedings of the 2001 ACM Symposium on Applied Computing, Special Track on Database Systems, Las Vegas, Nevada, Mar. 2001

A Framework for Customisable Schema Evolution in Object-Oriented Databases

Awais Rashid

Computing Department, Lancaster University, Lancaster LA1 4YR, UK
awais@comp.lancs.ac.uk

Abstract

This paper describes an evolution framework supporting customisation of the schema evolution and instance adaptation approaches in an object database management system. The framework is implemented as an integral part of an interpreter for a language with a versioned type system and employs concepts from object-oriented frameworks and aspect-oriented programming to support flexible changes. Some example customisations currently implemented with the framework are also described.

1. Introduction

The schema of an object-oriented database (OODB) is subject to change over its lifetime. A number of schema evolution approaches have been proposed to accommodate such changes. These range from basic *schema modification* (no versioning) [3, 9] to versioning of individual classes (*class versioning*) [14, 24] or whole schemas (*schema versioning*) [11, 16] through to mechanisms versioning partial, subjective views of the schema [1] or those based on superimposing one approach on another e.g. [18]. Similarly, a number of instance adaptation mechanisms – supporting simulated or physical conversion of objects upon schema evolution – have been proposed e.g. [9, 14, 22, 24]. Work has also been carried out to maintain behavioural consistency of applications as the schema evolves [4, 12, 13].

Traditionally, an object database management system (ODBMS) offers the maintainer one particular schema evolution approach coupled with a specific instance adaptation mechanism. For instance, CLOSQL [14] is a *class versioning* system employing *dynamic instance conversion* as the instance adaptation mechanism; ORION [3] employs *schema modification* and *transformation functions*; ENCORE [24] uses *class versioning* and *error handlers* to simulate instance conversion.

It has been argued that such "fixed" functionality does not serve "local" organisational needs effectively [21]. Organisations tend to have very specialised evolution requirements for their applications and these requirements can even vary across applications within an organisation. For one organisation (or application) it might be

inefficient to keep track of change histories, hence making *schema modification* the ideal evolution approach. For another organisation (or application) maintenance of change histories and their granularity might be critical. Similarly, in one case it might be sufficient that instance conversion is simulated while in another scenario physical object conversion might be more desirable. The requirements can be specialised to the extent that custom variations of existing approaches might be needed.

This paper describes a framework to support such customisations. The work builds upon our previous work on supporting customisations in database systems [21], in particular providing flexible instance adaptation mechanisms [22]. The framework employs its own language, Vejal, with a versioned type system to support instance adaptation across schema changes. Aspect-oriented programming (AOP) techniques [7] and hot spots, as in object-oriented frameworks [8], are employed to support customisation of the schema evolution and instance adaptation approaches.

The next section provides a brief introduction to object-oriented frameworks and AOP. Section 3 describes the Vejal language underpining the framework. Sections 4 and 5 discuss customisation of the instance adaptation and schema evolution approach respectively. Section 6 concludes the paper and identifies directions for future work.

2. AOP and OO frameworks

A framework provides a basic system model for a particular application domain within which specialised applications can be developed. It consists of already coded pieces of software which are reused, the so called *frozen spots* and the flexible elements, the *hot spots*, which allow the user to adjust the framework to the needs of the concrete application [15]. Object-oriented frameworks [8] employ object-oriented techniques to support customisation and are categorised into *white-box* and *black-box* frameworks. The former employ inheritance to configure the hot spots hence requiring that the architecture of the framework is known to the application developers who build upon it. The latter hide the internal structure of the framework by employing *composition* as the customisation mechanism hence requiring knowledge of the hot spots only and not the internal structure of the framework. Black-box frameworks, however, are harder to build than white-box frameworks. In practice there are few pure white or black box frameworks, and in most cases some hot spots are developed using a white-box approach while others use the black-box approach.

AOP [7] is a new programming paradigm which aims at separating concerns which cut across parts of a system. Examples of such crosscutting concerns include code handling synchronisation, persistence, debugging, security, resource sharing, distribution and memory management. Specific examples of crosscutting concerns in database systems include instance adaptation, change propagation and referential integrity semantics, and policies for version management, security, access control and cache management [19, 20, 22]. It is not possible to encapsulate such code within a single program module using conventional decomposition mechanisms – leading to tangled representations. For instance, in an object-oriented decomposition, code handling tracing, synchronisation or persistence is spread across several classes. With AOP crosscutting code is modularised using special constructs known as *aspects*. This promotes localisation of changes hence reducing development, maintenance and evolution costs. The links between aspects and classes are maintained by means of special reference points known as *join points*. An *aspect weaver* is used to compose the aspects and classes with respect to the join points. This composition may be carried out statically at compile time or dynamically at run time [10]. The join point specification and composition mechanism allow aspects to introduce additional behaviour into the program control flow at well-defined points. This makes AOP an ideal candidate to implement black-box customisations affecting a range of classes.

One of the leading AOP approaches is AspectJ [2], an aspect language for Java, developed at Xerox PARC and used in the implementation of the evolution framework described in this paper. In AspectJ, join points are nodes in a simple object call graph at run-time i.e. points at which an object receives a method call or has its fields referenced. Join points in AspectJ, therefore, include (among others) method/constructor calls and executions, field get and set, and exception handler execution. *Advices,* which are method-like constructs, are used to execute additional behaviour *before, after* or *around* a join point. Fig. 1 shows an example aspect in AspectJ (version 1.06) that displays tracing information (in this case the method signature) *before* and *after* executions of all the methods with any return type or arguments for objects of class `Main` and its subclasses (indicated by the "+" sign in the *pointcut* definition). Note that the class definitions, written in standard Java, do not require any special preparation e.g. hooks, for the aspect in fig. 1 to

be employed. The aspect can be compiled in when tracing is needed and compiled out when it is not desirable.

```
public aspect Tracing {

    pointcut methodExecutions(): execution(* Main+.*(..));

    before(): methodExecutions() {

        System.out.println("Entering " + thisJoinPointStaticPart.getSignature());

    }

    after(): methodExecutions() {

        System.out.println("Leaving " + thisJoinPointStaticPart.getSignature());

    }

}
```

Fig. 1: A tracing aspect in AspectJ (1.06)

3. Framework infrastructure

The framework has been implemented as an integral part of an interpreter for Vejal. Applications are written in Vejal, whereas the framework and its concrete instantiations are implemented in AspectJ and Java.

Vejal has a two-level versioning identifier system (analogous to that used by the popular free source code control system CVS [6]). `C[1]` indicates class version 1 of class C while `C[s=1]` implies the class version of C that occurs in schema version 1. In Vejal, one version of a class may be present in multiple schema versions. In order to prevent unworkable schema versions being created, a new version of a class can only be present in all the future schema versions in which it is still compatible with the contracts of the other classes in the schema.

Vejal aims to support the programmer to specify arbitrarily complex transformations between class versions, in the form of *instance adaptation aspects* [22]. These are essentially transparent view wrappers, written by the application programmer to present e.g. an instance of `Person[1]` as a `Person[2]`, which are invoked by the runtime environment automatically whenever an object needs to be adapted to a different class version. Crucially, they work by transforming data at the field level, and do not attempt to emulate methods (and nor do they require the application-specific evolution code to emulate methods) – the "real" methods are always used from the Vejal class version required by the application. Although this means an instance adaptation aspect breaks the encapsulation of the destination class version, this is arguably a good trade-off, because the alternative of emulating method behaviour leaves more room for error, and converting an object between class versions often requires knowledge of implementation details. There are no language restrictions on changes that can be made between one class version and the next. In particular, methods can be added, deleted and rewritten.

Vejal instance adaptation aspects are intended to support either simulated or physical conversions with exactly the same aspect. Thus, the real adaptation approach in use is abstracted out (cf. section 4). If the system is configured to use simulated conversions for a particular class, the instance adaptation aspect is used to project a compatible view. On the other hand, if physical conversion is required, the runtime environment "scans through" the aspect to physically convert the object to the new class. In either case, *hidden fields* are used, if required, to store data from previous schemas that is invisible now but may become visible upon another adaptation [14]. Thus no data is lost due to destructive conversions unless a previous schema is itself deleted.

4. Customisable instance adaptation

The framework supports plugging in different approaches to instance adaptation. As shown in fig. 2, the hot spots are exposed using the abstract class *Adapter* in a white-box fashion. In order to customise the instance adaptation approach subclasses of *Adapter* have to concretise two abstract methods:

— **public abstract** SysObj createObj(ClassRef classRef, Env env)

This method is overridden to create the new object in case of physical conversion or circumvent the creation in case of simulated conversion. *SysObj* is the object to be created upon adaptation; *classRef* refers to the class the object is to be an instance of; *env* is the current environment of the running thread in the Vejal interpreter.

— **public abstract** SysObj convert(SysObj old, ConversionE conv, Env env)

This method is called by the underlying Vejal converter (*conv*), which invokes the instance adaptation aspects. It encapsulates the main logic for the particular instance adaptation approach offered by the concrete subclass of *Adapter*.

The three customisations currently implemented using the framework include (cf. fig. 2):

— **View Adapter (non-materialised views):** recalculates the view for each read operation rather than storing it. An exception is the case of entirely new fields which have to be stored as hidden fields in the original object.

— **Converter Adapter (physical conversion):** converts the object in-place and physically changes its class.

— **Elastic Converter Adapter (elastic conversion):** a variation of the basic physical conversion approach hence implemented as an aspect inheriting from Converter Adapter (aspects in AspectJ can inherit from classes but not vice versa). The aspect does not override any functionality in its superclass. Therefore, the object is physically converted. However, an advice in the aspect traps the join point when the converted object is about to be written to disk at the end of the transaction (black-box customisation) and reverts it to its previous schema version.

The customisations are beneficial because non-materialised views might be more appropriate in situations requiring reduction in memory consumption, while physical or elastic conversion might be more suitable in others because of its caching behaviour.

Other customisations are possible and, at least for all the approaches we have considered, do not require any changes whatsoever to the instance adaptation aspects. This is because instance adaptation aspects are written in a field-view-oriented style i.e. specifying how to obtain any given field of the destination object. This means that they can be used as-is in non-materialised views, or in other approaches the list of fields in a class can be iterated through and all fields pulled through the instance adaptation aspect like a sieve. This is essentially a special case of separating core code from caching concerns.

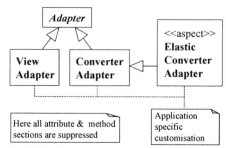

Fig. 2: UML diagram of classes and aspects for customisation of instance adaptation

5. Customisable evolution approach

Similar to customisation of instance adaptation, the framework exposes hot spots for customising the schema evolution approach in a white-box fashion (cf. fig. 3). However, instead of using a class hierarchy, an aspect hierarchy is employed. Advices in the aspects support the customisation by operating on other parts of the framework, mainly those pertaining to resolution of object references upon retrieval from the database (black-box customisation). The two abstract aspects, *Versioning Mode* and *Abstract N-Version Mode* expose a range of

344

abstract methods that are concretised by the sub-aspects to customise the schema evolution approach.

Currently three versioning modes for schema evolution are supported (cf. fig. 3):

— **N-Version Mode:** unrestricted schema evolution is allowed. Instead of duplicating every single class on disk each time a schema is updated, only the classes that have changed are allocated new version numbers. This means that references to classes have to be indirect (versionless) on disk, because `Person` could refer to `Person[1]` or `Person[2]` depending on the schema version in use by an application.

— **One Version Mode:** only one schema version exists in the database. This provides some optimisations in case of applications where change histories are undesirable. All on-disk references to classes now refer directly to resolved classes, rather than indirect references as in N-version mode.

— **N-to-1 Transition Mode:** to go from N-version mode to one version mode. This is essential as a significant amount of disk activity is required to get the database into one version mode. Note that there is no transition period to go from one version mode to N-version mode. The transition is virtually instantaneous.

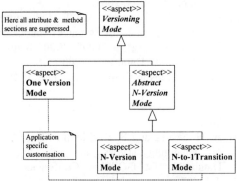

Fig. 3: UML diagram of aspects for customisation of schema evolution approach

6. Conclusion and future work

Existing schema evolution systems for object-oriented databases are inflexible resulting in organisations or applications having to adapt their evolution requirements to the functionality available. This leads to serious maintenance problems and evolution costs over the lifetime of the database with maintainers either opting for a cumbersome *dump and reload* approach or needing to develop an entirely new database to meet the evolution requirements [17]. The framework described in this paper

offers the maintainers the ability to evolve the evolution mechanism offered by the ODBMS itself in step with evolution requirements. It supports customisation of the instance adaptation and schema evolution approaches. The two customisations can be carried out independently of each other or the instance adaptation aspects (which perform the actual adaptation in line with the approach specified using the framework). This flexibility has been achieved through a combination of AOP, hot spots, a language with a versioned type system and field-view-oriented instance adaptation aspects.

The use of AOP has not only made it possible to introduce additional behaviour into the system control flow in a modularised fashion but also allowed us to expose hot spots for "advanced" customisation. For instance, when customising the instance adaptation approach, most basic customisations (e.g. view adapter, converter adapter) can rely on the hot spots exposed in a white-box fashion (using inheritance). However, advanced customisations (e.g. elastic adapter) can manipulate other points through AOP.

The customisability of the framework to support other schema evolution and instance adaptation approaches and its ability to cope with unanticipated evolution requirements need to be validated in real-life applications and case studies. Our future work will, therefore, focus on this validation. Furthermore, the current implementation of the framework is based on the underlying ODBMS exposing an ODMG Java binding [5]. We aim to migrate to the Java Data Objects (JDO) standard [23] in order to support customisable evolution for a range of database systems including object-relational systems.

Acknowledgements

This work is supported by UK Engineering and Physical Sciences Research Council (EPSRC) grant GR/R08612. The author wishes to thank Robin Green for his contribution to the framework implementation.

References

[1] J. Andany, M. Leonard, and C. Palisser, "Management of Schema Evolution in Databases", 17th International Conference on Very Large Databases, 1991, Morgan Kaufmann, pp. 161-170.

[2] AspectJ Team, "AspectJ Project", http://www.eclipse.org/aspectj/, 2003.

[3] J. Banerjee, H.-T. Chou, J. F. Garza, W. Kim, D. Woelk, and N. Ballou, "Data Model Issues for Object-Oriented Applications", *ACM Transactions on Office Information Systems*, Vol. 5, No. 1, pp. 3-26, 1987.

[4] P. L. Bergstein, "Maintenance of Object-Oriented Systems during Structural Evolution", *TAPOS -*

Theory and Practice of Object Systems, Vol. 3, No. 3, pp. 185-212, 1997.

[5] R. G. G. Cattell, D. Barry, M. Berler, J. Eastman, D. Jordan, C. Russel, O. Schadow, T. Stenienda, and F. Velez, *The Object Data Standard: ODMG 3.0*: Morgan Kaufmann, 2000.

[6] "Concurrent Versions System", http://www.cvshome.org/, 2003.

[7] T. Elrad, R. Filman, and A. Bader (eds.), "Theme Section on Aspect-Oriented Programming", *Communications of ACM*, Vol. 44, No. 10, 2001.

[8] M. E. Fayad and D. C. Schmidt, "Object-Oriented Application Frameworks", *Communications of the ACM*, Vol. 40, No. 10, pp. 32-38, 1997.

[9] F. Ferrandina, T. Meyer, R. Zicari, and G. Ferran, "Schema and Database Evolution in the O2 Object Database System", 21st Conference on Very Large Databases, 1995, Morgan Kaufmann, pp. 170-181.

[10] G. Kiczales, J. Lamping, A. Mendhekar, C. Maeda, C. Lopes, J. Loingtier, and J. Irwin, "Aspect-Oriented Programming", ECOOP, 1997, Springer-Verlag, Lecture Notes in Computer Science, 1241, pp. 220-242.

[11] W. Kim and H.-T. Chou, "Versions of Schema for Object-Oriented Databases", 14th International Conference on Very Large Databases, 1988, Morgan Kaufmann, pp. 148-159.

[12] G. N. C. Kirby, "Persistent Programming with Strongly Typed Linguistic Reflection", 25th International Conference on System Sciences, 1992, pp. 820-831.

[13] L. Liu, R. Zicari, W. Huersch, and K. J. Lieberherr, "The Role of Polymorphic Reuse Mechanisms in Schema Evolution in an Object-Oriented Database", *IEEE Transactions on Knowledge and Data Engineering*, Vol. 9, No. 1, pp. 50-67, 1997.

[14] S. Monk and I. Sommerville, "Schema Evolution in OODBs Using Class Versioning", *ACM SIGMOD Record*, Vol. 22, No. 3, pp. 16-22, 1993.

[15] W. Pree, *Design Patterns for Object Oriented Software Development*: Addison Wesley, 1994.

[16] Y.-G. Ra and E. A. Rundensteiner, "A Transparent Schema-Evolution System Based on Object-Oriented View Technology", *IEEE Transactions on Knowledge and Data Engineering*, Vol. 9, No. 4, pp. 600-624, 1997.

[17] A. Rashid, "A Database Evolution Approach for Object-Oriented Databases", *PhD Thesis*, Computing Department, Lancaster University, UK, 2000.

[18] A. Rashid, "A Database Evolution Approach for Object-Oriented Databases", IEEE International Conference on Software Maintenance (ICSM), 2001, IEEE Computer Society Press, pp. 561-564.

[19] A. Rashid, "A Hybrid Approach to Separation of Concerns: The Story of SADES", 3rd International Conference on Meta-Level Architectures and Separation of Concerns (Reflection), 2001, Springer-Verlag, Lecture Notes in Computer Science, 2192, pp. 231-249.

[20] A. Rashid and E. Pulvermueller, "From Object-Oriented to Aspect-Oriented Databases", 11th International Conference on Database and Expert Systems Applications (DEXA), 2000, Springer-Verlag, Lecture Notes in Computer Science, 1873, pp. 125-134.

[21] A. Rashid and P. Sawyer, "Aspect-Orientation and Database Systems: An Effective Customisation Approach", *IEE Proceedings - Software*, Vol. 148, No. 5, pp. 156-164, 2001.

[22] A. Rashid, P. Sawyer, and E. Pulvermueller, "A Flexible Approach for Instance Adaptation during Class Versioning", ECOOP 2000 Symposium on Objects and Databases, 2000, Springer-Verlag, Lecture Notes in Computer Science, 1944, pp. 101-113.

[23] R. Roos, *Java Data Objects*: Addison Wesley, 2002.

[24] A. H. Skarra and S. B. Zdonik, "The Management of Changing Types in an Object-Oriented Database", 1st OOPSLA Conference, 1986, pp. 483-495.

High Availability Solutions for Transactional Database Systems

Stella Budrean   Yanhong Li   Bipin C. Desai

Department of Computer Science Concordia University, Montreal, Canada
Steluta.Budrean@sita.int   yanho_li@cs.concordia.ca   bcdesai@cs.concordia.ca

Abstract

In our increasingly wired world, there is a stringent need for the IT community to provide uninterrupted services of networks, servers and databases. Considerable efforts, both by the industrial [1-13] and academic [14-17] community have been directed to this end. In this paper, we examine the requirements for high availability, the measures used to express it and the approaches used to implement this for databases. We present a high availability solution, using off the shelf hardware and software components, for transactions based applications and give our experience with this system.

1. Introduction

If availability is measured by the length of time during which a system can be used for uninterrupted production work, High Availability (HA) is an extension of that duration, perceived as extended functionality of the system, masking certain outages. This goal can be achieved through redundancy, allowing a system to take over when another one fails. Therefore, we can safely say that in a highly available system, unplanned outages do occur, but they are made transparent to the user [2].

The availability of a system is quantified differently depending on the type of processing done, such as batch processing and real-time. The requirements to insure availability of a batch processing system, compared to a real-time system are very different and hence a lot harder to achieve in the latter case, due to stringent time constraints. In a highly demanding environment in terms of throughput and transactional changes, the cost of a system that insures "continuous" availability could be very high.

Table 1. HA in terms of the number of "9s"

Availability	Downtime per year
99.9% (3 Nines)	525.6 min or 8.76 hrs
99.99% (4 Nines)	52.55 min
99.999% (5 Nines)	5.25 min

HA, expressed in the form of a number of "9s" [1], measures the percentage of uninterrupted service per year and hence the downtime. (Table 1)

There is a certain gray area in computing availability, given by the transparency of recovery, which may or may not be taken into account from the user's point of view. An interesting mathematical quantification in a multi-node/clustered architecture is given by Clustra database [1,2]. The factors that are taken into consideration for computing availability are the percent of time a node is unavailable and the likelihood of a node failure. The former is given as follows:

$$P_{unavailable} = \frac{N_{restart} \times T_{restart}}{24 \times 365} + \frac{N_{repair} \times T_{repair}}{24 \times 365} + \frac{N_{mnt} \times T_{mnt}}{24 \times 365} + \frac{N_{update} \times T_{update}}{24 \times 365}$$

where

$P_{unavailable}$ is the percentage of time a single node will be unavailable due to failure or maintenance,

$N_{restart}$ is the number of restartable node failures per year,

$T_{restart}$ is the time to recover from a retartable node failure,

N_{repair} is the number of node failures per year requiring repairing,

T_{repair} is the time to repair a node,

N_{mnt} is the number of maintenance operations per year,

T_{mnt} is the time a node is down due to maintenance operations,

N_{update} is the number of OS updates per year, and

T_{update} is the time a node is down during an OS update operation.

The likelihood of a node failure is given below:

$$I_{failure} = \frac{N_{restart} + N_{repair}}{24 \times 365} \times \partial$$

where

$I_{failure}$ is the likelihood of node failure,

$N_{restart}$ is the number of restartable node failures per year,

N_{repair} is the number node failures per year requiring repairing, and

∂ is the accelerator (increased likelihood of a

347

second node failure if the first one fails) ~ 2. Hence the Mean Time Between Failures (MTBF) can be calculated as follows:

$$MTBF = \frac{1}{P_{unavailable} \times I_{failure} \times N_{nodes}},$$

where

N_{nodes} is the number of node pairs in the system.

For a system with five "9s" availability, the maximum MTBF must be less than 330 seconds a year for a single downtime of about 5 minutes.

2. HA Methods

The cause for downtime of a database system can be divided into hardware problems and software problems; thus, the most common approach for HA system is to endow the system with redundant hardware and software components; however, this will lead to a dramatic increase in the cost. Thus, in practice, there is a trade-off between the system needs and an economically justifiable cost.

A system that deals automatically with failures passes through two stages: failover and fallback or recovery. Depending on the degree of availability required, a database is configured variously ranging from standby database to active replication. In the simplest failover situation, the failover schemes deployed are [6]:

- *Hot failover*: The standby node is on-line and ready to take over from the production node if there is a failure. It is the fastest recovery approach but the most complex to implement.
- *Warm failover*: It is similar to the hot failover. When the failover begins the standby node is already ready, but it requires configuring with the necessary operations and state information of the failed node.
- *Cold failover*: Failover begins when a node fails and the standby node is fired-up to take over the processing; the database is started and the recovery process begins. It is the least complex to implement but the slowest approach.

2.1. Redundant Components

Hardware producers have approached the problem of HA by making redundant components (disks, controllers, power supplies etc.) function together and by involving hardware/software embedded approach such as Storage Area Network (SAN) [4] and Server Clustering.

Hardware solutions that aim for "fault free" use technique such as disk mirroring, Redundant Array of Inexpensive Disks (RAID), SAN, and Server Clustering. RAID guarantees disk protection through different techniques (e.g. disk mirroring, disk strapping, disk spanning etc.). By grouping servers and storage devices together and using fiber optics connectivity, redundant components as well as failover technology, SANs protect the files throughout an enterprise, and increase the scalability, reliability and manageability of a system as well. Clustering is the technique of putting together multiple servers that may share the workload and if one of the nodes fails the others take over the workload. Appearing as a single server from the Client's point of view, the clustering technology is not so simple but mature enough to monitor different levels involved such as network clustering, data clustering and process clustering.

2.2. Database Replication

Database replication is the processing of copying and maintaining database objects on multiple servers that make up a distributed database system. Today, two major approaches for creating a replica of a database are available: asynchronous and synchronous replication.

The asynchronous replication usually is a built-in database feature and makes use of the transactions logs that are sent to the backup machines and applied online. Another method used for asynchronous replication is via triggers and/or snapshots, which are able to update objects in different databases.

The synchronous replication uses the two-phase commit (2PC) protocol that can be a built-in feature of the database or a middle-tier can be used to ensure that the transactions are committed or rollbacked-back at all sites.

In traditional systems, the replication is achieved by having a log-based standby system, which is a duplicate of a primary database and is updated after the event, thus making the standby system very close to the primary in case of failure. When the primary system goes down, the standby system takes over and continues the processing with minimal interruption for synchronizing the two databases, which will be within minutes of changes at best. Protection is limited to the database data instead of the file system. As for the network, adequate network bandwidth is necessary to insure the transfer of logs.

Another form of replication is achieved through distributed databases that encompass multiple database server nodes where each node runs a separate database with its own dictionary. One of the advantages of having distributed databases is the ability to replicate across multiple platforms, hence lowering the costs of standardizing the databases. This kind of replication improves the overall availability of a system by making the data available at multiple sites. If one site becomes unavailable then the data can be retrieved from other sites.

2.3. Parallel Server/Clustering

Parallel Servers are the database built-in capability to synchronously replicate the transactions processed by a database system. A database instance runs on each node and the data is stored on separate storage. Parallel Severs or Application Cluster can provide with load distribution and balancing, as well as HA and fail safety due to its architecture; clustered databases are either shared disk or share nothing databases. Good examples of shared-disk architecture are: Oracle Parallel Server where the database files are partitioned among the instances running in the nodes of a multi-computer system; and Informix with their Parallel Extended option for Dynamic Server proposes a shared-nothing architecture through partitioning of data, partitioning of control and partitioning of execution. A very interesting solution of shared nothing architecture with very high availability is provided by Clustra database [3], which is not that well known except in the telecommunication world.

2.4. Transactional Replication

In the pursuit of having data replicated at different sites, Transaction Processing (TP) is a widely accepted method to coordinate business transactions that modify databases; it keeps a log of all the modifications made to the database over a period of time in case of failure.

In distributed transactions processing, a Transaction Processing Monitor (TPM) helps facilitate distributed transactions processing by supplying functions, including naming services, security at the transaction level, recovery coordination and services, as well as fault tolerance features (e.g. failover redirection, transaction mirroring, and load balancing).

A transaction may involve changes on many different platforms and involve many different databases from different vendors. X/Open, a standard body, has developed the Distributed Transaction Processing (DTP) Model and the XA interface to solve the heterogeneous problem to allow a manager process to organize the behavior of databases [8]. An off-the-shelf transactional system is used as a middleware in a three-tier architecture for distributed transaction-processing systems. The part of the problem that is not addressed by the traditional Standby systems is the fine-grained synchronization after the failed system is recovered. By using transactional systems in conjunction with the database, the problem of synchronous writes in two or more databases is handled by the XA interface.

Example of middleware are: CICS [5] and ENCINA [9] by IBM, and Tuxedo [11] by AT&T Bell Laboratory[1]. For the DTP with the goal of achieving database

replication, Tuxedo represents one of the best candidates for a middle-tier due to the programming ease and well-defined architecture.

3. Proposed Architecture for HA

Choosing data replication technologies can be difficult because of the large number of products on the market with different implementation options and features. To add to this complexity, data replication solutions are specific to a database, file system OS or disk subsystem.

Depending on the amount of data that one is willing to sacrifice during an outage, the replication solutions vary from asynchronous replication when minutes of transactions can be lost, to synchronous when just the uncommitted work is lost and finally to transaction aware replication that offers the transaction level replication. Problems arise in a transactional environment, such as the telecommunication world, where no data can be lost and even the uncommitted/rolled back transactions have to be reapplied. The problem addressed by this paper is to find a solution, for a fast fallback and restart in such a fast changing transactional environment.

For a system with two databases that are updated at the same time using synchronous replication (i.e. the 2PC protocol), the goal, in case of failure, is to be able to resynchronize the two databases, without shutting down the system.

Consider the three-tier architecture shown in Figure 1, where the synchronous replication is handled by Tuxedo, the middleware. This method addresses just data related issues, the changes related to the database schema, or software upgrades are not addressed in this paper.

From functionality point of views there will be three modes that the system can be in:

- *Normal mode*, when both databases are available and transactions are committed to both databases.
- *Failsafe mode*, when one database is not available and the transactions will be committed to the available database and a journal (flat file).
- *Fallback mode*, when all the changes are applied from the journal to the restored database and the functionality is then resumed to Normal.

The aim of this system is to provide the client with a transparent access to the system, implicitly database, effectively presenting a single and stable interface. Hence, the server's availability will be decoupled from the database availability. Also, the main goal is that once a transaction has been taken in charge, and confirmed by the system it must not be lost, even if it is to be processed later. The following are some of the constraints implied by such an architecture:

---

[1] Tuxedo was originally built by AT&T and acquired by BEA.

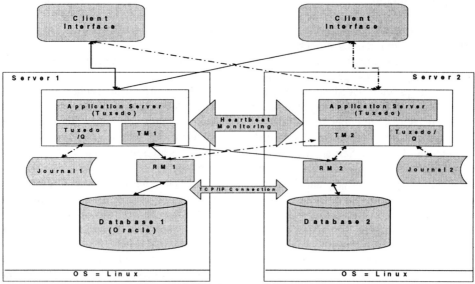

Figure 1. System architecture

- Minimum requirements in terms of hardware are two nodes to insure the failover and fallback procedures.
- There is a certain delay introduced by synchronous update that may affect the system depending on the bandwidth available.
- There is an extra burden of securing the journal, assessing its size and ensuring for space. The same goes for the queues that are used to store the messages while the systems are resynchronized.

We believe that this architecture is the answer for transaction-oriented systems, as a non-expensive solution but at the expense of adding another level of complexity represented by the middle-tier level. The components we used for the proof of concept consists of two PC based Servers running Linux RedHAT 7.2, TCP/IP network communication, Tuxedo 8.0 software to be used as a Transactional System to build the Application Server, and Oracle 8i database as the repository.

As depicted in Figure 1, the Client application is always connected to the active Application Server, in our case to Server 1. The Application Server via Tuxedo's Transaction Manager (TM) communicates with the Resource Managers (RMs) of the two databases, in order to commit all the changes (e.g. commands) required by one Client Application. When the system functions normally, a transaction would entail updating two databases via two RDBMS RMs using the 2PC protocol. In case of Server Application failure, all the processes are migrated to the second Server by the monitoring software allowing the system to resume operations. In case of Database failure, the operation continues with one Resource

Manager, and the TM updates instead of the failed database the journal file via the queuing mechanism provided by Tuxedo, called Tuxedo/Q queue[18].

The main part of the design for this system revolves around the Application Server that handles the updating of the databases and initiates the failure and fallback procedures in case of a failure. By using Tuxedo as a middleware, most of the design problems are solved by the X/Open interface. This interface provides the distributed transactions processing mechanism, reducing the design and implementation efforts.

As shown in Figure 2, the TM defines the transaction boundaries and provides the Application with API calls to inform it of the start, end and disposition of transactions. The Tuxedo System provides the components for creating the TM. The RM vendor (Oracle, Informix, etc.) provides an XA compliant library along with the Tuxedo utilities to build a TM program [8].

From a design point of view, the client and server applications in such a system can be described as follows:

- Client applications gather data from the outside world, which is then passed to the servers, for processing.

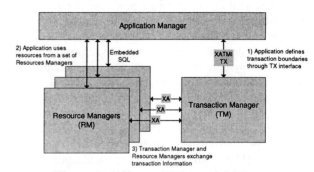

Figure 2. X/Open DTP model [8]

- Server applications are a set of business functions known as services that are then compiled along with the BEA TUXEDO binaries to produce a server executable. In our case, the servers manage the resources, update the databases or the queue, and manage the recovery process as well.

Each RM belongs to a Server Group that creates a transaction server, which will coordinate all the transactions directed towards this resource. Figure 3 below, shows an example of five server groups that handle the update of the two databases, the update of the database and a raw file, as well as the update of the failed database from the raw file, which are configured as follows:

- Two Server Groups for accessing the two databases.
- Two Server Groups for accessing the journal.
- One Server Group for handling the transactions from the Client.
- A group can run on either machine to handle the failover and also the load balancing.

Having to update multiple resources in the same transaction needs the use of global transactions, which are logged in the transaction log (TLOG) only when they are in the process of being committed [19].

For our application the Servers and implicitly the Tuxedo middleware will be distributed over the two machines as shown in Figure 4 below. The Client application, which will send information to the services that will update the databases, could reside on the same machine as the Server application or on workstations. The service advertised by the Server will be updated and its functionality will be transparent to the Client in case of database failure, meaning that the Client will always call this Service regardless of what happens behind the scene.

Since the system can be in three states, depending on the database availability, these states will be mapped into two Services that will have the name Update and a Recovery Service. From a functionality point of view, these services will have the following behavior:

- **Update Normal**: Update the two databases via the RM. The Client application calls the Update service advertised by the server, which results in the update of the two databases.
- **Update Degraded Mode**: In case of a database failure, the server will advertise a new Update service that will update one database and the queue, which is our journal.
- **Recovery Mode**: When the database has been restored up to the time of the failure, a new service will be called that updates the failed database from the queue. When the queue is

empty, it will advertise the Update Normal Service instead of the Update Degraded.

Figure 4 shows two types of processes: the automatic failover handled by the Update service and the manual Recovery called by the administrator. The Recovery is started when the failed database in our case the Database2 is recovered up to the time of failure, which is logged/enqueued by the Update Degraded service in a raw file and can be dequeued by the administrator via a special Client. When all the messages are dequeued from the raw file and the two databases are synchronized, the Update Degraded service is deadvertised and the Update Normal service is re-advertised. To avoid enqueuing more messages while the two services are switched, volatile queues can be used between the Client application and the Update service, making use of Tuxedo's Queue Forwarding mechanism. Hence, both Update1 and Update2 Services are made unavailable, while the Update Normal is advertised; thus, the incoming messages are stored in the volatile queue before being sent to the Update service, avoiding data inconsistency.

All the services described above are running on both machines, therefore regardless of which database goes down, the complementary service will take over. For safety purposes, the information will be saved in a raw file on the same machine as the database to avoid the loss of information in case of the second machine failure. All the servers are booted from the master machine, via the Bridge server provided by Tuxedo that uses the network connection and the tlisten process on both machines that listen on the same port. The Master/Backup role of the two machines (the *Distinguished Bulletin Board Liaison* or DBBL, and the bulletin board liaison or BBL [20]) can be switched between them via a script that monitors their sanity, avoiding the loss of the system in case of Master machine crash.

4. Experiment and Results

To implement the proposed Tuxedo application system, requires a binary version configuration file (TUXCONFIG), produced from an ASCII configuration file (UBBCONFIG), the latter defines the application with a set of parameters that the software interprets to create a viable application. [21] The TUXCONFIG file is copied on all participating machines along with the compiled servers and clients before the application can be booted.

For a request sent by the client application (*maincl*) to the system, there are the following four ways to handle it depending on the availability of the system:

- **Normal Mode**: The CALLRM service requested by the Client calls both database resource services UPDATE1(*dbupdt*) and UPDATE2(*dbupdt2*). The client can receive the confirmation if both services are successful. (Figure 5)

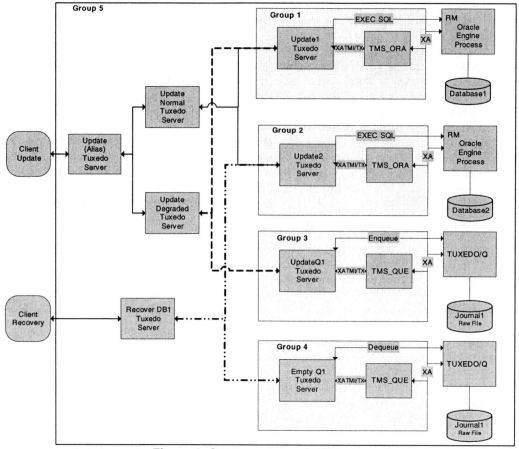

Figure 3. Server groups design

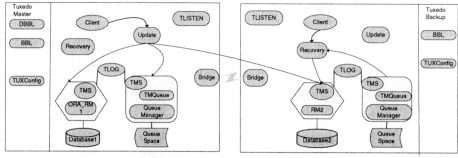

Figure 4. Application design

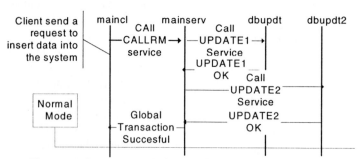

Figure 5. Sequence diagram for normal mode

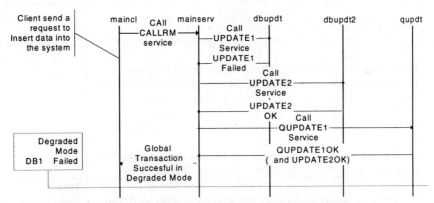

Figure 6. Sequence diagram for degraded mode

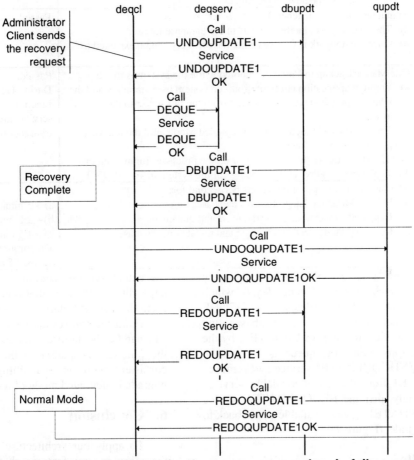

Figure 7. Sequence diagram for the recovery procedure in failure mode

- **Degraded Mode**: The CALLRM service calls QUPDATE1(*qupdt*) or QUPDATE2(*qupdt2*) service since one unavailable databases results in UPDATE1 or UPDATE2 service failure. If the queues are updated successfully, then the client can get the confirmation without noticing partial failure of the system. (Figure 6)

- **Failure Mode**: This is a total system failure when neither databases nor one database and a queue can be updated and the transaction is rejected. To insure that a queue is always available when a database/machine goes down, the system will always try to update the queue located on the same machine with the available database. In order to have the transaction done

353

Table 2. Testing scenarios and results

Test content	Scenario description	Results
Database Failure	Shutdown a database to simulate a database failure. Then, a) The system is automatically switched to Degraded Mode where the queue is updated. b) The database needs recovering up to the point in time of failure. c) The database update service is replaced by the queue update service. d) The messages forming the queue are applied via a special client. e) The services are switched again when the queue is emptied. f) The advertise/unadvertised mechanism for services works to make the switch transparent to the client. NOTE: The administrator has to ensure that the disk space is enough for the queues and to secure the transactions during the Degraded Mode.	Passed. Update services are not lost.
Server Process Failure	Kill multiple server processes on one of the machines randomly. a) The system restarts them automatically after they are declared dead. b) The transaction being executed will be rolled back but will success on retry using the new server process.	Passed. Restarting may introduce a 2 second delay.
Network Failure	Shutdown Tuxedo's listener (kill "*tlistener*" process). a) The recovery will be the same as in the database failure. b) Once the network is re-accessible, the recovery can be executed as usual.	Passed.
Node Failure	The Master/Backup machine is rebooted while the system is running. a) Through application configuration, the system is re-startable, and the whole application will be migrated from the fail server to the available one. b) The system will function in the Degraded Mode until the recovery process can be performed. NOTE: This case results in the loss of all the processes running on the Backup process, called a "Partitioning" of the system in Tuxedo [20].	Passed. During Degraded Mode, the system functions continuously without service interruption. And no transactions are lost.
Response time (10,000 messages)	Measure the number of transactions per second for: a) Normal Mode: update of the two databases b) Degraded Mode: update one database and one queue c) Recovery Mode: read from queue and update one database	Passed. a) ~ 3 minutes b) ~ 2.5 minutes c) ~ 1.5 minutes The throughput of the system in (a) is almost 55 transactions per second.

successfully, the system will do the recovery procedure by launching a new Client (*deqcl*), which will call the UNDOUPDATE1 (*dbupdt*) and DEQUE (*qupdt*) to synchronize the two databases via DBUPDATE1service (the alias of UPDATE1) by the administrator only. Once the queue is empty, the Client calls UNDOQUPDATE1 service that removes the QUPDATE1 from the list of available services and immediately after the REDOUPDATE1 service makes the UPDATE1 service available to get back to the Normal Mode. (Figure 7)

5. Test Results

In order to test the availability of our system, we implemented and tested it using a number of different scenarios. Our goal is to ensure that the database recovery mechanism could be performed without transaction loss. The scenarios and the results obtained for testing are shown in Table 2 above.

These measurements for testing response time are taken for an average loaded system, and give an idea of

the actual synchronization time of the failed database depending on the time that it takes to restore the database up to the time of failure.

From the test results we conclude that the prototype can handle the failures and most importantly can make the failures transparent to the users. These results are consistent with an availability of five "9s" with an upgrade in degraded mode of less than 330 seconds.

6. Conclusion

To apply our architecture to a real life application, there are several features that could be added to the proposed design in order to handle large volume of data. One feature is a load balancing option that allows the configuration of the percentage of load for each service and group while allowing the remaining to be routed to alternate resources. Certain services can have priority over the others, allowing the system to handle messages in a different manner. This is also configurable on a service/group basis. In a distributed environment, the management of different resources is made easier by enlarging the client-server model. Another feature that is very useful in a real-life scenario is the data-dependent routing. Thus, different number of databases can be used to store the data, depending on the data. Through this feature, the scalability of the system can be enhanced without diminishing the performance.

To enhance performance, the asynchronous update of the resources can be used within the same transaction, having as result, a faster access to various resources. In this case, the response has to be handled via programming as opposed to the synchronous update that is handled by the dual-commit protocol.

Generally, the system makes full use of the Tuxedo capacities in order to solve existing issues regarding the availability of the database system. This introduces an extra level of complexity, but nevertheless it provides a simple solution that is relatively easy to implement. As mentioned previously, the main effort is the application configuration on Tuxedo's side that requires good analysis skills in a distributed environment. The programming effort is minimal, being reduced to a number of C routines that make use of Tuxedo's ATMI library.

Acknowledgement: This work was supported in part by grants from the National Science and Engineering Research Council of Canada.

7. References

[1] "The five 9s Pilgrimage: Toward the Next Generation of High-Availability Systems ", 2000, Clustra Systems Inc.
Online achieve copy:
http://www.cs.concordia.ca/~faculty/bcdesai/grads/steluta/references/Clustra_5Nines_WP.pdf

[2] "Clustra Systems Availability Analysis-When 'five nines' is not enough", 2001 Clustra Systems Inc.
Online achieve copy:
http://www.cs.concordia.ca/~faculty/bcdesai/grads/steluta/references/Clustra_Availability_WP.pdf

[3] "Clustra Database-Technical Overview", 2000 Clustra Systems Inc.
Online achieve copy:
http://www.cs.concordia.ca/~faculty/bcdesai/grads/steluta/references /Clustra_Technical_WP.pdf

[4] Randy Kerns, *Open SANs An In-depth Brief*, Evaluator Group. Inc, December 2000
http://www.storage.ibm.com/ibmsan/whitepaper/open_san.pdf

[5] IBM CICS Family: *General Information (GC33-0155-05)-Copyright International Business Machines Corporation* 1982, 1995. All rights reserved.
http://www-1.ibm.com/software/ts/cics/about/

[6] "Linux and High-Availability Computing, Clustering Solutions for e-Business Today", Intel Corporation
http://www.intel.com/internetservices/intelsolutionservices/reference/index.htm

[7] Polyserve, "White Paper –Implementing Highly Available Commercial Systems under Linux using Data Replication", Dec. 2000 –Doug Delay
http://www.polyserve.com/

[8] Donald A. Marsh, Jr, "Global Transactions, X/Open XA – Resource Managers", January 2000, Aurora Information Systems Inc.
http://www.aurorainfo.com/wp3/

[9] "Encina Transactional Programming Guide", IBM Corporation 1997
http://www.transarc.ibm.com/Library/documentation/txseries/4.2/aix/en_US/html/aetgpt/aetgpt02.htm#ToC_182

[10] "Global Transactions in BEA TUXEDO System"
http://edocs.beasys.com/TUXEDO/tux65/proggd/tpg05.htm#997149

[11] BEA TUXEDO, "The programming model -White Paper", November 1996
http://www.bea.com/products/TUXEDO/paper_model.shtml

[12] "Comparing Replication Technologies", November 2002
http://www.peerdirect.com/library/index.php

[13] Juan M. Andrade, et al, *The Tuxedo System: Software for Constructing and Managing Distributed Business Applications,* Addison-Welsey Publishing Company.

[14] Robert Breton, "Replication Strategies for High Availability and Disaster Recovery", *Data Engineering* Vol. 21(4) pp.38-43

[15] Rosana S. G. Lanzelotte, Patrick Valduriez, Mohamed Zaït, Mikal Ziane, "Industrial-Strength Parallel Query Optimization: issues and lessons", *An International Journal*, 1994.
http://www-poleia.lip6.fr/~ziane/perso.html

[16] M. Tamer Özsu, Patrick Valduriez, "Distributed and Parallel Database Systems", *ACM Computing Surveys*, Vol.28, no. 1, pp 125-128, March 1996.

[17] L. Rodrigues and M. Raynal, "Atomic Broadcast in Asychronous Crash-Recovery Distributed Systems", *Proceedings of the 20th IEEE International Conference on Distributed Computing Systems*, Taipe, Taiwan, April 2000.

[18] BEA TUXEDO, "Using the BEA Tuxedo /Q Component - BEA Tuxedo Release 7.1, Document Edition 7.1", May 2000
http://edocs.bea.com/tuxedo/tux71/pdf/qgd.pdf

[19] BEA TUXEDO, "Setting Up a BEA Tuxedo Application - BEA Tuxedo Release 7.1, Document Edition 7.1", May 2000
http://edocs.bea.com/tuxedo/tux71/pdf/ads.pdf

[20] BEA TUXED, "Introducing the BEA Tuxedo System - BEA Tuxedo Release 7.1, Document Edition 7.1", May 2000
http://edocs.bea.com/tuxedo/tux71/pdf/int.pdf

[21] BEA TUXEDO, "Installing the BEA Tuxedo System -BEA Tuxedo Release 7.1, Document Edition 7.1", May 2000
http://edocs.bea.com/tuxedo/tux71/pdf/ins.pdf

[22] BEA TUXEDO, "Administering a BEA Tuxedo Application at Run Time -BEA Tuxedo Release 7.1, Document Edition 7.1", May 2000
http://edocs.bea.com/tuxedo/tux80/pdf/adminrun.pdf

Database Applications III

An Empirical Study of Commutativity in Application Code

Paul Wu
University of Sydney
pwu@it.usyd.edu.au

Alan Fekete
University of Sydney
fekete@it.usyd.edu.au

Abstract

A typical object database manages concurrency control by instance locking, based on the identification of instance operations as "read" or "write". An alternative theory shows that additional concurrency can be obtained based on operation commutativity. Under commutativity theory, activities can be allowed concurrently as long as they commute, that is, the effect is the same in either order. In this paper, we study an extensive commercial application from a telecommunications domain, and determine how much concurrency is actually present for commutativity theory to use. Our study extends to identify not only the operations that commute, but the reasons for their commutativity as well. We separated the commutative operations into three categories: those that commute because both are read operations, those that commute because different fields are accessed, and those that commute for semantic reasons. By doing this in our analysis we were able to show a comparison in concurrency potential between commutative locking and the two other common locking protocols in existence: instance locking and attribute locking.

1. Introduction

Many software applications need to maintain persistent data, which is available beyond the execution of the application. Databases are designed to store and manage such persistent data. Object databases can store and manipulate objects directly, and so have enjoyed success in certain niche markets such as telecommunications and the finance industry [1].

A survey of object databases in the industry by Doug Barry of Object Data Management Group (ODMG) shows that instance locking is the most commonly used protocol for concurrency control [2]. Alternatively, a different paradigm for concurrency control based on the notion of commutativity had been developed extensively in the research community. Commutativity makes use of the richer semantics of the operations (methods in Object Oriented terminology), as opposed to just simple read and write classifications, to further exploit the concurrency potential of conflicting operations.

These studies on concurrency control using semantically rich operations has been done since the 1980s by Weihl [3,4,5] and Schwarz and Spector [6]. In Schwarz and Spector, the use of call and return parameters for conditional commutativity was mentioned, while in Weihl [4], he pointed out the two different notions of commutativity; forward and backward commutativity. Exploiting method commutativity was discussed in Cart and Ferrie [7], and Muth et al. [8] presented a locking protocol for object databases that uses method commutativity. This locking protocol was further refined by Resende, Agrawal and El Abbadi [9] to deal with referentially shared objects. The textbook by Lynch et al. [10] discussed commutativity and commutativity-based locking algorithms in detail. In 1996 Jajodia and Mukkamala presented a probabilistic model that estimated the possible reduction in transaction conflicts when commutativity was used for concurrency control [11]. Topics on general commutativity, state-dependent commutativity, return value commutativity and commutativity based reducibility are all discussed comprehensively in a recent book by Weikum and Vossen [12].

The extensive research mentioned shows how commutativity can be exploited for concurrency control in theory, but no work to date has carried out an empirical analysis of commutativity in a real-world application domain. We wish to bridge this gap by investigating the applicability of commutativity in a commercial platform. The platform made available to us comes from the telecommunications industry; it is an IP-PBX switch called IP Exchange Systems, or IPES for short (IP-PBX switch is the newer generation of private branch exchanges that is IP-based and supports IP-telephony). IPES was developed by Lucent Technologies and is currently owned by Avaya Inc. The system is an object-oriented platform that uses an object-based data store called PSEPro™ to manage its persistent data.

We analysed the commutativity of operations on all persistent data stored in IPES. For each class in the data, we identify the commutative pairs of operations and separate them into three categories. The categories correspond to the concurrency obtainable by three different concurrency control protocols: instance locking, attribute locking, and commutative (semantic) locking. By doing this we are able to obtain empirical data on the extent to which each protocol can allow concurrent activity in this application, and we hope this will shed some light on the performance *potential* between commutative locking and the two other protocols in existence.

The rest of this paper is organised as follows: in Section 2 we define commutativity and introduce the commutativity categories, in Section 3 we discuss IPES and its persistent data set, in Section 4 we present the commutativity analysis of the data set, and in Section 5 we conclude with a discussion.

2. Background

We start our discussion of commutativity with its formal definition, then we introduce the three categories that commutative operations are separated into.

2.1. Commutativity defined

For a given object X, an operation pair (OPi, OPj) acting on X is *commutative* if the execution of OPi by transaction $T1$ followed by the execution of OPj by transaction $T2$ has the same final effect on X and the same results for the transactions as the execution in reverse order $(OPj$ followed by $OPi)$. Commutativity can be expressed by the equation below:

$$T1.OPi(X); T2.OPj(X) \sim T2.OPj(X); T1.OPi(X),$$

where $\sim$ denotes equivalence between the two execution orders. This equivalence means that subsequent operations can't distinguish the state X resulting from the two orders, and that each operation returns the same value independent of the presence or absence of the other operation.

A classical example of commutativity would be a bank account object with a deposit operation. The deposit operation is considered to be a write operation since it modifies the state of the bank account object, and under the traditional notions of conflict based on read and write operations, it follows that two deposit operations are in conflict. However, under the notion of commutativity, two deposit operations can be viewed as being commutative and not in conflict with each other, since running them in either order makes no difference to the final observable state of the bank account object (provided the return values of a deposit is a success indication, rather than, say, the new balance)

2.2. Commutativity categories

While commutativity theory has been explored in the research literature, available object databases use locking based on readlocks and writelocks. In most systems, these locks are taken on each instance of a class; however a few systems use locking on each attribute within an instance. (Instance locking corresponds to record locking in a relational database, while attribute locking corresponds to locking on separate fields within a record). Both instance locking and attribute locking ensure that non-commutative pairs can't run concurrently; that is, they allow some but not all of the concurrency available through commutativity analysis. The relationship between these different notions of conflict can be expressed as follows. For a given class, if we represent the set of operation pairs *not* in conflict under read/write locking at instance level as *NCF_INST*, the set of pairs not in conflict under read/write locking at attribute level as *NCF_ATTR*, and the set of pairs not in conflict under commutativity as *NCF_COMM*, then these three sets are related by the expression below:

$$NCF\_INST \subseteq NCF\_ATTR \subseteq NCF\_COMM.$$

As operation pairs are non-conflicting for different reasons under each of the three notions of conflict, and the set *NCF_COMM* embodies the set *NCF_ATTR*, which in term embodies the set *NCF_INST*, we can arrange the elements from set *NCF_COMM* into three disjoint categories using set difference: *NCF_INST*, *NCF_ATTR\NCF_INST* and *NCF_COMM\NCF_ATTR*. Each category would represent the unique reason for non-conflicting pairs of the three different notions of conflict. Arranging the elements from *NCF_COMM* in this fashion helps us to see the contribution of each category to a total across categories, and later we can compare easily the concurrency potential of commutativity to read/write locking at instance and at attribute granularity

2.2.1. Read/Read pairs. We start with the first category of commutative operation pairs; *NCF_INST*. Operation pairs in this category are two read operations, which is considered non-conflicting under read/write locking at instance granularity and also under commutativity. Two read operations will always commute. Take for example a class X with integer attributes A,B,C,D and two operations $M1()$ and $M2()$ below:

```
public int M1() {
    if (this.A) return this.B+this.C;
    else return this.B;
}
```

```
public int M2() {

    return this.A + this.C;

}
```

Both *M1()* and *M2()* are read-only operations; as there are only read accesses to retrieve the values of *A,B* and *C*. Since the values of *A,B,C* are not modified in any way, running *M1()* and *M2()* in either order on an instance object of *X* will produce the same results as far as the final object state and the operation return parameters are concerned.

2.2.2. Different Field pairs. Next we look at commutativity of operation pairs from accessing different fields; *NCF_ATTR\NCF_INST*. Read and write operations to different fields of an object will be commutative, and this is also what differentiate attribute locking from instance locking. Following from the previous example, if we now have a write operation *M3()* which reads the value of *C* and modifies the values *A* and *B*, and a read operation *M4()* which reads the value of *C*, running *M3()* and *M4()* on an instance of *X* in any order will still produce the same final state and the same return parameters because the two operations are both read-only for the shared fields (in this case, *C*), and modifications happen to different fields.

```
public void M3(int foo) {
    this.B += foo;
    this.A += this.C;
}
public int M4(int bar) {
    return (this.C*bar)/365;
}
```

Now if there is a write operation *M5()* such as below that modifies the value of *D*, it will be commutative with *M3()* as well because once again different fields are being accessed, except for fields where both operations are read-only.

```
public void M5(int foo) {
    if (this.C > 0)
        this.D *= foo;
}
```

2.2.3. Semantic Commutative pairs. Finally we look at commutativity for semantic reasons; *NCF_COMM\NCF_ATTR*. Two operations can commute, depending on their semantics, even if they are both acting on the same instance and same field and at least one of them is a write operation. For example, given a bank

account class with attribute *bal* for account balance and an operation *Deposit()* for adding money to the balance:

```
public void Deposit(float amount) {
    bal = bal + amount;
}
```

Two *Deposit()* operations on the same instance of a bank account in this case will be commutative, even though they are modifying the same field *bal* and they are both write operations. If the initial state of *bal* is 100, two *Deposit()* operations, one for 10 and another for 40, run in either order, will still achieve the same final state of *bal* being 150 and the same return parameters for both operations. Under read/write locking at instance granularity, these two operations are in conflict because they are both write operations. Even at attribute granularity of read/write locking, these two operations are still considered to be in conflict because they are both writes to the same attribute. Commutativity for semantic reasons, as this example shows, allows greater concurrency even beyond that of read/write locking at the fine attribute granularity.

3. Industry platform

The promise of greater concurrency potential than traditional read/write locking motivates us to explore commutativity in a real-world system. For our purpose we use a platform whose data set is object-based, so that the theories of commutativity could readily apply.

3.1. IP Exchange System

The industry platform chosen for our investigation is the IP-PBX switch IPES, made initially by Lucent Technologies, and later belonging to Avaya Inc. The version of IPES we examined is Release 2.0, which was made available in November 1999.

IPES is part of a new family of voice and data convergence solutions in the telecommunications industry. It is a software-based system developed by Lucent Bell Labs that allow small to mid-sized businesses to run voice and fax traffic over local and wide area networks. By converting voice and fax traffic to IP packets, this voice-over-IP system aims to eliminate the need for separate voice and data networks in the customer's organisations.

3.2. IPES data set

The IPES platform is developed in Java™ and C. It runs on a Microsoft® Windows NT® Server. Within the application, there is an administration module that

An Empirical Study of Commutativity in Application Code

Paul Wu
University of Sydney
pwu@it.usyd.edu.au

Alan Fekete
University of Sydney
fekete@it.usyd.edu.au

Abstract

A typical object database manages concurrency control by instance locking, based on the identification of instance operations as "read" or "write". An alternative theory shows that additional concurrency can be obtained based on operation commutativity. Under commutativity theory, activities can be allowed concurrently as long as they commute, that is, the effect is the same in either order. In this paper, we study an extensive commercial application from a telecommunications domain, and determine how much concurrency is actually present for commutativity theory to use. Our study extends to identify not only the operations that commute, but the reasons for their commutativity as well. We separated the commutative operations into three categories: those that commute because both are read operations, those that commute because different fields are accessed, and those that commute for semantic reasons. By doing this in our analysis we were able to show a comparison in concurrency potential between commutative locking and the two other common locking protocols in existence: instance locking and attribute locking.

1. Introduction

Many software applications need to maintain persistent data, which is available beyond the execution of the application. Databases are designed to store and manage such persistent data. Object databases can store and manipulate objects directly, and so have enjoyed success in certain niche markets such as telecommunications and the finance industry [1].

A survey of object databases in the industry by Doug Barry of Object Data Management Group (ODMG) shows that instance locking is the most commonly used protocol for concurrency control [2]. Alternatively, a different paradigm for concurrency control based on the notion of commutativity had been developed extensively in the research community. Commutativity makes use of the richer semantics of the operations (methods in Object Oriented terminology), as opposed to just simple read and

write classifications, to further exploit the concurrency potential of conflicting operations.

These studies on concurrency control using semantically rich operations has been done since the 1980s by Weihl [3,4,5] and Schwarz and Spector [6]. In Schwarz and Spector, the use of call and return parameters for conditional commutativity was mentioned, while in Weihl [4], he pointed out the two different notions of commutativity; forward and backward commutativity. Exploiting method commutativity was discussed in Cart and Ferrie [7], and Muth et al. [8] presented a locking protocol for object databases that uses method commutativity. This locking protocol was further refined by Resende, Agrawal and El Abbadi [9] to deal with referentially shared objects. The textbook by Lynch et al. [10] discussed commutativity and commutativity-based locking algorithms in detail. In 1996 Jajodia and Mukkamala presented a probabilistic model that estimated the possible reduction in transaction conflicts when commutativity was used for concurrency control [11]. Topics on general commutativity, state-dependent commutativity, return value commutativity and commutativity based reducibility are all discussed comprehensively in a recent book by Weikum and Vossen [12].

The extensive research mentioned shows how commutativity can be exploited for concurrency control in theory, but no work to date has carried out an empirical analysis of commutativity in a real-world application domain. We wish to bridge this gap by investigating the applicability of commutativity in a commercial platform. The platform made available to us comes from the telecommunications industry; it is an IP-PBX switch called IP Exchange Systems, or IPES for short (IP-PBX switch is the newer generation of private branch exchanges that is IP-based and supports IP-telephony). IPES was developed by Lucent Technologies and is currently owned by Avaya Inc. The system is an object-oriented platform that uses an object-based data store called PSEPro™ to manage its persistent data.

We analysed the commutativity of operations on all persistent data stored in IPES. For each class in the data, we identify the commutative pairs of operations and separate them into three categories. The categories correspond to the concurrency obtainable by three different concurrency control protocols: instance locking, attribute locking, and commutative (semantic) locking. By doing this we are able to obtain empirical data on the extent to which each protocol can allow concurrent activity in this application, and we hope this will shed some light on the performance *potential* between commutative locking and the two other protocols in existence.

The rest of this paper is organised as follows: in Section 2 we define commutativity and introduce the commutativity categories, in Section 3 we discuss IPES and its persistent data set, in Section 4 we present the commutativity analysis of the data set, and in Section 5 we conclude with a discussion.

2. Background

We start our discussion of commutativity with its formal definition, then we introduce the three categories that commutative operations are separated into.

2.1. Commutativity defined

For a given object X, an operation pair (OPi, OPj) acting on X is *commutative* if the execution of OPi by transaction $T1$ followed by the execution of OPj by transaction $T2$ has the same final effect on X and the same results for the transactions as the execution in reverse order (OPj followed by OPi). Commutativity can be expressed by the equation below:

$$T1.OPi(X); \ T2.OPj(X) \sim T2.OPj(X); \ T1.OPi(X),$$

where ~ denotes equivalence between the two execution orders. This equivalence means that subsequent operations can't distinguish the state X resulting from the two orders, and that each operation returns the same value independent of the presence or absence of the other operation.

A classical example of commutativity would be a bank account object with a deposit operation. The deposit operation is considered to be a write operation since it modifies the state of the bank account object, and under the traditional notions of conflict based on read and write operations, it follows that two deposit operations are in conflict. However, under the notion of commutativity, two deposit operations can be viewed as being commutative and not in conflict with each other, since running them in either order makes no difference to the final observable state of the bank account object (provided the return values of a deposit is a success indication, rather than, say, the new balance)

2.2. Commutativity categories

While commutativity theory has been explored in the research literature, available object databases use locking based on readlocks and writelocks. In most systems, these locks are taken on each instance of a class; however a few systems use locking on each attribute within an instance. (Instance locking corresponds to record locking in a relational database, while attribute locking corresponds to locking on separate fields within a record). Both instance locking and attribute locking ensure that non-commutative pairs can't run concurrently; that is, they allow some but not all of the concurrency available through commutativity analysis. The relationship between these different notions of conflict can be expressed as follows. For a given class, if we represent the set of operation pairs *not* in conflict under read/write locking at instance level as *NCF_INST*, the set of pairs not in conflict under read/write locking at attribute level as *NCF_ATTR*, and the set of pairs not in conflict under commutativity as *NCF_COMM*, then these three sets are related by the expression below:

$$NCF\_INST \subseteq NCF\_ATTR \subseteq NCF\_COMM.$$

As operation pairs are non-conflicting for different reasons under each of the three notions of conflict, and the set *NCF_COMM* embodies the set *NCF_ATTR*, which in term embodies the set *NCF_INST*, we can arrange the elements from set *NCF_COMM* into three disjoint categories using set difference: *NCF_INST*, *NCF_ATTR\NCF_INST* and *NCF_COMM\NCF_ATTR*. Each category would represent the unique reason for non-conflicting pairs of the three different notions of conflict. Arranging the elements from *NCF_COMM* in this fashion helps us to see the contribution of each category to a total across categories, and later we can compare easily the concurrency potential of commutativity to read/write locking at instance and at attribute granularity

2.2.1. Read/Read pairs. We start with the first category of commutative operation pairs; *NCF_INST*. Operation pairs in this category are two read operations, which is considered non-conflicting under read/write locking at instance granularity and also under commutativity. Two read operations will always commute. Take for example a class X with integer attributes A,B,C,D and two operations $M1()$ and $M2()$ below:

```
public int M1() {
    if (this.A) return this.B+ this.C;
    else return this.B;

}
```

```
public int M2() {

    return this.A + this.C;

}
```

Both *M1()* and *M2()* are read-only operations; as there are only read accesses to retrieve the values of *A,B* and *C*. Since the values of *A,B,C* are not modified in any way, running *M1()* and *M2()* in either order on an instance object of *X* will produce the same results as far as the final object state and the operation return parameters are concerned.

2.2.2. Different Field pairs. Next we look at commutativity of operation pairs from accessing different fields; *NCF_ATTR\NCF_INST*. Read and write operations to different fields of an object will be commutative, and this is also what differentiate attribute locking from instance locking. Following from the previous example, if we now have a write operation *M3()* which reads the value of *C* and modifies the values *A* and *B*, and a read operation *M4()* which reads the value of *C*, running *M3()* and *M4()* on an instance of *X* in any order will still produce the same final state and the same return parameters because the two operations are both read-only for the shared fields (in this case, *C*), and modifications happen to different fields.

```
public void M3(int foo) {
    this.B += foo;
    this.A += this.C;
}
public int M4(int bar) {
    return (this.C*bar)/365;
}
```

Now if there is a write operation *M5()* such as below that modifies the value of *D*, it will be commutative with *M3()* as well because once again different fields are being accessed, except for fields where both operations are read-only.

```
public void M5(int foo) {
    if (this.C > 0)
    this.D *= foo;
}
```

2.2.3. Semantic Commutative pairs. Finally we look at commutativity for semantic reasons; *NCF_COMM\NCF_ATTR*. Two operations can commute, depending on their semantics, even if they are both acting on the same instance and same field and at least one of them is a write operation. For example, given a bank

account class with attribute *bal* for account balance and an operation *Deposit()* for adding money to the balance:

```
public void Deposit(float amount) {
    bal = bal + amount;
}
```

Two *Deposit()* operations on the same instance of a bank account in this case will be commutative, even though they are modifying the same field *bal* and they are both write operations. If the initial state of *bal* is 100, two *Deposit()* operations, one for 10 and another for 40, run in either order, will still achieve the same final state of *bal* being 150 and the same return parameters for both operations. Under read/write locking at instance granularity, these two operations are in conflict because they are both write operations. Even at attribute granularity of read/write locking, these two operations are still considered to be in conflict because they are both writes to the same attribute. Commutativity for semantic reasons, as this example shows, allows greater concurrency even beyond that of read/write locking at the fine attribute granularity.

3. Industry platform

The promise of greater concurrency potential than traditional read/write locking motivates us to explore commutativity in a real-world system. For our purpose we use a platform whose data set is object-based, so that the theories of commutativity could readily apply.

3.1. IP Exchange System

The industry platform chosen for our investigation is the IP-PBX switch IPES, made initially by Lucent Technologies, and later belonging to Avaya Inc. The version of IPES we examined is Release 2.0, which was made available in November 1999.

IPES is part of a new family of voice and data convergence solutions in the telecommunications industry. It is a software-based system developed by Lucent Bell Labs that allow small to mid-sized businesses to run voice and fax traffic over local and wide area networks. By converting voice and fax traffic to IP packets, this voice-over-IP system aims to eliminate the need for separate voice and data networks in the customer's organisations.

3.2. IPES data set

The IPES platform is developed in Java™ and C. It runs on a Microsoft® Windows NT® Server. Within the application, there is an administration module that contains a persistent data set. This data set is the focus of our investigation.

The set contains system administration information and is stored and retrieved using the embedded object data store PSEPro™ for Java version 6.0 (patch number 15142). PSEPro is a small-footprint version of the object database ObjectStore®, both of which are products of eXcelon™ Corporation.

IPES system administration is done through secure web-based GUI using browsers Microsoft Internet Explorer and/or Netscape® Navigator. IPES can be administered remotely; the browser clients allow the display and modification of system administration data that are stored on the server side. This is achieved through a series of Java applet and servlet interactions and a number of database transaction calls on PSEPro.

The system administration is designed for different types of administrative users with varying degrees of access privileges. The administrative tasks include the following: configuring system-wide dial plan, configuring location sensitive parameters, configuring IPES gateway interface parameters, configuring outbound routing plans, configuring IP exchange adapters, configuring inbound routing plans, configuring advanced system features, managing passwords, configuring user accounts, configuring database backup parameters, and enabling system configurations [13].

The data set within the call manager is defined by a total of 47 Java classes. Each class consists of a number of attributes, which defines the state of the instances, and a number of methods, which are the operations on the instances. Together the instances of these 47 classes stored in PSEPro represent the state of IPES administration module at any given time.

4. Commutativity analysis

In this section, we examine the 47 classes to analyse the commutative potential of the IPES data set stored in PSEPro.

4.1. Commutativity matrix

To analyse the commutativity of operations, we draw up an N by N matrix for each class where N is the number of operations in the class. Within the matrix we analyse each operation conflict pair individually to determine whether they commute as read/read pairs, different field pairs, semantic commutative pairs, or that they do not commute.

In this paper we omitted our analysis of operations in one matrix against operations in other matrices since operations of a particular class will mostly have reads or writes that are relevant only to that class. Where an operation invokes other class's operations within its code, a properly designed commutative locking protocol should check for conflict by referring to other class's matrices. All possible classes and operations reachable by reference are included in our examination, and there are no instances of circular reference in the data set surveyed.

We now illustrate a matrix from one of the classes analysed. For confidentiality reasons all attribute and operation names have been replaced with generic names. In this class, there are two attributes A and B. A is of type Java String, and B is of type OSHashSet (it is similar and compatible to Java 1.2's API implementation of HashSet. More on OSHashSet's implementation and usage can be found in [14]). For attribute A, there is a read operation $gA()$ and a write operation $sA()$. For attribute B, there is a read operation $gB()$ which returns the hashset, and three write operations. The first write operation, abbreviated to $aB()$, adds an element to the hashset. The second write operation, abbreviated to $rB()$, removes an element from the hashset. The third operation, abbreviated to $raB()$, removes all elements from the hashset. All three write operations' return parameters are void. There is also a read operation $c()$, which makes a deep copy of attribute B but does not read attribute A.

Table 1: Commutativity with semantic operations

Class2	gA()	sA()	aB()	rB()	raB()	gB()	c()
gA()	r	n	d	d	d	r	r
sA()	n	n	d	d	d	d	d
aB()	d	d	s	n	n	n	n
rB()	d	d	n	s	s	n	n
raB()	d	d	n	s	s	n	n
gB()	r	d	n	n	n	r	r
c()	r	d	n	n	n	r	r

For the commutativity analysis, r means the operations commute because it is a read/read pair, d means the operations commute because they access different fields (except where both read a field and neither modifies it), s means the operations commute for semantic reasons, and n means the operations do not commute.

In this matrix, read operations such as $gA()$, $gB()$ and $c()$ commute with themselves and each other because they are all read operations, and executing them in any order will produce equivalent end states and return parameters. Operation pairs such as $[sA(),gA()]$, $[sA(),sA()]$, $[c(),rB()]$, $[aB(),raB()]$ etc. that are read/write or write/write to the same attribute do not commute because executing them in different order will produce different end results. On the other hand, operation pairs such as $[gA(),aB()]$, $[c(),sA()]$, $[rB(),sA()]$, etc. that are read/write or write/write to different attributes do commute because they access different fields. Some write operations commute for

364

semantic reasons. For example the two add element operations [*aB(),aB()*] commute since when two elements are added to a hashset, the final state of the set is the same regardless of the order of the add operations (and both return parameters are void). By definition elements in a set (OSHashSet included) have no ordering so the final states are the same whichever element is added first. A set also does not allow duplicates so if two elements being added to the set are the same, the final state of the set will just be a single instance of the element, whichever element is added first. The remove operation *rB()* and remove-all operation *raB()* commute with itself and with each other for the same reasons again; that any order of execution produces equivalent final results.

Note that in addition to operation semantics, operation return parameters play an important role in determining commutativity as well. For example, if the return parameter of *aB()* is the number of elements added successfully to the set instead of void, then the pair [*aB(),aB()*] will not commute because if the element to be added does not already exist in the set, the first *aB()* will return 1, whereas the second *aB()* will return 0. With

different return parameters depending on the order of execution, this operation pair will then not be commutative.

In Class 2, there are a total of 49 operation pairs; 30 of them are commutative, and 19 of them are not. Of the commutative pairs, 9 are read/read pairs, 16 are different field pairs, and 5 are semantic commutative pairs.

In the next section, we collate the commutativity statistics for all classes and present them in summary form.

4.2. Analysis summary

This table shows the summary data extracted from each commutativity matrix for all 47 classes. The commutative operation pairs are sorted into relevant categories, and class totals and grand totals for the entire data set are included in the table. For confidentiality reasons, real class names have been replaced by generic class names from Class1 to Class47.

Table 2: Commutativity analysis summary of all classes

Class	Read/ Read Pairs	Different Field Pairs	Semantic Commutative Pairs	Total Commutative Pairs	Non- Commutative Pairs	Total Pairs
Class1	225	828	13	1066	90	1156
Class2	9	16	5	30	19	49
Class3	16	38	5	59	22	81
Class4	81	184	0	265	24	289
Class5	81	184	0	265	24	289
Class6	25	44	0	69	12	81
Class7	289	870	5	1164	61	1225
Class8	36	70	0	106	15	121
Class9	64	140	0	204	21	225
Class10	36	52	0	88	12	100
Class11	81	160	16	257	32	289
Class12	1	0	0	1	0	1
Class13	100	234	0	334	27	361
Class14	64	114	0	178	18	196
Class15	25	30	0	55	9	64

Class16	225	30	0	255	34	289
Class17	4	0	0	4	5	9
Class18	169	278	2	449	35	484
Class19	1	0	0	1	0	1
Class20	4	2	0	6	3	9
Class21	1	0	0	1	0	1
Class22	1	0	0	1	0	1
Class23	9	10	0	19	6	25
Class24	4	2	0	6	3	9
Class25	1	0	0	1	0	1
Class26	25	42	0	67	14	81
Class27	9	4	0	13	3	16
Class28	36	70	0	106	15	121
Class29	1	0	0	1	0	1
Class30	16	24	0	40	9	49
Class31	25	0	0	25	24	49
Class32	16	22	0	38	11	49
Class33	9	8	0	17	8	25
Class34	16	0	0	16	0	16
Class35	576	1474	0	2050	66	2116
Class36	289	738	0	1027	62	1089
Class37	1	0	0	1	0	1
Class38	81	184	0	265	24	289
Class39	49	102	0	151	18	169
Class40	81	184	0	265	24	289
Class41	64	106	0	170	26	196
Class42	64	24	0	88	12	100
Class43	4	4	5	13	36	49
Class44	16	0	0	16	0	16
Class45	4	0	0	4	0	4

Class46	0	0	0	0	0	0
Class47	25	42	0	67	14	81
Grand Total	**2959**	**6314**	**51**	**9324**	**838**	**10162**

In this summary Class46 is exceptional in that it had only constructors and no other operations, and since constructors play no role in operation conflicts, they are not included in our commutativity analysis. Also, for all classes we focused our examination on operation conflict pairs, and not triplets or more because two is the minimum number of operations needed to identify conflicts. Any third or fourth operation that comes along during application execution can be evaluated by forming a pair with each of the operations individually and checking for the conflict again, and so on and so forth.

From the summary table above, we can see that for most classes the commutative pairs outnumber non-commutative pairs to form a majority of total operation pairs. The grand total for all commutative pairs, 9,324 out of a possible 10,162 pairs, is a very high ratio at 91.8%. This figure would seem to suggest that commutativity have a very high concurrency *potential* in this application domain. The individual statistics for the three commutative categories are: 2,959 read/read pairs which

constitute 29.1% of the total pairs, 6,314 different field pairs which constitutes 62.1% of the total pairs, and 51 semantic commutative pairs which constitutes a small 0.5% of the total pairs.

The three commutative categories can also be combined conveniently to represent different locking protocols. The read/read pairs column essentially represents the concurrency potential of read/write locking at instance granularity, and it stands at 29.1% of the total pairs as stated previously. The read/read pairs column combined with different field pairs column together represents the concurrency potential of read/write locking at attribute granularity, and this number is at 91.3% of the total pairs. These two figures, compared with the 91.8% of commutative locking, would suggest that commutative locking may have a large concurrency edge over instance locking, but it only has a minuscule edge over attribute locking in this application domain. We illustrate the difference in concurrency potential among the three locking protocols for each class in the graph below.

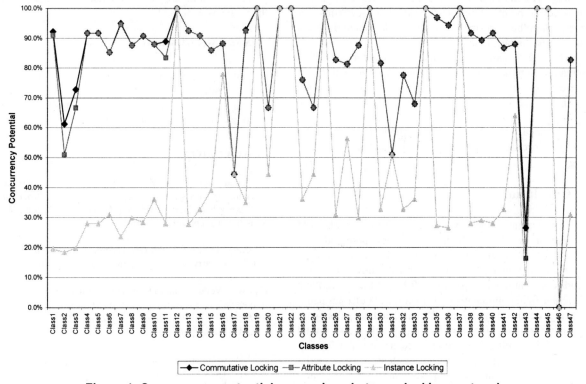

Figure 1. Concurrency potential comparison between locking protocols

The graph shows a comparison of concurrency potential between instance locking, attribute locking and commutative locking for the 47 classes. Data values of each class from Table 2 are combined as described earlier and translated into a percentage that is plotted accordingly on this graph. The maximum concurrency potential at 100% means all operations in the class commutes with each other. If serial execution (ie. no concurrency) is represented on this graph it would run along the 0% line.

From the graph we can see significant gains in concurrency potential going from serial execution to instance locking, and from instance locking to attribute locking. The gains are marginal going from attribute locking to commutative locking.

Of course, in dynamic executions of the application the actual difference in concurrency performance is dependent on numerous factors outside the scope of this static analysis. These factors include the particular transaction mix; which determines what operations are called and the frequency of their invocations. Vary the order of the transactions for one particular mix and that changes the equation yet again as the order in which operations are called will be different as well as the frequency of lock conflicts. There is also the overhead of different locking protocols to take into account when making comparisons, and different implementations of the same locking protocols may have different overheads as well. The importance of this graph, however, is that it provides a point of reference, statically speaking, for comparing the concurrency *potential* between different locking protocols in our study.

The 0.5% extra contribution to concurrency that semantic commutative pairs make may be marginal. But if these pairs happen to be in database hotspots or some tight loop that has a non-trivial effect on transaction throughput, then the contribution to concurrency performance during dynamic executions for these pairs will be more significant than the static analysis otherwise suggest.

5. Conclusion

Our empirical study of commutativity in a real-world system shows a very high concurrency potential - at 91.8% of total pairs, for commutativity in our chosen application domain. That figure breaks down to show read/read commutative pairs (at 29.1% of total pairs) and different field commutative pairs (at 62.1% of total pairs) making up the majority of all commutative pairs, with semantic commutative pairs making up only 0.5% of total pairs. This result can be interpreted as instance locking showing a higher concurrency potential over serial executions, attribute locking showing a significantly higher concurrency potential over instance locking, and

commutative locking showing marginally higher concurrency potential over attribute locking. This last point of course also implies that commutative locking shows a significantly higher concurrency potential over instance locking.

With instance locking being the most commonly used protocol in commercial databases today, the potentially significant concurrency edge of commutative locking over instance locking motivates us to investigate commutative locking further. Currently, work is in progress to construct a concurrency control mechanism that supports commutative locking on our platform. We hope to set up experiments that will benchmark commutative locking against instance locking and all other common locking protocols. By doing so we should get a better idea of how commutative locking performs in dynamic executions in the real world.

At present, there are no empirical analyses of commutativity in real-world systems other than our study, and more future work can be done in this regard to test the applicability of commutativity across a wider range of domains. During our commutativity analysis we have also noticed that operation return parameters play an important role in determining commutativity, and we have observed that semantic commutative operation pairs tend to occur in classes that contain complex data types. So a comprehensive investigation into the factors that lead to semantic commutativity could help shed some light on this issue as well.

6. Acknowledgment

Funding for this research was partially supported by the Australian Research Council, in partnership with Lucent Technologies, Bell Labs Australia from 1999-2000, and with Avaya Inc. afterwards.

7. References

[1] Chaudhri, A. and Zicari, R. (eds), E. Bertino, and G. Guerrini, *Succeeding with Object Databases: A Practical Look at Today's Implementations with Java and XML*, John Wiley & Sons Inc., Chichester, NY, 2001.

[2] Barry, D. and J. Duhl, *Object Storage Fact Book 5.0, Object DBMSs*, J. Barry & Associates Inc., Burnsville, MN, 2001.

[3] W. Weihl, "Data-Dependent Concurrency Control and Recovery", *Proceedings of the Second Annual ACM Symposium on Principles of Distributed Computing*, ACM Press, Montreal, Canada, 1983, pp. 63-75.

[4] W. Weihl, "Commutativity-Based Concurrency Control for Abstract Data Types", *IEEE Transactions on Computers*, IEEE, New York, 1988, pp. 1488-1505.

[5] W. Weihl, "Local Atomicity Properties: Modular Concurrency Control for Abstract Data Types", *ACM Transactions on Programming Languages and Systems*, ACM, New York, 1989, pp. 249-283.

[6] P.M. Schwarz and A.Z. Spector, "Synchronizing Shared Abstract Types", *ACM Transactions on Computer Systems*, ACM Press, Portland Oregon, USA, 1984, pp. 223-250.

[7] Bancilhon, F., Delobel, C., and Kanellakis, P. (eds), M. Cart, and J. Ferrie, *Building an Object-Oriented Database System: The Story of O2*, Morgan Kaufmann Publishers, San Mateo, CA, 1992.

[8] P. Muth, T.C. Rakow, G. Weikum, P. Brossler, and C. Hasse, "Semantic Concurrency Control in Object-Oriented Database Systems", *Proceedings of the Ninth IEEE International Conference on Data Engineering,* IEEE Computer Society, Vienna, Austria, 1993, pp. 233-242.

[9] R. Resende, D. Agrawal, and A. El Abbadi, "Semantic Locking in Object-Oriented Database Systems", *Proceedings of the Ninth Annual ACM Conference on Object-Oriented Programming, Systems, Languages, and Applications*, ACM Press, Portland Oregon, USA, 1994, pp. 388-402.

[10] Lynch, N., M. Merritt, W. Weihl, and A. Fekete, *Atomic Transactions*, Morgan Kaufmann, San Francisco, 1994.

[11] Kumar, V. (ed), S. Jajodia, and R. Mukkamala, *Performance of Concurrency Control Mechanisms in Centralized Database Systems*, Prentice-Hall Inc., Englewood Cliffs, NJ, 1996.

[12] Weikum, G. and G. Vossen, *Transactional Information Systems: Theory, Algorithms, and the Practice of Concurrency Control and Recovery*, Morgan Kaufmann, San Francisco, 2002.

[13] Lucent Technologies, *IP Exchange System R2 System Administrator Configuration Guide*, Communication Applications Group Technical Publications, Lucent Technologies, Denver, CO and Holmdel, NJ, 1999.

[14] Object Design, *ObjectStore PSE/PSE Pro for Java API User Guide*, Object Design Inc., Burlington, MA, 1999.

Fast Accurate Summary Warehouses with Distributed Summaries

Pedro Furtado, Joao Pedro Costa
CISUC DEI-UC / DEI-ISEC
pnf@dei.uc.pt, jcosta@mail.isec.pt

Abstract

Large Data warehouses (DW) put a major challenge in what concerns performance and scalability, as users request instant answers to their queries. Traditional solutions relying on very expensive architectures and structures cannot turn every complex aggregation query into minutes or seconds answers. The summary warehouse (SW) achieves such a speedup using only general-purpose sampling summaries well-fit for aggregated exploration analysis.

The major limitation of SWs results from the tradeoff between accuracy and speed: smaller, faster summaries cannot answer less-aggregated queries. We propose a simple and cheap strategy to meet these conflicting requirements and deliver unseen speedup by taking advantage of distributed computation ubiquity. The distributed summaries approach (DS) proposed in this paper manages a distributed set of summaries that are put in available computing nodes of a local area network to achieve very fast query processing, while guaranteeing enough accuracy.

1. Introduction

Today, data warehouses are no longer seen as an expensive luxury for occasional use in many organizations, but rather as a crucial day-to-day tool for controlling and deciding on issues in every field from sales and marketing to production and supply chain management. In many important organizations, the applications that allow users to analyze data (e.g. iterative exploration) have to deal with Giga or Terabytes of data, while those users require almost instant answers.

This issue has prompted investments in expensive special hardware architectures and complex distributed and parallel computation systems that improve query response time in the presence of such massive data sets. However, as return-on-investment considerations become crucial in technology investments, organizations worldwide become less willing to invest large sums and time in special architectures and consulting when much simpler and cheaper solutions can be found.

Sampling summaries [12, 7] are an alternative strategy that has proven to be very time effective for one of the most relevant class of OLAP queries – those that segment the data into groups and derive some aggregate information from those groups (group-by queries).

Instead of trying to manage the unmanageable, they reduce the amount of data that must be processed immensely and use the same DBMS storage and access structures as the DW, requiring only an independent middle layer that rewrites queries and collects results. The summary can be materialized using a one-pass sequential uniform sampling scheme [7] or the samples can be obtained "on-the-fly" [12], which is much slower but allows progressive refinement of the query results. The combination of estimations and confidence intervals [12, 10] returns a precise dimension of the results' accuracy and if a query cannot be answered satisfactorily with the summary, the intermediate layer simply redirects it to the original DW data.

Sampling summaries rely on statistical estimation to provide approximate answers, returning estimations together with confidence intervals. While this is the only possible way to deliver without requiring the whole data, it is prone to estimation problems related to what we call the "representation issue": does a sample represent the real data with sufficient accuracy? While very aggregated queries can be answered very quickly by extremely small summaries, less aggregated queries require larger, slower summaries. Larger summaries minimize representation limitations, but the speedup is also reduced. The conflicting requirements between accuracy and speed justify considering new summary strategies such as the one proposed in this paper.

We propose the use of a distributed summary structure and computing strategy that allows any candidate node in a local network to host a summary (or a set of summaries) and collaborate in the process of computing query result estimations. This is a significant proposal to solve the representation issue of summaries and deliver unseen speedup, as it allows the query processing layer to obtain estimations from a large summary base with enormous speedup, because the computation is done in parallel by the nodes. The approach is also cheap, as no special hardware is needed, and it is very simple to manage, as the configuration of nodes is flexible and completely dynamic.

The flexibility of DS also means that a single node being offline can still answer queries of certain granularities. There is the full range of possibilities: queries can be answered immediately by the node, by the DS network with the nodes that are available, redirected into the DW or even postponed to be answered when online if it is not possible to reach the network or DW at a given moment.

In this paper we present the Distributed Summaries (DS) strategy and show that it provides extremely fast answers in any DW environment, while also being able to return accurate answers to most queries. We provide comparisons with the most important alternative schemes.

The paper is organized as follows: section 2 discusses related work. Section 3 reviews the generic summary warehouse architecture (SW) and its limitations. Section 4 presents the Distributed Summaries approach (DS), including the specific summary warehouse structure used in DS, the query management functionality and the DS lifecycle and configuration management. Section 5 analyzes experimental results using the TPC-H decision support benchmark [14]. Section 6 contains concluding remarks.

2. Related Work

The time requirements imposed by data analysis in large data warehouses, which requires extensive scanning and joining of enormous data sets, has been a major driver for recent works in approximate query answering strategies, which include [12, 10, 11, 2, 15, 13, 1]. [12] proposed a framework for approximate answers of aggregation queries called online aggregation, in which the base data is scanned in random order at query time and the approximate answer is continuously updated as the scan proceeds. A graphical display depicts the answer and a confidence interval as the scan proceeds, so that the user may stop the process at any time. The Approximate Query Answering (AQUA) system [7, 8, 9] provides approximate answers using small, pre-computed synopsis of the underlying base data. The system provides probabilistic error/confidence bounds on the answer [2, 10].

There has also been considerable amount of work in developing statistical techniques for data reduction in large data warehouses, as can be seen in the survey [3].

Summaries reduce the amount of data that must be processed immensely. Materialized views (MVs) can also achieve this by pre-computing quantities, and they are quite useful for instance to obtain pre-defined reports. However, while summaries work well in any ad-hoc environment, MVs have a more limited scope. We mention a few reasons for that: MVs are inflexible in the sense that each one is specific to a given query pattern and corresponding rollups; They are only justifiable above a considerable aggregation granularity or dimensional subcube; It is not feasible to materialize a very large set of possible patterns into MVs in ad-hoc environments; a set of MVs can easily more than double the data warehouse space.

This means that summaries are useful in a broader context than MVs. However, summaries and MVs can coexist: the MV can be used if there is a suitable one to return an almost instant answer, otherwise the summary will be used instead.

The insufficiency of samples in summaries is considered an important issue and there has been previous work on the issue [2, 1, 5]. But while [1] and [5] use a query pattern perspective to reduce the problem, the DS approach does not assume any specific query pattern and is able to deliver desired scale-up and speedup in any context and at unseen speedups, as long as there are concurrent nodes.

The DS approach proposed in this paper also builds on our groups' previous work on Data Warehouse Striping (DWS) [4]. DWS has shown that it is possible to build a data warehouse (DW) with the data distributed into several nodes in such a way that the nodes are able to handle the bulk of query processing with relative independence, resulting in linear speedup with the number of nodes. DWS speedup relies entirely on the number nodes in the system. However, we describe some practical considerations that limit the speedup of DWS: The DWS replaces the DW entirely. As such, in practice it requires permanent availability of all nodes to be able to return exact answers when needed. This means that DWS should work on a dedicated cluster with a reasonably small number of nodes for high availability. The increase in data exchange overhead, load distribution and rebalancing overheads and complexity with the number of nodes also limits the number and dynamic configuration capacity of the system. DWS speedup is also severely limited in star schemas with large dimensions.

Although DWS can be configured to answer approximately when one or more nodes fail (DWS-AQA), the speedup of the system with the partial answer is approximately equal to the speedup with all nodes. Therefore the speedup is still at most approximately linear with the total number of nodes registered. The high availability constraint and additional overheads discussed above imply that the number of nodes is reasonably small. These two facts mean that the best speedup DWS can achieve when answering approximate queries is definitely limited when compared with summaries that do not need to represent the whole data warehouse. Therefore, DWS is a very interesting DW architecture, but is limited in what concerns the speedup that can be achieved when answering queries approximately.

DS was conceived to overcome the speedup limitations of DWS on approximate answering using a much more flexible and easy to manage system. It is based on a similar divide-to-conquer idea of distributing data into nodes, but it focuses and manages summaries instead of the whole data. While DWS must be viewed as a data warehouse architecture proposal to improve query processing speed, DS is a summary structure that provides orders-of-magnitude faster query processing times when applied to either a normal data warehouse or the DWS system. The speedup of DWS, DS and of a normal one-node summary are compared analytically in section 4.7 and experimentally in section 5.2, showing the relevance of DS.

3. Distributed Summaries

The DS system shown in Figure 1 is made of a set of 1..n nodes which receive summaries that must be registered into a DS registry. The DS registry is a simple directory maintaining a line per node with the address of the node together with the indication of which summaries are available in that node. The system is similar to the normal SW except that it is made of more than one node.

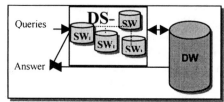

Figure 1 – The DS system

The DS registry is present in any node that requests it. This way, any node can submit and process queries to the DS network independently, at any time. Additionally, each node works completely independently and tries to send the query to the other nodes, but the approximate answer is computed regardless of the number of nodes that is available.

The DS system is completely flexible and dynamic: nodes can enter or leave the system, be online or offline at any given time. When a node enters the DS system, a star schema similar to the base data schema is created. The new, empty structure is loaded with samples from the DW facts, which are taken using a one-pass random sampling algorithm and the corresponding dimension values are also loaded. In this paper we assume sampling without replacement, which requires a simple bitmap index indicating, for each row of a fact table, whether the row has been extracted to a specific node (sampling with replacement could also be considered).

Each node that enters the system has one service waiting for query submission and another service listening for incoming queries, which processes the query and returns the partial answer to the submitting node. When a query is submitted in one node, the node becomes responsible for controlling the processing of the query, which involves submitting it to the DS system, collecting the results, computing the answers to the query and presenting those answers to the user.

4. Enabling Distributed Query Processing

In DS the query is first submitted, then rewritten and sent to n nodes. Nodes compute the answer independently and partial results are collected back to be merged at the collecting node. Computationally, this is possible thanks to the additivity property of the aggregation functions. If the sum of samples from all nodes is SP% of the original data set:

$$count=sum(count_{node\ i})/SP\%$$
$$sum=sum(sum_{node\ i})/SP\%$$
$$max=max(max_{node\ i})$$
$$min=min(min_{node\ i})$$
$$stdev=(sum(ssum_{node\ i})-sum(sum_{node\ i})^2)/sum(count_{node\ i})$$

The next sequence shows what each step does using an example.

Query submission:
Select sum(a), count(a), average(a), max(a), min(a), stddev(a)
From fact, dimensions
Group by grouping_attributes;

Query rewriting:
Select node_x, sum(a) suma, count(a) counta, sum(a x a) ssuma, max(a) maxa, min(a) mina
From fact, dimensions
Group by grouping_attributes;

Results merging:
Select sum(suma)/SP%, sum(counta) /SP%,
sum(suma) / sum(counta), max(maxa), min(mina)
$(sum(ssuma)-sum(suma)^2)/sum(counta)$,
From collected results (all_nodes)
Group by grouping_attributes;

The parameters collected from each node also provide confidence intervals directly.

5. DS Lifecycle

The structure and load process of an individual node entering DS was already explained in Section 3. As pointed out there, the star schema of the node is populated with random uniform samples taken from the base data using a one-pass algorithm. The initial setup of DS could be done similarly by entering nodes one-by-one into the system. However, it is faster to load the system by sampling only in one pass, using the sampling percentage SP% that corresponds to the sum of the nodes SPi%. A probability over the individual SPi% values is then used to direct extracted samples into nodes according to their

SPi%. Periodic loads can be handled using exactly the same algorithm, with the only difference that in this case the sequential sampling is from the stream of input data being imported into the data warehouse.

DS is conceived as a set of loosely-coupled autonomous and symmetric nodes. This means that the system works regardless of the availability of individual nodes at a given moment and any of the nodes can pose queries into the system, as long as they have such privilege. For DS to work like this, when a node enters the system it not only receives a summary as it also starts its own query processing service, so that it becomes able to receive requests. The node can also receive the DS directory and starts the query submission service to be able to pose queries. When a node leaves DS permanently, it must signal the leave so that the directories in other nodes are updated (unavailable nodes must be signaled later by one of the peers when they become online). Assuming that random sampling without replacement is being used, the bitmap structure described in section 3 must also be updated.

6. Expected Speedup of DS

In this section we show analytical formulas that give an approximate idea of the expected speedup of the distributed summaries approach (DS), the DWS approach and a normal one-node summary (SW) when compared with the base data (DW).

Consider a network with N nodes running DWS: DWS(N). Consider also a summary with sampling percentage SP%: SW(SP%). Finally, consider a distributed summary DS with N nodes: DS(N,SP%).

Intuitively, as well as from experiments in our previous works (e.g. [5]), the expected speedup of a normal one-node summary SW(SP%) answering a DW query is larger than 1/SP% (the summary has only SP% of the DW data). The expected speedup of DWS(N) is about N [4](approximately linear with the number of nodes, with limitations on N and on the speedup that were discussed in section 2). The distributed summaries approach has the advantage of both SW(SP%) and DWS(N). As a result, DS(SP%,N) obtains a speedup larger than N/SP%.

To arrive at these formulas, we used a simplifying assumption that the node data exchange and result merging overheads of DWS and DS are small and therefore can be disregarded in these approximate expressions.

Using the previous formulas for the expected speedup and considering at most 5 to 20 nodes (refer to the DWS limitations discussed in section 2) and SP% between 1%..5% (plus 0.1% if the summary is only for very aggregated queries), the DWS achieves speedups of 5 to 20 times, the SW achieves 20 to 100 times (1000 times if 0.1% is used) and DS achieves 100 to 2000 times (20000 times for the 0.1% summary)! But the most important aspect is that DS is able to be simultaneously extremely fast and very accurate and the speedup is orders of magnitude larger than either SW or DWS.

7. Future Work

The DS system opens up other future work possibilities which are part of our ongoing work on the subject and we only mention here. First of all, summary construction heuristics can be used to determine the size that each summary should have and/or the minimum number of nodes needed based on the speed/accuracy tradeoff. Nodes do not need to have the same SPi%, so that faster machines can house larger summaries. There can also be more than one summary in a node, possibly with different SPi%. In this case, it is possible to use some usage or selectivity estimation data to root a query into the summary that is as fast as possible while still guaranteeing enough accuracy. Finally, load balancing is also an interesting subject in the DS context.

8. Experimental Analysis

Using data from TPC-H decision support benchmark [14], we construct an experimental setup with schemas corresponding to the base DW, and some summary sizes.

The evaluation was conducted on a Intel Pentium III 866 MHz CPU with 120 GB IDE hard disk and 256 MB of RAM, running Windows 2000 professional with an Oracle 8i(8.1.7) DBMS, running the TPC-H benchmark. Scale factors (SF) of 10 (10GB) and 100 (100GB) were used.

A query template Qa was used which is a slightly modified version of a typical TPC-H query, to test varied granularities (degrees of detail). Qa computes aggregate quantities per brand, discount and a defined time period (e.g. year, quarter, month or week). Figure 2 shows the Qa query template.

SELECT p_brand, to_char(l_shipdate,'yyyy-mm') year_month, discount,

avg(l_quantity), sum(l_quantity), count(*), max(l_quantity)

FROM   lineitem, part

WHERE   l_partkey=p_partkey

GROUP BY   to_char(l_shipdate,'yyyy-mm'), p_brand, discount

ORDER BY 1,2

Figure 2 – Qa Query Template

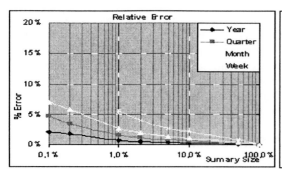 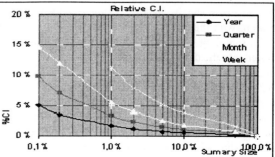

Figure 3 – Error and CI Results

8.1. Speedup

Our first experiment compares query processing time using distributed summaries(DS), the base data warehouse(DW) and the distributed data version(DWS). The objective is to show that DS is an effective strategy to obtain very fast query answers in exploration analysis. Each result was obtained by averaging over 5 runs of query Qa against the TPC-H data. For these experiments, notice that DS with one node is equivalent to a normal one node summary (SW).

Figure 4 shows results with SF=10(10GB). The query processing time (DW) varied between 3.9 hours(yearly aggregation) and 9 hours(weekly aggregation). From the figure it is possible to see that, although DWS with 15 or more nodes could deliver a significant improvement, DS can obtain almost instant answers to the same queries. For instance, the weekly aggregation took 9 hours against the DW, 54 minutes in DWS with 10 nodes and only 1 minute using DS(2%).

	N° of nodes						
	1	**2**	**3**	**5**	**10**	**15**	**20**
DW	546.4	---	---	---	---	---	---
DWS	546.4	273.2	182.1	109.3	54.72	36.55	27.48
DS(2)	8.81	4.42	2.96	1.80	0.96	0.71	0.61
DS(1)	5.35	2.69	1.81	1.11	0.62	0.48	0.43
DS(0.1)	0.51	0.27	0.20	0.14	0.13	--	--

Figure 4 – Speedup Results

8.2. Accuracy considerations

The previous results have shown that DS can be extremely fast and flexible. The speed/accuracy tradeoff means that the smaller the summary, the larger is the speedup, but with less accuracy guarantees. Figure 3 compares the accuracy (average error and confidence interval - CI - over returned group results) of alternative summary size (SP%) choices for DS considering aggregation levels over query Qa (year, quarter, month or week) run against TPC-H SF=10. Confidence intervals were set at a 90% level of confidence and individual group estimations were only returned if the maximum CI interval was within 15% of the actual group answer, otherwise a "no answer" was given.

9. Conclusions

In this paper we have proposed a solution to the need for almost instant answers to exploration analysis queries in very large data warehouses using approximate summaries. We have proposed the use of a distributed summary base to yield completely flexible and scalable speedup values. We have shown why DS solves the limitations of traditional summaries, by satisfying previously conflicting requirements of traditional summaries: that the summary must be sufficiently small to yield desired speedup and at the same time sufficiently large to yield necessary accuracy. DS uses a virtual larger summary from smaller ones in independent nodes, which compute in parallel, resulting in both extremely large speedup and good accuracy. By balancing the number of nodes and summary sizes, DS delivers both unseen speedups and enough accuracy.

We have presented the strategy of the "Distributed Summaries" approach (DS), showing that it is very flexible and loosely-coupled, with simple and flexible configuration and management strategies.

We have tested the speedup both analytically and experimentally against the data warehouse (DW), the DWS and normal summaries. We have also tested experimentally the accuracy of DS.

10. References

[1] S. Acharaya, P.B. Gibbons, and V. Poosala. "Congressional Samples for Approximate Answering of Group-By Queries", ACM SIGMOD Int. Conference on Management of Data, pp.487-498, June 2000.

[2] S. Acharaya, P.B. Gibbons, V. Poosala, and S. Ramaswamy. "Join synopses for approximate query answering", ACM SIGMOD Int. Conference on Management of Data, pp.275-286, June 1999.

[3] D. Barbara, W. DuMouchel, C. Faloutsos, P. J. Haas, J. M.Hellerstein, Y. Ioannidis, H. V. Jagadish, T. Johnson, R. Ng, V. Poosala, K. A. Ross, and K. C. Sevcik. The New Jersey data reduction report. Bulletin of the Technical Committee on Data Engineering, 20(4):3–45, 1997.

[4] Jorge Bernardino, Pedro Furtado, Henrique Madeira: DWS-AQA: A Cost Effective Approach for Very Large Data Warehouses. IDEAS 2002: 233-242.

[5] Pedro Furtado, João Pedro Costa: Time-Interval Sampling for Improved Estimations in Data Warehouses. DaWaK 2002: 327-338.

[6] Pedro Furtado, João Pedro Costa: The BofS Solution to Limitations of Approximate Summaries. DASFAA 2003.

[7] P. B. Gibbons, Y. Matias, and V. Poosala. Aqua project white paper. Technical report, Bell Laboratories, Murray Hill, New Jersey, December 1997.

[8] P. B. Gibbons and Y. Matias. New sampling-based summary statistics for improving approximate query answers. In Proc. ACM SIGMOD Int. Conference on Management of Data, pp.331–342, June 1998.

[9] P. B. Gibbons and Y. Matias. AQUA: System and Techniques for Approximate Query Answering. Bell Labs TR 1998.

[10] P. J. Haas. Large-sample and deterministic confidence intervals for online aggregation. In Proc. 9th Int. Conference on Scientific and Statistical Database Management, August 1997.

[11] Peter J. Haas. "Techniques for Online Exploration of Large Object-Relational Datasets". In Proc. 9th Int. Conference on Scientific and Statistical Database Management, SSDBM 1999, pp.4-12.

[12] J.M. Hellerstein, P.J. Haas, and H.J. Wang. "Online aggregation", ACM SIGMOD Int. Conference on Management of Data, pp.171-182, May 1997.

[13] Y. Ioannidis and V. Poosala. "Histogram-based techniques for approximating set-values query-answers", Proc. 25th Int. Conference On Very Large Databases, pp.174-185, September 1999.

[14] TPC Benchmark H, Transaction Processing Council, June 1999. Available at http://www.tpc.org/

[Vitter85] J. S. Vitter. Random sampling with a reservoir. ACM Transactions on Mathematical Software, 11(1):37-57, 1985.

[15] J. S. Vitter and M. Wang. "Approximate computation of multidimensional aggregates of sparse data using wavelets", ACM SIGMOD Int. Conference on Management of Data, pp.193-204, June 1999.

A Medium Complexity Discrete Model for Uncertain Spatial Data

Erlend Tøssebro and Mads Nygård
Department of Computer Science, Norwegian University of Science and Technology
Email: tossebro, mads@idi.ntnu.no

Abstract

This paper presents a method for representing uncertainty in spatial data in a database. The model presented requires moderate amounts of storage space. To compute the probability that an object is at a particular place, the representation employs probability functions that can be computed quickly and efficiently. This is different from an advanced model presented by the same authors. This medium complexity model is less powerful, but requires much less storage space, and computing probabilities is much less complicated.

1. Introduction

In many cases, one does not have accurate measurements of the position and shape of a geographic or spatial object. However, one often knows roughly where the object may be, and how uncertain its position or shape is. When storing such objects in a spatial or spatiotemporal database, it is therefore important not just to be able to store the fact that the object is uncertain, but to somehow store how uncertain the object is.

Spatial and spatiotemporal objects may be uncertain because the measurements needed to place the object accurately are too expensive, or because exact measurements are impossible. Two examples of this are given below. In the first example, it is theoretically possible but practically infeasible to make exact measurements. In the second example, it is impossible to measure the objects exactly.

Example 1: Imagine you have scientists who are driving around making measurements in the Sahara desert to determine the extent of underground water reservoirs. The scientists themselves are uncertain points due to the imprecision of the positioning system that they use. The roads are uncertain lines because the roads in the Sahara desert are more like routes that shift as the sand dunes move than paved roads. The water reservoirs that the scientists are studying are uncertain regions because they are located deep underground and it is therefore not feasible to do more than a few measurements at each site. The scientists there-

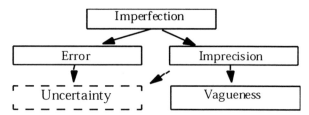

Figure 1 Hierarchy of the types of imperfection

fore lack the necessary information to define them precisely.

Example 2: In a historical spatial database[1] one may need uncertainty about all three spatial data types. The extents of ancient empires are uncertain regions, because one may not know precisely where the borders were. Rivers were important for both trade and agriculture in the past, and these rivers have shifted in their beds several times. Therefore, many rivers should be stored as uncertain lines. Some ancient cities may only be known from written records, which may be imprecise about the location of the city. Such a city should be stored as an uncertain point.

Our model should be useful in representing and manipulating cases like those described in Example 1 and Example 2.

In [2], an ontology of different kinds of uncertainty is defined. Imperfection is considered to be the general form of uncertainty. Error is when measurements do not reflect reality. Imprecision is when measurements are lacking in specificity or are incomplete. [2] considers vagueness[2], to be a subcategory of imprecision.

The basic goal of this paper is representing uncertainty in the position or extent of an object, regardless of the source of that uncertainty. In the rest of this paper, uncertainty therefore means either measurement error or imprecision due to incomplete knowledge. This definition of uncertainty is shown by the dashed box in Figure 1.

---

1. A database containing map data about ancient civilizations.
2. An example of a vague statement would be that Bergen is in the south of Norway, because the south of Norway is not clearly defined.

In [11], we gave an overview of our work on uncertainty in spatial and spatiotemporal databases. This paper will present a medium complexity discrete model, being one of three different discrete models designated in that paper. A discrete model is a model that is directly implementable, unlike abstract models that often use infinite point sets. The new model will be compared to the advanced discrete model from [12] with respect to storage requirement, how easy it is to implement some operations on them, processing speed of the operations and modelling capabilities.

The data model described in this paper has been partially implemented by the first author. All three data types have been implemented as java classes, which include some important operations on these types.

2. Related work

There are two basic discrete methods for storing spatial data, the raster and vector models. The raster model divides space into a partition (typically a grid) and stores one value in each cell. For vague data, [6] and [7] present raster models in which a fuzzy membership value is stored in each cell. Fuzzy sets [17] is a type of set in which the membership of an individual may be fuzzy, that is, have a value between 0 and 1. The problem with raster models is that the data volume quickly becomes very large if the spatial objects are to be stored accurately. The advantage of raster models is that the values of arbitrarily complex functions may be stored explicitly in the cells. Also, overlay operations in which the values from two functions are combined are much easier to compute for raster models than for vector models.

Vector models, on the other hand, store the boundary of a region as a set of line segments. This form of storage is more complex, but usually takes much less space. An example of a vector model for uncertain regions is presented in [9]. However, you cannot store probability functions with this model. One approach for storing distinct probabilities in such a model is to store a number of different regions, one inside the other, where each successive region has a higher probability than the one before. This method is used to compute fuzzy intersection in [10].

An early model for uncertain points and lines is presented in [4]. In this model, an uncertain point is stored as a central point with a circular deviation. The probability of a point being at any one place follows a bi-gaussian distribution over the deviation. Lines are made up of a series of such points. The probability of each of these potential line segments is the product of the probabilities of the two points being at those precise locations.

[8] describes a way to model uncertainty in the location of the boundary of a region that uses probabilistic error bands. This means that on each side of the estimated border there is an area with a certain width in which the border can be. Additionally, the probability that a point p is inside the area is a function of the distance from the estimated border to p.

[15] describes a model for fuzzy boundaries between regions in which the fuzzy membership function indicates how sharp the boundary is. A membership of 1.0 indicates a crisp boundary.

[1] describes several ways to extract fuzzy objects from observations. These methods use a combination of fuzzy sets and probability theory. The model that they use is a raster model because fuzzy membership values are stored in each cell. However, they also group the cells into objects according to different criteria.

[16] uses rough sets to define the outer and inner boundaries of possibly imprecise spatial objects. [16] defines resolution objects that are partitions on the underlying space, and shows how to convert objects from one resolution to another. This process may introduce imprecision even if the original representation was precise because the object may only partially overlap the new partition parts.

A discussion of the last five models compared to our work will be given in Section 7.

3. Basis for the new model

As mentioned in Section 2, there are two basic modelling techniques for creating a discrete model: raster and vector. The vector approach is chosen in this paper because rasters require much more storage space for regions, and lines may become inaccurate when stored in a raster format. Additionally, this paper presents ways to compute probability functions in a vector model, so that a raster model is no longer needed to store probability values or fuzzy set values.

Spatial data types in this paper are given names in the following format: The type name begins with an A for abstract or a D for discrete. For the uncertain types, DA means advanced discrete and DM means medium-complexity discrete. After these initial letters, the type name is given in subscript, with an initial U if the type is uncertain. For instance DM_{UPoint} is a medium-complexity discrete uncertain point.

The types for crisp spatial data listed in Table 1 will be used to define the types in this paper. These are taken from [5] with the exception of D_{Seg} and D_{Curve}. These two are different because a more specialized definition of lines is needed in the uncertain case. In this paper, the following terminology will be used for lines. A line segment is a

Table 1: Types for crisp spatial data

Type name	Type definition
D_{Point}	A single point
D_{Points}	A set of points
D_{Seg}	A single line segment consisting of a start point and an end point
D_{Curve}	A set of D_{Seg} forming a continuous line
D_{Cycle}	A D_{Curve} where the start point and end point are the same
D_{Face}	Area that has an outer cycle and a number of disjoint hole cycles
D_{Region}	Consists of a number of disjoint faces

straight line going between two points. A curve is a single continuous line that does not intersect itself. A curve consists of a set of line segments. A line is a set of curves.

The basic idea from [11] is that all uncertain objects, regardless of type, are known to be within a certain crisp region. It may also be known where the object is most likely to be. This is modelled as a function over the plane for all three types[1].

The abstract uncertain point (A_{UPoint}) is modelled as a region with a probability density function indicating where the point is most likely to be. The abstract uncertain curve (A_{UCurve}) is modelled as a core line with gradient lines crossing it, and probability functions for both of these. The probability distribution function along the core line represents uncertainty about the existence of the line and the length of the line. The probability density function along the gradient lines represents the fact that the exact location of the line is not known. These gradient lines must form a crisp face which is the area in which the line might possibly be.

The abstract uncertain face (A_{UFace}) is modelled as a probability distribution function over the plane. The set of points with function value above 0 must form a crisp face.

4. Medium complexity model

The model presented in [12] manages to model many aspects of uncertainty, but at the cost of increased complexity and increased storage space, especially for points. For applications which requires the full power of the model from [12], that model would be good. However, for many applications a simpler model may be sufficient. This section presents a model that is simpler than the model from

---

1. Points, lines and regions.

[12], while maintaining the goal of modelling all uncertain spatial data types.

In these definitions, $ProbMass(P)$ indicates that $P(x)$ is a probability mass function and $ProbFunc(P)$ indicates that $P(x)$ is a probability distribution function.

- Probability Mass Function:
$$ProbMass(P) \equiv (\forall x : P(x) \geq 0) \wedge \sum_x P(x) \leq 1$$
- Probability Distribution Function:
$$ProbFunc(P) \equiv \forall x : (P(x) \geq 0 \wedge P(x) \leq 1)$$

Probability mass functions are used whenever there is only one random variable. Because there is only one random variable, the sum of the probability masses of all possible singleton events should be at most one. For instance, an uncertain point can be at only one place. Therefore the probability distribution of an uncertain point should be a probability mass function. A simple way of storing a one dimensional probability mass function that is shaped as a series of steps is described in [3].

Probability distribution functions are used whenever there are multiple random variables. Each point that is a potential member of an uncertain region is a random variable of its own. Therefore the probability distribution of an uncertain region should be a probability distribution function.

Probabilities (DA_{Prob}) are floating point numbers between 0 and 1. In discussing the types, the number system used for coordinate values will be referred to as *CVS*. In these definitions, the *Core* is where the spatial object is known to exist. The *Support* is the region where the object has a probability greater than 0 of being. An *Alpha-Cut(object, alpha)* is the region in which the probability of the *object* being there is greater than *alpha*.

4.1. Uncertain Points

One major problem with the model for uncertain points from [12] is that the storage space needed may be far larger than that needed for crisp points. If the database models mainly points and if storage space is an issue, models requiring less storage space may be needed. One way to limit the amount of storage space needed is to limit the number of points that make up the boundary of support of the uncertain point. One natural way of doing this would be to store the distance from the central point to the boundary of the support at certain predefined angles, such as every 45 degrees. An example of such an uncertain point is shown in Figure 2.

The probability mass values of the uncertain point can now be computed based on the relative distance from the central point and the edge of the support.

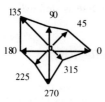

Figure 2: Medium complexity uncertain point with eight angles

Definition 1: The **uncertain point** is defined as follows:

$$DM_{UPoint} \equiv \{(a_0 a_1 a_2 \dots a_{N-1}, cp, ps, pe) |$$
$$a_{i|i=0\dots N-1} \in CVS \wedge cp \in D_{Point} \wedge$$
$$ProbMass(ps) \wedge pe \in DA_{Prob} \wedge$$
$$Increasing(ps)\}$$

The disadvantage of this model compared to the previous one is that it cannot model holes, and that it can only model uncertain points in which there is a straight line from the central point to any point in the support.

Another problem with this model is that the results of spatial set operations such as finding the intersection of an uncertain point and a face[1] are not necessarily members of the base type. They are not members because the result can have corners in different places than on the particular angles that are stored for the uncertain points. One solution is to store the normal point and to indicate that the probability mass function is the product of the normal probability mass function and the probability distribution function of the face. This problem does not occur in the advanced model from [12] because the support of the point can be an arbitrary face in that model.

One advantage of this model compared to the advanced one is that the storage space needed is known and bounded. Storing a single distance for every 45 degrees yields eight numbers. Because the central point needs two and the probability mass function requires one, this means that the uncertain point takes 11 numbers to store, or 5.5 times as much as a crisp point. For a number of angles n, the uncertain point takes $((n/2)+1.5)$ times as much space.

An alternative to this model might be to store a variable number of distances and angles. This would require that the angle was also explicitly stored and would have the problem of an arbitrary number of angles. This means that such a solution is essentially the same as the one presented in [12]. To conserve storage space, one would have to limit the number of angles and distances stored.

The **uncertain points** set type is a set containing only DM_{UPoint} values.

---

1. This is the part of the support of the uncertain point that is inside the face.

4.2. Uncertain Lines

The storage cost for an uncertain curve in the model from [12] is 3.75 times that of a crisp curve. This section will describe a model which takes somewhat less space. Another advantage is that it is very easy to compute probabilities for this model. The method for doing this will be described in Section 5. One disadvantage is that the model presented here does not allow holes in the support. Another problem is that spatial set operations, such as finding the parts of an uncertain line that is inside a given region, may require some additional support. This problem is further discussed in [14].

The basic idea is to store a central line, as well as crossing lines for each stored point along the central line. These crossing lines are equally long on each side of the central line, and determine the extent of the support of the line. These crossing lines are the "gradient lines" from [11] for the end points of each line segment. In the interior of the line segment, the gradient lines have an angle which is linearly interpolated between the two gradient lines at the end. The support of the uncertain curve is determined by taking straight lines between the ends of all the crossing curves. Straight lines are used to make it easier to run plane-sweep algorithms on the support.

One example of a line stored in this fashion is shown in Figure 3. From this figure, one can clearly see how the crossing lines determine the shape of the support of the uncertain line.

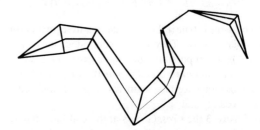

Figure 3: Medium complexity uncertain curve

The only aspects that need to be stored about the crossing lines (Hereafter called *CrossCurves*) are the length of the line and the angle between the line and the segment to which it belongs.

Definition 2: The **CrossCurve** is defined as follows:

$$D_{CCur} \equiv \{(a, b) | (a \in CVS \wedge b \in ANG)\}$$

In this formula, *ANG* is an angle. Angles are represented with floating-point numbers.

A line segment in this model may be defined as a single line segment of the central curve and the *CrossCurves* at each end of it. Each line segment contains a probability distribution function indicating how likely it is that the actual line exists in the various parts of the segment as well as its probability of existing at the beginning and end. The line segment also contains a probability mass function which applies along the *CrossCurves*. Storing the probability mass function in the segment rather than for the entire curve makes one able to use different functions for different parts of the curve. However, there will be discontinuities in the probability values if the function changes. Therefore, most curves should use a single function throughout the curve. The option to use different probability functions is there to enable union and intersection operations on uncertain regions with different probability functions (See Section 4.3).

Definition 3: The medium complexity **uncertain segment** is defined as follows:

$DM_{USeg} \equiv \{(cc, bc, ec, pb, pe, pf, pc) \mid$
$cc \in D_{Seg} \wedge bc \in D_{CCur} \wedge ec \in D_{CCur} \wedge pb \in DA_{Prob} \wedge$
$pe \in DA_{Prob} \wedge ProbFunc(pf) \wedge ProbMass(pc) \wedge$
$CenteredOn(bc, cc.sp) \wedge CenteredOn(ec, cc.ep)\}$

CenteredOn means that the given point is on the middle of the *CrossCurve*.

Definition 4: The medium complexity **uncertain curve** is defined as follows:

$DM_{Ucurve} \equiv \{(SS, pe) \mid$
$SS \subseteq DM_{USeg} \wedge pe \in DA_{Prob} \wedge$
$ContCurve(SS) \wedge$
$\forall a \in SS, \forall b \in SS, a \neq b \rightarrow \neg Ccross(a, b)\}$

ContCurve is true if the set of uncertain segments forms a continuous curve. They form a continuous curve iff for all $a \in SS$ except possibly one[1], there exists a $b \in SS$ such that $(a.cc.endpoint = b.cc.begpoint) \wedge (a.ec = b.bc)$ is true. *Ccross* for uncertain segments is true iff their central curves cross.

In Figure 3 the *CrossCurves* at the end have length 0. To model a crisp curve, all the *CrossCurves* should have length 0.

Compared to a crisp line, the *CrossCurves* and function references have an additional cost. A single *CrossCurve* contains two numbers. That means that the two crosscurves in the uncertain segment require four numbers. The uncertain segment requires four numbers. The probability values require two numbers. The probability functions require two numbers. Because a crisp line segment can be stored with four numbers, an uncertain line segments takes 12/4=3 times as much space as a crisp one. This is only slightly better than for the advanced model.

---

1. The last segment.

The **uncertain line** is defined as a set of uncertain curves.

4.3. Uncertain Regions

One problem with both the abstract model from [13] and the model presented in [12] is that the border of an uncertain region sometimes is not a valid uncertain line. This may be solved by defining the uncertain face the same way as the crisp face with the exception that uncertain cycles are used instead of crisp ones. An example of such a face is shown in Figure 4. An uncertain hole in the core can be stored in this model by using an uncertain cycle which is not certain to exist.

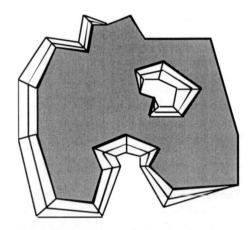

Figure 4: Medium complexity uncertain face

Definition 5: The **uncertain cycle** is defined as follows:

$DM_{UCyc} \equiv \{sc \in DM_{UCurve} \mid$
$IsCycle(sc.SS) \wedge ConstProb(sc.SS)\}$

In this definition, *IsCycle* means that the set of uncertain segments forms a cycle. A set of uncertain segments forms a cycle iff both the central line and the outer lines form cycles, all of the segments have $D_{USeg}pf = 1.0$ for all the points along the segment, and the probabilities of existence of all the segments are the same. *ConstProb* means that all the line segments in the set have the same constant probability of existing.

A hole in the support of an uncertain region is stored like a regular hole. When computing probabilities or isolines, one computes these for both the outer line and the uncertain hole. If one uses fuzzy set mathematics, which are less accurate but easier to compute, alpha-cuts can be produced by taking the alpha-cut of the main face and subtracting the same alpha-cut of the hole. When using probability theory it becomes more complex because the functions are multiplied together rather than taking the maximum or minimum.

This model cannot store a face with multiple core regions directly. This can only be done by storing several faces that have overlapping supports but non-overlapping cores in the same uncertain region.

However, it is very easy to determine the probability function at individual points as well as iso-lines of probability. In Section 5 it will be shown that this is even easier for these regions than it is for medium complexity uncertain lines.

The uncertain face also uses a different kind of probability function than the uncertain curve. In the gray area enclosed by the cycles, the probability of existence is always 1. Inside the supports of the uncertain cycles, the probability of existence is the sum of the probability mass function of the uncertain curve taken from outside and inward. To avoid having to compute this, it might be better to store this sum directly as a function rather than storing the probability mass function for the curves. If the function of the curves is also needed by the application, both may be stored together.

The definition of the uncertain face is taken from [5] and modified to use uncertain cycles.

Definition 6: The **uncertain face** is defined as follows:

$$DM_{UFace} \equiv \{(bc, HS, ps, pe) |$$
$$bc \in DM_{UCyc} \land HS \subseteq DM_{UCyc} \land$$
$$ProbFunc(ps) \land pe \in DA_{Prob} \land$$
$$\forall a \in HS \rightarrow EdgeInside(a, bc) \land$$
$$\forall a \in HS, \forall b \in HS, a \neq b \rightarrow EdgeDisjoint(a, b) \land$$
$$bc.sc.pe \equiv 1\}$$

In this definition, *EdgeInside* means that all the line segments of *a* are in the interior of the cycle defined by *bc* with 100% certainty, and *EdgeDisjoint* means that the interiors of two cycles are certainly disjoint. The sum of a probability mass function is a probability distribution function. Therefore, *ps* is a probability distribution function. *Existence* is the probability that an uncertain object exists.

The definition of the **uncertain region** is a set of non-overlapping uncertain faces.

To make this model computationally closed under normal set operations, ways of dealing with uncertain curves that cross each other must be introduced. In Figure 5, the union and intersection of two example objects are shown. From this figure, one can see that the results of such set operations contain places in which one have to use just parts of some uncertain segments. The dotted lines from the figure shows where the segments are divided. This line also separates between segments that originated in the two curves.

However, this does not solve the problem when there is one or more *CrossCurves* inside the area in which the lines may possibly intersect. The solution to this problem is omitted due to space constraints. It is described in [14].

The increase in storage space for an uncertain region compared to a crisp region in this model is the same as for the uncertain curve (3X). This means that it actually costs slightly more storage space to store an uncertain region in this model than one stored in the model from [12].

However, for this slight increase in storage space, we gain the ability to compute alpha-cuts and the probability that a given crisp point is inside the region in an efficient and consistent manner. This is very difficult for the model from [12].

5. Storing and computing probability functions

The goal of this section is to find ways of using one-dimensional functions to compute the probabilities or probability densities rather than two-dimensional ones. This is done because one-dimensional functions are much easier to define for the user of the system and much easier to store and compute for the computer.

For the following algorithm to work, the probability functions should be functions that accept input values from

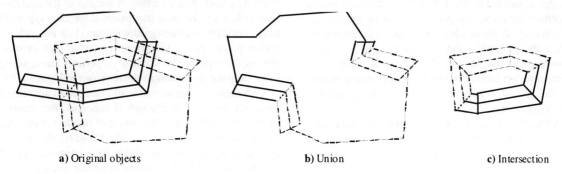

a) Original objects   b) Union   c) Intersection

Figure 5: Union and intersection of medium complexity regions

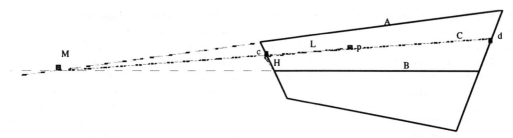

Figure 6: Computing probability values for medium complexity uncertain segments

0 to 1. The actual distances should be scaled to be between 0 and 1.

For the **lines** and **regions** in the medium complexity model, computing the probability functions is easy. In the end points of each uncertain line segment, the probability is computed along the *CrossCurves*. In the interior of **regions**, the function value for a point p should be computed as follows:

1. Take the lines A and B (the central line) from Figure 6 and compute the point M in which they intersect
2. Compute the line C from M to p.
3. Compute the point c or d where the line C crosses the *CrossCurves*.
4. Compute the distance H between the point c and the central curve B along the *CrossCurve*.
5. Find how long H is compared to the *CrossCurve*. This ratio determines the value of the probability distribution function for point p.

Two special cases need to be considered. The first is if the lines A and B are parallel, because in this case there is no meeting point M. In this case, the line C should be parallel to A and B and go through p.

The second is if the line A has length 0. In this case the line A becomes the point a. Compute the line K that passes through both a and p. H is now the distance from p to the line B along K, and the ratio from 5) uses the length of K instead of the length of the *CrossCurve*.

This method of computing probabilities has several advantages compared to other models. In Dutton's model for uncertain lines, one would need to take the sum of the probabilities of all the possible lines that might cross p to determine the probability that the line was in p. This is much more costly than the procedure outlined above.

Computing iso-lines of the probability is also simple in the model presented here. The iso-line passing through point p in Figure 6 is line C.

For **lines**, the process to compute individual probability values is similar to the process for regions described above. The process for lines requires one more step:

6. Find how long the distance L is compared to the distance between c and d. This ratio is used to find the probability that the curve exists at point p.

This probability is then multiplied with the probability value from step 5.

One also uses a probability mass function along the gradient lines rather than a distribution function. This mass function needs to be normalized to yield a sum of 1 regardless of the length of the gradient. Instead of using H and the length of the *CrossCurve* to determine the probability function, one has to find the length of the gradient that passes through p. The angle between this line and line B is linearly interpolated. Because the length of L is known, this ratio is easy to determine. One then needs to find where this gradient crosses A and B. Then the distance between A and B along the gradient and the location of p on the gradient is used to determine the value of the probability mass function.

For lines, computing iso-lines of a given probability is only slightly harder than for regions as long as the probability functions are linear. If both $DM_{USeg}.pf$ and $DM_{USeg}.pc$ are linear, the iso-lines will be straight lines. Then one just needs to compute the location of the iso-lines along the *CrossCurve*s.

6. Implementation

The model presented in this paper has been implemented as a set of java classes. A number of the operations from [14] have also been implemented for these types. The implementation was designed with one class for each type (point, points, curve, line, face, region) as well as superclasses for types with common properties. Some screenshots from the implementation are shown in Figure 7.

Although set operations for all types are fundamentally based on the same mathematical concepts, they must be implemented differently. The union of two sets of uncertain points can be performed normally. However, the union of two uncertain regions must check for overlaps between the member faces and join together those that overlap. This is because the semantics of union for regions is a union of the

a) Two uncertain curves   b) Support of one of the uncertain curves   c) Core of an uncertain face

Figure 7: Screen shots from the implementation

set of points that is contained in the region, not a union of the face sets.

As we have used fuzzy set mathematics instead of the more complex probability theory, some operations are fairly easy to implement. For instance, it is possible to handle holes in uncertain faces that overlap with the support. However, fuzzy set mathematics yields less accurate results for uncertainty. The full discussion on this is omitted due to space constraints, but may be found in [14].

7. Discussion

This paper has presented a new discrete model for storing uncertain spatial data. The advantages of this model over the advanced model from [12] is that it takes much less storage space and that the probability functions are much easier to compute. One problem with this model is that it cannot model holes in lines. It also cannot easily model faces with disjoint cores but single support. Thus it is less expressive than the advanced model. It also has the problem that a special construct has to be defined to make them computationally closed for regions. The advanced model does not need any special considerations for this.

Compared with earlier models, the major advantage of the new model for spatial data is that it can model all the normal spatial data types. [4] only describes modelling points and lines, although it is simple to extend his model to regions. An advantage of the model presented here over the model from [4] is that it is much easier to compute the probability values. In [4], only the points have a probability function, and to compute the probabilities of the line passing through a given point, one has to take the integral of all possible placements of the two end points which would yield a line passing through the given point. This integral is infeasible to perform in practise in a database system, although it could be done numerically in a simulator in which one has a lot of time available.

The approaches for storing imprecise regions in [8] and [15] are similar to our approach in that they store the uncertainty in the border line. However, they cannot store lines and points. These models are also more abstract in nature than this model as they base themselves on continuous lines rather than line segments.

The models from [1] and [16] are essentially rasters, which means that they can store complex functions but take a lot of storage space.

Compared to [9], our model is able to store more types of data and is also able to store probability functions. The method for computing fuzzy intersection from [10] is very costly if one desires high accuracy because one would have to store many regions, one inside the other. Our method produces fairly accurate results with a much lower storage requirement.

The different advantages and drawbacks of the model presented here and the advanced model presented in [12] show that none of the two models are obviously superior to the other. One should choose which to use based on what data one has and which functionality and operations one needs.

Storing spatial uncertainty takes more space than only storing crisp data. How much depends on the model chosen. For the model presented here, uncertain lines and region require three times as much space and uncertain points take 5.5 times more space than crisp ones. This is a smaller increase than in [12], but still significant.

Because the model presented here models points, lines and regions in a uniform way, it is better suited to databases like Example 1 than previous models which handles only one or two of the types. The types presented here are better integrated than a system consisting of a point model, a line model and a region model from different authors chosen because they are good models for the individual types. We are currently working on the issue of the completeness and computational closeness of this model. Converting from line to region (*enclosed_by* operation) and from region to line (*border* operation) is trivial in this model because the border line of an uncertain face is explicitly stored in the face. Such conversion from point to line (*connecting_line* operation) and line to point (*end_points* operation) will be published elsewhere. Of course, conversion from point to region and vice versa is not applicable.

The time taken to process data depends on the operation. Plane-sweep algorithms typically take $O(n*\log(n))$ time. However, these do not usually run on all the points at once. For regions with only spatial uncertainty, they run on the core region and the support region separately. Therefore the increase in processing cost is proportional to the increase in data stored. This is also true for uncertain lines, although the support here normally takes twice as much space as a crisp line. This means that an operation on the core will take somewhat longer compared to the size of the line than operations on crisp lines would. Only for points is there an increase in processing cost significantly greater than the data increase, because operations that before only had to operate on a single point now have to operate on the support of the point, which consists of eight points.

References

[1] T. Cheng, M. Molenaar, T. Bouloucos: Identification of Fuzzy Objects from Field Observation Data. In S. C. Hirtle and A. U. Frank (eds.) *Spatial Information Theory: A Theoretical Foundation for GIS*, LNCS vol. 1329, Springer-Verlag, 1997, pages 241-259.

[2] M. Duckham, K. Mason, J. Stell, M. Worboys: A formal approach to imperfection in geographic information. In *Computers, Environment and Urban Systems*, 25, 2001, pages 89-103.

[3] C. E. Dyreson and R. T. Snodgrass: Supporting Valid-time Indeterminacy. In *ACM Trans. on Database Systems*, vol. 23, no. 1, pages 1-57.

[4] G. Dutton: Handling Positional Uncertainty in Spatial Databases. In *Proc. SDH'92*, vol. 2, pages 460-469

[5] L. Forlizzi, R. H. Güting, E. Nardelli and M. Schneider: A Data Model and Data Structures for Moving Objects Databases. In *Proc. ACM SIGMOD Int. Conf. on Management og Data* (Dallas, Texas), pages 319-330, 2000

[6] P. Lagacherie, P. Andrieux and R. Bouzigues (1996): Fuzziness and Uncertainty of Soil Boundaries: From Reality to Coding in GIS: In *Geographic Objects with Indeterminate Boundaries*, GISDATA series vol. 2, Taylor & Francis, 1996, pages 155-169.

[7] K. Lowell: An Uncertainty-Based Spatial Representation for Natural Resources Phenomena. In *Proc. SDH'94* vol. 2, pages 933-944.

[8] D. M. Mark and F. Csillag: The nature of boundaries of 'area-class' maps. In *Cartographica*, 26, 1989, pages 65-77.

[9] M. Schneider: Modelling Spatial Objects with Undeterminate Boundaries using the Realm/ROSE Approach. In *Geographic Objects with Indeterminate Boundaries*, GISDATA series vol. 2, Taylor & Francis, 1996, pages 155-169.

[10] M. Schneider: Fuzzy Spatial Querying Based on Topological Predicates for Complex Crisp and Fuzzy Regions. In *Proc. ER2001 Conference*, pages 103-116.

[11] E. Tøssebro and M. Nygård: Abstract and Discrete Models for Uncertain Spatiotemporal Data. In *Proc. 14th Int. Conf. on Scientific and Statistical Databases (SSDBM)*, page 240, July 2002.

[12] E. Tøssebro and M. Nygård: An Advanced Discrete Model for Uncertain Spatial Data. In *Proc. 3rd Int. Conference on Web-Age Information Management (WAIM02)*, pages 37-51, 2002.

[13] E. Tøssebro and M. Nygård: Representing Uncertainty in Spatial Databases. *Submitted for publication*.

[14] E. Tøssebro: Representing uncertainty in spatiotemporal databases. Ph.D. Thesis.

[15] F. Wang and G. B: Hall: Fuzzy representation of geographical boundaries in GIS. In *Int. Journal of Geographical Information Systems*, 10(5), 1996, pages 573-590.

[16] M. F. Worboys: Imprecision in Finite Resolution Spatial Data. In *GeoInformatica*, 2(3), 1998, pages 257-279.

[17] L. A. Zadeh (1965): Fuzzy sets. In *Information and Control*, 8, pages 338-353, 1965

A CBIR-framework:
using both syntactical and semantical information
for image description

Laurent Besson, Arnaud Da Costa
Eric Leclercq, Marie-Noëlle Terrasse
Laboratoire LE2I - Université de Bourgogne - France
E-mail:firstname.lastname@u-bourgogne.fr

Abstract

Content-based image retrieval systems can use classification or indexing based on syntactical and/or semantical features of images. We aim at providing a framework which can be instantiated for each specific application: a framework which combines syntactical and semantical information for image description. We believe that a model which integrates syntatical and semantical descriptions, together with its similarity measure between images, is the core of such a framework. In this paper, we propose an integrated model with two example applications on which expressiveness of our model have been tested.

1 Introduction

Expressiveness of modeling languages and increasing power of computers have made it possible for images to become essential for information exchange in many different fields. Such a wide use of images makes their retrieval one of the major issues in image databases. Image retrieval remains a difficult task since it has to cope with a two-fold problem of information volume. First, an image database contains a huge number of images, with multiple images of a database referring to the same event of the real world. Second, each image itself is complex and thus it corresponds to a significant amount of data. Image databases generally provide users with two types of tools (i.e., classification and indexing), each of them solving one of the above volume problems. Classification and indexing replace an actual database with a virtual one. Classification represents similar images within an actual database by a single image, while indexing replaces actual images by simplified images. Classification is well adapted to users that need an overview of a database content, while indexing is well adapted to users that search databases for a particular image.

In order to classify an image database, it is necessary to define criteria for similarity of images. In the same way, in order to index an image database, it is necessary to define criteria for simplification of images. Thus implementations of classification or indexing need to define a measure of distance between images. Such a mechanism must reflect the chosen criteria (for classification or indexing). Criteria for similarity or simplification of images can be based either on syntactical or semantical features of images. Syntactical information is extracted from physical representation of images [3, 5, 12] (e.g., color histograms, textures, shapes). Semantical information must be attached to images by users (typically experts) through image annotations (objects and their relationships, keywords, etc.). Syntactical information is an objective criterium in the sense that it is easily computed from an image, yet it may be difficult to use since it does not agree with the human perception model of images. Semantical information is a subjective criterium which is well adapted to users sharing the annotation perspective with annotating experts. Since extraction of images can be invoked by different types of users (experts or non-experts of image retrieval systems, experts or non-experts of the domain, having or not having a common point of view), it would be harmful to rely extensively on annotations. Various systems have been designed by choosing basic mechanisms (indexing or classification) and features of images (syntactical or semantical) [6, 7, 9, 10, 11, 13].

Our framework, which is illustrated in Figure 1, aims to provide image database designers with convenient tools for image retrieval (classification or indexing based on syntactical or semantical features of images). These tools can be combined according to the needs of a given application. Our framework is meant to be instantiated for each specific application. Based on such an objective, the core of our framework is a model of images which can support integrated descriptions of syntax and semantics of images, together with a corresponding measure of similarity between

385

images. Such an integrated model can receive information from various pre-defined information extractors. Physical extractors search images for physical parameters such as average values of color, energy, etc. Geometrical extractors search images for plain geometrical shapes (e.g., circles, triangles, rectangles) which have a continuous border or a uniform color or texture. Semantical extractors –working under control of a domain expert– enable users to attach meta-data to images. We require our framework to allow a combination of several different extractors for a given application: all pieces of information provided by the chosen extractors being integrated into our model. We plan to develop –as soon as possible– a library of strategies for extractor combination and combined retrieval.

The rest of the paper is organized as follows: Section 2 presents our integrated model and its similarity measure. Section 3 presents two examples of prototype design by instantiating our framework. These prototypes have been used for validation of expressiveness of our model for geometrical, spatial and semantical features.

2 The core of our framework: a model and its similarity measure

Within our model images are described at two different levels. The global level describes an image in terms of global attributes, i.e. attributes which apply to the whole image. The local level describes an image as a collection of objects with their individual, i.e. local, attributes. Both levels contains syntactical and semantical descriptions. Our model, as well as the similarity function associated with it, are generic and are thus usable for a large number of applications. Some issues (relevant only to special applications domains) are not developed in this article: we just illustrate such application-related issues on two examples.

First, consider the issue of choosing fundamental features of images. For example, in our archaeological database (see Section 3.2), color is not used to describe objects. On one hand, our database is composed of air photographs taken using various techniques and during different seasons, thus the same object can appear in different colors in different images. On the other hand, in this application, shape is an essential parameter.

Second, relevance of the use of certain relations can vary from one application to another. For example, direction relations may not have any interest. As a consequence, it is necessary to instantiate our model for each specific application.

In the following sections, we first present main features of image descriptions (Section 2.1), the basis of formal definition of our model (Section 2.2), and the computation of the similarity measure (Section 2.3).

2.1 Main features of image descriptions

Global syntactic descriptions of images are sets of physical attributes which can be automatically extracted from images. A global syntactic attribute of an image is either an average value or a representative value. Global semantic descriptions of images are provided by experts who are in charge of image annotations. Local descriptions of images are defined through a set of objects that appear in an image. Since objects that compose an image can be very complex, local descriptions rely upon the hierarchy of objects: an image is decomposed into inter-related objects (level-one objects and their relations). Each level-one object can be decomposed into related objects (level-two objects and relations), etc. At any level of the hierarchy, local descriptions of images have two components: objects and relations among them. In order to structure local descriptions of images, we propose a three-fold perspective on images, i.e., syntactical, spatial, and semantical descriptions.

Syntactical description of an image contains all syntactical objects that can be found within the image. Syntactical objects are discovered by shape detection. Depending on the application, detection of shapes can rely on contour or texture detection, etc. Our choice is to enable more or less accurate shape-based detection of syntactical objects, e.g., we allow the use of fuzzy objects.

Spatial description of images are given in terms of spatial relations between pairs of objects: topological relations, distances, and direction relations. Spatial relations need to be extended in order to be applicable to fuzzy objects. In [1] we have presented our definition of fuzzy direction relations.

Semantical descriptions of images consist of semantical annotations of objects and semantic relations between objects. Since both syntactical and spatial levels of descriptions can be fuzzy, guarding conditions to semantical annotations may be necessary.

2.2 Towards formalization of image descriptions

Image descriptions rely upon object descriptions by tuples consisting of: an object identification (denoted by idf), a level (denoted lev), a geometry (denoted by geo), tuples of physical and semantical attributes (denoted by $PAtt$ and $SAtt$, respectively), a set of component objects (denoted by S) which lie at the $lev + 1$ level, and a multi-relation between component objects (denoted by $\Re$). Let us denote by Obj an object with such a description:

$$Obj =< idf, lev, geo, PAtt, SAtt, S, \Re > \quad (1)$$

The multi-relation $\Re$ of an image description contains both spatial and semantic relations. For a given image database, we denote by p and m the numbers of spatial and semantic relations, respectively. Thus, the multi-relation tuple is divided in two parts: $\mathfrak{R}_{sp} =< sp_1, ..., sp_p >$ whose elements are spatial relations and $\mathfrak{R}_{sem} =< sem_1, ..., sem_m >$ whose elements are semantical relations:

$$\mathfrak{R} =< sp_1, ..., sp_p, sem_1, ..., sem_m > \qquad (2)$$

We consider two special cases of structure of a multi-relation. If a multi-relation is such that $m = 0$, then $\mathfrak{R}_{sem}$ is an empty set and we have a purely spatial model for an image database. If a multi-relation is such that $p = 0$, then $\mathfrak{R}_{sp}$ is an empty set and we have a purely semantic model for an image database.

We also distinguish simple objects (whose set of component objects S is empty) from composed objects (whose set of components is non-empty). We note that the multi-relation $\mathfrak{R}$ of a simple object is an empty tuple.

Finally, an image I is described as an object at level zero:

$$I =< idf, 0, geo, PAtt, SAtt, S, \mathfrak{R} > \qquad (3)$$

One of our short-term objectives is to introduce a partially automated tool for propagation of attribute values for objects that are linked by a whole-part relation or by an inclusion relation.

2.3 Computing similarity between images

In order for our model to be useful, we need to define how to compare two images described in our model. Such a similarity function assigns a similarity index to a pair of images. A similarity index is a real value in $[0, 1]$. If two images are identical, the similarity index is 1. The similarity index decreases with differences between images. In this section, we consider the case of a query by image content and we compute a similarity between two images: a query image Q given by the user and an image I from the database.

Consider two images, denoted by Q and I, that are represented –in our model– by a hierarchy of composed and simple objects connected by relations. Q is the query-image and I is a database-image. The similarity $S(Q, I)$ between Q and I is a weighted sum of two partial similarities. The first partial similarity, which we call object similarity, $s_o(Q, I)$ is based on the objects of Q and I. The second partial similarity, which we call relation similarity, $s_r(Q, I)$ is due to the relations of Q and I. As the model uses both a decomposition of the image into objects and a a description of the relations between these objects the image modeled can be consedered as a graph in which the nodes are the objects and the arcs are the relations. Thus we use graph-matching approaches [2] to compute our partial similarities/ We associate each object of the query image Q

with one object from I, based upon their locations in the hierarchies of objects composing Q and I. The object similarity of images Q and I is based on object associations. Their relation similarity is computed recursively by using elementary distances between pairs of associated relations.

We presume that we have already defined –depending on the application domain– similarity functions for each attribute, as well as for each type of relation (direction, topological, etc.).

3 Experimentation

We have conducted two experiments to validate instantiation of the generic platform for specialized applications. Corresponding architectures are described in Figure 1. Our first instantiation has been directed towards the use of syntactic features for classifying images from a paleontological image database. Such a prototype provides users with an automatic classification mechanism (which enables non-expert users to browse the database). The syntactic extractor relies upon earlier research work on wavelet transform developed in our laboratory. Our second experiment consists in integrating semantic, spatial, and geometric data. Such experiment has been carried out on an image database of air photographs of archaeological sites of Burgundy.

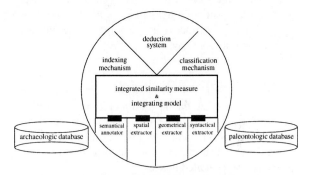

Figure 1. Two example architectures produced by instantiating our framework

3.1 Syntactic classification

The work carried out by Arnaud Da Costa (Master Thesis in French) aims to develop and validate the syntactic part of our framework. It has been conducted by validating the syntactic extractor level and the physical component of our model. This work is based on multi-level descriptions of images computed using wavelet transform. The extraction of physical features based on wavelet transform has been developed by J. Landré [5]. We have used a subset of the Burgundy University's paleontological image database[1]. The goal is to use multi-resolution capabilities of wavelet transform in order to produce a summary of images for classification of the database. The database is classified by using visual resolution and physical parameters extracted from each image at a given resolution level.

3.1.1 Extraction of syntactic features

The wavelet transform provides a multi-level physical description images: when we increase the level of the transform, visual resolution of images decreases. Thus, the volume of data characterizing the image also decreases. The extraction of physical parameters is based on this property.

Let us denote an image by I and the corresponding approximative image at resolution i by I_i. We use three levels of resolution for the wavelet transform (with approximative images denoted by A_1, A_2, and A_3). On each level, we obtain three descriptions representing the horizontal, vertical and diagonal details of the image. Physical parameters characterizing an image are then extracted from the approximative images A_1, A_2, A_3. Physical parameters such as standardized energy or average of the color histogram are extracted from detailed images.

The syntactic extractor provides a triple of physical parameters for each image. Each element of the triple matches one level of the wavelet transform. Our model is instantiated as follows in order to realize a prototype. For a given image I, its approximative image at the resolution i is represented in our model by:

$$I_i = <A_i, i, null, <PAtt>, <SAtt>,$$
$$\{I_{i+1}, V_{i+1}, H_{i+1}, D_{i+1}\}, null >$$

where $<PAtt>$ are physical attributes extracted from the image at the resolution i (i.e., I_i itself) and $\{I_{i+1}, V_{i+1}, H_{i+1}, D_{i+1}\}$ represents the next level of the wavelet transform. For this precise instantiation of the model, semantical attributes are used to discriminate approximate and detailed images:

$$SAtt \in \{'small\ image', 'horizontal\ details',$$
$$'vertical\ details', 'diagonal\ details'\}.$$

Since the component $\mathcal{R}$ is null in this instantiation of the model, the similarity between two images Q and I is reduced to object similarity, i.e., $S(Q, I) = s_o(Q, I)$. The object similarity of images Q and I is a similarity between physical attributes of the components I_i, V_i, H_i, D_i. Distance between physical attributes is not defined for attributes extracted from components of different types (see semantical attributes) or from different levels of resolution. Thus evaluation of the similarity measure of Q_i and I_i can be performed only if $SAtt_{Q_i} = SAtt_{I_i}$.

[1] U.M.R. 5561 CNRS, Université de Bourgogne. URL *"http://www.u-bourgogne.fr/BIOGEOSCIENCE/ttf2.html"*.

3.1.2 Syntactic extractor

Our syntactic extractor uses physical parameters extracted from the wavelet transform in order to compute summaries of images. The syntactic extraction proceeds in four phases: conversion of the images into levels of gray, transformation of images to reduce the number of pixels to 256×256 pixels[2], wavelet transform to obtain three levels of resolution (Figure 2, top), and computation of physical parameters on each level of the transformed images.

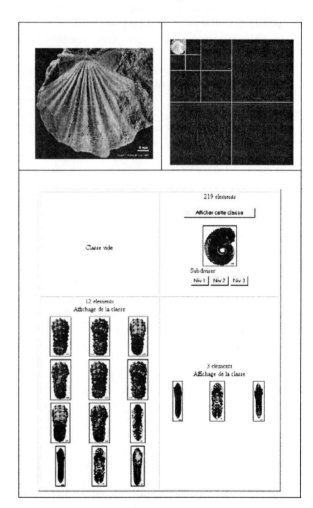

Figure 2. Top: an image of a shell transformed into gray and scaled to 256×256 **pixels; the 3 levels wavelet transform of the image. Bottom: screenshot of the user interface representing a step of the classification algorithm**

[2] In the general case, images are reduced to $2^n \times 2^n$ pixels.

3.1.3 Classification and navigation

The purpose of classification mechanisms is to dynamically divide the whole database into classes of images — if possible homogeneous and clearly discriminated. We use n parameters computed by the syntactic extractor to build a characteristic vector for each image. Then, we use the k-means algorithm to obtain a first partitioning of the space of characteristic vectors. At each iteration of the algorithm we present c classes to users. For each class, either we choose a representative image[3] for the class (if the number of elements in a class is larger than a given threshold) or we display all the images of the class. This process is performed each time the user selects a class. A change of the level of resolution is carried out manually by the user when he/she thinks that the level of resolution is no longer sufficient to discriminate classes produced by two successive steps of the algorithm. Figure 2 (bottom) presents a screenshot of the user interface during the navigation.

3.2 Archaeological experimentation

We have been working on a project of building an image database from a collection of slides and paper notes. Slides represent views of potential archaeological sites in Burgundy. These pictures have been taken from planes, over a period of more than thirty years, using various types of photography (e.g., standard or infra-red photography). Each picture has been annotated: description sheets contain meta-data (e.g., precise locations and dates), as well as archaeological information. We have chosen to build our specific model for this application by decomposing an image into geometrical objects (since we are interested in components of buildings). Spatial relationships (e.g., distance, direction, and adjacency) between objects are automatically calculated. Semantic annotations of objects and semantical relationships are specified by domain experts.

The particular architecture we propose is based on a *geometrical extractor* for extraction of geometric objects. Such objects are visible within the image: they can either be modern infrastructures or archaeological remains (e.g., traces of walls, parts of cobbling or paving). Modern infrastructures are generally fully visible. Archaeological remains are generally partially visible. Geometrical extractors can be based on various proposals [4, 8].

A *semantical annotator* is used to associate archaeological keywords with objects. Semantic annotations are partially produced from paper records associated with images, under control of a domain expert.

A *spatial extractor* is used to evaluate distances and direction relations between objects. In this particular case,

---

[3]E.g., an image nearest to the center of gravity of the class.

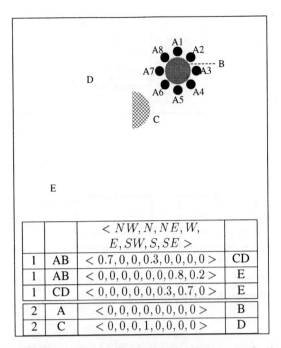

		$< NW, N, NE, W,$ $E, SW, S, SE >$	
1	AB	$< 0.7, 0, 0, 0.3, 0, 0, 0, 0 >$	CD
1	AB	$< 0, 0, 0, 0, 0, 0, 0.8, 0.2 >$	E
1	CD	$< 0, 0, 0, 0, 0, 0.3, 0.7, 0 >$	E
2	A	$< 0, 0, 0, 0, 0, 0, 0, 0 >$	B
2	C	$< 0, 0, 0, 1, 0, 0, 0, 0 >$	D

Figure 3. Archaeological image: geometrical extraction and direction relationships

grouping of objects into a complex object is based on distance (we propose to group objects that are close to each other). Since objects associated with archaeological remains have very imprecise borders, we have developed a set of fuzzy direction relations [1] based on bounding boxes of X and Y coordinates of objects. As depicted in Figure 3, a direction measure between objects contains eight values (all between 0 and 1) which correspond to North-West, North, North-East, West, East, South-West, South, and South-East, respectively.

Our combination strategy for extractors is based on our strategy for image modeling: our geometrical extractor is used first; then our spatial extractor is used to evaluate distance and direction relationships, a proposition of object grouping is carried out from evaluation of distances; and finally, our semantical annotator is used to introduce domain keywords.

Our example image (Figure 3a) is modeled by the following steps (we limit this example to objects $A1$ to $A8$ and B). Simple objects are extracted by a geometrical extractor which combines border and texture analyses. Simple objects in our image are: objects $A1$ to $A8$, B, etc. First, domain keywords (e.g., pillar, cella, etc.) are associated with these objects. Second, distances between objects are evaluated. Based on distance evaluations, one group of objects is proposed: group AB from objects $A1$ to $A8$ and B. Third, a domain expert validates objects for the next step: com-

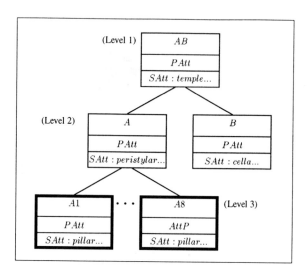

Figure 4. Hierarchical composition of the archaeological image

plex object *A* (from objects *A1* to *A8*), object *B*, etc. Our image is then represented by a hierarchy of objects (given in Figure 4). Simple objects are represented by thick boxes. Finally, direction relationships are evaluated (see Figure 3) and integrated into our image description.

4 Conclusion

In this paper we argue that a framework with plug-in extractors and an integrated model is well suited to tackle the problem of domain-dependent CBIR (content-based image retrieval) applications. We have proposed such a framework for combining syntactical and semantical features of images, as well as for using classification and indexing mechanisms. We describe the core of our framework which includes an integrated model and its similarity measure. Two application prototypes from paleontological and archaeological domains have been developed to validate the core framework.

Our work continues in two directions. First, we plan to build a deduction system and to specify interfaces for inclusion of different kind of extractors. Second, we intend to include a set of strategies for combining different extractors, a specific indexing mechanism for the archaeological database and a tool to insert images in the database.

References

[1] L. Besson, M.N. Terrasse, and K. Yétongnon. A fuzzy approach to direction relations. In *CBMI 2001, Content-Base Multimedia Indexing*, pages 169–176, Brescia, Italy, September 2001.

[2] H. Bunke. Recent Advances in Structural Pattern Recognition with Applications to Visual Form Analysis. In *Visual Form 2001, Springer Verlag, LNCS 2059*, pages 11–23, 2001.

[3] C.-C. Chen and J.Z. Wang. Large-scale Emperor Digital Library and Semantics-sensitive Region-based Retrieval. In *Proc. of the Int. Conf. on Digital Library – IT Opportunities and Challenges in the New Millennium*, pages 454–462, July 2002.

[4] Q. Ke, T. Jiang, and S.D. Ma. A Tabu Search Method for Geometric Primitive Extraction. *Pattern Recognition Letters*, 18:1443–1451, 1997.

[5] J. Landré, F. Truchetet, S. Montuire, and B. David. Content-based multiresolution indexing and retrieval of paleontology images. *SPIE Proc. of Storage and Retrieval for Media Databases - San Jose - CA - USA*, 4315:482–489, 2001.

[6] V. Ogle and M. Stonebraker. Chabot: Retrieval from a relational database of images. *IEEE Computer*, 28(9):40–48, September 1995.

[7] G. Petraglia, M. Sebillo, M. Tucci, and G. Tortora. Virtual Images for Similarity Retrieval in Image Databases. *Transactions on Knowledge and Data Engineering*, 13(6), November/December 2001.

[8] G. Roth and M. Levine. Geometric primitive extraction using a genetic algorithm. *Trans. on Pattern Anal. and Mach. Intell.*, 16(9):901–905, 1994.

[9] R. K. Srihari and D. T. Burhans. Visual semantics: Extracting visual information from text accompanying pictures. In *Proc. of AAAI '94, Seattle, WA*, August 1994.

[10] R. K. Taira, A. F. Cardenas, W. W. Chu, C. M. Breant, J. D. N. Dionisio, C. C. Hsu, and I. T. Ieong. An object-oriented data model for skeletal development. In *Proc. of the SPIE*, February 1994.

[11] W. Al-Khatib, Y. Francis Day, A. Ghafoor, and P. B. Berra. Semantic Moldeing and Knowledge Representation in Multimedia Databases. *Transactions on Knowledge and Data Engineering*, 11(1), January/February 1999.

[12] D.A. White and R. Jain. Imagegrep: Fast visual pattern matching in image databases. In *Proc. SPIE: Storage and Retrieval for Image and Video Databases*, volume 3022, pages 96–107, 1997.

[13] X.M. Zhou, C.H. Ang, and T.W. Ling. Image Retrieval Based on Object's Orientation Spatial Relationship. *Pattern Recognition Letters*, 22, 2001.

Operations on metamodels in the context of a UML-based metamodeling architecture

Marie-Noëlle Terrasse, George Becker, Marinette Savonnet, and Eric Leclercq
Laboratoire LE2I, Université de Bourgogne
B.P. 47870, 21078 Dijon Cedex, France
E-mail: {terrasse,becker,savonnet,leclercq}@khali.u-bourgogne.fr

Abstract

In the context of information system engineering, we propose a four-layer metamodeling architecture with a comprehensive set of operations on metamodels. Our architecture enables modelers to use a three-step modeling process: first, giving an informal description of the universe of the discourse (in terms of modeling paradigms); then, defining a corresponding UML dialect (in terms of metamodels); and finally –using the chosen dialect– describing a model of an information system. By using specific properties of our metamodeling architecture, we define formal and semantical operations on metamodels, e.g., integration of metamodels. In this paper we focus on a measure of a semantical distance between metamodels.

1 Introduction

Information system engineering is turning into an increasingly complex process [7] which has to take into account complexity of information systems, deployment environments, exploitation environments, and users' requirements. In order to cope with such demanding requirements, information system engineering has been using sophisticated abstraction mechanisms: abstraction by conceptualization (four-layer metamodeling architectures) and abstraction by projection (multi-view models). These abstraction mechanisms are implemented by metamodeling environments. These environments also provide modelers with formal languages (logics, set theory, Z notation or VDM languages, etc.) and formal methods (model checking, theorem proving, etc.). Nevertheless, many metamodeling environments additionally provide modelers with more intuitive languages, such as natural languages. Many metamodeling environments are based on UML. In such metamodeling environments, the UML metamodel forms the core of both abstraction mechanisms. The UML metamodel is used for defining a set of views and a modeling language which can satisfy the specific needs of a given application domain. For example, Koch & al. (UWE project for hypermedia design [4]) define additional diagrams and UML-constructs for these diagrams[1]. In practice, searching for a convenient metamodel could be really difficult: it would be necessary to know all earlier metamodel extensions (in order to decide whether an existing metamodel can be used or whether a new metamodel needs to be defined), and it would be necessary to master the manner in which existing metamodels have been built (in order to be able to extend them properly). Furthermore, when studying modelers' practice, it appears that modelers do not work directly with metamodel descriptions: information is provided to them in the form of "semi-formal" descriptions (which can be ambiguous but tend to be more readable). We call such a description a *modeling paradigm*. The modeling process –in practice– is a three-step process: 1) defining a modeling paradigm (by identifying a modeling paradigm which is close to the needed paradigm, and then building a variant of such a modeling paradigm); 2) instantiating the modeling paradigm into a metamodel; and 3) instantiating the metamodel into a model. As a consequence, metamodels and models do not provide comprehensive information about the actual modeling process: all the initial work (in defining modeling paradigms) is lost. Such an "elimination" of meaningful information from a metamodeling architecture can lead to metamodel proliferation since the easier choice for a modeler is to derive his/her own metamodel directly from the UML metamodel (without reusing existing extensions of the UML metamodel). The first effort to avoid

---

[1] Koch & al. propose to model web-systems by navigational space, navigational structure, static and dynamic presentational diagrams. A *navigational space diagram* describes classes that users are allowed to visit, together with links available for navigation between these classes. A *navigational structure diagram* describes which types of navigation are available for each link (e.g., guided tour, index). A *static presentational diagram* describes how objects are presented to users (i.e., interfaces), etc. Koch & al. propose new stereotypes such as ≪*navigational class*≫, and ≪*guided tour*≫ which are stereotypes of class.

metamodel proliferation has been made by the OMG which defined specific "profiles" for various application domains [8, 9]. Another approach is to organize existing metamodels into a hierarchy [1, 2]: each extension is a heir of an existing metamodel. In such a case, quality of the hierarchy of metamodels (which must reflect semantical links between metamodels) is a major requirement. Thus, we need to organize metamodels into a structure that makes them easy to reuse by modelers. Our proposal is based on a mirroring descriptive structure: the first part of the description is unformal and easily usable by any modeler, the second part of the description is formal and can thus form a basis for application of formal methods. In order to make such a two-fold description meaningful, the two parts of a description must be closely tied together.

2 Overview of our metamodeling architecture

Modeling paradigms describe –in terms of concepts that are interrelated by constraints– the semantics modelers assign to the real world. Our hypothesis is that there is a one-to-one correspondence between modeling paradigms and metamodels. This hypothesis leads to the metamodeling architecture described in the following paragraphs and depicted in Figure 1. We first present, using an example, the two uppermost layers of our metamodeling architecture (i.e., a poset of modeling paradigms and an inheritance hierarchy of metamodels). Then we give more details on the mirroring structure and its features: subsumption of modeling paradigms, instantiation function of modeling paradigms in metamodels, and partitionning of UML-constructs and OCL-constraints for a given metamodel.

A poset of modeling paradigms Modeling paradigm descriptions possibly mix several different languages: the English language, logics, the set theory, the Z notation, etc. Modeling paradigms may use a various number of concepts, e.g., class and abstract class, each of them being described with more or less precision. A modeling paradigm mp is described by two sets, $\mathcal{E}l^3(mp)$ and $\mathcal{C}^3(mp)$. The set $\mathcal{E}l^3(mp)$ contains descriptions of elementary concepts, while the set $\mathcal{C}^3(mp)$ contains constraints between concepts of $\mathcal{E}l^3(mp)$.

We define a partial order between modeling paradigms by using a subsumption relation and we obtain a poset (i.e., partially ordered set) of modeling paradigms.

We denote by gmp the generic modeling paradigm which corresponds to the standard UML semantics. We restrict ourselves to a set of modeling paradigms that are subsumed by gmp: we denote this set by $Restrict_{MP}$.

In Figure 1 we depict several examples modeling paradigms of $Restrict_{MP}$. Modeling paradigms mp_2 and

mp_4 provide time descriptions. mp_4 which has an additional constraint (i.e., time model uniqueness) is subsumed by mp_3 which supports several time models. Modeling paradigm mp_3 supports the C2 Architecture Description Language. There is no subsumption between mp_2 and mp_3.

A mirroring inheritance hierarchy of metamodels Our objective is to build the metamodel layer of our architecture as a mirror of the poset of modeling paradigms: the generic modeling paradigm gmp is instantiated into the UML metamodel itself (which we denote by mm_{UML}), and all other modeling paradigms are instantiated into specializations of the UML metamodel (by using UML's extension mechanisms: constraints, tag-values, and stereotypes). Furthermore, we require that each metamodel instantiates some modeling paradigm, and that each inheritance link between metamodels instantiates a subsumption link between modeling paradigms. For example, in Figure 1, the general modeling paradigm gmp is instantiated into the UML metamodel mm_{UML} and mp_3 is instantiated into a metamodel mm_3. Large grey arrows, denoted with $\mathcal{E}^{3,2}$, represent instantiations of modeling paradigms into metamodels.

We denote by L^0, L^1, L^2, and L^3 the instance, model, metamodel, and meta-metamodel layers, respectively. Consistently with this notation, we will attach a superscript (from 0 to 3) to each element that is localized on the corresponding layer of the metamodeling architecture.

An example using ADL (Architecture Description Language) Medvidovic & al. [5] describe the C2-style Architecture Description Language in English[2]: "connectors *transmit messages between components, while* components *maintain state, perform operations, and exchange messages with other components via two interfaces (named "top" and "bottom"). ... Inter-component messages are either* requests *for a component to perform an operation or* notifications *that a given component has performed an operation or changed state*". Let us call by mp_3 the described modeling paradigm. As depicted in Figure 1, the description of mp_3 includes concepts (e.g., *connector, component, interface, message*) and constraints (e.g., "components may not directly exchange messages; they may only do so via connectors").

Robbins & al. [11] propose an extension of UML's metamodel for C2-ADL. Their extension is an instantiation of the Medvidovic's modeling paradigm in terms of a metamodel which we denote by mm_3. They define $\ll C2 - interface \gg$ as a stereotype of the UML *interface* with a tagged value (*top, bottom*). $\ll C2 - operation \gg$ (which can be either a request for operation or a notification message) is defined as a stereotype of the UML *operation* with

---

[2]A formal description of C2 in language Z is given in [6].

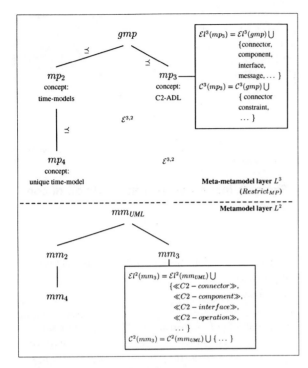

$\mathcal{E}l^3(mp_3) = \mathcal{E}l^3(gmp) \bigcup$
{connector,
component,
interface,
message, ... }
$\mathcal{C}^3(mp_3) = \mathcal{C}^3(gmp) \bigcup$
{ connector
constraint,
... }

$\mathcal{E}l^2(mm_3) = \mathcal{E}l^2(mm_{UML}) \bigcup$
{ $\ll C2 - connector \gg$,
$\ll C2 - component \gg$,
$\ll C2 - interface \gg$,
$\ll C2 - operation \gg$,
... }
$\mathcal{C}^2(mm_3) = \mathcal{C}^2(mm_{UML}) \bigcup \{ ... \}$

Figure 1. Our mirroring structure of meta-metamodel and metamodel layers

a constraint forbidding any return value. The tagged values *request, notification* are used to distinguish requests from notifications. The set of UML-constructs of mm_3 is depicted in Figure 1. The set of OCL-constraints of mm_3 contains instantiations of constraints of modeling paradigm mp_3.

Subsumption of modeling paradigms is intended to express a relationship between a modeling paradigm and one of its variants. For example, Koch & al.'s modeling paradigm for hypermedia design [4] subsumes Fröhlich & al.'s modeling paradigm [3] which imposes more explicit restrictions, namely a restriction allowing only binary associations, and an inter-diagram constraint (a limitation of types of navigation –in the navigational structure diagram– depending on multiplicities of associations in the navigational space diagram).

A modeling paradigm mp_1 *is subsumed by* a modeling paradigm mp_2 if both *extended inclusion of concepts* and *subsumption of constraints* are satisfied. Extended inclusion of concepts means that each concept of $\mathcal{E}l^3(mp_2)$ is either a member of $\mathcal{E}l^3(mp_1)$ or a generalization of a concept of $\mathcal{E}l^3(mp_1)$, where a generalized concept may have fewer features than its specialization has. Subsumption of constraints means that by using $\mathcal{C}^3(mp_1)$ as a hypothesis, it is possible to prove that each constraint of $\mathcal{C}^3(mp_2)$ holds.

Given two modeling paradigms mp_1 and mp_2, we denote by $mp_1 \preceq mp_2$ the subsumption of mp_1 by mp_2. We denote by $\mathcal{E}l^3(mp_2) \subseteq_e \mathcal{E}l^3(mp_1)$ the extended inclusion of concepts of mp_2 in concepts of mp_1. We denote by $\mathcal{C}^3(mp_1) \Rightarrow_s \mathcal{C}^3(mp_2)$ the subsumption of constraints of mp_1 by constraints of mp_2.

For example, there is an extended inclusion (which we denote by $\{t2\} \subseteq_e \{t1\}$) between a concept of time $t2$ with features *model, unit* and a concept of time $t1$ with features *model, unit, interpolation* [10].

We note that the subsumption relation $\preceq$ is a partial order relation. Given two modeling paradigms mp and mp' such that $mp \preceq mp'$, we use our definition of subsumption of modeling paradigms ($mp \preceq mp'$) for partitionning the sets of concepts and constraints of the subsumed modeling paradigm (mp). As an example, we will consider the above modeling paradigm for C2-ADL, mp_3, which is subsumed by the general modeling paradigm gmp. We obtain:

- A partition of the set of elementary concepts of mp into three subsets:

  - The set of common concepts: $Com(mp, mp')$ contains all concepts belonging to the intersection $\mathcal{E}l^3(mp) \cap \mathcal{E}l^3(mp')$.

    For example, the concept of class is common to mp_3 and gmp.

  - The set of specialized concepts $Spe(mp, mp')$ contains all concepts of mp that specialize concepts of mp'.

    For example, the gmp's concept of interface is specialized in mp_3: "*A C2 interface has a tagged value identifying its position. All C2 interface operations must be C2 operations*".

  - The set of new concepts that contains all other concepts of mp: $New(mp, mp') = \mathcal{E}l^3(mp) - (Com(mp, mp') \cup Spe(mp, mp'))$

    For example, the concept of message is a new concept which is introduced in mp_3.

- A partition of the set of constraints of mp in three subsets:

  - The set of shared constraints: $Sh(mp, mp')$ that contains all constraints belonging to $\mathcal{C}^3(mp) \cap \mathcal{C}^3(mp')$.

    For example, the constraint "*Any object belongs to a class*" is common to mp_3 and gmp.

  - The set $Ded(mp, mp')$ of constraints of mp that are used to deduce non-shared constraints of mp'.

    For example, the constraint "*Both ends of a C2 attachment must be to a C2 component*" of

$\mathcal{C}^3(mp_3)$ implies that "*Both ends of a C2 attachment are to a class*" since C2 attachments are stereotypes of class.

- The set of new constraints that contains all other constraints of mp: $Add(mp, mp') = \mathcal{C}^3(mp) - (Sh(mp, mp') \cup Ded(mp, mp'))$

  For example, the constraint "*Each C2 component and connector has exactly one instance*" is a new constraint which is introduced into mp_3 and gmp.

Definition of an instantiation function An instantiation function

$$\mathcal{E}^{3,2} : Restrict_{MP} \rightarrow \{UML - metamodel\ extensions\}$$

is defined for building metamodels from modeling paradigms. Let us consider a modeling paradigm mp. $\mathcal{E}^{3,2}$ associates each concept of $\mathcal{E}l^3(mp)$ with one or more elementary components of the UML language. Such components are either standard UML constructs or stereotypes. We further assume that mp's corresponding metamodel $mm = \mathcal{E}^{3,2}(mp)$ is described by a set of UML-constructs and a set of OCL-constraints (denoted by $\mathcal{E}l^2(mm)$ and $C^2(mm)$, respectively). Some constraints of $\mathcal{C}^3(mp)$ are included into stereotype definitions. For example, the constraint "*messages have no return value*" is included in stereotype $\ll C2 - operation \gg$. Thus $C^2(mm)$ contains instantiations of all other constraints of $\mathcal{C}^3(mp)$, as well as additional constraints due to the instantiation process itself.

Partitionning of UML-constructs and OCL-constraints of a metamodel Let us consider two metamodels mm_1 and mm_2 where mm_1 is a direct heir of mm_2. Due to our mirroring structure, their corresponding modeling paradigms mp_1 and mp_2 are related by our partial order $\preceq$ (i.e., $mp_1 \preceq mp_2$). Thus we have –as defined above– a partition of the concepts of mp_1: $Com(mp_1, mp_2)$, $Spe(mp_1, mp_2)$, and $New(mp_1, mp_2)$; and a partition of the constraints of mp_1: $Sh(mp_1, mp_2)$, $Ded(mp_1, mp_2)$, and $Add(mp_1, mp_2)$.

By applying the instantiation function $\mathcal{E}^{3,2}$ to concepts of mp_1, we induce several subsets of UML-constructs and OCL-constraints. These subsets are depicted in Figure 2. Large grey arrows represent instantiations of concepts and constraints. Double-headed arrows represent inclusion of some constraints of a modeling paradigm in stereotypes of its corresponding metamodel. A thin dark-grey arrow represents instantiation of new concepts/constraints as part of a stereotype defined for specialization: an example is given is Section 3 where two new concepts (for C2-ADL modeling paradigm mp_3), namely connector and component, are

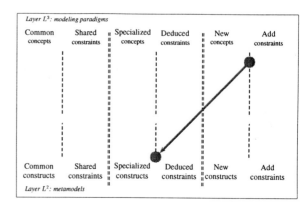

Figure 2. Instantiation of the partition of concepts

instantiated as specialization of UML-constructs (as stereotypes of class).

We obtain:

- A subset of constructs of mm_1 containing all common constructs. This subset is defined by $Com_{UML}(mm_1, mm_2) = \mathcal{E}^{3,2}(Com(mp_1, mp_2))$.

- A subset of all pairs of constructs of mm_1 and mm_2 (i.e., a subset of $\mathcal{C}(mm_1) \times \mathcal{C}(mm_2)$), denoted by $Spe_{UML}(mm_1, mm_2)$, which contains all pairs of specialized-generalized constructs such that the specialized construct of the pair belongs to mm_1 and the generalized construct of the pair belongs to mm_2. These pairs of constructs correspond either to the instantiation of specialized concepts (which belong to $Spe(mp_1, mp_2)$) or to some of the additional elementary concepts (which belong to $New(mp_1, mp_2)$).

- A subset of the constructs of mm_1, denoted by $New_{UML}(mm_1, mm_2)$, containing the new constructs introduced by the instantiation of mp_1 into mm_1. These new constructs instantiate some of the additional elementary concepts (which belong to $New(mp_1, mp_2)$).

By applying the same approach to constraints of mp_1, we induce three subsets of the constraints of mp_1: the subset of shared constraints $Sh_{UML}(mm_1, mm_2)$; the subsets of constraints mp_1 which are used to deduce constraints of mp_2, namely $Ded_{UML}(mm_1, mm_2)$; and the subset of new constraints $Add_{UML}(mm_1, mm_2)$. This construction is more complex than the construction of subsets of concepts since a constraint of mm_2 can be deduced from several constraints of mm_1. We do not give full details in this paper since the only subset we will use is $Add_{UML}(mm_1, mm_2)$.

3 Semantical distance between metamodels

In order to be able to evaluate semantical quality, we need to measure semantical distances between metamodels. Our proposal for such an evaluation is to build a measure of semantic distance as a weighted sum of elementary distances between corresponding elements of metamodels (i.e., corresponding constructs and corresponding constraints). The main difficulty in such an approach is how to determine corresponding pairs of elements. For that, we use subsets of UML-constructs and of OCL-constraints induced by our subsumption relationship and instantiation function.

In the rest of this section, we provide a generic method for defining a measure of semantic distance between two metamodels. Elementary distances between paired elements, as well as weights used for combination of these elementary distances, are not discussed in the general case: they need to be fine-tuned in the context of a specific application domain.

Let us consider two metamodels mm_1 and mm_2 and their corresponding modeling paradigms mp_1 and mp_2, respectively. We assume that mm_1 is a direct heir of mm_2 (i.e., $mp_1 \preceq mp_2$). Our strategy for measurement of semantical distance is defined separately for each of the subsets of UML-constructs:

- Elementary measure due to $Com_{UML}(mm_1, mm_2)$ is based on the fact that common constructs implement common concepts. The only variation may be in the way common concepts have been translated by $\mathcal{E}^{3,2}$ into UML-constructs. This part of the measure is a syntactical measure and can be ignored in most cases.

- Elementary measure due to $Spe_{UML}(mm_1, mm_2)$: we work with pairs of constructs corresponding to a general concept and a specialization of this general concept. For every such a pair, evaluation of distance has to take into account both semantical variations due to added features and syntactical variations (due to $\mathcal{E}^{3,2}$-instantiation).

- Elementary measure due to $New_{UML}(mm_1, mm_2)$: new components correspond to concepts that have been introduced in mp_1, thus we have to evaluate the semantical cost of the concept itself. We believe that –in most cases– such evaluation can rely on the semantical distance between the new construct and the initial UML-construct that it originates from.

Let us present an example using metamodels mm_3 and mm_{UML} (see Figure 1). Metamodel mm_3 is a specialization of mm_{UML}, and mp_3 is subsumed by gmp. In order to evaluate a semantical distance between mm_3 and mm_{UML}, we build the following sets:

- At the meta-metamodel level, the set of common concepts:
$$Com(mp_3, gmp) = \mathcal{E}l^3(gmp)$$

- At the meta-metamodel level, the set of specialized concepts:
$$Spe(mp_3, gmp) = \{interface, message\}$$

- At the meta-metamodel level, the set of new concepts:
$$New(mp_3, gmp) = \{connector, component\}$$

- At the metamodel level, the pairs of initial UML-constructs and specialized constructs:
$$Spe_{UML}(mm_3, mm_{UML}) =$$
$$\{(\ll C2 - operation \gg, operation),$$
$$(\ll C2 - interface \gg, interface),$$
$$(\ll C2 - component \gg, class),$$
$$(\ll C2 - connector \gg, class)\}.$$

We note that the two new concepts of mp_3 are instantiated as specializations of the UML class: their instantiations belong to $Spe_{UML}(mm_3, mm_{UML})$. Thus, $New_{UML}(mm_3, mm_{UML}) = \emptyset$.

Analogously to the above, we use subsets of UML constraints of mm_1 and mm_2. We assume that the distance due to shared constraints, as well as to deduced constraints, is not significant[3]. We consider several types of constraints: 1) constraints which introduce a slight variation (e.g., $\ll C2 - interface \gg$ are limited to have only $\ll C2 - operation \gg$); 2) weak constraints which cannot weaken a fundamental feature (e.g., a constraint "$\ll C2 - operation \gg$ has no return value" added to the UML-construct $operation$ to define a $\ll C2 - operation \gg$ stereotype); and 3) strong constraints which modify a fundamental feature of the corresponding element (e.g., a constraint "each $\ll C2 - component \gg$ has exactly one instance in the running system" induces a major change when going from the UML-construct $class$ to the stereotype $\ll C2 - component \gg$).

We have shown how to determine pairs of corresponding elements (either concepts or constraints) for measurement of a semantical distance between two metamodels when one of the metamodels is a heir of the other. In the general case, we define a more complex partition of sets of constructs and constraints (hints about such a partition can be found in [12]).

---

[3]This assumption relies on the fact that modeling paradigms are defined by modelers who use OCL as a common foundation for expression of constraints.

4   Conclusion

Our metamodeling architecture takes advantage of the knowledge of modelers' behaviors, abstract approaches to information system engineering, and formal methods. Modeler's behavior is represented by a poset of modeling paradigms at the meta-metamodel level. Abstraction in information system engineering is represented by metamodels which also form the core of our architecture and support formal methods. Cohesion of the two uppermost layers of our architecture (i.e., modeling paradigms and metamodels) is guaranteed by the hypothesis of *one-to-one correspondence of modeling paradigms and metamodels* as well as by *mirroring structure of the poset of modeling paradigms and the inheritance hierarchy of metamodels*. Such a hypothesis is somewhat restrictive but it allows to "induce" properties of modeling paradigms from properties that have been formally defined on metamodels.

We present formal operations on metamodels. We then extend these operations into semantical ones: semantical integration of metamodels and a measure of a semantical distance between metamodels. These semantical operations form the basis of two frameworks which employ metamodeling in the context of interoperability of information systems and of the Semantic Web. We continue our work on several technical issues related to this project:

- Providing modelers with a convenient interface for using our mirroring structure in the form of a library of domain descriptions (for describing modeling paradigms and instantiating corresponding metamodels). One of the more important part of such an interface is a support for analysis of modeling paradigm descriptions. Such an analyzer must accept as input multi-notation descriptions (which encompass a natural language). It must be able to extract from these descriptions concepts (and constraints) that form the modeling paradigm.

- Providing domain experts with a methodology for adaptation of our generic measure of a semantical distance between metamodels to domain experts' application domains.

- Defining generic rules for quality measurement of the sub-poset of modeling paradigms that correspond to closely related application domains.

Finally, we believe that the extensive use of our proposal would open a "standardization" issue, namely the need for a new organization of domain modeling. Modelers would be responsible for "local semantics" (i.e., for describing their own application domain as a variation of an existing domain description). Domain experts would be responsible for the global semantics (i.e., for validating semantical dependencies between domain descriptions).

References

[1] S. Cook, A. Kleppe, R. Mitchell, B. Rumpe, J. Warmer, and A. C. Wills. Defining UML Family Members Using Prefaces. In C. Mingins and B. Meyer, editors, *Proceedings of "Technology of Object-Oriented Languages and Systems", TOOLS 32*, pages 102–114. IEEE, November 1999.

[2] E. D. Falkenberg and J. Han Oei. Meta Model Hierarchies from an Object-Role Modeling Perspective. In *Proceedings of the 1st International Conference on Object-Role Modeling, ORM-1, Magnetic Island, Australia*, 1994.

[3] P. Fröhlich, N. Henze, and W. Nejdl. Meta-Modeling for Hypermedia Design. In *Proceedings of the Second IEEE Metadata Conference, MD97*, 1997.

[4] N. Koch, H. Baumeister, R. Hennicker, and L. Mandel. Extending UML for Modeling Navigation and Presentation in Web Applications. In *Proceedings of the Workshop Modeling Web Applications in the UML, UML'00*, 2000.

[5] N. Medvidovic and D. S. Rosenblum. Assessing the Suitability of a Standard Design Method for Modeling Software Architectures. In *Proceedings of the 1st IFIP Working Conference on Software Architecture, San Antonio, Texas, USA*, pages 161–182, 1999.

[6] N. Medvidovic, R. N. Taylor, and J. E. James Whitehead. Formal Modeling of Software Architectures at Multiple Levels of Abstraction. In *Proceedings of the California Software Symposium 1996*, pages 28–40, 1996.

[7] UML4MDA, Response to the omg RFP Infrastructure for UML2.0, Report 2003-01-13. Available at URL http://www.omg.org, January 2003.

[8] Roadmap for the Business Object Initiative: Supporting Enterprise Distributed Computing, OMG Report 98-10-09. Available at URL http://www.omg.org.

[9] A UML Profile for CORBA, OMG Report 99-08-02, 1999. Available at URL http://www.omg.org, Version 1.0, August 2, 1999.

[10] R. Price, B. Srinivasan, and K. Ramamohanarao. Extending the Unified Modeling Language to Support Spatiotemporal Applications. In C. Mingins and B. Meyer, editors, *Proceedings of TOOLS 32, Conference on Technology of Object-Oriented Languages and Systems*, pages 163–174. IEEE, November 1999.

[11] J. E. Robbins, N. Medvidovic, D. F. Redmiles, and D. S. Rosenblum. Integrating Architecture Description Languages with a Standard Design Method. In *Proceedings of the 1998 International Conference on Software Engineering*, pages 209–218. IEEE, April 1998.

[12] M.-N. Terrasse. A Metamodeling Approach to Evolution. In H. Balsters, B. de Bruck, and S. Conrad, editors, *Database Schema Evolution and Meta-Modeling*. Springer-Verlag, LNCS 2065, ISBN 3-540-42272-2, 2001. 9th International Workshop on Foundations of Models and Languages for Data and Objects, Schloss Dagstuhl, Germany, September 2000.

Poster Papers

Issues in Object-Based Notification

Paul Kim and Dorothy Curtis
paulhkim@alum.mit.edu, dcurtis@lcs.mit.edu
Massachusetts Institute of Technology
Laboratory for Computer Science
Cambridge, MA

Abstract

Integrating notification with shared memory applications is an interesting problem. This paper looks at implementing notification in a shared memory, object-oriented, distributed transaction environment.

1 Introduction

As software applications move from stand-alone entities to interdependent components in increasingly distributed systems, software designers must focus more attention on integrating distributed components. A common scenario involves one application waiting for another to update or modify the value of some shared object. An example of this is a flight arrival notification system, in which a user calls in to an application requesting to be notified once the flight arrival time reaches a given threshold. The application, in turn, waits for some third party application to modify the time-to-arrival value before calling the user back. Assuming the application is connected to the rest of the system via a network connection, the question arises as to how the application can be made aware of a change to time-to-arrival.

One possible solution is to have the client poll the system to check whether the value of time-to-arrival has changed. Repeatedly making calls over a network connection to inquire about the value could potentially waste network bandwidth or be expensive. Alternatively, having the system notify the waiting client application upon change of time-to-arrival requires only one network call at the precise time that the value is actually modified. provides two benefits over polling: preservation of network bandwidth as well as providing a new value at time closer to that at which the value was changed. Combining notification with polling improves the latency at which data is refreshed.

We seek to provide the notification mechanism within

The remainder of the paper is as follows: Background on notification and invalidation will be in Section II. Section III will provide an overview of the implementation environment. Section IV will discuss the details and implementation details of the notification mechanism. Section V will explore related work, and Section VI will conclude with possible future projects that may benefit from notification.

2 Background

This section describes the issues and concepts involved in notification. Further, we examine the definition of notification itself, and identify the applications that use notification as well as the various types of notifications that are possible.

The discussion of notification for this paper will be in the context of a multi-user, multi-application distributed environment. We will assume that all applications run on top of a shared database, and are connected to the database via a network connection. Furthermore, we will assume that applications work on locally cached copies of data from the database. Notification refers to the update of an application's data with the changes made by another application. Notification is application specific. Each application running on the database may be interested in notification for different subsets of the centralized data objects. In some cases, a multi-cast notification may be appropriate. For the purposes of this paper, however, notifications will use a one-message-per-application approach. The types of applications for which notification is provided for has an impact on the design and implementation of the mechanism. Two distinct types of applications exist for notification: waiting and non-waiting applications.

2.1 Waiting Applications

Waiting applications are those applications that, while waiting to be notified of a change, do not require any other access to or modifications of data. The example of the flight arrival notification system mentioned in the Section I is such an application.

2.2 Non-waiting Applications

Non-waiting applications encompass those applications that actively read and write data, while expecting some local data to be updated. In non-waiting applications, the benefit of notification is that applications can better ensure that the data being used in a transaction is fresh, and thus the result of the transaction is more likely to be valid. An example of a non-waiting application that uses notification is a calendar application that can be accessed by two different parties, for example, a doctor and his secretary. In the event where a secretary commits an appointment to a day on the doctor's schedule, that day becomes invalid to the doctor's application. Without notification, the doctor may not know about the change until he tries to add another event to that day, at which point, the transaction will abort, and he can request the new copy of the day. In contrast, if the system were to notify the doctor of the secretary-entered appointment before the doctor tried to modify the date, the doctor would be aware of the change and be able to act accordingly on a valid piece of data. In such cases, notification can eliminate the need for unnecessary transaction aborts by providing updated and valid copies of data.

2.3 Notification Propagation

There are three levels of the client to which the notification message may propagate: the application cache, the application, or the user. The application and its usage determine how far notifications must propagate for correct behavior. Generally, the more frequently that notifications are expected, the less propagation is necessary. A message that propagates to only the application cache results in the cache updating the application's data without the application having any knowledge of a change. Applications in which the rate of data change is extremely fast, such as real-time stock quoting applications can assume that data is constantly changing, thus do not need to be notified very time a member of its cache is updated. Indeed, application notification would be burdensome and not particularly useful. Applications that explicitly wait for a change in a specific piece of data, however, do require to be notified when the data is modified. Such applications require application-level notification. For example, an application that waits for a temperature to exceed a certain threshold before acting, must know when the notification is received to be able to proceed. Blindly updating the application's data is not sufficient. Propagating the notification message all the way to the user consists of the application conveying an update through its interface to the user. This is needed when

changes may impact the user's interaction with his/her application. An application that would need to notify its user is the aforementioned calendar application.

2.4 Notification and Polling

While notification may exist as an alternative to polling in situations where conservation of network bandwidth is desirable, situations in which this is not an issue could couple notification with polling to improve the likelihood of obtaining a fresher value of a particular piece of data. For example, if an application were to poll a database for an updated value every 20 seconds, the value of the data could be as old as 20 seconds by the time the application had access to the value (disregarding the network latency). If polling were then augmented by a notification mechanism, we could ensure the following: in the case that the notification is successfully transferred to the application via the network, the application would have access to the new updated value faster than through simple polling.

3 THOR: the Implementation Environment

The implementation of notification in this paper uses THOR[3], a distributed object-oriented database system.

The THOR environment provides objects. Each object has a unique identifier and a set of methods for access and modification. The architecture is in the form of a client-server model that maintains the persistent state of each object, see Figure 1. All persistent objects are stored at the Object Repository (OR), which is the server side of THOR. The OR contains a root object, through which all objects are reachable. The OR is responsible for checking the validity of any potential transaction and committing the transaction if valid. The client side of THOR consists of a Front End

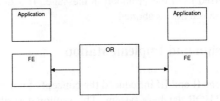

Figure 1. Thor Architecture

(FE), which serves as a local cache for the application that runs on top of it. An application's FE contains copies of a subset of the objects stored at the OR. The application accesses objects as if they were local objects. The FE/OR infrastructure provides, essentially, a shared memory model for accessing the database objects. Commiting changes to the objects is managed through transactions. request on to the OR. The FE and OR communicate through a network connection. If an application requires an object that is not stored at its FE, the FE can request the object from the OR, which will send the object back to the FE. The application can then read and/or modify the object. The application invokes the FE interface to commit a transaction, and the FE will send the commit message on to the OR. If the OR determines the transaction is valid, it will commit the updated values, otherwise it will return an abort message back to the FE. The application then determines the appropriate course of action in the case of an abort, i.e, abort or retry. Additionally, the OR sends invalidation messages to FE's that contain new values for stale copies of objects.

FE's each have a Resident Object Table (ROT) that maps an object id to a location in local memory, through a process called swizzling.

The FE keeps track of an application's transaction by maintaining a Read Object Set (ROS), Modified Object Set (MOS), and New Object Set (NOS). The NOS is made up of those objects that are created during the course of the transaction. Each set consists of a list of the relevant objects. some member in the MOS. When the application decides to commit, the FE gathers the information from the MOS, NOS, and ROS and sends a commit message to the OR.

The OR will determine whether or not to commit or abort the transaction from the FE. For each FE, the OR keeps track of which objects are stale. If the objects from the FE commit message are contained in the set of the FE's invalid objects, the FE's transaction is aborted, and an abort message is returned to the FE.

The OR uses an invalidation mechanism to inform the FE about stale objects. Upon receiving a valid commit from one FE, it sends invalidation messages to all other FE's that have copies of the committed object cached. Upon receipt of an invalidation message, the FE will check to see if any of the members of its MOS or ROS match the object that was referred to in the invalidation message. If it does, the current transaction is aborted.

4 Design and Implementation

Sections II and III introduced the concept of notification and the THOR database system. This section describes the enhancements made to the THOR architecture that allow applications to be notified of changes made to relevant objects.

4.1 Enhancing the OR for Notification

Additional data structures are required to allow the OR to implement notification. A class called Notification_set is created to allow a collection of object ids to be stored. Notification_set's store the object ids for which an FE wishes to be notified. Two sets of Notification_set's are kept. The first, called wanted_objs contains those objects for which the FE desires notification. The other, called notify_objs represents a subset of the wanted_objs objects that have been modified by the commit of another FE's transaction.

The FE sends an FE_recv_notify_msg to the OR to indicate which objects' modifications are of interest.

Once the OR has registered the FE's requests for notification it is ready to send the actual notification message. At the appropriate time it creates an FE_send_notification_msg message. This message will contain the new value for each object that has been modified and is on the FE's wanted_objs list.

The notification mechanism that was implemented for the purposes of this paper as described above has a potential scalability flaw that may be addressed in future work. Currently, the OR loops through each FE and checks which object ids are registered for notification, before sending out the notification message. The data for notification is essentially stored on a per-FE basis. In a scenario where there are few objects shared across numerous FE's, the performance could potentially suffer. It seems a more efficient means of notifying FE's would be to design a data structure that stores the notification configuration on a per-object id basis.

4.2 Enhancing the FE for Notifications

In order to request send a notification of changes to a particular object, the FE creates a message of type FE_Send_Notify. This message contains the object ids for which the application wishes notification.

In handling notification messages from the OR, the goal of the FE is preserve data consistency and correctness of the system. This entails not only updating the values of the modified objects, but also ensuring that transactions involving modified objects are aborted. There are potentially three situations in which the FE can pick up the notification message: an explicit call by the application to check for notification messages, a waiting mechanism in which the FE waits on the network for any notification messages, and a check for notification in the process of a commit by the application, in which the contents of notification messages are checked to determine whether the transaction being committed is valid. An explicit check for notification is initiated by the application running on the FE. A waiting mechanism is also provided by the FE to "wait" for any notification messages to appear on the network queue. Such a mechanism is ideal for applications whose continuity depends on receiving a notification message. The waiting can be interrupted when either a message is received on the network queue, or the application interrupts the wait process. Allowing the wait to be interrupted enables the application to perform transactions and process information. The third place where the notification messages are retrieved is when a transaction commit is processed by the FE. If any of the object ids contained in the notification message match any of the objects in the transaction's MOS or ROS, then the contents of the transaction are invalid. The FE discontinues the commit process before a commit message is sent to the OR. Furthermore, the FE informs the application of the unsuccessful commit attempt and provides object ids that were modified from the notification message.

The FE stores any notification messages, but does not update the values until a later convenient time. In order to ensure that data for which notification messages are received are not modified in the lag time between receipt and update, the FE locks all the pages that were sent in the notification message. Any subsequent access attempts to the page result in aborting the transaction. As will be seen in the next section, the pages are unlocked after the update is completed.

4.3   Writing an Application to Use Notification

An application must explicitly request notification from the central data repository for the relevant pieces of data. When designing an application to receive and incorporate notification messages, the responsibilities of the application consistency are twofold. First, the application must regularly check the network queue for the presence of notification messages. Secondly, the application should correctly incorporate the messages. The application must regularly check for notification messages in order to realize benefit from the notification mechanism. If an application were to ignore notification messages until the time of transaction commit, the transaction could potentially be invalidated. For example, an application "A" may be interested in changes made to a member "x" of its data set. A notification message informing of a change to "x" may be sent "A", but if the application does not check for the message, then it may continue to perform invalid transactions on "x". Upon attempting to commit the transaction, the application will then be informed of the invalidity of its object set. The application must check for notification messages in order to avoid performing invalid transactions, thus realizing a key benefit of the notification mechanism. Upon receiving the notification messages, the application must then correctly integrate the message into its own behavior. If the notification message is for data involved in an uncommitted transaction, then the application must undo the results of the transaction, while also informing the application user of the invalidation if necessary. If the notification message is for data that has yet to be accessed in a transaction by the application, then the application can simply update the relevant data without affecting the validity of its transaction. Again, notifying the end user is an application-dependant

issue.

4.4   Application Support for Notifications

The degree of involvement of the application in supporting the notification mechanism varies significantly with the type of application as well as the type of notification the application is interested in. From a high level perspective, the application identifies those objects for which it is interested in receiving notification messages. Upon receiving a notification message from the OR, the FE updates the object values as described in the previous section. A list of the modified objects is passed back to the application layer. At this point, the applications use of the modified orefs is dependent on the context in which the application is used. It can inform the user of the changes, or hide the changes altogether. There are some situations, however, where the application desires not only a single object, but any new entities related to the object. For example, the calendar application described earlier might request Notifcation for modifications made to a single calendar object. It is reasonable to assume that modifications could include adding a notice or an object. Depending on the object representation of the calendar, an added notice may be assigned a new oref from that of the calendar itself. The application's calendar class, when requesting notification, must have knowledge of which orefs will change when new objects are added and include those in the notification message. It is thus necessary for applications, or some of their classes, to be aware of the object representations to properly request notification. The next section shows how the calendar application would be modified to support notification.

4.4.1   Identifying the Calendar Objects to Notify

The Calendar application consists of a collection of calendar objects. Each calendar object is a representation of scheduled events for a given individual. Within the context of the calendar application, we desire the ability to receive notifications of modifications made to individual calendars. The request for notification about a specific calendar is accomplished by deriving the oref of the individual calendar object. This in itself, however, is not sufficient to achieve successful update via notification. An oref is assigned to each calendar object, as well as its member variables. The items in the calendar object that represent each of the scheduled events are stored in an array called "Items", which is one of the calendar object's member variables. "Items" is itself a pointer to the array. By simply requesting notification of changes made to the calendar object itself, objects added to "Items" will not be included in the notification because although the contents of "Items" have changed, the the array has not.

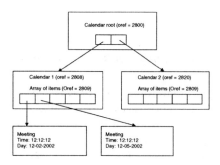

Figure 2. Object Representation of Calendar Application with two Calendars

It is thus necessary to send the oref of the array "Items" along with the calendar object oref in the notification request message. Figure 2 displays the object representation of a calendar application with two separate calendar objects.

4.4.2 Receiving Notification for Calendar Objects

In the calendar application, it seems reasonable to require notifications of modified objects to be conveyed directly to the user via the user interface. This is accomplished via a notification dissemination mechanism within the application. It is first necessary to identify all the areas within the application that a notification message may be received. As discussed earlier, the application can invoke a wait-for-change as well as a direct request to check for notification messages on the queue. The third area of notification receipt is potentially after a failed commit. The FE is further modified to keep track of which objects were modified by notifications. The interface between application and FE allows the calendar application to access these modified. Once the list of modified orefs is obtained by the calendar application, the application must distribute the notification to the appropriate calendar objects.

5 Related Work

Notification is not a new concept. GARDEN [5] provides a server with persistent, shared object-oriented data storage and retrieval. GARDEN uses pessimistic locking while THOR uses optimistic locking. THOR's notification system is more efficient because it includes all objects and their new values while GARDEN's notification indicates that a single object has changed.

ORION [2] is an object-oriented database system that supports versioning and change notification. ORION supports both message and flag-based notification while the THOR implementation supports only message-based notification. The message-based notification infrastructure in

ORION relies on an object representation that differs significantly from that of THOR. Notification messages are sent from object-to-object. In contrast, notification in THOR uses the existing messaging architecture in which the server (the OR in this case) sends notification messages out to the clients, who in turn modify the objects. ORION was designed with a local environment in mind, as opposed to a globally distributed environment.

Microsoft SQL Server Notification Services [4] and IBM Everyplace Intelligent Notification Services [1] provide notification mechanisms. The applications that use these systems receive notifications as messages, while, in Thor, the application sees the database objects as local objects, i.e., the Thor applications appear to have shared memory with the OR.

6 Conclusions

We have described a notification mechanism in a distributed database environment that notifies clients of modifications made to shared data. This notification mechanism increases the flexibility and efficiency of applications to run in a distributed data environment.

We are grateful for support from members of the MIT Project Oxygen partnership: Acer, Delta, Hewlett Packard, NTT, Nokia, and Philips. We would like to thank the reviewers for their comments. For readers interested in more information, please see http://nms.lcs.mit.edu/papers/pkim-thesis.pdf.

References

[1] V. Bennett and A. Capella. *Extending Intelligent Notification Services to Monitor New Sources.* "http://www7b.software.ibm.com/wsdd/library/techarticles/0303_bennett/benne%tt.html".

[2] H.-T. Chou and W. Kim. Versions and change notification in an object oriented database system. In *25th ACM/IEEE Design Automation Conference*, pages 275–281, 1988.

[3] B. Liskov, M. Castro, L. Shrira, and A. Adya. Providing persistent objects in distributed systems. In R. Guerraoui, editor, *ECOOP '99 — Object-Oriented Programming 13th European Conference, Lisbon Portugal*, volume 1628, pages 230–257. Springer-Verlag, New York, NY, 1999.

[4] Notification_Services_Product_Team. *Microsoft SQL Server Notification Services Technical Overview*, 2002. "http://www.microsoft.com/sql/techinfo/development/2000/sqlnsto.asp".

[5] A. H. Skarra, S. B. Zdonik, and S. P. Reiss. An object server for an object-oriented database system. In *ACM Transactions on Database Systems*, pages 196–204, January 1986.

A Portable Interoperation Module for Workflow System

Wooseok Jun, Dongsoo Han

School of Engineering

Information and Communication University

Yusong P.O. Box 77, Yusong, Deajon

305-600, Korea South

holos@icu.ac.kr, dshan@icu.ac.kr

Abstract

The interoperation between workflow management systems in different organization became indispensable. If the interfaces between the two have standardized specification, it will be easy to add module to workflow system. Therefore, we suggest a Workflow engine independent interoperability module for workflow system using workflow interface 2. This approach will provide the portability with the interoperation support module.

1. Introduction

At the beginning of using WfMS, the interoperability of WfMS was not an important issue than other functions such as interfaces for applications, process definitions, monitoring and administration. Nowadays WfMS, however, is used not only as a tool of business process automation in a single organization but as one of solutions supporting inter-organizational process. Therefore, it is essential to support interoperation ability - interoperability - among different workflow management systems.

Many researches are adding interoperation modules to Workflow systems. The problem is that there are no standardized requirements the interfaces between the Workflow system and the interoperation module. Therefore, the interoperation modules have the dependence to specific Workflow engine where the module is applied. And for the same reason, it may get troubles when modification is needed. To the contrary, if there is a standardized interface between them, it will be easy to adapt the module to any Workflow engine.

To make it easier to use, the interoperability components should be completely separated from WfMS. By this way we can provide the portability to the module. The portability means how easy it can be applied to different Workflow engine. That is the reason we try to suggest the Workflow application connected through interface 2&3 as an interoperability supporting module.

Based on the approach above, we designed and implemented an interoperation module. We designed it to have three sub-modules, each of which work as communicating with Workflow engine, creating and parsing the Wf-XML messages and transmitting messages. We also designed an example scenario and tested it. In the scenario we designed chained sub-process model and nested sub-process model.

2. Supporting Interoperability for WfMS

2.1 Problem Definition

To provide the interoperation ability for the workflow system, the researches have been carried out such as Interworkflow and AFRICA. Those researches are adding interoperation modules to workflow systems. The problem is that there are no standardized requirements of the interfaces between the Workflow system and the interoperation module. Therefore, the interoperability modules have dependence to the specific Workflow engine where the module is applied. Therefore we can define the problems as below:

• **Disunity of interface**

- **Dependency to workflow system**
- **Not fully supporting standard requirements**

2.2 The Requirements

According to the definition of Workflow Relevant data, an application can access the data as Workflow engine can, while the other two types of data can be accessible only by the applications or Workflow engine. It means that Workflow relevant data can be a means of interaction between Workflow engine and applications. Unlike other data types, Workflow relevant data may be manipulated by workflow applications as well as by the Workflow engine.

For an application to access and manipulate workflow relevant data at run time, it must be defined which relevant data can be accessible to the activity, which controls that application at build time. All these definitions should be described by a process definition tool at build time. As we can see at the Workflow data type, if parameters are defined as relevant data at build-time, the interoperation module we design can access and use them when creates the Wf-XML messages. Therefore, it is required to define required parameters as Workflow relevant data.

From the problems of referred researches, we aim the following objectives for a module supporting interoperability for WfMS. The objectives are portability, flexibility, supporting Workflow standards and minimizing effect on existing Workflow engine and WfMS.

- **Portability**: It means that the module is independent to workflow engine, thus easy to apply to any Workflow engine. To develop an interoperability module with portability, the module should be designed as a separate component to workflow engine.
- **Minimizing effect on existing workflow engine**: This can be met by achieving portability. It is required for reducing problems by affecting various components of WfMS, such as process definition tool, client applications and monitoring tool, when a new component for interoperation is added.
- **Supporting Workflow standards**: This should be accomplished

for supporting interoperability between heterogeneous workflow engines from different vendors.

To achieve above objectives, we designed a module which supports the interoperability as a client application of WfMS. In other words, the module should have functions for satisfying interface 2&3 for acting as an application and for satisfying interface 4 for supporting WfMS's interoperability. Therefore, the module is completely separated from the workflow engine. And for that reason, there will be no effects on the workflow engine when the module is adopted.

3. Design

The module consists of three parts, named WAPI sub-module, Operation sub-module and Transport sub-module. This layered architecture makes it easy to fit heterogeneous environments. For example, if a organization would like to change its transmission protocol, just changing the Transport sub-module will do without any changes to other sub-modules.

The WAPI sub-module communicates with workflow engine. It has two sub-components named Remote Process Handler and Local Process Handler. The Remote Process Handler receives orders to create process instance at remote WfMS. The Local Process Handler receives the order of creating process instance and request to create it to the workflow engine that it belongs to. Basically, an organization, which requests uses Remote Process Handler and one, which provides services uses Local Process Handler.

The Operation Sub-module consists of two sub-components named, Operation Manager and Wf-XML Manager. Operation Manager receives orders from Remote Process Handler. It decides which messages to create based on the orders it received and calls Wf-XML Manager to create Wf-XML message. When a message is received from the other organization, the Operation Manager sends the message to Wf-XML Manager to parse it. When the result is returned, Operation Manager calls Local Process Handler to do jobs according to the message.

The Transport sub-module has Sender and Receiver, which sends and receives messages respectively. The Sender is ordered by the Operation Manager and the Receiver passes the messages to Operations Manager when it receives them.

To use the parameters required for Wf-XML operation messages, we defined them as relevant data. These parameters are used in Wf-XML document as XML elements.

Some parameters like *ObserverKey* should gain value in run-time, the value is passed when the application invoked. Some, however, can be defined to have default value, e.g. value of *StartImmediately* can be set when process definition is defined.

To use an application in a process, it must be registered and defined in process definition. Also the relevant data that the application can access should be defined. Because the interoperation module we design is not different from other applications that workflow engine generally uses, the definition is not different from that of other activity for applications.

One operation requires four phases to complete the operation. That means that if one workflow engine requests an operation for interoperation, the interoperation module takes the order and send Wf-XML message to partner workflow engine (Phase 1). The interoperation module at partner workflow engine receives the message, and requests the operation to its workflow engine (Phase 2). This interoperation module receives the result of operation from its workflow engine and sends the message contains the result (Phase 3). The interoperation module at requesting workflow engine receives the message, and passes it to workflow engine (Phase 4).

The required functions can be classified as the sub-module is divided; performing or requesting the operation, generating and parsing XML messages and transmitting and receiving the messages.

The WAPI sub-module should have functions for supporting the four operations that Wf-XML binding standard defined. Each function is in pair, requesting and performing. For example, Remote Process Handler has

functions for request of CreateProcessInstance, and Local Process Handler has functions for performing CreateProcessInstance. In case of response, Local Process Handler has functions for requesting and Remote Process Handler performing reaction.

The operation sub-module should have functions to create Wf-XML messages according to passed parameters and to parse messages received from partner workflow engine. If it receives parameters form WAPI sub-module, operation sub-module decides which message to create and verifies the created message.

The transmission sub-module should have functions to send and receive messages. More important function for this sub-module, however, is to support various transmission protocols. Therefore, frames of functions should be designed.

4. Summary

As the need of cross-organizational process has been increased, workflow systems are also required interoperability. Because the interoperability was not a significant function when workflow system was initially used, most WfMS does not have functions for interoperation. Therefore, there have been many researches about workflow interoperation including the standard and the referred researches.

We focused on the portability of interoperability module. And to achieve our aim, we used the workflow application for supporting interoperability. The workflow applications are completely separated from the workflow engine and communicate through the standard Tool Agents. Therefore, the module can be easily adapted to any workflow engine that follows the standard.

To implement the suggested interoperation module, parameters required for Wf-XML messages were defined as workflow relevant data. And we designed the module to have three sub-modules. The WAPI sub-module communicates with workflow engine, the operation sub-module generates the Wf-XML messages and manipulates them and the transport sub-module sends and receives the messages. Using the interoperation module, we also designed a scenario that shows nested sub-process model and chained sub-process model.

For now only two models were simulated, however, the rest should be supported. Therefore, implementing whole scenario models is required in next research, and the monitoring system for the suggested model is also required.

5. References

[1] Workflow Management Coalition, *The Workflow Reference Model*, Document Number TC00-1003, 1995.

[2] Workflow Management Coalition, *Workflow Standard – Interoperability Abstract Specification*, Document Number WFMC-TC-1012, 1999.

[3] James G. Hayes, Effat Peyrovian, Sunil Sarin, Marc-Thomas Schmidt, Keith D. Swenson, Rainer Weber, *Workflow Interoperability Standards for the Internet*, Internet Computing, 2000.

[4] Workflow Management Coalition, *Workflow Management Standard–Interoperability Wf-XML Binding version 1.1*, Document Number WFMC-TC-1023, 2001.

[5] Casati, Dayal and Shan, *Business Operation Intelligence, Databases in Networked Information Systems*, 2002.

[6] OMG, *Workflow Management Facility Specification V1.2*.

[7] Keiko Hiramatsu, Ken-ichi Okada, Yutaka Matushita and Haruo Hayami, *Interworkflow System: Coordination of Each Workflow System Among Multiple Organizations*, 1998.

[8] Hayami, Haruo, *Development and Experimental Proof of an Interworkflow Management System*, Presentation at the Workflow Management Coalition Meeting in Tokyo, 1999.

[9] Michael zur Muehlen, Florian Klein, *AFRICA: Workflow Interoperability based on XML-Messages*, 2001.

[10] Michael zur Muehlen, *A Framework for XML-based Workflow Interoperability–The AFRICA Project*, 2001.

[11] Workflow Management Coalition, *Terminology & Glossary*, Document Number WFMC-TC-1011, 1999.

[12] Workflow Management Coalition, *Interface 1: Process Definition Interchange Process Model*, Document Number WfMC TC-1016-P, 1999.

[13] Dongsoo Han, Jeayong Shim and Chansu Yu, *ICU/COWS: A Distributed Trnasactional Workflow System Supporting Multiple Workflow Type*, IEICE Transactions of Information and Systems, E83-D(7), 2000.

An Object-Oriented Representation and Reasoning Model to Rewriting Queries using Views

Abdelhak SERIAI

Ecole des Mines de Douai, Département GIP
941, rue Charles Bourseul, BP 838 - 59508 Douai Cedex, France
email : seriai@ensm-douai.fr

Abstract

We propose in this article an object-oriented approach to rewriting queries using views. Our approach aims to mitigate certain limitations of existing query rewriting approaches. Among these limitations, the inconsideration of certain types of object-oriented complex queries or the lack of uniformity of this approaches compared to the object-oriented model.

1. Introduction

The importance of query rewriting using views is not any more to be illustrated [3]. This technique has multiple applications for data integration, query optimisation or for maintenance of physical data independence. Consequently, many approaches were proposed to rewriting queries using views in object-oriented contexts. From them, we distinguish mainly three categories: the by-transformation [5], the algorithmic [4] and the heterogeneous approaches [2].

The disadvantage of the transformation approach is that it requires the translation of object concepts to be left towards a target representation (logical or descriptive). Moreover, it's limited to queries, which can be expressed via logical or descriptive representations.
However, the disadvantage of the algorithmic approach is that the related reasoning is carried out through ad-hoc algorithms. Algorithmic reasoning is known, among other, to be difficult to check, to adapt and to re-use.
Disadvantage of the heterogeneous approach is the heterogeneity of the used query and view models.

Considering these limitations, we propose in this article an object-oriented approach to rewriting queries using views. Our approach aims to mitigate these limitations.

2. The proposal principle

We think that weaknesses underlined above can be alleviate by exploiting all power of the object-oriented representation and reasoning. Thus, we propose, on one hand, an object-oriented representation model of queries and views, and on other hand, the exploitation of the object-oriented classification mechanism to rewrite, using views, complex OQL queries. Accordingly, our model includes two parts: an object-oriented representation and organisation architecture of queries and views, and a query containment and rewriting reasoning mechanism.

2.1 Query and view object-oriented representation model

Our representation model is based on one hand, on three concepts: *query*, *query-result* and *view,* and in other hand, on object-oriented representation of these concepts as object-oriented classes and their organisation in specific inheritance hierarchies.

A Query-class is the result of an object-oriented representation of a query. It's a composite class whose components are classes representing algebraic operations used in this query (e.g. restriction, join, projection, etc.). As an example, figure 1_a and figure 1_b represent respectively, using UML notation [1], the corresponding object-oriented representation model of OQL *Select-From-Where* and *Intersection* queries.
An *intersection* query-class is composed of two query-classes representing used operands.

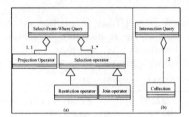

Figure 1 *Select-From-Where and Intersection query-classes*

A query-result class is the representation model of data selected by a query. Figure *4* represents the query-result class related to query presented in *Example 1*.

Figure 2 *Example of a query-result class*

We consider that a view is defined through two parts: the query defining this view (view intension) and data resulting from its evaluation (view extension). Thus, we represent a view as a composite class, whose components are classes representing equivalent queries defining this view, and at most one class representing the corresponding query-result data.

2.2 Complex query containment

Query containment permits to detect link between, in one side, collection representing result of a query to be rewritten, and in other side, collections representing extensions of existing views. To determine these containment links, we proceed following two steps. First, canonical transformation of queries which determine semantically equivalences between queries, which can be syntactically different. Next, the classification of classes, representing these ones in an inheritance hierarchy, to detect links between query-class representing a query to be rewriting and query-classes representing queries defining existing views. These links are used to deduce inclusion relationships existing between the corresponding query-result collections.

2.3 Query rewriting reasoning

We have based the rewriting of a query on deduced links of this query. Therefore we distinguish, followings these links, two types of rewriting: elementary and complex rewritings[6].

2.3.1 Elementary query rewritings

Elementary rewriting of a query consists of exploiting views which are directly related to query to be rewritten.

Exemple 1. Are $Q1_{view}$, $Q2_{view}$ two queries defining views representing respectively "*Associate teachers*" and "*Employees older than 25 year*". The corresponding query-result classes of $Q1_{view}$ and $Q2_{view}$ are respectively C_{Q1} and C_{Q2}.

$Q1_{View}$: *SELECT* x *FROM* x *in Teachers*	
WHERE $x.$ *status= «associate»*	

$Q2_{View}$: *SELECT* $y.name, y.age, y.MaritalStatus$	
FROM y *in Employees* *WHERE* $y.age > 25$	

Let consider Q_{user}, a query where its corresponding query-class is classified as sub-class of those representing $Q1_{view}$ and $Q2_{view}$.

Thus, Q_{user} can be rewritten using $Q1_{view}$ and $Q2_{view}$ as it's illustrated by $Q_{ByRewriting}$ query described below.

Q_{user} : *SELECT* $z.name, z.age,$	*FROM*	z *in Teachers*
WHERE $z.statut = «associate»$ *AND*		$z.age > 50$

$Q_{ByRewriting}$:
SELECT $z.name, z.age$
FROM z *in Teachers, x in Extent(C_{Q1}), y in Extent(C_{Q2})*
WHERE $z = x$ *AND* $z.name=y.name$
AND $z.age = y.age$ *AND* $z.age > 50$

2.4 Recursive query rewriting

Compared to elementary query rewriting, recursive one is characterized by considering all existing views. These ones can be directly or indirectly linked to the query to be rewritten. In fact, we propose to exploit links concerning component-classes to rewrite sub-query expressions forming part of a query to be rewritten and which are represented by components.

Exemple 2. Let consider Q_{user} and Q_{view} two queries, where the first one calculates "*Names of temporary teachers intervening in a Master formation*", and the second calculates "*Courses given in all Master formations*".

Q_{user}	*SELECT* *teacher. name*
	FROM *teacher in Teachers,*
	formation in Formations, course in Courses
	WHERE *Teacher. status= « Temporary »*
AND	*course in teacher. courses*
AND	*course in formation. courses*
AND	*formation. name=«Master»*

Q_{view} :	*SELECT* *course*
FROM	*course in Courses, formation in Formations*
WHERE	*course in formation. Courses*
AND formation. type=«Master»	

Using recursive query rewriting principle, Q_{user} can be rewritten by exploiting Q_{view}, as it's shown by $Q_{byRewriting}$ query. This is possible because the object collection resulting from the evaluation of Q_{view} is an intermediate result in the calculation of Q_{user}. This situation is deduced from the result of the classification of query-class corresponding to Q_{user} (cf. Figure 8).

$Q_{ByRewriting}$:	
SELECT	*teacher. name*
FROM	*course in Extent(C_{QView}), teacher in teachers*
WHERE	*teacher. status= « Temporary »*
AND	*course in teacher. course*

3. Conclusion

We have proposed in this paper an object-oriented approach to rewrite queries using views. Our approach is based on the object-oriented classification reasoning mechanism which is possible thanks to the representation of queries as classes. In our approach, we used results of classification of query-classes, to generate possible rewritings for the corresponding queries. We have proposed two types of rewritings: elementary rewritings and recursive rewritings.

References

[1] G. Booch, J. Rumbaugh, I. Jacobson *The UML user guide* ISBN 0-201-57168-4, Addison-Wesley.

[2] M. Bucheit, M.A Jeusfled, W. Nutt, M. Staudt: *Subsumption between Queries to Object-Oriented Databases.* EDBT 1994: 15-22

[3] D. Calvanese, G. Giacomo, M. Lenzereni, M.Vardi: *What is View-Based Query Rewriting?* KRDB 2000: 17-27

[4] D. Florescu, L. Raschid, P. Valduriez: *Answering Queries Using OQL View Expressions.* VIEWS 1996: 84-90

[5] A. Y. Levy, A. O Mendelzon, Y. Sagiv, D. Srivastara: *Answering Queries Using Views.* PODS 1995: 95-104

[6] A. Seriai, *QUERYAID : an Object-Oriented model for query and query-result representation and management,* PHD thesis, Nantes university (in French).

Implementation Issues of Bio-AXS: An Object-oriented Framework for Integrating Biological Data and Applications

Luiz Fernando Bessa Seibel, Melissa Lemos and Sérgio Lifschitz

{seibel, melissa, sergio}@inf.puc-rio.br

Pontifícia Universidade Católica do Rio de Janeiro
Departamento de Informática
Rio de Janeiro - Brazil

Abstract

Bio-AXS is an object-oriented framework tool that aims at integrating genomic databases as well as related applications. This approach provides the expected flexibility, reusability and extensibility requirements of this domain. We present here an overview of Bio-AXS implementation issues that show how this tool may be effectively used in practice.

1 INTRODUCTION

In [1] we have proposed the use of an object-oriented framework [2, 3] approach to deal with these genomic data integration problem. A framework is an incomplete software system, which contains many basic pre-defined components (frozen spots) and others that must be instantiated (hot spots) for the implementation of the desired and particular functionality. Our proposed framework may be considered specific to the application domain, in our case, molecular biology and the genomic area.

The basic idea for choosing a framework approach is that we need a tool for integrating genomic information that is spread in a distributed environment (mostly available in the web). This information is constantly changing and used by distinct (and at the same time similar), applications. Therefore, flexibility, extensibility and software reusability are required.

Our proposed framework, whose static part is described in [1], was actually implemented and has become an effective tool called Bio-AXS [4]. Its functionalities and implementation details will be further explained in this paper.

This paper is organized as follows: we first give an overview of Bio-AXS framework. Then we detail the Bio-AXS implementation and the choices we have made. Finally, we conclude with contributions.

2 BIO-AXS OVERVIEW

This section describes briefly the BIO-AXS specification, which is the proposed architecture for the integration of the molecular biology data and applications through the use of the object-oriented framework technology. A complete presentation of the Bio-AXS architecture, with class and sequence diagrams, is available in [5].

2.1 Framework Architecture

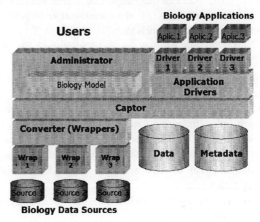

Figure 1 - The Bio-AXS Architecture

The Bio-AXS tool is divided in four main modules: Administrator, Captor (architecture mediator [6]), Application Driver and Converter. Their relationship and an overview of the framework architecture are depicted in Figure 1. The hot spots of our framework are the wrappers associated to biology data sources and the application drivers. Their instantiation implements a particular functionality, defining an application over the molecular biology application domain.

The administrator module acts as the interface with end users to provide the biological data model management, which include schemas and/or data capturing requests or even the execution of algorithms instantiated in the framework. Therefore, this module contains a biology class model that is committed with the existing data sources, as well as with the methods that are associated to these classes. The captor module is responsible for the data and schema repositories. The converter provides access to the biology data sources, translates their own schemas to XMLSchema and data to XML. Finally, the application drivers' module is the interface between biological applications and Bio-AXS.

2.2 Semi-structured Data Model

At this point it is important to explain our decision about using XML [7] and XMLSchema [8] as the chosen data model for Bio-AXS. A lot has been questioned with respect to adequate data models to represent the molecular biology data. The relational model does not enable an easy comprehension of the biological object (biologists and other end users would have problems to understand the meaning of a 200 tables database). Object-oriented models have difficulties to adapt to design changes and schema evolution. Usually data sources represent data in a text format, where special markers indicate the beginning and the end of the attributes. This has been shown easier for user's comprehension.

The XML standard has important characteristics to solve some problems of the computational biology community [9, 10, 11], such as:

- it is flexible because one can easily modify the DTD, or the XMLSchema, adding new elements or attributes with no further effects on the corresponding data;
- It has facilities for interconnection of data sources through links among the data instances (for example, in the construction of crossed references between data sources). The semi-structured data model is widely used in computational biology area for information change among data sources;
- It is used for definitions and standardized specifications of data;
- an XML file can be read and interpreted by any text editor, what does not occur, for example, with the ASN.1 [12] format.

Due to the above reasons, it has been decided that the repository should store data and schemas using the XML

2.3 Architecture General Description

Our Bio-AXS framework is enable to provide, then, the following functionalities:

- Schemas capture of existing and different data sources;
- Matching of the architecture objects to those objects in the captured schema;
- Definition of new ad-hoc schemas;
- Capture of data belonging to the data sources;
- Data generation in a format required by a molecular biology application;
- Execution of algorithms instantiated as methods of the biology classes.
- Information of the update of a schema, verified in a given data source;

- Update of the data instances as long as they are being updated in their original source.

Bio-AXS integrates molecular biology data from any data source. Indeed, wrappers that capture the schema, and also the data from specific data sources, are made available. These wrappers also translate the data source schemas to XMLSchema and data to XML. Both schemas and data are stored in a repository that uses the semi-structured model.

A special user, named system administrator, is responsible for the comprehension of the schema captured from the data sources and the definition of a biological information global schema. The administrator needs a visualization tool for captured objects, where the object descriptions (object name, data type, description and domain) are incorporated in order to enable their understanding and the use by other researchers. After the complete object description, the administrator must add them to the global schema. It leads to the definition of relationships with other objects of the global schema, with the description of the cardinalities, identification of synonymous and the definition of the conversion rules (of unities and or values, for example, an attribute named sex may be stored as 0/1 in a data source and "m"/"f" in another).

With the Bio-AXS tool, the administrator can define a specific schema (e.g., the schema used in GUS [13]) for a given research project that will be later instantiated. The data instantiation facilitates the schema comprehension, the formulation of queries and reduce the response time.

If the administrator decides to instantiate the local data warehouse, the architecture mediator must choose, from the global schema definition, which data sources must be searched to obtain the schema objects to be instantiated and the way associations among the object instances are done. The conversion rules that were defined for the objects are executed at the mediator's level, as well as type conversions.

With an instantiated schema, the users may access the data warehouse through a given query language, such as XML-QL, Xquery or Xpath, in databases that admit a data type specific for XML, such as the XMLType defined in the SGBD Oracle 9i [14].

It is important to observe that the global schema registers the ontology that is effectively used in the molecular biology data sources. A more detailed and complete ontology is directly dependent of the number of captured data sources. It can be also noted that is not necessary to build instances of the captured schemas: only the needed schemas should be instantiated.

The administrator can also define data converters (or drivers) to enable the use, through the Bio-AXS, of multiple applications that are available for molecular biology research projects. The global schema of the architecture contemplates the classes' methods used in molecular biology. Thus, our tool allows users to execute those methods directly over the instantiated data.

The architecture also monitors the schemas of captured data sources in order to inform the administrator of any the change (schema evolution) through software agents that act in the same level as the wrappers. A similar mechanism for monitoring data sources, based in agents, updates the data instances that have been changed in the original source. The choice of XML makes this task easier because many data sources also use XML-bases storage structures. However, data updates are harder but could be easier if the data sources had independent files containing only updated data, with timestamps for each registration. Some data sources already implement this kind of update mechanisms.

We claim that the Bio-AXS architecture is flexible because data source wrappers and application drivers may be included with no restrictions or limitations. The capture of schemas allows the definition of a global schema and makes it possible to define an ontology. The low query performance, very common in some studied architectures, is solved through the data warehouse instantiation. The architecture has also mechanisms to update schemas and data.

The implemented architecture intends to be an important support tool for the research in molecular biology, as it presents innovative solutions for the limitations of known integration tools. Bio-AXS deals with integration based on a meta-model, which makes it different from approaches in the literature. The integration is executed through a mediator that captures the data source schema and data, makes necessary conversions and materializes the information in the repository.

3   BIO-AXS IMPLEMENTATION

In this section we describe the implementation details of the Bio-AXS functionalities and a few examples of the actual use of our tool.

The implementation of the data source schema capture is obviously dependent on the data model used by the source. For a data source that uses the semi-structured model, the schema capture can be done as follows:

• It is first defined a grammar for the language used;

• Next it is executed a syntactic analyzer generator (for example, YACC [15]);

• The syntactic analyzer is changed to generate XML code. Thus, an output can be automatically generated in XML format;

• Finally the SPY program [16,17] is used to generate the corresponding XMLSchema from the XML code

For data sources implemented in object-oriented or relational DBMS, the schema can be generated through a sequence of queries to the database data dictionary. Our implemented tool has used so far data sources exclusively in the semi-structured model. This has happened because the semi-structured model is widely present in the molecular biology area. Also, even for those data sources implemented in a DBMS, they may export data in semi-structured files.

The wrappers were implemented for a data source of nucleotides sequence (GenBank) and two sources of proteins sequence (PIR [18, 19] and Swiss-Prot). For the Swiss-Prot, the schema was defined manually from the documentation available in [20]. PIR provides data in XML as well as the correspondent DTD. The SPY tool generates the PIR schema description in XML schema from the DTD.

For the generation of the GenBank schema we have used a public domain parser that transforms data into XML and also generate the correspondent DTD. Once more SPY was used to convert the DTD to the correspondent representation in XMLSchema. Unfortunately the XMLSchema document generated from SPY is not very clear because the data definitions are automatically generated from instances or the DTD. Thus, it was necessary to edit the XMLSchema document in order to simplify it and improve its comprehension.

3.1   Global Schema Creation/Extension

The idea here is to create and extend the global conceptual schema of biological information. The natural way to implement this functionality is to start with a previously defined schema and increase it with data source schemas that are captured with Bio-AXS.

This can be done through a visual tool that shows the global schema and a captured schema and allows the administrator user to manipulate the schemas in order to represent the information that is being integrated. In this process, new objects can be identified and incorporated to the global schema, as well as new relationships. For each object of the global schema, properties can be assigned with their respective information (name, type, domain, default values and obligation indication), methods and relationships with other objects (with the corresponding cardinalities).

Besides, concepts can be associated to objects so that they can be better understood. It is important that the object contains references to the data sources that store their instances. This way it is possible, in the future, to instantiate the global schema. Synonyms can also be identified among objects and the need of data type or domain conversion. The objects can be simple or composed and can be organized in different ways. The organization must contemplate the ones typically used in biology (for example, the CPL types [21], list, bag, registration and variant). The schema integration produces the data source ontology. Our implementation contemplates the described integration form. The XMLSchema language has made possible the representation of the supra-mentioned metadata.

For example, to represent information of an object and its respective properties, clauses have been used with direct correspondence in XMLSchema (*name*, *type* from *element*; *restriction*; *use*, *value*, *required/optional* from *attribute*). The relationships with other objects, and the correspondent cardinalities, have been mapped in XMLSchema in the clauses *ref*, *minoccurs / maxoccurs* from *element*.

For the definition of concepts related to an object, we have added a new attribute in XMLSchema to the object, implemented through the clause *name* = "desc" and *value* = "concept description" of an *attribute*. Likewise, to identify to which data source the object belongs, a new attribute was added to the object, implemented through the clause *name* = "source" and *fixed* ="data source name" of *attribute*. Analogously, attributes were added in order to identify synonyms between objects and to identify type conversion of data.

The clauses *simpleType* and *complexType* were used to represent simple and complex objects. The different ways for object organization can also be represented using special clauses of XML Schema. For example, the clause *sequence* of *element* can be used to represent the CPL list and the clause *choice* can be used to represent the CPL variant.

Bio-AXS has a friendly web-like interface for building a global schema from other existing data source schemas. These are represented in a tree structure: users may not understand XML Schema and still work well with it. This feature was implemented using Oracle packages found in [22], particularly oracle.xml.parser.schema, oracle.xml.parser.v2 and oracle.xml.treeviewer. These packages parse a XML Schema file and show its corresponding tree view.

We have defined classes to control events and business rules in a layer on top of these Oracle packages. These classes accomplish the following tasks:

• Definition of object concepts;
• Synonyms implementation;
• Implementation of semantic rules that manage the construction of the global schema tree (create, remove, rename object(s) of the tree);
• Construction of the XML Schema from the global schema tree;
• Encapsulation of the DBMS information and also schemas that are used by our tool (it is possible to read schemas from any DBMS and also text files);
• Application Graphic interface is responsible for tree format exhibition from the XML Schema.

3.2 Specific Schema Creation

We may create with Bio-AXS specific schemas starting with the biology global schema. This functionality is a particular situation of the previous functionality. There is a single class that deals with the initial system interface where the operation mode is defined to be either the creation/extension of a general schema or creation of a specific schema. When the administrator user makes the choice, schemas that must be represented are known.

3.3 Data Capture

The data instantiation is related to its schema (the object can belong to one or more data sources and it can be instantiated in the repository). In the case of one single data source, if it uses the semi-structured model, data is captured in the following way:

• If already in XML format, the syntax must be checked and store the data in the repository;
• If data is not in XML, we first define a grammar for the language being used. Next, we execute a syntax analyzer generator (YACC), indicating the grammar previously defined. Finally, the syntax analyzer is modified in order to generate XML code.

For the data sources stored in relational DMBS there are many ways to generate data in XML. The most convenient form for Bio-AXS requires the assembly of the biological object, which is different than the simple conversion of the data at each table to XML. For object-oriented DBMS, data in XML format can be generated through search operations in the database.

To instantiate data from objects that are stored in the repository, we start from the global schema (which defines objects, relationships and locations) and search the object instances stored in the repository to build the specific schema instance. If they are not stored in the repository, we use the global schema (which defines the location of the objects in the data sources) and the data source wrappers to capture object instances that belong to the schema.

Finally, for generating data for an external application, this requires drivers that know the data format specifically required by the application. Thus, for each application (or family of applications), we need to develop a specific driver. For example, we have implemented and tested a driver for FASTA format. The driver reads the sequences (nucleotides or amino acids) from the repository and builds a file in the format expected by the BLAST and other applications.

3.4 Execution of Bio-AXS Own Applications

The biology global schema classes or even the captured schemas classes, may be associated to methods that are instantiated in the architecture through the use of software components, implemented through mechanisms like Java Beans [23].

In our current version of Bio-AXS there is a components repository. This is read by the Administrator Module and exhibited to the users, which can choose the component to be executed on the data. For example, the sequence class of the global schema has the method Alignment that executes the algorithm of optimal global alignment [24] between sequence pairs. One sequence is obtained in the repository and the other is given as parameter.

3.5 Schema and Data Monitoring

This functionality aims at keeping schemas and data in the Bio-AXS repository up to date with respect to the data sources. The implementation of this functionality is done through a software agent that is inside the data source wrapper. The agent monitors constantly the data source schema and reports the change events to the administrator user, so that the administrator can (re)capture the new schema. This way we can deal with schema evolution. Analogously, a software agent notices the changes in the data instances and may update the repository.

4   CONCLUSIONS

This work presents an architecture, which has solutions for the integration of molecular biology data sources and applications. The architecture, whose specification, project and implementation are in this paper, proposes the integration of any data source previously existent and the available applications. The architecture allows to instantiate new data sources and to incorporate new applications.

With the first version of Bio-AXS developed, studies were and are still being done by molecular biology researchers aiming at solving problems like integrity, data quality and new knowledge discovery. Bio-AXS has been used already by biologists that normally waste a long time while searching, capturing, formatting and analyzing information gathered from multiple data sources.

REFERENCES

[1]   Seibel, L.F.B., Lifschitz, S.. "A Genome Databases Framework". Proc. 12th Database and Expert Systems Applications (DEXA), pp. 319-329, 2001.

[2]   Fayad, M.E., Schmidt, D.C.. "Object-Oriented Application Frameworks". Communications of the ACM, vol 40, n. 10, pp.32-38, 1997.

[3]   Fayad M.E., Schmidt D.C. Johnson R.E., Building Application Frameworks, Addison-Wesley, 1999.

[4]   Seibel, L.F.B., "Bio-AXS: An Architecture for Integrating Data Sources and Molecular Biology Applications", PhD Thesis, Depto Informática, Pontifícia Universidade Católica do Rio de Janeiro, 2002.

[5]   Seibel, L.F.B., Lifschitz, S. "A Genome Databases Framework". Tech Report MCC 20/01, Dept Informática, Pontifícia Universidade Católica do Rio de Janeiro, 2001.

[6]   Wiederhold, G.. "Mediators in the Architecture of Future Information Systems". IEEE Computer, pp. 38-49, 1992.

[7]   "XML". http://www.w3.org/XML/, 2002.

[8]   "XML Schema". http://www.w3.org/XML/Schema, 2002.

[9]   Achard, F., Vaysseix, G., Birfllot, E.. "XML, bioinformatics and data integration". Bioinformatics, 17, pp. 115-125, 2001.

[10]   Guerrinia, V, Jackson D.. "Bioinformatics and XML". On Line Journal of Bioinformatics, 1(1), pp. 1-13, 2000.

[11]   Mello, R., Heuser, C.. "A Bottom-up Approach for Integration of XML Sources". Proc. of the International Workshop on Information Integration on the Web - WIIW, pp. 118-124, 2001.

[12]   Dubuisson, O. "ASN.1 - Communication between heterogeneous systems". Morgan Kaufmann Publishers. http://www.oss.com/asn1/dubuisson.html, 2000.

[13]   Davidson, S. B., Crabtree, J., Brunk, B. P., Schug, J., Tannen, V., Overton, G. C., C. J. Stoeckert, Jr.. "K2/Kleisli and GUS: Experiments in integrated access to genomic data sources".IBM Systems Journal, 40(2), 2001. http://www.research.ibm.com/journal/sj/402/davidson.html

[14]   "Oracle 9i". http://www.oracle.com/, 2002.

[15]   "The LEX & YACC Page". http://dinosaur.compilertools.net/, 2002.

[16]   "XML Spy". http://www.xmlspy.com/, 2002.

[17]   "The World Wide Web Consortium (W3C)". http://www.w3.org/, 2002.

[18]   Barker W.C., Garavelli J.S., Huang H., McGarvey P.B., Orcutt B.C., Srinivasarao G.Y., Xiao C., Yeh L.L., Ledley R.S., Janda J.F., Pfeiffer F., Mewes H., Tsugita A., Wu C., The Protein Information Resource (PIR), Nucleic Acids Research 28(1), pp. 41-44, 2000.

[19]   "Protein Information Resource". http://pir.georgetown.edu/, 2002.

[20]   "ExPASy - SWISS-PROT and TrEMBL". http://www.expasy.ch/sprot/, 2002.

[21]   "Collection Programming Language - Penn DB Research Group". http://db.cis.upenn.edu/, 2002.

[22]   Oracle XML packages: http://technet.oracle.com/docs/ tech/xml/xdk_java/doc_library/Production9i

[23]   JavaBeans(TM). http://java.sun.com/products/javabeans/, 2002

[24]   Needleman, S.B., Wunsch, C.D.. "A general method applicable to the Search for Similarities in the Amino Acid Sequence of TwoProteins". Journal of Molecular Biology, 48, pp. 443-453, 1970.

CONFSYS: The CINDI Conference Support System

Zhengwei Gu
Dept. of Computer Science
Concordia University
Montreal, Canada
zgu@csc.com

Xin Jin
Dept. of Computer Science
Concordia University
Montreal, Canada
xjin@cs.concordia.ca

Bipin C. Desai
Dept. of Computer Science
Concordia University
Montreal, Canada
bcdesai@cs.concordia.ca

1. Introduction

In managing an academic conference, the program chair (PC) is required to deal with many repetitive administrative tasks such as: interaction with authors and program committee members (reviewers), paper collection, paper allocation, distributing the paper to the reviewers, collating, sorting and tabulating the evaluations, orchestrating the debate of controversial evaluation of some of the papers, making the final tabulation and preparing the notification and comments to the reviewers and authors.

A number of web-based systems for automating the above tasks have been reviewed in [1]. Some of the systems are no longer supported. Most of these systems use script programming languages and CGI technology. However, Java Servlet technology has better performance. Most of this software requires some efforts to handle different situations. So, system administrators are required for set-up; a service offered by the commercialization of these systems. The user interface is non-existence in many systems especially for administration and requires running scripts.

The Conference Management System (ConfSys) presented here is a entirely a Web-based system which provides facility for the Program chair(s) to set up the details for a meeting, allows authors to register and submit papers to the system on-line; records the topic of expertise of the members of the program committee members (reviewers); helps the PC by performing an automatic allocation of the submitted papers to the reviewers. The reviewers have a facility to bid in an auction for papers to review and later to download and review the assigned paper via the Internet. The ConfSys uses the DBLP database [2] in the automatic assignment of papers to avoid any conflict of interest and thus helps in the allocation of papers to the reviewers for a fair and impartial review of each paper.

2. Architecture and Sequence of Events

The major part of this system is a web-based application, which uses a 3- tier framework. The system supports three groups of users: authors, reviewers and program (co) chair(s) (PC). We assume that the reviewers may use external referees, however the reviewers are responsible for the actual evaluations and would participate in their debate. For clear and easy notation, we assume that authors and PC are female and the reviewers are male.

On the client side, the web browser is the only tool to allow users of the system, including paper authors, reviewers and PC, to communicate with server. The server side stores the business logics for the system. By reviewing the client's request, the server will produce an appropriate response. Finally the database supports the server and keeps all information sent by clients.

In the figure below, we outline the flow of events, the actors involved and the actions that are orchestrated by ConfSys; it thus indicates the interaction of each group and shows the manual and automatic actions supported by it.

For the functions of the authors and reviewers, we need to consider concurrency, synchronization and database locks. Functions for program chair(s) involve complex logic for example, in the algorithm for automatic papers allocation to reviewers; however, because of the limited number of users, they require minimal multi-user consideration.

3. Implementation

Since this is a web-based application, it makes sense that users can use browsers (IE or Netscape) to communicate with the server. Other function to be added are the ability to upload papers by authors, and the ability of the reviewers to download the papers they are to evaluate and submit their score and comments on them. They also need to debate the reviews and if needed modify some scores in case of contradictions in the evaluation of a given paper. The application allows authors to upload file from client side to server side, not only in HTML format but also MIME format. In order to handle non-HTML package sent by clients using browser, there is a need of an additional tool on the server side. For ConfSys system we use two java classes called MultiRequest and MultiRequestServlet [3].

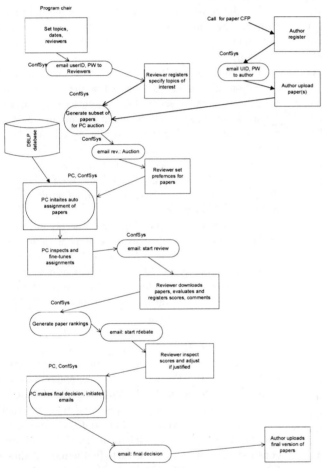

Since this application uses Java Servlet as middleware, a servlet engine needs to be deployed on the server side. We have implemented the current version using Tomcat as the servlet engine. Though Tomcat includes function of a web server, it is not advisable to use it as both web server and servlet engine due its poorer performance as a web server. ConfSys hence uses Apache as the HTML server and Tomcat as the servlet engine extension of Apache to support Java servlet classes.

The back end is the database server. MySQL is used as the database server in this application; it is suitable for medium size application and it interfaces easily with Java or C/C++. In the case users try to query the database, the request finally will be passed to the servlet engine and a Java class will do the job for the query.

4. ConfSys Sequence of Events

4.1 File Uploads

We allow the author the flexibility in uploading a file; this includes canceling an uploaded file or replaces it by another. However, since the embedded part in a multipart request can only be from a web client to a web server, there is no way for a web server to send back the embedded part to a web browser. This causes a problem to propagate the name of the uploaded file from one web page to another web page needed for the above feature. To solve this problem, we use a child window for the uploading page instead of using an upload button directly in the main window. The child window is used to select the file to be uploaded; this file is stored in a temporary folder on the server and the file name is written to the main window on the client screen. File name can be carried from page to page and get to be verified. If the client makes the final confirmation for the uploaded file and submitted related information, then the file will be moved from a temporary folder to the regular folder for uploaded files. If the author decides to delete the uploaded file during processing, the file in the temporary folder would be deleted. If the author aborts the submission process, the uploaded file will remain in the temporary folder. If an author returns to resubmit a file with the same name as an aborted upload of a file in the temporary folder, it will be overwritten.

File upload function is a multi-user function and requires concurrency control to avoid file with the same name submitted by more than one user overwriting each other[1]. To avoid the file being overwritten, one of the users will be requested to change the file name. Once an author clicks to confirm the upload, the server saves the file into regular folder with the user specified name that is guaranteed to be unique.

4.2 DBLP System and its conversion to MySql table

---

[1] Many authors tend to use name for files such as paper03.pdf or ideas03.pdf

Digital Bibliography & Library Project (DBLP)[2] contains information on conference papers, journals papers, books and thesis etc. Each DBLP file, in XML, represents one item; there being thousands of such files in tree-structured directories. Since searching XML files in such a tree-structured directories is time consuming with Java, we have pre-processed the information from these files into a relational database; this pre-processing step is needed only once; after which it can be used efficiently. For conflict avoidance, we only need to verify the co-author relationship; hence we create a table with three columns. One is key, which is an incremental number. Another is the path of the file, which we need to verify during the automatic assignment process. The last is a string, which contains the authors of each item in the DBLP database. If the reviewer's name and the author's name appear in the same tuple of this table, then it is considered a conflict.

Pre-processing the DBLP files is straightforward since all the authors are tagged. We used a C program for this process and insert the result directly in the MySql database. This approach has excellent performance since querying a table in the database is much faster than searching XML files in a tree structure directories using a Java program.

4.3 Paper allocation algorithm

ConfSys has three paper allocation schemes. These are:
  (a) Manually by the PC,
  (b) Automatic followed by fine-tuning by the PC,
  (c) PC auction followed by an automatic allocation followed by fine-tuning.

For the PC auction, ConfSys uses a scheme where reviewers, indicate via web forms, their areas of expertise from the list of topics for the conference. The authors are required to indicate the topics for their papers as well. Once the call for paper (CFP) deadline is over, the system generates a list of papers, which match their expertise and/or a random subset of papers for each reviewer and the reviewer is requested to indicate their priority (high, average, low) for reviewing the papers.

In the case GC member uses the automatic allocation, several constrains will be applied to this function. There is no limitation for GC's manual allocation or for the fine-tuning stage.

Following are the constraints for the automatic allocation:
  i. The same paper should not be allocated to same reviewer more than once.

ii. A paper cannot be allocated to a reviewer if either the limit of papers for the reviewer or the number of reviewers assigned to the paper is reached.

iii. A paper can be allocated to a reviewer if the intersection of the set of the paper's topics and reviewer's interests is not empty.

iv. A paper can't be allocated to a reviewer if one of the authors and the reviewer are from the same organization.

v. A paper can't be allocated to a reviewer if one of the authors and the reviewer were co-authors in the past.

For the constraints i to iv, we can use the information from the system database; for constraint v, we use the information generated from the DBLP database for the decision.

For the constraint i, the system can check the allocation table in the database. For the constraint ii, it uses the parameters set by PC to indicate the number of reviewers for a paper and the maximum number of papers for each reviewer. For the constraint iii, the system uses the paper's topics, a required field when an author submits a paper, with the reviewer's area of interests. If there is an match, then the paper can be allocated the reviewer. For the constraint iv, we can use the information provided by paper author and reviewers.

The problem of expressing the same organization in different ways is resolved using a number of heuristics such as matching the initial letters of a multiword organization or using different abbreviations etc. For example, University of Quebec at Montreal in French is written as Université du Quebéc à Montréal, UQAM, or Univ. du Que. à Montréal. For authors we need to use similar heuristics for names; for example, Hong Feng Lee can be written as H. F. Lee or as Hong F. Lee.

The automatic allocation algorithm also considers the preference of the PC as well as the above-mentioned constraints. An optimal allocation algorithm based on preferences could be very complex and time consuming to execute. The algorithm used in ConfSys is sub-optimal but much simpler to implement and the allocation constraints, in most cases, are satisfied without additional fine-tuning by the PC. The algorithm attempts to assign most reviewers their preferences unless there is an apparent conflict of interest.

The algorithm gives higher priority to reviewer's first preference before considering a match of topics. The automatic algorithm assigns a paper to a reviewer who has indicated a high priority for a paper, even though the author specified topics for the paper and the reviewers' interests are not matching. During the setup of ConfSys, the PC assigns the number of reviews for each paper (called reviewer limit, R_l); and the maximum number of paper to assign to each reviewer (called paper limit, P_l)

In the auction process, the reviewer can assign high, average, and low preference or no interest, for each paper. The automatic allocation algorithm, categorizes all submitted papers into four groups: paper with at least one or more high, average, low priorities and the same topic.

Once the auction process is over, the automatic allocation algorithm sorts the paper in each category based on their count. For example, papers assigned high preferences are sorted on paper id and the total number of high priority for the paper. The algorithm will attempt to allocate papers to reviewers who have assigned high priority. Thus a paper having the largest number of high priority will be allocated earlier in the process.

If the number of priorities assigned to a paper is $\geq R_l$, then the paper can be assigned based only on the priorities. If the number of high priority assigned to a paper is $\leq R_l$, then the algorithm can assign paper directly to those reviewers with high priority followed by lower priority until the limit R_l is reached. If the number of reviewers assigned to a paper based on the priority is $< R_l$ then matching of topics of the paper with the reviewers' interests is used.

For each assignment, the algorithm checks if one of the authors and the reviewer is working in the same organization, or if one of the authors and the reviewer were co-author of paper using DBLP.

For each assignment, the algorithm checks both R_l and P_l

In choosing to assign a paper to a reviewer, the algorithm chooses a reviewer with the minimum assignment number; each time a reviewer is assigned a paper, his assignment number is incremented.

The remaining papers, which are not in any of the four categories, would not be assigned by the algorithm; PC is required to allocate them manually during the fine-tuning stage.

4.4 Database connection strategy

To connect to the MySQL database using Java, we must use a JDBC driver for MySQL. Since there is a lot of common code for initiating a JDBC connection, a better way to implement the DB connection is to use a centralized Java class to do all database operations. Thus setting database connection in each Java class where we need to communicate with database is avoided. The common Java class is called ConferenceSql. When we need a database connection in a class we need to first "instance" the ConferenceSql class then simply use its functions. This not only centralizes the connection

functions in one class but also makes these functions reusable. One requirement is that all ConferenceSql's functions that are to be accessed from other classes must be made "static". This is because the JDBC driver is "static" class and we can't wrap a static class with a non-static class in Java.

5. Major functions of ConfSys

The PC sets up the parameter for a conference by interacting with the ConfSys via the PC menu. Details of some of these are given below.

5.1 Topic control

Since every conference has its own topics, the PC must have a way to insert the topics, the reviewers and other parameters for the event. These functions give the PC a way to add, delete and modify the topics.

5.2 Reviewer control

The program committee members (reviewers) are entered in the ConfSys using a Web-based interface. The program chair can add a new reviewer, delete an existing reviewer who could not participate or modify the details for an existing reviewer. The details entered are the reviewer's name and email address. The system generates a random user ID and a password. These are sent by email to reviewers who can interact with ConfSys through the reviewer Web page and are required to register their topics of interests.

5.3 Setting up parameters for automatic allocation

For the automatic allocation function, the PC needs two parameters to limit the number of papers a reviewer can review and the number of reviewers for each paper P_l and R_l.

5.4 Paper allocation, review and debate

Once the paper submission deadline is over, the PC can use the auto allocation function, discussed earlier. At the start of the process, the number of reviewers for each paper is 0. The auto-allocation function would attempt to assign reviewers for most of the papers and the most of reviewers would be assigned some of the papers. If the PC clicks the detail button for each paper she will see the names of reviewers for the paper. Notice that it is possible that some papers would have very few or no reviewers assigned. This is because these papers do not match the interests of reviewers or those who can review these papers have already been allocated other papers by the allocation algorithm or there may be conflicts. In this case, the PC must fine-tune the allocation manually and assign these papers to reviewers regardless of the allocation rules used for automatic allocation. Also the PC may not be satisfied with the result of automatic allocation. In which case, she can use the manual allocation function to do some adjustment. Once the PC feels comfortable with the allocation, she can set the start review date to let reviewers review the papers.

Once the PC has allocated the papers to a reviewer, she can set the start review date to enable the reviewer to download the files for papers allocated to them. There is a security concern for downloading the files for papers. If the files are put in a folder that is accessible by the web server it is possible for any one, who knows the name of the directory and file name, to download it. To avoid this drawback, we don't put the files in a web server accessible folder but let the servlet read the files from a non-web directory and return the stream for downloading by the client. Since the download servlet can only be accessed by the reviewers, only they can download the assigned files.

A reviewer can use a link from the reviewer web page to register the evaluation information including score, and comments both for the author and the program chair(s). The result will be sent to the server and the values will be refreshed in the main evaluation window. The comments and scores are modifiable by the reviewer (during the debate stage of the evaluation process) until the PC makes a final decision on a paper. Once a final decision on a paper is made, that paper could not be evaluated by any reviewers who had not submitted the review for the paper nor can an already submitted review be modified. A message will be displayed to indicate that a final decision on this paper has been made.

5.5 Final decision and communication to authors

Once the reviews have been made and debated, the program chair needs to make a decision on each paper. Based on the reviewers' scores, weights and comments the program chair can either accept a paper as full, short or poster paper or simply reject the paper. Once a final decision is made, the program chair(s) initiate ConfSys to send emails to inform authors and reviewers to check the final results of papers. The comments made by the reviewers meant only for the program chair(s) will not be displayed to the authors.

The author can only view the reviews of her paper(s); this includes the reviewers' IDs, comments, score,

confidence, and the weighted score as well as the final decision for the paper. The final result is only available after program chair(s) makes final decision and sends e-mail to them. If the paper is accepted, author can make recommended changes and resubmit the paper.

Reviewers can view final results of papers that they reviewed. Other reviewers' comments, scores, weight, etc. will be also be shown in the window without the names of any reviewers. The final result is only available after the program chair(s) makes final decision and the system sends emails to the authors and reviewers.

6. Conclusions

Confsys can coordinate the authors, reviewers and PC to process conference paper via Internet. It also reduces the manual operation normally to be done by the PC and streamline the paper allocation operation as well as the collecting of reviews and tabulating the final results. All the software packages used in this application are Open Source. These software packages are very stable and proved by the Open Source community to be reliable.

ConfSys has been used in a test environment and successfully in production environment. It is a component of the Cindi Digital library [4]; our goal is to provide not only a conference management system but also to add the papers submitted to the digital library for better dissemination. ConfSys is in the process of being released to support academic conferences and symposia.

Acknowledgement:

This work was supported in part by grants from the National Science and Engineering Research Council of Canada.

Reference

[1] R. Snodgrass. Summary of Conference Management Software. http://www.acm.org/sigs/sgb/summary.html
[2] DBLP Reference Site, http://dblp.uni-trier.de/db/
[3] MultiRequest and MultiRequestServlet, www.geocities.com/jasonpell
[4] Bipin C. Desai, Rajabihan Shayan Nader, R. Shinghal, Youquan Zhou, ``CINDI: A System for Cataloging Searching and Annotating Documents in Digital Libraries''. Library-trend, Vol. 48-1, Summer 1999.

Author Index

Seventh International Database Engineering and Applications Symposium (IDEAS 2003)

Notes

IEEE Computer Society Publications

The world-renowned IEEE Computer Society publishes, promotes, and distributes a wide variety of authoritative computer science and engineering texts. These books are available from most retail outlets. Visit the CS Store at *http://computer.org* for a list of products.

IEEE Computer Society Proceedings

The IEEE Computer Society also produces and actively promotes the proceedings of more than 160 acclaimed international conferences each year in multimedia formats that include hard and soft-cover books, CD-ROMs, videos, and on-line publications.

For information on the IEEE Computer Society proceedings, please e-mail to csbooks@computer.org or write to Proceedings, IEEE Computer Society, P.O. Box 3014, 10662 Los Vaqueros Circle, Los Alamitos, CA 90720-1314. Telephone +1-714-821-8380. Fax +1-714-761-1784.

Additional information regarding the Computer Society, conferences and proceedings, CD-ROMs, videos, and books can also be accessed from our web site at *http://computer.org/cspress*

Revised 11 March 2002